Making Work Pay

Making Work Pay

The Earned Income Tax Credit and Its Impact on America's Families

Bruce D. Meyer and Douglas Holtz-Eakin, Editors

Russell Sage Foundation ◆ New York

The Russell Sage Foundation

The Russell Sage Foundation, one of the oldest of America's general purpose foundations, was established in 1907 by Mrs. Margaret Olivia Sage for "the improvement of social and living conditions in the United States." The Foundation seeks to fulfill this mandate by fostering the development and dissemination of knowledge about the country's political, social, and economic problems. While the Foundation endeavors to assure the accuracy and objectivity of each book it publishes, the conclusions and interpretations in Russell Sage Foundation publications are those of the authors and not of the Foundation, its Trustees, or its staff. Publication by Russell Sage, therefore, does not imply Foundation endorsement.

Library of Congress Cataloging-in-Publication Data

Making work pay : the earned income tax credit and its impact on America's families / Bruce D. Meyer, Douglas Holtz-Eakin, editors.
    p. cm.
Includes bibliographical references and index.
ISBN 0-87154-599-3
    1. Earned income tax credit—United States. 2. Public welfare—United States.
I. Meyer, Bruce D. II. Holtz-Eakin, Douglas.
HJ4653.C73 M35 2002
336.24'16'0973—dc21   2001041784

The paper used in this publication meets the minimum requirements of American National Standard for Information Sciences—Permanence of Paper for Printed Library Materials. ANSI Z39.48–1992.

Text design by Suzanne Nichols.

RUSSELL SAGE FOUNDATION
112 East 64th Street, New York, New York 10021
10 9 8 7 6 5 4 3 2 1

To our children
Robert, Benjamin, Jacob, Colin, Eleanor and Austin

Contents

Contents

Contributors

BRUCE D. MEYER is professor of economics at Northwestern University and a faculty affiliate of the Northwestern University/University of Chicago Joint Center for Poverty Research. He is also research associate of the National Bureau of Economic Research.

DOUGLAS HOLTZ-EAKIN is professor of economics at Syracuse University and research associate of the National Bureau of Economic Research.

LISA BARROW is an economist at the Federal Reserve Bank of Chicago.

DAVID T. ELLWOOD is Lucius N. Littauer Professor of Political Economy at Harvard's John F. Kennedy School of Government and research associate of the National Bureau of Economic Research.

JANET HOLTZBLATT is deputy director of the Individual Tax Division in the U.S. Department of the Treasury's Office of Tax Analysis.

JEFFREY B. LIEBMAN is associate professor of public policy at Harvard's John F. Kennedy School of Government and a faculty research fellow at the National Bureau of Economic Research.

JANET MCCUBBIN is an economist in the Office of Tax Analysis of the U.S. Department of Treasury.

LESLIE MCGRANAHAN is lecturer in economics at the University of Warwick and a consultant at the Federal Reserve Bank of Chicago.

MICHAEL A. O'CONNOR is an attorney and public benefits consultant for government agencies, foundations, and nonprofit organizations. He also serves on the IRS Advisory Council.

KATHERIN ROSS PHILLIPS is a research associate in the Urban Institute's Income and Benefits Policy Center.

ROBERT REBELEIN is assistant professor of economics at the University of Cincinnati.

Contributors

JENNIFER L. ROMICH is a doctoral candidate in human development and social policy at Northwestern University.

DAN T. ROSENBAUM is assistant professor of economics at the University of North Carolina, Greensboro.

TIMOTHY M. SMEEDING is Maxwell Professor of Public Policy, professor of economics and public administration, and director of the Center for Policy Research, the Maxwell School, at Syracuse University.

DENNIS J. VENTRY, JR. is Samuel I. Golieb Fellow in Legal History at New York University School of Law.

THOMAS S. WEISNER is professor of anthropology in the Department of Psychiatry at the Center for Culture and Health and the Department of Anthropology at the University of California, Los Angeles.

Acknowledgments

This book grew out of a conference on the Earned Income Tax Credit that took place at Northwestern University on November 11–12, 1999 and was sponsored by the Northwestern University/University of Chicago Joint Center for Poverty Research. We would like to thank the staff of the Joint Center for their outstanding organizational and logistical support, including Audrey Chambers, Ilana Cohen, Julie Daraska, Johana Owens-Ream, and Laura Pepol. We would also like to thank Fay Cook, Julie Daraska, Greg J. Duncan and Susan E. Mayer for their essential role in encouraging and supporting this endeavor.

Several organizations quickly and generously provided support for the conference—in particular the Annie E. Casey Foundation, the Joyce Foundation, the John D. and Catherine T. MacArthur Foundation, the Russell Sage Foundation, and the U.S. Department of Health and Human Services.

We would like to thank the authors of the chapters whose intellectual efforts, promptness and diligence are most responsible for the book. A superb group of researchers and policy analysts participated in the conference as discussants and greatly improved the manuscripts. These include Joseph Altonji, Lisa Barrow, Rebecca Blank, Fay Lomax Cook, Stacy Dickert-Conlin, Nada Eissa, David Ellwood, Robert Greenstein, Douglas Holtz-Eakin, Hillary Williamson Hoynes, Marvin Kosters, Jeffrey B. Liebman, Thomas MaCurdy, Leslie McGranahan, David Neumark, Elizabeth Powers, Joel Slemrod, Timothy M. Smeeding, John Karl Scholz, Christopher Taber, Eric Toder, and James Ziliak.

In putting the book together, the Russell Sage Foundation and its staff were invaluable. In particular, Suzanne Nichols and Emily Chang provided outstanding editorial assistance. Denise Paul at the National Tax Journal assisted with the manuscripts, while James Sullivan provided the data analysis for the introduction in his usual excellent fashion. We would also like to thank reviewers at the National Tax Journal and the Russell Sage Foundation for their comments that have been incorporated in these studies.

Bruce D. Meyer and Douglas Holtz-Eakin

Introduction

Bruce D. Meyer and Douglas Holtz-Eakin

S ince its inception in 1975, the federal Earned Income Tax Credit (EITC) has grown dramatically in size, and it is now the largest antipoverty program for the nonaged in the United States. In 1998, 19.7 million families received EITC payments totaling $31.6 billion. As a result, in 1999 the EITC lifted 3.7 million individuals above the poverty line. In addition to directly raising incomes, the EITC has sharply changed work incentives, increasing the after-tax wage by up to 40 percent for those with low earnings. Since the credit is refundable, a person without a tax liability receives it as a payment that, by 2001, could exceed $4,000.

The rapid growth in the EITC in the 1990s left researchers with the challenge of understanding its impact. This book constitutes a large share of the recent efforts, with chapters examining the history of the EITC, its effects on work and marriage, and how the credit is used by recipients. These studies also describe problems with noncompliance and marriage penalties and evaluate the implications of potential changes to the credit.

WHO RECEIVES THE EARNED INCOME TAX CREDIT

The EITC provides an earnings subsidy to family members who satisfy three criteria. First, a family must have a wage earner, since only those who work are eligible. Second, the family must have low income. In 2001, a family with one child could receive the EITC if its income was below $28,281, while a family with two children could earn up to $32,121 and receive the credit. Third, while a small EITC (up to $364 in 2001) is available to the childless, to receive a significant EITC a family has to have children. The maximum credit for a family with one child was $2,428 in 2001, while that for a family with two or more children was $4,008. Since the EITC is refundable, a family can receive the credit even if they do not have an income tax liability. In the vast majority of cases, the credit is received as a lump sum as part of a tax refund early the following year. In summary, the credit subsidizes work by poor parents as it transfers income to them.

FIGURE I.1 / Federal Earned Income Tax Credit Schedule for Families With Children, 2001

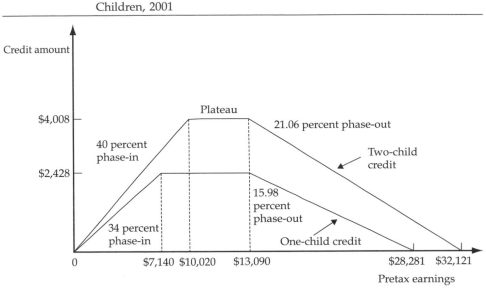

Source: Authors' configuration.

The EITC schedule for families with children in 2001 is illustrated in figure I.1. The schedule for families with two or more children (represented by the upper line) provides a larger credit at all income levels than that for families with only one child (the lower line). Both schedules provide a large earnings subsidy initially as the credit is phased in: forty cents for each dollar earned for the first $10,020 in earnings for those with two or more children. For example, a single mother with two children who earned $10,000 in the previous year would receive a credit of $4,000. At the flat part of the schedule, the plateau, the total credit received does not change with earnings. With additional earnings beyond the plateau, however, the credit is decreased, resulting in an implicit tax on earnings at a rate just over 21 percent for those with two or more children. For those with one child there are somewhat lower earnings subsidies, credits, and implicit taxes.

To paint a statistical portrait of recipients, we examine their characteristics from several angles and with two data sets. The two sources of data do not perfectly agree, but they lead to roughly similar conclusions. Table I.1 is calculated from the Current Population Survey (CPS), the largest in-depth survey of the economic status of American households.[1] The table shows that a majority of EITC dollars go to single mothers. Adding in single fathers, one can see that 60 percent of EITC dollars go to single parents. Since poor families with children are disproportionately headed by single parents, such families receive the preponderance of EITC payments. The vast majority of remaining dollars go to married couples with children, who receive 37 percent of the credit dollars. While a substantial number of recipient couples or individuals are childless (24

TABLE I.1 / EITC Benefits Received and Number of Recipients, by Family Type, 1999

Recipient Category	EITC (Millions)	Distribution of EITC (Percentage)	Average Benefit Received
Single women with children			
Total benefits	$12,138	52.95	$1,903
Number of recipients	6.379	39.41	
Single men with children			
Total benefits	$1,570	6.85	$1,701
Number of recipients	0.923	5.70	
Married couples with children			
Total benefits	$8,522	37.17	$1,682
Number of recipients	5.066	31.30	
Individuals without qualifying child			
Total benefits	$623	2.72	$184
Number of recipients	3.384	20.91	
Couples without qualifying child			
Total benefits	$72	0.31	$166
Number of recipients	0.435	2.69	
Total			
Total benefits	$22,926	100.00	$1,416
Number of recipients	16.187	100.00	

Source: Authors' calculations using the Current Population Survey, annual demographic file 2000. All numbers are weighted.

percent), they receive only 3 percent of the credit dollars. This concentration of 97 percent of EITC dollars in families with children reflects the program design that provides larger credits to these families.

The EITC is also targeted toward large families. Table I.2 reports total benefits received and the number of recipient families for families with different numbers of children. More than two-thirds of payments go to families with two or more children. Thirty-eight percent of dollars go to families with two children, while 27 percent of dollars go to families with three or more children.

Table I.3 reports descriptive information on the age, race, and education of recipients and the ages of their children. Single-mother EITC recipients are disproportionately young, less educated, and white. Their children are fairly evenly spread across the age ranges. Married mothers are slightly older, with even less education, more likely to be white, and have disproportionately young children. Recipients without children tend to be even older, but their other characteristics are similar to those with children.

While the CPS is the best source of detailed information on the characteristics of families receiving the EITC, data from the Internal Revenue Service (IRS) provide better information on numbers of recipients and credit amounts. Table I.4

TABLE I.2 / EITC Benefits Received and Number of Recipients, by Number of Children in Family, 1999

Recipient Category	EITC (Millions)	Distribution of EITC (Percentage)	Average Benefit Received
Recipients without a qualifying child			
Total benefits	$696	3.03	$182
Number of recipients	3.819	23.59	
Recipients with one qualifying child			
Total benefits	$7,300	31.84	$1,432
Number of recipients	5.096	31.48	
Recipients with two qualifying children			
Total benefits	$8,789	38.34	$2,046
Number of recipients	4.296	26.54	
Recipients with more than two qualifying children			
Total benefits	$6,141	26.79	$2,064
Number of recipients	2.976	18.38	
Total			
Total benefits	$22,926	100.00	$1,416
Number of recipients	16.187	100.00	

Source: Authors' calculations using the Current Population Survey, annual demographic file 2000. All numbers are weighted.

TABLE I.3 / Demographic Characteristics of EITC Recipients, 1999

Recipient Characteristic	With Children		Without Children	
	Single	Married	Single	Married
Average age (years)	34.839	37.432	40.458	56.055
Educational attainment (percentage)				
High school dropout	23.1	36.3	26.9	37.7
High school graduate	40.5	35.2	37.6	37.7
Some college	30.2	20.4	22.8	16.5
College graduate	06.1	08.1	12.7	08.1
Black (percentage)	24.0	07.7	15.4	07.6
Average number of children, by age				
0 to five years old	0.506	0.725	—	—
Six to seventeen years old	1.051	1.248	—	—
Total	1.557	1.974	—	—

Source: Authors' calculations using the Current Population Survey, annual demographic file 2000. All numbers are weighted.

TABLE I.4 / EITC Benefits and Number of Recipients, 1998, Comparisons of IRS Data to CPS Data

Recipient Characteristic	IRS		CPS		Ratio (CPS $EITC / IRS $EITC)
	EITC (Millions)	Distribution of EITC (Percentage)	EITC (Millions)	Distribution of Credit (Percentage)	
By filing status of recipient					
Head of household					
Total benefits	$21,215	67.15	$13,634	59.94	0.64
Number of recipients	10.42	52.88	7.318	45.00	0.70
Joint					
Total benefits	$9,683	30.65	$8,532	37.51	0.88
Number of recipients	5.73	29.10	5.589	34.37	0.97
Single					
Total benefits	$694	2.20	$581	2.55	0.84
Number of recipients	3.549	18.01	3.357	20.64	0.95
Total					
Total benefits	$31,592	100.00	$22,747	100.00	0.72
Number of recipients	19.71	100.00	16.264	100.00	0.83
By number of qualifying children					
Returns without a qualifying child					
Total benefits	$694	2.20	672	2.95	0.97
Number of recipients	3.549	18.01	3.894	23.94	1.10
Returns with one qualifying child					
Total benefits	$11,818	37.41	$6,860	30.16	0.58
Number of recipients	7.803	39.60	4.949	30.43	0.63
Returns with more than one qualifying child					
Total benefits	$19,080	60.40	$15,215	66.89	0.80
Number of recipients	8.353	42.39	7.421	45.63	0.89
Total					
Total benefits	$31,592	100.00	$22,747	100.00	0.72
Number of recipients	19.705	100.00	16.264	100.00	0.83

Source: Authors' calculations using data from Current Population Survey, annual demographic file 1999; IRS 2000, figure H; U.S. House 1998, table 13-13.

provides a less detailed breakdown of the characteristics of EITC recipients and compares CPS and IRS data.[2] The IRS data indicate that an even larger share of EITC dollars go to single parents (those filing as heads of households): 67 percent of all payments in 1998. Almost all of the remaining dollars go to married couples, who receive 31 percent of all payments. Again, families with more than one child receive most of the credit dollars, but the IRS data indicate that they receive 60 percent of payments, a somewhat lower share than that indicated by the CPS. Overall, we can see from table I.4 that the IRS paid out $31.6 billion dollars under the EITC in 1998.[3]

HOW THE EITC AFFECTS THE DISTRIBUTION OF INCOME

Because its effect on the income distribution is among the most important consequences of the EITC, we provide a brief description of the distributional effects of the credit.[4] Figure I.2 reports mean income with and without the EITC for single parents in various income groups. For those with incomes under $6,000, the EITC raises average income by about 30 percent. For those with incomes between $6,000 and $12,000, the increase in mean income is about 25 percent. Together, these two income groups include 23 percent of families with children that are headed by a single parent. For single-parent families with incomes between $12,000 and $20,000, the EITC raises mean income by between 3 and 4 percent. For other income groups the effects are smaller, with little discernible effect on the incomes of those with pretax income of more than $35,000. In short,

FIGURE I.2 / Mean Family Income With and Without the EITC, Single Parents

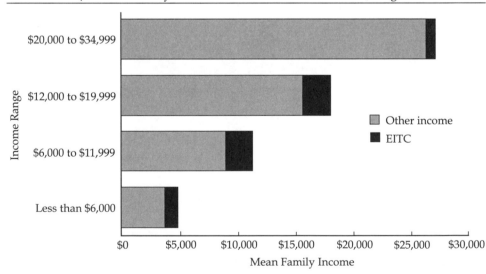

Source: 1999 income data from the Current Population Survey, annual demographic file 2000.

the EITC goes primarily to very low-income single parents, and it amounts to a large share of the resources this group has available to consume.[5]

A second way to gauge the distributional effects of the EITC is to ask how many people it raises above the poverty line or other target income levels. As shown in table I.5, in 1999 the EITC lifted almost 1.0 million families with more than 2.0 million children above the poverty line.[6] The credit lifted 3.7 million people above the poverty line, reducing the overall poverty rate by 13 percent and the poverty rate among children by 21 percent. While no other antipoverty program approaches these poverty-reduction numbers, one caution is that the effects of the EITC are concentrated around the poverty line (see Liebman 1998). Table I.5 also shows that the number of families or children below other target levels, such as 50 percent of the poverty line or 200 percent of the poverty line, is also sharply reduced by the EITC, although the largest effects occur around the poverty line itself. Other programs such as Temporary Assistance for Needy Families or the Food Stamps program are targeted more toward those with the very lowest incomes.

THE COVERAGE OF THIS BOOK

The chapters of this book cover four broad areas of interest. One chapter outlines the history of the EITC and examines how research has informed the political debate regarding its expansion. Four studies examine the extent of work and marriage incentives inherent in the EITC and how tax policy could be altered in light of these incentives. Two chapters address whether the tax credit goes to its intended recipients and examine the extent of noncompliance in the EITC. Finally, three studies identify how EITC recipients view the credit and what types of expenditures are made with the funds.

The History of the Earned Income Tax Credit

In chapter 1, Dennis J. Ventry Jr. outlines the emergence of the EITC from the political debates surrounding failed-negative-income tax and guaranteed-annual-income proposals during the Nixon administration. He describes how forces coalesced around an antipoverty program that was perceived as pro-work, pro-growth, and low cost. These forces led to the introduction of the Earned Income Tax Credit in 1975, fostered its expansion though the 1980s and early 1990s, and came to its defense in the late 1990s.

Work and Marriage Incentives

Owing to the design of the EITC, with its combination of work subsidies and implicit taxes for families with children and low earnings, incentives to work

TABLE I.5 / Number of Families, Individuals, and Children in Poverty With and Without the EITC, 1999 (In Thousands)

Recipient Income Level	Without EITC	With EITC	Difference (Without EITC − With EITC)	Ratio (Without EITC / With EITC)
Families				
Below 50 percent of poverty line	2,621.67	2,332.72	288.94	1.12
Below 75 percent of poverty line	4,486.47	3,762.89	723.59	1.19
Below the poverty line	6,675.82	5,694.26	981.56	1.17
Below 150 percent of poverty line	12,259.67	11,357.94	901.73	1.08
Below 200 percent of poverty line	18,166.54	17,891.13	275.42	1.02
Individuals				
Below 50 percent of poverty line	13,146.44	12,024.81	1,121.63	1.09
Below 75 percent of poverty line	21,797.60	18,866.13	2,931.46	1.16
Below the poverty line	32,302.25	28,574.93	3,727.32	1.13
Below 150 percent of poverty line	56,975.27	53,889.70	3,085.57	1.06
Below 200 percent of poverty line	81,490.25	80,452.91	1,037.34	1.01
Children under the age of eighteen				
Below 50 percent of poverty line	4,659.60	4,004.55	655.05	1.16
Below 75 percent of poverty line	8,055.56	6,390.59	1,664.97	1.26
Below the poverty line	11,607.58	9,567.64	2,039.94	1.21
Below 150 percent of poverty line	19,503.70	18,001.90	1,501.81	1.08
Below 200 percent of poverty line	26,842.22	26,382.19	460.02	1.02

Source: Authors' calculations using the Current Population Survey, annual demographic file 2000. All numbers are weighted.
Note: The poverty line refers to the standard measure reported by the U.S. Census Bureau. Calculations based on money income of families and individuals before taxes (excluding capital gains).

and marry are altered. In chapter 2, Bruce D. Meyer and Dan T. Rosenbaum put the EITC's work incentives in the larger context of recent tax and welfare program changes that have promoted work. The authors show that the EITC was the most important change in work incentives for single mothers from 1984 to 1996, during which period the employment rate of single mothers rose sharply. The authors then compare employment rates of groups affected by the EITC and other policies and conclude that recent EITC expansions have led to a large increase in the labor force participation of single mothers.

David T. Ellwood, in chapter 3, examines the effects of the EITC on the employment of single and married women and on marriage and living arrangements. He argues that welfare reform and a strong economy, in combination with the EITC, have been responsible for the unprecedented recent increase in the employment of single mothers. Ellwood concludes that social policy changes have had a dramatic impact on the labor force participation of low-income single parents but that the EITC also has dampened the increase in work by low-wage married parents. He also considers the possible effect of the EITC and other social policy changes on marriage behavior, finding little effect of these policies on marriage patterns.

Further focusing on the marriage penalties and bonuses created by the EITC, Janet Holtzblatt and Robert Rebelein, in chapter 4, measure the prevalence and magnitude of EITC marriage penalties and bonuses and consider the effects of possible reform proposals. They show how measures of penalties are sensitive to assumptions regarding income, living arrangements, and child custody agreements if a couple were not married. Their preferred approach indicates that on net the EITC increases marriage penalties by approximately $3.5 billion. They then show how various reform proposals differ in their targeting of low-income taxpayers and their reduction in marriage penalties. They find that a two-earner deduction is the best targeted of these proposals but that it is somewhat more complicated than the alternatives.

These early chapters focus largely on the EITC in its current form and study its effects on labor supply and marriage. In chapter 5, Jeffrey B. Liebman examines what would be the optimal level of the maximum credit, the phase-in rate, and the phase-out rate. Taking into account the increased work and reduced welfare receipt that occurs as a result of the EITC, he finds lower efficiency costs of the EITC than past authors. While he finds that optimal parameters depend crucially on society's taste for redistribution, the results suggest that a credit close to the current EITC is optimal.

Compliance Problems

In addition to concerns about work and marriage disincentives embodied in the EITC, some policymakers are also concerned about what they consider a high incidence of "cheating" on taxes by people who claim the credit. Chapters 6 and 7 address this issue and examine more closely who wrongly claims the EITC and how such noncompliance can be prevented.

In chapter 6, Janet McCubbin uses U.S. Treasury tax data to estimate a model of noncompliance. McCubbin finds that reducing the size of the EITC would have only a modest effect in decreasing the EITC error rate. She suggests other methods of improving noncompliance, including simplifying eligibility requirements for qualifying children, tightening social security number requirements for claiming a child, and adding new penalties.

Jeffrey B. Liebman, in chapter 7, also examines EITC noncompliance. Liebman reports that according to IRS tabulations from the 1980s, one-third of EITC recipients were not eligible for the credit, primarily because they did not have eligible children. Using household survey data matched to 1990 tax returns, Liebman finds that overall, between 11 and 13 percent of EITC recipients had no children in their households when they claimed the credit (in 1990 there was no credit for the childless). He also finds that a large share of overpayments went to low-income families with children.

How Recipients Use Their Credit

The remaining chapters turn to a final question: how do recipients use their EITC dollars? For many EITC recipients, the tax refund check constitutes a large part of their annual income. Three chapters address how this "lumpiness" in their income affects EITC recipients.

In chapter 8, Timothy M. Smeeding, Katherin Ross Phillips and Michael O'Connor examine a large sample of individuals filing 1997 income tax returns in Chicago. Most EITC recipients, they argue, expect to receive a tax refund. These recipients plan to use their credit for purposes that extend beyond current consumption, including savings, car purchases, tuition payments, residential moves, and other uses that lead to economic and social mobility. They also find that families with more children are more likely to use the credit for current consumption. The authors conclude that the EITC does more than increase consumption; it also allows recipients to make changes in economic status.

In contrast with social programs that pay benefits evenly over the year, the vast majority of EITC recipients receive their benefits in a single check averaging more than $1,500. In chapter 9, Lisa Barrow and Leslie McGranahan ask whether the lumpy nature of EITC payments induces changes in expenditure patterns among recipients. This issue is particularly important given recent congressional proposals to alter the timing of EITC payments. Barrow and McGranahan find that consumption rises, particularly for durable goods, in the months in which EITC refunds are received. Thus, the evidence suggests that the EITC facilitates the purchase of big-ticket items by low-income families.

In chapter 10, Jennifer Romich and Thomas Weisner examine how low-income participants in Milwaukee's New Hope Project have perceived and used the EITC. They find that the families generally know about the EITC and other programs. Still they do not know much about how to receive the EITC on a monthly basis rather than as a single lump-sum payment—or they choose not to do so. Romich and Weisner also find that recipients use their refund checks for such things as furniture, transportation, housing, and savings. They conclude that families use the lump-sum delivery as a form of forced savings and that the lump-sum option enables families to save for asset purchases.

Taken together, the studies in this volume provide a broad summary of the state of knowledge on the Earned Income Tax Credit. They describe a large program that appears to have mostly favorable incentive effects and is used for valuable purposes by its recipients. They assess the degree of noncompliance, discuss how it has changed, and put it in perspective relative to other programs. Finally, the studies provide directions for future efforts to explore the effects of the EITC and improve its design.

NOTES

1. The CPS imputes EITC receipt using family composition and income information and an algorithm that is checked against IRS records. One might reasonably suppose that the CPS overstates EITC receipt since the algorithm assumes that all eligible recipients receive the credit. However, comparisons of CPS and IRS data suggest that the CPS sharply understates receipt, particularly for single parents.

2. The CPS numbers here are slightly different from those in table I.2 because 1998 data are used, to allow comparability with the IRS numbers.

3. For total EITC payments as well as dollars received by single parents or those with one child, the IRS numbers are substantially larger than comparable CPS numbers. These discrepancies suggest substantial EITC noncompliance, an issue discussed in two of the chapters in this volume. These discrepancies also potentially raise questions about the CPS coverage of low-income groups.

4. For earlier discussions of the effects of the EITC on the distribution of income, see Hoffman and Seidman 1990, Burkhauser, Couch, and Glenn 1996, Liebman 1998, and Hotz and Scholz 2001.

5. See also Hotz and Scholz 2001, especially figure 3, which shows that EITC payments are primarily received by those with incomes between $5,000 and $20,000.

6. It should be emphasized that these calculations are made under the assumption that the EITC has no effect on pretax income or family formation, both of which assumptions are challenged in the chapters of this book. Nevertheless, the direct effect of the transfers on incomes are probably much larger than effects through earnings and marriage, making these descriptions useful.

REFERENCES

Burkhauser, Richard V., Kenneth A. Couch, and Andrew J. Glenn. 1996. "Public Policies for the Working Poor: The Earned Income Tax Credit Versus Minimum Wage Legislation." *Research in Labor Economics* 15: 65–109.

Hoffman, Saul D., and Laurence S. Seidman. 1990. *The Earned Income Tax Credit: Anti-*

poverty Effectiveness and Labor Market Effects. Kalamazoo, Mich.: W. E. Upjohn Institute for Employment Research.

Hotz, V. Joseph, and John Karl Scholz. 2001. "The Earned Income Tax Credit." Working Paper 8078. Cambridge, Mass.: National Bureau of Economic Research (January).

Licbman, Jeffrey B. 1998. "The Impact of the Earned Income Tax Credit on Incentives and Income Distribution." In *Tax Policy and the Economy 12*, edited by James M. Poterba. Cambridge, Mass.: MIT Press.

U.S. Department of the Treasury. Internal Revenue Service (IRS). 2000. "Individual Income Tax Returns, 1998." *Statistics of Income Bulletin* (Fall). Washington: U.S. Government Printing Office.

U.S. House of Representatives. 1998. *1998 Green Book: Background Material and Data on Programs Within the Jurisdiction of the Committee on Ways and Means*. Washington: U.S. Government Printing Office.

Part I

The History of the Earned Income Tax Credit

Chapter 1

The Collision of Tax and Welfare Politics: The Political History of the Earned Income Tax Credit

Dennis J. Ventry, Jr.

Over the course of the past thirty years, tax expenditures have become increasingly visible components of the U.S. tax transfer system. Although they do not require annual review by the appropriations process, tax expenditures are subject nevertheless to the whims of politics and national mood.[1] The Earned Income Tax Credit (EITC) is a case in point. Enacted in 1975 as a refundable tax offset for low-income workers, the EITC appeared to politicians an attractive, work-oriented alternative to existing welfare programs. It was both an antipoverty and an antiwelfare instrument. It complemented national concerns over welfare caseloads, unemployment rates, and the working poor. By the 1990s, however, the same political forces that had nurtured the EITC threatened to eliminate it. The EITC was now part of the problem; it had begun to look more like a welfare subsidy (replete with work disincentives, poor targeting, and high costs) and less like a tax offset. It had become simply another federal handout, a welfare program administered through the tax system.[2]

This chapter describes the "collision" of tax and welfare politics. It examines the political history of the EITC to show how the politics of welfare reform influence tax policies that function as social policy. It explains the creation and development of the EITC in relation to a welfare reform consensus that emphasized pro-work, pro-growth, low-cost policies. This paper also uses the EITC to show how economic tradeoffs inherent in the formulation of tax-transfer programs are also political tradeoffs. It examines policy choices between costs and labor supply incentives (or targeting and labor supply disincentives), as well as those between ease of participation and compliance rates. Thus, it highlights a fundamental social policy conundrum of the last 30 years; that is, whether to favor programs with high budgetary costs (that is, high break-even points), less-targeted benefits, and small marginal labor supply disincentives, or those with low budgetary costs (that is, low break-even points), more-targeted benefits, and large marginal labor supply disincentives. This study places the dilemma in historical context, illuminating the relationship between technical policy options and the political process.

WELFARE DEPENDENCY AND TAX TRANSFERS: THE EARLY YEARS

President Lyndon Johnson's Great Society identified poverty as the social problem of the 1960s. By contrast, welfare dependency became the social problem of the 1970s.[3] While policymakers in the 1960s talked of entitlement-oriented guaranteed annual incomes, in the 1970s they debated work-oriented programs. Of course, the dichotomy between the two decades was not this neat; calls for a guaranteed annual income persisted into the 1970s, for example, and social policies that reinforced work predated the English Poor Laws. Nonetheless, the perceived social crises of the two decades were distinct.

The debates surrounding President Richard Nixon's Family Assistance Plan (FAP) illuminate this distinction. They represent a transitional period between the perceived social ills of poverty on the one hand and welfare dependency on the other. Moreover, the political discussions of Nixon's welfare initiative highlight trade-offs in tax transfer programs that not only doomed the FAP but also engaged policymakers for the next thirty years. The fight over the FAP alerted politicians to how the tax system could alleviate or, conversely, perpetuate social problems. It also spawned alternative tax transfer proposals, including the EITC.

A Developing Intellectual Vanguard

The United States "rediscovered" poverty in the early 1960s.[4] Once poverty had been exposed, the federal government addressed itself to the elimination of what many considered a poverty epidemic. Social policy experts attempted to fill the "poverty gap." Defined as the income deficiency between a family's income level and a specified poverty level, the poverty gap informed social policy discussions in the early 1960s.[5] Prompted by President Johnson's declaration of war on poverty in 1964, social policymakers set about formulating various anti-poverty schemes.

These formulations, Johnson declared, would not dole out cash grants. "The majority of the Nation," the president argued in his 1964 *Economic Report*, "could simply tax themselves enough to provide the necessary income supplements to their less fortunate citizens. . . . But this 'solution' would leave untouched most of the roots of poverty. It will be far better, even if more difficult, to equip and permit the poor of the Nation to produce and earn the additional" money required to escape from poverty (Council of Economic Advisers 1964, 4). Johnson's emphasis on work-oriented programs was rooted in a historical national aversion to federal handouts. The antiwelfare, pro-work sentiment pervaded the national culture. It emphasized work over dependency, distinguishing between poverty (which was seen as a temporary condition of the working poor and a permanent condition of the disabled and aged) and welfare dependency (which was seen as a pathological and voluntary condition of the indolent).[6] Put simply, it conflated social policy with morality. This national consensus, moreover, persisted across time. In 1937, for instance, with the nation immersed in a protracted depression and with millions of Americans lacking jobs, public opinion favored "work relief" over "cash relief" by a nine-to-one margin (Gallup 1972, 1: 84). A year later, in 1938, as the economy underwent what President Franklin Roosevelt euphemistically termed a "recession," 68 percent of respondents opposed paying unemployed citizens "script money" (Gallup 1972, 1: 124). Even in the hardest of times, Americans supported work- over cash-relief programs.

Imbued with this pro-work sentiment, the Johnson administration sought to remove obstacles that prevented individuals from attaining self-sufficiency. Policymakers soon identified the tax system as one of those impediments. In 1965, Joseph Pechman, senior fellow at the Brookings Institution and consultant to the Treasury Department throughout the 1960s, observed that "the government has launched a program to alleviate poverty. In such a situation," he reasoned, "it is clearly undesirable to maintain a tax system that subjects the 'poor' as officially defined to taxes."[7] Rather than perpetuate the poverty cycle, the tax system could be a useful "device" in removing individuals from poverty and in keeping them from turning to welfare.[8]

Fiddling with the tax system in the traditional manner (reducing positive tax rates or raising personal exemptions) would not help low-income individuals whose federal income tax bill was already zero. Reformers needed to alter the tax law to pay out benefits directly. Enter the negative income tax (NIT). By applying negative rates to unused exemptions and deductions, as the early proposals suggested, or by applying a negative rate per capita credit—a structure later plans employed—a negative income tax could close, and even eliminate, the poverty gap.[9] By running the program from the tax system, moreover, an NIT could improve on existing welfare services. First, it reduced administrative costs by displacing most social workers, which, in turn, complemented the prevailing notion among experts that poverty had more to do with deficiencies in income than character.[10] Second, a negative income tax improved horizontal equity on the transfer side of the tax transfer system; that is, it equalized state differences in benefit levels by providing a national, federally subsidized payment.[11] Third, and perhaps most important, an NIT encouraged individuals, once out of poverty, to earn their way toward self-sufficiency. Traditional welfare programs imposed 100 percent marginal tax rates on earnings. An NIT, on the other hand, could avoid these prohibitive work disincentives by using fractional marginal rates, thereby "ensur[ing] that those who work will not remain in poverty."[12] In acknowledgment of these myriad benefits, President Johnson's Office of Economic Opportunity made the negative income tax the capstone of its ambitious 1966 antipoverty program, which promised to "finish the job of ending poverty by the end of 1976."[13]

As NIT plans proliferated, and as they became more costly, critics associated them with a guaranteed annual income scheme. By most accounts, guaranteed-annual-income plans provided benefits "as a matter of right" with constitutional guarantees.[14] They resembled "social dividend" plans, contemporaneously under consideration in Britain, that placed an income floor under every family—again, as a matter of right (Rhys-Williams 1943, 1953). Neither guaranteed-annual-income plans nor social dividend plans contained phase-out rates. In addition, although both plans proposed to close all or most of the poverty gap, they were prohibitively expensive;[15] worse yet, they seemed to take the form of a demeaning dole.

Milton Friedman (1962), whose articulation of a negative income tax in 1962 made it a viable policy option, feared the confusion between an NIT and existing plans for a guaranteed annual income.[16] He argued that the use of fractional tax rates distinguished negative income taxation not only from guaranteed incomes but also from conventional welfare programs. Friedman's NIT utilized a 50 percent phase-out rate, substantially lower than the 100 percent rate used by the Aid to Families with Dependent Children (AFDC) program. Friedman also showed that the marginal rates in an NIT could be graduated to preserve work incentives even further. In fact, the parameters of an NIT could be set so differently from the parameters of a guaranteed annual income that Friedman publicly denounced the connection between an NIT and "superficially similar but basically very different guaranteed minimum income plan[s]." According to Friedman, the existing "grab bag of relief and welfare measures," not an NIT, amounted to a "government guaranteed annual income."[17]

Despite Friedman's efforts, many observers continued to associate the negative income tax with guaranteed-annual-income plans. President Johnson, for one, did not perceive the distinctions between the two policy instruments as parameterized by NIT advocates within his administration. In Johnson's eyes, each program amounted to a cash benefit, and thus a work disincentive. He opposed the Office of Economic Opportunity's proposal for a negative income tax, for example, on the grounds that it undermined the self-help principles of his War on Poverty (Moynihan 1973, 131). He preferred more explicit pro-work, rehabilitative policies. The legislative foundation of Johnson's Great Society, the Economic Opportunity Act of 1964, contained six parts, each of which "reaffirmed the central and traditional objective of extending opportunities for individual initiative"; they provided a hand up, not a handout (Davies 1996, 34). Johnson opposed cash supplements in any form and preferred "opening to everyone the opportunity for education and training, [and] the opportunity to work" (Economic Opportunity Act of 1964, 377).

The American people also favored work over income programs. In a 1966 Gallup Poll, 67 percent of respondents opposed a "guaranteed minimum annual income" (Gallup 1972, 3: 1965). By 1968, public opinion had warmed slightly to a guaranteed annual income; 36 percent favored and 58 percent opposed a federally guaranteed family income. Tellingly, however, 78 percent of respondents favored guaranteeing a job rather than a cash grant (2133). Poverty may have been the social crisis of the 1960s, but avoiding dependency on the government remained a top priority for Americans and their elected officials. Who better to continue the pro-work legacy than tough, conservative Richard Nixon?

Politics, Economic Research, and the Family Assistance Plan

President Nixon's Family Assistance Plan, introduced in August 1969, provided a bold alternative to existing public assistance programs. Philosophically, it attempted to strike a balance between "the mutually inconsistent goals of adequate benefit levels and work incentives" (Davies 1996, 214). Its federal minimum cash guarantee, in the form of a negative income tax, would replace the much-maligned AFDC program with a uniform national payment that states could supplement at their discretion. Through the use of an income disregard, fractional phase-outs, and a requirement that all recipients either maintain employment or seek work, the FAP would keep work disincentives to a minimum.[18] Most important, the FAP would reverse the rising welfare rolls. In 1960, before President Johnson deployed his forces for a war on poverty, 3.1 million people were receiving AFDC. By 1969, that number had risen to 6.7 million, and it would jump again to 9.0 million by 1970 (Berkowitz 1991, 116, 93). Johnson's self-help programs failed to curb the swelling welfare rolls and in fact seemed to fuel a developing welfare "crisis."[19] His War on Poverty had amounted to "little more than a modestly financed skirmish"; it was oversold, underfunded, and wrong-headed (Esterly and Esterly 1971, 26). It promised economic opportunity through work, but failed to pave the road to self-sufficiency with income supports or jobs. It was now Nixon's turn. The Family Assistance Plan, the new president stated, would address the crisis of welfare dependency with a radical new income strategy that lifted individuals out of poverty and at the same time reinforced the work ethic. His choice of an NIT, however, would make it difficult for him to sell his proposal as a pro-work measure.

The public responded warmly to the FAP. One week after its introduction, Gallup found that of those familiar with it, 65 percent favored the plan, 20 percent opposed it, and 15 percent recorded no opinion (Moynihan 1973, 268). Eighty-one percent of the telegrams sent to the White House on the subject expressed support, and 95 percent of newspaper editorials praised the proposal (Small 1999, 188). In an informal White House survey of four hundred editorials, the counselor to the president, Daniel Patrick Moynihan, proudly reported that "the merging of a work requirement with a general income scheme was far and away the single most praised aspect of the President's proposal."[20]

The FAP initially enjoyed congressional enthusiasm, as well; but opposition formed quickly.[21] Liberals thought the plan inadequate and demanded higher benefit levels. The Nixon proposal provided a national floor of $1,600 for a family of four, more generous than existing AFDC benefit levels in almost every state. Liberals made it known they would accept nothing less than $5,500, a figure originally derived by the National Welfare Rights Organization (NWRO) and its campaign against the FAP, "Fifty-five Hundred or Fight" (Davies 1996, 223).[22] Although the $5,500 plan was estimated to cost $71 billion and cover 150 million people, the welfare rights group increased the proposed benefit to $6,500 in 1971, a demand that presidential hopeful George McGovern endorsed.[23] Conservatives, meanwhile, professed shock that a Republican president supported what amounted to "a national guaranteed income arrangement" (Reichley 1981, 144). The Nixon proposal, they argued, contained weak work requirements that made its benefits resemble cash giveaways. The FAP would perpetuate, not abolish, existing work disincentives. Al Ullman (Dem.-Ore.) complained to administration officials that the proposal "open[ed] up the Treasury of the United States in a way it has never been opened up" (Burke and Burke 1974, 152). Moreover, the FAP would add 10 million recipients to the welfare rolls and cost $2 billion more than existing public assistance programs (Haveman 1973, 35).

The Nixon administration countered. It argued that the bill's price tag was modest compared to the extravagant alternatives. The president carefully differentiated between the work incentive features of his NIT plan and the disincentives of guaranteed-annual-income schemes. "This national floor under incomes for working or dependent families," he emphasized, "is not a 'guaranteed income'" (quoted in O'Connor 1998, 113). Nixon expressly reiterated his proposal's work requirements. "The family assistance plan that I propose increases the incentive to work," he wrote George Bush in 1970.[24] It allowed recipients to keep their first $720 of earnings, above which point it taxed additional earnings at 50 percent up to a phase-out of $4,000. In comparison to AFDC, which used 67 percent marginal tax rates, the FAP boasted more positive work incentives.[25] Moreover, the FAP required that "every adult in the assisted families register at the employment office for work or training or sign up for vocational rehabilitation if handicapped."[26] The plan also included expanded day care and transportation services so that claimants could more easily get to and from work. Despite these assurances, Nixon found it difficult to mobilize support for the FAP among congressional allies. They ignored the FAP's work requirements and confused the plan's NIT component with more liberal income maintenance schemes.

Adding to these difficulties, empirical evidence indicated that the FAP did not make work pay. The Senate Finance Committee staff produced tables exposing the FAP's work disincentives. Committee chair Russell Long (Dem.-La.) used the data to show that under the administration's bill, a father in a four-person family who earned $2,000 annually would receive benefits that raised his total annual income to $2,960. This amount, however, "is less than what he would get if he were totally unemployed," Long reported. "In other words, he can increase his family's income by . . . quitting work entirely" (quoted in Moynihan 1973, 465). Indeed, under both AFDC and the FAP, an unemployed father with no earnings received $3,000 in benefits from the federal government. Was the administration's plan no better than the system it proposed replacing, Long asked?

The White House responded lamely. During congressional testimony, Senator Herman Talmadge (Dem.-Ga.) asked Robert Finch, the secretary of the Department of Health, Education, and Welfare (HEW), about the effects of the FAP. A man "could do a little casual labor on somebody's yard from time to time," Talmadge hypothesized, "maybe sell a little heroin or do a little burglary and he would be in pretty good shape, wouldn't he?" Finch responded, "He would be in about the same shape as under the present program." In a similar exchange, Long asked Robert Patricelli of HEW the logic behind penalizing individuals for choosing work over welfare: "There is none, Senator," Patricelli admitted (Moynihan 1973, 473, 481).

Nor did the administration have a response to Senator John Williams (Rep.-Del.). In a relentless attack on the labor supply effects of the FAP, Williams showed that work did not pay under the Nixon plan. Using data produced by HEW, he demonstrated how the plan exacerbated existing benefit reduction rates.[27] When combined with food stamps, social security taxes, Medicaid payments, public housing subsidies, and federal and state taxes, the Family Assistance Plan created an even more perverse system of social provision. Although it replaced AFDC's 67 percent phase-out rate with a 50 percent rate, its benefits extended much further up the income scale and affected individuals not eligible for AFDC or other welfare programs, particularly the working poor. It worsened what was referred to as "notch" problems, and it raised cumulative tax rates in the tax transfer system. Williams belabored these notches. A four-person family with no earned income in New York City, he told the Senate Finance Committee, could claim $7,435 in benefits. If the same family earned $6,000, its total income would increase by only $1,750; it faced a marginal tax rate of 70 percent. If it managed to earn an additional $279, its income would *decrease* by $1,656. In an even more extreme case, a seven-person family with no earned income could claim $10,207 in benefits. If the same family earned $8,658, its income would fall $405, to $9,802 (Moynihan 1973, 480).[28]

The Family Assistance Plan was wounded but not dead. In February 1970, the Nixon administration produced evidence that the FAP would increase work effort among recipients. Beginning in 1968, the University of Wisconsin Institute for Research on Poverty and Mathematica, Inc., under the auspices of the Office of Economic Opportunity (OEO), initiated the first of four income maintenance experiments, the New Jersey Graduated Work Incentive Experiment.[29] Like the other studies (Denver-Seattle, Iowa–North Carolina, and Gary, Indiana), the New Jersey experiment tested the influence of income supplements on work, consumption, borrowing, saving, and family stability. It was to be completed by 1972. By 1970, however, the Nixon administration needed data to support its case for a negative income tax. At the request of the Office of Economic Opportunity, the groups conducting the experiments "broke into" the data. In a report entitled, "Preliminary Results," they summarized the early findings. "There is no evidence," the report stated, "that work effort declined among those receiving income support payments. On the contrary, there is an indication that work effort of participants receiving payments increased relative to the work effort of those not receiving payments" (quoted in Moynihan 1973, 192). The White House immediately released these findings to the press.

The report, although preliminary, began to win over converts to the viability of the NIT-driven Family Assistance Plan. Wilbur Mills, chair of the House Ways and Means Committee, threw his influence behind the proposal, while other legislators stopped talking about the plan's possible work disincentives.

By the summer of 1970, the report was receiving less favorable treatment, and consequently, so too was the FAP. A *New York Times Magazine* article, citing the assistant director of the Office of Economic Opportunity, John O. Wilson, as its source, reported that the Nixon administration had "rigged" the preliminary data (Cook 1970). Senator Williams called it a "political report to justify a conclusion," and journalists Clark Mollenhoff and Richard Wilson wrote that White House official Daniel Patrick Moynihan had "pressured" Wilson to prepare the report. The U.S. General Accounting Office, however, audited the findings and verified the report's conclusions. The available evidence suggested that the episode merely reflected welfare politics as usual. Nevertheless, the "case [for the FAP's work incentives] was shaken simply in that it was challenged" (Moynihan 1973, 511). With the New Jersey experiment discredited and no other alternative data sources to validate an NIT, the Nixon administration awaited the inevitable defeat of the FAP.

Indeed, the end was near. It seemed that the FAP could neither reverse the cycle of welfare dependency nor move welfare claimants into paid employment. Senator Russell Long concluded that the FAP would "reward idleness and discourage personal initiative of those who can provide for themselves." In a meeting with the president, Long made this point more colorfully. His committee, he told Nixon, objected "to paying people not to work" and to instead "lay about all day making love and producing illegitimate babies" (quoted in Moynihan 1973, 515, 523).

Long's political acumen perceived another trend: the preference among legislators for assisting low-income working families. Acting on his instincts, Long proposed an alternative to the FAP that directed benefits toward the "deserving" poor, that is, those willing to work.[30] His proposal, part of a larger public jobs program, called for wage subsidies to low-income workers and a "work bonus" equal to 10 percent of wages subject to social security taxation. The work bonus rose to a maximum credit of $400, declined at a 25-percent rate from $4,000, and phased out at $5,600. Long argued that it would offset social security taxes, act as an earnings subsidy, and "prevent the taxing of people onto the welfare rolls" (Long 1972). His plan differed from both negative-income-tax and guaranteed-annual-income plans in that it conditioned benefits on work. Moreover, whereas the negative-income-tax and guaranteed-annual-income proposals gave their highest benefits to those with no earned income, Long's work bonus phased in benefits. In addition, although an NIT phased out benefits, Long's alternative declined at 25 percent as opposed to 50 percent for most NIT plans. Senate Finance Committee members expressed interest in Long's work-bonus proposal. In 1972, however, Congress rejected it, along with the FAP.

The debate over the FAP accentuated the trade-offs inherent in tax transfer programs. It focused on whether a reformed social welfare system would be entitlement oriented or work conditioned, permanent or temporary. In defeat, the FAP portended the future course of welfare reform. "Welfare" connoted indolence, a way of life; "poverty" implied hard luck, a temporary condition of the down-and-out and a permanent condition of the disabled and aged. After the

FAP, successful social policy proposals would have to meet both antipoverty and antiwelfare goals. They would have to fulfill pro-work, pro-growth, low-cost requirements.

Helping the Working Poor

Despite its defeat in 1972, the work bonus remained on the policy agenda because of Russell Long's indefatigable efforts. He attached the plan to various pieces of legislation and explained to his colleagues how it rewarded work while NITs, guaranteed annual incomes, and existing welfare services promoted dependency. Long perceived his work bonus as a substitute for conventional welfare programs—in particular, for AFDC. He sympathized with the poor but differentiated sharply between the working and the nonworking poor. As a preliminary to his more sophisticated work-bonus proposal of 1972, Long unveiled in 1970 a "workfare" alternative to the FAP that distinguished between employables and unemployables (defined as the aged, blind, and disabled and single mothers with preschoolers). For the unemployables, Long's plan offered a modest guaranteed income. For the employables, it provided work and training opportunities. It also allowed income maintenance payments when no work was available, as well as wage subsidies for the workfare participants whose hourly wage fell below the minimum.[31]

The work bonus came later and reflected an evolving political consensus that payroll taxes fell heavily, even regressively, on the poor.[32] Throughout the 1960s, the Treasury Department and various executive-commissioned antipoverty task forces had noted the regressive effects of social security taxation.[33] They also showed that future refinancing of the social security system might encumber the poor even more.[34] Congress, too, became increasingly aware of payroll tax burdens. It considered amendments to the Social Security Act in 1967, 1970, 1971, and 1972. The emergent national debate over the future of social security focused Congress's attention on payroll taxation and prompted legislators to introduce legislation that relieved the poor from future refinancing of the system.[35] Between 1972 and 1973, the employee payroll tax experienced its sharpest one-year jump, rising from 5.2 to 5.8 percent. The longer trend was even more arresting: the worker's share of the tax rose from 1.5 percent in 1950 to 3.0 percent in 1960 and to 4.8 percent in 1970 (Pechman 1987, 332). The surges heightened reform pressures and made legislative relief of payroll taxes imminent. Russell Long's long-running advocacy on this score made his work bonus the front-runner.

While Long advocated a tax credit for the working poor, others rejuvenated the negative income tax. The FAP's demise had not stopped many policy experts from continuing to support an NIT.[36] These analysts—housed within universities, Washington think tanks, and the federal bureaucracy—produced economic data that indicated the viability of an NIT-driven income security system. They pioneered modeling techniques that simulated the effects of various NIT designs.[37]

They helped conduct the income maintenance experiments. Perhaps most important, they enjoyed institutional ties to the federal bureaucracy. HEW's assistant secretary for planning and evaluation created a subdivision called Income Security Policy. Michael Barth, a former member of the Office of Economic Opportunity and a designer of the Family Assistance Plan, staffed the division with economists from the recently reorganized OEO. Under his direction, the Income Security Policy division funded research on poverty and welfare reform and maintained close links with the policy research community, which included the University of Wisconsin's Institute for Research on Poverty and the Urban Institute.

The network of social policy experts in and around government provided data for several comprehensive welfare reform proposals in the mid-1970s. It contributed to the work of the Subcommittee on Fiscal Policy of the Joint Economic Committee (JEC), for example, which conducted a three-year, nineteen-volume study on the U.S. tax transfer system. Begun in 1972, this study addressed itself to improving the equity, simplicity, incentives, and multiprogram interaction of the existing system. It examined a number of antipoverty alternatives, including comprehensive income supplements, demogrants, in-kind programs, minimum-wage increases, wage subsidies, earnings subsidies, and public employment programs (Joint Economic Committee 1974, 129). Ultimately, the subcommittee, chaired by Martha Griffiths (Dem.-Mich.), recommended a dual approach to welfare reform that replaced public assistance programs with a federal system of tax credits and income allowances. In 1974, Griffiths introduced the Tax Credit and Allowances Act (H.R. 17574), a bill that embodied the JEC's recommendations. Griffiths's proposal, which she dubbed "Income Security for Americans," replaced deductions and personal exemptions for low-income families with refundable tax credits. It abolished AFDC and the food stamps program, moreover, in favor of a guaranteed-income program administered by the Internal Revenue Service (IRS). Also in 1974, the secretary of HEW, Caspar Weinberger, proposed on behalf of the Ford administration the Income Supplement Plan, a comprehensive negative-income-tax proposal that would replace all existing welfare programs (see HEW 1974; Weinberger 1976). The proposal ensured that a "family would no longer both pay taxes and receive benefits at the same time, but instead would have either a tax liability or eligibility for a transfer" (HEW 1974, 7).

Despite the extensive research behind both proposals, critics argued that neither advanced the welfare reform debate. In fact, some individuals charged that the two plans amounted to guaranteed annual income schemes reminiscent of the failed Family Assistance Plan. It "was like going back in time five years," observed Martin Anderson, chair of the ad hoc White House task force charged with evaluating the Ford administration's Income Supplement Plan (Anderson 1976, 10).[38] Opponents felt that President Gerald Ford's and Representative Griffiths's alternatives did not move the discussion beyond unproved and widely criticized income guarantees, on the one hand, and disproved public assistance measures, on the other. Policymakers seemed neglectful of the lessons provided by the FAP, critics believed: they did not acknowledge the extent to which Americans had grown weary of comprehensive welfare proposals that "tax[ed] the many on behalf of the few" (Phillips 1970, 37).

Congress ultimately rejected both Ford's and Griffiths's plans because they did not fit the pro-work, pro-growth, low-cost mold. To be sure, both alternatives emphasized work and economic growth, but not satisfactorily. Moreover, they were too expensive, costing $15.4 billion and $4.6 billion, respectively (1974 dollars) (Joint Economic Committee 1974, 162; HEW 1974, F-1). Although each plan explicitly targeted "dependency," neither convinced Congress that it did enough to alleviate the welfare problem.

The Earned Income Tax Credit

Russell Long's work bonus presented a more attractive policy alternative and a path toward economic independence. It contained implicit work incentives, and it conformed to budgetary constraints. Moreover, by putting money in the hands of low-income consumers, it complemented President Ford's pledge to stimulate the flagging economy. The Senate passed versions of Long's work bonus each year from 1972 to 1974, but the House rejected them on each occasion. With the economy slipping into recession in 1974, President Ford introduced the Tax Reduction Act of 1975, hoping that tax cuts would bring stimulative effects. Congress responded to Ford's cue by refunding $8.1 billion in 1974 individual income taxes and reducing 1975 income taxes by an additional $10 billion (U.S. Senate 1975). As part of the bill's tax-cutting features, Congress established section 32 of the Internal Revenue Code for one year, a refundable credit for taxpayers with incomes below $8,000. The Earned Income Credit (EIC) equaled 10 percent of the first $4,000 of earned income, or $400.[39] It phased out at 10 percent and vanished completely at $8,000. The Finance Committee report suggested that the EIC would "assist in encouraging people to obtain employment, reducing the unemployment rate and reducing the welfare rolls" (U.S. Senate 1975, 33). It would also offset payroll tax burdens for low-income families.[40]

The EITC embodied Long's vision of a program that moved individuals off welfare and into paid employment while keeping others off the welfare rolls. It covered only working poor families with children and forced the "undeserving" poor either to choose paid employment or resort to stigmatized and inadequate AFDC services.[41] It neglected nonworking Americans, including childless low-income individuals.[42] In short, the EITC's modest responsibilities and cost ($1.25 billion) reflected the prevailing welfare reform consensus that carefully circumscribed its parameters. The credit would reduce welfare dependency, not poverty.[43]

INTERSTICE

For three years, the EITC underwent only slight modification, adhering to its pro-work, antiwelfare charter.[44] In an effort to tie the credit more directly to work, Congress allowed EITC eligibles an advance payment option as opposed to year-end, lump-sum payments. The 1978 law also made the EITC a permanent provision of the Internal Revenue Code. The "new" EITC still phased in at 10 percent, but it now rose until $5,000 in income and provided a maximum benefit of $500 at incomes between $5,000 and $6,000.[45] Beyond $6,000, the credit declined at 12.5 percent, zeroing out at $10,000. These increased thresholds nearly restored the credit's original value, which had been eroded by inflation (Campbell and Peirce 1980, 6) (see the appendix to this chapter for EITC parameters from 1975 to 1999).

The Joint Committee on Taxation attributed the EITC's popularity to how it provided both tax relief and work incentives for low-income families (1979, 51). In this way, the EITC fulfilled its original tenets as set forth by Congress; that is, it served as "an added bonus or incentive for low-income people to work," and as a way to reduce welfare dependency by "inducing individuals with families receiving Federal assistance to support themselves" (U.S. Senate 1975, 11).

A cohort of liberal bureaucrats and academic researchers expressed less excitement for the EITC. They believed the program's antipoverty effectiveness quite limited. Despite widespread antiwelfare rhetoric and the popularity of pro-work programs, many economists and social policy officials supported comprehensive cash assistance in the form of a negative income tax. Others, citing the persistent unemployment and eroding wages of the 1970s, advocated ambitious public jobs programs. The EITC did not address these ambitions. It remained small and inexpensive, categorical and limited.

Given the early design of the EITC, neither its proponents nor its critics could have anticipated the program's next stage of development. Indeed, much to everyone's surprise, the EITC would emerge from the welfare reform discussions at the end of the 1970s forever transformed. It would no longer constitute simply a modest work subsidy; rather, it would represent an antipoverty device that could potentially raise the income of all working Americans above the poverty line.

WELFARE REFORM AND THE EITC:
THE PROGRAM FOR BETTER JOBS AND INCOME

In May 1977, President Jimmy Carter announced that his administration was in the process of designing a consolidated income security system. The new tax transfer system would "scrap" existing public assistance programs and deliver "jobs, simplicity of administration, financial incentive to work, [and] adequate assistance for those who cannot work."[46] Moreover, it would narrow the differences in benefit levels among states by providing a uniform federal payment, increase work incentives for mothers with young children, and provide benefits to low-income two-parent families. During the development of Carter's welfare initiative, HEW and the Department of Labor (DOL) collaborated on a proposal to combine a federal jobs program for the able-bodied, with a modest guaranteed income for the nonworking poor. In an effort to make work more attractive than welfare and to keep subsidized jobs to a minimum, HEW and the DOL proposed more than tripling the size of the EITC for workers in unsubsidized jobs. The internal discussions over an expanded EITC provide insights into how deeply the pro-work, pro-growth, low-cost welfare reform consensus influenced policy alternatives at the end of the 1970s.

Bureaucratic Infighting and Economic Research

Carter's Program for Better Jobs and Income took shape on two separate tracks. The DOL and HEW agreed that the plan should differentiate between those expected to work and those not expected to work. However, the two departments differed in how they extended coverage to these groups. HEW advocated comprehensive cash grants, a scheme that most politicians considered a poor alternative to existing welfare programs but one that many academics and policy analysts still supported. The DOL, on the other hand, believed that only those not expected to work should receive cash subsidies. For those expected to work, the DOL advocated expanding federal training programs and liberalizing the EITC. Its recommendations followed the assumption that individuals should "turn first to . . . employment and training or the tax system for support."[47]

The two departments differed not just philosophically but also analytically. For several years, HEW had employed various microsimulation models, such as MATH (microanalysis of transfer to households) and TRIM (transfer income model), to test the impact of income maintenance reforms on the federal budget and poverty populations (Kraemer et al. 1987). Although the DOL did not possess MATH or TRIM, several economists in the Office of the Assistant Secretary for Policy and Evaluation Research were familiar with the modeling techniques. Despite their effectiveness in simulating income transfer programs, neither MATH nor TRIM could simulate the pure-cash approach of HEW or the pure-jobs approach of the DOL. Analysts had to design new models. Rather than cooperate in this endeavor, however, the two agencies created their own models. HEW developed a variant of TRIM, which it named KGB for its designers, Rick Kasten, David Greenberg, and Dave Betson. Meanwhile, the DOL settled on a variation of MATH called JOBS, which simulated a service employment program.

The differences in modeling exacerbated differences in agency ideology. As one observer explained, "'Counter-modeling' by DOL and HEW analysts . . . seemed to fuel agency rivalries and competitiveness" (Kraemer et al. 1987, 130). HEW's model generated numbers that suggested a jobs program would cost substantially more than a cash-assistance program. Alternatively, the DOL's model forecasted that its jobs and training strategy not only would cost less than the HEW's cash approach, but would stand a better chance of reducing the welfare rolls.

Politics and the EITC, Part 1

Presented with two distinct welfare reform visions, as well as conflicting micro-simulation data, President Carter and his Domestic Policy Staff (DPS) combined the HEW and DOL proposals. The administration's initiative would include both a jobs and a cash component, Carter told the nation on May 2, 1977.[48] He would unveil a more detailed plan in August. That left him three months to produce a bill he could send to Congress. The presence of a deadline, and the political necessity to present a united front, forced HEW and the DOL to put aside their differences. The two agencies accepted the need to cooperate and even agreed to use the same simulation model (KGB).

The détente between HEW and the DOL reflected an awareness of politics. So, too, did the decision to recommend an expanded EITC. Recall that opponents of Nixon's FAP objected to the number of recipients the plan added to the welfare rolls, its insufficient work requirements, its implicit work disincentives, and its cost. The DOL argued that a more liberalized EITC would correct similar deficiencies in the HEW proposal and increase the likelihood that Congress would pass welfare reform. Unless officials wanted the Program for Better Jobs and Income to join the Family Assistance Plan in the dustbin of failed welfare proposals, they should avoid guaranteed annual incomes and negative income taxation.

Under these assumptions, HEW's cash subsidy promised failure. Tom Joe, a widely respected policy consultant, called the HEW plan "a thinly disguised comprehensive negative income tax system." Likewise, Jodie Allen, the DOL's deputy assistant secretary for policy evaluation and research, observed that the proposal amounted to "a high guarantee, high tax rate universal NIT in disguise" (quoted in Lynn and Whitman 1981, 153, 154). Such an arrangement, Carter's DPS observed, would mobilize the opposition immediately. Both Russell Long and House Ways and Means chair Al Ullman could be expected to oppose "the large numbers of persons added to the welfare rolls."[49] They would also object to the high cumulative marginal tax rates created by HEW's negative-income-tax plan. Moreover, Congress would reject the program's cost. An expanded EITC, officials suggested, suffered from none of these liabilities.

Theoretically, the EITC could reduce the welfare rolls. In a July 1977 letter to White House official Stuart Eizenstat, Tom Joe suggested that "by expanding the EITC as a major mechanism for supplementing the income of the working poor, the desired distribution of benefits could be obtained without this rapid expansion of the welfare caseload."[50] Eizenstat, in turn, told President Carter that the EITC could "provide all or most assistance to a significant number of families through a tax credit rather than through the cash assistance system."[51] Administration analysts also argued that by reducing cumulative marginal tax rates, the EITC could "alleviate the disincentives to work for poor families."[52] The phase-in range of the program reduced marginal tax rates and provided positive work incentives. Unlike HEW's negative income tax, moreover, the EITC's maximum benefit went to low-income working taxpayers. The phase-out range of the credit initially presented officials with problems, however. Just as the phase-in reduced cumulative marginal tax rates, the phase-out increased them.[53] HEW suggested eliminating the EITC and replacing it with a work-expense deduction. For their part, the DOL suggested the phase-out could begin at the welfare break-even point (the point at which welfare benefits become zero), reducing additional work disincentives for welfare recipients (Lynn and Whitman 1981, 187). Alternatively, the EITC could phase in up to the tax entry point (the point at which taxpayers enter the positive tax system) and phase down at a low rate (10 percent in most proposals). Structurally, this latter option pulled middle-income families into the program, making it appear to be "welfare for the middle class." The DOL did not seem to consider this a political liability, except for its effect on cost (Lynn and Whitman 1981, 221, 201–26).

In the frenetic three months between May and August 1977, an expanded EITC garnered crucial support. Although the administration possessed only preliminary data from its simulation models (and not actual microdata), it believed the EITC reduced the number of people on welfare while at the same time increasing incentives to work. As testament to the triumphant effort to liberalize the EITC, the Treasury Department, the Council of Economic Advisers, HEW, the DOL, and DPS all recommended expanding the program on July 31, 1977—only seven days before the president unveiled his welfare initiative to the American people.

POLITICS AND THE EITC, PART 2

Administration officials were confident in the proposal's political attractiveness. Tom Joe affirmed that the EITC would "improve the legislative feasibility of the plan by using a tax rather than a welfare mechanism."[54] It rewarded work, not dependency. It was not "welfare," observed the DPS, but rather "closely related to the 'Workfare' proposal which Russell Long advanced in 1972."[55] It would assist the working poor "without labeling them as welfare recipients."[56] An expanded EITC, moreover, could alleviate other deficiencies in the tax transfer system. It helped the poor without "requiring that they undergo a means test," for instance, and it provided aid "in a form relatively less stigmatizing" than traditional public assistance programs.[57] Although an expanded EITC phased out at higher income levels, Carter officials insisted that the credit was hardly "middle-income tax relief."[58] They argued that it removed individuals from the welfare rolls while keeping would-be welfare claimants in the paid workforce. To its supporters, an expanded EITC was a reward for "playing by the rules" and choosing self-reliance over dependency. In addition, a portion of the EITC could be scored in the budget as a loss in tax receipts (as opposed to revenue outlays), thus making Carter's welfare proposal appear less costly.[59]

Carter's welfare bill, unveiled on August 7, did not liberalize the EITC as much as some participants had hoped. It contained lower phase-in and phase-out rates than those agreed upon by officials as late as July 25. Flattening the rates lowered benefit levels and provided less relief to low-income taxpayers and more to middle-income families. According to a staff member of HEW's Income Security Policy division, the last-minute changes to the EITC "had all the disadvantages of the large-scale EITC [cost] and really none of its advantages [antipoverty effectiveness]" (quoted in Lynn and Whitman 1981, 221). Joe expressed his "disappoint[ment] that attention was not devoted to more creative use of the EITC."[60] He suggested that before the White House present the Program for Better Jobs and Income to Congress, it explore "EITC alternatives that could more completely accomplish the goals of welfare as well as tax reform."[61]

The administration did not heed Joe's advice, but its welfare proposal was well received, nonetheless. Russell Long praised its "laudable objectives," while Daniel Patrick Moynihan (by this time a U.S. senator from New York) declared it "the most important piece of social legislation since the New Deal."[62] Media coverage was equally positive. The *New York Times* wrote, "Mr. Carter's plan . . . turns out to be bold, intelligent, and humane," and the *Washington Post* predicted that "this time around there is a better chance that a decent version of welfare reform will be enacted" (quoted in Lynn and Whitman 1981, 229).

The *Post's* forecast proved premature. Interest groups lined up to oppose the Program for Better Jobs and Income. Conservatives considered the plan profligate, while liberals thought it penurious. It did not contain a strict work requirement, it contained too strict a work requirement. The National Welfare Rights Organization was at it again, too, labeling the Carter bill "JIP," an acronym suggestive of Nixon's FAP.

Hostility to Carter's plan did not simply represent a replay of resistance to Nixon's welfare proposal, however. Unemployment and inflation in the late 1970s posed a dual threat. Economic uncertainty fueled the pervasive sentiment that welfare reform must reward work, stimulate economic growth, and keep costs to a minimum. Equally important, the "datawars" between competing executive agencies and the legislative branch introduced a pall of confusion and deception to the reform process (Kraemer et al. 1987). The Carter administration originally estimated that its bill would cost $2.8 billion. The Congressional Budget Office, however, using the same KGB model as that used by HEW and the DOL, pegged the figure at $14 billion, five times the administration's initial estimate.[63] The conflicting estimates gave the impression that the administration "had intentionally placed a deceptively low price tag" on the Program for Better Jobs and Income (Lynn and Whitman 1987, 238).[64] To make matters worse, the administration released new estimates, claiming that its program would cost $8.8 billion, not $2.8 billion. The Congressional Budget Office released new forecasts, as well: $17.4 billion. In the end, the opposition of interest groups, the high costs of welfare reform, persistent stagflation, and the political suspicion surrounding Carter's proposal killed the bill.

In March 1978, Carter dropped the welfare proposal from his agenda. However, the end of comprehensive welfare reform in 1978 signaled a beginning for the EITC. Opponents of the bill rarely attacked the EITC's proposed liberalization. In fact, most observers praised it as positive antipoverty reform directed at the "deserving" poor. After Carter abandoned the Program for Better Jobs and Income, a number of members of Congress introduced welfare reform bills, each of which included an expanded EITC.[65] None of the bills became law, but Congress enlarged the EITC in 1978, making it one of only three welfare-related provisions passed that year.[66] Recall, too, that the Revenue Act of 1978 raised the maximum credit to $500, allowed for an advance-payment option, and made the credit a permanent section of the tax code. And in 1979, Carter included an expanded EITC as part of his Work and Training Opportunities Act (Lynn and Whitman 1981, 252).[67] Indeed, by the end of the 1970s, the EITC had become "everybody's favorite program" (Lynn and Whitman 1981, 247).

Surviving Welfare Retrenchment

For six years, Congress made only minimal changes to the EITC. The Technical Corrections Act of 1979 addressed the EITC's interaction with federal welfare programs. It required that both the advance and lump-sum payments be treated as earned income for individuals who also received AFDC or Supplemental Security Income Benefits. The Omnibus Budget Reconciliation Act of 1981 (OBRA 81) preserved this change but required welfare agencies to assume that individuals eligible for both AFDC and the EITC received their EITC benefits through the advance-payment option. This stipulation had the effect of reducing an individual's AFDC monthly payment by the amount of the assumed EITC benefit.[68] The Deficit Reduction Act of 1984 reversed this provision, allowing states to count the EITC when calculating AFDC benefits only when they could verify that individuals actually received the EITC payment.[69] The 1984 act also raised the maximum benefit to $550, the length of the plateau range by $500, and the end of the phase-out to $11,000 (see the appendix to this chapter). Despite these changes, inflation continued to erode the real value of the EITC.

Congress's alterations to the EITC might appear minor. In the context of general welfare retrenchment during the late 1970s and early 1980s, however, the changes loom large. Evidence of an expanding attack on the welfare state abounded (Piven and Cloward 1982; Champagne and Harpham 1984; Block 1987). President Carter lost interest in an expensive substitute for the tax transfer system, and the crusade for comprehensive income maintenance was forgotten. In its place emerged an economical welfare initiative for 1979.[70] Whereas Carter had stemmed social welfare spending, President Ronald Reagan cut it. The Omnibus Budget and Reconciliation Act of 1981 slashed federal and state welfare expenditures by $4 billion and in the process cut AFDC funding by 17.4 percent (Patterson 1994, 212–13). It eliminated the earnings-disregard formula for AFDC, the so-called "30 and 1/3" rule. And it reduced the value of allowable monthly deductions for work-related expenses. These and other features of OBRA 81 had the effect of removing more than four hundred thousand families from the welfare rolls and increasing the nation's poverty rate by 2 percentage points (Patterson 1994, 213).

The EITC, however, survived this retrenchment. As other programs fell victim to the budgetary knife, the EITC escaped relatively unscathed. Legislators and analysts alike viewed the program as a viable alternative to conventional social welfare services. While they worked to maintain the EITC's integrity, they also devised plans for a substantial expansion of the credit, an expansion that produced a mature antipoverty program.

MATURITY OR TRANSFORMATION?

The Tax Reform Act of 1986 initiated this maturation process. Between 1975 and 1984, the EITC's maximum credit had fallen by 35 percent in real terms. The 1986 tax bill offset this erosion and raised the maximum benefit to $1,174, slightly more than the 1975 level of $1,165 (1996 dollars).[71] It also increased the point at which the credit phased out, to $21,287 (slightly less than the 1975, inflation-adjusted, $23,301 break-even point). Moreover, the Tax Reform Act of 1986 guaranteed the future integrity of the EITC by indexing it for inflation. Reminiscent of the spirit that imbued the original credit, the 1986 changes to the EITC assured that "low-income citizens [were] no longer taxed into poverty" (Senator Spark Matsunaga [Dem.-Hawaii], quoted in Storey 1996, 7). The 1986 law reaffirmed the program's mandate as a tax offset for low-income families and upheld Senator Long's 1972 desire to "prevent the taxing of people onto the welfare rolls."

The 1986 alterations to the EITC sprang from efforts on behalf of the Treasury Department and elsewhere to remove working poor families from the income tax rolls (Conlan, Wrightson, and Beam 1988; Steuerle 1992). In its 1984 *Report on Fundamental Tax Simplification and Reform* (Treasury I), the Treasury Department noted that inflation had eroded the real value of the "tax-free amount," the point at which tax is first paid (U.S. Department of the Treasury 1984, 1: 5). Although the overall burden of federal taxes had risen only slightly since 1950 (from 17.3 percent of GNP in 1950 to 18.7 percent in 1983), the poor experienced disproportionately higher tax burdens. As corporate income taxes fell (a trend that accelerated in the early 1980s), social security taxes rose sharply. The combined employee and employer payroll tax increased from 3 percent in 1950 to 14 percent by 1984 (Pechman 1987, 318). Rising payroll taxes shifted the tax burden "toward the poor—particularly the working poor" (Blank and Blinder 1986, 198).

In addition to lower tax-free thresholds and rising payroll taxes, the poor faced deteriorating wages. Beginning in the early 1970s, real earnings reversed their post–World War II upward trend. As the economy worsened, earnings inequality accelerated, creating a "hollowed out" earnings distribution that produced large percentages of workers at the top and bottom of the distribution and smaller percentages in the middle (Levy and Murnane 1992, 1371). The value of the minimum wage, moreover, deteriorated dramatically between 1981 and 1986, falling in real value from $4.50 to $3.35 an hour (1986 dollars). During the 1970s a full-year, full-time minimum-wage job kept a family of three above the poverty line. By 1986, the minimum wage had fallen short of this plateau by 20 percent (Ellwood 1988, 110).

Policymakers endeavored to curb these disturbing trends. Wage subsidies, increases in the minimum wage, and child-care tax credits or child allowances all loomed large on the policy agenda. Ultimately, politicians and experts abandoned these alternatives. Wage subsidies faced administrative difficulties, while the minimum wage poorly targeted low-income groups and contained potentially adverse labor demand effects. Child-care tax credits faced similar targeting problems, and child allowances resembled too closely the kind of guaranteed-income arrangements that Congress had rejected in both 1971 (Nixon's Family Assistance Plan) and 1978 (Carter's Program for Better Jobs and Income). Officials sought alternative ways to address deteriorating wages and income inequality.

Both the Treasury Department and Congress chose the EITC. An expanded EITC could raise the income tax threshold to approximately the poverty level. In conjunction with a larger personal exemption, the EITC could provide greater equity and "fairness for families" (U.S. Department of the Treasury 1984, 1:37, 66–67; 2:15–16). An indexed EITC could address the erosion of low-income wages as well as rising income inequality. By the mid-1980s, and with the help of the Treasury, Congress had identified the tax system as both the problem and the solution to rising rates of inequality. From 1984 to 1986, congressional committees examined the tax treatment of families, in particular, the increased tax burdens of poor families (U.S. House 1984, 1985a, 1985b, 1985c, 1985d, 1986; U.S. Senate 1985). Politicians introduced bills designed to alleviate taxes on low-income taxpayers.[72] Most of these plans recognized the antipoverty effectiveness of the EITC, while many of them called for significant increases in the credit.[73] By the time President Reagan unveiled his second major tax bill in May 1985, the congressional majority believed that poor Americans should be freed from burdensome tax obligations. It also named the EITC as the primary vehicle of this reform. The Tax Reform Act of 1986 removed more than 6 million impoverished Americans from the income tax rolls by raising the standard deduction and personal exemption and liberalizing the EITC (Conlan, Wrightson, and Beam 1988, 3).

The success of the 1986 tax law, particularly its expansion of the EITC, complemented a political and professional consensus surrounding tax reform as well as welfare reform. By the early 1980s, this political and professional issue network gathered together liberals such as Senator Bill Bradley (Dem.-N.J.) and "populist conservatives" such as Representative Jack Kemp (Rep.-N.Y.).[74] The idea of reducing income tax burdens on the poor resonated with liberals who were drawn to the idea of tax fairness. An enlarged EITC, by supplementing the incomes of the working poor, addressed deteriorating wages and rising income inequality. It also made the tax system more progressive, balancing out the recent increases in social security and excise taxes. Conservatives, too, felt the need to remedy unfair tax burdens. Endorsing a larger EITC ameliorated conservative responsibility for the growing disparity between rich and poor, which the

Reagan administration accelerated with its early tax and social policy changes.[75] Along with increases in the standard deduction and personal exemption, a liberalized EITC also benefited middle-class families. Finally, the EITC assuaged anxiety over welfare dependency by theoretically keeping would-be welfare recipients off the welfare rolls and in the workforce.

The EITC enjoyed bipartisan support for another reason: it elided the pitfalls of budget politics. Increased defense spending in the 1980s, along with supply-side tax changes, created huge federal deficits. Shortly after passing the Economic Recovery Tax Act of 1981, Congress began trying to undue its harm.[76] The Tax Equity and Fiscal Responsibility Act of 1982 and the Deficit Reduction Act of 1984 raised tax revenues. In 1985, the Gramm-Rudman Act mandated automatic spending cuts if budget targets were not met beginning in 1991. By controlling direct expenditures, Gramm-Rudman and other deficit reduction acts increased pressure on legislators to channel spending programs through the tax system.[77] The EITC complemented these new budget rules perfectly. Its cost could be scored in both the tax expenditure and direct expenditure budgets. During the political odyssey of the 1986 Tax Reform Act, the EITC also used budget politics to its advantage by improving the bill's distributional neutrality. It offset tax preferences for high-income taxpayers and corporations and balanced out the all-important distribution tables.

"IT'S JUST WELFARE, IT'S A SUBSIDY"

While alterations to the EITC in 1986 reduced taxes for low-income families, changes made in the early 1990s signaled to some observers that the program was headed in the direction of welfare. The 1990 and 1993 Omnibus Budget Reconciliation Acts expanded the EITC's maximum benefit and phase-out rates, and the 1993 law also raised the break-even point. The 1990 bill distinguished for the first time between families with one and two or more qualifying children, and the 1993 law extended the credit to childless low-income workers. Critics considered the benefit levels overly generous, the phase-out an implicit work disincentive, and the higher break-even point a form of welfare for the middle class. Under the changes produced by the 1990 and 1993 bills, the cost of the EITC almost tripled, jumping from $7.5 billion in 1990 to $21.1 billion in 1994 (current dollars) (U.S. House 1999, 872). When examined over a longer period, the expansion appeared more dramatic. From 1986 to 1996, EITC expenditures grew by 1,191 percent (computed from U.S. House 1999, 872). The credit's break-even point, again in current dollars, increased from $11,000 in 1986 to $28,495 by 1996; the break-even point had risen from 37 percent of median family income to 67 percent (U.S. Bureau of the Census 2000). Although these changes appeared less dramatic when adjusted for inflation, the EITC's critics focused on its nominal growth. The program, once a Washington darling, now represented "too much of a good thing."[78]

The EITC had not only grown too big and too fast; it also had begun to look less like tax policy and more like welfare policy. Generous benefits extended the program well beyond its mandate. Only a fraction of EITC benefits, opponents argued, offset income and self-employment taxes, while the rest amounted to direct outlays ("Senate Continues Budget Debate" 1995; Kosters 1993b). Senator Don Nickles (Rep.-Okla.) insisted that "in almost 99-plus percent of the cases, it is a check paid as a refund to people in lump sum payment" ("Senate Continues Budget Debate" 1995). The federal government, it seemed, was back in the business of "taxing the many on behalf of the few." As Bill Archer (Rep.-Tex.) complained, "Is it fair to ask middle-income taxpayers to give additional public assistance to those who pay little or no taxes?" (U.S. House 1997a).

Noncompliance

The charges against the EITC gained credence when other negative side effects of the program surfaced. Particularly damaging were studies released by the IRS, which reported unusually high error rates for the EITC. Critics of the program interpreted these findings to mean that a large proportion of EITC beneficiaries were defrauders and cheats. The EITC, they concluded, amounted to "a tax credit for crooks" (Aley 1993, 24).

The first episode in the EITC compliance story played out in 1990. In the spring, both the House and Senate passed child-care bills that included an expanded EITC. In the weeks before the Conference Committee met, Congress debated whether the IRS could handle an enlarged, more complex EITC. It was particularly concerned about compliance rates. The best available compliance data, the IRS's Taxpayer Compliance Measurement Program (TCMP) study, revealed that in tax year 1985, 46 percent of taxpayers who claimed the EITC may not have been entitled to the benefit amount received; and the overclaim rate (the dollar amount claimed in error divided by the total dollar amount claimed) was 39.1 percent (Scholz 1994, 69, table 2). The Treasury responded with a simplification package designed to increase compliance rates by clarifying EITC eligibility rules and enhancing IRS verification of claims (Holtzblatt 1991). Congress included this proposal in the 1990 Omnibus Budget Reconciliation Act, a law that significantly expanded the EITC.

The 1988 Taxpayer Compliance Measurement Program study, released in 1992, indicated a drop in the overclaim rate, from 39.1 percent to 35.4 percent (Scholz 1994, 69, table 2). Congress still considered the error rates too high, however, and wondered if noncompliance would rise in response to increased benefit levels set in 1990 and 1993. Some analysts cautioned that EITC error rates might reach 50 percent (Sparrow 1993), while others argued that the program facilitated a "superterranean economy" by encouraging taxpayers to overstate their earnings (Steuerle 1991, 1993, 1995b).[79]

Congress mobilized its forces to investigate the EITC's compliance problems. Both houses conducted numerous hearings on the EITC between 1993 and 1997.[80] In 1994, Senator William Roth (Rep.-Del.) asked the General Accounting Office to investigate the noncompliance charges and determine what the IRS was doing to reduce the error rates (Roth 1994b). Legislators considered suggestions designed to reform, simplify, and even repeal the credit (Roth 1994a; Petri 1994, 1996; Yin 1995).[81] No stone was left unturned in the effort to locate perpetrators of EITC fraud. Congress went after EITC claimants, the IRS, the Treasury Department, and even health insurance agents who sold policies to low-income taxpayers eligible to claim the health insurance component of the EITC.[82] Critics tied the EITC to a host of national problems, including reduced economic growth, the growing tax gap (the yearly difference between federal income taxes owed and federal income taxes collected), and rising taxes for the middle class (Godfrey 1995b; U.S. House 1997a, 1997c; GAO 1994).

Some critics believed the IRS so incapable of administering the EITC that the program might be better run through welfare offices.[83] They cited the substantially lower error rates in the AFDC and food stamp programs: 6.1 percent for AFDC in 1994, and 7.3 percent for food stamps in 1995 (McCubbin 1999, 56; also see chapter 6, this volume). Meanwhile, the EITC overclaim rate hovered well above 20 percent. Not only were welfare offices more efficient than the IRS, EITC critics argued, but caseworkers could also more easily evaluate qualifying characteristics for EITC eligibles.

Labor Supply Effects

In addition to compliance and administrative problems, the EITC's parameters implied work disincentives. When combined with other taxes and transfer phaseouts, the EITC benefit reduction rate resulted in marginal tax rates that could exceed 50 percent (Browning 1995; Steuerle 1995a, 1995c; National Center for Policy Analysis 1995). Analysts warned that the EITC could push marginal tax rates for the tax and transfer system to 65 percent for families with two or more children and 60 percent for families with one child (Browning 1995). Researchers attempted to determine the extent to which these tax rates reduced work effort.

Economic theory predicts that the EITC influences some individuals to enter the labor force and some secondary workers to leave the labor force. For individuals already in the labor force, the theory predicts an ambiguous (positive substitution, negative income) effect in the phase-in range of the credit, a negative (no substitution, negative income) effect in the plateau, and a negative (negative substitution and negative income) effect in the phase-out. Researchers attempted to measure the cumulative effects of the EITC based on how many individuals fell into each range of the credit and how individuals responded to different incomes. By examining tax data, researchers determined the number of EITC recipients in each group: roughly 15 percent in the phase-in range, 25 percent in the plateau, and 60 percent in the phase-out (Hoffman and Seidman 1990, 88; Scholz 1994, 78). Several analysts—basing their conclusions on the high number of taxpayers in the phase-out and on predicted income and substitution effects estimated by other researchers, and without considering changes in labor force participation—concluded that the EITC created aggregate work disincentives (Kosters 1993a, 1993b; Browning 1995). Studies that examined microdata predicted a less severe effect on the number of hours worked by persons already in the labor force (Hoffman and Seidman 1990; GAO 1993; Holtzblatt, McCubbin, and Gillette 1994), while some predicted that the EITC might have "a beneficial effect on labor supply" (Dickert, Houser, and Scholz 1994, 622). Until very recently, however, the evidence remained mixed. Through the mid-1990s, legislators seemed more influenced by the apocalyptic warnings that highlighted the EITC's potentially significant work disincentives.

Although much of the case against the EITC was constructed without microdata, politicians made it part of their rhetorical attack against the EITC. Out of control growth, error rates, and work disincentives, according to critics, plagued the program. With such features, how could the EITC be considered tax policy and not welfare policy? Indeed, as Senator Phil Gramm (Rep.-Tex.) bluntly stated in 1995, "It's just welfare, it's a subsidy."[84]

Counterattack

The EITC's supporters recognized the danger in this charge and defended the credit. They argued that by expanding, the EITC was "doing exactly what Congress intended it to do" (U.S. Senate 1997). To the accusation that the EITC was "out of control," the program's advocates cried foul play. Senator John Rockefeller (Dem.-W.V.) called such claims "totally misleading," while Senator Ted Kennedy (Dem.-Mass.) considered the accusations not only untrue but also unmindful of the EITC's growth relative to inflation.[85] In relation to pre-1990 law, the 1990 and 1993 expansions did not increase eligibility up the income scale for families with one child; for families with two or more children, the income cutoff increased only slightly ($3,700, in 1999 dollars) relative to the 1986 tax law.[86] Supporters emphasized that in 1990 and 1993, Congress altered the credit to cover increased payroll taxes (which had jumped 25 percent from 1980 to 1990), real reductions in the minimum wage, higher excise taxes (particularly the gas tax), and certain "deficit reduction provisions" (Storey 1996, 11).

The EITC had expanded, moreover, in response to bipartisan efforts. George Bush initiated the 1990 expansion, while Bill Clinton, who considered a larger EITC the cornerstone of his first-term pledge to "make work pay," endorsed the 1993 expansion.[87] "We wanted the EITC to grow," recalled Rockefeller, "because of its fundamental role in helping parents who are teetering on the economic edge to be able to choose work over welfare, independence over dependence, dignity over the indignities of the welfare system" (U.S. Senate 1997, 7). Far from growing beyond its mandate, the EITC respected the original intent of the credit, which the Senate Finance Committee in 1975 said would provide "an added bonus or incentive for low-income people to work" and an inducement for "families receiving Federal assistance to support themselves" (U.S. Senate 1975, 11).

By 1996, the EITC's responsibilities had changed in one important respect: it was all that kept millions of individuals out of poverty. Beginning in the late 1980s, the nation's social safety net—as it was traditionally conceived—started to shrink. Public assistance programs gave way to work-oriented programs. States received "waivers" of federal welfare rules, allowing them to experiment with alternative ways of administering welfare services. States responded by imposing strict requirements on welfare recipients in an effort to reduce caseloads. In 1996, the Personal Responsibility and Work Opportunity Reconciliation Act replaced AFDC with a new program, Temporary Assistance for Needy Families, which eliminated open-ended federal matching grants in favor of block grants, thereby devolving welfare responsibility still further to the state level. In exchange for the block grants, the new welfare program required that claimants work (or that states reduce welfare caseloads) and that states impose a five-year lifetime limit on receipt of benefits. It also allowed states to set shorter time limits and add other requirements. The combination of the 1996 welfare reform act and the new welfare program it instituted dramatically decreased welfare caseloads. In addition to the unusually strong economic expansion of the late 1990s, time limits, work requirements, reduced benefits, and administrative actions reduced caseloads by as much as 80 percent in some states. While federal and state welfare programs pushed one-time (and would-be) welfare claimants toward work, the EITC eased the transition. It provided individuals entering the labor force an earnings subsidy as well as an incentive to remain employed.[88] The EITC had not grown beyond its mandate; it had merely assumed new responsibilities thrust upon it by the work-oriented welfare reform consensus. The program was working as planned.

Neither was the credit a welfare subsidy. The assistant Treasury secretary for tax policy, Leslie B. Samuels, testified in 1995 that the EITC should still be considered a tax refund. When one accounted for payroll taxes, he revealed, 78 percent of the EITC offset tax obligations, while only 22 percent of benefits exceeded total tax liabilities (Samuels 1995). Earlier estimates that ignored payroll tax burdens misrepresented the true nature of the EITC. The credit offset the social security tax and provided an added bonus for low-income families to choose work over welfare. Moreover, it accrued primarily to those working families most in need of assistance, those with incomes between 50 and 150 percent of the poverty line (Liebman 1998, 7).

The "Real" Compliance Rates

It was not enough to differentiate the EITC from welfare. If the program were to survive, researchers would have to address its high error rates. It was difficult to deny that the program provided incentives for individuals in the phase-in range to overreport income and for those in the phase-out range to underreport income. So, too, did it include incentives to overclaim dependents. These incentives could increase noncompliance and raise administrative costs.

Between 1994 and 1995 the IRS conducted two studies that measured the rate of EITC noncompliance.[89] The first study included EITC claims filed electronically in January 1994 for tax year 1993. The second study included EITC claims filed both electronically and on paper and received by the IRS through April 21, 1995, for tax year 1994. The tax year 1993 study found an overclaim rate of 26.1 percent (IRS 1995b). It also estimated that IRS enforcement techniques (matching returns to information reports, for example) and legislative and administrative changes effective for the 1995 filing season would have further reduced the overclaim rate to 19.1 percent (IRS 1995b). The study of tax year 1994 reached similar conclusions (IRS 1997). It estimated a 25.8 percent overclaim rate and indicated that enforcement activities conducted during the 1995 filing season would have reduced the overclaim rate to 23.5 percent. Moreover, subsequent legislation and administrative actions that took effect during the 1997 filing season (especially the authority, granted in 1996, to treat missing and invalid social security numbers as math errors) would have reduced the error rate to 20.7 percent.

Additionally, the IRS studies showed that some EITC eligibles failed to claim the full amount to which they were entitled. This amount totaled $293 million, or 1.7 percent of the total EITC claimed for the 1995 filing period. Other studies suggested that nonparticipants (eligibles who do not claim the credit) constituted an even larger source of underclaimed benefits. Between 13.6 and 19.5 percent of filers eligible for the EITC did not receive the credit for tax year 1990 (Scholz 1994). The failure to account for nonparticipation, researchers argued, made it impossible for the IRS to measure the amount of overpayments net of the amount not paid, and could overstate the importance of the EITC compliance problem. Even without these additional adjustments, the evidence suggested that EITC overclaim rates declined relative to the 1980s and that efforts to reduce noncompliance were succeeding.

The legislature, the executive branch, and the IRS attacked noncompliance from every angle. In 1990, the Treasury Department determined a relationship between EITC overclaims and errors in filing status and dependency claims. The Treasury presented a proposal to Congress (which it subsequently enacted) that simplified the qualifying-child criteria and filing status and made it easier for the IRS to verify EITC eligibility based on information reporting (Holtzblatt 1991). The IRS was given the authority to match names and taxpayer identification numbers on tax returns to individual social security numbers, including those of qualifying children under the age of one. Moreover, the 1996 welfare reform act allowed the IRS to deny the EITC to undocumented workers. It also allowed the IRS to reject electronic returns with missing, invalid, or duplicated social security numbers and to delay refunds for paper returns with similar problems until it could further investigate the cases.

Officials scrutinized electronic filing of the EITC, using field personnel to check electronic return originators. The IRS discovered that a significant number of these returns included falsified EITC claims (Richardson 1994). Based on these findings, the IRS stopped issuing the direct deposit indicator, which showed whether a taxpayer's refund could be used to offset other liabilities (in which case the taxpayer could be issued a refund anticipation loan). Lenders had relied on the direct deposit indicator to screen loan applicants who used the expected tax refund as collateral on short-term debt (Godfrey 1994).

By 1998, the IRS could also levy penalties against individuals who abused the EITC. The Taxpayer Relief Act of 1997 contained provisions that disqualified abusive filers for various lengths of time depending on the infraction. The bill also granted the IRS authority to recover excess refund payments or unpaid taxes by garnishing a percentage of unemployment and means-tested benefits. In addition, it provided the IRS two new data sources (the Federal Case Registry of Child Support Orders and data culled by the Social Security Administration) that will aid in assessing the accuracy of future EITC claims.[90]

The IRS also used outreach programs to combat error rates. It established partnerships with state and local government agencies, national and local community service groups, and social welfare, religious, professional, business, labor, and ethnic organizations. It produced instructional workbooks, nationwide tax forums, and explanatory videos to assist in filing for the credit (IRS 1994a, 1994b, 1994c, 1995a, 1996). The IRS also provided training for volunteers to help EITC-eligible taxpayers. It distributed promotional information in both English and Spanish and worked with local school systems to increase awareness among students' families (Taxpayer Advocate 1997).

At the behest of the Clinton administration, and through the Balanced Budget Act of 1997, the IRS received special discretionary appropriations for fiscal years 1997 through 2002. In both 1998 and 1999, the funds ($138 million and $143 million, respectively) went toward EITC compliance activities. The additional funding yielded a significant return. In 1998, the IRS spent $101 million adjusting EITC math errors and auditing and conducting criminal investigations related to EITC claims (IRS 1999). These activities, the IRS reported in 1999, prevented or recovered $977 million in EITC overpayments (McCubbin 1999, 61; see chapter 6 of this volume).

In addition to reducing EITC noncompliance, the IRS also kept administrative costs below those of other programs. Recall that some individuals suggested the IRS should transfer administrative oversight of the EITC to welfare offices. Although the EITC experienced higher error rates than other programs, the General Accounting Office has estimated that EITC administrative costs equal only 1 percent of payments (GAO 1995, 1997). Comparatively, administrative costs for AFDC equaled 16 percent of total claims for fiscal year 1995, and for food stamps, 15.4 percent of total claims (McCubbin 1999, 77; see chapter 6 of this volume). It is impossible to determine an optimal administrative cost, but at least by comparison, the EITC appears an administratively efficient tax transfer program.

The "Real" Labor Supply Effects

While efforts to reduce EITC error rates and instill confidence in the IRS's administrative capabilities progressed, new studies revealed that the program's work disincentive effects were not as severe as its critics insisted. Early research had concluded that with a majority of recipients in the phase-out range, the EITC reduced cumulative hours worked for low-income individuals (Kosters

1993a, 1993b; Browning 1995). New research using tax-return microdata reached different conclusions. Although the majority of EITC eligibles reside in the phase-out range and experience marginal tax rates that can exceed 50 percent, recent studies suggest that the phase-out has little or no impact on hours worked (Eissa and Liebman 1996; Liebman 1998; Meyer and Rosenbaum 1998).[91] The credit provides unambiguous incentives for single workers to participate in the labor force, moreover, and it produces statistically significant increases in aggregate labor force participation (Scholz 1997; Liebman 1998; Blank, Card, and Robins 1999; chapters 2 and 3, this volume). Also, the EITC only slightly reduces total number of hours worked by individuals already in the labor force (Hoffman and Seidman 1990; GAO 1993; Holtzblatt, McCubbin, and Gillette 1994; Dickert, Houser, and Scholz 1994), and it raises labor force participation rates among single women who might otherwise choose welfare over work (Dickert, Houser, and Scholz 1994; Eissa and Liebman 1996; Liebman 1998; Meyer 1998; Meyer and Rosenbaum 1998; Blank, Card, and Robins 1999). The program raises labor force participation among married men, as well (Eissa and Hoynes 1998). Of course, not all the evidence is positive. Recent analysts have warned that the EITC might reduce cumulative hours worked among married women (Eissa and Hoynes 1998). It is important to qualify this last finding, however, by pointing out that it is sensitive to the selection of instrumental variables.[92]

The preponderance of economic evidence suggests that the EITC constitutes a uniquely effective and viable antipoverty program (CEA 1998; Greenstein and Shapiro 1998; Liebman 1998; Blank, Card, and Robins 1999; CEA 1999). It responds directly to the economic changes of the past few decades, "explicitly supplementing the wages received by low-wage workers" (Blank 1997, 111). It offsets the tax burden, which has fallen increasingly on the working poor, accounting especially for rising excise and payroll taxes. It shrinks the income gap between rich and poor (Greenstein and Shapiro 1998). As reported by the Council of Economic Advisers, the EITC lifted 4.3 million persons out of poverty in 1997, including 2.2 million children under the age of eighteen—more than any other government program (CEA 1999, 114). The EITC has proven such an effective antipoverty program at the federal level that eleven states have enacted their own EITCs.[93] According to recent studies, state-level EITCs produce the same kind of positive benefits as their federal counterpart (Johnson and Lazere 1999; Madden 1999; Rust 1999).

THE INFLUENCE OF ECONOMIC RESEARCH ON TAX-TRANSFER PROGRAMS

With the help of economic research, the intense political debate surrounding the EITC has subsided. Studies on the EITC's labor supply effects, for instance, have helped diffuse criticism and mobilize support for the credit. Economic research has also mitigated concerns regarding EITC compliance. Although error rates remain unsatisfactorily high, the evidence indicates they are dropping. Further enforcement efforts promise to lower the overclaim rate still further.[94] Once the

Omnibus Budget Reconciliation Act of 1993 completely phased in, and as more researchers discussed the EITC as an integral part of a new, work-oriented welfare state, critics stopped calling the credit a welfare program. More generally, economic research has provided an educative function by emphasizing that designing a tax transfer system involves making tough choices between policy outcomes. If officials wish to keep the EITC narrowly targeted, they must accept attendant high marginal tax rates, which in turn will theoretically increase the likelihood that recipients trade benefits for work. Similarly, if policymakers want the tax system to perform social policy functions, they must acknowledge that ease of participation might increase error rates. Indeed, economic research has contributed to a more knowledgeable debate over the tax and transfer system.

The debate itself is far from over, however. Compliance problems and cost remain highly political issues. The EITC poses questions that do not yield to clarification by scientific research alone. The trade-offs in tax transfer programs require political solutions. No matter how many studies analysts produce, no matter how much evidence is amassed, policymakers will continue to debate the EITC's work incentives, its relationship to the private economy, and its cost.

It should come as no surprise that politics influence national social provision. However, exactly when has politics mattered in the development of the tax and transfer system? More important, how and why has politics mattered, particularly in relation to economic analysis? During the past thirty years, economic research has influenced how politicians use tax provisions as substitutes for direct expenditure programs. But to what extent did politics affect, and even compromise, tax policies that functioned as social policy? The balance of this chapter uses the foregoing history of the EITC to analyze the relationships among tax policy, politics, and economic research. It borrows a theoretical framework from political science—the multiple streams model—to clarify how, why, and to what extent economic research, as opposed to political rhetoric, mattered in the creation and development of the EITC. Three separate "streams" constitute the most common articulation of this model: problem recognition (where a sufficient number of individuals identify a "condition" as a "problem"); the development of policy solutions (where a policy community generates solutions for the identified problem); and politics (such as swings in national mood, public opinion, or election results) (Kingdon 1984). As John Kingdon notes, "A problem is recognized, a solution is available, the political climate makes the time right for change, and the constraints do not prohibit action" (Kingdon 1984, 93). Issues rise and fall on the policy agenda in relation to whether or not the streams merge (or "couple") and whether issue advocates ("policy entrepreneurs") take advantage of certain opportunities (or "policy windows") (Kingdon 1984, 129–30 and 173–204).[95]

Swimming Upstream: The Case of the Negative Income Tax

Interpreting how and why the EITC rose on the policy agenda requires understanding the policy alternatives that preceded it. The negative income tax was the intellectual and political antecedent to the EITC. Its short-lived but intense popularity, followed by its sudden departure from atop the policy agenda and then temporary reemergence, helps explain the success of a work-oriented tax credit like the EITC.

In the early 1960s, "poverty" the condition came to be defined as "poverty" the problem. The Johnson administration developed an arsenal of antipoverty proposals, including a negative income tax. By 1966, the Office of Economic Opportunity believed an NIT could help eliminate poverty within a decade. A number of disparate interest groups supported the NIT concept. "It [was] endorsed by the left-leaning Americans for Democratic Action and by the right-leaning Ripon Society, by the National Association of Social Workers . . . and by a committee of business leaders" (Wilcox 1969, 248). It also had the support of experts. In 1968, twelve hundred economists signed a petition encouraging the White House to consider an NIT. Despite these endorsements, the NIT did not rise to the top of the policy agenda, because the president, a critical agenda-setting actor, withheld his support.

Only a year later, Richard Nixon gave the NIT new life. "Welfare dependency" had joined "poverty" as a pressing national problem. Rising welfare rolls indicated that the existing system of social assistance extended the time individuals spent on the public "dole." The Family Assistance Plan, with its NIT and work requirements, promised to eliminate both poverty and welfare dependency. Powerful interest groups supported the concept of an NIT, and experts evaluated various parameters for an NIT program, all while a new president was looking for a ready-made solution to a national "crisis." In the language of political scientists, the policy streams converged, and the NIT percolated to the top of the policy agenda in 1969.

As quickly as the NIT rose, it also fell. After President Nixon proposed the FAP, divergence, rather than convergence, characterized the ensuing political debate. Of the many factors that knocked the NIT from atop the policy agenda, two predominate: the highly publicized congressional debate over "notches" and the perceived obfuscation behind the administration's use of the New Jersey negative-income-tax experiment. In both instances, credible economic voices challenged the NIT plan. Credible countervoices alone, however, cannot remove an issue from the policy agenda (Cook 1990, 408). It can remain on the agenda if its advocates respond adequately. The Nixon administration neither remedied the notch problems in its NIT program nor convinced anyone that it had not compromised the integrity of the New Jersey experiment. Indeed, it was difficult to muster counterevidence for a program that contained fundamental flaws: the administration could not parameterize its NIT in such a way as to contain an adequate income guarantee, maintain all the characteristics of the tax system, and provide work incentives, all at an acceptable cost.

The credible countervoices shook the administration's proposal, but it took additional, "micromediating" factors to knock it from the policy agenda (Cook 1990, 408–9). Interest groups openly criticized the program. Experts, too, withdrew their allegiance.[96] Even the president abandoned his initiative. To make matters worse, results from the Seattle-Denver NIT experiments indicated that low-income husbands and wives, presumably in an effort to receive larger cumulative benefits, were more likely to split up in the presence of an NIT. All of this was reported in the media, which chronicled the FAP's disintegrating support as well as the charges that an NIT amounted to a perverse guaranteed annual income that perpetuated the cycle of welfare dependency and undermined family values. In short, the policy community that had muscled negative income taxation onto the policy agenda cracked; the streams diverged; the policy window closed on the NIT; and negative income taxation fell from the policy agenda.[97]

In the final analysis, the economic research that the administration had hoped would support income supplements helped destroy them. Officials failed to demonstrate to politicians the difficult trade-offs inherent in the design of tax transfer programs. Moreover, by inadequately addressing the notch problems and inappropriately breaking into the New Jersey experiment, the Nixon White House discredited social science inquiry and experimentation. It politicized economic research and, for at least the duration of the FAP debates, blurred the distinction between empirical analysis and theoretical prediction.

Convergent Streams: The Case of the EITC

Although the agenda-setting streams diverged in the early 1970s, they did not fundamentally reconstitute themselves. Welfare dependency remained a national problem. The political environment, too, remained constant; public opinion and elected officials preferred pro-work social programs. The list of policy solutions sounded familiar, as well. None of the ideas captured the attention of Congress, however, and none of the solutions addressed new problems on the policy agenda. Payroll taxes and social security refinancing preoccupied legislators in the early 1970s. As the decade progressed, economic growth and unemployment were added to the list, as was tax reduction. A welfare reform initiative that sufficiently appreciated the problem stream as well as the political stream could jump through the policy window.

In 1975, the EITC emerged from the policy stream as the perfect complement to the other two streams. Its benefits accrued to workers, and it provided incentives for individuals outside the labor force to enter. It offset rising payroll taxes, and it reduced income tax liability for low-income individuals. It was run through the tax system, not welfare offices, and it boasted a modest price tag. Moreover, critical policy entrepreneurs supported the EITC and convinced legislators that it could remedy several prevailing national problems (Michael Stern, Russell Long's key staff member for the EITC, deserves especial comment). They also demonstrated the relative structural simplicity of the EITC; it phased up to a certain income level and phased out at an agreeable point. Its modest size kept it from raising cumulative marginal tax rates too high. The streams converged, and policy entrepreneurs pushed the EITC through the policy window.

For the next several years, a group of policy entrepreneurs nurtured the EITC, while another group fought to replace it. The first policy community envisioned an expanded EITC that provided more substantive economic support to individuals moving from welfare to unsubsidized work. A second policy community de-emphasized work-oriented policies and reincarnated a comprehensive, high-rate NIT. In an effort at compromise, the two policy communities merged their proposals, but with disastrous results. Jimmy Carter's Program for Better Jobs and Income spoke of work incentives, but it also contained a cash subsidy. It was a workfare bill, and at the same time, it was a guaranteed annual income. Moreover, it was confusing. Charles Schultze, chair of Carter's Council of Economic Advisers, acknowledged its complex nature. "The thing got so goddamned complicated," he complained, "that nobody in the world but the three or four people who put it together fully understood it, and I doubt if they did fully" (quoted in Lynn and Whitman 1981, 191).

Economic research might have clarified the policymaking process by attaching numbers to predicted behavioral responses, but it only served to confuse the Carter proposal. Modeling data, for instance, divided the administration in the early planning stages and then later confounded the political process by producing inconsistent cost estimates. Although much of the cost discrepancies were attributable to political disagreements regarding which program savings should be offset against the costs of the Program for Better Jobs and Income,[98] economic analysis, it seemed, not politics, complicated the policy process. Not only did economic data attach an aura of confusion and carelessness to the bill, it also left the impression that the administration was deceptively fiddling with the economics of its initiative. Reminiscent of the FAP, economic research politicized rather than clarified the political discussion. Of course, other factors contributed to the demise of the Program for Better Jobs and Income—divergence of interest groups, poor presidential leadership, a heightened antiwelfare sentiment—but the improvident use of economic data killed the Carter welfare bill.

The EITC remained a viable policy solution despite the defeat of the Program for Better Jobs and Income. Although it had contributed to the proposal's confusion (complicating break-even points, phase-outs, and marginal tax rates), politicians identified the NIT, not the EITC, as the cause of that confusion. Into the 1980s, policy entrepreneurs advocated the EITC as complementary to both the political and problem streams. It provided an incentive for individuals to leave welfare for work, and it satisfied a political conservatism that required pro-work, pro-growth, low-cost social programs. By the mid-1980s, the visible policy participants (the president, members of Congress, and high-level appointees), as well as the hidden policy participants (experts, bureaucrats, and staffers), recognized that the EITC complemented emergent national problems. It could help policymakers address rising tax burdens on working families, for example, and decrease sharpened inequalities between rich and poor. New budget rules, too, worked to the advantage of those desiring an expanded EITC. By 1986, the program enjoyed the support of liberals and conservatives, the president, congressional leaders, disparate political interests, and powerful policy communities.

If that were not enough, the EITC provided the glue that held together one of

President Reagan's most important legislative accomplishments: the 1986 Tax Reform Act. Specifically, the EITC helped policymakers achieve distributional and revenue neutrality in the final bill. As a tax credit for low-income individuals, it offset tax cuts for high-income taxpayers and balanced the incidence of the tax reform package. Also, the EITC's cost could be split between the direct expenditure and tax expenditure budgets. Equally important, policy entrepreneurs kept the EITC simple. They did not confuse the political debate with the program's structural or administrative technicalities but rather referred to it as a tax offset for the working poor. They showed how the credit's expansion, although significant, merely reestablished original benefit levels.

To explain the EITC's expansion in 1986, we need look no further than this conflation of interests and careful lobbying effort. A consensus formed around the EITC. The streams merged, and they remained together. No credible counter-voice challenged the program. Policy communities defended the credit to their constituents. No viable policy alternatives emerged. The credit remained relatively simple for the media to report: it was a tax credit that removed millions of low-income, working Americans from poverty. Thrust onto the national stage, the EITC was transformed from an obscure tax credit to a more visible social instrument with significant antipoverty responsibilities.

Economic Research Helps Save the EITC

For the next several years, the "new" EITC enjoyed bipartisan support. However, the bubble burst in the early 1990s. According to critics, the program suffered from high error rates, significant work disincentives, and skyrocketing costs. The EITC was in serious trouble, but it survived for two reasons: first, it complemented the political stream by providing a coherent, pro-work, pro-growth, low-cost, antipoverty program; second, economic research indicated the extent to which it upheld the principles of the welfare reform consensus.

The Treasury identified causes of taxpayer error and responded with a series of simplification and compliance proposals. They strained resources to improve and update enforcement techniques. They educated taxpayers on how and when to claim the credit. Their administrative efforts, as we have seen, proved successful. Other researchers dispelled rumors that the EITC reduced work effort. They showed that the credit provided unambiguous incentives for single workers to participate in the labor force. It also produced statistically significant increases in aggregate labor force participation. The evidence indicated that the credit raised labor force participation among married men and (more important politically) among single women who might otherwise choose welfare over work.

Collectively, economic research provided a valuable educative function, as well. Economic analysts carefully articulated the policy trade-offs involved in programs like the EITC. They taught legislators about the design and interaction of a comprehensive tax transfer system. They admitted that although it was far from perfect, the EITC represented the best available policy solution (Steuerle

1995b). Most important, it embodied the "make work pay" consensus that had come to dominate social policymaking in the 1990s (Blank, Card, and Robins 1999, 4–5).

CONCLUSION

For much of the EITC's history, political rhetoric, not economic research, dominated the debate over tax transfers. As this chapter has demonstrated, economic analysis helped at least one tax transfer program survive. In the 1990s, it depoliticized what was otherwise a highly political battle over the EITC. It responded quickly to credible countervoices (Taxpayer Compliance Measurement Program data, theoretical labor supply effects, rapid growth) with even more credible empirical research; it explained the complexities of tax transfer policymaking to a nonexpert audience; it generated consensus about the EITC as a policy solution among various policy communities; and it spoke to national problems and the political environment. In a sense, economic analysts finally learned to appreciate the politics of welfare reform; they "saved" the EITC by helping merge the three policy streams. In another sense, experts got lucky. The EITC's survival depended more on a receptive political environment than on economists becoming more effective political actors. The EITC represented the perfect policy solution to a set of social problems and a welfare reform consensus that favored pro-work, pro-growth, low-cost alternatives. Indeed, economic research was a necessary, but not sufficient, component of the EITC's survival.

The future of the EITC will depend on the relative flow of the problem, policy, and political streams. Economic analysis will influence whether the streams remain together or diverge. The political process, however, will continue to challenge and distill economic research. More generally, politics, not economics, will dominate future discussions of the U.S. tax transfer system. The foregoing history of the EITC exposes the powerful influence that national politics and values have on tax transfer programs like the EITC. It is not the historian's role to make predictions or to suggest policy prescriptions based on these observations. Rather, it is incumbent on the historian to identify political, social, and cultural trends and continuities that might inform policy discussions. This chapter describes the intersection of tax policy, politics, and economic analysis. More pointedly, it explores the political uses and abuses of economic theory and research, with specific reference to the EITC. If future social policymaking follows the pattern described here, policy alternatives, regardless of their theoretical or analytical appeal, will have to complement rather than conflict with social and cultural forces to prove successful.

APPENDIX

TABLE 1.A1 / Earned Income Tax Credit Parameters, from 1975 to 1999

Year	Phase-In Rate (Percentage)	Phase-In Range (Dollars)	Maximum Credit (Dollars)	Phase-Out Rate (Percentage)	Phase-Out Range (Dollars)
1975 to 1978	10.0	0 to 4,000	400	10.0	4,000 to 8,000
1979 to 1984	10.0	0 to 5,000	500	12.5	6,000 to 10,000
1985 to 1986	14.0	0 to 5,000	550	12.22	6,500 to 11,000
1987	14.0	0 to 6,080	851	10.0	6,920 to 15,432
1988	14.0	0 to 6,240	874	10.0	9,840 to 18,576
1989	14.0	0 to 6,500	910	10.0	10,240 to 19,340
1990	14.0	0 to 6,810	953	10.0	10,730 to 20,264
1991[a]	16.7[b] 17.3[c]	0 to 7,140	1,192 1,235	11.93 12.36	11,250 to 21,250
1992[a]	17.6[b] 18.4[c]	0 to 7,520	1,324 1,384	12.57 13.14	11,840 to 22,370
1993[a]	18.5[b] 19.5[c]	0 to 7,750	1,434 1,511	13.21 13.93	12,200 to 23,050
1994	26.3[b] 30.0[c] 7.65[d]	0 to 7,750 0 to 8,425 0 to 4,000	2,038 2,528 306	15.98 17.68 7.65	11,000 to 23,755 11,000 to 25,296 5,000 to 9,000
1995	34.0[b] 36.0[c] 7.65[d]	0 to 6,160 0 to 8,640 0 to 4,100	2,094 3,110 314	15.98 20.22 7.65	11,290 to 24,396 11,290 to 26,673 5,130 to 9,230
1996	34.0[b] 40.0[c] 7.65[d]	0 to 6,330 0 to 8,890 0 to 4,220	2,152 3,556 323	15.98 21.06 7.65	11,610 to 25,078 11,610 to 28,495 5,280 to 9,500
1997	34.0[b] 40.0[c] 7.65[d]	0 to 6,500 0 to 9,140 0 to 4,340	2,210 3,656 332	15.98 21.06 7.65	11,930 to 25,750 11,930 to 29,290 5,430 to 9,770
1998	34.0[b] 40.0[c] 7.65[d]	0 to 6,680 0 to 9,390 0 to 4,460	2,271 3,756 341	15.98 21.06 7.65	12,260 to 26,473 12,260 to 30,095 5,570 to 10,030
1999	34.0[b] 40.0[c] 7.65[d]	0 to 6,800 0 to 9,540 0 to 4,530	2,312 3,816 347	15.98 21.06 7.65	12,460 to 26,928 12,460 to 30,580 5,670 to 10,200

Source: U.S. House 1999, U.S. Department of the Treasury, RG 59.
[a]Basic credit only. Does not include supplemental young-child credit or health insurance credit.
[b]Families with one qualifying child.
[c]Families with two or more qualifying children.
[d]Taxpayers with no qualifying child.

NOTES

1. The political scientist Christopher Howard (1997) has argued that tax expenditures slip through the policymaking process; they are, he concludes, the result of surreptitious and undemocratic policymaking. Perhaps the complexities of the Internal Revenue Code influence some politicians to cede authority on tax issues to the tax-writing committees. But Howard's view of tax expenditures is more true of the tax policymaking process thirty or forty years ago than of recent tax expenditure history. Indeed, since at least the mid-1970s, when Congress began requiring the Treasury Department to produce an annual list of tax expenditures, politicians have examined tax expenditures alongside direct expenditures. Many direct expenditure programs are no less technical or confusing than tax expenditures, and politicians understand perfectly well the distributive features of tax programs. With the tax expenditure budget approaching $700 billion for 1999, politicians cannot afford to ignore its economic and social influences. Therefore, I agree with John Witte that "it seems unlikely" that tax expenditures "are enacted or modified without full congressional knowledge of the intent and effects of the legislators" (Witte 1985, 335).

2. The Republican Contract with America associated the EITC with the old, failed regime of social provision (Gillespie and Schellhas 1994). Commentators in the popular press voiced similar criticisms, calling it "a program that pays taxpayer dollars to people who don't even earn enough to be taxpayers" (Paul C. Roberts, "Revenge of the Unheards . . . Rising: Clinton's Deception," Washington Times, May 27, 1993, G1; see also James Bovard, "Clinton's Biggest Welfare Fraud," Wall Street Journal, May 10, 1994, A18). Others went further. They identified the EITC as "the biggest . . . transfer swindle in the history of the nation" (Gross 1995, 137). Legislators, too, attacked the program. In 1995, Senator Don Nickles (Rep.-Okla.) called the EITC "the fastest growing, most fraudulent program that we have in Government today" (Nickles 1995). Such federal largesse, argued Senator William Roth (Rep.-Del.), created a tax and transfer system that allowed individuals to make "millions of dollars off [the EITC] by scam" (U.S. Senate 1995a, 13).

3. Alice O'Connor has written that "welfare, not poverty, was the social problem of the 1970s" (O'Connor 1998, 99).

4. Historians have identified several studies from the late 1950s and early 1960s that spurred this "rediscovery" of poverty, particularly John Kenneth Galbraith's *The Affluent Society* (1958) and Michael Harrington's *The Other America* (1962). See Brauer 1982, 103; Matusow 1984, 119. Although historians correctly identify the importance of these studies, they overlook earlier work on poverty and income distribution, which laid the foundation for later "rediscoveries" of poverty. See Lampman 1954, 1957; Goldsmith 1957; Lydall and Lansing 1959.

5. According to Robert Lampman, the University of Wisconsin economist who animated the modern war on poverty, the aggregate poverty gap in 1963 reached $12 billion. Robert J. Lampman, "Negative Rates Income Taxation," U.S. Department of the Treasury, Records of the Office of Tax Analysis (hereafter, OTA), Box 53. The OTA estimated in late 1964 that the poverty gap had climbed to $16 billion; see "Social Security, Financing, Taxation and Welfare, and Income Maintenance," 10, August 10, 1964, OTA, Box 41. Filling the poverty gap remained a goal of social policymakers through-

out the 1960s. See, for example, Brookings Research Report, "Using Negative Taxes to Narrow the Poverty Gap," 1967, OTA, Box 53.

6. For more on the moral perceptions of poverty, see Katz 1986, 1989; Handler and Hasenfeld 1991; Hirschman 1991; Fraser and Gordon 1994.

7. Joseph Pechman to Stanley Surrey, October 13, 1965, 3, OTA, Box 53. Stanley Surrey, assistant secretary of the treasury for tax policy from 1961 to 1969, perceived the same kind of illogic regarding tax policies in 1965. "At the present moment we are considering easing the income tax on low income groups," Surrey observed. "However at the same time we are increasing payroll taxes under Social Security. And thus in this sense we are working in contradictory directions." Surrey to the Secretary, July 25, 1965, Stanley S. Surrey Papers (hereafter, SSP), Box 199, Folder 2.

8. Stockfisch to Surrey, January 6, 1964, "Administration's Anti-poverty Campaign," OTA, Box 7. The Treasury Department investigated the effect of federal and state taxes on the poor. Brannon to Stockfisch, "Tax Relief for Very Low Incomes," January 16, 1964, OTA, Box 52; Stockfisch to the Secretary of the Treasury, "Effect of Tax Bill on Poverty Income Classes," January 27, 1964, OTA, Box 7; Surrey to Stockfisch, "Taxes and Poverty," March 23, 1964, OTA, Box 7; Stockfisch to Mr. Lusk, "Estimating tax liabilities for poverty levels of income," March 26, 1964, OTA, Box 52; Surrey to Stone and Brannon, "List of Substantive Tax Matters Requiring Consideration," July 7, 1965, SSP, Box 180, Folder 5; OTA, "Two-Year Carryforward and Two-Year Carryback of Unused Exemptions and Minimum Standard Deduction," August 23, 1965, OTA, Box 53.

9. "Negative Tax," September 1, 1964, Treasury Department discussion paper for Income Maintenance Task Force Meeting, OTA, Box 53; "Negative Tax Systems: Report of Technical Working Committee, Task Force on Income Maintenance," September 14, 1965, prepared by the staffs of the Treasury and the Council of Economic Advisers, OTA, Box 41.

10. For social science expertise in the 1960s, see O'Connor 2001.

11. I am indebted to one of the referees from the Russell Sage Foundation for this observation.

12. OTA, "An Explanation of a Negative Income Tax," February 9, 1967, OTA, Box 52; Lampman, "Negative Rates Income Taxation," OTA, Box 53.

13. Office of Economic Opportunity, "Program Memorandum on Income Maintenance, FY 1968–72," June 1966, OTA, 1, Box 53. The Office of Economic Opportunity produced a separate report discussing the implementation of a negative income tax. OTA, "Office of Economic Opportunity Program for a Negative Income Tax," July 28, 1966, OTA, Box 53. For reaction to the OEO's plan, see Tobin 1967.

14. For NIT benefits "as a matter of right," see Education, Manpower, and Science Division (Bureau of the Budget) to Charles J. Zwick, "The Income Maintenance System," October 17, 1966, OTA, Box 52. For a constitutional right to a federally guaranteed livelihood, see Schwartz 1964; "Report of the Task Force on Income Maintenance: Summary and Recommendations," September 18, 1965, OTA, Box 41; OTA, "An Explanation of a Negative Income Tax," February 9, 1967, OTA, Box 52. For a slightly different variant of an NIT as a guaranteed annual income for unemployed workers displaced by technological gains, see Theobald 1963, 155–56.

15. Social dividend plans after the British models would have cost well over $50 billion. By contrast, negative-income-tax schemes designed to close the poverty gap in the United States cost much less, ranging from $3 billion to $15 billion.

16. For the development of the negative income tax concept, see Green 1967; Lenkowsky 1986; Ventry 1997.

17. Friedman, "The Case for a Negative Income Tax: A View from the Right," speech given at Chamber of Commerce, National Symposium on Guaranteed Income, Washington, D.C., December 9, 1966, Milton Friedman Papers, Box 49, 1. Although other supporters of negative income taxation were also careful to emphasize the differences between an NIT and a guaranteed annual income, the distinction between the two policy options was less real than political. "Properly stated," Friedman has written, an NIT and a guaranteed annual income "are identical. At least they can be made to be identical if the proper parameters are chosen. For every guaranteed income plus tax structure, there is an identically equivalent negative income tax and vice versa." Milton Friedman to Dennis Ventry, December 3, 1996, personal correspondence.

18. Income disregards provided an exemption level below which the program's marginal tax rates could not reduce earned income.

19. For the "failed" war on poverty, see Matusow 1984, 217–71; Patterson 1994, 171–84; Davies 1996, 219–20. For the welfare "crisis," see Moynihan 1968; "Welfare Out of Control" 1971; "Welfare: The Shame of a Nation" 1971; O'Connor 1998, 101–7.

20. Daniel P. Moynihan to Art Klebanoff, September 5, 1969, 1, Richard M. Nixon Presidential Materials Staff (hereafter NPM), Subject: Welfare, Box 61.

21. As testament to the FAP's early appeal, the House Ways and Means Committee reported it out of committee, 21 to 3, and the full body of the House approved it, 243 to 155 (Small 1999, 188).

22. According to Moynihan, the National Welfare Rights Organization plan became "a talisman of advanced liberalism" (Moynihan 1973, 250).

23. The figures are from Moynihan 1973, 247. The original data came from an unnamed study by Charles Schultze and Andrew Brimmer.

24. Nixon to George Bush, October 23, 1970, 1, NPM, Subject: Welfare, Box 21. For similar correspondence, see Robert Finch to Lester Maddox, draft letter for the President, November 30, 1970, NPM, Subject: Welfare, Box 63. Despite these assurances, the president felt compelled by political pressures to direct his administration to use the term "workfare" when referring to the FAP. Tod R. Hullin to Staff Secretary, July 14, 1971, NPM, Subject: Welfare, Box 62.

25. In 1967, Congress had reduced marginal tax rates for the AFDC program as part of that year's social security amendments. The new "30 and 1/3" rule allowed AFDC recipients to keep the first $30 they earned and one-third of additional earnings without having to count them against AFDC benefits.

26. Nixon to George Bush, October 23, 1970, 1, NPM, Subject: Welfare, Box 21.

27. The Department of Health, Education, and Welfare's tables depicted the "combined benefits and reduction rates under selected income-tested programs for a four-person, female-headed family" in four cities: Phoenix, Arizona; Wilmington, Delaware; Chicago, Illinois; and New York, New York. For the complete tables, see Moynihan 1973, 475–79.

28. According to Frank C. Porter of the *Washington Post*, Williams's testimony "torpedoed" the Nixon plan, while Moynihan concluded that the Delaware senator killed the FAP (Moynihan 1973, 474, 534). It should be noted that HEW's tables did not reflect reality. They assumed, for example, that all welfare families lived in public housing, but only a fraction (18 percent in Chicago and 8 percent in New York) lived in public housing units. The department also assumed that each member of welfare families collected Medicaid. Thus, by overstating the benefits lost to the FAP, HEW implied a much larger notch problem (Moynihan 1973, 480).

29. For the income maintenance experiments, see Pechman and Timpane 1975; Palmer and Pechman 1978; Munnell 1986.

30. For an animated summary of Long's distinction between the deserving and undeserving poor, see U.S. Senate 1972.

31. "Outline for Workfare Proposal," no date, no author, NPM, Subject Files: Welfare, Box 52, 1–2. See also "Possible Amendments to Family Assistance," September 2, 1970, and, "Briefing Paper: Meeting with Senate Finance Committee Members on Family Assistance," September 3, 1970, both from NPM, Subject Files: Welfare, Box 52.

32. A handful of scholars resisted the conclusion that social security taxes were regressive. They argued that the contributory nature of the system assured wage earners "deferred income commensurate with, or in excess of . . . their contributions" (Riesenfeld 1955, 235). They also maintained that social security benefits were progressive, with the poor receiving higher payments as a percentage of their income (Harvey 1965).

33. Stockfisch to Surrey, January 6, 1964, "Administration's Anti-poverty Campaign," OTA, Box 7; Assistant Commissioner to Mr. J. A. Stockfisch, "Materials Relating to Impact of Taxes on Poverty," May 4, 1964, OTA, Box 53; Surrey to Files, "Possible Presidential Tax Programs," 4, June 8, 1964, SSP, Box 180, Folder 6; OTA, "Social Security, Financing, Taxation and Welfare, and Income Maintenance," August 10, 1964, 10, OTA, Box 41; Surrey to Stockfisch, October 9, 1964, OTA, Box 53; Surrey to Secretary of the Treasury, "Income Maintenance Task Force Recommendations," November 14, 1964, OTA, Box 41.

34. The 1964 Presidential Task Force on Sustaining Prosperity argued that "further increases in payroll taxes will force an increasingly large share of the total federal tax burden to fall on lower income families." Task Force on Sustaining Prosperity, Draft of Task Force's Final Report," 11, October 28, 1964, SSP, Box 207, Folder 3. See also Surrey to Arthur M. Okun, "Tax Aspects of Post-Vietnam Plans," May 28, 1968, SSP, Box 206, Folder 1. With social security taxes rising rapidly, the poor's tax burden could no longer be justified simply by reference to the contributory aspect of the social security system. Task Force on Sustaining Prosperity, "Draft of Task Force's Final Report," 12; Surrey to Arthur M. Okun, "Tax Aspects of Post-Vietnam Plans"; Surrey to Stone and Brannon, June 23, 1965, SSP, Box 111, Folder 1. The Treasury Department considered ways to relieve, and even exempt, low-income workers from payroll tax obligations. OTA, "Social Security, Financing, Taxation and Welfare, and Income Maintenance," 10, August 10, 1964, OTA, Box 41; OTA, "Exemption of Employee Social Security Tax for the Poor," December 6, 1968, Box 52; Albert Brisbin to Deputy Assistant Secretary Helmuth, December 5, 1968, SSP, Box 196, Folder 1.

35. Various legislators, predominantly Democrats, proposed their own legislation designed to relieve low-income workers from social security taxes. A number of plans

provided refundable tax credits similar to Long's work bonus (H.R. 12646, 1974, by Representative Barbara Jordan [Dem.-Tex.], and S. 918, 1975, Senator Hubert Humphrey [Dem.-Minn.]), while others provided a tax deduction for social security taxes (H.R. 9000, 1973, Representative William R. Cotter [Dem.-Conn.]; H.R. 15281, 1974, Representative Bertram Podell [Dem.-N.Y.]; and H.R. 1141, 1975, Representative Joseph Waggonner [Dem.-La.]). Still other proposals lowered the social security tax rate (H.R. 12489, 1974, Representative James A. Burke [Dem.-Mass.] and 125 cosponsors; H.R. 13803 and H.R. 13804, 1974, Representative Henry S. Reuss [Dem.-Wisc.]; S. 1838, 1974, Senator Vance Hartke [Dem.-Ind.]; and S. 2055, 1975, Senator Vance Hartke [Dem.-Ind.], cosponsored by Senators George McGovern [Dem.-S.D.], James Abourezk [Dem.-S.D.], and Hugh Scott [Rep.-Pa.], Senate minority leader). A few plans called for the abolition of social security taxes altogether (H.R. 13019, 1974, Representatives Henry S. Reuss [Dem.-Wisc.] and William D. Ford [Dem.-Mich.]. Other proposals extended more general tax relief for the working poor by increasing personal exemptions (H.R. 13048, 1974, Representative John Matthew Zwach [Rep.-Minn.]; and H.R. 13092, 1974, Representative Wright Patman [Dem.-Tex.]) or allowing an optional tax credit in lieu of personal exemptions (H.R. 13197, 1974, Representative Martha Griffiths [Dem.-Mich.]; and H.R. 13741, 1974, Representative Lionel Van Deerlin [Dem.-Calif.]).

36. This paragraph borrows heavily from O'Connor 1998.

37. Washington policy organizations developed many of these models. The Urban Institute, for example, created RIM (reform in income maintenance), TRIM (transfer income model), and DYNAMISM, while Mathematica Policy Research produced MATH (microanalysis of transfers to households). See Kraemer et al. 1987, 38–62.

38. Anderson had witnessed the debates over the FAP, too, while acting as special assistant to Arthur F. Burns, Nixon's counselor for domestic affairs.

39. Although the Tax Reduction Act of 1975 named the new tax credit the "Earned Income Credit," politicians and experts referred to it interchangeably as the "Earned Income Credit" (EIC), or the "Earned Income Tax Credit" (EITC). To this day, both designations are acceptable and understood, but "EITC" is more widely used.

40. The Ways and Means Report that first included the EITC stated that "it is appropriate to use the income tax system to offset the impact of the Social Security taxes on low-income persons in 1975 by adopting for this one year only a refundable income tax credit against earned income" (U.S. House 1975, 10). See also Long 1975.

41. As part of this vision, Long introduced an amendment to the Tax Reduction Act of 1975 that would have reduced AFDC payments to EITC recipients by amounts equal to the credit. Although Long's amendment failed to pass in conference, the bill's final language did not require state welfare agencies to disregard the EITC from income when calculating AFDC benefits. The result was that most states considered EITC benefits as income and reduced AFDC payments accordingly.

42. The House Ways and Means Committee proposed extending the EITC to all low-income workers, regardless of their family responsibilities. The Senate Finance Committee, however, concentrating on out-of-work welfare mothers and determined to minimize the cost of the proposal, voted to restrict EITC eligibility to low-income individuals with children. The House acceded to the Senate in conference (U.S. Senate 1975, 33).

43. In theory, Long's plan extended "a substantial new application of the principle of taxation according to 'ability-to-pay'" ("Tax Credit for Low-Income Workers with Families" 1974). By refunding more than 85 percent of the total tax on workers, it implied that workers bore both the employee and the employer portion of the payroll tax. Long argued that the credit would "provide tax relief to people who are too poor to pay income tax, but who still pay Social Security tax and bear the burden of the Social Security tax paid by their employers" (Long 1975). But in practice, the EITC was hardly radical.

44. Congress extended the Earned Income Tax Credit through 1976 (the Revenue Adjustment Act of 1975), 1977 (the Tax Reform Act of 1976), and 1978 (the Tax Reduction and Simplification Act of 1977).

45. The Revenue Act of 1978 instituted these modifications to the EITC.

46. Statement by the President, May 2, 1977, 1, Jimmy Carter Library (hereafter JCL), Box 318, May 1977.

47. Tom Joe to Stu Eizenstat, "HEW's Proposed Welfare Reform Plan," July 27, 1977, 3, JCL, Eizenstat, Box 318, July 1977.

48. Carter did not detail the proposal at his press conference on May 2 but instead provided a set of twelve goals for welfare reform. Notably, Carter explicitly recommended continued use of the EITC to help the working poor.

49. Stu Eizenstat, Bert Carp, Bill Spring, and Frank Raines to President Carter, April 26, 1977, 1, JCL, Eizenstat, Box 317, April 1977. The Department of Health, Education, and Welfare's own estimate indicated that those covered by direct cash assistance under its program would increase 67 percent, from 23.67 million to 39.58 million individuals.

50. Tom Joe to Stu Eizenstat, July 27, 1977, 7, JCL, Eizenstat, Box 318, July 1977.

51. Stu Eizenstat to the President, July 31, 1977, 11, JCL, Eizenstat, Box 318, August 1977.

52. Charles Schultze to the President, July 27, 1977, 4, JCL, Eizenstat, Box 318, July 1977.

53. As parameterized late in the design of the welfare initiative, the EITC would have increased the combined benefit-reduction rate (including social security taxes) in states that supplemented cash assistance "to a maximum of 68 percent for those 'expected to work' and to a maximum of 86 percent for those 'not expected to work.'" The DPS demanded that HEW and the DOL reduce these "serious work disincentives." Eizenstat to the President, July 31, 1977, 11, JCL, Eizenstat, Box 318, August 1977.

54. Tom Joe to Stu Eizenstat, July 27, 1977, 4, JCL, Eizenstat, Box 318, July 1977.

55. Eizenstat, Carp, Spring, and Raines to the President, April 26, 1977, 2, JCL, Eizenstat, Box 317, April 1977.

56. Jack Watson and Jim Parham to the President, May 23, 1977, 1, JCL, Eizenstat, Box 318, May 1977.

57. Watson and Parham to the President, May 23, 1977, 1, JCL, Eizenstat, Box 318, May 1977; Jack Watson and Jim Parham to the President, April 26, 1977, 1, JCL, Eizenstat, Box 317, April 1977.

58. Compare the administration's conclusions with a 1978 Urban Institute study (Hoffman 1978, xi).

59. Joe to Eizenstat, July 27, 1977, 4, JCL, Eizenstat, Box 318, July 1977. A few individuals on the welfare reform planning team warned, somewhat prophetically, that expanding the EITC would undercut its advantages. The domestic policy staff argued, for example, that "folding into the 'welfare system' the Earned Income Tax Credit . . . will appear to be an expansion of the welfare system and will label as 'welfare recipients' people who are not now so perceived." Jim Parham to Jack Watson, April 15, 1977, 1, JCL, Eizenstat, Box 317, April 1977.

60. Tom Joe to Stu Eizenstat, August 2, 1977, 3, JCL, Eizenstat, Box 319, August 1977.

61. Joe to Eizenstat, August 2, 1977, 3, JCL, Eizenstat, Box 319, August 1977.

62. Long quoted in Lynn and Whitman 1981, 230. Moynihan quoted in Link 1977, 1701.

63. Never mind that the different estimates were easily explained: the Congressional Budget Office used 1982 dollars, while HEW estimated using 1978 dollars, a difference that accounted for $7 billion of the discrepancy; the Congressional Budget Office refused to include the CETA VI, the wellhead tax, HEW savings from reduced fraud, and reductions in extended unemployment insurance as legitimate offsets; and it did not charge the expanded EITC to tax reform.

64. For a fuller description of the discrepancies in costs, see Demkovich 1978, 633; Lynn and Whitman 1981, 231–40; and Kraemer et al. 1987, 141–43.

65. These bills included the House Welfare Reform Subcommittee revisions of the Program for Better Jobs and Income (H.R. 10950), the Ullman Welfare Reform Act (H.R. 10711), the Job Opportunities and Family Security Act of 1978 (S. 2777, also known as Baker-Bellmon-Ribicoff), the State and Local Welfare Reform and Fiscal Relief Act (also known as Moynihan-Cranston-Long), and the Welfare Reform and Fiscal Relief Act (sponsored by Senator Edward Kennedy).

66. The other two were (1) eliminating the purchase requirement in the food stamps program and creating tighter eligibility requirements for high income recipients and (2) renewing CETA and tightening eligibility to target only low-income workers.

67. Congress never passed the 1979 jobs bill.

68. Recent studies suggest that fewer than 1 percent of EITC eligibles opt for the advance payment. If these studies are any indication of the rate at which individuals chose the advance credit in the late 1970s, state welfare agencies were unfairly reducing AFDC benefits for individuals eligible for both the EITC and AFDC programs. See GAO 1992 and Yin et al. 1994.

69. The 1990 Omnibus Budget Reconciliation Act affirmed this requirement and also prohibited the counting of EITC as income in determining eligibility for Medicaid, food stamps, Supplemental Security Income, and low-income housing benefits.

70. The 1979 welfare legislation amounted to two bills, the Work and Training Opportunities Act and the Social Welfare Reform Amendments, both of which failed to pass. Despite the program's modest cost ($5.7 billion), Carter warned his staff, "Do not ask me to approve a higher figure in the future" (Patterson 1998, 130).

71. Unless otherwise noted, the statistics in this paragraph are from Storey (1996, 16–17) and refer to 1996 dollars.

72. These bills included H.R. 200 (introduced by Siljander), H.R. 373 (Moore), H.R. 416 (Quillen), H.R. 623 (Young, of Alaska), H.R. 794 (Frank), H.R. 800 (Gephardt), H.R.

1040 (Rangel), H.R. 1057 (Lloyd), H.R. 1165 (Heftel), H.R. 1551 (Coats), H.R. 2222 (Kemp), H.R. 2472 (Schroeder and others), H.R. 2477 (Kennelly), H.R. 2480 (Rangel), H.R. 2585 (Ford and Rangel), S. 321 (DeConcini and Symms), S. 409 (Bradley and others), S. 411 (Roth), S. 556 (Chafee), S. 888 (Durenberger), S. 909 (Quayle), S. 1006 (Kasten and Wallop), and S. 1194 (Moynihan).

73. Those plans that increased the EITC included H.R. 373, H.R. 1040, H.R. 2472, H.R. 2480, H.R. 2585, S.R. 411, and S.R. 1194. Those that maintained the credit or simply modified it to more explicitly offset social security taxation included H.R. 200, H.R. 800, H.R. 2222, S.R. 409, S.R. 556, and S.R. 1006.

74. Conlan, Wrightson, and Beam (1988, 62) describe this consensus in detail.

75. The drastic cuts in social services, in combination with the Economic Recovery Tax Act of 1981, drastically reduced progressivity in the tax system (Kasten, Sammartino, and Toder 1996) and increased inequality (Gramlich, Kasten, and Sammartino 1993) between 1980 and 1985.

76. In fairness to President Reagan, the looming deficit was the product of years of fiscal mismanagement as well as changing macroeconomic forces (including reduced inflation that resulted in lower federal revenues), not merely the direct consequence of Reaganomics. Indeed, as Gene Steuerle has shown, the "era of easy financing" that characterized postwar fiscal policy ended before Reagan took office (Steuerle 1992, 1996). Nevertheless, the Economic Recovery Tax Act of 1981 and Reagan's increased defense spending accelerated the day of reckoning.

77. Deficit reduction efforts began as early as 1974 with the Congressional Budget and Impoundment Control Act. They also included the Tax Equity and Fiscal Responsibility Act of 1982 and the Deficit Reduction Act of 1984, as well as the Omnibus Budget Reconciliation Acts of 1987 and 1989 and the Budget Enforcement Act of 1990. For the way deficit reduction influenced tax policy, see Gutman 2000.

78. The full citation is from floor comments Senator William Roth made in October 1995: "The EITC was to create incentives for low-income parents to work. It was that simple. But as they say about too much of a good thing becoming dangerous, such is what happened to this once well-intended program" (Roth 1995). Similar criticism emanated from the popular press. During the 1995 budget debate, columnist James Glassman argued that the EITC "like many other good ideas in Washington, [has] gotten completely out of hand" (James K. Glassman, "A Program Gone Bonkers," *Washington Post*, October 26, 1995, A25).

79. Sparrow did not use microdata and characterized his conclusions as "moderately informed guesses." Steuerle's suggestion that the EITC encourages a superterranean economy remains a theoretical prediction; the 1993 and 1994 IRS data provide no indication that overreporting of income constitutes a significant compliance problem.

80. For these investigations, see U.S. House (1993a, 1993b, 1994, 1997b) and U.S. Senate (1995b, 1995c).

81. Suggestions included replacing the EITC with an exemption for payroll taxes; providing the EITC benefit to low-income workers through a tax credit awarded to employers; disallowing EITC claims filed electronically; denying the EITC to illegal aliens; eliminating the health care and young child supplemental credits; raising the amount of disqualified income for EITC claimants; and denying the EITC to childless families.

82. The Omnibus Budget Reconciliation Act of 1990 added a health insurance credit to the basic EITC credit. Available to EITC eligibles who purchased health insurance that included child coverage, the health insurance credit varied with a claimant's income and offered a maximum benefit of $451 in 1992. In 1993, the Clinton administration proposed repealing the supplemental credit, a suggestion Congress acted on in the 1993 Omnibus Budget Reconciliation Act. For a discussion of abusive insurance sales and marketing techniques involving the EITC, see U.S. House 1993a and Greenstein 1993.

83. See Congressman Rob Portman's comments, for example, in U.S. House 1997b.

84. Comment by Senator Phil Gramm (Rep.-Tex.) during Senate Finance Committee debate over the EITC in 1995 (Godfrey 1995a). Although the EITC is indeed an earnings subsidy, Senator Gramm most likely did not have that distinction in mind when he called the EITC a "subsidy."

85. For Rockefeller's comment, see U.S. Senate 1997. The program's projected 4.5 percent growth rate in 1996, Kennedy argued, barely kept pace with increases in the consumer price index (Kennedy 1995).

86. I am indebted to Janet Holtzblatt for the information relating to the EITC's expansion in the 1990 and 1993 bills.

87. The presidential initiative to expand the EITC in 1993 was inspired by David Ellwood's three-pronged attack on poverty: (1) making work pay (by enlarging the EITC); (2) enforcing child support orders; and (3) setting welfare time limits. See Ellwood's last chapter in Bane and Ellwood 1994.

    In selling the EITC in 1993, Clinton argued that posterity would remember favorably his proposed expansion of the program. "By expanding the refundable earned income tax credit," he declared, "we will make history; we will reward the work of millions of working poor Americans by realizing the principle that if you work 40 hours a week and you've got a child in the house, you will no longer be in poverty" (Shapiro and Greenstein 1993, 4).

88. For a discussion of the EITC's growth relative to the dramatic changes in welfare policy during the 1980s and 1990s, see Ellwood 2000.

89. For a more detailed examination of these studies, see chapter 6, this volume.

90. For a more detailed accounting of the authority granted to the IRS, see chapter 6, this volume. Unfortunately, the two new data sources only partially compensate for the lack of a recent Taxpayer Compliance Measurement Program study, last conducted in 1988. Congress has cut funding for the exhaustive study, and in 1998 the Senate explicitly prevented the IRS from conducting another TCMP study. The lack of a current TCMP study prevents not only an accurate picture of EITC compliance rates but also a whole array of additional tax compliance issues.

91. Studies using microdata have found that even in the presence of the EITC, "typical tax rates on the poor are not particularly high—they rarely exceed 40 percent." Dickert, Houser, and Scholz 1994, 636.

92. I am indebted to one of the referees from the *National Tax Journal* for this observation.

93. The eleven states are Colorado, Iowa, Kansas, Maryland, Massachusetts, Minnesota, New York, Oregon, Rhode Island, Wisconsin, and Vermont. Eight of the eleven state EITCs are refundable.

94. Janet McCubbin, in chapter 6 of this volume, offers evidence to suggest that concentrating on improving enforcement techniques—rather than scaling back the EITC—will most effectively reduce the program's overclaim rate.

95. In addition to Kingdon's multiple-streams model, political scientists have described the agenda-setting process with the help of other theoretical frameworks, including the convergent- and divergent-voice models and punctuated equilibrium model. See Cook 1981, 1990, for the convergent- and divergent-voice models, and Baumgartner and Jones 1993 for the punctuated equilibrium model.

96. In 1970, Milton Friedman, a one-time FAP supporter, called the proposal "a striking example of how to spoil a good idea" (Friedman 1970, 89).

97. Although Congress rejected negative income taxation in 1972, it enacted the first federally subsidized guaranteed income in the form of the Supplemental Security Income program. Restricted to the aged, blind, and disabled, the program originally provided a monthly income of up to $210 for each couple.

98. See note 64.

REFERENCES

Aley, James. 1993. "A Tax Credit for Crooks?" *Fortune*, October 4: 24.

Anderson, Martin. 1976. *Welfare: The Political Economy of Welfare Reform in the United States.* Stanford, Calif.: Hoover Institution.

Bane, Mary Jo, and David Ellwood. 1994. *Welfare Realities: From Rhetoric to Reform.* Cambridge, Mass.: Harvard University Press.

Baumgartner, Frank R., and Bryan D. Jones. 1993. *Agendas and Instability in American Politics.* Chicago: University of Chicago Press.

Berkowitz, Edward D. 1991. *America's Welfare State: From Roosevelt to Reagan.* Baltimore: Johns Hopkins University Press.

Blank, Rebecca. 1997. *It Takes a Nation: A New Agenda for Fighting Poverty.* New York: Russell Sage Foundation.

Blank, Rebecca M., and Alan S. Blinder. 1986. "Macroeconomics, Income Distribution, and Poverty." In *Fighting Poverty: What Works and What Doesn't*, edited by Sheldon H. Danziger and Daniel H. Weinberg. Cambridge, Mass.: Harvard University Press.

Blank, Rebecca M., David Card, and Philip K. Robins. 1999. "Financial Incentives for Increasing Work and Income Among Low-Income Families." Working Paper 6998. Cambridge, Mass.: National Bureau of Economic Research.

Block, Fred. 1987. *The Mean Season: The Attack on the Welfare State.* New York: Pantheon Books.

Brauer, Carl. 1982. "Kennedy, Johnson, and the War on Poverty." *Journal of American History* 69(2): 98–119.

Browning, Edgar K. 1995. "Effects of the Earned Income Tax Credit on Income and Welfare." *National Tax Journal* 48(1): 23–43.

Burke, Vincent J., and Vee Burke. 1974. *Nixon's Good Deed: Welfare Reform.* New York: Columbia University Press.

Campbell, Colin D., and William L. Peirce. 1980. *The Earned Income Credit.* Washington, D.C.: American Enterprise Institute.

Carter, Jimmy. Domestic Policy Staff Files. Welfare Reform, Boxes 317, 318, 319. Jimmy Carter Library, Atlanta, Georgia.

Champagne, Anthony, and Edward J. Harpham. 1984. *The Attack on the Welfare State.* Prospect Heights, Ill.: Waveland Press.

Conlan, Timothy J., Margaret T. Wrightson, and David R. Beam. 1988. *Taxing Choices: The Politics of Tax Reform.* Washington, D.C.: Congressional Quarterly Press.

Cook, Fay Lomax. 1981. "Crime and the Elderly: The Emergence of a Policy Issue." In *Reactions to Crime*, edited by D. A. Lewis. Beverly Hills, Calif.: Sage Publications.

———. 1990. "Agenda Setting and the Rise and Fall of Policy Issues: The Case of Criminal Victimization of the Elderly." *Environment and Planning: Government and Planning* 8: 395–415.

Cook, Fred J. 1970. "When You Just Give Money to the Poor." *New York Times Magazine,* May 3.

Council of Economic Advisers. 1964. *Economic Report of the President.* Washington: U.S. Government Printing Office.

———. 1998. "Good News for Low-Income Families: Expansions in the Earned Income Tax Credit and the Minimum Wage." Washington, D.C. (December).

———. 1999. *Economic Report of the President.* Washington: U.S. Government Printing Office.

Davies, Gareth. 1996. *From Opportunity to Entitlement: The Transformation and Decline of Great Society Liberalism.* Lawrence: University of Kansas Press.

Demkovich, Linda E. 1978. "The Numbers Are the Issue in the Debate over Welfare Reform." *National Journal* 10(16): 633–37.

Dickert, Stacey, Scott Houser, and John Karl Scholz. 1994. "Taxes and the Poor: A Microsimulation Study of Implicit and Explicit Taxes." *National Tax Journal* 47(3): 621–38.

Economic Opportunity Act of 1964. 1964. *Findings and Declaration of Purpose.* H.R. 10440, sec. 2. *U.S. Code Congressional and Administrative News.* 88th Cong., 2d sess., vol. 1. St. Paul, Minn.: West Publishing.

Eissa, Nada, and Hillary Williamson Hoynes. 1998. "The Earned Income Tax Credit and the Labor Supply of Married Couples." Working Paper 6856. Cambridge, Mass.: National Bureau of Economic Research.

Eissa, Nada, and Jeffrey Liebman. 1996. "Labor Supply Response to the Earned Income Tax Credit." *Quarterly Journal of Economics* 111(2): 605–37.

Ellwood, David T. 1988. *Poor Support: Poverty in the American Family.* New York: Basic Books.

———. 2000. "Anti-Poverty Policy for Families in the Next Century: From Welfare to Work—and Worries." *Journal of Economic Perspectives* 14(1): 187–98.

Esterly, Stanley, and Glenn Esterly. 1971. *Freedom from Dependence: Welfare Reform as a Solution to Poverty.* Washington, D.C.: Public Affairs Press.

Fraser, Nancy, and Linda Gordon. 1994. "A Genealogy of Dependency: Tracing a Keyword of the U.S. Welfare State." *Signs: Journal of Women in Culture and Society* 19(21): 309–36.

Friedman, Milton. 1962. *Capitalism and Freedom.* Chicago: University of Chicago Press.

———. 1970. "Milton Friedman on Welfare: Back to the Drawing Board." *Newsweek,* May 18, 89.

———. Papers. Hoover Institution Library, Stanford University, California.

Galbraith, John Kenneth. 1958. *The Affluent Society.* Boston: Houghton Mifflin.

Gallup, George H. 1972. *The Gallup Poll: Public Opinion, 1935–1971.* 3 Vols. New York: Random House.

Gillespie, Ed, and Bob Schellhas, eds. 1994. *Contract with America: The Bold Plan by Repre-*

sentative Newt Gingrich, Representative Dick Armey, and the House Republicans to Change the Nation. New York: Random House.

Godfrey, John. 1994. "IRS Crackdown on EITC May Hurt Refund Anticipation Loans." *Tax Notes* 65: 511–12.

———. 1995a. "Finance Republicans Agree on EITC Tax Cuts." *Tax Base,* September 22. *taxbase.tax.org/* (citation 95 TNT 186-1).

———. 1995b. "Finance Wraps Up Tax Bill Mark: GOP Crows, Democrats Criticize." *Tax Notes* 69: 391.

Goldsmith, Selma F. 1957. "Changes in the Size Distribution of Income." *American Economic Review* (Papers and Proceedings of the Sixty-eighth Annual Meeting of the American Economic Association) 47(2): 504–18.

Gramlich, Edward M., Richard Kasten, and Frank Sammartino. 1993. "Growing Inequality in the 1980s: The Role of Federal Taxes and Cash Transfers." In *Uneven Tides: Rising Inequality in America,* edited by Sheldon Danziger and Peter Gottschalk. New York: Russell Sage Foundation.

Green, Christopher. 1967. *Negative Taxes and the Poverty Problem.* Washington, D.C.: Brookings Institution.

Greenstein, Robert. 1993. *Statement Before the U.S. House of Representatives, Committee on Ways and Means, Oversight Committee.* Washington, D.C. (March 4).

Greenstein, Robert, and Isaac Shapiro. 1998. "New Research Findings on the Effects of the Earned Income Tax Credit." Washington, D.C.: Center on Budget and Policy Priorities (March 11).

Gross, Martin L. 1995. *The Tax Racket: Government Extortion from A to Z.* New York: Ballantine Books.

Gutman, Harry L. 2000. "Reflections on the Process of Enacting Tax Law." *Tax Notes* 86: 93–101.

Handler, Joel, and Yeheskel Hasenfeld. 1991. *The Moral Construction of Poverty: Welfare Reform in America.* Newbury Park, Calif.: Sage Publications.

Harrington, Michael. 1962. *The Other America: Poverty in the United States.* New York: McGraw-Hill.

Harvey, Ernest C. 1965. "Social Security Taxes: Regressive or Progressive?" *National Tax Journal* 18(4): 408–14.

Haveman, Robert H. 1973. "Work-Conditioned Subsidies as an Income Maintenance Strategy: Issues of Program Structure and Integration." In *Studies in Public Welfare,* Paper 9 (pt. 1), *Concepts in Welfare Program Design.* Washington: U.S. Government Printing Office for the Joint Economic Committee, Subcommittee on Fiscal Policy.

Hirschman, Albert O. 1991. *The Rhetoric of Reaction: Perversity, Futility, Jeopardy.* Cambridge, Mass.: Harvard University Press/Belknap Press.

Hoffman, Saul D., and Laurence S. Seidman. 1990. *The Earned Income Tax Credit: Antipoverty Effectiveness and Labor Market Effects.* Kalamazoo, Mich.: W. E. Upjohn Institute for Employment Research.

Hoffman, Wayne Lee. 1978. *The Earned Income Tax Credit: Welfare Reform or Tax Relief? An Analysis of Alternative Proposals.* Washington, D.C.: Urban Institute.

Holtzblatt, Janet. 1991. "Administering Refundable Tax Credits: Lessons from the EITC Experience." In *Proceedings of the Eighty-fourth Annual Conference on Taxation.* Washington, D.C.: National Tax Association.

Holtzblatt, Janet, Janet McCubbin, and Robert Gillette. 1994. "Promoting Work Through the EITC." *National Tax Journal* 42(3): 591–607.

Howard, Christopher. 1997. *The Hidden Welfare State: Tax Expenditures and Social Policy in the United States.* Princeton: Princeton University Press.

Johnson, Nicholas, and Ed Lazere. 1999. "State Earned Income Tax Credits." *Poverty Research News* 3(1): 23–25.

Joint Committee on Taxation. 1979. *General Explanation of the Revenue Act of 1978.* Washington: U.S. Government Printing Office (May 12).

Joint Economic Committee. Subcommittee on Fiscal Policy. 1974. *Income Security for Americans: Recommendations of the Public Welfare Study.* Washington: U.S. Government Printing Office.

Kasten, Richard, Frank Sammartino, and Eric Toder. 1996. "Trends in Federal Tax Progressivity, 1980–1993." In *Tax Progressivity and Income Inequality*, edited by Joel Slemrod. Cambridge, Mass.: Cambridge University Press.

Katz, Michael B. 1986. *In the Shadow of the Poorhouse: A Social History of Welfare in America.* New York: Basic Books.

———. 1989. *The Undeserving Poor: From the War on Poverty to the War on Welfare.* New York: Pantheon Books.

Kennedy, Edward. 1995. "The Balanced Budget Reconciliation Act of 1995." *Congressional Record,* October 26, S15707–840.

Kingdon, John W. 1984. *Agendas, Alternatives, and Public Policies.* New York: HarperCollins.

Kosters, Marvin. 1993a. "The Earned Income Tax Credit and the Working Poor." *American Enterprise* 4(3): 64–72.

———. 1993b. *Statement Before the U.S. House of Representatives, Committee on Ways and Means, Subcommittees on Select Revenue Measures and Human Resources.* Washington, D.C. (March 30).

Kraemer, Kenneth L., Siegfried Dickhoven, Susan Fallows Tierney, and John Leslie King. 1987. *Datawars: The Politics of Modeling in Federal Policymaking.* New York: Columbia University Press.

Lampman, Robert J. 1954. "Recent Changes in Income Inequality Reconsidered." *American Economic Review* 44(3): 251–68.

———. 1957. "The Effectiveness of Some Institutions in Changing the Distribution of Income." *American Economic Review* (Papers and Proceedings of the Sixty-eighth Annual Meeting of the American Economic Association) 47(2): 519–28.

Lenkowsky, Leslie. 1986. *Politics, Economics, and Welfare Reform: The Failure of the Negative Income Tax in Britain and the United States.* New York: University Press of America.

Levy, Frank, and Richard J. Murnane. 1992. "U.S. Earnings Levels and Earnings Inequality: A Review of Recent Trends and Proposed Explanations." *Journal of Economic Literature* 30(3): 1333–81.

Liebman, Jeffrey B. 1998. "The Impact of the Earned Income Tax Credit on Incentives and Income Distribution." *Tax Policy and the Economy* 12: 80–119. Cambridge, Mass.: National Bureau of Economic Research and MIT Press.

Link, Mary. 1977. "Carter, Congress, and Welfare: A Long Road." *Congressional Quarterly* 35(33): 1699–1707.

Long, Russell. 1972. Remarks in the Senate. *Congressional Record,* Sept. 30, 33010.

———. 1975. Remarks in the Senate. *Congressional Record,* March 18, 7230.

Lydall, Harold, and John B. Lansing. 1959. "A Comparison of the Distribution of Personal Income and Wealth in the United States and Great Britain." *American Economic Review* 49(1): 43–67.

Lynn, Laurence E., Jr., and David deF. Whitman. 1981. *The President as Policymaker: Jimmy Carter and Welfare Reform.* Philadelphia: Temple University Press.

Madden, Nan. 1999. "Minnesota: Expansion of State Tax Credit Makes Work Pay for Welfare Families." *Poverty Research News* 3(1): 25–27.

Matusow, Allen. 1984. *The Unraveling of America: A History of Liberalism in the 1960s.* New York: Harper and Row.

McCubbin, Janet. 1999. "Non-Compliance and the Optimal Design of the Earned Income Tax Credit." Paper presented at the Conference on Earned Income Tax Credit: Early Evidence. Evanston, Ill.: Northwestern University (October 7–8).

Meyer, Bruce D. 1998. "Single Mothers, Work, and the EITC." *Poverty Research News* 2(3): 1–4.

Meyer, Bruce D., and Dan T. Rosenbaum. 1998. "Welfare, the Earned Income Tax Credit, and the Labor Supply of Single Mothers." Northwestern University (October 26). Mimeo.

Moynihan, Daniel Patrick. 1968. "The Crisis in Welfare." *Public Interest* 10: 3–31.

———. 1973. *The Politics of a Guaranteed Income: The Nixon Administration and the Family Assistance Plan.* New York: Random House.

Munnel, Alicia H., ed. 1986. *Lessons from the Income Maintenance Experiments.* Boston: Federal Reserve Bank of Boston.

National Center for Policy Analysis. 1995. "Taxes, Welfare, and Work." Washington, D.C.: National Center for Policy Analysis (September 14).

Nickles, Don. 1995. Remarks in the Senate. "U.S. Senate Begins Debate on Budget Bill." *Congressional Record,* October 25, S15599–682.

Nixon, Richard M. Presidential Materials Staff. White House Central Files. National Archives Branch Depository. College Park, Maryland.

O'Connor, Alice. 1998. "The False Dawn of Poor-Law Reform: Nixon, Carter, and the Quest for a Guaranteed Income." *Journal of Policy History* 10(1): 99–129.

———. 2001. *Poverty Knowledge: Social Science, Social Policy, and the Poor in Twentieth-Century U.S. History.* Princeton: Princeton University Press.

Palmer, John L., and Joseph A. Pechman. 1978. *Welfare in Rural Areas: The North Carolina–Iowa Income Maintenance Experiment.* Washington, D.C.: Brookings Institution.

Patterson, James. 1994. *America's Struggle Against Poverty, 1900–1994.* Cambridge, Mass.: Harvard University Press.

———. 1998. "Jimmy Carter and Welfare Reform." In *The Carter Presidency: Policy Choices in the Post–New Deal Era,* edited by Gary M. Fink and Hugh Davis Graham. Lawrence: University Press of Kansas.

Pechman, Joseph A. 1987. *Federal Tax Policy.* 5th ed. Washington, D.C.: Brookings Institution.

Pechman, Joseph A., and P. Michael Timpane. 1975. *Work Incentives and Income Guarantees: The New Jersey Negative Income Tax Experiment.* Washington, D.C.: Brookings Institution.

Petri, Thomas. 1994. "EITC Reform." *Congressional Record,* October 25, E2109.

———. 1996. "Replacing the EITC." *Congressional Record,* August 1, H9705.

Phillips, Kevin P. 1970. *The Emerging Republican Majority.* New York: Doubleday.

Piven, Frances Fox, and Richard A. Cloward. 1982. *The New Class War: Reagan's Attack on the Welfare State and Its Consequences.* New York: Pantheon Press.

Reichley, A. James. 1981. *Conservatives in an Age of Change: The Nixon and Ford Administrations.* Washington, D.C.: Brookings Institution.

Rhys-Williams, Juliette Evangeline. 1943. *Something to Look Forward To.* London: MacDonald.

———. 1953. *Taxation and Incentive.* New York: Oxford University Press.

Richardson, Margaret Milner. 1994. *Treasury Press Conference on the Earned Income Tax Credit.* Washington, D.C. (October 26).

Riesenfeld, Stefan A. 1955. "The Place of Unemployment Insurance Within the Pattern, and Policies of Protection Against Wage Loss." *Vanderbilt Law Review* 8(2): 218–44.

Roth, William. 1994a. "The Illegal Alien Credit Denial Act." *Congressional Record.* October 7, S14830, S14876–77.

———. 1994b. "Letter to GAO." *Tax Base,* March 10. *taxbase.tax.org/* (citation 94 TNT 57-79).

———. 1995. "Senate Debate on the Budget Bill." *Congressional Record,* October 25, S15599–682.

Rust, Bill. 1999. "Tax Relief for Working Poor Families: State Earned Income Tax Credits." *Advocacy* 1(2): 22–26.

Samuels, Leslie. 1995. *Statement Before the U.S. Senate, Committee on Governmental Affairs.* Washington, D.C. (June 15).

Scholz, John Karl. 1994. "The Earned Income Tax Credit: Participation, Compliance, and Antipoverty Effectiveness." *National Tax Journal* 47(1): 63–87.

———. 1997. *Statement Before the U.S. House of Representatives, Committee on Ways and Means.* Washington, D.C. (May 8).

Schwartz, Edward E. 1964. "A Way to End the Means Test." *Social Work* 9(3): 3–12.

"Senate Continues Budget Debate." 1995. *Congressional Record,* May 23. 57820–73.

Shapiro, Isaac, and Robert Greenstein. 1993. *Making Work Pay: The Unfinished Agenda.* Washington, D.C.: Center on Budget and Policy Priorities (May).

Small, Melvin. 1999. *The Presidency of Richard Nixon.* Lawrence: University Press of Kansas.

Sparrow, Malcolm K. 1993. *Fraud in the Electronic Filing Program: A Vulnerability Assessment Prepared for the Internal Revenue Service.* Washington, D.C. (September).

Steuerle, C. Eugene. 1991. "The 'Superterranean' Economy." *Tax Notes* 51: 647–48.

———. 1992. *The Tax Decade: How Taxes Came to Dominate the Public Agenda.* Washington: D.C.. Urban Institute Press.

———. 1993. "The IRS Cannot Control the New Superterranean Economy." *Tax Notes* 59: 1839–40.

———. 1995a. "Combined Tax Rates and AFDC Recipients." *Tax Notes* 69: 501–3.

———. 1995b. "The Future of the Earned Income Tax Credit." Pt. 2, "Distortions and Compliance Problems." *Tax Notes* 67: 1819–20.

———. 1995c. "Giving Jobs to Welfare Recipients: The Tax Rates They Face." *Tax Notes* 69(5): 641–44.

———. 1996. "Financing the American State at the Turn of the Century." In *Funding the Modern American State, 1941–1995: The Rise and Fall of the Era of Easy Finance,* edited by W. Elliot Brownlee. New York: Woodrow Wilson Center Press and Cambridge University Press.

Storey, James R. 1996. "The Earned Income Tax Credit: A Growing Form of Aid to Low-Income Workers." CRS Report to Congress. Washington, D.C.: Congressional Research Service (December 5).

Surrey, Stanley S. Papers (SSP). Harvard Law School Library, Cambridge, Massachusetts.

"Tax Credit for Low-Income Workers with Families." 1974. *Tax Notes,* September 23: 23–24.

Taxpayer Advocate. 1997. "Taxpayer Advocate's Annual Report to Congress, FY 1996." *Tax Base.* Accessed in May 1998 at: *taxbase.tax.org* (citation 97 TNT 11-4).

Theobald, Robert. 1963. *Free Men and Free Markets.* New York: Doubleday.

Tobin, James. 1967. "It Can Be Done! Conquering Poverty in the United States by 1976." *New Republic,* June 3, 14–18.

U.S. Department of Commerce. U.S. Bureau of the Census. 2000. *Table F6—Regions: Families (All Races) by Median and Mean Income, 1953–1998.* Available at: census.gov/hhes/income/histinc/fo6.htm.

U.S. Department of Health, Education, and Welfare (HEW). 1974. *Income Supplement Program: 1974 HEW Welfare Replacement Proposal.* Washington, D.C.

U.S. Department of the Treasury. 1984. *Tax Reform for Fairness, Simplicity, and Economic Growth.* 2 vols. Washington, D.C. (November).

———. Internal Revenue Service (IRS). 1994a. "Earned Income Tax Credit (EITC)/Advance EITC." FS-94-9. Washington, D.C. (December 28).

———. 1994b. "Eligible Workers Can Boost Their Take-Home Pay." IR-94-46. Washington, D.C. (April 22).

———. 1994c. "IRS Sponsors Nationwide Tax Forum." IR-94-53. Washington, D.C. (May 25).

———. 1995a. "Advance Earned Income Tax Credit Can Raise Monthly Take Home Pay by $105." IR-95-3. Washington, D.C. (January 11).

———. 1995b. *Study of EIC Filers for Tax Year 1993.* Appendix to Statement of Margaret Milner Richardson, Commissioner of Internal Revenue. *Statement Before the U.S. House of Representatives, Committee on Ways and Means, Subcommittees on Oversight and Human Resources.* Washington, D.C. (June 15).

———. 1996. "The Advance Earned Income Tax Credit." IRS Publication 1844. Washington, D.C. (February 1).

———. 1997. *Study of EITC Filers for Tax Year 1994: 1995 Earned Income Tax Credit Compliance Study.* Washington, D.C. (April 22).

———. 1999. *IRS Tracking, Earned Income Tax Credit Appropriation, Annual Report: FY 1998.* Document 9383. Washington, D.C.

———. Records of the Office of Tax Analysis (OTA). Record Group 59. National Archives Branch Depository. College Park, Maryland.

U.S. General Accounting Office (GAO). 1992. *Earned Income Tax Credit: Advance Payment Option Is Not Widely Known or Understood by the Public.* Washington, D.C.

———. 1993. *Earned Income Tax Credit: Design and Administration Could Be Improved.* GAO/GGD-93-145. Washington, D.C. (September).

———. 1994. *Tax Gap: Many Actions Taken, But a Cohesive Compliance Strategy Needed.* Washington, D.C. (May).

———. 1995. *Earned Income Credit, Noncompliance, and Potential Eligibility Revisions: Statement of Lynda D. Willis Before the U.S. Senate, Committee on Finance.* GAO/T-GGD-95-179. Washington, D.C. (June 8).

———. 1997. *Earned Income Credit Noncompliance: Statement of Lynda D. Willis Before the U.S. House of Representatives, Committee on Ways and Means.* GAO/T-GGD-97-105. Washington, D.C. (May 8).

U.S. House of Representatives. 1975. Committee on Ways and Means. *Tax Reduction Act of 1975.* H. Rept. 94-19. Washington: U.S. Government Printing Office (February 26).

———. 1984. Committee on Ways and Means. Subcommittee on Oversight. *Federal Tax Treatment of Low Income Persons.* Washington: U.S. Government Printing Office (April 12).

———. 1985a. Committee on Ways and Means. Select Committee on Children, Youth, and Families. *A Family Report Card: Comparing Seven Critical Tax Issues for Families as Treated Under Current Law, Kemp-Kasten, Bradley-Gephardt, and Treasury II.* Washington: U.S. Government Printing Office (August).

―――. 1985b. Committee on Ways and Means. Select Committee on Children, Youth, and Families. *Tax Policy: How Do Families Fare?* Washington: U.S. Government Printing Office (October).

―――. 1985c. Committee on Ways and Means. Select Committee on Children, Youth, and Families. *Tax Policy: What Do Families Need?* Washington: U.S. Government Printing Office (April 24).

―――. 1985d. Committee on Ways and Means. Subcommittee on Select Revenue Measures. *Federal Tax Treatment of Individuals Below the Poverty Level.* Washington: U.S. Government Printing Office (June 6).

―――. 1986. Committee on Ways and Means. Select Committee on Children, Youth, and Families. *A Family Report Card, Round II: Comparing Seven Critical Tax Issues for Families as Treated Under Current Law, Kemp-Kasten, Bradley-Gephardt, and Treasury II, and Ways and Means.* Washington: U.S. Government Printing Office (December 1985).

―――. 1993a. Committee on Ways and Means. Subcommittee on Oversight. *Hearing on Abusive Insurance Sales and Marketing Techniques Involving the Earned Income Tax Credit.* Washington: U.S. Government Printing Office (March 4).

―――. 1993b. Committee on Ways and Means. Subcommittees on Select Revenue Measures and Human Resources. 1993. *Hearing on Selected Aspects of Welfare Reform.* Washington: U.S. Government Printing Office (March 30).

―――. 1994. Committee on Ways and Means. Subcommittee on Oversight. *Hearing on Treasury's Tax Refund Fraud Task Force.* Washington: U.S. Government Printing Office (October 6).

―――. 1997a. Committee on Ways and Means. *Charts Comparing Middle-Income and EITC Families' Tax Burdens.* Washington: U.S. Government Printing Office (July 14).

―――. 1997b. Committee on Ways and Means. *Hearing on the Internal Revenue Service's 1995 Earned Income Tax Credit Compliance Study.* Washington: U.S. Government Printing Office (May 8).

―――. 1997c. Committee on Ways and Means. Press Release on Earned Income Tax Credit. Washington, D.C. (July 10).

―――. 1999. Committee on Ways and Means. *1998 Green Book.* Washington: U.S. Government Printing Office.

U.S. Senate. Committee on Finance. 1972. *Hearing on Welfare Cheating.* Address of Hon. Russell B. Long. Washington: U.S. Government Printing Office.

―――. 1975. *Tax Reduction Act of 1975: Report to Accompany H.R. 2166.* Washington: U.S. Government Printing Office (March 17).

―――. 1985. *Federal Tax Treatment of Individuals Below the Poverty Level.* Washington: U.S. Government Printing Office (June 17).

―――. 1995a. *Earned Income Tax Credit.* Washington: U.S. Government Printing Office (June 8).

―――. 1995b. *Hearing on the Earned Income Tax Credit Program.* Washington: U.S. Government Printing Office (June 8).

―――. Subcommittee on Governmental Affairs. 1995c. *Hearing on Earned Income Tax Credit.* Washington: U.S. Government Printing Office (April 4).

―――. Committee on the Budget. 1997. *Senate Budget Committee Report on Fiscal Year 1997 Concurrent Budget Resolution.* S. Rept. 104-271. Washington: U.S. Government Printing Office.

Ventry, Dennis J., Jr. 1997. "The Negative Income Tax: An Intellectual History." *Tax Notes* 77: 491–500.

Weinberger, Caspar. 1976. "The Reform of Welfare: A National Necessity." *Journal* (of the Institute for Socioeconomic Studies) 1(1): 1–27.

"Welfare Out of Control." 1971. *U.S. News and World Report,* February 8, 32.

"Welfare: The Shame of a Nation." 1971. *Newsweek,* February 8, 23.

Wilcox, Clair. 1969. *Toward Social Welfare: An Analysis of Programs and Proposals Attacking Poverty, Insecurity, and Inequality of Opportunity.* Homewood, Ill.: Richard D. Irwin.

Witte, John F. 1985. *The Politics and Development of the Federal Income Tax.* Madison: University of Wisconsin Press.

Yin, George K. 1995. *Statement Before the U.S. Senate, Subcommittee on Governmental Affairs: Hearings on Effectiveness and Design of the Earned Income Tax Credit.* Washington, D.C. (April 5).

Yin, George K., John Karl Scholz, Jonathan Barry Forman, and Mark J. Mazur. 1994. "Improving the Delivery of Benefits to the Working Poor: Proposals to Reform the Earned Income Tax Credit Program." *American Journal of Tax Policy* 11(2): 225–98.

Part II

Work and Marriage Incentives

Chapter 2

Making Single Mothers Work: Recent Tax and Welfare Policy and Its Effects

Bruce D. Meyer and Dan T. Rosenbaum

Between 1984 and 1996 there were enormous changes in many of the tax and transfer programs that affect single mothers. These changes dramatically increased the incentive to work. During that period, real dollars received through the Earned Income Tax Credit (EITC), which go primarily to working families with children, increased more than tenfold. The number of children receiving Medicaid increased 72 percent, while the number of covered adults with dependent children increased 27 percent. These Medicaid expansions primarily affected nonwelfare families with incomes near the poverty line, making work more attractive for low-income single mothers. Since 1993, nearly every state has experimented with changes in its welfare programs, often under waivers of the existing program rules. Many of these changes imposed work requirements, time limits, or other measures that encouraged single mothers to work. Finally, child-care funding for single mothers was increased. These program changes combined to greatly increase the incentive for single mothers to enter the workforce.

At the same time, there was a substantial increase in the employment of single mothers. The annual employment of all single mothers increased by about 9 percentage points between 1984 and 1996, while that for single mothers with children under the age of six increased 13.5 percentage points. Nearly all of this increase occurred after 1991. We should emphasize that all of these changes took place before the elimination of "welfare as we knew it" under the Personal Responsibility and Work Opportunity Reconciliation Act of 1996, which replaced Aid to Families with Dependent Children (AFDC) with Temporary Assistance for Needy Families.

Many papers have described one element of the changes in tax and welfare policy after 1984 until the passage of the 1996 welfare act that have affected the employment of single mothers, but no past work has described in detail the larger pattern of policy change. In this chapter, we seek to address this deficit by describing federal and state EITCs and other federal and state tax changes; the effects of changes in welfare programs; the expansions of Medicaid coverage to low-income non-AFDC children; and the recent flurry of welfare waivers. We also discuss the effects of changes in child-care programs during this period.[1] Because the Personal Responsibility and Work Opportunity Reconciliation Act changed many features of welfare in ways that are difficult to characterize, we end our analysis in 1996.

We then examine whether the changes in employment rates over time for different demographic groups and states are consistent with a causal effect of these policies on employment. These comparisons provide a transparent way of examining the plausibility of our findings elsewhere, based on a simple structural approach, that about 60 percent of the increase in single mothers' employment between 1984 and 1996 was in response to the EITC expansions (Meyer and Rosenbaum 2001).[2] In our earlier work, smaller though substantial roles were found for welfare benefit cuts and welfare waivers, while child care played an even smaller role. Though more structural approaches have advantages, transparency is not one of them.[3]

With many influences interacting to produce the variables, combined with functional form assumptions, it is often hard to see what leads to structural coefficient estimates. This chapter provides simple comparisons that examine the plausibility of the claim that the EITC was the main source of the employment changes, and examines the plausibility of alternative hypotheses, as well. Combined with the evidence in our "Welfare, The Earned Income Tax Credit, and the Labor Supply of Single Mothers" (Meyer and Rosenbaum 2001) and other papers, we can provide a convincing picture.

POLICY CHANGES THAT AFFECTED LABOR SUPPLY

In this section, we describe the major policy changes between 1984 and 1996 that affected the labor supply of single mothers. For each policy or program, we first provide some brief background information and outline major changes between 1984 and 1996. Next, we describe how and when the policies affected different groups. Finally, we analyze the theoretical effects of these changes on the choice of whether or not to work. The summary measures we use to describe the policy changes capture their overall effects on the budget sets of single women. We calculate the taxes and welfare benefits of single women at thirty different earnings levels and then average these values to get an overall effect for each policy that we examine.[4]

The EITC and Federal and State Income Taxes

In recent years, the most important change for single mothers in the financial incentive to work has probably come from the Earned Income Tax Credit.[5] The total amount of the EITC increased fifteenfold over the period under study, from $1.6 billion in 1984 to $28.8 billion in 1996. Single parents received more than two-thirds of these EITC dollars (U.S. House Committee on Ways and Means 1996; IRS, *Statistics of Income*, 1999).[6] In 1996, a single woman with two children who earned less than $8,890 (the phase-in range) received a 40 percent credit on dollars earned, up to a maximum of $3,556. Because the credit is refundable and a mother of two with those earnings was not subject to any federal income tax (owing to the standard deduction and personal exemptions), she would have received a check from the Internal Revenue Service for the credit amount. With additional earnings up to $11,610 the credit amount did not change. Additional earnings beyond $11,610 and up to $28,495 (the phase-out range) resulted in a reduction in the credit by 21.06 percent of the additional earnings, until the credit was reduced to zero at earnings of $28,495. This credit schedule meant that a woman with two children earning between $5,000 and just under $19,000 received at least a $2,000 credit.

The current EITC is the result of several legislative changes (summarized in figure 2.1) that greatly expanded the EITC after 1984. Between its beginning in 1975 and the passage of the Tax Reform Act of 1986, the EITC was small, and the credit amounts did not keep up with inflation. Beginning with the 1986 act, the EITC was expanded in a number of dimensions.

First, credit rates, phase-in ranges, and phase-out ranges were increased considerably. For a mother of one child in 1984, for example, the credit rate was 10 percent for earnings up to the end of the phase-in range at $5,000, implying a maximum credit of $500. In 1987 the credit rate rose to 14 percent on earnings up to $5,080, implying a maximum credit of $851. In 1988 the beginning and end of the phase-out range were increased by about $3,000. The credit parameters were then unchanged in real terms for several years, but beginning in 1991 the credit rates rose in small steps, up to 18.5 percent in 1993. In 1994 and 1995 there were large increases in the credit rates, to 26.3 and 34.0 percent respectively, though the phase-in range was reduced. The resulting maximum credit for a mother of one child was $2,094 in 1995.

Second, in 1991 the credit was expanded to provide a larger credit for families with two or more children and families with very young children. The increment to the maximum credit for a second child was small through 1993, never exceeding $77. Beginning in 1994, however, the difference began to rise sharply; it rose to $490 in 1994, $1,016 in 1995, and $1,404 in 1996. From 1991 through 1993, there were also small refundable credits for child health insurance premiums and for children under the age of one.[7]

Third, before 1991 children generally had to be claimed as dependents in order to be qualifying children, which required that the taxpayer provide more than half of their support. This requirement meant that low-income mothers who received more in AFDC than in earnings would not qualify for the EITC. Since 1991, to qualify the taxpayer must have a child who is under the age of nineteen or is a full-time student under the age of twenty-four who lived with the taxpayer for more than half of the year, regardless of who supported the child or children.[8]

Fourth, the relationship of the EITC with other programs has changed over time. Before October 1984, the EITC was counted as earned income in AFDC and food stamp calculations at the time it was earned. Between October 1984 and October 1989, it was counted at the time it was received, thereby typically

FIGURE 2.1 / Major Tax and Welfare Policy Changes Affecting Low Income Women, from 1984 to 1997

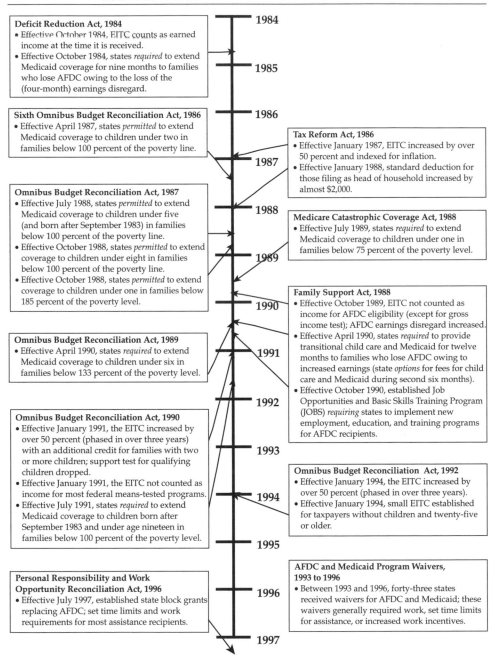

Deficit Reduction Act, 1984
- Effective October 1984, EITC counts as earned income at the time it is received.
- Effective October 1984, states *required* to extend Medicaid coverage for nine months to families who lose AFDC owing to the loss of the (four-month) earnings disregard.

Sixth Omnibus Budget Reconciliation Act, 1986
- Effective April 1987, states *permitted* to extend Medicaid coverage to children under two in families below 100 percent of the poverty line.

Omnibus Budget Reconciliation Act, 1987
- Effective July 1988, states *permitted* to extend Medicaid coverage to children under five (and born after September 1983) in families below 100 percent of the poverty line.
- Effective October 1988, states *permitted* to extend coverage to children under eight in families below 100 percent of the poverty line.
- Effective October 1988, states *permitted* to extend coverage to children under one in families below 185 percent of the poverty level.

Omnibus Budget Reconciliation Act, 1989
- Effective April 1990, states *required* to extend Medicaid coverage to children under six in families below 133 percent of the poverty level.

Omnibus Budget Reconciliation Act, 1990
- Effective January 1991, the EITC increased by over 50 percent (phased in over three years) with an additional credit for families with two or more children; support test for qualifying children dropped.
- Effective January 1991, the EITC not counted as income for most federal means-tested programs.
- Effective July 1991, states *required* to extend Medicaid coverage to children born after September 1983 and under age nineteen in families below 100 percent of the poverty level.

Personal Responsibility and Work Opportunity Reconciliation Act, 1996
- Effective July 1997, established state block grants replacing AFDC; set time limits and work requirements for most assistance recipients.

1984
1985
1986
1987
1988
1989
1990
1991
1992
1993
1994
1995
1996
1997

Tax Reform Act, 1986
- Effective January 1987, EITC increased by over 50 percent and indexed for inflation.
- Effective January 1988, standard deduction for those filing as head of household increased by almost $2,000.

Medicare Catastrophic Coverage Act, 1988
- Effective July 1989, states *required* to extend Medicaid coverage to children under one in families below 75 percent of the poverty level.

Family Support Act, 1988
- Effective October 1989, EITC not counted as income for AFDC eligibility (except for gross income test); AFDC earnings disregard increased.
- Effective April 1990, states *required* to provide transitional child care and Medicaid for twelve months to families who lose AFDC owing to increased earnings (state *options* for fees for child care and Medicaid during second six months).
- Effective October 1990, established Job Opportunities and Basic Skills Training Program (JOBS) *requiring* states to implement new employment, education, and training programs for AFDC recipients.

Omnibus Budget Reconciliation Act, 1992
- Effective January 1994, the EITC increased by over 50 percent (phased in over three years).
- Effective January 1994, small EITC established for taxpayers without children and twenty-five or older.

AFDC and Medicaid Program Waivers, 1993 to 1996
- Between 1993 and 1996, forty-three states received waivers for AFDC and Medicaid; these waivers generally required work, set time limits for assistance, or increased work incentives.

Source: Authors' compilation.
Note: Medicaid expansions covering children cover pregnant women as well.

affecting AFDC and food stamp benefits only when the tax return check was received. Between October 1989 and January 1991, the EITC was not counted as income in AFDC calculations (except for the gross income test), and effective January 1991, the EITC was not counted at all in most means-tested programs, including AFDC, food stamps, and Medicaid.[9] By not counting the EITC in these means-tested programs, these reforms have increased the value of the credit for very low-income women.

We should note that there were other changes in federal income taxes during this period that affected single women. In particular, in 1987 the personal exemption was increased by $820, and in 1988 the standard deduction for household heads rose by $1,860. These changes, in conjunction with the many changes in EITC credit rates and phase-in and phase-out ranges, make it hard to picture the changes in taxes at various earnings levels. To aid this evaluation, we plot in figure 2.2 the difference in after-tax earnings (earnings minus federal income taxes plus the EITC) between a woman with two children and a woman with no children for various pretax earnings levels in 1984, 1988, 1992, and 1996.[10] We focus on the difference between a woman with two children and a childless woman because this comparison is used in our later analysis of employment trends. As table 2.1 indicates, changes over time in this difference were almost entirely a response to changes in taxes paid (or credits received) by single mothers.

Figure 2.2 illustrates several important aspects of the EITC expansions. First, between 1984 and 1988, single mothers of two with earnings between $10,000 and $20,000 experienced increases in take-home pay (relative to single women without children) that ranged from $500 to $1,500.[11] Thus, the reward to working

FIGURE 2.2 / Difference in After-Tax Income of Single Women With and Without Children, Selected Years

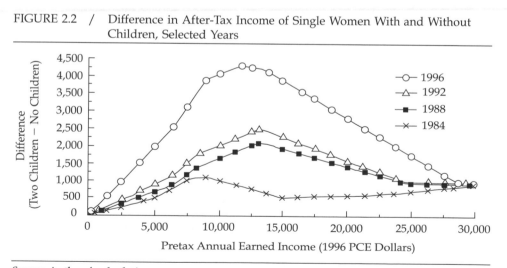

Source: Authors' calculations.
Note: All women are assumed to have only earned income and to take the standard deduction. Single women with children and without children are assumed to file as heads of households and single, respectively. *After-tax income* is income after federal taxes or credits.

TABLE 2.1 / Summary Characteristics of Policies Affecting Single Mothers and Single Women Without Children, 1984, 1988, 1992, and 1996

| | 1984 | | 1988 | | 1992 | | 1996 | |
| | With Children | Without Children | With Children | Without Children | With Children | Without Children | With Children | Without Children |
Variable								
Annual federal and state income taxes, EITC, and one-half Social Security taxes								
At $5,000 earnings	−165	352	−331	376	−530	408	−1,472	194
At $10,000 earnings	96	954	−361	1,356	−687	1,427	−2,032	1,432
At $15,000 earnings	1,582	2,075	705	2,589	456	2,687	−533	2,706
At $20,000 earnings	2,704	3,325	2,391	3,844	2,335	3,980	1,626	4,009
At $30,000 earnings	5,438	6,326	5,368	6,538	5,549	6,666	5,580	6,668
Annual AFDC and Food Stamp benefits								
At $0 earnings	7,705	0	7,603	0	7,464	0	7,089	0
At $5,000 earnings	4,856	0	4,940	0	4,866	0	4,619	0
At $10,000 earnings	1,977	0	2,059	0	2,078	0	2,013	0
At $15,000 earnings	557	0	566	0	654	0	635	0
At $20,000 earnings	95	0	95	0	111	0	136	0

Medicaid: number of family
members covered

At $0 earnings	2.65	0.00	2.65	0.00	2.65	0.00	2.65	0.01
At $5,000 earnings	2.53	0.00	2.58	0.00	2.54	0.00	2.48	0.01
At $10,000 earnings	1.13	0.00	1.50	0.00	1.65	0.00	1.75	0.01
At $15,000 earnings	0.34	0.00	0.42	0.00	0.74	0.00	0.88	0.01
At $20,000 earnings	0.05	0.00	0.06	0.00	0.29	0.00	0.46	0.01
At $25,000 earnings	0.01	0.00	0.01	0.00	0.09	0.00	0.18	0.01
AFDC waivers								
Any time limit	0.00	0	0.00	0	0.01	0	0.40	0
Any terminations	0.00	0	0.00	0	0.00	0	0.20	0
Extended transitional	0.00	0	0.00	0	0.01	0	0.12	0
Major waiver application	0.00	0	0.02	0	0.22	0	0.84	0
Annual child care dollars per eligible recipient	0	0	0	0	243	0	294	0
Number of observations	126,750	18,914	126,750	18,612	126,750	19,311	126,750	15,846

Source: The data are from the Current Population Survey Outgoing Rotation Group files (ORG) from 1984 to 1996.

Note: The sample consists of single women (divorced, widowed, or never married) aged nineteen to forty-four who are not in school. These weighted means are calculated using the characteristics of the ORG sample for the given year for single women without children and for a sample with a fixed distribution of children for single mothers. Women are assumed to be in their first four months of work, to have no unearned income, and to claim no child care expenses. Also, single women with and without children are assumed to file as head of household and single, respectively, and to claim the standard deduction. Taxes and welfare are adjusted for state cost of living differences, and all dollar amounts are expressed in 1996 dollars. See text for details.

increased substantially for single mothers relative to single childless women. Most of this increase was due to large increases in both the maximum credit and the earnings level before the credit phase-out began. Between 1988 and 1990, tax and EITC parameters were adjusted only for inflation, so the after-tax earnings difference remained the same. Between 1990 and 1992, the moderate increase in the credit rate is evident.

The most striking feature of figure 2.2 is the effect of the expansions from 1994 to 1996, which particularly affected women with two or more children.[12] For example, the take-home pay difference for women with $7,500 of earnings increased only about $600 between 1984 and 1993 but increased more than $1,500 between 1993 and 1996. Unlike the earlier expansions, those since 1993 dramatically increased the take-home pay difference for very low-income women (with earnings of less than $10,000) because of large increases in the credit rate and maximum credit. Thus, these EITC expansions sharply increased over a short period of time the reward for working, particularly for women with two or more children.

In addition to federal income tax changes, there were changes in state income taxes, including state EITCs, during this period. By 1994, seven states had their own EITCs. The largest five of these states introduced the credits from 1984 to 1996, the period under examination here. All of the state EITCs were set as a fraction of the federal EITC and thus increased when it did.[13] Four states (Minnesota, New York, Wisconsin, and Vermont) had refundable tax credits, while three other states (Iowa, Maryland, and Rhode Island) had nonrefundable credits. The size of these credits ranged from Iowa's nonrefundable credit set at 6.5 percent of the federal EITC (a maximum of $231 in 1996) to Wisconsin's refundable credit, which in 1996 was set at 43 percent of the federal EITC for a family with three or more children (a maximum of $1,529). Other state income tax changes during our sample period reduced taxes for single mothers. More than a dozen states increased their personal exemption, increased their child credit, added a higher standard deduction, or added a separate tax schedule for household heads. Quantitatively, though, these changes were not nearly as important as the institution and expansion of state EITCs.

To summarize these changes in federal and state taxes, we calculate the average taxes a single mother would pay if she worked. We obtain this measure by averaging taxes over the earnings distribution for single women. We use separate earnings distributions for women with and without children from the March Current Population Survey, which we average over all years from 1984 to 1996. We use this earnings distribution to calculate several other variables. To illustrate the changes in the variable for average income taxes over time, in figure 2.3 we plot its mean for single women with no children, one child, and two or more children by year from 1984 to 1996. Figure 2.3 and table 2.2 indicate that the taxes of a typical single mother with one child fell about $1,000 over the twelve-year period. About 40 percent of that fall had occurred by 1990, and about 60 percent occurred over the next six years. For a single mother with two or more children, the fall was almost $1,900, with more than 55 percent of that fall occurring between 1993 and 1996. Over the same period, from 1984 to 1996,

FIGURE 2.3 / Federal and State Income Taxes Paid If Working, Single Women With and Without Children, 1984 to 1999

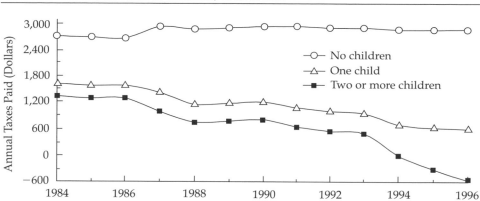

Source: The data are from the CPS Outgoing Rotation Group files (ORG), from 1984 to 1996.
Note: Taxes include federal and state income taxes, including federal and state EITCs. Dollar amounts are in 1996 PCE dollars.

the taxes paid by a single woman with no children rose slightly. Overall, the taxes paid by a single mother fell $1,629 between 1984 and 1996 relative to that of a single childless woman. Almost all of the fall was due to federal tax changes. Only $31 of the fall was due to state taxes, entirely owing to state EITCs. However, in the seven states with state EITCs the role of state taxes was much greater. In these jurisdictions, state EITCs accounted for a $224 drop in the taxes of single mothers relative to single women without children.

The theoretical effect of the EITC expansions on the annual labor force partici-pation decision of single parents is unambiguously positive. Since the EITC ex-pansions have increased the after-tax return to work at all earnings levels, some work during the year is unambiguously more attractive for single mothers. The effect of the EITC and its expansions on the hours of work among those working is much less clear and depends on where a person would choose to work on the precredit or postcredit budget sets. The higher income that one receives under the credit will discourage work through the income effect. While additional hours or weeks of work are encouraged as the credit is phased in, the phase-out of the credit adds an implicit tax, which discourages additional work through the substitution effect. Overall, since more people are expected to be on the phase-out range than the phase-in range, this negative substitution effect com-bined with the income effect is likely to reduce the hours and weeks worked of those who do work.

One might wonder if these income tax incentives for low-income households were ineffective because households were unaware of the incentives or did not bother to file tax returns (for evidence on knowledge of the EITC, see chapters 8 and 10, this volume). However, EITC take-up appears to be high and rising. John Karl Scholz (1990, 1994) estimates that 75 percent of EITC eligibles in 1988 and

TABLE 2.2 / Summary Measures of Incentives to Work from Different Sources, Single Mothers and Single Childless Women, 1984 to 1996

	1984	1986	1988	1990	1991	1992	1993	1994	1995	1996	1996 to 1990	1996 to 1984
When working												
Income taxes paid												
Single mothers with one child	1,625	1,580	1,157	1,210	1,083	1,001	955	702	633	609	−601	−1,016
Single mothers with two or more children	1,336	1,291	751	808	651	554	501	19	−291	−548	−1,356	−1,884
All single mothers	1,484	1,438	960	1,015	873	784	735	369	181	42	−973	−1,442
Single childless women	2,719	2,635	2,903	2,968	2,973	2,935	2,934	2,901	2,901	2,907	−61	187
AFDC + food stamps received, all single mothers	1,543	1,598	1,567	1,610	1,596	1,575	1,511	1,500	1,490	1,510	−101	−34
Medicaid received (at cost), all single mothers	1,224	1,402	1,397	1,601	1,647	1,746	1,817	1,915	1,972	1,996	394	752
When not working (single mothers only)												
AFDC + food stamps received	7,705	7,711	7,603	7,610	7,550	7,464	7,298	7,214	7,150	7,089	−520	−616
Medicaid received (at cost)	4,294	4,294	4,294	4,294	4,294	4,294	4,294	4,294	4,294	4,294	0	0

Gain from working for single mothers (working – not working)

Wages + welfare – taxes	10,519	10,614	11,169	11,151	11,339	11,492	11,643	12,082	12,324	12,543	1,392	2,024
Wages + welfare + medicaid – taxes	7,469	7,722	8,272	8,458	8,692	8,943	9,166	9,703	10,002	10,245	1,787	2,776

Relative gain from working (single mothers – single childless women)

Wage + welfare – taxes	−4,927	−4,866	−4,093	−4,047	−3,854	−3,738	−3,588	−3,182	−2,942	−2,715	1,332	2,212
Wages + welfare + medicaid – taxes	−7,997	−7,758	−6,990	−6,739	−6,500	−6,286	−6,065	−5,561	−5,264	−5,013	1,726	2,964
Wages + welfare + medicaid + child care – taxes	−7,997	−7,758	−6,990	−6,701	−6,327	−6,043	−5,810	−5,228	−4,966	−4,719	1,982	3,258

Source: The data are from the Current Population Survey Outgoing Rotation Group (ORG) files for 1984 to 1996 and are weighted.

Note: The sample consists of single women aged nineteen to forty-four who are not in school. These weighted means are calculated using the characteristics of the ORG sample for the given year for single women without children and for a sample with a fixed distribution of children for single mothers. Wages for all single women are assumed to be $18,165 a year. Medicaid coverage is assumed to be worth $1,900 for each eligible child and $1,083 for each eligible adult. All dollar amounts are expressed in 1996 dollars. See text for details.

between 80 and 86 percent of EITC eligibles in 1990 received the credit.[14] One of the reasons for this high take-up rate is the common use of paid tax preparers by low-income women (Olson and Davis 1994). With the increases in the EITC after 1990, one might expect that the participation rate would have risen further, though tougher compliance efforts may have discouraged some filers.

Aid to Families with Dependent Children and Food Stamps

The two programs most commonly thought of as welfare are Aid to Families with Dependent Children (AFDC) and Food Stamps.[15] We discuss the two programs together because nearly 90 percent of AFDC recipients also receive food stamps (U.S. House Committee on Ways and Means 1996). Both of these programs are large relative to other means-tested programs, but neither has grown much since 1984. Real spending on AFDC benefits fell slightly between 1984 and 1996, from $21.7 billion to $20.4 billion, even though the number of recipients increased by 15 percent, from 10.9 million to 12.6 million. Expenditures for the Food Stamp program increased by more than 35 percent during this same period, from $20.0 billion to $27.3 billion, though most of this increase resulted from the rise in the number of recipients, from 20.9 million to 25.5 million. Even if some measures of overall spending did not change a great deal, there have been changes in the benefits and implicit tax rates under these programs over time, and in recent years there has been experimentation with many other features of these programs. Before describing these recent changes, it is useful to summarize how the programs work.

The AFDC program provides cash payments to families with children who have been deprived of support because of the absence or unemployment of a parent. The Food Stamp program provides low-income households with coupons with which to purchase food. The parameters of the AFDC program are set by the states, while most Food Stamp parameters are the same in all states. Nevertheless, because of the interaction of the eligibility and benefit calculations of the two programs, there are interstate differences in the amount of food stamps received by people in similar situations.

Eligibility and benefit calculations under the two programs follow roughly similar rules. A monthly benefit or guarantee that varies with family size is provided to recipients with no income. After an initial earnings exemption (earnings that result in no benefit reduction), benefits are reduced by the amount of the additional income times a fraction, called the implicit tax rate, until benefits are zero and the family is no longer eligible for the program. The full details of the calculations are quite involved.

Several things should be noted about the calculations. First, there are complicated interactions between the two programs, because the Food Stamp program counts AFDC benefits as income in its benefit calculations (but the AFDC program does not count food stamp amounts as income in its benefit calculations). This rule implies that in states with sufficiently high AFDC benefits an implicit food stamp tax rate is applied to the first dollar of earnings, while in other states initial earnings result in no benefit reduction. This rule also implies that for some states the implicit tax rate used in calculating food stamps will fall when earnings are sufficiently high that AFDC benefits have been reduced to zero. Second, state AFDC programs differ in their earnings exemptions and implicit tax rates, though this point is not widely understood.[16] For example, since October 1989, in most states the earnings exemption for AFDC has been $120 during the first four months of work, $120 again during the fifth through eighth months, and $90 thereafter, but in Mississippi the earnings exemptions for the same periods have been $372, $288, and $258, respectively. Furthermore, the AFDC implicit tax rate in most states is 0.67 during the first four months of work and 1.00 thereafter, but in Mississippi these figures are 0.40 and 0.60, respectively. Third, the implicit tax rates can be substantial. Once AFDC and food stamp disregards are exhausted, a typical implicit tax rate is 0.71.

To illustrate these calculations, figure 2.4 presents the 1996 benefit schedules for AFDC, Food Stamps, and Medicaid for women with two children in Alabama, Mississippi, and Pennsylvania. These states have been chosen to highlight the difficulty with the common approach of measuring the combined effect of AFDC and food stamps using only the combined maximum benefit.[17] Measuring the AFDC and Food Stamp programs using the combined maximum benefit ignores these interstate differences in earnings exemptions and implicit tax rates, which are likely to be important for working AFDC recipients or those considering work. For example, in 1996 a woman with two children who works part-time (eighty hours a month) at a low wage ($5 an hour) receives $355 a month in combined AFDC and food stamp benefits in Mississippi but in Alabama the same woman would receive $295 in food stamps only, even though the maximum benefit in Alabama ($468) is higher than that in Mississippi ($424).[18] Consequently, summarizing these benefit schedules using only the maximum combined benefit completely ignores this large source of variation in state AFDC benefit schedules. Figure 2.5 shows the time pattern of the mean maximum welfare benefit and the mean benefit if a single mother works (averaging over the earnings distribution described earlier). Owing to cuts in AFDC, the mean maximum combined AFDC and food stamp benefit fell about 7 percent over the sample period. Over the same period mean benefits for a working single mother remained roughly constant as implicit tax rates were reduced.

Theory predicts that the AFDC and Food Stamp programs decrease labor supply for two reasons. First, the income effect of the guarantee amount (the maximum benefit) should make participation less likely and reduce hours worked if a woman participates. A cut in the maximum benefit unambiguously increases the likelihood of working. Second, the implicit tax rate resulting from the reduction in benefits as earnings increase, that is, the substitution effect, reduces the return to work. However, for someone working, the effect of reducing the implicit tax rate on additional work is ambiguous since a reduction in the implicit tax rate means that the welfare benefits received when working are higher, which can lead people who were not receiving welfare to reduce their

FIGURE 2.4 / Benefit Schedules for AFDC, Food Stamps, and Medicaid for Mothers with Two Children in Alabama, Mississippi, and Pennsylvania, 1996

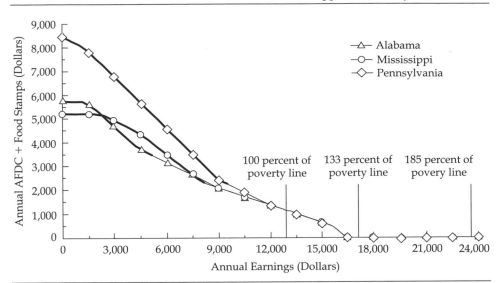

Source: Authors' calculations.

Note: Women are assumed to be in their first four months of work, to have no unearned income, and to claim no child care expenses. Annual shelter costs are assumed to be at the mean for food stamp households in the given state: Alabama, $2,820; Mississippi, $2,424; and Pennsylvania, $3,984. Bold lines indicate both AFDC receipt and Medicaid coverage for the entire family.

FIGURE 2.5 / Welfare When Working and Not Working for Single Mothers

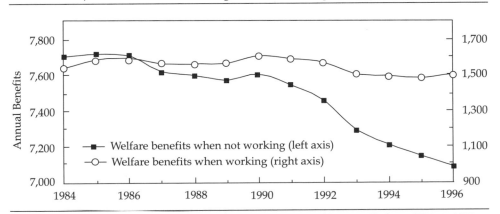

Source: The data are from the CPS Outgoing Rotation Group files (ORG), from 1984 to 1999.

Note: "Welfare when not working" gives the average AFDC and Food Stamp benefit (in 1996 PCE dollars) when a single mother does not work. "Welfare when working" gives the average AFDC and Food Stamp benefit (in 1996 PCE dollars) when a single mother works.

working hours in order to do so. In summary, it is expected that cuts in the maximum benefit and reductions in the implicit tax rate on earnings while on AFDC will increase the likelihood that a woman will work, though the effect of tax-rate cuts on hours is uncertain.

Medicaid

Medicaid is the biggest and most costly program that aids single mothers and their children. Medicaid expenditures for those not aged or disabled (those remaining are predominately single mothers and their children) totaled $29.8 billion in 1996 and went to 24.1 million people (U.S. House Committee on Ways and Means 1996, 897–902). Unlike the Food Stamp program and especially AFDC, Medicaid eligibility has expanded dramatically since 1984, resulting in a more than threefold increase in Medicaid expenditures (and a 60 percent increase in the caseload) on families with dependent children between 1984 and 1994.

Before 1987, Medicaid eligibility for single mothers and their children required receipt of AFDC, except in the special cases of families with very large medical expenses, those receiving Supplemental Security Income, and those leaving AFDC and receiving transitional Medicaid. In a series of expansions, Medicaid coverage was extended to low-income pregnant women and children (see figure 2.1). Beginning in April 1987, states were permitted to extend Medicaid coverage to children under the age of two in families with incomes below 100 percent of the federal poverty line.[19] Medicaid coverage was subsequently extended to older children and to those in higher-income families. In October 1988, states were permitted to cover children under the age of one in families with incomes below 185 percent of the poverty line. Later legislation often replaced state options with state requirements. Hence, since April 1990, states have been required to cover all children under the age of six living in families with incomes below 133 percent of the poverty line and, since July 1991, all children under the age of nineteen (and born after September 1983) with family incomes below 100 percent of the poverty line. This last provision expanded the coverage of poor children each year to those one year older, so that by the year 2000 even seventeen-year-olds were covered if their family incomes were below the poverty line.

These rules describe what can be done with Medicaid dollars that are matched by the federal government. Some states expanded medical coverage for children, and sometimes adults, with their own funds. Furthermore, the differences across states in the extent to which they took advantage of the permitted coverage options generated large differences in who was covered in different years in different states. Moreover, state AFDC rules interacted with the Medicaid expansions to determine the additional families covered. For example, in Alabama in 1996 (see figure 2.4) a family consisting of a woman with two children was eligible for both AFDC and Medicaid provided that the woman's earnings each month were below $366. Her children born after September 1983 were eligible for Medicaid if the family's monthly income was below 100 percent of the federal poverty line (about $1,050). Children under the age of six were covered if the family's monthly income was below 133 percent of the federal poverty line (about $1,400). In a state like Pennsylvania (see figure 2.4), the effect of the Medicaid expansions was less dramatic, since families with monthly earnings below $752 were already eligible for Medicaid on the basis of their AFDC receipt. Thus, in states with higher AFDC payment standards, the Medicaid expansions affected a smaller fraction of children.

Medicaid also was extended under transitional Medicaid programs to families who left AFDC. Beginning in October 1984, families who lost AFDC benefits because of the loss of the four-month earnings disregard were granted nine months of Medicaid coverage. Later, as part of the Family Support Act of 1988, states were required to extend Medicaid coverage (and provide child care) for twelve months to families who lost AFDC because of increased earnings. During the second six months, states had the option to charge fees for child care or to charge premiums or limit available services for Medicaid.

One can summarize the Medicaid expansions by calculating the number of total family members that would be covered if a woman were working. Figure 2.6 shows that Medicaid coverage for working single mothers increased on average by 0.26 family members between 1984 and 1996. The theoretical effect of Medicaid expansions on the decision to work is unambiguously positive, since those newly covered are those with earnings that would make them ineligible for AFDC. This conclusion should be qualified slightly given the low take-up rate of Medicaid under many expansions and the potential for the expansions to cause employers to drop health insurance coverage for their workers or to make it less generous.

FIGURE 2.6 / Medicaid Coverage and Child Care for Single Mothers, from 1984 to 1996

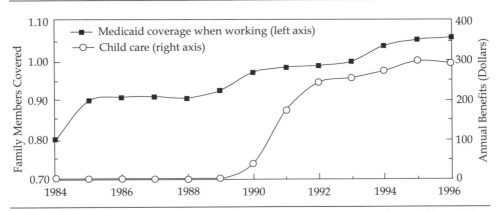

Source: The data are from the CPS Outgoing Rotation Group files (ORG), from 1984 to 1996.
Note: "Medicaid coverage when working" gives the number of family members covered when a single mother works. "Child care" gives the average child-care dollars (in 1996 PCE dollars) for each eligible single mother.

AFDC Program Waivers

Under the AFDC, the Secretary of Health and Human Services was authorized to waive certain program requirements to allow states to experiment with program changes that were judged to promote the objectives of the program. This waiver authority had rarely been used before the late 1980s, but its use accelerated during the Bush administration and continued under President Bill Clinton. Between January 1993 and August 1996, the Department of Health and Human Services approved welfare waivers in forty-three states.

While states experimented with changes in nearly every aspect of AFDC, many provisions applied to small parts of states or would not be expected to have a substantial effect on the employment of single mothers. We focus here on a few types of waiver provisions that were tried in many states. These provisions strengthened work and training requirements (in twenty-seven states), set time limits for welfare receipt (in twenty-four states), or extended transitional child care or Medicaid benefits for those leaving AFDC (in sixteen states). Some common types of provisions, such as expanded income disregards, have been incorporated in our summary of the AFDC program. Others, such as family caps (which limit the benefits for additional children) or increased resource limits (which loosened the asset restrictions for AFDC eligibility), most likely had small or ambiguous effects on employment.

Unlike several other recent studies, we focus on implementation dates of waiver provisions and actual beginning dates of terminations. For illustrative purposes, we also report whether a state had made a major statewide waiver application in case this indicates a tightening of administrative requirements in a state. In figure 2.7 we report the fraction of single women living in states that had applied for or implemented various types of waivers. One can see that very few women lived in states that had implemented significant waivers through at least 1994. The fraction of women in states that had made a major waiver application, however, was much higher, at 0.22 percent in 1992 and 0.85 percent in 1996.

Child Care

The cost and quality of child care is likely to have an important effect on whether a mother works. A large number of federal and state programs affect the availability and cost of child care.[20] Several federal programs, such as the Dependent Care Tax Credit and Title XX Social Services Block Grants, have existed for decades, though they have declined in importance in recent years. Another program, Head Start, has not declined in expenditures or enrollment but usually provides only part-day care and serves three- and four-year-olds almost exclusively.

The federal role in child care for low-income women expanded greatly fol-

FIGURE 2.7 / AFDC Waivers for Single Mothers

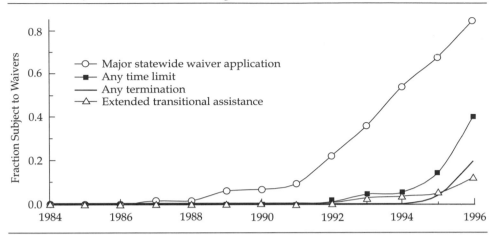

Source: The data are from the Current Population Survey Outgoing Rotation Group files (ORG), from 1984 to 1996.
Note: The AFDC waiver variables give the fraction of single mothers in states with a given AFDC waiver.

lowing the Family Support Act of 1988 and the Omnibus Budget Reconciliation Act of 1990. Four large programs started during this period: AFDC Child Care, Transitional Child Care, At-Risk Child Care, and Child Care and Development Block Grants. We focus on these programs because they were likely to be particularly important for single mothers. AFDC Child Care was provided to AFDC recipients who were employed or in training. Former recipients were eligible for Transitional Child Care for the first twelve months following termination of benefits. At-Risk Child Care was for low-income families not on AFDC who needed child care to work and were at risk of becoming eligible for AFDC. The Child Care and Development Block Grants program provided funds for child-care services for low-income families as well as for activities to improve the overall quality and supply of child care for all families. Total expenditures on these four federal programs by state and year are scaled by the number of single women in each state with children under the age of six. These numbers can be seen in figure 2.6, which shows a steep rise in child-care expenditures between 1989 and 1992, followed by a slower rise in later years. By 1992, federal expenditures under the four programs averaged more than $250 for each single mother with young children.

Summarizing the Changes in Work Incentives

Tables 2.1 and 2.2 provide summary measures of the changes from 1984 to 1996 in the incentives for single mothers to work. Table 2.1 reports taxes paid and welfare and Medicaid benefits received at different earnings levels as well as some summary measures of waivers and child care. Table 2.2 provides summary measures of changes in work incentives by combining the changes in taxes and benefits and averaging them over the earnings distributions of single women. Note that these earnings distributions do not vary over time, implying that changes over time reflect policy changes rather than changes in the wages or hours worked of single women. Annual tax payments by working single mothers fell by $1,442, while those for single women without children rose $187—a decrease of $1,629 in the taxes of single mothers relative to single women without children. The sharpest decreases in taxes were for single mothers with two or more children, whose taxes fell $868 more than those of the average single mother with only one child.

Over the same time period, the welfare benefits (AFDC and Food Stamps) for working single mothers rose $582 relative to nonworking single mothers. In other words, between 1984 and 1996 the increased incentive to work attributable to tax changes was about three times as large as that attributable to changes in welfare benefits. Medicaid coverage for the families of single mothers increased by about 0.26 family members over this same period. Valued at the average cost of Medicaid coverage for adults ($1,083) and children ($1,900) during this period, the changes in Medicaid eligibility increased single mothers' relative incentive to work by about $752 between 1984 and 1996. The change in average child-care benefits for those with young children was smaller, at about $294. Combining the changes in taxes with changes in welfare, Medicaid, and child-care benefits increased the financial return to working by a total of $3,258 over the period from 1984 to 1996. This change was almost 18 percent of the average annual pretax and transfer earnings of working single mothers ($18,165). As a percentage of the financial gain from working ($7,270 in 1984), this change was nearly a 45 percent increase. Overall, the policy changes between 1984 and 1996, especially the tax changes, dramatically increased the incentive for single mothers to work.[21]

DATA

The data used in this chapter come from the Current Population Survey (CPS), a nationally representative monthly survey of approximately sixty thousand households. We use two types of the CPS data, the March CPS files and the merged Outgoing Rotation Group (ORG) data. During each interview household members are asked whether they worked during the previous week and, if so, how many hours they worked, as well as many other questions. In the March interviews, individuals are asked to provide detailed retrospective information, including hours worked, earnings, and weeks worked during the previous year. The ORG files come from all twelve months of the year but include an individual only once in a given year.

The March CPS data used here are from interviews conducted between 1968 and 1997 and therefore provide information on the years 1967 through 1996. The ORG data used here are from all twelve months during the period from 1984 to

1996. We report two different measures of employment: whether a woman worked during the previous week (the ORG data) and whether a woman worked at all during the previous year (from the March CPS data). Each measure has its advantages. Whether a woman worked during the previous week is probably a better measure of labor supply to use as an input to policy decisions, since its average captures the fraction of women working in a given week. This variable will be especially useful if those who move in or out of the workforce on the margin work few weeks during the year. On the other hand, the EITC unequivocally increases the probability of working at all in a given tax year, though for some it could decrease weeks worked. If our goal is to provide a sharp test of theoretical predictions, whether a woman worked during the previous year is a better outcome measure. We report both measures with the expectation that the effects of many of the recent policy changes on the weekly employment measure will be smaller than those for the annual measure.

CHANGES IN EMPLOYMENT AND WELFARE RECEIPT

Table 2.3 summarizes long-term patterns in employment, welfare receipt, and single motherhood among women between the ages of nineteen and forty-four, using the March CPS data.[22] We also report, in the last column, the overall U.S. unemployment rate. The table indicates an increase in the employment rate of single mothers starting in the late 1980s that accelerated in recent years. Between 1984 and 1996 the employment rate of single mothers rose 8.7 percentage points, with a 6 percentage point increase after 1990. While we do not discuss hours worked here, there were even larger percentage increases in hours worked (see Meyer and Rosenbaum 1999b). There were some earlier periods, before 1984, in which the employment rate of single mothers was high, particularly from 1969 to 1970 and from 1978 to 1980. Neither of the earlier periods of increase were nearly as pronounced as the recent increase. The employment of single mothers appears to be cyclical, as their employment tends to rise as the overall unemployment rate falls. However, these two variables do not track each other that closely, as the unemployment troughs of 1973 and 1989 were not associated with substantial employment rate increases for single mothers. The recent rise in the employment of single mothers appears to have little precedent in the past. However, since we have not thoroughly studied the policy changes that occurred before 1984 (such as the provisions of the 1981 Omnibus Budget Reconciliation Act, which effectively discouraged work by welfare recipients), we cannot be much more definitive about the employment rates in these much earlier years.

Table 2.3 also shows that the recent increases in the employment of single mothers were mirrored by changes in welfare receipt of a similar magnitude and the opposite sign. This pattern is not sufficient, however, to conclude whether it was changes in work incentives or welfare itself that led to the behavioral changes. With this in mind, it is striking that 1996 is the first year in which most women who received welfare also worked during the year.

TABLE 2.3 / Employment Rates and Welfare Receipt for Single Mothers, Single
Motherhood, and Unemployment Rates, 1967 to 1996

	Fraction of Single Mothers, Aged Nineteen to Forty-Four, Who During the Year						Single Mothers As Fraction of Women Aged Nineteen to Forty-Four	National Unemployment Rate
	Worked		Did Not Work			Total Received Welfare		
Year	Total	No Welfare	Received Welfare	Received Welfare	No Welfare			
1967	0.7426	0.6515	0.0911	0.1320	0.1254	0.2231	0.0400	3.8
1969	0.7581	0.6545	0.1037	0.1312	0.1107	0.2348	0.0431	3.5
1971	0.7335	0.5910	0.1425	0.1719	0.0947	0.3144	0.0509	5.9
1973	0.7223	0.5778	0.1445	0.1845	0.0932	0.3291	0.0591	4.9
1975	0.7251	0.5853	0.1398	0.1985	0.0764	0.3384	0.0742	8.5
1977	0.7446	0.5967	0.1479	0.1999	0.0555	0.3478	0.0831	7.1
1979	0.7871	0.6543	0.1328	0.1601	0.0528	0.2929	0.0905	5.8
1981	0.7387	0.6214	0.1173	0.1882	0.0731	0.3055	0.1026	7.6
1983	0.7140	0.6189	0.0951	0.2090	0.0770	0.3041	0.1090	9.6
1984	0.7322	0.6509	0.0813	0.2066	0.0612	0.2879	0.1155	7.5
1985	0.7302	0.6358	0.0945	0.2036	0.0662	0.2981	0.1123	7.2
1986	0.7310	0.6303	0.1007	0.2051	0.0639	0.3058	0.1144	7.0
1987	0.7382	0.6331	0.1052	0.1885	0.0733	0.2937	0.1136	6.2
1988	0.7482	0.6491	0.0991	0.1943	0.0575	0.2934	0.1173	5.5
1989	0.7577	0.6690	0.0888	0.1811	0.0611	0.2699	0.1159	5.3
1990	0.7591	0.6518	0.1074	0.1806	0.0603	0.2880	0.1191	5.6
1991	0.7428	0.6397	0.1031	0.1934	0.0638	0.2965	0.1261	6.8
1992	0.7387	0.6321	0.1066	0.1924	0.0689	0.2990	0.1256	7.5
1993	0.7511	0.6350	0.1161	0.1852	0.0637	0.3013	0.1310	6.9
1994	0.7907	0.6681	0.1226	0.1470	0.0623	0.2696	0.1286	6.1
1995	0.8072	0.6966	0.1106	0.1254	0.0674	0.2360	0.1306	5.6
1996	0.8191	0.7046	0.1146	0.1107	0.0702	0.2250	0.1303	5.4

Source: The data are from the March Current Population Survey (March CPS) from 1968 to 1997 and
are weighted.
Note: The sample includes single mothers aged nineteen to forty-four (child under nineteen or
under twenty-four and a student) who are not in school, disabled, or ill. Those reporting positive
earned income but zero hours of work are excluded. "Worked" equals one for those who worked in
the preceding calendar year, and "received welfare" equals one for those who report receiving
public assistance income in the preceding calendar year. "Single mothers as fraction of women"
gives the fraction of all women aged nineteen to forty-four who satisfy the above school, disability,
and earnings criteria who are single mothers. See text for details.

HAS THE EMPLOYMENT OF OTHER GROUPS RISEN WITH THAT OF SINGLE MOTHERS?

To determine whether these policy changes are the likely cause of recent changes
in the employment of single mothers, we compare the employment trends of
single mothers with those of other groups. If the increases in employment were
not shared by other groups, it is more likely that policies that affected single
mothers, but not others, were responsible. We use multiple comparison groups

because each of the groups has strengths and weaknesses. While no single comparison provides a compelling picture, the weight of the evidence from the many different comparisons provides strong evidence of behavioral effects. In tables 2.4 through 2.6, we report raw employment differences for the various treatment and comparison groups. As a check on these comparisons, we have also estimated probit equations, which account for differences in the characteristics of members of the groups and changes in these characteristics over time. We also include a measure of macroeconomic conditions (the state unemployment rate) as well as its interaction with educational group and treatment group. We report the year × single mother estimates from these probit equations (1984 normalized to zero) in figures 2.8 and 2.9 for our main comparisons; other comparisons are described in the text.

Single Mothers Versus Single Women Without Children

We begin by comparing the employment rates of single mothers and single women without children.[23] In the left panel of table 2.4, we report these employment rates during a typical week from the ORG data, and in the right panel we report the rate for having worked at all during the year from the March data. We report rates for single women with and without children and the difference in employment rates between single mothers and single women without children. We report this difference because many determinants of employment that change over time—in particular, wages—might be expected to affect the two groups similarly. However, other determinants of employment—in particular, the tax and transfer programs described earlier—specifically affect single mothers.

The employment rates reported in table 2.4 show a striking time pattern. In the ORG sample, weekly employment increased by almost 6 percentage points for single mothers between 1984 and 1996 but declined by 0.75 percentage points for single women without children. In the March CPS, annual employment rose by 8.70 percentage points for single mothers but declined by more than a full percentage point for single women without children over the same time period. Furthermore, nearly all of the relative increase in employment for single mothers took place between 1991 and 1996. These results suggest that the rising employment of single mothers was not a result of better work opportunities for all women, since single women without children had slight declines in employment. Moreover, the timing of the increase in employment suggests that policy changes in the 1990s are likely to have played a role.

The changes in employment over time for single mothers compared with single women without children might be partly explained by differential changes over time in characteristics such as age and education for single women with and without children. Moreover, business cycles may differentially affect single women with and without children, thereby leading to employment shifts unrelated to policy changes. However, the results are little changed when we account for a wide range of demographic and business-cycle characteristics, including

TABLE 2.4 / Employment Rates, Differences, and Differences in Differences for Single Women With and Without Children, ORG and March CPS

Year	CPS Outgoing Rotation Group, Employed = Worked Last Week				March CPS, Employed = Worked During Year			
	Single Mothers	Single Women Without Children	Difference	Standard Error	Single Mothers	Single Women Without Children	Difference	Standard Error
1967	—	—	—	—	0.7426	0.9246	−0.1820	0.0153
1969	—	—	—	—	0.7581	0.9120	−0.1539	0.0148
1971	—	—	—	—	0.7335	0.9068	−0.1734	0.0143
1973	—	—	—	—	0.7223	0.9166	−0.1942	0.0138
1975	—	—	—	—	0.7251	0.9298	−0.2047	0.0120
1977	—	—	—	—	0.7446	0.9288	−0.1842	0.0103
1979	—	—	—	—	0.7871	0.9381	−0.1510	0.0084
1981	—	—	—	—	0.7387	0.9415	−0.2028	0.0088
1983	—	—	—	—	0.7140	0.9337	−0.2197	0.0087
1984	0.5854	0.8014	−0.2160	0.0059	0.7322	0.9399	−0.2077	0.0083
1985	0.5861	0.8048	−0.2187	0.0058	0.7302	0.9439	−0.2137	0.0083
1986	0.5891	0.8131	−0.2240	0.0057	0.7310	0.9450	−0.2141	0.0082
1987	0.5941	0.8179	−0.2238	0.0056	0.7382	0.9473	−0.2091	0.0081
1988	0.6027	0.8215	−0.2188	0.0058	0.7482	0.9485	−0.2003	0.0084
1989	0.6136	0.8150	−0.2015	0.0058	0.7577	0.9409	−0.1831	0.0080
1990	0.6007	0.8155	−0.2148	0.0056	0.7591	0.9424	−0.1832	0.0079
1991	0.5790	0.8031	−0.2242	0.0056	0.7428	0.9418	−0.1990	0.0079
1992	0.5790	0.7957	−0.2167	0.0057	0.7387	0.9299	−0.1913	0.0081
1993	0.5875	0.7918	−0.2044	0.0057	0.7511	0.9356	−0.1845	0.0080
1994	0.6053	0.7921	−0.1868	0.0057	0.7907	0.9312	−0.1405	0.0078
1995	0.6265	0.7971	−0.1707	0.0058	0.8072	0.9340	−0.1268	0.0080
1995	0.6450	0.7958	−0.1488	0.0060	0.8191	0.9290	−0.1098	0.0079
1995 − 1984	0.0596	−0.0075	0.0671	0.0084	0.0870	−0.0109	0.0979	0.0114

Source: The data are from the Current Population Survey Outgoing Rotation Group file (ORG) from 1984 to 1996 and the March Current Population Survey (March CPS) from 1968 to 1997. The data are weighted.

Note: The samples are composed of single women aged nineteen to forty-four who are not in school. The March CPS sample excludes disabled or ill persons and those with positive earned income but zero hours of work.

the unemployment rate as well as its interaction with whether or not a woman has children.[24] To illustrate this result, we show in figures 2.8 and 2.9 the difference in employment rates between single mothers and single women without children for the years 1984 to 1996, after accounting for these demographic and business-cycle characteristics. Figure 2.8 reports the pattern of weekly employment from the ORG, while figure 2.9 shows the pattern of annual employment from the March CPS. Both figures show a relative increase in single mothers' employment that accelerated after 1991. As we expected, the relative increases in single mothers' employment are larger for annual employment from the March CPS than for weekly employment from the ORG data.

One concern in interpreting changes in employment for single mothers during the years 1992 to 1994 is that beginning in January 1994 the CPS used a redesigned questionnaire. In appendix 2B, we assess the extent of any bias owing to the redesign using the parallel survey, which provides contemporaneous responses using the new and old surveys. We also employ comparisons between ORG and March CPS data, using the fact that redesign affected the two data sets at different points in time. Overall, these comparisons indicate that the CPS redesign had a small effect, which, if it leads to any bias, suggests that we slightly understate the recent employment increases of single mothers.

FIGURE 2.8 / Weekly Employment Estimates, Controlling for Individual Characteristics and Macroeconomic Conditions

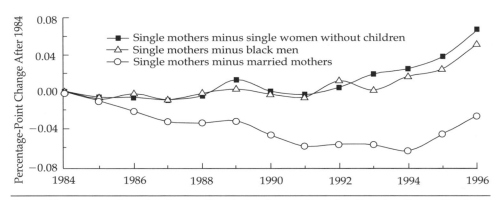

Source: The data are from the Current Population Survey Outgoing Rotation Group files from 1984 to 1996.

Note: Estimates are derivative estimates averaged over the single-mother observations from interactions of year and single-mother status. They are normalized so that the 1984 value equals zero. Standard errors range from 0.006 to 0.0016. The sample is composed of women aged nineteen to forty-four who are not in school. The following controls are included: indications for race, ethnicity, age group, education group, marital status, marital status interacted with any children, year, state, calendar month, and calendar month interacted with single-mother status. Continuous variables are included for the number of children under the age of six and the number of children under the age of eighteen, the state unemployment rate, the state unemployment rate interacted with single-mother status, and the state unemployment rate interacted with education group.

FIGURE 2.9 / Annual Employment Estimates, Controlling for Individual
Characteristics and Macroeconomic Conditions

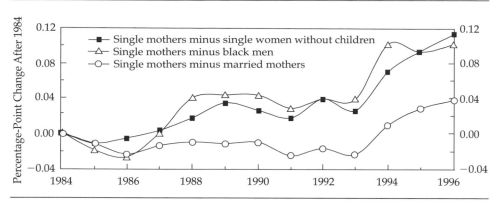

Source: The data are from the March Current Population Survey from 1985 to 1997.
Note: Estimates are derivative estimates averaged over the single-mother observations from
interactions of year and single-mother status. They are normalized so that the 1984 value
equals zero. Standard errors range from 0.006 to 0.0016. The sample consists of women aged
nineteen to forty-four who are not in school. The sample excludes disabled or ill persons and
those with positive earned income but zero hours worked. The following controls are
included: indicators for race, ethnicity, age group, education group, marital status, marital
status interacted with any children, pregnancy, central city, year, and state. Continuous
variables are included for the number of children under six and under eighteen, unearned
income, the state unemployment rate, the state unemployment rate interacted with single-
mother status, and the state unemployment rate interacted with education group.

Employment Among Single Mothers Versus Married Mothers

Table 2.5 provides a second set of comparisons: single mothers versus married
mothers. This comparison is useful because there have been legislative changes
other than welfare and tax policy, such as revisions in child-care programs and
family leave rules, that might be expected to affect mothers but not women
without children. Thus, the previous results could derive partially from the presence of such programs rather than from changes in tax and transfer programs.
When examining the employment rate of married mothers, however, one needs
to keep in mind that, unlike the rate for single women without children, the
employment rate of married women has been rising steadily for nearly a century. The left-hand side of table 2.5 shows that work in a typical week rose 10.7
percentage points between 1984 and 1996, almost 1 percentage point a year.
Over the longer period of the March CPS data, from 1967 to 1996, work anytime
during the year rose 27.5 percentage points, again almost a percentage point
each year, on average. One must somehow abstract from this trend if one is
going to use married women as a comparison group for single mothers. First of
all, while the employment of single mothers increased after 1984 and accelerated
after 1991, the trend increase in the employment rate of married women slowed

TABLE 2.5 / Employment Rates, Differences, and Difference in Differences for Single and Married Mothers, ORG and March CPS, 1967 to 1996

Year	CPS Outgoing Rotation Group, Employed = Worked Last Week				March CPS, Employed = Worked During Year			
	Single Mothers	Married Mothers	Difference	Standard Error	Single Mothers	Married Mothers	Difference	Standard Error
1967	—	—	—	—	0.7426	0.4820	0.2606	0.0149
1969	—	—	—	—	0.7581	0.5022	0.2560	0.0143
1971	—	—	—	—	0.7335	0.4973	0.2362	0.0139
1973	—	—	—	—	0.7223	0.5337	0.1886	0.0135
1975	—	—	—	—	0.7251	0.5474	0.1777	0.0118
1977	—	—	—	—	0.7446	0.5949	0.1497	0.0103
1979	—	—	—	—	0.7871	0.6458	0.1413	0.0085
1981	—	—	—	—	0.7387	0.6633	0.0754	0.0090
1983	—	—	—	—	0.7140	0.6657	0.0483	0.0088
1984	0.5854	0.5272	0.0582	0.0056	0.7322	0.6836	0.0485	0.0085
1985	0.5861	0.5386	0.0475	0.0056	0.7302	0.6934	0.0368	0.0086
1986	0.5891	0.5563	0.0329	0.0055	0.7310	0.7188	0.0121	0.0085
1987	0.5941	0.5754	0.0186	0.0055	0.7382	0.7288	0.0095	0.0084
1988	0.6027	0.5845	0.0182	0.0057	0.7482	0.7338	0.0144	0.0087
1989	0.6136	0.5946	0.0190	0.0056	0.7577	0.7355	0.0222	0.0082
1990	0.6007	0.6021	-0.0014	0.0054	0.7591	0.7384	0.0207	0.0082
1991	0.5790	0.5999	-0.0210	0.0055	0.7428	0.7465	-0.0038	0.0082
1992	0.5790	0.6051	-0.0261	0.0054	0.7387	0.7431	-0.0045	0.0083
1993	0.5875	0.6085	-0.0210	0.0054	0.7511	0.7523	-0.0012	0.0082
1994	0.6053	0.6299	-0.0247	0.0055	0.7907	0.7580	0.0327	0.0080
1995	0.6265	0.6320	-0.0056	0.0055	0.8072	0.7569	0.0503	0.0082
1996	0.6450	0.6344	0.0106	0.0058	0.8191	0.7571	0.0620	0.0081
1996 – 1991	0.0661	0.0345	0.0316	0.0080	0.0764	0.0106	0.0658	0.0115
1996 – 1984	0.0596	0.1073	-0.0476	0.0081	0.0870	0.0735	0.0135	0.0117

Source: The data are from the Current Population Survey Outgoing Rotation Group file (ORG) from 1984 to 1996 and the March Current Population Survey (March CPS) from 1968 to 1997. The data are weighted.
Note: Both samples consist of single (divorced, widowed, or never married) and married (with spouse present) mothers aged nineteen to forty-four who are not in school. The March CPS sample excludes disabled or ill persons and those with positive earned income but zero hours of work.

considerably over this period. This pattern indicates that the forces increasing the employment for single mothers did not have a similar effect on married mothers. Furthermore, in the 1990s the employment of single mothers rose relative to that of married mothers. Recall from earlier in this chapter that the year 1991 began a period of continuous expansion of the EITC. Between 1991 and 1996 the employment of single mothers rose faster than that of married mothers by 3.2 percentage points in a typical week and 6.6 percentage points during the year.[25]

Again, figures 2.8 and 2.9 illustrate the rise in single mothers' employment relative to that of married mothers, after accounting for demographic and business cycle factors. The figures indicate that the long-term trend of a relative decrease in single mothers' employment was reversed by 1986 for annual employment and by 1991 for weekly employment. The relative employment of single mothers then rose sharply starting in 1994 or 1995. Thus, the recent rise in employment of single mothers does not appear to result from factors affecting all mothers.

Employment Among Single Mothers Versus African American Men

In table 2.6, employment patterns of single mothers are compared with those of African American men. We examine black men because relatively disadvantaged groups may respond similarly to macroeconomic conditions and other changes in the low-wage labor market. There are only small changes over time in the employment rates for black men, particularly for work at any time in the year from the March CPS. Therefore, again there are large increases in the relative employment rate of single mothers from 1984 to 1996, again especially since 1991. Probit equations that control for individual characteristics (we now interact all the controls with being a black man as well as include the main effects) do little to alter the patterns in the 1990s, though they do increase the relative rise in single mothers' employment over the full period from 1984 to 1996. These results can be seen in figures 2.8 and 2.9. The weekly employment rate of black men in the ORG data is low (only about 10 percentage points higher than that of single mothers), thus the constancy of the black male employment rate is not the result of a lack of room for it to rise. Overall, changes in the economic conditions affecting disadvantaged groups do not appear to be an explanation for the recent increases in the employment of single mothers.

High-School-Dropout Single Mothers and Single Women Without Children

In table 2.7, we compare high-school-dropout single mothers with high-school-dropout women without children. Single mothers who did not finish high school are likely to be disproportionately affected by the EITC, given their low wages

TABLE 2.6 / Employment Rates, Differences, and Difference in Differences Between Single Mothers and African American Men

	CPS Outgoing Rotation Group, Employed = Worked Last Week				March CPS, Employed = Worked During Year			
Year	Single Mothers	Black Men	Difference	Standard Error	Single Mothers	Black Men	Difference	Standard Error
1984	0.5854	0.7108	−0.1254	0.0074	0.7322	0.8936	−0.1614	0.0101
1985	0.5861	0.7288	−0.1427	0.0073	0.7302	0.9175	−0.1872	0.0098
1985	0.5891	0.7286	−0.1394	0.0072	0.7310	0.9193	−0.1883	0.0097
1987	0.5941	0.7459	−0.1519	0.0071	0.7382	0.9285	−0.1903	0.0094
1988	0.6027	0.7469	−0.1442	0.0073	0.7482	0.9175	−0.1693	0.0100
1989	0.6136	0.7607	−0.1471	0.0072	0.7577	0.9201	−0.1624	0.0094
1990	0.6007	0.7482	−0.1475	0.0071	0.7591	0.9248	−0.1656	0.0093
1991	0.5790	0.7375	−0.1586	0.0072	0.7428	0.9034	−0.1606	0.0097
1992	0.5790	0.7144	−0.1355	0.0073	0.7387	0.8956	−0.1570	0.0099
1993	0.5875	0.7256	−0.1382	0.0073	0.7511	0.9109	−0.1598	0.0097
1994	0.6053	0.7282	−0.1229	0.0074	0.7907	0.9031	−0.1124	0.0097
1995	0.6265	0.7495	−0.1231	0.0073	0.8072	0.9086	−0.1014	0.0101
1996	0.6450	0.7386	−0.0936	0.0078	0.8191	0.9113	−0.0922	0.0098
1996 − 1984	0.0596	0.0278	0.0318	0.0107	0.0870	0.0177	0.0693	0.0141

Source: The data are from the Current Population Survey Outgoing Rotation Group files (ORG) for 1984 to 1996 and the March Current Population Survey (CPS) for 1985 to 1997. The data are weighted.
Note: Both samples consist of persons aged nineteen to forty-four who are not in school. The March CPS sample excludes disabled or ill persons and those with positive income but zero hours worked.

and the recent expansions in the credit for those with the lowest earnings that we see in figure 2.2. Furthermore, among high school dropouts the wages and other characteristics of single mothers and single women without children are strikingly similar (see figure 2.10). Finally, single childless women who did not finish high school have quite low employment rates, implying that they should be responsive to favorable changes in working conditions that affect all low-educated single women. When we compare work in a typical week over the period from 1984 to 1996, the employment rate of single mothers rises 9.8 percentage points relative to that of single women without children. For employment anytime during the year, the relative rise is 14.7 percentage points. In both cases, most of the rise occurs in the 1990s. When we control for individual characteristics in a probit equation as described earlier (we now drop the education controls), the relative increases in single mothers' employment are about one-third larger. However, over the period since 1991, the controls have little effect, barely affecting the large rise in single mothers' employment. Overall, there are particularly large increases in the relative employment of high-school-dropout single mothers during the period of EITC expansions.

TABLE 2.7 / Employment Rates, Differences, and Difference in Differences Between Single Women With and Without Children, by Education

	CPS Outgoing Rotation Group, (Employed = Worked Last Week)				March CPS (Employed = Worked During Year)			
	Dropout Single Mothers	Dropout Single Women Without Children	Difference	Standard Error	Dropout Single Mothers	Dropout Single Women Without Children	Difference	Standard Error
1984	0.3199	0.4876	−0.1678	0.0153	0.4699	0.7446	−0.2747	0.0263
1988	0.3298	0.5173	−0.1875	0.0161	0.4613	0.7520	−0.2907	0.0280
1992	0.3005	0.4766	−0.1761	0.0152	0.4481	0.6524	−0.2043	0.0278
1996	0.3640	0.4335	−0.0695	0.0174	0.5646	0.6919	−0.1273	0.0308
1996 − 1984	0.0441	−0.0542	0.0983	0.0232	0.0946	−0.0528	0.1474	0.0405

Source: The data are from the Current Population Survey Outgoing Rotation Group files (ORG) for 1984 to 1996 and the March Current Population Survey (CPS) for 1985 to 1997. The data are weighted.
Note: Both samples consist of persons aged nineteen to forty-four who are not in school. The March CPS sample excludes disabled or ill persons and those with positive income but zero hours worked.

FIGURE 2.10 / The Distribution of Hourly Earnings for High-School-Dropout Single Women With and Without Children

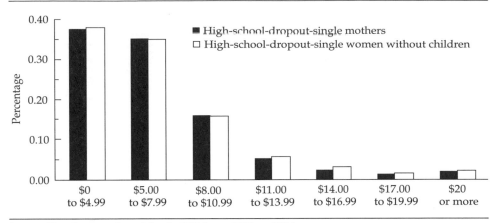

■ High-school-dropout-single mothers
□ High-school-dropout-single women without children

Source: The data are from March CPS from 1985 to 1997.
Note: Hourly wages are expressed in 1996 personal consumption expenditure deflated dollars.

DO THE PATTERNS OF EMPLOYMENT CHANGE SUGGEST THAT POLICY LED TO THE CHANGES?

As we have already emphasized, the changes in tax and welfare policy in recent years should have particularly affected certain groups. In this section we examine some of these hypotheses in order to determine which are likely to have been responsible for the increases in employment. In table 2.8, we begin by looking at the employment changes for women with two or more children relative to those with only one child. Recall that the EITC differed only trivially by the number of children until 1994. By 1996, however, the maximum credit for families with two or more children had risen to $3,556, while that for one-child families was $2,152 and had remained constant in real terms since 1994. The effect of these EITC changes on expected taxes for women who work can be seen in table 2.2 and figure 2.3. Between 1993 and 1996, income taxes when working fell an average of $1,049 for single mothers with two or more children but by only $346 for those with one child.

We see in table 2.8 that the employment of single mothers with two or more children was steady or falling through 1993, both on an absolute level and relative to single mothers with one child. Between 1984 and 1993, the difference between the employment rate of single mothers with two or more children and that of single mothers with one child fell 3.6 percentage points in a typical week. For work anytime during the year, the difference in employment fell 6.3 percentage points. Beginning in 1994, this trend was sharply reversed, with single mothers with two or more children increasing their relative employment. Between 1993 and 1996, the relative employment in a typical week of those with

TABLE 2.8 / Employment Rates, Differences, and Difference in Differences Between Single Mothers With One Child and Single Mothers With Two or More Children

	CPS Outgoing Rotation Group, Employed = Worked Last Week				March CPS, Employed = Worked During Year			
Year	Two or More Children	One Child	Difference	Standard Error	Two or More Children	One Child	Difference	Standard Error
1984	0.5328	0.6392	−0.1064	0.0101	0.6634	0.8028	−0.1393	0.0151
1988	0.5194	0.6801	−0.1607	0.0101	0.6664	0.8315	−0.1651	0.0153
1992	0.5080	0.6508	−0.1427	0.0096	0.6643	0.8144	−0.1502	0.0146
1993	0.5169	0.6597	−0.1428	0.0096	0.6518	0.8537	−0.2019	0.0141
1996	0.5831	0.7068	−0.1237	0.0101	0.7697	0.8697	−0.1000	0.0138
1993 − 1984	−0.0159	0.0205	−0.0364	0.0139	−0.0116	0.0509	−0.0626	0.0207
1996 − 1993	0.0662	0.0471	0.0191	0.0139	0.1179	0.0160	0.1020	0.0198
1996 − 1984	0.0503	0.0675	−0.0172	0.0143	0.1063	0.0669	0.0394	0.0204

Source: The data are from the Current Population Survey Outgoing Rotation Group files (ORG) for 1984 to 1996 and the March Current Population Survey (CPS) for 1985 to 1997. The data are weighted.

Note: Both samples consist of persons aged nineteen to forty-four who are not in school. The March CPS sample excludes disabled or ill persons and those with positive income but zero hours worked.

two or more children rose 1.9 percentage points. For work anytime during the year, the increase was a very large 10.2 percentage points. This pattern closely fits what would be expected if the EITC had a substantial causal effect on employment.

Two alternative explanations for this pattern of employment change by number of children are not supported by the evidence. It is possible that a given dollar tax cut could have different quantitative effects on one- and two-child families, complicating the use of family size as a source of identification. However, the pattern of tax and employment changes is fortuitous in allowing us to distinguish the effects on families with one child as distinct from families with two or more children. The EITC expansions through 1993 cut taxes equally for the two groups and coincided with relative decreases in the employment of single mothers of two or more children, suggesting a smaller average effect of each dollar on those with two or more children. After 1993, however, the expansions were focused on mothers with two or more children, and it is only then that we see relative increases in the employment of this group. Note that changes in the incremental welfare benefits for additional children are also not a plausible alternative explanation. Over the full period from 1984 to 1996, or the recent period from 1993 to 1996, the difference in welfare benefits between those with one child and those with two or more children did not change in percentage terms, and the absolute differences in the changes were small.

To examine further whether tax policy was the cause of the employment increase, table 2.9 compares employment changes in low- and high-cost-of-living states.[26] A tax credit of a given dollar amount should be valued more and have a greater behavioral response in states with a low cost of living than in states with a high cost of living. Our calculations indicate that taxes fell $357 more in real terms between 1984 and 1996 in the states with a low cost of living.[27] Employ-

TABLE 2.9 / Employment Rates, Differences, and Difference in Differences Between Single Mothers in Low-Cost-of-Living and High-Cost-of-Living States

	CPS Outgoing Rotation Group (Employed = Worked Last Week)				March CPS (Employed = Worked During Year)			
	Low Cost of Living	High Cost of Living	Difference	Standard Error	Low Cost of Living	High Cost of Living	Difference	Standard Error
1984	0.5951	0.5740	0.0211	0.0102	0.7426	0.7203	0.0223	0.0153
1988	0.6135	0.5906	0.0229	0.0103	0.7739	0.7204	0.0535	0.0157
1992	0.5973	0.5589	0.0384	0.0097	0.7625	0.7113	0.0511	0.0149
1996	0.6716	0.6155	0.0560	0.0102	0.8540	0.7801	0.0739	0.0140
1996 − 1984	0.0765	0.0415	0.0350	0.0144	0.1114	0.0598	0.0516	0.0208

Source: The data are from the Current Population Survey Outgoing Rotation Group files (ORG) for 1984 to 1996 and the March Current Population Survey (CPS) for 1985 to 1997. The data are weighted.
Note: Both samples consist of persons aged nineteen to forty-four who are not in school. The March CPS sample excludes disabled or ill persons and those with positive income but zero hours worked.

ment rates increased more in the states with a low cost of living through most of the period from 1984 to 1996, as predicted. However, the employment increase is not focused in the last few years of greatest expansion of the EITC, and it is probably larger than is plausible. Nevertheless, the increase does begin in 1988 or 1989, which is roughly consistent (especially with a lagged response) with the longer period of increases in the EITC from 1987 through 1996. We have also examined the change in employment in states with high and low costs of living for single mothers relative to that for single women without children. In this case, the changes in employment between the two sets of states are less sharp, particularly for work in a typical week, but they still go in the expected direction. Overall, the differences in cost of living are further evidence in favor of a tax effect on employment, though the differences reported in table 2.9 are probably too large to be purely a result of the interaction of living costs and taxes.

In table 2.10, we continue to probe whether the evidence is consistent with a substantial effect of tax changes on employment. Here we examine the change in employment among single mothers in states that had a state EITC sometime during our sample period compared with that of women in those states that never had state EITCs. By 1996, seven states had their own EITCs, all of which had enacted their credit by 1994. While this comparison does not use the timing of specific states' EITCs, our calculations of average state taxes indicate that state EITCs did not significantly reduce taxes until 1994. In table 2.10, there is weak evidence of a small effect of the state EITCs on the employment of single mothers. In the ORG data the relative employment of single mothers rises 2.3 percentage points in EITC states after 1992. In the March CPS data there is little change in EITC states in later years. We also examined the difference in employment changes between single mothers and single childless women in states with their own EITC relative to women in non-EITC states. These estimates suggest

TABLE 2.10 / Employment Rates, Differences, and Difference in Differences Between Single Mothers in States With and Without State EITCs

	CPS Outgoing Rotation Group, Employed = Worked Last Week				March CPS, Employed = Worked During Year			
Year	State EITC	No State EITC	Difference	Standard Error	State EITC	No State EITC	Difference	Standard Error
1984	0.5247	0.5953	−0.0706	0.0149	0.6793	0.7412	−0.0619	0.0229
1988	0.5463	0.6125	−0.0662	0.0158	0.6849	0.7598	−0.0749	0.0255
1992	0.5286	0.5871	−0.0585	0.0145	0.6782	0.7481	−0.0699	0.0234
1996	0.6146	0.6500	−0.0354	0.0150	0.7674	0.8276	−0.0603	0.0219
1996 − 1992	0.0860	0.0629	0.0231	0.0208	0.0891	0.0796	0.0096	0.0320
1996 − 1984	0.0899	0.0546	0.0352	0.0212	0.0881	0.0864	0.0016	0.0317

Source: The data are from the Current Population Survey Outgoing Rotation Group files (ORG) for 1984 to 1996 and the March Current Population Survey (CPS) for 1985 to 1997. The data are weighted.
Note: Both samples consist of persons aged nineteen to forty-four who are not in school. The March CPS sample excludes disabled or ill persons and those with positive income but zero hours worked.

an increase of 1 to 2 percentage points in single mothers' employment after 1993 in EITC states. Overall, there is some evidence in support of a state EITC effect.

In table 2.11, we examine single mothers with children under the age of six compared with single women without children. For women with young children the increase in employment in the ORG data is even larger than it was for all single mothers: 10.9 percentage points. In the March CPS data the increase in employment is larger still: 14.6 percentage points. As noted earlier, there are only small changes in the employment of single childless women. Since many of the policy changes might be expected to particularly affect mothers of young children,[28] this result is interesting but does not rule out or confirm any particular policy. This comparison of two groups also partly reflects the effect of having two or more children, since a mother with a young child is more likely to have more than one child under the age of eighteen.

Tables 2.12 and 2.13 provide comparisons of employment change for states with different changes in welfare and Medicaid policies. Table 2.12 compares employment in states with large and small increases in the difference in welfare benefits for a woman who works relative to those for a woman who does not work. There was little difference between states with large and small increases in the incentive to work under welfare programs. The employment rate difference between the states was fairly constant over time, though there was a slight dip in the difference in the middle of the time period from 1984 to 1996. The point estimates indicate a relative increase in employment where the welfare incentives were changed less, but the estimates are not significantly different from zero.

Table 2.13 compares states with large Medicaid expansions with those that experienced small expansions in their Medicaid eligibility rules. The table indicates that from 1984 to 1996 employment rose more in states with large Medicaid expansions than in states with small expansions. However, the timing of the employment changes is not favorable to a causal interpretation of this finding. Medicaid coverage increased the fastest in states with large increases relative to those with small increases from 1986 to 1991 and from 1993 to 1996. In the ORG sample, the employment of single mothers fell in states with large increases relative to those with small increases during both of these periods. In the March CPS, relative employment increased during the first period but fell during the second period.

We also examined states with major statewide welfare applications by 1994. There was a relative increase in both measures of employment for these states, but it appears that the increase in employment began well before the states even applied for the waivers, and application usually preceded implementation by a year or more.

To assess the relative contribution of changes in different policies in causing the recent employment increases, some form of multivariate analysis is probably the best approach. A multivariate approach, such as that which we used earlier (Meyer and Rosenbaum 2001), can account for the many dimensions of policy change, the differential impact of the policies on different types of families, and the timing of the specific changes. The approach taken in this chapter is a complement, not an alternative, to this earlier approach.

TABLE 2.11 / Employment Rates, Differences, and Difference in Differences Between Single Mothers With at Least One Child Under the Age of Six and Single Women Without Children

Year	CPS Outgoing Rotation Group (Employed = Worked Last Week)				March CPS (Employed = Worked During Year)			
	Single Mothers, Child Under Six	Single Women Without Children	Difference	Standard Error	Single Mothers, Child Under Six	Single Women Without Children	Difference	Standard Error
1984	0.4382	0.8014	−0.3632	0.0083	0.6122	0.9399	−0.3277	0.0131
1988	0.4634	0.8215	−0.3581	0.0084	0.6277	0.9485	−0.3207	0.0132
1992	0.4330	0.7957	−0.3627	0.0078	0.6273	0.9299	−0.3027	0.0124
1996	0.5396	0.7938	−0.2543	0.0085	0.7476	0.9290	−0.1813	0.0119
1996 − 1984	0.1014	−0.0075	0.1089	0.0119	0.1335	−0.0109	0.1464	0.0177

Source: The data are from the Current Population Survey Outgoing Rotation Group files (ORG) for 1984 to 1996 and the March Current Population Survey (CPS) for 1985 to 1997. The data are weighted.

Note: Both samples consist of persons aged nineteen to forty-four who are not in school. The March CPS sample excludes disabled or ill persons and those with positive income but zero hours worked.

TABLE 2.12 / Employment Rates, Differences, and Difference in Differences Between Single Mothers in States With Large and Small Increases in Welfare Payoffs to Working

	CPS Outgoing Rotation Group, Employed = Worked Last Week				March CPS, Employed = Worked During Year			
Year	States With Large Increases	States With Small Increases	Difference	Standard Error	States With Large Increases	States With Small Increases	Difference	Standard Error
1984	0.5979	0.5725	0.0255	0.0102	0.7600	0.7057	0.0543	0.0153
1988	0.6076	0.5978	0.0098	0.0103	0.7550	0.7414	0.0137	0.0157
1992	0.5862	0.5713	0.0149	0.0098	0.7325	0.7453	−0.0129	0.0149
1996	0.6543	0.6361	0.0182	0.0103	0.8327	0.8058	0.0270	0.0140
1996 − 1984	0.0564	0.0637	−0.0073	0.0145	0.0728	0.1001	−0.0273	0.0207

Source: The data are from the Current Population Survey Outgoing Rotation Group files (ORG) for 1984 to 1996 and the March Current Population Survey (CPS) for 1985 to 1997. The data are weighted.

Note: Both samples consist of single mothers aged nineteen to forty-four who are not in school. The March CPS sample excludes disabled or ill persons and those with positive earned income but zero hours worked. The table compares states in which the difference between working and not working increased by more than or less than $600 between 1984 and 1996.

TABLE 2.13 / Employment Rates, Differences, and Difference in Differences for Single Mothers in States With Large and Small Increases in Medicaid When Working

Year	CPS Outgoing Rotation Group (Employed = Worked Last Week)				March CPS (Employed = Worked During Year)			
	States With Large Increases	States With Small Increases	Difference	Standard Error	States With Large Increases	States With Small Increases	Difference	Standard Error
1984	0.5814	0.5888	−0.0074	0.0102	0.7287	0.7353	−0.0066	0.0153
1986	0.5881	0.5900	−0.0019	0.0100	0.7177	0.7424	−0.0246	0.0154
1988	0.6025	0.6028	−0.0003	0.0102	0.7646	0.7344	0.0302	0.0156
1991	0.5745	0.5828	−0.0083	0.0098	0.7559	0.7321	0.0238	0.0147
1992	0.5934	0.5672	0.0262	0.0097	0.7490	0.7300	0.0189	0.0149
1993	0.5975	0.5790	0.0186	0.0097	0.7775	0.7293	0.0481	0.0146
1996	0.6514	0.6394	0.0120	0.0102	0.8423	0.7988	0.0435	0.0139
1991 − 1986	−0.0136	−0.0072	−0.0064	0.0140	0.0382	−0.0102	0.0484	0.0213
1996 − 1993	0.0539	0.0604	−0.0065	0.0141	0.0648	0.0694	−0.0047	0.0201
1996 − 1984	0.0700	0.0505	0.0194	0.0144	0.1135	0.0635	0.0501	0.0207

Source: The data are from the Current Population Survey Outgoing Rotation Group files (ORG) for 1984 to 1996 and the March Current Population Survey (CPS) for 1985 to 1997. The data are weighted.

Note: Both samples consist of single mothers aged nineteen to forty-four who are not in school. The March CPS sample excludes disabled or ill persons and those with positive earned income but zero hours of work. The table compares states with large increases from 1984 to 1996 in the number of family members eligible for Medicaid to states with small increases. Large increases are defined as those greater than 0.28 persons. See text for details.

The EITC might be expected to have a lagged effect on employment if some recipients do not learn about changes in the credit until after they have filed their taxes or received a refund. There is some hint that EITC changes have a lagged effect on employment in the overall time pattern of employment changes and in the cost of living results. Two studies (Eissa and Liebman 1996 and Meyer and Rosenbaum 2001) find some evidence in favor of a lagged effect. In addition, the elasticities in our forthcoming paper, which are based on a more structured analysis of the data presented in this chapter, are not large relative to those in the literature and thus may be consistent with imperfect perception of taxes.

ARE THE COMPARISON GROUPS VALID?

To assess the accuracy of our findings, we examine whether single mothers and the comparison groups are comparable in a number of dimensions. In particular, we examine the wages of the different groups, "ceiling effects" that could lead to the differential impact of omitted factors on the groups, and the potential endogeneity of single motherhood. The primary determinant of employment for single mothers and the comparison groups is wages. We examined the wage distributions of single mothers and the comparison groups using the March CPS data averaged over the period from 1984 to 1996. While single women without children have higher wages on average than single mothers, there is a high degree of overlap between the two distributions. The same high degree of overlap is true for the wage distributions of single and married mothers. In figure 2.10 we show the distributions for single women with and without children after restricting the sample to those with less than a high school education. The wage distributions for these two groups are almost indistinguishable. Thus, the wage levels of single mothers and the comparison groups, especially when conditioned on education, are quite comparable. One might then ask if there have been disproportionate changes in the wages of single mothers and the comparison groups over time. We focus on single women with and without children, since they are our primary comparison group. If the wages of single mothers rose more in recent years than the wages of single women without children, it would provide an alternative explanation for the rise in single mothers' employment. As mentioned earlier, the reverse is true: the wages of single childless women rose about 6 percent between 1984 and 1996, while those of single mothers only rose about 1 percent. A similar pattern holds if one looks at single women without a high school education. Overall, the pattern of wage levels and changes suggests that we are not overstating the rise in single mothers' employment.

Another potential criticism of some of our comparison groups is that their employment rates are so high that it is unreasonable to expect them to respond to changes in economic conditions and other factors in the same way that single mothers do. In our probit estimates, this argument is not compelling because we include as controls the unemployment rate as well as its interaction with being a single mother, which accounts for a differential effect of economic conditions on the two groups. This argument is also not compelling because employment rates are not particularly high for several of our comparison groups, especially for work in a typical week. Married mothers and single mothers have similar employment rates, and the weekly employment of black men is only about 10 percentage points higher than the rate for single mothers. Most important, in the comparison of low-educated single women with and without children, the employment rates of both groups are not high at all. Only 33 percent of high-school-dropout single mothers and 48 percent of high-school-dropout single women without children worked in a typical week. Nevertheless, the relative changes in employment are larger for high school dropouts than for all single mothers.

Yet another potential criticism is that using variation across women in their marital status and presence of children implicitly assumes that marriage and fertility decisions are exogenous to the policy changes that we examine. The evidence on the effects of policy changes on these decisions is mixed, making the exogeneity assumption more plausible. For example, in her review of work and marriage incentives, Hilary Hoynes notes that "together this evidence suggests that marriage decisions are not sensitive to financial incentives. . . . Overall [the effects of welfare on out-of-wedlock births] are often insignificant, and when they are not, they are small (Hoynes 1997, 129–30)." On the other hand, in another review, Robert Moffitt (1997) suggests that the weight of the evidence implies some effect of welfare benefits on marriage and fertility. The second-to-last column of table 2.3 reports the fraction of women aged nineteen to forty-four who are single mothers for the years 1967 to 1996. This rate shows a steep increase over the period as it more than triples from 1967 to 1991. In recent years, the rate of increase has slowed, suggesting that the large recent increases in work by single mothers are not the result of working women changing their fertility or marriage behavior. However, the appropriate counterfactual rate of single motherhood is unclear. Aggregate data may also hide increases in marriage for some groups and decreases for others. Eissa and Hoynes (1999) conclude that recent tax and welfare changes increased marriage rates for very low-income couples but decreased marriage among those with somewhat higher incomes.[29] However, given that we expect only small changes in marriage and fertility, it is unlikely that employment rates are sufficiently different across these groups to lead to a substantial increase in measured employment for single mothers. Overall, it is likely that endogenous single motherhood exerts a small bias on our results.

CONCLUSION

Between 1984 and 1996, there were enormous changes in many of the tax and transfer programs that affect single mothers. The Earned Income Tax Credit was expanded, welfare benefits were cut, welfare time limits were added and cases were terminated, Medicaid for the working poor was expanded, training programs were redirected, and programs providing subsidized or free child care were expanded. All of these changes would be expected to encourage single mothers to work.

These changes were followed by large increases in the employment rates of single mothers. The employment of single mothers in a typical week rose 6 percentage points, while employment at any time during the year rose 8.5 percentage points. These employment increases were not shared by other low-wage groups, such as single women without children, married mothers, or black men. This evidence suggests that policy changes specific to single mothers are likely to be responsible for the recent rise in their rate of employment.

Large relative increases were seen in the employment rate of single mothers with two or more children beginning in the year when there was a substantially higher EITC for those with two or more children. There were also larger increases in employment rates in states with a low cost of living, where a given dollar EITC would be expected to have a larger effect. We find some evidence of larger employment increases in states with their own EITCs. States with larger Medicaid expansions had larger employment increases, but the timing of the employment changes fits poorly with that of the policy changes. Furthermore, there is little evidence for an effect of changes in welfare benefits. However, welfare and Medicaid may be better evaluated in a multivariate structural approach such as we present elsewhere (Meyer and Rosenbaum 2001). Overall, the findings are supportive of our earlier conclusion that the EITC had a major role in spurring the recent increase in the employment rate of single mothers.

APPENDIX

TABLE 2.A1 / Effect of CPS Redesign on the Employment of Single Women, ORG and March CPS Comparisons

| | CPS Outgoing Rotation Group | | | | March CPS | |
Year	Children	No Children	Difference	Standard Error	Children	No Children
Employment rate (from table 2.2)						
1992	0.5790	0.7957	−0.2167	0.0057	0.7387	0.9299
1993	0.5875	0.7918	−0.2044	0.0057	0.7511	0.9356
1994	0.6053	0.7921	−0.1868	0.0057	0.7907	0.9312
Yearly differences						
1993 − 1992	0.0085	−0.0039	0.0124	0.0080	0.0125	0.0057
1994 − 1993	0.0178	0.0003	0.0175	0.0080	0.0396	−0.0044
Effect of Redesign on March CPS ([1993 March CPS−1992 March CPS] − [1993 ORG − 1992 ORG])					0.0040	0.0096

TABLE 2.A1 / *Continued*

Year	CPS Outgoing Rotation Group				March CPS	
	Children	No Children	Difference	Standard Error	Children	No Children
Effect of Redesign on ORG ([1994 ORG – 1993 ORG] – [1994 March CPS – 1993 March CPS])					−0.0218	0.0047

Source: The data are from the Current Population Survey Outgoing Rotation Group files (ORG) from 1992 to 1994 and the March Current Population Survey (March CPS) from 1993 to 1995 and are weighted.

Note: Both samples include single women aged nineteen to forty-four who are not in school. The March CPS sample excludes disabled or ill persons and those with positive earned income but zero hours of work.

APPENDIX 2A: THE CPS REDESIGN

One caveat in interpreting changes in employment during the years 1992 to 1994 is that beginning in January 1994, the CPS used a redesigned questionnaire.[30] We use two methods to assess the extent of any bias is the employment rate of single women attributable to the redesign.

First, we take advantage of the fact that the March CPS reports retrospective employment information, so the redesign first affects the 1993 employment rates. Conversely, for the contemporaneous employment information used in the ORG, the redesign first affects the 1994 rates. We compare the seam in each of these two data sets to unbroken data from the other data set to provide an estimate of the bias owing to the redesign.[31] Note that we focus on the difference in differences, that is, the one-year change in the employment rate for single mothers minus the one-year change for single women without children. The redesign is not a concern for our results unless the redesign affected single mothers and control groups differently. In table 2.A1, we compare the March CPS difference in differences from 1992 to 1993 (single mothers minus single women without children) that spans the redesign to that in the unbroken ORG data. This comparison suggests that the redesign has led to an understatement of the increase in single mothers' employment in the March CPS, but the bias is small and insignificant. Similarly, we compare the ORG difference in differences from 1993 to 1994, that spans the redesign, to that in the unbroken March CPS data. This comparison suggests that the redesign has led to a substantial understatement of the increase in single mothers' employment in the ORG, though the bias estimate is only marginally significant. Since the changes attributable to the redesign mostly affected questions from the monthly questionnaire (the basis for the ORG data) rather than those from the supplemental questionnaires (the basis for the March CPS data), it is not surprising that the effects of the redesign are larger in the ORG.

The second method of estimating the redesign bias exploits the parallel survey of twelve thousand households that was conducted using the new collection procedures and questionnaire between July 1992 and December 1993. Table 2.A2 reports comparisons of the difference in differences (single mothers minus single women without children) in the parallel survey to those in the ORG. These estimates suggest a small but insignificant positive bias in the ORG attributable to the redesign. Hence, this analysis suggests that the redesign resulted in a small overstatement of the increase in the employment rate of single mothers in the ORG.[32] Overall, these comparisons indicate that the CPS redesign is not the source of the recent increases in the rate of employment of single mothers.[33]

TABLE 2.A2 / Effect of CPS Redesign on the Employment of Single Women, ORG and Parallel Survey Comparisons

	Children		No Children		Difference	
	Mean	Standard Error	Mean	Standard Error	Mean	Standard Error
1993 Parallel Survey	0.5926	0.0055	0.7915	0.0033	−0.1988	0.0064
1993 ORG	0.5875	0.0048	0.7918	0.0029	−0.2044	0.0057
Effect of Redesign on ORG	0.0052	0.0073	−0.0004	0.0044	0.0055	0.0086

Source: The data are from the 1993 Current Population Survey Outgoing Rotation Group files (ORG) and the 1993 Current Population Survey and are weighted.
Note: The sample includes single women aged nineteen to forty-four who are not in school.

APPENDIX 2B: SOURCES OF INFORMATION ON POLICY CHANGES

We obtain the federal income tax schedules from the U.S. Department of the Treasury, *Tax Guide* (IRS, various years). The state tax information was obtained from four sources: the Advisory Committee on Intergovernmental Relations (various years), the Commerce Clearing House (various years), unpublished data from the Center on Budget and Policy Priorities, and Feenberg and Coutts (1993).

The AFDC program parameters are obtained from the U.S. Department of Health and Human Services (various years) and unpublished data from the Urban Institute. The Food Stamp parameters come from the U.S. House Committee on Ways and Means (various years) and the U.S. Department of Agriculture (various years). The Medicaid program information is obtained from three sources: the National Governor's Association (various dates), the Intergovernmental Health Policy Project (various years), and the U.S. House Committee on Energy and Commerce (1988, 1993).

The AFDC waiver variables we used are based on our reading of the waiver summaries in U.S. General Accounting Office (1997), the U.S. Department of Health and Human Services (1997b), and Savner and Greenberg (1997). These sources generally have the implementation dates of waivers. We also consulted American Public Welfare Association (1996), Levine and Whitmore (1998), and U.S. Department of Health and Human Services (1997a). Child-care expenditures come from unpublished U.S. Department of Health and Human Service tabulations.

NOTES

1. We do not try to examine every government program that affects single women and their families. Other relevant programs we omit include training programs (see Meyer and Rosenbaum 1999a), public and subsidized housing, child support enforcement, food and nutrition programs other than Food Stamps, and Supplemental Security Income.

2. Related work in Bishop 1998 and in chapter 3 of this volume examines the effects of the EITC on employment and other outcomes. Nada Eissa and Jeffrey Liebman (1996) examine the EITC changes that were part of the Tax Reform Act of 1986.

3. Advantages of structural approaches include implications regarding what variables should influence outcomes and the form in which they do so, as well as improved validity for simulations.

4. The assumptions and data used in these calculations are described in Meyer and Rosenbaum 2001. See table 2.1 for the average values of the policy variables at various earnings levels. Note that for single mothers we compute policy variables for each year using the sample of single mothers from the entire 1984 to 1996 sample. This approach accounts for changes in policies but holds constant over time each state's distribution of family sizes and child ages.

5. See Liebman 1998 for a history of the EITC and a survey of many of the key economic issues.

6. Most of the remaining dollars are received by married taxpayers.

7. In 1993 (the last year of these credits), the total credit received for child health insurance premiums was $0.46 billion, the total credit for children under the age of one was $0.76 billion, and the value of the basic credit was $14.3 billion (IRS, *Statistics of Income,* 1994).

8. Beginning in 1994, childless taxpayers could receive a small credit.

9. Beginning in 1997, some states chose to count the EITC in benefit calculations for their welfare programs.

10. Note that figure 2.2 illustrates only the differences in after-tax earnings owing to federal income taxes and the EITC. Other programs and work expenses, especially child-care expenses, would need to be taken into account to fully characterize differences in disposable income between single women with and without children.

11. Unless noted, all dollar amounts are in 1996 dollars, indexed by the personal consumption expenditure (PCE) deflator.

12. Figure 2.2 does not incorporate the small credit, instituted beginning in 1994, available to taxpayers aged twenty-five and older without qualifying children. This credit is incorporated in the tax variable used in the empirical work that follows.

13. Wisconsin used a slightly different rule, but only in 1994.

14. Because of these high participation rates, a significant literature (Scholz 1990; Liebman 1995; chapter 7, this volume) has focused on ineligible EITC recipients.

15. With the passage of the Personal Responsibility and Work Opportunity Reconciliation Act of 1996, AFDC has been replaced by welfare block grants to states under the Temporary Assistance for Needy Families program.

16. For most states (Alabama and Pennsylvania, for example), the payment standard (the level of income after disregards at which AFDC benefits are zero) is the same as the maximum benefit. Furthermore, the ratable reduction (the fraction paid to AFDC recipients of the difference between the payment standard and income after disregards) is one, making the AFDC implicit tax rate identical to the benefit reduction rate and the AFDC earnings exemption equal to the earnings disregard. However, in 1996, fifteen states had ratable reductions different from one, or maximum benefits different from their payment standards, or both. For example, in Mississippi the ratable reduction equaled 0.60, and the maximum benefit was set at less than a third of its payment standard.

17. Some research has used the implicit tax rate in addition to the maximum benefit to parameterize AFDC and Food Stamps; see Moffitt 1992 and Danziger, Haveman, and Plotnick 1981 for excellent reviews of the AFDC literature.

18. Women are assumed to be in their first four months of work, to have no unearned income, and to claim no child-care expenses.

19. Medicaid expansions covering children under the age of one typically covered pregnant women for services related to the pregnancy.

20. The Congressional Research Service has identified forty-six programs operating in 1994 that were related to child care (U.S. House Committee on Ways and Means 1996, 640). Most of the programs were small; thirty-two of the forty-six provided less than $50 million in annual funding.

21. Wage changes over this period may have slightly favored the employment of single women without children relative to single mothers. Hourly wages rose by 1 percent for single mothers but increased by 6 percent for single women without children. Note, however, that the changes in the composition of single mothers working attributable to their increased employment may have affected these simple comparisons of means. When we account for changes in the observed characteristics of single mothers and single women without children in a log wage regression, the changes over time in hourly wages are similar for the two groups of single women.

22. We report only March CPS results here since children were not identified in the ORG data before 1984. The ORG data also do not include welfare receipt.

23. This approach is the one taken by Eissa and Liebman (1996), who use the March CPS data to compare single women with and without children from 1984 to 1990.

24. For example, between 1984 and 1996, probit average derivatives indicate that the weekly employment of single mothers relative to single women without children rises 7.1 percentage points without controls and 6.8 percentage points with controls. For annual employment, the corresponding numbers are 11.7 percentage points without controls and 11.5 percentage points with controls. The controls include state, race, ethnicity, age, education, marital status, marital status interacted with a children indicator. We also include the number of children under the age of six and the number of children under the age of eighteen, the state unemployment rate, the state unemployment rate interacted with education group, the state unemployment rate interacted with a children indicator, controls for pregnancy, central city, and unearned income (for the March CPS only), controls for month and month interacted with a children indicator (for the ORG only). See Meyer and Rosenbaum 1999b, section 5.3, for details.

25. The EITC expansions may be partly responsible for the slower growth of married mothers' employment, but the likely impact is small relative to the changes for single mothers. Eissa and Hoynes (1998) conclude that the EITC has reduced the employment of high-school-dropout single mothers by 1.2 percentage points.

26. We divide states into high and low cost of living using the index described in detail in Meyer and Rosenbaum 2001. This index incorporates housing cost differences across states, using Census data to calculate the price of a standardized apartment in each state.

27. This calculation incorporates the differences in the wage distributions between states with high and low costs of living.

28. The changes in the AFDC training programs particularly affected women with young children, and the child-care programs might be expected to have the largest effects on preschool children. However, even the changes in welfare and the EITC might have the largest impact on those with young children, if this group is disproportionately located close to the margin between work and nonwork.

29. On the other hand, David Ellwood, in chapter 3 of this volume, finds little or no marriage effect of the EITC and welfare.

30. For a description of this CPS redesign, see Cohany, Polivka, and Rothgeb 1994 and Polivka and Miller 1998.

31. One caution regarding this procedure is that the March CPS measures annual employment, while the ORG records weekly employment. However, table 2.2 indicates that year-to-year changes in the two surveys tend to be in the same direction and of a similar magnitude, though the March CPS changes tend to be slightly larger.

32. The difference between the ORG and March CPS data and the parallel survey may be a result of differences between the parallel survey and the regular CPS. In particular, the parallel survey interviewers had lower caseloads, and the interviews were longer and were supervised more carefully.

33. A final source of evidence is the Survey of Income and Program Participation employment rate change between 1993 and 1994 reported in Liebman 1998. Liebman finds that employment rose 4.5 percentage points over this period. The comparable change in the ORG was 1.8 percentage points, again suggesting that the ORG understates the rise in single mothers' employment.

REFERENCES

American Public Welfare Association. 1996. "Summary of Approved AFDC Waiver Actions." Report. Washington, D.C.

Advisory Committee on Intergovernmental Relations. Various Years. *Significant Features of Fiscal Federalism*. Washington, D.C.

Bishop, John H. 1998. "Is Welfare Reform Succeeding?" Cornell University. Mimeo.

Cohany, Sharon, Anne Polivka, and Jennifer Rothgeb. 1994. "Revisions in the Current Population Survey Effective January 1994." *Employment and Earnings* 41(2): 13–37.

Commerce Clearing House. Various years. *State Tax Handbook*. Chicago, Ill.

Danziger, Sheldon, Robert Haveman, and Robert Plotnick. 1981. "How Income Transfers Affect Work, Savings, and the Income Distribution: A Critical Review." *Journal of Economic Literature* 19(3): 975–1028.

Eissa, Nada, and Hilary Williamson Hoynes. 1998. "The Earned Income Tax Credit and the Labor Supply of Married Couples." Working Paper 6856. Cambridge, Mass.: National Bureau of Economic Research.

———. 1999. "Good News for Low-Income Families? Tax-Transfer Schemes, and Marriage." University of California, Berkeley (November). Mimeo.

Eissa, Nada, and Jeffrey B. Liebman. 1996. "Labor Supply Response to the Earned Income Tax Credit." *Quarterly Journal of Economics* 112(2): 605–37.

Feenberg, Daniel, and Elisabeth Coutts. 1993. "An Introduction to the TAXSIM Model." *Journal of Policy Analysis and Management* 12(1): 189–94.

Hoynes, Hilary. 1997. "Work and Marriage Incentives in Welfare Programs: What Have We Learned?" In *Fiscal Policy: Lessons from Economic Research*, edited by Alan J. Auerbach. Cambridge, Mass.: MIT Press.

Intergovernmental Health Policy Project. Various years. *Major Changes in State Medicaid and Indigent Care Programs*. Report. Washington, D.C.

Levine, Phillip B., and Diane M. Whitmore. 1998. "The Impact of Welfare Reform on the AFDC Caseload." In *Proceedings of the Ninetieth Annual Conference on Taxation*. Washington, D.C.: National Tax Association.

Liebman, Jeffrey B. 1995. "Noncompliance and the Earned Income Tax Credit: Taxpayer Error or Taxpayer Fraud?" Harvard University. Mimeo.

———. 1998. "The Impact of the Earned Income Tax Credit on Incentives and Income Distribution." In *Tax Policy and the Economy 12*, edited by James M. Poterba. Cambridge, Mass.: MIT Press.

Meyer, Bruce D., and Dan T. Rosenbaum. 1999a. "Medicaid, Private Health Insurance, and the Labor Supply of Single Mothers." Northwestern University. Mimeo.

———. 1999b. "Welfare, The Earned Income Tax Credit, and the Labor Supply of Single Mothers." Working Paper 7363. Cambridge, Mass.: National Bureau of Economic Research.

———. 2001. "Welfare, The Earned Income Tax Credit, and the Labor Supply of Single Mothers." *Quarterly Journal of Economics* 116(3): 1063–2014.

Moffitt, Robert. 1992. "Incentive Effects of the U.S. Welfare System." *Journal of Economic Literature* 30(1): 1–61.

———. 1997. "The Effect of Welfare on Marriage and Fertility: What Do We Know and What Do We Need to Know?" Johns Hopkins University. Mimeo.

National Governor's Association. Various dates. *MCH (Maternal and Child Health) Update*. Washington, D.C.

Olson, Lynn M., and Audrey Davis. 1994. "The Earned Income Tax Credit: Views from the Street Level." Working Paper Series. Evanston, Ill.: Northwestern University, Center for Urban Affairs.

Polivka, Anne E., and Stephen M. Miller. 1998. "The CPS After the Redesign: Refocusing the Economic Lens." In *Labor Statistics Measurement Issues*, edited by John Haltiwanger, Marilyn E. Manser, and Robert Topel. Chicago: University of Chicago Press.

Savner, Steve, and Mark Greenberg. 1997. "The CLASP Guide to Welfare Waivers, 1997." Washington, D.C.: Center for Law and Social Policy.

Scholz, John Karl. 1990. "The Participation Rate of the Earned Income Tax Credit." Discussion Paper 928-90. Madison: University of Wisconsin, Institute for Research on Poverty.

———. 1994. "The Earned Income Tax Credit: Participation, Compliance, and Antipoverty Effectiveness." *National Tax Journal* 48(1): 59–81.

U.S. Department of Agriculture. Various years. *Characteristics of Food Stamp Households*. Alexandria, Va.: U.S. Department of Agriculture, Food and Consumer Service, Office of Analysis and Evaluation.

U.S. Department of the Treasury. Internal Revenue Service (IRS). 1994. *Statistics of Income, Individual Income Tax Returns*. Washington: U.S. Department of the Treasury, Internal Revenue Service.

———. 1999. *Statistics of Income, Individual Income Tax Returns*. Washington: U.S. Department of the Treasury, Internal Revenue Service.

———. Various years. *Your Federal Income Tax: Tax Guide for Individuals*. Washington: U.S. Department of the Treasury, Internal Revenue Service.

U.S. Department of Health and Human Services. Various years. *Characteristics of State Plans for Aid to Families with Dependent Children*. Washington: U.S. Department of Health and Human Services, Administration for Children and Families, Office of Family Assistance.

———. 1997a. *HHS Fact Sheet: State Welfare Demonstrations*. Washington: U.S. Department of Health and Human Services.

———. 1997b. *Setting the Baseline: A Report on State Welfare Waivers*. Washington: U.S. Department of Health and Human Services Office of the Assistant Secretary for Planning and Evaluation.

U.S. General Accounting Office. 1997. *Welfare Reform: States' Early Experiences with Benefit Termination*. GAO S-97-74. Washington, D.C. (May).

U.S. House of Representatives. Committee on Energy and Commerce. 1988. *Medicaid Source Book: Background Data and Analysis*. Washington: U.S. Government Printing Office.

———. 1993. *Medicaid Source Book: Background Data and Analysis*. Washington: U.S. Government Printing Office.

U.S. House of Representatives. Committee on Ways and Means. Various years. *Green Book: Background Material and Data on Programs within the Jurisdiction of the Committee on Ways and Means*. Washington: U.S. Government Printing Office.

Chapter 3

The Impact of the Earned Income Tax Credit and Social Policy Reforms on Work, Marriage, and Living Arrangements

David T. Ellwood

A ll social policies create incentives, and most create at least some that are undesirable in the eyes of policymakers. The Earned Income Tax Credit (EITC) is unusual in that it creates sharply different incentives for different individuals. For some it serves as a strong work incentive; for others it is a work disincentive. Similarly, the EITC rewards marriage among some and penalizes it among others. In contrast, traditional means-tested benefits usually create unambiguous work disincentives and marriage penalties.

In this chapter, I exploit the fact that work and marriage incentives have changed differentially for various groups in order to test the ramifications of these changed incentives. I use an intuitively straightforward methodology to allow both graphical and statistical "difference in difference" estimators to track work and marriage behavior of different subgroups over time. Significantly, this chapter is one of the first attempts to examine the impact of changing economic incentives on marriage and to look specifically at their impact on marriage as against nonmarried cohabitation.

The results suggest that the EITC, welfare reforms, and the strong economy have had a strong positive effect on work by single parents and a somewhat more modest negative effect on the work of some married mothers. They also suggest that marriage and cohabitation have not changed dramatically, but there is at least a hint of some changes, though these effects are far more tentative and sensitive.

ALTERED ECONOMIC AND SOCIAL POLICY

Several dramatic policy changes occurred during the late 1980s and early 1990s that profoundly shifted the incentives for work and marriage for low- and moderate-income parents. Welfare reform began in earnest at the state level in the late 1980s and early 1990s, with many states receiving "waivers" of federal rules that allowed them to experiment with alternative reforms. In 1996, in the midst of already sharp falls in the caseload since 1993, the Personal Responsibility and

Work Opportunity Reconciliation Act was passed. Temporary Assistance for Needy Families (TANF) replaced Aid to Families with Dependent Children (AFDC), changing what had been an open-ended federal matching grant into a block grant to states. It added requirements that a sizable share of recipients be working (or that state caseloads be reduced equivalently) and imposed a five-year lifetime limit on benefits for most recipients. States were given the option of adding whatever other restraints they chose, including setting even shorter time limits.

States have responded in a myriad of ways. Some have imposed strict time limits. Others require work immediately. Some have reduced benefits. Many have altered the effective tax rate on earnings when people go to work. Perhaps the most dramatic changes, however, have been administrative. States have used a variety of mechanisms to push people off welfare and toward work. Some states have experienced caseload reductions as large as 70 or 80 percent, something completely unprecedented in the sixty-plus-year history of the program.

Yet as dramatic as the shift in welfare has been, expansions in supports for low-income working families are perhaps even more remarkable. Whereas in the late 1980s low-income working families were eligible for about $5 billion (1998 dollars) annually in federal aid, by the late 1990s the total expenditures were more than $50 billion (see Ellwood 2000). About half of this growth can be traced to expansions in the Earned Income Tax Credit. By 1996, inflation-adjusted federal expenditures on the EITC alone exceeded the combined real state and federal benefit expenditures on AFDC benefits in any year. Starting in 1998, a nonrefundable child tax credit has been in place ($400 maximum for each child in 1998, $500 thereafter). As a family's income pushes them into the range in which they owe taxes, this credit can be used to offset these taxes.

Most of the rest of the growth is traced to expansions in medical assistance programs for low-income working families. Whereas Medicaid coverage once was limited primarily to people receiving means-tested cash assistance such as AFDC, states are now required to provide coverage for all children born after October 1983 with family income at or below the poverty line. Many states have chosen to cover children who are older and whose families are considerably above the poverty line either through Medicaid or the newly adopted Children's Health Insurance Program (CHIP), which offers still more money for covering children. Some expansion in federal support for child care has also occurred.

THE NEW WORK AND MARRIAGE INCENTIVES

Figure 3.1 shows how EITC benefits vary with earnings. At first, each new dollar of earnings brings added benefits, since each dollar of earnings generates up to 40 percent in refundable tax benefits up to a maximum benefit of $3,756 in 1998. When earnings exceed a cutoff, however ($12,260 in 1998), benefits are reduced as earnings rise. The phase in, where benefits rise along with earnings, creates an incentive to work, while the phase-out, where benefits decrease as earnings

FIGURE 3.1 / Earned Income Tax Credit Payments in 1998, by Level of Earnings and Number of Children (1998 Dollars)

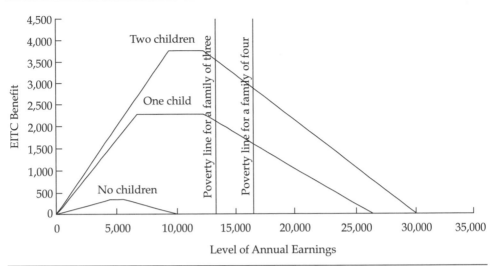

Source: Author's tabulations based on statutes in 1998.
Note: Calculations assume no other income.

grow above a certain level, creates disincentives. Moreover, the nature of the incentives also varies depending on whether a family has only one potential earner or two.

The overall incentive effects are a reflection of taxes, means-tested benefits, work expenses, and the like. To understand the changes, let us begin by looking at the situation as it stood in 1986, when a small EITC existed. Consider a low-skilled woman with two children who might have earned $10,000 annually (1998 dollars) if she had chosen to work. She might also have married a man who earned $15,000.[1] Table 3.1 shows what her family's disposable income would have been in 1986 under different combinations of work and marriage. In deriving this table and subsequent ones, I ignore any housing benefits and assume people collect benefits to which they are entitled.

Suppose the single parent was considering whether or not to work. If she had not worked, she would have received $8,804 in means-tested aid, and she and her children would have been covered by government health insurance (Medicaid). If she had gone to work at a job paying $10,000, her AFDC and food stamp benefits would have fallen dramatically, she would have incurred child-care costs, and she would have been expected to pay taxes. Her overall after-tax income would have grown by only $1,860, to $10,664. In effect her tax rate was 81 percent. In addition, her family would have lost Medicaid benefits, which would easily be worth more than $2,000, so the effective tax rate may well have exceeded 100 percent.

Table 3.2 shows how dramatically things had changed by 1998. A large EITC

TABLE 3.1 / Earnings, Taxes, and Benefits Under Differing Scenarios for Work and Marriage, 1986 (1998 Dollars)

	Total Earnings	Federal Taxes[a]	Means-Tested Benefits[b]	Child-Care Expense[c]	Earned Income Tax Credit	Child-Care Support[d]	Total Disposable Income	Government-Paid Health Insurance? (Medicaid)
Unmarried woman with children, woman does not work	0	0	8,804	0	0	0	$8,804	Yes
Unmarried woman with children, woman earns $10,000	10,000	−879	2,602	−2,000	777	164	$10,664	No
Married couple with children, man earns $15,000, woman does not work	15,000	−1,415	1,862	0	166	0	$15,613	No
Married couple with children, man earns $15,000, woman earns $10,000	25,000	−3,316	62	−2,000	0	532	$20,279	No
Unmarried man, no children, man earns $15,000	15,000	−2,376	0	0	0	0	$12,624	No

Source: Author's calculations based on 1986 statutes.
[a]Social Security, Medicare, and income taxes before EITC.
[b]AFDC and food stamps.
[c]If all parents worked.
[d]Dependent child-care credit.

TABLE 3.2 / Earnings, Taxes, and Benefits Under Differing Scenarios for Work and Marriage, 1988 (1998 Dollars)

Scenario	Total Earnings	Federal Taxes[a]	Means-Tested Benefits[b]	Child-Care Expense[c]	Child Tax Credit	Earned Income Tax Credit	Child-Care Support[d]	Total Disposable Income	Government-Paid Health Insurance? (Medicaid)
Unmarried woman with children, woman does not work	0	0	7,717	0	0	0	0	$ 7,717	Yes
Unmarried woman with children, woman earns $10,000	10,000	−765	2,602	−2,000	0	3,756	1000	$14,593	At least children under fifteen, older in some states
Married couple with children, man earns $15,000, woman does not work	15,000	−1,148	1,862	0	0	3,179	0	$18,894	At least children under fifteen, older in some states
Married couple with children, man earns $15,000, woman earns $10,000	25,000	−2,978	62	−2,000	800	1,073	265	$22,223	Children covered in some states
Unmarried man, no children, earns $15,000	15,000	−2,355	0	0	0	0	0	$12,645	No

Source: Author's calculations based on 1998 statutes.
[a]Social Security, Medicaid, and income taxes before EITC.
[b]AFDC and food stamps.
[c]If all parents worked.
[d]Dependent child-care credit.

had been instituted, means-tested benefits had been cut, medical care was usually offered to children of poor working families, and child-care aid was often available. As a result, the income of a similar single parent going to work in 1998 would rise from $7,717 to $14,593. The EITC and other benefits helped overcome the negative incentives of means-tested benefits. Her children under the age of fifteen would retain their Medicaid, and in many states, even older children would be covered.[2]

Next consider a husband-and-wife family with a single $15,000 wage earner. In 1986, the family would have had $15,613 and no medical benefits. By 1998 this working poor family would have gained an additional $3,281, primarily from the EITC, and Medicaid would cover the children. The EITC and other targeted benefits for working families clearly reward working poor and near-poor families.

Yet the EITC has also changed work incentives in the opposite direction for a mother married to a low-income working man. If her husband earned $15,000 a year, a mother who entered the workforce in 1998 and earned $10,000 would have pushed up the family income well into the phase-out range of the EITC, so that the returns to going to work would have been reduced by the falling EITC benefits. The impact of the EITC and other programs on work incentives is illustrated in table 3.3. The last columns in the table illustrate that for a single parent considering a low-wage job, the payoff to taking a $10,000 a year job rose from roughly $2,000 in 1986, coupled with the loss of Medicaid, to almost $7,000 in 1998, with only the adult losing Medicaid coverage. Even the adult can get coverage in some circumstances. By contrast, for a low-wage mother married to a low-income man, rewards to working have been cut sharply, with the net increase in income from a $10,000 job falling from $4,700 in 1986 to $3,300 in 1998. Married mothers in 1998 faced an effective tax rate of 67 percent. The situation was even worse in the previous year, before a new child tax credit offset a large share of federal taxes for this family. The family also faces a potential loss of medical coverage. Note that there is also a large income effect created by the EITC. Tables 3.1 and 3.2 show that the disposable income of a married couple with one $15,000 earner would rise from $15,600 in 1986 to $18,900 in 1998. Thus both the marginal tax rate (substitution) effects and the income effects would reduce incentives to work for low-wage married mothers. Of course, one could just as easily say that if the mother works, the father faces strong work disincentives.

Is it likely that people will even be aware of these work incentives and therefore respond to them? Welfare recipients often go to work for brief periods, return to welfare, and then return to work. They should notice how their income changes. Moreover, the EITC typically arrives in a visible lump sum as a tax refund or credit. Indeed, chapters 8 and 10 in this volume indicate considerable knowledge of the program among potential participants. Also, some newspaper accounts suggest that while low-income families do not really understand the EITC in detail, they do realize that if they go to work, they will get a big refund, in part because tax preparers are offering large immediate refunds (see Jason

TABLE 3.3 / Work Incentives for Married and Unmarried Mothers, 1986 and 1998 (1998 Dollars)

	Change in Earnings	Change in Federal Taxes	Change in Means-Tested Benefits	Change in Child-Care Expenses	Change in Earned Income Tax Credit	Change in Child Tax Credit	Change in Child-Care Subsidies	Net Increase in Income[a]	Effective Tax Rate on Earnings (Percentage)	Change in Government-Paid Medical Coverage
Unmarried mother with two children begins working and earns $10,000										
1986	10,000	−879	−6,202	−2,000	777	0	164	1,861	81	Loses all coverage
1998	10,000	−765	−5,115	−2,000	3,756	0	1,000	6,876	31	Children under the age of sixteen remain covered
Mother with two children, married to a man earning $15,000, begins working and earns $10,000										
1986	10,000	−1,900	−1,800	−2,000	−166	0	532	4,665	53	No effect
1998	10,000	−1,830	−1,800	−2,000	−2,106	800	265	3,329	67	Children under the age of sixteen may lose coverage

Source: Author's calculations.
[a] Excluding medical benefits.

DeParle, "Life After Welfare: First-Time Filers; On a Once Forlorn Avenue, Tax Preparers Now Flourish," *New York Times,* March 21, 1999, A1). It is reasonable to suppose that single parents, at least, might be influenced by the work incentives.

The situation is more complicated for married mothers. The combination of multiple incomes and the fact that the family may get a tax credit that will mainly just offset other taxes owed, rather than producing a big refund check, seems more likely to obscure the overall impact of the EITC. Still, if a family experiments by sending a second earner to work or keeping him or her at home, they should notice just how much their living circumstances change. Perhaps more important, in the years when the EITC was being increased the after-tax income of families with one low-wage worker would be rising rapidly, and this dramatic difference in income would surely be noticed and might well diminish work by the second earner.

The EITC creates some bipolar incentives for or against marriage as well. Table 3.4 illustrates the marriage penalties. Looking at the last columns, we see that in all years and in all circumstances, clear marriage penalties were created, largely as a result of the means-tested programs, though regular taxes play some role as well. There will, of course, be some compensating economic advantages, including economies to scale achieved by having to support only one household (though these could be achieved by living together outside of marriage). The size of the marriage penalty varies greatly by type of situation and year. In 1986, a *nonemployed* single mother faced a $5,815 penalty by marrying a man earning $15,000. By 1998, the penalty was sharply reduced to just under $1,500. The reduction in penalty is partially caused by the decline in means-tested benefits available to unmarried parents. Most of the improvement, however, can be traced to the nearly $3,000 increase in the EITC since 1986. In this case, the EITC serves as a marriage bonus.

The *working* single mother who considers marrying a working man faces a much larger marriage penalty in 1998 than she would have in 1986. As the combined income of the husband and wife push people into the phase-out range, the EITC now serves as a marriage penalty. Whereas a working mother marrying a working man suffered a roughly $3,000 marriage penalty in 1986, by 1998 that penalty had grown to more than $5,000—virtually all of it owing to the loss of EITC and child-care aid to lower-income working families. Indeed, this situation was worse in 1997 before the child tax credit offered some additional tax relief. Note that so-called marriage penalties could influence both decisions to marry and decisions to end a marriage.

This analysis of marginal marriage incentives misses a couple of critical issues, including income effects and the feedback from altered work behavior. Consider the situation facing a struggling low-income married couple with children, in which both parents are working. The expansion of the EITC does create a marriage penalty—the mother could potentially get a larger EITC by divorcing. That same EITC would also provide extra income to the household, however, and reduce work incentives for the second earner. The added income may

TABLE 3.4 / Marriage Penalties and Rewards for Employed and Nonemployed Mothers, 1986 and 1998 (1998 Dollars)

	Combined Disposable Income If Couple Does Not Marry	Change in Federal Taxes	Change in Means-Tested Benefits	Change in Child-Care Expenses	Change in Earned Income Tax Credit	Change in Child Tax Credit	Change in Child-Care Subsidies	Net Increase in Income[a]	Marriage Penalty as a Percentage of Combined Disposable Income If Unmarried	Change in Government-Paid Medical Coverage
Nonemployed mother with two children marries childless man with $15,000 in earnings										
1986	21,428	961	−6,941	0	166	0	0	−5,815	−27	Loses all coverage
1998	20,362	1,208	−5,855	0	3,179	0	0	−1,468	−7	Children under the age of sixteen remain covered
Employed mother with two children and $10,000 in earnings marries childless man with $15,000 in earnings										
1986	23,288	−60	−2,540	0	−777	0	368	−3,010	−13	No effect
1998	27,238	143	−2,540	0	−2,683	800	−735	−5,015	−18	May lose coverage for children under the age of sixteen

Source: Author's calculations.

[a]Excluding medical benefits.

reduce stress in the household and increase the likelihood that the family will stay together. The altered work incentives may lead the mother to spend less time in the workforce, which, according to a model of marriage like that of Gary Becker (1981), might increase the comparative advantages of marriage.

This analysis also misses altered incentives for childless couples. In particular, suppose a couple considers marriage with the expectation that they will have a child at some point and that they have no intention of having a child outside of marriage. For this couple, the EITC also serves as a marriage inducement. At worst they can get nothing; at best, they will receive some money from the tax credit once they start raising a family.

Moreover, couples who face a marriage reward or penalty may at a later point face the opposite incentives if their economic status or parental status changes, given the duration of marriage. Thus short-term incentives may not reflect couples' expectations regarding the effects of social policy over the life of the marriage. Finally, the EITC might also influence fertility, encouraging some married and unmarried women to have children who might otherwise have been reluctant to do so. This too could influence the stock of married and unmarried mothers.

Once again it is fair to ask if people would notice the marriage incentives. It is apparent that people notice the incentive effects of means-tested programs. Few who marry expect to continue receiving welfare, so its loss is quite clear. The EITC incentives may be more obscure, however. Since marriages tend to last for extended periods, there is almost no way to implicitly learn about the tax consequences of being married or not by repeated marriages and divorces. Still, one group—couples with children who are cohabiting but unmarried—might be unusually sensitive to marriage incentives. The marriage penalties or rewards of the EITC might be particularly important in influencing decisions about marriage among these couples.

THE IMPACT OF THE POLICY CHANGES ON WORK

Three broad methods are used to estimate the effect of the altered work incentives. The first involves the estimation of structural models, in which the kinks and other features of the budget constraints created by the EITC and other programs are explicitly modeled. One can either use existing estimates of labor supply elasticities or estimate new ones based on actual work behavior to determine the structural parameters (or both). This is essentially the methodology used by Thomas MaCurdy, David Green, and Harry Paarsch (1990) and Robert Moffitt (1986). Stacy Dickert, Scott Houser, and John Karl Scholz (1995) estimate 1990 cross-sectional elasticities of labor supply response to net income after accounting for multiple program effects and then use these estimates to simulate the marginal effects of the expanded EITC. Orazio Attanasio and Thomas MaCurdy (1997) seek to estimate the effect of the EITC on the entire life cycle of labor supply. One difficult problem is modeling the complex combination of means-tested benefits, the EITC, and tax rates facing individuals. The changes in welfare policy are particularly difficult to model.

A second strategy is to quantify the various changed incentives facing potential workers and to use these to estimate a fairly straightforward reduced-form model of labor supply. The most sophisticated use of this strategy is the model presented by Bruce Meyer and Daniel Rosenbaum (1999). These authors go to considerable effort to parameterize altered incentives created by both state and federal EITC policies and by changes in AFDC, including benefit rule changes, time limits, and some state Medicaid extensions, child-care, and training benefits. Nada Eissa and Hilary Hoynes (1999) estimate a reduced-form model of labor supply for married women relying on variation in tax treatment (primarily the EITC) to judge the influence of the EITC on labor supply.

Although such methods hold the hope of fairly precise behavioral estimates, they suffer limitations. First the models usually explicitly assume that the response to a one-dollar increase in the EITC (or any other financial benefit) will be the same as a one-dollar increase in earnings. Indeed, the model is estimated by assuming that sample individuals fully understand the true multiple incentives they face. Yet the complexities of such incentives suggest that recipients may not fully understand them or respond appropriately. To model the incentive effects properly, one really should also take account of the wide range of kinks and slopes in the budget set, as the structural models attempt to do, though the complexity of the incentives makes this a daunting task.

Perhaps more important, however, the recent changes in the incentives facing those who would previously have received means-tested benefits (welfare) and changes in Medicaid policies are virtually impossible to characterize quantitatively. Some states have dramatically increased pressure to leave welfare. Their methods have generally not involved dramatically lowering benefits. Rather, they have sought other means to divert people from getting aid or to move people off welfare quickly.

Consider two examples. In Georgia, before she can even begin the application process, a woman seeking aid is required to get a form signed by six employers saying that she applied in good faith for a minimum-wage job and was turned down.[3] Once enrolled, if she is penalized twice for failure to meet some key administrative or work requirement, she is barred for life from seeking aid in the state. In Wisconsin, no aid is provided unless the person is already working. When applicants claim they really cannot find a job, the providers of TANF will, in some cases, provide a subsidized job for a limited duration, but aid remains tied to working. In both states, caseloads have dropped dramatically—nearly 80 percent in Wisconsin.

In chapter 2 of this volume, Meyer and Rosenbaum examine a host of measures ranging from benefit levels to elements in waivers. They have done about as well as can be imagined. Yet no measures can really capture the crucial administrative elements in Georgia or Wisconsin or most other states. Indeed, in the measures used by those authors, Georgia shows up as essentially unchanged. Administrative changes, such as a greater emphasis on sanctioning or increasing the difficulty of getting aid by making it more unpleasant or stig-matizing, are probably impossible to measure. Even if we could somehow cap-ture them, modeling would still be a bit of a mystery. Administrative changes interact with the economy and the availability of other benefits. States appear far more willing to sanction people or refuse them aid if jobs are perceived to be relatively plentiful.

This discussion suggests that state-to-state variations in the structure of AFDC or TANF are measured with considerable error, downwardly biasing the appar-ent impact of welfare "reforms." Since these changes occurred almost simul-taneously with EITC expansions, the mismeasurement will most likely create an upward bias in the apparent impact of EITC and tax changes.

Few authors have tackled the hardest issue of all—the changed availability of Medicaid for children.[4] I have previously noted that the federal cost of growing health coverage for children of the working poor and some adults has been almost as great as the cost of the EITC. But should such benefits be treated as the insurance value of Medicaid? Should it vary by the health of family members? What value do potential beneficiaries of such aid place on it when they are healthy?

The alternative methodology is to exploit the natural experiments created by the timing of the rapid expansion in the EITC and changes in social policy and the fact that they did not affect all persons equally. This method is used by Nada Eissa and Jeffrey Liebman (1996) and Robert Schoeni and Rebecca Blank (2000), and it underlies much of the analysis in Meyer and Rosenbaum (1999; chapter 2, this volume). For each group, subjected to sharply different incentives, the au-thors seek a control group that faces fewer changes, and this can be problematic. Eissa and Liebman (1996), Meyer and Rosenbaum (1999; chapter 2 of this vol-ume), and Eissa and Hoynes (1999) rely heavily on childless women as controls, which has some appeal but also some obvious problems. A much larger fraction of childless single women already worked even before EITC expansions, so their employment would not be expected to grow as much. Moreover, the temporal trends in labor force participation of the women with and without children are often different before the enactment of the EITC, so drawing inferences from differential trends afterward is troubling. An alternative, also used by Eissa and Liebman (1996), is to use mothers at higher education levels as controls for less skilled ones, but they too start at much higher levels of work. Probably the best strategy is to explore a variety of potential control groups.

While one would be unwilling to treat such "difference in differences" esti-mates as highly precise, they can offer powerful and straightforward evidence of the behavioral impacts. In the past, such methods made it difficult to disentangle the separate impact of the multitude of policy changes from one another or from the impact of the economy. One could mostly test the overall impact of the com-bination of policies in a strong economy. While important in its own right, such a conclusion is distinctly frustrating to economists and policymakers interested in looking at the margin. Moreover, it seems that the remarkable variation in state welfare policies ought to provide some leverage for decomposing things.

This chapter seeks to extend and exploit the difference-in-difference method to determine behavioral impacts of the changed policies for both unmarried and married mothers at various skill and potential wage levels. Moreover, it explores ways to measure welfare reform aggressiveness in hopes of comparing changes in work in states with more and less aggressive welfare reform policies. Hypothetically, if there were a group of states that had done little in the way of serious reform, one might look to difference-in-difference estimates of work behavior in those states as a measure of the impact of the EITC alone. The additional changes in the more aggressive states could indicate the impact of welfare reforms.

Using the Current Population Survey from March 1999,[5] I first ran a basic wage equation based on average hourly earnings in 1998 for women aged eighteen to forty-four who worked at least twenty-six weeks, using characteristics including age, education, race, and number of children as independent variables.[6] I then take women aged eighteen to forty-four in each March CPS survey from 1975 to 1999 and use the wage equation to predict a potential 1998 wage for them, whether or not they worked. Finally, I use that predicted wage to place the women into predicted wage and skill quartiles for their survey year.[7] Note that each predicted wage quartile for each year contains 25 percent of all women.

Thus I have created a consistent set of four equal skill and wage groups in each year based on characteristics highly correlated with pay, such as education and age. Since I use this same equation to create wage and skill quartiles each year, I can track what happens to quartiles of similar women over time. If incentives changed differentially for women in the bottom skill and wage quartile as against those in the top quartile over time, by tracking the behavior of women in each quartile I have a natural experiment. I can compare, for example, the work of the single parents in the lowest wage quartile to work by women in the next highest quartile. I can also compare what happens to the lowest-wage and lowest-skill single women with children in relation to the lowest-wage and lowest-skill women without children.

One might have chosen, as Eissa and Liebman (1996) have, to track people over time based on education levels. The mix of education changes over time, however. In 1975, my first sample year, 23 percent of women aged eighteen to forty-four were high school dropouts. By 1998, that figure had fallen to 13 percent. Thus I would be comparing the behavior of the bottom 23 percent of women in 1975 with that of the bottom 13 percent in 1998. My method also largely obviates the need to do regression-corrected estimates, because I have already grouped people according to their measured characteristics.

Measuring Welfare Reform Aggressiveness

Finding a legitimate measure of welfare reform aggressiveness is remarkably difficult given the nature of the program changes and the extremely close linkage between work and welfare. Yet the obvious desire to disentangle the impact of welfare reform from the economy and the EITC pushes toward the development of mechanisms to at least establish some reasonable bounds. In this chapter I examine two different measures, one programmatic and one statistical.

PROGRAMMATIC MEASURES   Meyer and Rosenbaum (1999) have compiled a considerable list of measures that might be used to determine the particular programmatic changes that could influence caseload. Ultimately they select a few measures for inclusion in their analysis. Based on their work and supplemented with my own experiments, I determined that four measures seem particularly good candidates as indications of the states' aggressiveness: whether the state had a real benefit decline of more than 25 percent between 1986 and 1997, whether the state had imposed a time limit of any sort under a waiver by 1996, whether the state used full-family sanctions for AFDC recipients who did not comply with the requirements of the Jobs Opportunities and Basic Skills Training Program (an earlier welfare reform), and whether any persons were terminated for failure to meet a requirement created under an AFDC waiver. All of these are for the period immediately preceding the passage of national welfare reform, since state data are not yet available after that period.

The benefit level is the most obvious and powerful financial incentive; the other measures are all indications of administrative or time-limited measures that are not otherwise captured. I experimented with different weights for each of these, based on their impacts on caseload changes, but ultimately concluded that a simple sum was the cleanest method of classifying. States that made none of these changes are least aggressive; states that enacted at least three out of four of them are considered the most aggressive.

STATISTICAL MEASURES   A state that aggressively pursues welfare reform through economic and administrative actions will most likely have two possible observable effects: it will increase work among single parents, thereby raising their earnings, and it will reduce the odds that someone with a given level of earnings receives aid. The incentives built into the EITC will also pull people into higher earnings categories, but it should have no impact on the odds that someone with a given level of earnings receives benefits. The distinction suggests that a measure that captures the changing odds that people of given earnings receive aid in a state would be a plausible measure of administrative aggressiveness that is not automatically correlated with EITC and other incentive changes. It is also likely to be closely linked to other features of welfare reform, since administrative and nonadministrative methods of discouraging welfare and encouraging work seem likely to go hand in hand.

Using CPS data for each state over the period from 1984 to 1992, I estimated fifty-one state probit models of AFDC participation among single parents, conditional on age categories, education categories, racial categories, the state unemployment rate, four earnings categories, and a time trend.[8] I use this period because it was not a time of particularly dramatic changes in policy at the national level. Thus this model simulates the eligibility and participation structures for each state in the late 1980s and early 1990s.

Then, using the actual earnings and education of single mothers and the state unemployment rates in 1997 and 1998, I predict the fraction of sample participants one would have expected to collect AFDC in 1997 and 1998 had the eligibility and participation structures been the same as during the base period (1984 to 1992). Because earnings had risen and unemployment rates had fallen, the model predicts declines in welfare use in virtually all states. The actual declines in many states were even greater, however, presumably because they had become more aggressive in deterring welfare participation among persons of a given level of earnings. The difference between the actual and the predicted change in participation from 1991 and 1992 to 1997 and 1998 is thus an indicator of how aggressively states sought to reduce the roles through changes in eligibility.[9]

As expected, in virtually every state, the model predicts less of a decline in participation than was actually observed, even after accounting for the rise in work and earnings of single parents. Welfare reform had changed the rules. The states that had pushed caseloads down even further than one would have expected, given the rise in work by single parents, are presumably the ones that are acting most aggressively to move people off welfare.

One might be concerned that this is simply a measure of the decline in participation in AFDC in the state over time. That is precisely why we are conditioning on the level of work and earnings of people in the later period. If nonwelfare factors were pushing up employment and earnings and those rises were in turn reducing caseloads in a welfare environment that was unchanged, our model should accurately predict the change in participation. Only if the structure of welfare had changed for single parents of given earnings should the prediction deviate. The more aggressively the state has reduced participation for a given level of income, the greater the deviation from the prediction. Indeed, the correlation between changes in the actual and predicted participation is "just" .36, revealing that this measure is not simply a measure of caseload change.[10]

Inevitably, this measure suffers from some potential weaknesses. There are dangers that deviation from predicted participation is capturing unmeasured changes in the state environment that might be affecting both caseloads and employment patterns simultaneously. Although the functional form is rather loose for each state, it does impose some structure. If local economic conditions that are not captured by the state unemployment rate altered the likelihood that people of given earnings would apply for welfare, the measure might be biased. It is unclear what the direction of the bias would be, however. On the one hand, people might be more optimistic and thus less likely to seek out aid (meaning the prediction will include a positive correlation with unmeasured economic conditions). On the other hand, the newly working group has previous exposure to welfare and thus might be more likely to apply for welfare than previous low- to moderate-earning workers (creating a negative correlation between the trend and unmeasured economic conditions).

Another potential source of concern involves any correlation between AFDC aggressiveness and state EITCs. If states that are unusually aggressive are also more likely to have state EITCs, then aggressiveness may artificially capture some EITC effects. In fact, the reverse appears to be true. By 1996, seven states had EITC programs. Three of these were states are classified as least aggressive, three as intermediate; only one state, Wisconsin, was both aggressive in AFDC or TANF policy and had a state EITC.

The most serious concern may be that unmeasured individual characteristics may influence both employment and welfare participation. Thus if our sample for a particular state in 1997 and 1998 had a disproportionate share of single parents who were more inclined to work and were disinclined to accept welfare for any given level of their earnings, work rates would be higher and rates of welfare use lower than we might have predicted—even given the higher level of work. This potential bias can be avoided by using one sample to generate the statistical aggressiveness measure and another to examine its link to earnings.

Inevitably this measure of aggressiveness is subject to error. Thus it would be a mistake to use this aggressiveness measure in any precise way. Instead, I use it to break states into three categories. There seem to be a couple of natural break-points, at $-.04$ and $-.10$. In other words, the least aggressive states show less than a 4 percent difference between actual and predicted participation, and the most aggressive show at least a 10 percent difference. Using these breaks, roughly one-fourth of single parents were in the less aggressive states, 40 percent were in moderately aggressive states, and one-third were in the more aggressive ones.

Incentive Effects by Predicted Wage Quartile

Table 3.5 illustrates the difference in the work incentives in 1986 and in 1998 for people in different quartiles of the wage distribution. The first rows show the median level of earnings for all women (regardless of marital or family status) in the quartile who actually worked at least twenty-six weeks, based on annual CPS data. These rows provide a rough estimate of what a woman in that quartile would earn if she went to work. The second set of rows shows the median income earned by the husbands of married women with children in this wage quartile. These are not perfect estimates of what people might actually earn if they went to work. I use these figures only to illustrate roughly how different the incentives have been across the groups and over time.

Look first at the situation facing single parents in the lowest potential wage quartile. Reinforcing the earlier finding, the table shows that a low-skill single mother going from welfare to work could hope to earn just $2,800 more in 1986 (not counting the lost Medicaid). Her effective tax rate was 76 percent. By 1998, the gains to work had risen to nearly $7,600, and her effective tax rate had fallen to 31 percent.

Incentives for women in the next quartile also improved dramatically, with the tax rate falling from 70 percent to 35 percent. Still, this is not as great a change as for the lowest-skill group. The incentives for women with the highest

TABLE 3.5 / Work Incentives for Women in Different Family Situations and at
Potential Wage Levels, 1986 and 1998

	Lowest Quartile	Second Quartile	Third Quartile	Highest Quartile
Median earnings of women who work more than twenty-six weeks[a]				
1986	11,600	14,872	19,334	27,346
1998	11,000	15,000	20,000	30,100
Median earnings of husbands for mothers who are married[a]				
1986	19,334	29,745	36,392	44,617
1998	18,720	30,000	35,000	45,000
Work incentives if single parent goes to work				
Net earnings				
1986	2,767	4,489	6,716	12,341
1998	7,559	9,716	12,081	19,080
Effective tax rate (percentage)				
1986	76	70	65	55
1998	31	35	40	37
Work incentives if married mother goes to work				
Net earnings				
1986	6,894	9,676	12,310	16,732
1998	4,300	10,383	14,270	20,307
Effective tax rate (percentage)				
1986	41	35	36	39
1998	61	31	29	33

Source: Author's calculations using March Current Population Surveys, 1987 and 1999.
[a]Based on annual CPS data.

wages and skills changed the least. There was still an increased payoff, but the
tax rate fell "only" from 55 percent to 37 percent.

Thus one should expect to see employment rates rising for unmarried
mothers in all groups but also far greater increases at the bottom than at the top.
I also compare the work patterns of low-skilled unmarried mothers with those
of low-skilled unmarried women without children.

Next consider what happened to work incentives of married women. As we
have already seen, incentives to work were sharply reduced for low-income
women. By contrast, effective tax rates actually fell slightly for women in the
other quartiles (mostly owing to other tax changes). Women in the second quartile were affected the least. Thus I have a particularly good natural experiment. I

can explore whether married mothers in the lowest quartile alter their work behavior relative to married mothers in the second and other quartiles.

Table 3.5 presents comparisons for only two years, 1986 and 1998. The EITC, originally instituted in 1975, has risen in several increments. There was a modest jump in benefits in 1987, followed by sizable annual increases throughout the 1990s. Given the gradual ramping up of benefits and the potentially delayed response as people learned of the incentives, one would expect the behavioral responses to show up most dramatically in the 1990s.

Empirical Estimates of Work Effects for Single Mothers

Results for work among single persons with and without children are presented in figures 3.2 through 3.5. The figures relate to the fraction of persons who were working in March in each year from 1980 to 1999. Figure 3.2 shows large changes in work by the lowest-wage group of unmarried mothers. After virtually no change in employment patterns from 1980 to the early 1990s, employment rates suddenly shot upward, rising from roughly 34 percent in 1992 to 55 percent in early 1999. This truly unprecedented rise, which has been noted by numerous others including Liebman (1998), Dickert, Houser, and Scholz (1995), Meyer and Rosenbaum (chapter 2, this volume), and Rebecca Blank, David Card, and Philip Robins (2000), seems to offer powerful evidence that incentives can play a major role in the decision to work. As predicted, the levels of work also rose for women in the second quartile, though less so than for women in the first, and so on up to the highest quartile. Work patterns changed little for one potential comparison group—unmarried women without children—as shown in figure 3.3.

I perform a more formal test of the proposition that behavior really did change in a statistically meaningful way. I compare March 1986 with March 1999, based on the theory that the former survey was just before the beginning of the big growth in the EITC and the economy was stronger than in the preceding couple of years. The first four rows of table 3.6 show what figure 3.2 also reveals: employment rose for all quartiles, but it rose more for the lower quartiles. There was no growth in employment among unmarried low-wage childless women.

I then perform several treatment-control comparisons. I compare the behaviors of women in the lowest and highest wage quartiles, women in the lowest and the third quartiles (which would give a lower bound, since both groups are affected by the incentives), and single women with and without children. Each of these comparisons yields an estimated effect of between 13 and 23 points. All are statistically significant.

Next I turn to the question of how significant a role welfare policy played in influencing this expansion in work among single parents. Figure 3.4 shows what happened to work by single mothers in the lowest predicted-wage quartile (in

FIGURE 3.2 / Employment Rate of Unmarried Mothers With Children, by Predicted
Wage Quartile

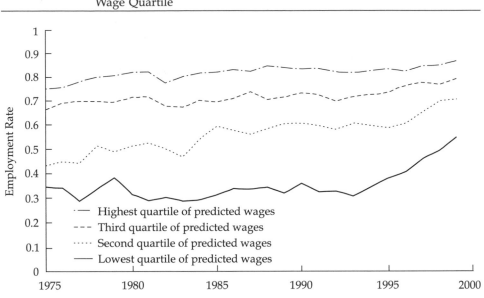

Source: March Current Population Surveys, 1975 to 1999.

FIGURE 3.3 / Employment Rate of Unmarried Women Without Children, by
Predicted Wage Quartile

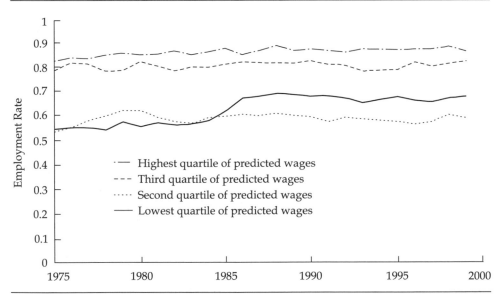

Source: March Current Population Surveys, 1975 to 1999.

TABLE 3.6 / Changes in Work by Unmarried Mothers and Estimated Impact of Social Policy Between March 1986 and March 1999

Category	Fraction Working		Difference
	1986	1999	
Unmarried women with children			
Women with characteristics that would place them in the lowest quartile of potential wages in 1998	0.34	0.55	0.21
	(0.01)	(0.01)	(0.02)
Second quartile of potential wages	0.57	0.71	0.13
	(0.01)	(0.01)	(0.02)
Third quartile of potential wages	0.71	0.79	0.08
	(0.01)	(0.02)	(0.02)
Highest quartile of potential wages	0.83	0.87	0.04
	(0.02)	(0.01)	(0.02)
Unmarried women without children			
Women with characteristics that would place them in the lowest quartile of potential wages in 1998	0.60	0.59	−0.01
	(0.01)	(0.01)	(0.01)
Differences between groups			
Bottom as compared to highest quartile among unmarried mothers	−0.49	−0.32	0.18[a]
	(0.01)	(0.02)	(0.02)
Bottom as compared to third quartile among unmarried mothers	−0.37	−0.24	0.13[a]
	(0.02)	(0.02)	(0.03)
Bottom wage quartile unmarried women with children as compared to unmarried women without children	−0.26	−0.04	0.23[a]
	(0.01)	(0.02)	(0.02)

Source: March Current Population Surveys, 1986 and 1999.
Note: Standard errors are in parentheses.
[a]This figure represents the difference in the differences, the estimated impact of social policies.

three-year moving averages) in states ranked by my statistical measures of reform aggressiveness. Moving averages are used because the annual samples become rather thin. Similarly, I pool years in determining aggressiveness because sample sizes make most estimates of single-year aggressiveness subject to considerable error. Pooling and using moving averages does pose a problem, however. The period from 1997 to 1999 was a time of most rapid change in welfare policies. While some states had begun reform years earlier through the waiver process, others were just becoming aggressive in 1999. Thus it is probably best to examine the impact of state aggressiveness through March 1998, particularly since I am using three-year moving averages.[11] If, as seems plausible, some states that were previously less aggressive become more so over the period from 1998 to 1999, we would expect to see some convergence in employment patterns after 1998.

Patterns of work are relatively similar across the states until the late 1980s, but they then diverge. Employment rates (three-year moving averages) for the most

FIGURE 3.4 / Employment Rate of Single Mothers in the Lowest Predicted Wage Quartile, by Aggressiveness of State Welfare Reform, Statistical Estimation Method (Three-Year Moving Averages)

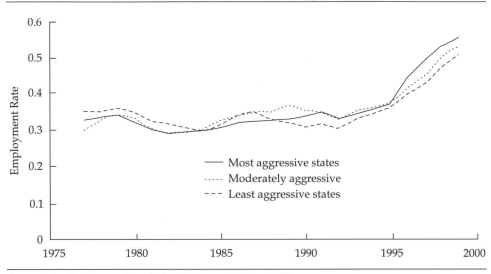

Source: March Current Population Surveys, 1975 to 1999.
Note: Beginning and end years represent two-year averages with the beginning or end year weighted double.

aggressive states rise from .32 in 1986 to .53 in 1998. Employment starts at .34 in the least aggressive states but rises only to .47.[12] Table 3.7 indicates that this eight-point difference in differences was statistically significant.

One concern with our measure of aggressiveness is that it may be biased because of sampling errors owing to correlations in unmeasured propensities to work and to collect welfare at a given level of earnings. One can test for this problem by using the welfare aggressiveness measure on an alternative data source. Using data from outgoing rotation groups (ORG) of the CPS for January and February and for July to December from 1985 onward, one can explore employment patterns for single mothers who were never present in the March surveys—and thus represent a completely independent sample.[13] I broke single parents into groups using the same wage model and examined the differences in employment gains in more and less aggressive states, using the state aggressiveness measure generated by the March data. Table 3.7 indicates that the outgoing rotation group shows a nine-point difference in differences—virtually identical to the eight-point gain found earlier.

Still, a closer inspection of figure 3.4 suggests the results are not as robust as they might at first appear. If, for example, one used 1991 as a base year, one finds far less divergence in employment between the more and less aggressive states. Other years can heighten the effect. Moreover, there is some convergence in employment rates between more and less aggressive states in 1999 in both

TABLE 3.7 / Changes in Work Among Poor Single Mothers Between 1985 and 1987 and 1997 and 1999, by Aggressiveness of State Welfare Reform

Category	1985 to 1987	1997 to 1999	Difference
Fraction working, March CPS data			
Living in least aggressive states	0.34	0.47	0.13
	(0.01)	(0.01)	(0.02)
Living in moderately aggressive states	0.33	0.50	0.17
	(0.01)	(0.01)	(0.02)
Living in most aggressive states	0.32	0.53	0.21
	(0.01)	(0.01)	(0.02)
Fraction working, ORG data[a]			
Living in least aggressive states	0.39	0.50	0.11
	(0.01)	(0.01)	(0.02)
Living in moderately aggressive states	0.33	0.51	0.18
	(0.01)	(0.01)	(0.02)
Living in most aggressive states	0.33	0.53	0.21
	(0.01)	(0.01)	(0.02)
Differences between groups			
Most − Least Aggressive	0.02	−0.06	−0.08[b]
March data	(0.02)	(0.02)	(0.03)
ORG data	0.06	−0.03	−0.09[b]
	(0.02)	(0.02)	(0.03)

Source: March Current Population Surveys, 1985 to 1987 and 1997 to 1999, and Outgoing Rotation Groups.

Note: Standard errors are in parentheses. Poor single mothers are defined here as those whose characteristics at the time of sampling would have placed them in the lowest wage quartile in 1990.

[a]Sample excludes persons in the ORG data who were also present in the March CPS sample.
[b]This figure represents the difference in the differences, the estimated impact of social policies.

CPS and ORG data. While this convergence in 1999 can quite plausibly be attributed to simple sampling variation or to the efforts of formerly less aggressive states finally to act on reform, it may indicate that aggressiveness is changing rapidly, and thus an average measure for the six-year period selected may be subject to considerable error.

I tried using these measures to conduct various decompositions of the relative magnitude of the economic strength (low unemployment), state aggressiveness, and the EITC and other work incentives. These proved to be quite sensitive to the comparison groups used and the time periods chosen.

I also explored other measures of aggressiveness: programmatic measures, in a manner similar to that of Meyer and Rosenbaum (1999). The programmatic aggressiveness measures used to create figure 3.5 show differences between more and less aggressive states, but the patterns over time show considerable variation, a finding that is consistent with the view that it is difficult to measure accurately the real changes in AFDC based on programmatic measures. More-

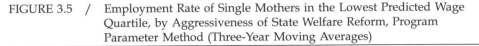

FIGURE 3.5 / Employment Rate of Single Mothers in the Lowest Predicted Wage Quartile, by Aggressiveness of State Welfare Reform, Program Parameter Method (Three-Year Moving Averages)

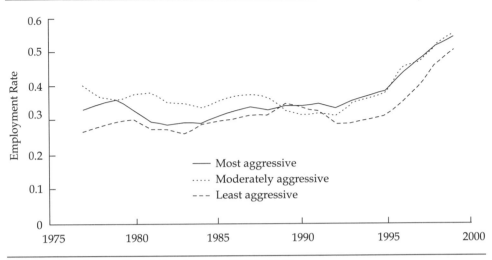

Source: March Current Population Surveys, 1978 to 1999.
Note: Beginning and end years represent two-year averages with the beginning or end year weighted double.

over, in the period preceding 1989, the trends in these states differed greatly. This pattern reveals that the measured impact depends a great deal on which year is taken as the base. Since this measure mostly captures state changes up to 1996, one should not necessarily expect it to predict well after that period, but even in 1996, the moderately aggressive states seem to have had more impact on employment than the most aggressive ones.

State policies are changing rapidly over time. The methodology proposed here for determining statistical aggressiveness could, in principle, be used to create separate aggressiveness estimates for each state and year, but given the sample sizes, these would be subject to sizable measurement error. Indeed, any measure of state reform—whether it be statistical or programmatic—is certain to be subject to considerable measurement error, given the current state of data available for each. I suspect this renders the attempt to decompose the relative impacts of welfare reform, the economy, and the EITC perilous to impossible. One should be particularly cautious about attempts that begin by estimating the impacts of measured state variation in welfare and measured economic conditions and then attributing the residual impacts to the EITC. Given the inherent difficulties in measuring state policy, such methods seem likely to understate the role of welfare changes.

In the end, the whole exercise seems problematic in any case. State and federal policymakers would almost certainly have adopted a different set of policies under different economic conditions. The impact of the EITC will surely be different at a time when low-paying jobs are plentiful than it would be when jobs are scarce. Recipients may be far more sensitive to welfare reform policies designed to get them working when the economy is strong and the rewards to work have grown so significantly. Finally, the whole tenor of welfare reform, the changing social climate, and the strong economy may have dramatically increased the stigma associated with welfare receipt and failure to be working outside the home in all states—leading to changed behavior of recipients and caseworkers alike, regardless of any actual changes in state policy. Thus the question of the marginal impact of particular policies may not even be meaningful—at least not in a sense that can be determined from existing behavior. Indeed, it is quite logical that the combination of welfare sticks, EITC carrots, and a remarkably strong economy had a multiplicative effect that is far greater than any one or two of these policies would have had on their own.

Empirical Estimates of Work Effects for Married Mothers

Figure 3.6 examines the work behavior of married mothers. Once again the responses are remarkably consistent with the altered incentives. Up until roughly 1988, the employment rates of married mothers at all potential wage levels were rising pretty much in tandem. Then the rises abruptly ceased for the low-wage group—the only group whose incentives were sharply altered by the EITC.

This change is particularly surprising in light of two other facts. The earnings of husbands in the lowest-wage group were falling somewhat as the wage of

FIGURE 3.6 / Employment Rate of Married Mothers, by Predicted Wage Quartile

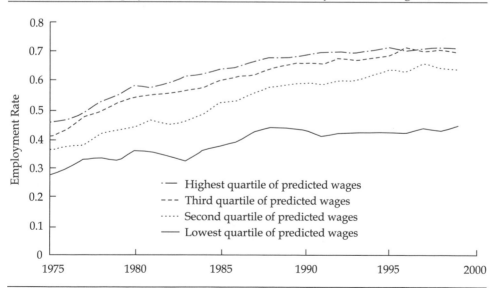

Source: March Current Population Surveys, 1975 to 1999.

FIGURE 3.7 / Employment Rate of Married Women Without Children, by Predicted Wage Quartile

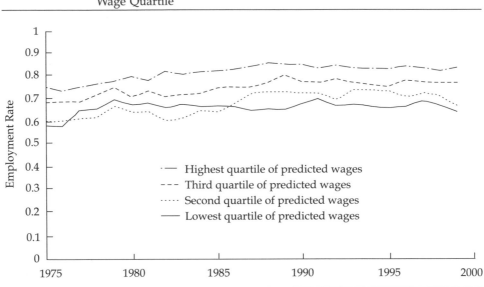

Source: March Current Population Surveys, 1975 to 1999.

less skilled men fell. That decline would ordinarily have been expected to lead to a disproportionate rise in the employment rate among low-wage women. Second, the strong economy might have been expected to disproportionately benefit low-skill married mothers, just as it seemed to help work by single mothers. Indeed, as shown in figure 3.7, work among childless married women in the bottom quartile rose relative to work among childless wives in higher quartiles. This change seems likely to have been caused by changes in the EITC, especially since changes in the welfare system are not much of a factor. Married mothers virtually never would qualify for benefits before or after this period.

There is an alternative and even more powerful way to test the significance of the EITC. Some married women with low predicted wages are married to men with high enough earnings that the family does not qualify for the EITC, whether or not the woman works. In other cases, the man's income is so low that work by the mother would actually increase the EITC benefits. One can exploit this natural experiment by comparing the employment patterns over time of low-wage women whose incentives are adversely affected by the EITC with comparably skilled women who have neutral or positive work incentives. I simulated for all married women with children in my sample whether their EITC payments would rise, fall, or be unchanged if they earned $10,000 and faced the EITC rules as they existed in 1998. Thus I track over time the low-wage women for whom the expanding EITC discourages work and compare them with other low-wage women.

Throughout the sample period roughly 54 percent of married women in the

FIGURE 3.8 / Employment Rate of Married Mothers, Indexed to 1986, With and Without EITC Disincentives to Work, for Women in the Lowest Quartile of Predicted Wages (Three-Year Moving Average)

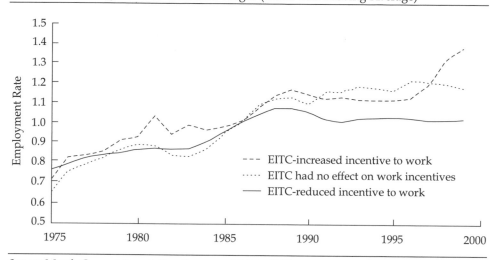

Source: March Current Population Surveys, 1975 to 1999.
Note: Beginning and end years represent two-year averages with the beginning or end year weighted double. Base year is 1986.

bottom quartile would have faced 1998 EITC earnings penalties averaging $1,288 (had they earned $10,000 and faced the 1998 EITC provisions). These are typically women with working husbands who earn less than the EITC maximum. Another 28 percent would have had no work incentives from the EITC because their husbands' incomes were above the maximum. Finally, 18 percent would have had work incentives averaging $2,678 because their husbands had low earnings.

Figure 3.8 shows what happened to the employment rates of women in each group over the period. Because married women in the three categories start with somewhat different levels of work in 1986, I have normalized the patterns relative to what they were for each group in that year, to make visual interpretation easier. These results again appear to confirm strongly the earlier findings.

As compared with 1986, work by married mothers in the bottom quartile by predicted wages, where the EITC had a positive incentive on work, rose the most; those for whom the EITC was neutral rose considerably less, and work rose least for those wives where the EITC penalized their work. I should note that this result is somewhat more sensitive to estimation methods than others in this chapter, and one can see higher and lower estimates depending on the method used. In addition, the timing is somewhat odd. Some divergences occurred in the late 1980s, before the EITC was very large. The biggest changes have been in the past several years, somewhat after the time when EITC expansions occurred. Still, it seems reasonable to presume that the effects of the dramatically expanded EITC in the mid-1990s would take some time to become more fully understood and experienced by married women, for whom the impacts were less obvious. The divergence in work by those with incentives to work less and others is also striking.

In table 3.8, I once again perform more rigorous statistical tests of what these graphs show. Here the tests are strong, but they are not quite as conclusive as

TABLE 3.8 / Changes in Work by Married Mothers and Estimated Impact of Social Policy Between March 1986 and March 1999

Category	Fraction Working		Difference
	1986	1999	
Married women with children			
Women with characteristics that would place them in the lowest quartile of potential wages in 1998	0.39 (0.01)	0.44 (0.01)	0.05 (0.01)
Second quartile of potential wages	0.53 (0.01)	0.63 (0.01)	0.11 (0.01)
Third quartile of potential wages	0.61 (0.01)	0.69 (0.01)	0.08 (0.01)
Highest quartile of potential wages	0.64 (0.01)	0.70 (0.00)	0.06 (0.01)
Married women with children in the lowest potential wage quartile			
Women for whom the 1998 EITC created work disincentives	0.42 (0.01)	0.43 (0.02)	0.01 (0.02)
Women for whom the 1998 EITC had no effect on incentives	0.39 (0.02)	0.47 (0.03)	0.08 (0.03)
Women for whom the 1998 EITC created positive work incentives	0.28 (0.02)	0.43 (0.03)	0.15 (0.04)
Married women without children			
Women with characteristics that would place them in the lowest quartile of potential wages in 1998	0.66 (0.02)	0.64 (0.02)	−0.02 (0.03)
Differences between groups			
Bottom as compared to third quartile among married mothers	−0.22 (0.01)	−0.25 (0.01)	−0.03[a] (0.02)
Bottom as compared to second quartile among married mothers	−0.14 (0.01)	−0.19 (0.01)	−0.05[a] (0.02)
Married mothers in bottom with disincentives versus married mothers with no effect on incentives	0.11 (0.02)	0.04 (0.03)	−0.07[a] (0.04)
Bottom married women with children as compared to bottom married women with children	−0.28 (0.02)	−0.20 (0.02)	0.08[a] (0.03)

Source: March Current Population Survey, 1986 and 1999.
Note: Standard errors in parentheses.
[a]This figure represents the difference in the differences, the estimated impact of social policies.

before. All except the comparison with childless married women (a comparison that seems highly questionable, given the already high rates of work in this latter group) show a depression of work from 3 to 7 percentage points. The seven-point estimate reflects the impact of the negative incentives only, while the three- to five-point estimate is for the low-wage group as a whole, including women facing positive and negative incentives (though negative incentives vastly outnumber positive in this group).

One estimate goes in the wrong direction: the comparison between low-wage married women with and without children. A comparison of figures 3.6 and 3.7 suggests that this is likely to be a highly problematic comparison group. Employment rates were vastly higher for the group without children, and there has been essentially no growth in work for any of the wage quartiles since the mid-1980s, in sharp contrast with the pattern for married mothers. Thus I am inclined to accept the three- to five-point estimated range for low-wage married women.

These results are consistent in direction with the projections of Dickert, Houser, and Scholz (1995) and the findings of Eissa and Hoynes (1999). The magnitudes are larger than the estimates of the latter, however, who estimate that the labor force participation of married high school dropouts would have declined by somewhat more than 1 percentage point. This may reflect the fact that Eissa and Hoynes used married women without children as the control group, with its attendant concerns.

One obvious question is whether the EITC, on net, increased or decreased work by women when the positive work effects for single mothers is combined with the negative ones for married mothers. Based on the number of mothers in each group affected, the EITC still results in a net increase in work by women.

THE IMPACT OF POLICY CHANGES ON MARRIAGE AND COHABITATION ARRANGEMENTS

I now turn to an examination of how policy changes altered marriage patterns and cohabitation among single parents. My basic methodology is quite similar to that used for work. I begin by examining how incentives change for mothers in different quartiles of the potential wage distribution and then examine how those patterns changed.

The EITC creates a strong marriage bonus for low-skill, nonworking single parents. It creates an equally large penalty for a working single parent. An obvious question is whether the marriage rewards outnumber the marriage penalties. Nicholas Bull and colleagues (1999) point out that any attempt to fully parameterize marriage penalties requires a comparison of how an existing or potential couple would behave if they were married or unmarried. Janet Holtzblatt and Robert Rebelein (chapter 4, this volume), Daniel Feenberg and Harvey Rosen (1995), Leslie Whittington and James Alm (1997), and the U.S. Congressional Budget Office (1997) all estimate the size of the marriage penalty based on the observed work earnings of men and women who are married, with the assumption that these would be unchanged if the couple were not married. They then make further assumptions about how the children, deductions, and unearned income of the couple would be divided after marriage. Stacy Dickert-Conlin (1999) simulates marriage among low-income unmarried women and men and separation among married couples and compares their tax liabilities before and after the change in marital status, under the assumption that their work behavior would not change.

As an empirical matter, people's behavior clearly does change with marriage, and some couples have children only after they marry. Thus, in determining how many people might actually face penalties or bonuses, I find a variant on a method by Alm and Whittington (1997) particularly helpful. Use of the data from the Panel Study of Income Dynamics allows observation of reported income for each person in the year preceding the marriage and the year following the marriage. In a sample of people who married before the EITC expansions had taken place, one can explore how many would have been rewarded or penalized by the EITC that was in place in 1996, based on their actual observed work behavior and family patterns before and after marriage. Had they been married in 1996, would their 1996 EITC have grown or diminished in the year following their marriage? Since the 1996 EITC was not yet in place in the years we examine, it cannot yet have influenced behavior, and thus we can ask about the impact of the EITC absent behavioral change.

I observed 1,671 marriages (first or later) for women in the Panel Study of Income Dynamics between 1983 and 1991 that could be used in this analysis.[14] I limited the sample to marriages before 1992 to minimize the danger that their behavior had already been altered by the EITC changes that came later. I used information on income from the last full year before the year of marriage and the first full year after it to determine whether the couples would have been EITC winners or losers had the 1996 EITC provisions been in place when they married. I calculated what their combined EITCs would have been before marriage and compared that with their joint EITC following it.

One important feature of this method is that changes in the earnings or parental status of the partners following marriage may also affect the EITC. I would argue that the right question regarding the EITC for a couple contemplating marriage is whether or not their combined benefits will change after marriage after taking account of their likely choices regarding children and work in the event they do marry; this method allows for behavioral changes that occur after marriage absent the high EITC of the middle to late 1990s. By looking only one year forward, however, the method surely understates eventual winners because many people will wait a year or more to have children. Moreover, behavioral changes induced by the EITC would also tend to increase rewards and reduce penalties in actuality.

Table 3.9 is drawn from the Panel Study of Income Dynamics.[15] The results are rather striking. Marrying couples facing EITC marriage penalties outnumber couples getting EITC marriage rewards. The reason is simple enough. In 29 percent of the marriages in the sample, one or the other partner was living with a

TABLE 3.9   /   Projected Effect of EITC Receipt on Marriages Between 1983 and 1991, Under 1996 EITC Rules

Work and Family Situation Before Marriage	EITC Benefits Would Have Been Lower in Year After Marriage	EITC Benefits Would Have Been Unchanged in Year After Marriage	EITC Benefits Would Have Been Higher in Year After Marriage	Total
At least one partner was living with a child in year before marriage (percentage)				
At least one partner with child and did not work in year before marriage (percentage)	0	3	2	6
Both partners worked in year before, marriage (percentage)	16	4	3	23
Neither partner was living with a child in the year before marriage (percentage)	0	65	6[a]	71
Total	16	72	11	100
Mean gain (dollars)	−$1,505	$0	$1,367	−$92

Source: Based on author's tabulations of 1,671 marriages in the Panel Study of Income Dynamics.

Note: The table presents a comparison of the sum of what the partners could have individually received from the 1996 EITC based on their earnings and child status in the last full survey year before their marriage with the 1996 EITC the couples could have received based on the couples' earnings and child status in the first full survey year after marriage. The table does not include the impact of the very small EITC available in 1996 for persons without children.

[a]Each couple had a child in the year after marriage and thus became newly eligible for the EITC.

child before the observed marriage. In the large majority of those cases, both partners worked in the year preceding marriage. In the bulk of those cases, marriage led to a decline in EITC benefits, as the spouse's income reduced the benefits. Among couples in which at least one partner is living with a child, losers outnumber winners, 16 percent to 5 percent.

There is another group that benefits from the EITC after marriage, however. Childless couples who marry and have a child in the year following marriage are often EITC winners. Thus in roughly 6 percent of marriages, the arrival of a child in the first year leads them to benefit from the EITC in ways they otherwise would have missed.

Overall, 16 percent of marriages would have been EITC losers and 11 percent would have been winners. The size of the potential EITC penalties and benefits is not trivial, averaging almost $1,400 in gains for the winners and $1,500 in losses for the losers.

Holtzblatt and Rebelein (chapter 4, this volume) also find that among existing married couples, the presence of the EITC creates many more filers with marriage penalties in the tax system and fewer receiving marriage bonuses. On net, they report that the EITC increases marriage penalties by $3.6 billion, though as noted, their method assumes no behavioral change among existing married couples.

The important question is whether these penalties and bonuses have had any behavioral impact. It has proved remarkably difficult for social scientists to reach a definitive consensus about the influence of social policies on marriage and family formation. In his fine review of the literature, Moffitt (1998) concludes that the impact of AFDC on family structure is at best mixed, with somewhat inconsistent cross-sectional and time-series patterns. He believes that the evidence hints at some modest impacts of social policy on family structure, but the findings remain scattered and often contradictory. The only randomized experiment that found an impact of financial incentives was the negative income tax, and even its findings remain highly controversial.

Unlike the case of labor supply, relatively little work has been done on the impact of the EITC on marriage and separation. In perhaps the most important work to date, Dickert-Conlin (1999) examines the impact of taxes and transfers on the decision to end a marriage. Using longitudinal data, she tracks divorce patterns, exploring whether persons with high marriage penalties are more likely to divorce. She finds that divorces are indeed slightly more common in the penalized group. With this methodology, she can examine only the behavior of those already married, not whether people marry more or less in the first place. With this sort of longitudinal work, since marriage penalties chiefly arise when the incomes of husband and wife are similar, it may be hard to correctly model the impact of tax penalties as against labor supply patterns of the couple, though Dickert-Conlin attempts to do so using instrumental variables.

Dickert-Conlin and Houser (1999) seek to examine the overall female-headship decision. They seek to parameterize financial incentives in AFDC and the EITC and examine the connection between these changes and female headship, using a rather limited set of independent variables. They use aggregate measures of AFDC and EITC generosity. They find little impact of the EITC on female headship of either whites or African Americans. They use a reduced-form specification, and the results appear to be somewhat sensitive to specification.

Most recently, Schoeni and Blank (2000) have compared the changes in marriage and female headship rates between waiver and nonwaiver states among women with low levels of education and find evidence that early welfare reforms influenced marriage. On the other hand, they find little evidence that TANF welfare reforms had any impact on family formation.

Here I once again use the natural experiment created by EITC expansion and

AFDC contraction to look for behavioral effects in CPS data. Indeed, the 1990s seem to have been a time of changed marriage incentives as well as work incentives. The EITC expansion was accompanied by a dramatic change in welfare policy. Thus, for very low-income women on welfare who are not working, there is far more incentive to marry than before; welfare is less available, and the EITC rewards marriage between a nonworking parent and another working childless individual. Meanwhile, somewhat higher-skill women, who would probably work if they were single, face suddenly increased marriage penalties.

Table 3.10 illustrates marriage penalties and rewards for people of different wage quartiles under different conditions in the CPS. For the purposes of developing this table, I again assume that women who work earn the median for their wage group and that if they marry, they will marry a man who earns the median-level income of husbands of currently married women. In reality, currently married men are undoubtedly a select group, and their wages may be somewhat higher than what an unmarried woman might expect from the remaining men, but for simple illustrative purposes, these estimates seem adequate.

The first and second panels of the table show marriage penalties under different conditions. Two striking features emerge immediately. First, in every case there is a financial penalty to marriage, whether or not the mother works, regardless of whether the working mother is in the top or bottom quartile of wages. Of course this is not entirely the result of the EITC. The impacts of means-tested transfer programs at the bottom and tax policies at the top are an important part of the story. Second, incentives for working and nonworking mothers changed dramatically over time and in opposite directions. After 1986, one sees a significant reduction in marriage penalties for nonworking mothers and a modest rise in them for working ones.

What is the overall impact of policy changes on women in each group? That depends on the probability that a woman in each category would be working if she were a single parent. Very-low-skill women are less likely to work if they are single parents. For such women, the expanded EITC creates, on net, an incentive to marry. Higher-skill women are more likely to work. For them the penalty is dominant.

The bottom line on marriage incentives by wage group in 1986 and 1998 is shown in the bottom rows of table 3.10. For the lowest quartile of women, on average marriage penalties have been reduced over time. In 1986 marriage meant enduring a marriage penalty equal to 20 percent of combined net income. By 1998, the penalty was down to 14 percent. Note this reduction in penalties would be even greater if the potential mates had lower incomes than those of currently married men. For all other quartiles, the marriage penalties have increased since 1986. In absolute terms, these increases were quite large. As a percentage of combined income, however, the changes were relatively modest—from 1 to 3 percent of net income.

Since marriage incentives grew by 4 percent of combined income (or nearly $1,000) for the bottom quartile and fell by 3 percent for the second, and since welfare reform was sharply reducing opportunities for low-wage women to sup-

TABLE 3.10 / Marriage Penalties for Women in Different Family Situations and Potential Wage Levels, 1986 and 1998

	Lowest Quartile	Second Quartile	Third Quartile	Highest Quartile
Marriage penalty for nonemployed single parent with two children who marries an employed childless man (1998 dollars)				
1986	−6,854	−7,075	−6,527	−5,888
1998	−2,710	−6,055	−5,724	−4,424
Marriage penalty for employed single parent with two children who marries an employed childless man (1998 dollars)				
1986	−2,727	−1,888	−934	−1,497
1998	−5,846	−4,988	−3,134	−2,797
Probability women will work if they are single parents (percentage)				
1986	0.34	0.57	0.71	0.83
1998	0.49	0.70	0.77	0.85
Average or expected marriage penalty (penalty for nonemployed × probability nonemployed + penalty for employed × probability employed) (1998 dollars)				
1986	−5,461	−4,096	−2,565	−2,242
1998	−4,258	−5,309	−3,734	−3,040
Average or expected marriage penalty as a share of combined male and female disposable income if partners remain unmarried (percentage)				
1986	−20	−11	−6	−4
1998	−14	−13	−8	−5

Source: Author's calculations based on March Current Population Survey, 1987 and 1999.

port themselves through welfare, it appears that marriage incentives for the bottom quartile increased relative to those in higher quartiles. We should thus expect marriage to grow in the bottom group relative to the others.

These incentives should operate both on marriage and divorce. The fraction of persons who are married and living with a spouse reflect the impact of both these flows. If these incentives are influencing marriage, one should see the fraction married in the bottom group to grow relative to the others.

It is important to recall the earlier discussion suggesting that the true influence of the EITC and other policies is likely to be far more complex than the simple calculated marriage penalties shown here. The added income and reduced stress from an EITC might actually stabilize a low-income married couple, even if it creates an apparent marriage "penalty."

Still, it seems natural to compare the marriage patterns of mothers at the bottom with those of other mothers to see if there is any evidence of changing marital behavior in the face of the rather monumental changes in social policy. Figure 3.9 shows the fraction who are married and living with their spouses in each of the wage groupings. There is little evidence here that marriage patterns are changing in response to the new incentives. Instead of rising relative to the other marriage rates, the marriage rates for those in the bottom wage category seem to be still falling. There is some possibility that the trend has slowed somewhat in the past few years, but certainly no dramatic changes have been seen. One striking feature of figure 3.9 is that marriage rates among women with

FIGURE 3.9 / Fraction Married With Spouse Present Among Women Aged Eighteen to Forty-Four With Children, by Predicted Wage Quartile

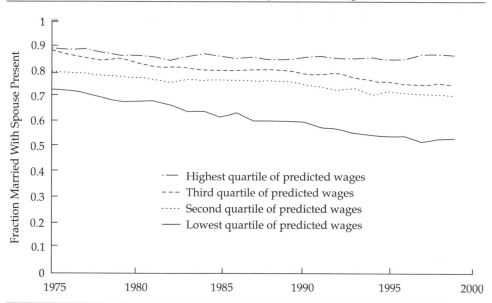

Source: March Current Population Surveys, 1975 to 1999.

FIGURE 3.10 / Fraction Married With Spouse Present Among Childless Women
Aged Eighteen to Forty-Four, by Predicted Wage Quartile

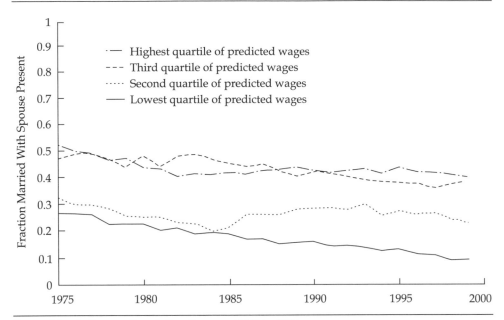

Source: March Current Population Surveys, 1975 to 1999.

children are rapidly becoming more unequal. The marriage patterns at the top of the wage distribution have changed little, but at the bottom they are in sharp decline.

It is also possible that the incentives have slowed what would have been an even faster decline. The only way to test that is to find an adequate control group. Figure 3.10 shows the marriage patterns for childless women. The pattern is less consistent than for women with children, but there is a spreading here, as well. For a variety of reasons, including the fact that marriage proportions among childless women are vastly smaller, I do not think this is a good control group for this purpose.

One can also look to see if the aggressiveness of welfare reform has influenced marriage patterns. If welfare is powerfully influencing marriage, then the sharp cutbacks in aggressive states would be expected to influence family structure. I also find no relevant difference in the change in the odds of marriage or cohabitation between states with more aggressive welfare reforms and less aggressive ones, illustrated in table 3.11. The table statistically confirms what is already evident from the graphs. Generally one finds insignificant results when one tries to compare the marriage patterns of the lowest-wage group with other wage groups or with childless women. The results all have the opposite sign of what was expected.

In interpreting these results, however, one should keep in mind that age is

TABLE 3.11 / Levels and Changes in Fraction Married, Spouse Present, Among Women Aged Eighteen to Forty-Four in Various Situations Between March 1986 and March 1999

Category	Fraction Married, Spouse Present		
	1986	1999	Difference
Women with children			
Women with characteristics that would place them in the lowest quartile of potential wages	0.63	0.53	−0.10
	(0.01)	(0.01)	(0.01)
Second quartile of potential wages	0.76	0.70	−0.06
	(0.01)	(0.01)	(0.01)
Third quartile of potential wages	0.80	0.75	−0.06
	(0.01)	(0.01)	(0.01)
Highest quartile of potential wages	0.85	0.86	0.02
	(0.01)	(0.00)	(0.01)
Women with children in the lowest potential wage quartile			
Women in states with the most-aggressive welfare reform policies	0.59	0.49	−0.10
	(0.01)	(0.01)	(0.01)
Women in states with the least-aggressive welfare-reform policies	0.66	0.60	−0.06
	(0.01)	(0.01)	(0.01)
Women without children			
Women with characteristics that would place them in the lowest quartile of potential wages	0.17	0.10	−0.07
	(0.01)	(0.01)	(0.01)
Differences between groups			
Bottom quartile as compared to third quartile among women with children	−0.17	−0.21	−0.04[a]
	(0.01)	(0.01)	(0.01)
Bottom quartile as compared to second quartile among women with children	−0.13	−0.17	−0.04[a]
	(0.01)	(0.01)	(0.01)
Bottom quartile women in most-aggressive compared to least-aggressive welfare-reform states	−0.06	−0.10	−0.04[a]
	(0.01)	(0.01)	(0.02)
Bottom women with children as compared to bottom women without children	0.46	0.44	−0.03[a]
	(0.01)	(0.01)	(0.02)

Source: March Current Population Surveys, 1986 and 1999.
Note: Standard errors in parentheses.
[a]This figure represents the difference in the differences, the estimated impact of social policies.

used in determining predicted wages, so that women in the lower wage quartiles tend to be younger than those in higher quartiles. Thus in comparing lower- and higher-wage women, one is partly comparing younger and older women.[16] If younger women were postponing marriage for reasons unrelated to the EITC, the age differences might obscure EITC patterns. To test this hypothesis I generated figure 3.11, limiting the sample to women aged twenty-five to forty-four.[17] Here a somewhat more interesting pattern emerges. Although there is year-to-

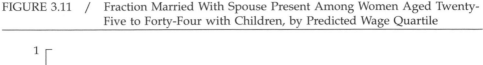

FIGURE 3.11 / Fraction Married With Spouse Present Among Women Aged Twenty-Five to Forty-Four with Children, by Predicted Wage Quartile

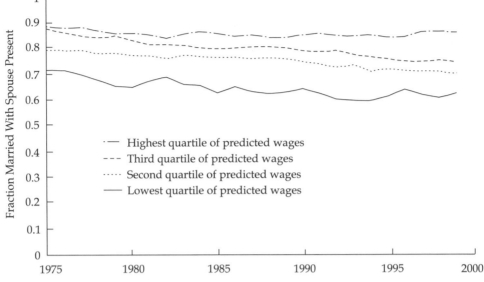

Source: March Current Population Surveys, 1975 to 1999.

year fluctuation, after falling until the early 1990s the fraction married among the lowest wage quartile does seem to have flattened out in the past six or seven years. By contrast, marriage percentages continued falling for the second and third quartiles. The differences in these trends are simply too tenuous to draw strong conclusions. Yet there is at least some possibility that the decline in marriage among the lowest-skill women has been slowed among women older than twenty-four by the social policies of recent years. Note that confining the sample to this group of older women does not affect the finding that welfare aggressiveness seems unrelated to marriage patterns.

The spreading of marriage patterns shown in figure 3.9 and the differences in patterns for the young and old strongly suggest that our model is incomplete and that other factors are influencing marriage and may be obscuring the results. For example, if the declining fortunes of low-skill men, especially younger men, have reduced the appeal of marriage, then trends in male earnings may obscure the impact of tax policy. It may also be that the combination of marriage rewards and penalties are confounding our estimation. Fortunately there is another more powerful way to test the power of the EITC and AFDC incentives to marriage.

THE INFLUENCE OF THE EITC ON THE CHOICE OF MARRIAGE VERSUS UNMARRIED COHABITATION

Couples often cohabit without being formally married and are doing so in increasing numbers. In general, if they live together without being married, they will be treated by the AFDC-TANF system and the tax system as single individuals.[18] This offers a wonderful experiment. With CPS data it is possible to observe couples with children who are living together—either married or as unmarried cohabiters. Since this latter group has already taken the step of living together, many factors influencing choices of adults to live together have already been accounted for. One question often remains, however: whether to formally marry or not. This group seems the one most likely to be sensitive to economic incentives for marriage.

I begin by creating a consistently defined series on cohabitation from the CPS. (The rules I used for cohabitation are described in the appendix.) For each couple with children (whether married or unmarried cohabiters) I calculate whether the couple would have faced a marriage penalty or reward under the 1998 EITC rules. In this work I assume that each person's earnings would be the same regardless of whether the couple was formally married, that only the mother is the legal guardian of the children, and that she is the one claiming the EITC if the partners are not legally married.[19]

If the EITC influences behavior, one would expect marriage to decline and unmarried cohabitation to rise among couples living together who begin to face a large EITC penalty in the later years. Conversely, one would expect marriage to rise or at least fall less sharply among couples who face an EITC marriage reward. Figure 3.12 and table 3.12 show the results. Among couples living together with children, marriage (as opposed to unmarried cohabitation) fell just as much in settings in which the EITC rewarded marriage as in those in which the EITC penalized it until 1996. Then, rather dramatically, marriage rates turned up among cohabiting couples who would experience a marriage reward.

The trend illustrated in figure 3.12 among those getting rewards only really becomes evident with the addition of the last year's data. The rise relative to those with penalties is statistically significant. The timing is slightly odd, since most of the EITC changes had peaked by 1996, but this may be another case of people learning about the incentives only gradually. Still these data do seem to suggest that EITC incentives may influence decisions about cohabitation as against marriage.

These results should be treated cautiously. The proportion of married persons among cohabiters rose from 89 to 93 percent in these data, certainly not a massive change. The change is only seen in the last two years of data, and it mostly represents greater marriage rates among the group of single mothers who are cohabiting and not working. This may simply be the result of changing work patterns of unmarried women—fewer nonworking women were single, so fewer nonworking cohabiters were single.

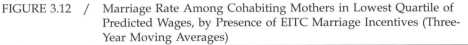

FIGURE 3.12   /   Marriage Rate Among Cohabiting Mothers in Lowest Quartile of Predicted Wages, by Presence of EITC Marriage Incentives (Three-Year Moving Averages)

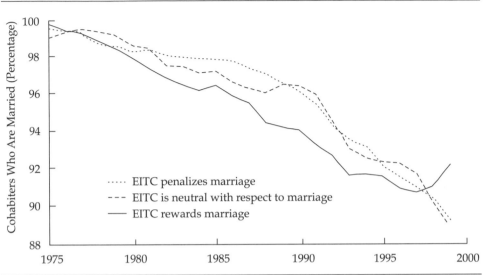

Source: Current Population Surveys, 1975 to 1999.
Note: Beginning and end years represent two-year averages with the beginning or end year weighted double.

This same question can be looked at another way, by comparing the cohabitation rates of working and nonworking low-skill unmarried mothers. A working single parent now faces a larger marriage penalty than in previous years; thus a woman who would like to live with a man would often be financially better off cohabiting outside of marriage. By contrast, a nonworking single mother faces far less marriage penalty than before and thus would be better off marrying rather than cohabiting. Thus we might expect the fraction of single mothers who were cohabiting to diverge between the working and nonworking mothers.

Figure 3.13 shows this pattern. Interestingly, after running together until the early 1980s, the rates of cohabitation diverge sharply in the mid-1980s (when Reagan-era welfare cuts and tightening rules regarding eligibility may have played a role); they then rise in parallel and finally diverge again in the past few years. A more convincing test will await longitudinal data to examine how marriage patterns of individuals changed over time as the incentives they faced changed. Nonetheless, the changes in apparent cohabitation patterns are intriguing. It is possible that marriage and cohabitation patterns are changing slowly.

In contrast with the changes in work, changes in marriage and living arrangements are more subtle. So far, there has been no dramatic change in marriage patterns, especially among the young. Nonetheless, there is the hint of possible family change beginning to occur in these results, at least for older women and

TABLE 3.12   /   Levels and Changes in Fraction of Cohabiting Couples Who Are
Married Among Couples in Which the Woman Is in the Lowest
Predicted Wage Quartile, March 1985 to March 1987 and March 1997 to
March 1999

Category	Fraction of Cohabiters Who Are Married		
	1985 to 1987	1997 to 1999	Difference
Couples with children and woman is in lowest predicted wage quartile			
Couples for whom the 1998 EITC creates a marriage penalty	0.959 (0.004)	0.911 (0.006)	−0.047 (0.007)
Couples for whom the 1998 EITC is neutral with respect to marriage	0.966 (0.004)	0.903 (0.009)	−0.064 (0.010)
Couples for whom the 1998 EITC creates a marriage reward	0.978 (0.003)	0.905 (0.006)	−0.072 (0.007)
Differences between groups			
Couples facing EITC marriage penalty as compared to couples facing a marriage reward, bottom quartile as compared to third quartile among women with children	−0.019 (0.005)	0.006 (0.009)	0.025[a] (0.010)

Source: March Current Population Surveys, 1985 to 1987 and 1997 to 1999.
Note: Standard errors in parentheses.
[a]This figure represents the difference in the differences, the estimated impact of social policies.

women who are already cohabiting. The large EITC, perhaps coupled with welfare reform, may yet lead to somewhat greater marriage rates.

CONCLUSION

This examination of incentives and behavioral responses points to several findings regarding the EITC and welfare reform.

- The combination of the higher EITC, welfare reform, and a strong economy
  has led to a truly unprecedented increase in labor market activity by low-
  income single parents.

- Since the late 1980s, labor market work by low-wage married mothers has not
  increased in the way that work by other categories of married mothers has.
  Neither social policy changes nor the economy should have produced reduced
  work rates, so the income effects and adverse work incentives of EITC seem
  the most likely cause.

- Although the EITC sharply reduced marriage penalties and welfare reform has
  pushed many people off welfare, there is no dramatic increase in marriage or
  decrease in cohabitation among the lowest-skill single mothers. There is at

FIGURE 3.13 / Share of Unmarried Mothers in the Lowest Wage Quartile Who Are Cohabiting, by Work Status (Three-Year Moving Averages)

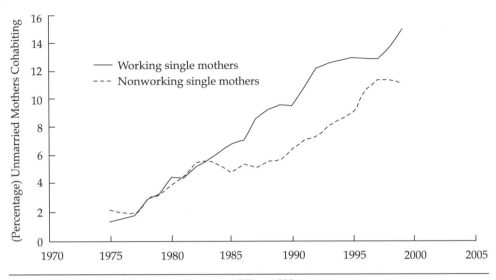

Source: March Current Population Surveys, 1975 to 1999.

least some possibility that marriage and cohabitation patterns have been changed slightly, however, especially among older women.

The interpretation of whether these results are reassuring or somewhat troubling depends on one's attitudes toward work and marriage among mothers. The fact that the EITC really does help working poor and near-poor families is consistent with recent public opinion in the United States that the working poor are among the most deserving. In the U.S. context, where the nation seems to have concluded almost unequivocally that single mothers should work outside the home, the first finding in the foregoing list should be welcome news. After years of being employed in lower proportions, single mothers are now employed at the same rate as married mothers. However, some observers may rightly worry about whether children are being helped or harmed by this rapid move into the labor market.

Whether the apparent reduction in work among married mothers is seen as good news or bad is likely to vary. Some believe that social policy ought to do more to enable married mothers to remain at home and nurture their children. Others will be troubled by the distortions in behavior and the danger that married mothers may lose out in the long run.

The possible results on marriage coupled with reductions in work by married women seems to echo a recent finding of the Minnesota Family Investment Program as evaluated by Manpower Demonstration Research Corporation and reported by Virginia Knox and colleagues (2000). In that experiment, a program of strong encouragement to work coupled with higher benefits to working two-parent families led to somewhat reduced work by wives and to lower levels of divorce and separation as compared with a randomized control group.

I did not find any real evidence that the EITC marriage penalties were reducing marriage rates. Nonetheless, social policymakers may still want to remove penalties to marriage based as much on symbolism and fairness as on any observed behavioral response.

Some might use the existence of marriage penalties as an argument for cutting back the EITC. Such a plan would have significant consequences. The EITC supports low-income working families with children. In an era of welfare reform, such aid may be especially important. The EITC clearly creates a marriage reward for the poorest single parents. The other alternative for fixing marriage penalties is to work on modifications in the design of the EITC.

The EITC's positive work and marriage incentives result from the fact that people with no earnings get nothing, while those with modest earnings get significant benefits. One needs to work or be married to someone who works in order to qualify for the credit. The negative incentives mostly come as a result of the phase-out—specifically, the fact that the income from one spouse can lead to a reduction in the EITC for the other spouse. Exploring alternative designs is beyond the scope of this chapter. At a time when removing marriage penalties in tax policy affecting higher-income families is a popular notion, it seems strange to ignore marriage penalties for those at the bottom of the income range.

Note that the incentives reported for the EITC apply to a host of other programs designed to provide aid to low-income working families where low income is based on the combined income of the family. Any targeted program of this sort will show incentives like the EITC. Incentives for a first parent to find employment, incentives for a second parent to remain at home, incentives for a nonworking parent to marry, and incentives for a working single parent to remain single will all be present. Since social policy in the United States is rapidly moving out of the traditional "welfare" programs and into supports for low-wage workers, it behooves policymakers to look closely at this mixed group of incentives when designing new programs.

APPENDIX: RULES FOR CREATING SINGLE PARENTS AND COHABITERS

Single mothers with children can in principle be classified as primary family heads, related subfamily heads, or unrelated secondary family (now called unrelated subfamily) heads. Unfortunately, before 1982 there were errors in the way related subfamilies were defined, owing to the fact that the relation to the head variable created ambiguous situations (see U. S. Bureau of the Census 1985). A mother, her two daughters, and her grandchild would be classified as a head, two children of the head, and an "other relative of the head" (who was under the age of eighteen). Thus it was unclear which of the two daughters was the grandchild's mother or even if some other nonresident was the parent. For many years, it appears that coders faced with this ambiguity often did not define such family groups as subfamilies even when they should have. The situation was corrected in 1982 and 1983, when more detailed information on relationships was collected. As a result, there is a sudden jump in subfamilies in the data after 1981. In time-series work, this creates potential inconsistencies.

Thus as a starting point, I assigned related persons under the age of eighteen (who were not children of the head and not already in a related subfamily) to potential parents within the household. Children were assigned first to daughters of the head who were at least fourteen years older than the child and no older than forty-four themselves. When more than one daughter was a possible mother, the oldest qualifying daughter was chosen. If no daughters were found, the procedure next looked for sons and then to other relatives who met the stated age criterion. This procedure undoubtedly creates some additional related subfamilies that would not be so defined after 1983, when full data was available. Since we are interested in tracking trends, for consistency, I created additional "subfamilies" in the post-1983 period, using this procedure, as well.

The procedure seems to have worked well. In the years just preceding 1982, the procedure increased the number of subfamilies by close to 50 percent. In the post-1984 period, the procedure added just 7 percent to the total, and time-series trends now look sensible.

Various definitions have been used to denote "persons of the opposite sex in shared living quarters" (POSSLQs) over the years. After the mid-1990s, more information was collected on the nature of relationships within the household. Before that time, however, the POSSLQ relationship had to be inferred. The standard Census Bureau procedure called for forming POSSLQs when there were two and only two unrelated adults in a household. The reason for this restriction was to exclude cases where groups of roommates were living together. One weakness in this formulation, however, is that any family that included related adults (over the age of fifteen) could not have a POSSLQ. Thus a mother and her seventeen-year-old son could never be assigned to the POSSLQ category. Since adult children are living at home in greater and greater numbers, this restriction seems problematic. Moreover, it is quite possible for two POSSLQ couples to share an apartment. Thus I prefer a methodology similar to that of Robert Moffitt, Robert Reville, and Anne Winkler (1998), one that does not limit POSSLQs to cases in which there are only two adults or to families with only one unrelated adult, as does the POSSLQ definition in the work of Lynne Casper, Philip Cohen, and Tavia Simmons (1999).

Moreover, since I am seeking to create a consistent series over time, I use the same procedure to form POSSLQs after 1995 even though more complete data is available after that time. A POSSLQ couple is formed if and only if two or more unrelated adults of the opposite sex separated in age by no more than twenty years are living in the same household. In cases in which there was more than one possible POSSLQ couple, the pair closest in age were designated. A POSSLQ couple may be formed with unmarried family heads, primary individuals, related subfamily heads, unrelated individuals, and unrelated secondary heads.

The classification specifically allows for a POSSLQ relationship to be formed in cases in which an individual listed as the head of household is living with an unrelated secondary family. Thus a man and his girlfriend and her daughter living in "his" house could be designated as a POSSLQ group. Similarly, in rare cases a related subfamily can have a POSSLQ relationship if there is an appropriate unrelated secondary individual or family of the right age and sex in the family and such a relationship cannot be formed with the household head.

Using this procedure, in later years I can examine the self-reported status of persons who were earlier designated as POSSLQs. Roughly 94 percent of those who classified themselves as a "partner" in 1999 were classified as POSSLQs using this procedure. Of those classified as POSSLQs, 64 percent report themselves as "partners," 24 percent report the somewhat more ambiguous designation, "roommate," 8 percent report the nonspecific "nonrelative of the head," and 4 percent report themselves as boarders. Not surprisingly then, some designated POSSLQs are simply "roommates," though one cannot be certain whether some of the "roommates" and "nonrelatives" preferred not to report themselves as "partners." I know of no reason to believe this upward bias varies over time. Note that limiting POSSLQs to cases in which there is only one unrelated adult in the household excludes roughly the same number of self-designated "partners" (who one would want to include) as "roommates" (who one would like to exclude), and among families with children it mostly excludes persons who were self-designated "partners."

TABLE 3.A1 / Regression Coefficients for Working Women in 1998

Variable	Coefficient	Standard Error
Age twenty-five to thirty-four	0.332	0.012
Age thirty-five to forty-four	0.445	0.012
Black	−0.048	0.012
Other	−0.017	0.019
High school graduate	0.263	0.016
Some education beyond high school	0.413	0.016
College graduate	0.736	0.017
More than college	0.900	0.021
Number of children under the age of eighteen	−0.025	0.004
Constant	1.593	0.016
R squared	.251	
Number of observations	17,402	
Standard error of the estimate	.533	

Source: March Current Population Survey 1999.
Note: Sample includes all women, regardless of marital status, who worked at least twenty-six weeks in 1998. Wage is defined as total earnings divided by annual hours worked (weeks worked times usual hours worked). The sample excludes persons with calculated wages of less than $1.00 an hour or more than $75.00 an hour.

TABLE 3.A2 / Measures of Welfare Reform Aggressiveness, by State

State	Probability That a Single Mother Received AFDC in 1991–1992	Actual Change in Probability 1991–1992 to 1997–1998	Predicted Change in Probability 1991–1992 to 1997–1998	Difference	Standard Error of Difference	Statistical Aggressiveness (1 = less aggressive)	Program Aggressiveness Derived from Meyer and Rosenbaum (1 = less aggressive)
Alabama	0.28	−0.14	−0.01	−0.14	0.06	3	1
Alaska	0.34	0.00	0.01	−0.01	0.06	1	1
Arizona	0.30	−0.12	−0.09	−0.02	0.05	1	3
Arkansas	0.35	−0.19	−0.19	0.00	0.05	1	2
California	0.37	−0.10	−0.09	−0.02	0.02	1	3
Colorado	0.36	−0.24	−0.06	−0.18	0.05	3	2
Connecticut	0.46	−0.35	−0.25	−0.09	0.05	2	3
Delaware	0.33	−0.16	0.00	−0.16	0.07	3	3
District of Columbia	0.34	−0.02	0.02	−0.04	0.05	1	1
Florida	0.30	−0.14	−0.10	−0.04	0.02	2	1
Georgia	0.30	−0.14	0.01	−0.15	0.04	3	2
Hawaii	0.31	0.08	0.23	−0.15	0.06	3	2
Idaho	0.17	−0.09	0.03	−0.12	0.05	3	3
Illinois	0.39	−0.18	−0.08	−0.10	0.02	3	3
Indiana	0.32	−0.22	−0.09	−0.13	0.04	3	3
Iowa	0.32	−0.10	−0.03	−0.08	0.06	2	3
Kansas	0.34	−0.20	0.04	−0.24	0.05	3	3
Kentucky	0.43	−0.18	−0.15	−0.03	0.06	1	1
Louisiana	0.43	−0.21	−0.10	−0.11	0.05	3	3
Maine	0.42	−0.18	−0.06	−0.11	0.07	3	2
Maryland	0.30	−0.16	−0.07	−0.08	0.06	2	2
Massachusetts	0.43	−0.16	−0.02	−0.14	0.03	3	3
Michigan	0.44	−0.18	−0.08	−0.10	0.03	2	3
Minnesota	0.49	−0.13	−0.15	0.02	0.06	1	2
Mississippi	0.36	−0.27	−0.10	−0.17	0.04	3	3
Missouri	0.37	−0.10	0.00	−0.10	0.06	3	3
Montana	0.32	−0.18	−0.02	−0.16	0.05	3	3

TABLE 3.A2 / *Continued*

State	Probability That a Single Mother Received AFDC in 1991–1992	Actual Change in Probability 1991–1992 to 1997–1998	Predicted Change in Probability 1991–1992 to 1997–1998	Difference	Standard Error of Difference	Statistical Aggressiveness (1 = less aggressive)	Program Aggressiveness Derived from Meyer and Rosenbaum (1 = less aggressive)
Nebraska	0.49	−0.23	−0.09	−0.13	0.08	3	3
Nevada	0.13	−0.05	−0.04	−0.01	0.04	1	1
New Hampshire	0.38	−0.18	−0.25	0.06	0.07	1	3
New Jersey	0.32	−0.10	−0.10	0.00	0.03	1	3
New Mexico	0.48	−0.23	−0.06	−0.18	0.06	3	1
New York	0.48	−0.15	−0.07	−0.07	0.02	2	1
North Carolina	0.29	−0.16	−0.07	−0.08	0.03	2	3
North Dakota	0.41	−0.23	−0.13	−0.10	0.05	3	1
Ohio	0.36	−0.09	−0.05	−0.05	0.03	2	3
Oklahoma	0.31	−0.14	−0.18	0.04	0.06	1	2
Oregon	0.41	−0.19	−0.02	−0.17	0.06	3	3
Pennsylvania	0.40	−0.16	−0.12	−0.04	0.03	2	1
Rhode Island	0.65	−0.15	−0.22	0.08	0.09	1	1
South Carolina	0.30	−0.23	−0.19	−0.03	0.04	1	2
South Dakota	0.25	−0.09	0.02	−0.12	0.06	3	3
Tennessee	0.41	−0.29	−0.11	−0.18	0.05	3	3
Texas	0.25	−0.12	−0.05	−0.07	0.02	3	3
Utah	0.27	−0.10	−0.03	−0.07	0.06	2	2
Vermont	0.45	−0.24	−0.22	−0.02	0.07	1	3
Virginia	0.35	−0.13	−0.04	−0.10	0.08	2	3
Washington	0.42	−0.19	−0.08	−0.10	0.05	3	1
West Virginia	0.52	−0.31	−0.16	−0.15	0.06	3	3
Wisconsin	0.55	−0.36	−0.14	−0.22	0.08	3	3

Source: Author's calculations based on data from the March Current Population Surveys, 1992, 1993, 1998, and 1999.
Note: Wyoming omitted due to small sample size.

NOTES

1. In fact, the median woman in the bottom quartile of the predicted wage distribution earned roughly $10,000 in 1998 if she worked at least twenty-six weeks; if a woman in the same bottom quartile was married, her husband earned a median of $18,000.

2. Note, however, that although EITC use is very high, use of food stamps and Medicaid is hardly universal among working families eligible for such aid. This is especially true of Medicaid enrollment. See Guyer, Broaddus, and Cochran 1999. Thus the table gives a sense of what people could qualify for, not necessarily the amounts that any individual actually collects.

3. LaDonna Pavetti, personal communication (July 2000, Washington, D.C.).

4. Ham and Shore-Sheppard 1999 is one of the few papers that do so.

5. This is the CPS survey conducted in March of 1999 that asked about income in the previous calendar year.

6. The results of that equation are provided in table 3.A1, in the appendix. The preferred way to estimate potential wages is to use a Heckman correction for selection bias owing to the fact that some women do not work because their wages are lower. I tried such a correction in several years and predicted wages again. Although the levels differed as a result of the correction, the rank order changed little. The correlation between the corrected and uncorrected wage predictions exceeded .95. Since we only seek to group people into quartiles, and since I want to estimate equations for well over 350,000 women over the age of eighteen, I relied on the simpler ordinary least squares regressions.

7. One could also create new wage equations in every year. I prefer using the 1998 model since it guarantees I will be tracking similar people over time. However, I have done all the estimates presented in this chapter using separate-year wage equations as well, and the results are virtually identical.

8. The age, race, and education categories are the same as those used in table 3.A1. The annual earnings categories are 0, $7,500, $15,000, and more than $15,000. State unemployment rates were taken from the Bureau of Labor Statistics. Earnings do not include EITC or similar benefits as these were not counted as income in calculating AFDC benefits or eligibility.

9. In making these projections I set the trend value at 1992, effectively simulating eligibility patterns for 1992.

10. The state-by-state differences in actual as against predicted caseload declines and their standard errors are shown in table 3.A2, in the appendix. Because of space limitations I do not report the full probit results for each state.

11. For 1999, the value represents two-thirds of the 1999 value plus one-third of the 1998 value.

12. As a test of whether these aggressiveness measures were somehow capturing other aspects of the state economic environment, I tabulated work patterns of unmarried women without children and of married mothers. As expected, I found no significant differences in work patterns by welfare reform aggressiveness in these groups.

13. The CPS sample includes a given household for four consecutive months, then skips it for eight months, and then includes it for another four months. In effect respondents are interviewed for the same four months over two consecutive years. At the end of both of these four-month interview periods, they are members of the outgoing rotation group, and special information is collected that, at least after 1984, allows one to determine the potential wage quartile and whether the heads of household were female. Because of the nature of this sampling design, outgoing rotation groups from March to June include members who were included in the monthly March CPS data. But those in outgoing rotations in other months were never a part of the March samples.

14. A small portion of women married more than once in our sample period—all marriages are included.

15. In deriving this table, I ignored the very small EITC available to low-earning childless individuals.

16. Note that unlike marriage results, work results described earlier are essentially unaffected by limiting the sample to particular age groups.

17. Further segregating the sample into women twenty-five to thirty-four years old and those thirty-five to forty-four years old reveals patterns that are similar to the one shown here.

18. Not surprisingly, the story can get complicated. Alm, Dickert-Conlin, and Whittington (1999) and Moffitt, Reville, and Winkler (1998) note that in theory both the AFDC-TANF system and the tax system distinguish between cohabitation with the father of the children and cohabitation with an unrelated male, though my understanding of actual AFDC practice differs from their interpretation of the actual rules. Rather than include the father as part of the filing unit when the couple is not married, states may often elect to establish paternity and collect child support. States rarely look carefully at the contributions of other relatives in the home for AFDC cases, but benefits could be reduced somewhat if the family reported that a cohabiting adult was contributing money toward the rent. As Alm, Dickert-Conlin, and Whittington properly note, the IRS has rules about who can claim the EITC when a child is living with two adults. If the man is the father and lives with the child for at least six months, or if he is "caring for the child as his own" and lives with the child for a full twelve months, he can claim an EITC on the child if the mother has no earnings. If the mother has earnings, the person with the higher earnings must claim the child for purposes of the EITC. Note that unlike the married case, however, the other partner's income is not counted in determining the level of the EITC—thus there remains a marriage penalty in cases where both adults have income. I know of no information on the number of cases where an unmarried father is legally claiming the EITC of a child who is legally in the custody of the mother or men who claim it for children they "care for as their own." Paternity has been legally established in a minority of cases of single parents. Moreover, I suspect these rules are rarely applied in practice, and they still leave EITC marriage rewards and penalties in place for unmarried couples. Finally, I know of no reliable data on the fraction of cohabiters who are fathers of the children among low-income couples, much less a breakdown by earnings of each partner.

19. Using the table from Alm, Dickert-Conlin, and Whittington (1999), one can see that this assumption will roughly lead to the correct measure of marriage versus cohabita-

tion rewards in every case except when the cohabiting man is the father of the child, the mother is not working, and the father claims the EITC for the child. While I have no evidence on the incidence, I would suspect such cases are quite rare. I experimented with assuming that the high earner always claimed the EITC if a child was living with two adults of the opposite sex and recalculating penalties and rewards. The results were similar to those reported.

REFERENCES

Alm, James, Stacy Dickert-Conlin, and Leslie A. Whittington. 1999. "Policy Watch: The Marriage Penalty." *Journal of Economic Perspectives* 13(3): 193–204.

Alm, James, and Leslie A. Whittington. 1997. "Income Taxes and the Timing of the Marital Decision." *Journal of Public Economics* 64(2): 219–40.

Attanasio, Orazio, and Thomas MaCurdy. 1997. "Interactions in Family Supply and Their Implications for the Impact of the EITC." Stanford University. Mimeo.

Becker, Gary. 1981. *A Treatise on the Family.* Cambridge, Mass.: Harvard University Press.

Blank, Rebecca, David Card, and Philip Robins. 2000. "Financial Incentives for Increasing Work and Income Among Low-Income Families." In *Finding Jobs: Work and Welfare Reform,* edited by Rebecca Blank and David Card. New York: Russell Sage Foundation.

Bull, Nicholas, Janet Holtzblatt, James Nunns, and Robert Rebelein. 1999. "Defining and Measuring Marriage Penalties and Bonuses." Paper 82. Washington: U.S. Department of the Treasury, Office of Tax Analysis.

Casper, Lynne M., Philip N. Cohen, and Tavia Simmons. 1999. "How Does POSSLQ Measure Up? Historical Estimates of Cohabitation." Working Paper 36. Washington: U.S. Bureau of the Census, Population Division.

Dickert, Stacy, Scott Houser, and John Karl Scholz. 1995. "The Earned Income Tax Credit and Transfer Programs: A Study of Labor Market and Program Participation." In *Tax Policy and the Economy,* edited by James M. Poterba. Cambridge, Mass.: MIT Press.

Dickert-Conlin, Stacy. 1999. "Taxes and Transfers: Their Effect on the Decision to End a Marriage." *Journal of Public Economics* 73(2): 217–40.

Dickert-Conlin, Stacy, and Scott Houser. 1999. "EITC, AFDC, and the Female Headship Decision." Syracuse University. Mimeo.

Eissa, Nada, and Hilary Hoynes. 1999. "The Earned Income Tax Credit and the Labor Supply of Married Couples." University of California, Berkeley. Mimeo.

Eissa, Nada, and Jeffrey B. Liebman. 1996. "Labor Supply Response to the Earned Income Tax Credit." *Quarterly Journal of Economics* 112(2): 605–37.

Ellwood, David T. 2000. "Anti-Poverty Policy for Families in the Next Century: From Welfare to Work—and Worries." *Journal of Economic Perspectives* 14(1): 187–98.

Feenberg, Daniel R., and Harvey S. Rosen. 1995. "Recent Developments in the Marriage Tax." *National Tax Journal* 48(1): 91–101.

Guyer, Jocelyn, Matthew Broaddus, and Michelle Cochran. 1999. "Missed Opportunities: Declining Medicaid Enrollment Undermines the Nation's Progress in Insuring Low-Income Children." Washington, D.C.: Center on Budget and Policy Priorities (October).

Ham, John, and Lara Shore-Sheppard. 1999. "The Impact of Public Health Insurance on Employment Transitions." University of Pittsburgh. Mimeo.

Knox, Virginia, Cynthia Miller, Lisa A. Gennetian, Martey Dodoo, Jo Anna Hunter, and Cindy Redcross. 2000. "Reforming Welfare and Rewarding Work: Final Report on the

Minnesota Family Investment Program." New York: Manpower Demonstration Research Corporation (May).

Liebman, Jeffrey B. 1998. "The Impact of the Earned Income Tax Credit on Incentives and Income Distribution." In *Tax Policy and the Economy,* edited by James M. Poterba. Cambridge, Mass.: MIT Press.

MaCurdy, Thomas E., David A. Green, and Harry J. Paarsch. 1990. "Assessing Empirical Approaches for Analysing Taxes and Labour Supply." *Journal of Human Resources* 25(3): 415–90.

Meyer, Bruce, and Daniel Rosenbaum. 1999. "Welfare, the Earned Income Tax Credit, and the Labor Supply of Single Mothers." Northwestern University. Mimeo.

Moffitt, Robert. 1986. "The Econometrics of Piecewise-Linear Budget Constraints: A Survey and Exposition of the Maximum Likelihood Method." *Journal of Business and Economic Statistics* 4(3): 317–27.

———. 1998. "The Effect of Welfare on Marriage and Fertility." In *Welfare, the Family, and Reproductive Behavior,* edited by Robert Moffitt. Washington, D.C.: National Academy Press.

Moffitt, Robert A., Robert Reville, and Anne E. Winkler. 1998. "Beyond Single Mothers: Cohabitation, Marriage, and the U.S. Welfare System." *Demography* 35(3): 259–78.

Schoeni, Robert F., and Rebecca M. Blank. 2000. "What Has Welfare Reform Accomplished? Impacts on Welfare Participation, Employment, Income, Poverty, and Family Structure." Working Paper W7627. Cambridge, Mass.: National Bureau of Economic Research.

U.S. Congressional Budget Office. 1997. "For Better or For Worse: Marriage and the Federal Income Tax." Washington: U.S. Congress (June).

U.S. Department of Commerce. U.S. Bureau of the Census. 1985 and various years. "Marital Status and Living Arrangements: March 1984." *Current Population Reports,* P-20, no. 399. Washington: U.S. Government Printing Office.

Whittington, Leslie A., and James Alm. 1997. "Til Death or Taxes Do Us Part: The Effect of Income Taxation on Divorce." *Journal of Human Resources* 32(2): 388–412.

Chapter 4

Measuring the Effect of the Earned Income Tax Credit on Marriage Penalties and Bonuses

Janet Holtzblatt and Robert Rebelein

According to the U.S. General Accounting Office (1996), there are fifty-nine provisions in the income tax code that either penalize or reward marriage.[1] The presence of marriage penalties and bonuses in the income tax code raises at least three concerns. First, one goal of tax policy is horizontal equity, or the equal tax treatment of equals. The presence of marriage penalties and bonuses, however, implies that two couples who are similar except for the existence of a marriage license can be taxed differently on the same amounts of income. Second, marriage penalties and bonuses may affect taxpayers' behavior by distorting decisions to marry or to work. Third, marriage penalties and bonuses may encourage taxpayers to evade tax liabilities by misreporting marital status and other family characteristics to tax authorities.

These concerns are particularly important when considering the impact of the Earned Income Tax Credit (EITC). The EITC is a refundable tax credit that has been supported by many because they view it as fair, pro-family, pro-work, and relatively simple to administer. If the design of the EITC results in marriage penalties and bonuses and these penalties and bonuses adversely affect equity, taxpayer behavior, or compliance, then the credit may not be fully achieving the goals of its supporters.

Because the EITC initially increases and then declines with taxpayers' income, a marriage license can make a significant difference in the amount of the credit received by a couple. For example, two very-low-wage workers with a child may receive a marriage bonus if they file a joint return, because their combined income will entitle them to a larger EITC than they can receive, in combination, as two unmarried filers. On the other hand, a two-earner couple with children and $35,000 of combined income will be ineligible for the credit if married, but may be eligible for a sizable credit if they do not marry and, instead, live together and raise a family. Although their income and family responsibilities may be similar, these married and unmarried couples are not treated in the same way under the income tax code.

Marriage penalties and bonuses in the EITC raise further questions because the credit is targeted to low-income families. These families are also subject to marriage penalties associated with needs-based transfer programs. As the number of single-parent families has grown over the past three decades, concern has also grown that transfer programs may have spurred this growth by discouraging marriage. Marriage bonuses in the EITC may partially or fully offset the marriage penalties caused by the transfer system. The credit may also give rise to marriage penalties, however, which can compound the effects of the transfer system. Thus, it is critical to take into account both the tax system and the transfer system when studying family formation decisions, as some recent research has (Dickert-Conlin 1999; Eissa and Hoynes 1999).

Another source of concern are the findings from an Internal Revenue Service study that more than 20 percent of the credit was claimed in error in 1994 and that nearly one-third of EITC overclaims were attributable to married taxpayers' misreporting their filing status on tax returns (Scholz 1997; chapter 6, this volume). Some of the errors may simply reflect taxpayer confusion over the rules regarding filing status. It is also possible, however, that some taxpayers may respond to marriage bonuses and penalties by misreporting filing status in order to evade taxes. If true, understanding marriage penalties and bonuses in the tax system may provide further insight into ways to improve tax compliance. Since EITC noncompliance has been the subject of much scrutiny in recent years, particular attention is warranted to the marriage penalties and bonuses caused by the credit's design.

Each of these concerns is generated by the same fundamental issue: the relative tax treatment of single and married taxpayers. In spite of this common issue, it is unfortunately not possible to derive a unique measure of marriage penalties and bonuses that can simultaneously address concerns as complex and diverse as horizontal equity, decisions to marry or work, or taxpayer compliance.

For example, measuring the effect of marriage penalties and bonuses on horizontal equity requires comparing tax liabilities of couples who are similar in all regards except for the existence of a marriage license. Thus, we assume that a couple, if not married, would still live together and make consumption, investment, and child-rearing decisions jointly. Using this method, the EITC is found to increase total marriage penalties in the income tax by $3.1 billion (10.4 percent) and reduce marriage bonuses by $439 million (1.5 percent) in 2000. Nearly 63 percent of the EITC-related marriage penalties accrue to couples who are ineligible for the EITC as joint filers because their combined income, which may be as much as $60,000, is too high.

This may also be a logical starting point for examining the impact of marriage penalties and bonuses on the decision to cohabit rather than marry. An analysis of other family formation choices, however, such as the decision to separate or divorce, may require different measures of marriage penalties and bonuses. The income tax code does not simply distinguish between married and single statuses by the existence of a marriage license; it also accounts for differences in living arrangements among couples, particularly among those who have children. If we instead assume that the couple, if not married, would live apart and that the lower-wage earner would have custody of the children, the EITC is found to increase total marriage penalties by $9.9 billion (31.7 percent) and reduce marriage bonuses by $5.7 billion (9.8 percent). This method increases the impact of the EITC on marriage penalties because even couples with incomes over $60,000 could qualify for the credit if eligibility were based only on the lower-earning spouse's income. Under this measure, nearly all (93 percent) of the EITC-related marriage penalties are incurred by couples whose incomes exceed the current EITC eligibility cutoff.

The preceding measures assume that taxpayers would not reorganize their living arrangements simply to avoid income taxes. These measures also assume taxpayers would comply with the tax code. Measuring the impact of marriage penalties and bonuses on tax avoidance or evasion requires a third method that allows taxpayers to either reorganize or misreport their living arrangements to the tax authorities in order to minimize their tax liabilities. Some taxpayers would find that their combined tax liabilities as unmarried filers will be minimized by allocating children to the higher earner, while others would find it more beneficial to assign custody of the children to the lower earner. This measure also gives taxpayers the option to divide custody of their children and thus both spouses, if eligible, can claim the EITC. Using such a measure, the EITC is found to increase marriage penalties by $12.8 billion (29.7 percent) and reduce marriage bonuses by $1.5 billion (5.7 percent). Under this measure, more than 83 percent of the EITC-related marriage penalties are attributable to couples whose combined incomes are too high to qualify for the EITC as joint filers.

SOURCES AND IMPLICATIONS OF MARRIAGE PENALTIES AND BONUSES

In the United States, the personal income tax is based on the income of the individual or, if married, the couple.[2] Since 1948, spouses have been effectively allowed to split income when filing a joint return. Married couples can file separate income tax returns, but most file joint returns because their income taxes are generally lower than if they opted for the "married filing separate" status. For example, married taxpayers are ineligible for the EITC or the child and dependent care tax credit if they file separately.

A couple has a marriage penalty if they owe more income tax filing a joint return than they would if they were unmarried and each were taxable as a single or head-of-household filer. Conversely, a couple has a marriage bonus if they owe less income tax filing a joint return than they would if they were unmarried and each were taxable as a single or head-of-household filer.

Marriage penalties and bonuses are difficult to eliminate because they are often the by-products of trade-offs among many policy goals. By treating the married couple as a distinct tax unit, the personal income tax recognizes that spouses share resources and make consumption and savings decisions together. From a practical perspective, it may be difficult to disentangle the income or expenses of one spouse from those of the other. The current tax code achieves horizontal equity among married couples because couples with equal combined incomes generally pay the same amount of taxes, regardless of the allocation of income between spouses.[3] However, as Boris Bittker (1975) and many others have shown, a tax system cannot simultaneously have neutrality toward marriage, progressivity, and equal taxation of couples with the same total incomes. Graduated tax rate schedules and phase-outs of deductions and credits contribute to the progressivity of the tax code but also can lead to marriage penalties when spouses' incomes are combined. Social policy considerations may also affect both the design of tax systems and the magnitude of marriage penalties and bonuses. During recent policy debates on the federal role in the provision of child-care assistance, tax cuts that enhance marriage bonuses have been proposed for families with stay-at-home parents.

The design of the EITC provides further evidence of the trade-offs that are made between the goal of marriage neutrality and other tax and social policy goals. For example, two of the fundamental goals of the EITC are to encourage work, particularly among those with little or no attachment to the labor force, and to lift working families out of poverty. Three design features of the EITC contribute toward the achievement of these goals. First, individuals must have earned income to qualify for the credit. Second, the EITC initially increases with earned income at a maximum rate of 40 percent, thus offsetting the disincentive effects that may be associated with a 15 percent social security tax rate and a 24 percent reduction rate in food stamp benefits. Third, the maximum amount of the EITC was raised in 1993 with the goal of reducing the likelihood that a family of four with one full-time minimum-wage worker lived in poverty. In 2000, the maximum EITC will be $3,888.

In addition to encouraging work, the first two features also create marriage bonuses, and the third feature—the size of the maximum credit—affects the magnitude of these bonuses. For example, by marrying an unemployed single parent with little or no taxable income, a low-income childless worker will always qualify for a much larger EITC than if he or she remained unmarried.

Another goal of tax policy is to raise sufficient revenues to pay for spending programs. Concerns about fiscal responsibility prevent policymakers from extending eligibility for this nearly $4,000 tax credit to all taxpayers, but limiting benefits to those with the greatest needs causes marriage penalties. The magnitude of these penalties depends on the size of the credit and the extent to which eligibility for the credit is limited to those with the greatest needs.

Eligibility for the EITC is limited in two ways. First, after reaching a maximum value, the EITC decreases with modified adjusted gross income (or earned income, if greater) until it is fully phased out at an income of $31,152 (for a taxpayer with two or more children). Second, taxpayers are also ineligible for the EITC if their investment income, including interest, dividends, net capital gains, net rents, and net royalties, exceeds $2,400.

Finally, policymakers have used the EITC to adjust for differences in ability to pay among taxpayers based on their family responsibilities. Until 1994, the EITC was available only to taxpayers if they resided with children for more than half the year, although the amount of the credit did not vary with the number of children in the family. This had two consequences. On the one hand, the EITC could result in a significant bonus when a childless worker married a nonworker with children. On the other hand, it created a sizable penalty when two low-income workers, each with at least one child, married; instead of qualifying for two credits, the married couple would only be eligible for one credit.

Recent legislative changes have reduced the magnitude of both these effects. Legislation in 1990 and 1993 entitled families with two or more children to a somewhat larger EITC than those with one child. At the maximum credit amounts, a family with two or more children receives a credit that is 165 percent of the amount received by families with only one child. This differential reduces—but does not eliminate—the marriage penalty caused by the cap on the number of EITC-qualifying children.

In addition, since 1994, very-low-income taxpayers who do not reside with children have been eligible for a small EITC that equals, at most, the employee contribution for social security taxes. This provision reduces EITC-related marriage bonuses that occur when a very-low-wage childless worker marries a nonworker with children but may increase penalties when two very-low-wage childless workers marry.

DISTINGUISHING BETWEEN HOUSEHOLDS

As has already been noted, the tax code treats married couples with the same total income equally, thus achieving a measure of horizontal equity. Horizontal equity comparisons can encompass other types of households as well. Harvey Brazer (1980) has observed that a household might consist only of single individuals who share resources and otherwise appear to act as an economic unit in much the same manner as the marital unit. He argues that such households can be economically equivalent to marital units and that treating married couples, but not similar types of households, as the unit of taxation can lead to another type of horizontal inequity in the tax code.

Brazer suggests that horizontal equity could be improved if the basic filing unit were the household, but he recognizes that this would be difficult to administer because of the absence of an easily identifiable and readily verifiable group outside marriage. Alternatively, these inequities could be eliminated if the individual were the filing unit. Under a progressive income tax, however, married couples with the same combined income could pay vastly different amounts of taxes if the income tax were based on an individual filing unit.

There is a third option that Brazer does not consider. Even within the context of a progressive income tax with joint filing for married couples, special rules have been created that recognize certain similarities between married couples and other types of households but that apply only in limited situations. As a result, in some circumstances married individuals may be treated as if they were unmarried, and in others unmarried individuals may have to take into account the income (or support) of others in their household when computing their tax liability.

First, while married individuals generally cannot file for the EITC on separate returns unless they are legally separated from their spouses, there is an exception for "abandoned spouses." The abandoned spouse rules apply to certain provisions in the tax code (such as head-of-household filing status) and predate the EITC. The rules were enacted to address concerns about low-income taxpayers who did not live with their spouses and who could not afford the legal expenses associated with divorce or legal separation, although they are also applicable to higher-income taxpayers. Under the rules, abandoned spouses are married individuals who have not lived with their spouses for the second half of the tax year, have not obtained a legal separation, and pay more than half the costs of maintaining the homes in which they and their dependent children reside. If they meet these conditions, they may file as heads of households and, if eligible, claim the EITC. Thus, some married individuals can be treated, for EITC purposes, as if they were single. Their spouses, however, would be required to file as "married filing separate" unless they also meet the abandoned spouse conditions, and thus the effect of the abandoned spouse rule on the couple's combined tax liability is ambiguous.

Second, an adjusted gross income (AGI) tiebreaker rule can affect EITC eligibility among individuals who share a home and the responsibility for the care of a child. For example, if two unmarried individuals live together and have a child, both could potentially be eligible to claim the child and receive the EITC. The AGI tiebreaker determines which of the two parents receives the credit. Under this rule, only the parent with the higher modified adjusted gross income can claim the EITC on behalf of the child.[4] The lower earner may not claim the childless EITC.

Through the AGI tiebreaker, the EITC eligibility rules recognize that households consisting of two single individuals who live together and care for children may make economic decisions as a unit.[5] Their circumstances are different from those in which the separated or divorced parents live apart. Because the AGI tiebreaker rule does not treat cohabiting single parents and married parents exactly alike, however, marriage penalties and bonuses may still occur, although their magnitude may be smaller than for couples who live apart.

Consider the effects of marriage on the tax liability of two workers, one with earnings of $18,000 a year and the other with earnings of $12,000 a year. The couple initially lives apart, and the lower earner is the custodial parent of the couple's two children. When the couple marries and their incomes are combined, their combined adjusted gross income falls within the credit's phase-out range, and the EITC is reduced by $3,645, from $3,888 to $243. If, instead, the unmarried couple initially lived together with their children, the couple would be entitled to a smaller EITC—only $2,770—than if they had lived apart; marriage would reduce their EITC by $2,527, to $243.

Undeniably, abandoned spouse rules and AGI tiebreakers add complexity to the tax code. As Brazer notes, it is difficult to recognize and verify informal household arrangements. A recent Internal Revenue Service (IRS) compliance study shows that failure to comply with the AGI tiebreaker rule is a significant source of EITC errors, either because taxpayers do not understand the rules or because they purposely ignore them (Scholz 1997; also see chapter 6, this volume). The study also reveals that some married taxpayers claim head-of-household status even when they do not meet the abandoned spouse criteria, although again the data do not reveal the extent to which such errors are caused by intent or confusion.

David Ellwood, in chapter 3 of this volume, speculates that the AGI tiebreaker is rarely applied in practice. When examining the effect of the EITC on cohabitation, he assumes that the woman, regardless of her income relative to the income of the man in the house, would claim the EITC. However, while the findings of the IRS compliance study show that some taxpayers disregard the AGI tiebreaker, there is little if any data with which to test Ellwood's speculation that the rules are rarely applied. Taxpayers do not check boxes on their tax return to indicate that they "won" the AGI tiebreaker or that they are abandoned spouses, and the IRS compliance study does not contain extensive information on the characteristics or living arrangements of compliant taxpayers. Thus, neither the compliance study nor any other IRS data reveal the important converse: the number of individuals who are accurately complying with either the AGI tiebreaker or abandoned spouse rules.

MEASURING MARRIAGE PENALTIES AND BONUSES

Aggregate measures of marriage penalties and bonuses can be derived by "divorcing" married couples or by "marrying" single individuals. Starting with married individuals requires making assumptions about how they would allocate income, expenses, and children and other dependents if they were not married. Assumptions must also be made regarding whether or not the couple would reside together and, if not, who would have custody of the children. Starting with single individuals requires either estimating the earnings of their potential (but unobservable) spouses (Dickert-Conlin and Houser 1998) or focusing only on those single individuals for whom something may be known about their prospective spouses (Feenberg and Rosen 1995; Alm and Whittington 1997; chapter 3, this volume). Under either scenario, assumptions must also be made regarding how marital status affects behavior such as work effort or child-care expenditures.

Most studies of marriage penalties and bonuses have taken the former approach, "divorcing" married couples (Feenberg and Rosen 1995; Alm and Whittington 1996; Congressional Budget Office 1997; Bull et al. 1999). However, these studies have differed in how they reorganize the family unit and its financial and living arrangements under the assumption that the couple is no longer married.

For example, some studies have assumed taxpayers would reorganize the family unit in ways that would minimize their tax liability. The tax minimization method assumes that if taxpayers could file as single, they would allocate their income, exemptions, adjustments, deductions, and credits in a manner that minimizes their combined tax liability. Daniel Feenberg and Harvey Rosen (1995) assume that couples would minimize tax liability by allocating all but one child exemption to the higher-income spouse; if there are two or more children, the lower-earning spouse is assumed to claim one child exemption. Spouses with child exemptions would then be allowed head-of-household filing status and, if eligible, the EITC.

Other studies have adopted an empirical method. Under the empirical method, marriage penalties and bonuses are estimated using information about the effects of actual life events—such as marriage, divorce, or cohabitation—on the allocation of children, income, and expenses. Observing that most single-parent households are headed by a female, James Alm and Leslie Whittington suggest that the wife be assumed to claim the child exemptions, head-of-household filing status, and the EITC. They find that during the 1980s, their empirical method generated net marriage bonuses, while a tax minimization method similar to the one used by Feenberg and Rosen resulted in net marriage penalties. By 1994, that disparity had disappeared, and Alm and Whittington (1996) estimated an average net marriage penalty of $375 under both methods.

Few studies look at the effect of the EITC, in isolation, on marriage penalties and bonuses. The U.S. Congressional Budget Office (1997) has measured marriage penalties and bonuses under 1996 law using a sample of married couples who filed joint returns. They reject both the empirical and tax minimization methods and instead allocate income and dependents based on specific rules thought to reflect those that might be included in possible congressional marriage-penalty relief bills. Nonetheless, some of their assumptions, particularly those dealing with the allocation of child exemptions and filing status, are the same as those used by Feenberg and Rosen. The Congressional Budget Office finds that the EITC increased total marriage penalties by about $11.8 billion (or more than 40 percent) but had a negligible effect on marriage bonuses.

Using the Panel Survey of Income Dynamics, Ellwood measures the change in the EITC among couples between the year preceding marriage and the first full year following marriage (chapter 3, this volume). While marriage does not affect EITC eligibility for most newlyweds, Ellwood finds that the EITC declines an average of $1,505 for 16 percent of couples after marriage and increases by an average of $1,367 for 11 percent of couples. Unlike most studies, Ellwood's estimates of marriage penalties and bonuses reflect nontax factors that change after marriage. For example, among the couples who experience an increase in the EITC, more than half also had their first child after marriage.

Choosing Among Approaches

We estimate marriage penalties and bonuses using the Treasury Department's Individual Tax Model (ITM), a microsimulation model based on the Statistics of

Income sample of tax returns for tax year 1995 (Cilke 1994). Because the Statistics of Income sample is a cross-sectional sample, the ITM does not contain any information regarding the marital history of taxpayers. It also does not contain the demographic data that would be required to predict the earnings of an unmarried individual's potential spouse. Without such information, it is difficult to estimate marriage penalties and bonuses using the single filers in the ITM. We therefore follow the more conventional approach of "divorcing" married couples to estimate marriage penalties and bonuses. This approach allows us to measure marriage penalties and bonuses among those couples who have chosen to marry. It may not, however, be adequate for measuring potential marriage penalties and bonuses observed by single individuals as they consider the tax consequences of marriage. This is particularly true if unmarried individuals differ in fundamental ways (such as earnings and presence and number of children) from those who are married.

In an earlier paper (Bull et al. 1999), we considered and rejected the empirical method for allocating income, expenses, dependents, and living arrangements between the two spouses. Information on how cohabiting or divorced couples split assets and family responsibilities could be used to derive assumptions on how married couples might act if they were not married, but those who already cohabit or divorce may be fundamentally different from those who remain married and subject to either marriage penalties or bonuses under the tax code. We also rejected a tax minimization strategy. A complete tax minimization model would be conceptually quite complex because of the simultaneity of many variables. Most studies avoid much of this computational complexity and instead use fixed allocation rules. It is difficult (perhaps impossible), however, to come up with one rule that minimizes taxes for all taxpayers or a set of rules that is consistent with compliant behavior.

Instead of the tax minimization or empirical methods, we first consider a "resource pooling" method to measure marriage penalties and bonuses. This is also the method used by the Treasury Department's Office of Tax Analysis. This measure is best suited for addressing horizontal equity concerns. We then compare the results of this measure to those obtained using methods that are more similar to the empirical or tax minimization methods used in earlier studies. We find that these alternative measures can be used to address other concerns, such as the impact of marriage penalties and bonuses on family formation and taxpayer compliance.

Resource Pooling Method

The resource pooling method tries to isolate the effects of marriage on tax liabilities by assuming that married couples could—through implicit and explicit contractual arrangements—duplicate the same pooling of assets and expenses that occurs within their marriages without actually being married. The couple is assumed to live together even if they are not married. Both spouses are assumed to contribute to the family's expenses based on their ability to pay. We measure ability to pay using each spouse's share of gross income. In addition, taxpayers are assumed to act honestly and to understand the tax laws (at least as well as they currently comply with and understand the tax laws). Because the couple is assumed to act similarly whether married or unmarried, this measure provides insight into the effects of marriage penalties and bonuses on horizontal equity.[6]

LIVING ARRANGEMENTS Current law allows only one taxpayer (if otherwise eligible) to claim head-of-household filing status for a household. This means that at most one taxpayer would be allowed to claim head-of-household filing status if the couple continues to share a residence and pool resources. To qualify as a head of household, the taxpayer must provide more than half the costs of maintaining the home shared with the taxpayer's children or dependents. While tax return data do not contain much information regarding expenditures on the household or family, it seems reasonable to assume that the individual with the highest income is responsible for most of the costs of maintaining the home and is thus able to claim head-of-household filing status. We assume this individual is also most likely to provide more than half the support for the couple's dependents and can thus claim the exemptions. The spouse with the lower income claims single filing status.

Following the rules described earlier for cohabiting couples, we also assume that only the taxpayer with the higher adjusted gross income may claim the EITC when children are present. If there are no children, then current law allows both spouses, if eligible, to claim the EITC if they file as single taxpayers.

DIVISION OF EARNED INCOME AND CERTAIN TRANSFERS Our measure, like most measures of marriage penalties and bonuses, assumes that returns to human capital are retained by the earner. While some studies have shown that the labor supply of wives is particularly sensitive to marginal tax rates, these second-order effects are generally not accounted for in measures of marriage penalties and bonuses and are not included in our estimates.

Information from the W-2 form and the schedule SE is used to allocate wages and self-employment income to the appropriate earner. We also use information reports (1099s) from the Social Security Administration to attribute social security and disability insurance benefits to the appropriate beneficiary. Unemployment benefits and miscellaneous forms of earned income are assumed to be retained by the earner.

Some deductions and adjustments can be incurred only if the taxpayer has wage or self-employment income. These include deductions for contributions to a Keogh pension plan, self-employment taxes, self-employment health insurance, and moving expenses. Allocation of these items depends on the spouse's share of self-employment earned income (or, in the case of moving expenses, earned income).

DIVISION OF UNEARNED INCOME Unearned income is divided in proportion to each spouse's share of earned income.[7] The assumption regarding the ownership of assets may also affect the division of other itemized deductions or adjustments. We assume most expenses included in itemized deductions or adjustments are allocated according to ability to pay and that for this purpose gross income is the appropriate proxy for ability to pay. Changes in the definition of gross income therefore affect the allocation of these deductions and adjustments.

Marriage Penalties and Bonuses Using the Resource Pooling Method

In 2000, of the 50.4 million joint returns expected to be filed, 24.4 million (48.3 percent) will have a marriage penalty attributable to the individual income tax, 21.1 million (41.9 percent) will have a marriage bonus, and the remaining 5.0 million (9.8 percent), many of whom have no tax liability, will have neither a penalty nor bonus (see table 4.1). Aggregate marriage penalties in 2000 will total $30.0 billion, and aggregate marriage bonuses will be $28.5 billion. On net, the marriage penalty will amount to $1.5 billion.

The second set of columns in table 4.1 contains estimates of marriage penalties and bonuses for all individual income tax provisions except for the EITC. To obtain these estimates, we assume that the couple would be entitled to the same EITC as unmarried filers as they receive when they file a joint return.[8] Under this measure, there would be 22.5 million joint filers (44.6 percent) with a marriage penalty, 21.8 million (43.3 percent) who will have a marriage bonus, and 6.1 million (12.1 percent) with neither. Aggregate marriage penalties in 2000 would be $26.9 billion, while aggregate marriage bonuses would be $28.9 billion. On net, there would be a marriage bonus—not a marriage penalty—of $2.0 billion.

The third set of columns in table 4.1 shows the difference between the first two sets, which is the contribution of the design of the EITC to marriage penalties and bonuses. The EITC increases the number of couples with marriage penalties by 1.9 million while reducing the number of couples with marriage bonuses by 710,000. The number of couples with neither a penalty nor a bonus falls by 1.2 million. The EITC adds $3.1 billion to aggregate marriage penalties (about 10.4 percent of total penalties) while reducing aggregate marriage bonuses by $439 million (or about 1.5 percent of total bonuses). Thus, net aggregate marriage penalties increase by $3.6 billion owing to the design of the EITC.

The EITC affects marriage penalties and bonuses differently over the income distribution. For couples with positive adjusted gross incomes below $15,000 (including the entire phase-in range as well as the plateau and portions of the phase-out range), the EITC increases marriage bonuses by $144 million while reducing marriage penalties by $90 million. For those with adjusted gross incomes between $15,000 and $30,000 (covering much of the phase-out range of the EITC), the credit increases marriage penalties by $1.3 billion and reduces marriage bonuses by $191 million. However, most of the effect of the EITC on marriage penalties and bonuses occurs at incomes above the cutoff for EITC eligibility. For couples with adjusted gross incomes between $30,000 and $50,000, the EITC causes marriage penalties to increase by $1.6 billion and marriage bo-

TABLE 4.1 / Marriage Penalties and Bonuses With and Without EITC Under Resource-Pooling Method, All Taxpayers (2000 Law and Income Levels)

	Attributable to Individual Income Tax (Including EITC)				Attributable to Individual Income Tax (Excluding EITC)				Effect of EITC on Penalties and Bonuses (Difference)			
	Penalties	Bonuses	Neither	Total	Penalties	Bonuses	Neither	Total	Penalties	Bonuses	Neither	Total
Number of returns (thousands), by adjusted gross income												
$0 to $15,000	302	1,355	2,675	4,332	30	1,093	3,209	4,332	272	262	−534	0
$15,000 to $30,000	3,100	3,885	821	7,807	2,041	4,445	1,321	7,807	1,059	−560	−500	0
$30,000 to $50,000	5,608	4,627	216	10,451	5,141	5,016	293	10,451	467	−389	−77	0
$50,000 to $100,000	10,301	8,082	865	19,248	10,240	8,112	895	19,248	61	−30	−30	0
$100,000 and over	5,021	3,147	35	8,203	5,021	3,147	35	8,203	0	0	0	0
Total	24,352	21,109	4,956	50,418	22,474	21,819	6,124	50,418	1,878	−710	−1,168	0
Amount of penalty (−) or bonus (millions of dollars), by adjusted gross income												
$0 to $15,000	−93	596	0	503	−3	452	0	449	−90	144	0	54
$15,000 to $30,000	−1,872	2,109	0	237	−563	2,300	0	1,737	−1,309	−191	0	−1,500
$30,000 to $50,000	−3,882	3,827	0	−55	−2,260	4,046	0	1,786	−1,622	−219	0	−1,841
$50,000 to $100,000	−9,981	12,845	0	2,864	−9,895	12,984	0	3,089	−86	−139	0	−225
$100,000 and over	−14,164	9,067	0	−5,097	−14,164	9,105	0	−5,059	0	−38	0	−38
Total	−30,005	28,472	0	−1,534	−26,887	28,911	0	2,024	−3,118	−439	0	−3,558

Source: Cilke 1994.

Note: Totals include returns with negative adjusted gross incomes.

nuses to fall by $219 million. In total, nearly 55 percent of EITC-related marriage penalties will be attributable to couples whose incomes are between $30,000 and $60,000. The EITC has a negligible effect on marriage penalties and bonuses at higher income levels since the income of the higher-earning spouse must be less than $31,000 to qualify for the EITC as an unmarried filer.

Table 4.2 looks at marriage penalties and bonuses among EITC claimants only. In total, about one in four EITC claimants currently file a joint return. Among the 4.6 million EITC claimants filing jointly in 2000, 1.4 million (30.1 percent) will have a marriage penalty, 1.3 million (28.7 percent) will have a marriage bonus, and the remaining 1.9 million (41.2 percent), most of whom are one-earner couples, will have neither. Aggregate marriage penalties in 2000 will be $1.2 billion (4.1 percent of aggregate marriage penalties for all filers), and aggregate marriage bonuses will be $554 million (1.9 percent of aggregate marriage bonuses for all filers). Filers who claim the credit would experience net marriage penalties of $682 million.

The EITC increases the total number of credit claimants with marriage penalties by 1.1 million while reducing the number with bonuses by more than one hundred thousand and the number with neither a penalty nor bonus, many of whom are one-earner couples, by almost 1 million. For EITC claimants, the EITC is responsible for nearly all—$1.2 billion, or 94.1 percent—of aggregate marriage penalties caused by the individual income tax. Nonetheless, a comparison of the findings in tables 4.1 and 4.2 shows that nearly 63 percent of EITC-related marriage penalties are attributable to couples who do not qualify for the EITC as joint filers because their combined income exceeds the eligibility cutoff. Not surprisingly, marriage penalties among EITC claimants are primarily found among those with adjusted gross incomes between $15,000 and $30,000. Table 4.2 also shows that the EITC increases aggregate marriage bonuses among claimants by only $31 million (5.6 percent). Marriage bonuses among credit claimants with adjusted gross incomes of less than $15,000 are also largely attributable to the EITC.

As shown in table 4.3, only two-earner couples have marriage penalties.[9] Furthermore, the effect of the EITC on marriage penalties and bonuses is generally concentrated among two-earner couples. These results reflect the assumptions, in the resource pooling model, that the higher earner would claim the children if the two spouses filed separate returns.

Estimates of Marriage Penalties and Bonuses Under Alternative Assumptions

A unique measure of marriage penalties and bonuses that can simultaneously address concerns as complex and diverse as horizontal equity, decisions to marry or work, or taxpayer compliance may not exist. While the resource pooling method is best-suited to measuring the impact of marriage penalties and bonuses on horizontal equity, analysis of other issues may require alternative measures of marriage penalties and bonuses.

TABLE 4.2 / Marriage Penalties and Bonuses With and Without EITC Under Resource-Pooling Method, EITC Claimants Only (2000 Law and Income Levels)

	Attributable to Individual Income Tax (Including EITC)				Attributable to Individual Income Tax (Excluding EITC)				Effect of EITC on Penalties and Bonuses (Difference)			
	Penalties	Bonuses	Neither	Total	Penalties	Bonuses	Neither	Total	Penalties	Bonuses	Neither	Total
Number of returns (thousands), by adjusted gross income												
$0 to $15,000	180	418	1,318	1,916	1	118	1,797	1,916	179	300	−479	0
$15,000 to $30,000	1,129	854	532	2,515	249	1,272	994	2,515	880	−418	−462	0
$30,000 to $50,000	55	28	0	84	32	50	2	84	23	−22	−2	0
$50,000 and over	0	0	0	0	0	0	0	0	0	0	0	0
Total	1,373	1,308	1,877	4,559	282	1,441	2,836	4,559	1,091	−133	−959	0
Amount of penalty (−) or bonus (millions of dollars), by adjusted gross income												
$0 to $15,000	−48	181	0	133	0	24		24	−48	157	0	109
$15,000 to $30,000	−1,103	358	0	−745	−65	478		413	−1,038	−120	0	−1,158
$30,000 to $50,000	−79	12	0	−66	−8	21		13	−71	−9	0	−79
$50,000 and over	0	0	0	0	0	0		0	0	0	0	0
Total	−1,237	554	0	−682	−73	523		450	−1,164	31	0	−1,132

Source: Cilke 1994.

Note: Totals include returns with negative adjusted gross incomes.

TABLE 4.3 / Marriage Penalties and Bonuses With and Without EITC Under Resource-Pooling Method, by Number of Earners (2000 Law and Income Levels)

	Attributable to Individual Income Tax (Including EITC)				Effect of EITC on Penalties and Bonuses			
	Penalties	Bonuses	Neither	Total	Penalties	Bonuses	Neither	Total
All taxpayers								
Total								
Number of returns	24,352	21,109	4,956	50,418	1,878	−710	−1,168	0
Amount of penalty (−) or bonus	−30,005	28,472	0	−1,534	−3,118	−439	0	−3,558
No-earner and one-earner couples								
Number of returns	0	9,678	2,211	11,889	0	20	−20	0
Amount of penalty (−) or bonus	0	18,080	0	18,080	0	12	0	12
Two-earner couples								
Number of returns	24,352	11,431	2,747	38,530	1,878	−730	−1,148	0
Amount of penalty (−) or bonus	−30,005	10,391	0	−19,614	−3,118	−452	0	−3,570
EITC claimants only								
Total								
Number of returns	1,373	1,308	1,877	4,559	1,091	−133	−959	0
Amount of penalty (−) or bonus	−1,237	554	0	−682	−1,164	31	0	−1,132
No-earner and one-earner couples								
Number of returns	0	718	1,603	2,321	0	20	−20	0
Amount of penalty (−) or bonus	0	315	0	315	0	12	0	12
Two-earner couples								
Number of returns	1,373	591	274	2,239	1,091	−153	−939	0
Amount of penalty (−) or bonus	−1,237	241	0	−996	−1,164	19	0	−1,145

Source: Cilke 1994.
Note: Number of returns in thousands; amounts are in millions of dollars. Earnings include income from wages, self-employment, and certain transfers.

SEPARATE RESIDENCES Under the first alternative, we assume that each spouse maintains a separate residence. This method measures the penalty or bonus associated with two decisions: the decision to marry and the decision to share a residence. It may be a more appropriate measure than the joint residence method when considering the impact of the EITC or other tax provisions on the decisions to separate or divorce, net of other factors (such as the costs of maintaining two residences) (Holtzblatt 1997).

When assuming separate residences, tax law alone does not provide guidance as to which spouse might be eligible to claim dependents or file as head of household. For purposes of this measure, we assume the lower-earner spouse becomes the custodial parent and claims head-of-household filing status, the dependents, and the EITC. These assumptions are similar to those used by Alm and Whittington (1996) for allocating dependents under their empirical approach, since the lower-earner spouse tends to be the wife. Alm and Whittington (1999), Stacy Dickert-Conlin (1999), and Nada Eissa and Hilary Hoynes (1999) also use similar assumptions when examining the effects of the EITC or tax system on family formation decisions.

This alternative method results in an aggregate net marriage bonus of $27.2 billion, in contrast to the $1.5 billion net marriage penalty under our first measure (alternative 1 in table 4.4). While aggregate marriage penalties are only $1.1 billion larger ($31.1 billion under the separate residences method as against $30.0 billion under the resource sharing method), aggregate marriage bonuses ($58.3 billion) are more than twice those found using the resource pooling method. The large difference in marriage bonuses occurs because the head-of-household status, exemptions, and child-related credits generally provide less benefit to the lower-earner spouse than to the higher-earner spouse (who is often in a higher tax bracket and has greater tax liability with which to absorb credits).[10]

Under this alternative method, the EITC will increase marriage penalties by $9.9 billion and reduce marriage bonuses by $5.7 billion in 2000. Net penalties will increase by nearly $15.6 billion. The EITC is responsible for a greater share of both marriage penalties and bonuses than under the resource pooling method: 31.7 percent of total marriage penalties instead of 10.4 percent and 9.8 percent of total marriage bonuses instead of 1.5 percent.

The choice of assumptions also affects the distribution of the marriage penalties and bonuses attributable to the EITC. Under the separate residency assumption, the EITC increases marriage bonuses by $3.5 billion and has a negligible effect on marriage penalties for couples with adjusted gross incomes of less than $15,000. This is largely the effect of nonworkers (or very-low-income earners) with children marrying workers with earnings within the EITC range. For couples with adjusted gross incomes between $30,000 and $50,000, the EITC increases marriage penalties by $4.6 billion and reduces marriage bonuses by $3.1 billion. Among those with adjusted gross incomes of more than $50,000 (a group largely unaffected by the EITC under the resource pooling method), marriage penalties increase by $4.3 billion as a consequence of the EITC, while marriage bonuses fall by $7.8 billion.

TABLE 4.4 / Marriage Penalties and Bonuses With and Without EITC Under Alternative Assumptions, All Taxpayers (2000 Law and Income Levels)

	Alternative 1: Separate Residences				Alternative 2: Allocate Dependents to Minimize Tax				Alternative 3: Unearned Income Evenly Divided			
	Penalties	Bonuses	Neither	Total	Penalties	Bonuses	Neither	Total	Penalties	Bonuses	Neither	Total
N^a	23,354	24,682	2,382	50,418	26,769	19,252	4,396	50,418	28,249	17,173	4,996	50,418
Amount of penalty (−) or bonus (millions of dollars) under individual income tax (including EITC), by adjusted gross income												
$0 to $15,000	−59	4,517	0	4,457	−173	508	0	335	−161	529	0	368
$15,000 to $30,000	−1,368	8,399	0	7,031	−2,848	2,068	0	−780	−2,300	1,653	0	−647
$30,000 to $50,000	−6,156	9,009	0	2,853	−7,771	3,630	0	−4,141	−4,539	2,875	0	−1,664
$50,000 to $100,000	−10,347	22,645	0	12,298	−15,486	12,054	0	−3,432	−12,053	9,828	0	−2,225
$100,000 and over	−13,150	13,633	0	483	−16,594	8,702	0	−7,892	−19,815	5,714	0	−14,101
Total	−31,105	58,274	0	27,169	−42,908	26,985	0	−15,923	−38,889	20,642	0	−18,247
Effect of EITC on penalties and bonuses: amount of penalty (−) or bonus (millions of dollars), by adjusted gross income												
$0 to $15,000	−56	3,495	0	3,438	−170	60	0	−110	−151	145	0	−6
$15,000 to $30,000	−929	1,622	0	693	−2,268	−147	0	−2,415	−1,395	−199	0	−1,594
$30,000 to $50,000	−4,601	−3,079	0	−7,680	−5,266	−288	0	−5,554	−1,676	−213	0	−1,889
$50,000 to $100,000	−3,794	−6,387	0	−10,181	−4,449	−807	0	−5,256	−88	−110	0	−198
$100,000 and over	−469	−1,393	0	−1,862	−566	−346	0	−912	0	−14	0	−14
Total	−9,872	−5,706	0	−15,578	−12,753	−1,526	0	−14,279	−3,327	−387	0	−3,714

Source: Cilke 1994.
Note: Totals include returns with negative adjusted gross income. Under all three alternatives, all assumptions other than the stated alternative are standard assumptions.
[a]Number of returns (in thousands) with marriage penalties or bonuses under individual income tax, including EITC.

The magnitude of the EITC's effect on marriage penalties and the distributional results reflect the assumption that the lower-earner spouse could qualify for an EITC if his or her income is not combined with the income of a high-earning spouse. Under this method, couples with combined incomes that exceed $60,000 could incur an EITC-related marriage penalty as long as the lower-earning spouse's income was less than $31,000.

Under this alternative, 3.8 million (83.4 percent) couples claiming the EITC will have marriage bonuses, and the amount of total marriage bonuses will be $9.9 billion (see table 4.5). Only 583,000 couples (12.8 percent) claiming the EITC will have a marriage penalty, and the aggregate amount of marriage penalties is $650 million. With relatively few EITC claimants incurring a marriage penalty owing to the credit, more than 93 percent of EITC-related marriage penalties under this measure are accrued by couples whose combined income is too high to qualify for the credit as joint filers. On net, EITC claimants are estimated to have $9.3 billion of marriage bonuses, of which nearly half—$4.7 billion—is attributable to the EITC.

MINIMIZING TAX LIABILITY BY CHANGING THE ALLOCATION OF CHILDREN As discussed earlier, it is difficult to derive assumptions that would minimize taxes for all couples if they filed as unmarried but would still be consistent with compliant behavior and be computationally simple. Under the second alternative, we allow couples to allocate dependents, but not income and expenses, in the manner that would minimize their combined income tax liability when filing separate returns without being constrained by the rules governing dependency, household maintenance, or the residency of EITC-qualifying children. As a result, the dependents may be claimed by either spouse or divided between them, and both spouses are allowed to claim head-of-household filing status if eligible. Both may claim the EITC (even if children are present), and they may each claim up to two EITC-qualifying children.

This method is consistent with either one of the following scenarios. Under the first scenario, a couple divorces, and the former spouses move into separate residences. They divide custody of their children and other dependents in the manner that minimizes their combined separate income tax liabilities. Under the second scenario, they do not divorce. However, they fail to comply (either intentionally or unintentionally) with the tax code provisions governing dependents, filing status, and EITC-qualifying children. Instead, they claim to be unmarried and living separately. Under this scenario, the alternative does not measure marriage penalties and bonuses under current law but may, instead, be an estimate of what some married couples perceive their penalties or bonuses to be without fully understanding how tax laws would actually apply if they were not married.

These alternative assumptions do not affect the tax liability for the 24 million couples who do not have dependents. Among the remaining 26.5 million couples, 14.7 million (55.4 percent) would minimize taxes when filing separate returns by allocating all of the dependents to the higher earner, 7.5 million (28.4

TABLE 4.5 / Marriage Penalties and Bonuses With and Without EITC, Under Alternative Assumptions, EITC Claimants Only (2000 Law and Income Levels)

	Alternative 1: Separate Residences				Alternative 2: Allocate Dependents to Minimize Tax				Alternative 3: Unearned Income Evenly Divided			
	Penalties	Bonuses	Neither	Total	Penalties	Bonuses	Neither	Total	Penalties	Bonuses	Neither	Total
N^a	583	3,802	174	4,559	1,514	1,180	1,864	4,559	1,548	1,281	1,729	4,559
Amount of penalty (−) or bonus (millions of dollars) under individual income tax (including EITC), by adjusted gross income												
$0 to $15,000	−16	4,034	0	4,018	−121	96	0	−25	−51	184	0	133
$15,000 to $30,000	−574	5,751	0	5,177	−1,915	344	0	−1,571	−1,153	341	0	−812
$30,000 to $50,000	−56	89	0	33	−158	12	0	−146	−81	11	0	−70
$50,000 and over	0	0	0	0	0	0	0	0	0	0	0	0
Total	−650	9,911	0	9,261	−2,208	453	0	−1,755	−1,292	539	0	−753
Effect of EITC on penalties and bonuses: amount of penalty (−) or bonus (millions of dollars), by adjusted gross income												
$0 to $15,000	−16	3,509	0	3,493	−121	72	0	−49	−51	159	0	108
$15,000 to $30,000	−570	1,876	0	1,306	−1,839	−73	0	−1,912	−1,069	−129	0	−1,198
$30,000 to $50,000	−56	−74	0	−130	−146	−3	0	−149	−72	−9	0	−81
$50,000 and over	0	0	0	0	0	0	0	0	0	0	0	0
Total	−646	5,348	0	4,702	−2,120	−3	0	−2,123	−1,199	24	0	−1,175

Source: Cilke 1994.

Note: Totals include returns with negative adjusted gross income. Under all three alternatives, all assumptions other than the stated alternative are standard assumptions.

[a] Number of returns (in thousands) with marriage penalties or bonuses under individual income tax, including EITC.

percent) would minimize taxes by somehow splitting the child dependents, and 4.3 million (16.1 percent) would fare better under the income tax system if the lower-earner spouse could claim all of the dependents.[11] Nearly half (49.1 percent) of those who benefit by splitting dependents or allocating them to the lower earner have an adjusted gross income of less than $60,000.

Under this alternative, 26.8 million (53.1 percent) couples would have a marriage penalty, 19.3 million (38.2 percent) would have a marriage bonus, and 4.4 million (8.7 percent) would have neither a penalty nor bonus (alternative 2 in table 4.4). Couples would incur a total of $42.9 billion of marriage penalties and $27.0 billion of marriage bonuses. On net, there would be a total of $15.9 billion in marriage penalties.

Assuming couples could receive the same total EITC as unmarried filers as they would receive as joint filers dramatically affects the benefits to reallocating children between the spouses. More than three-quarters of couples with dependents (20.1 million) would minimize their combined income tax liability if the higher-earner spouse claimed the dependents. The number who benefit from splitting their dependents falls by 2.3 million to 5.3 million, while the number who minimize income tax liability by allocating dependents to the lower-earner spouse declines by 3.2 million to 1.1 million. Among those who split dependents or allocate them to the lower earner, nearly two-thirds have an adjusted gross income of more than $60,000. Although the dependent exemptions would be valued at a higher marginal tax rate, higher-income taxpayers may benefit from shifting dependents because of the phase-out of the dependent exemption, the alternative minimum tax, and the "kiddie" tax, which applies when a child's unearned income is taxed as if it were the parent's income.

Under this alternative, the EITC will increase aggregate marriage penalties by $12.8 billion (29.7 percent of aggregate penalties), while total marriage bonuses will be reduced by $1.5 billion (5.7 percent of aggregate bonuses) in 2000. On net, the EITC will increase marriage penalties by $14.3 billion.

Thus, the effects of the EITC on total marriage penalties are greatest when taxpayers are assumed to be able to reorganize their actual or reported living arrangements so as to minimize their combined tax liabilities as unmarried individuals. Under this alternative, they can choose to allocate their children in the way that will result in the lowest income tax liability. For example, many two-earner couples would find it advantageous to allocate the children to the lower earner if the higher earner's income is in the EITC phase-out range or higher and both spouses are in the 15 percent tax bracket (that is, the value of most other child tax benefits is the same regardless of which spouse claims the children). As tax minimizers, couples would also have a choice that is not available to them under the resource sharing or separate residence alternatives: by splitting custody of their children, each spouse could claim the EITC to which they would be entitled if they were not married, and thus the magnitude of EITC-related marriage penalties would be increased.

This alternative measure also affects the distribution of marriage penalties and bonuses. In contrast to the resource pooling method, the EITC increases marriage penalties by more than marriage bonuses among those with adjusted gross incomes of less than $15,000. Marriage penalties increase by $2.3 billion among joint filers with adjusted gross incomes between $15,000 and $30,000, or $959 million more than under the resource pooling method. The most significant differences occur among joint filers with adjusted gross incomes between $30,000 and $100,000, where marriage penalties increase by $9.7 billion, or $8.0 billion more than under the resource pooling method.

Among EITC claimants, the number of taxpayers with marriage penalties and bonuses is similar to that under the resource pooling method. However, aggregate marriage penalties, and the amount attributable to the EITC, will be nearly $1 billion higher under this alternative (see table 4.5). Furthermore, these results, in combination with the findings in table 4.4, imply that a greater share (more than 83 percent) of EITC-related marriage penalties are attributable to couples who do not qualify for the credit as joint filers under this alternative than under the resource pooling method.

UNEARNED INCOME EVENLY DIVIDED   Splitting unearned income evenly tends to equalize spouses' income. This, in turn, increases marriage penalties and reduces marriage bonuses relative to assumptions that allocate unearned income in proportion to earned income. When unearned income is assumed to be divided evenly if the couple were not married, marriage penalties amount to $38.9 billion, and marriage bonuses would total $20.6 billion (alternative 3 in table 4.4).

Assumptions regarding the allocation of unearned income do not significantly change the effect of the EITC on marriage penalties and bonuses relative to the resource pooling method. The EITC will reduce marriage penalties by $3.3 billion, or by $209 million more than under the resource pooling method, and will reduce marriage bonuses by $387 million, or by $52 million less than under the resource pooling method. Among credit claimants, the EITC will reduce marriage penalties by $1.2 billion, or by $35 million more than under the resource pooling method (see table 4.5).

ANALYSIS OF RECENT PROPOSALS TO REDUCE MARRIAGE PENALTIES IN THE EITC

From 1998 through 2000, the Clinton administration and Congress introduced proposals that would reduce marriage penalties caused by the standard deduction, rate brackets, and the EITC. In this section, we consider the impact of several congressional proposals to reduce marriage penalties in the EITC, using the resource pooling method.

Proposal 1: Increase Phase-Out Range by $2,000

In 1999, Congress passed the Taxpayer Refund and Relief Act of 1999, which was subsequently vetoed by President Bill Clinton. Under this bill, the starting point of the EITC phase-out range would have been extended by $2,000 for married couples filing joint returns, beginning in 2006. Because the phase-out rate would not be changed, the EITC would phase out at income levels that are $2,000 higher than under current law. The $2,000 amount would be adjusted for inflation after 2006. (All proposals are evaluated at calendar year 2000 levels. At 2000 levels, the EITC phase-out range would be extended by $1,740.)[12]

For example, consider a married couple with two children. Both spouses work. One spouse earns $18,000, the other $12,000. They have no other forms of income. Under current (2000) law, they receive an EITC of $243 and pay income taxes of $475. Their marriage penalty (as a result of both the EITC and other factors) is $2,525. Under the proposal, their EITC would increase by $366 to $609, and their income taxes would fall to $109. Their marriage penalty would also drop by $366, to $2,159.

At a cost of $1 billion a year, the EITC provision in the Taxpayer Refund and Relief Act of 1999 would primarily have benefited low- and moderate-income taxpayers (see table 4.6). At 2000 levels, 3.6 million couples would have had an average tax cut of $275, with nearly all of the benefits (93.2 percent) going to couples with adjusted gross incomes of less than $30,000, who are already eligible for the EITC. About five hundred thousand taxpayers would have become eligible for the EITC.

Less than half ($406 million or 40.6 percent) of the benefits of the proposal would have reduced marriage penalties. Of the 3.6 million couples who would have benefited from the proposal, one-third would have received a larger bonus than under current law, and nearly one-fourth, who currently do not have either a bonus or penalty, would have received a bonus. The proposal would also have added some complexity to the current EITC instructions by adding several columns to lookup tables and a few additional lines to the instructions.

An examination of two variants of the congressional proposal illustrates the trade-off between two tax policy goals: marriage neutrality and tax simplicity. In the first variant, a greater share of the costs of the proposal could be used to reduce marriage penalties by limiting the expansion to couples in which both spouses earn at least $2,000. This would reduce the costs of the proposal by more than 60 percent (to $394 million a year), with $366 million (or 92.9 percent of the costs) reducing marriage penalties. While this proposal would be more efficient than the congressional proposal in reducing marriage penalties, it would be more complicated and difficult for the IRS to verify eligibility during initial return processing because spouses' wage and salary incomes are not shown separately on tax returns. (Sometime later in the year after refunds are paid out, the IRS would be able to verify each spouse's share of earned income using the edited and matched W-2 forms.)

The second variant would extend the plateau by $2,000 for all taxpayers. Unlike the preceding two options, this variant would not require any fundamental changes to the tax instructions or forms. Taxpayers would determine their eligibility for the EITC and compute the amount of the credit using tax forms and lookup tables that are identical to those they currently use except for containing

TABLE 4.6 / Summary of the Impacts of Recent Proposals to Address Marriage Penalties in the EITC (2000 Law and Income Levels)

	Impact (Millions of Dollars)			Reduction in Penalties as Percentage of Total	Ratio of Total to Couples with AGI (Percentage)[a]		
Proposed Law	Reduction in Penalties	Increase in Bonuses	Total Cost		Under $15,000	$15,000 to $30,000	$30,000 to $60,000
Impact using resource pooling method							
Increase EITC phase-out range by $2,000 for joint filers ($1,740 in 2000 dollars)	406	593	1,000	40.6	13.5	79.7	6.3
Increase limited to two-earner couples	366	28	394	92.9	8.4	81.7	9.1
Increase extended to all filers	−685	−95	3,230	−21.2	19.0	77.5	3.3
Increase EITC phase-out range by $3,500 for joint filers	780	1,269	2,050	38.0	10.0	79.6	10.0
Allow joint filers to deduct portion of earned income of lower-earner spouse in EITC phase-out range							
Deduct 20 percent of income	295	14	310	95.2	6.5	80.6	12.3
Deduct 100 percent of income	2,741	381	3,123	87.8	2.1	42.5	55.0
Impact using alternative assumption 1 (separate residences)							
Increase EITC phase-out range by $2,000 for joint filers ($1,740 in 2000 dollars)	183	816	1,000	18.3	13.5	79.7	6.3
Increase limited to two-earner couples	182	212	394	46.2	8.4	81.7	9.1
Increase extended to all filers	−1,736	496	3,230	−53.7	19.0	77.5	3.3
Impact using alternative assumption 2 (allocate dependents to minimize tax)							
Increase EITC phase-out range by $2,000 for joint filers ($1,740 in 2000 dollars)	439	561	1,000	43.9	13.5	79.7	6.3
Increase limited to two-earner couples	386	8	394	98.0	8.4	81.7	9.1
Increase extended to all filers	−1,851	−87	3,230	−57.3	19.0	77.5	3.3

Source: Cilke 1994.

Note: Owing to rounding, percentages may not add up to 100 percent.

[a] Returns with negative adjusted gross income are not shown in the AGI distribution.

higher credit amounts. However, this option is costlier and provides no relief for marriage penalties. It would cost three times as much ($3.2 billion a year) and provide tax cuts to 2.4 million single filers and 7.1 million heads of households as well as the 3.6 million couples covered by the congressional proposal. It would increase aggregate marriage penalties by $685 million while reducing aggregate marriage bonuses by $95 million.

Proposal 2: Increase the Phase-Out Range by $3,500

During consideration of the tobacco bill in 1998, Senator Phil Gramm (Rep.-Tex.) offered an amendment that would, among other things, allow married taxpayers to deduct $3,500 of income in the phase-out range of the EITC (proposal 2 in table 4.6). This proposal effectively extends the beginning and end points of the phase-out range by a total of $3,500, which is equal to the difference between the standard deduction for a couple filing a joint return and the combined standard deduction for a single filer and a head of household. This amount was chosen because the amendment also provided all joint filers with combined incomes of less than $50,000 with an additional deduction of the same amount. The following analysis considers only the effects of the EITC expansion.

The proposal would increase the EITC for the two-earner couple described earlier by $737 to $980. On net, they would receive a tax refund of $262, and their marriage penalty would fall to $1,788. This option would cost more than $2 billion a year, or twice the cost of the conference agreement. Under this option, 4.2 million taxpayers would receive an average tax cut of $488. About 90 percent of the benefits would go to taxpayers with adjusted gross incomes of less than $30,000, with 1 million couples becoming eligible for the EITC. As with the proposal contained in the 1999 tax bill, only about 38 percent of the benefits of the proposal actually reduce marriage penalties.

Proposal 3: Allow Two-Earner Deduction

Senator Tom Daschle (Dem.-S.D.) introduced S. 8 in January 1999. It contains a provision to reinstate the two-earner deduction that existed before enactment of the Tax Reform Act of 1986. His bill went further than prior law by extending a two-earner deduction explicitly to the EITC. Under the bill, married couples could deduct 20 percent of the earnings of the lower-earner spouse from income when computing the EITC in the phase-out range. The following analysis examines only the proposed changes to the EITC (proposal 3 in table 4.6).

Under this proposal, the two-earner couple described earlier would be able to deduct 20 percent of the lower earner's earnings, or $2,400 (.2 × $12,000), from income in the EITC phase-out range. As a consequence, the couple's EITC would increase by $505, to $748, and they would receive a net income tax refund of $30. The marriage penalty would fall to $2,020.

At a cost of roughly $300 million a year, this proposal would provide 1.6 million couples with an average tax cut of $192. Most (87.1 percent) of the benefits would go to couples with adjusted gross incomes of less than $30,000. The rest of the benefits would go to couples with adjusted gross incomes between $30,000 and $40,000. The majority of those who would benefit already receive the EITC; the option would extend EITC eligibility to fewer than two hundred thousand new claimants. More than 95 percent of benefits would reduce marriage penalties. Of the 1.6 million couples who would benefit from the proposal, 1.5 million would see a reduction or elimination of their marriage penalties.

We also consider a variant that would allow two-earner couples to deduct 100 percent of the earned income of the lower-earning spouse when computing the EITC. This option effectively treats married couples in roughly the same manner as if they were single but cohabiting. If they were not married and were living in the same residence, the higher earner would generally win the AGI tiebreaker and claim the EITC. The lower earner would not be eligible for any EITC. Under this option, eligibility for the EITC would be based on the earnings of the higher earner, and the earnings of the lower-earning spouse would be disregarded entirely for EITC eligibility determinations.[13]

Under this variant, 3.5 million couples would have an average tax cut of $878 at a cost of $3.1 billion a year. Nearly 88 percent of benefits would reduce marriage penalties. Most of the benefits (55 percent) would go to couples with adjusted gross incomes between $30,000 and $60,000. The rest of the benefits would go to couples with adjusted gross incomes of less than $30,000, with 42.5 percent of benefits accruing to couples with adjusted gross incomes between $15,000 and $30,000. Eligibility for the EITC would be extended to 2.1 million couples with incomes up to $60,000.

A two-earner deduction demonstrates some of the trade-offs between the various goals of the EITC. A two-earner deduction is well targeted to reducing marriage penalties. Furthermore, by increasing the return to work, a two-earner deduction may increase labor force participation by the lower-earner spouse, particularly among those already eligible for the EITC. Since only two-earner couples would receive the deduction, however, the option violates the principle in current law that couples with the same total incomes pay the same total taxes. By extending the EITC phase-out range, it also increases marginal tax rates on taxpayers with adjusted gross incomes roughly between $30,000 and $60,000. Finally, it increases filing burdens by requiring an additional worksheet or form for the computation of the two-earner deduction.

Effects of Alternative Assumptions on Measures of Proposals

The bottom half of table 4.6 shows the effects of the various proposals under the alternative assumptions of separate residency and allocation of dependents to minimize tax. As has been shown by Bull and colleagues (1999), the change in the level of aggregate marriage penalties net of bonuses is the same for the proposals that change the EITC only for married couples. Thus, estimates of the change in net marriage penalties are invariant to the assumption used, when measuring the effect of proposals that affect joint filers only. However, the choice of assumptions may affect the allocation between marriage penalties and bonuses.

Moreover, between 1975 and 2000, the credit has never been changed for joint filers only. When the EITC phase-out range is extended by $2,000 for all taxpayers, the change in net marriage penalties differs greatly under the two sets of assumptions. Under the resource pooling method, marriage penalties net of bonuses increase by $780 million, while they rise by $1.2 billion under the separate residence assumption and by $1.9 billion under the tax minimization method. This result follows from the fact that the computation of the EITC changes for both married and unmarried filers under this variant, and the amount received by unmarried filers is sensitive to the assumptions made regarding living arrangements and custody of the children. Studies that examine the effect of comprehensive changes in the income tax, including the EITC, on marriage penalties and bonuses should test the sensitivity of their estimates to alternative measures of marriage penalties and bonuses.

CONCLUSIONS

Measures of aggregate marriage penalties and bonuses are very sensitive to the underlying assumptions used to allocate a married couple's income, living arrangements, and dependents if they were able to file separate returns. Estimates of marriage penalties and bonuses attributable to the EITC—both in the aggregate and relative to total marriage penalties and bonuses—are also sensitive to the assumptions used to allocate living arrangements and dependents. However, the estimates of EITC-related penalties and bonuses are not very sensitive to the division of unearned income.

Estimates of EITC-related marriage penalties and bonuses are smallest under the assumption that the couple would continue to live together if they were not married. This is not surprising, given that the EITC eligibility rules effectively reduce marriage penalties and bonuses among married and unmarried couples who are the most similar—those who live together with their children. Using this measure, we find that the EITC will increase total marriage penalties by $3.1 billion (10.4 percent) and reduce total bonuses by $439 million (1.5 percent) in 2000. Among those who claim the EITC, the credit will increase marriage penalties by $1.1 billion and will account for nearly all—about 94 percent—of the marriage penalties imposed by the individual income tax on these taxpayers. However, couples who currently are ineligible for the EITC will incur nearly 63 percent of EITC-related marriage penalties because their combined income exceeds eligibility limits under current (2000) law. More than half of EITC-related marriage penalties will be attributable to couples who are ineligible because their combined income is more than $30,000.

This measure provides the best estimate of marriage penalties and bonuses when considering the effect of the EITC on horizontal equity—the relative tax treatment of couples who are similar in all ways except for the existence of a marriage license. Other measures of marriage penalties and bonuses may be better suited to studying the effect of the EITC on family formation decisions or tax avoidance or evasion. Under these alternative measures, the EITC is found to increase marriage penalties by between $9.9 billion and $12.8 billion and reduce marriage bonuses by between $1.5 billion and $5.7 billion. Regardless of the assumptions used to allocate family responsibilities or income, the EITC is responsible for most of the marriage penalties associated with the income-tax among EITC claimants, while most EITC-related marriage penalties are attributable to higher-income taxpayers who are currently not eligible for the EITC.

Recent proposals to reduce EITC marriage penalties are well targeted to lower-income taxpayers. Proposals that would extend the length of the EITC phase-out range for married couples are relatively simple to administer, but less than half of their costs go to the reduction of marriage penalties. A two-earner deduction would be a more target-efficient way of reducing EITC-related marriage penalties but would add some complexity to the EITC schedule and instruction.

Most recent proposals eliminate only a small portion of total marriage penalties attributed to the EITC. It is not possible to eliminate all marriage penalties attributable to the EITC unless eligibility is extended to couples with incomes of $60,000 (or more, depending on the assumptions used to measure marriage penalties). In the past, however, there has been some resistance (from both sides of the political spectrum) to expanding the EITC to middle-income families rather than targeting additional assistance to those with lower incomes, many of whom are headed by a single parent or by a one-earner couple (chapter 1, this volume).

Does this mean that the current proposals do not address concerns caused by EITC-related marriage penalties and bonuses? Although most EITC-related marriage penalties are incurred by higher-income taxpayers, the EITC is responsible for most of the marriage penalties experienced by low-income couples as a result of the individual income tax. Targeting lower-income families may also have indirect effects that are not observed in our sample of married couples. About three-quarters of EITC claimants are not counted as incurring a marriage penalty precisely because they are unmarried. If the EITC affects marriage decisions, reducing the credit's marriage penalties or increasing its marriage bonuses may affect family formation decisions among these single individuals in ways that policymakers view as beneficial. However, the evidence of the effect of the EITC on marriage is mixed, and the results of prior studies may be sensitive to their specification of marriage penalties and bonuses. Further research on the effect of the EITC on family formation decisions should take into account all of the ways—such as the AGI tiebreaker and the abandoned spouse rules—in which the tax code distinguishes among families.

Views and opinions expressed in this chapter are those of the authors and do not necessarily represent the policies or positions of the Department of the Treasury.

NOTES

1. Since the 1996 publication of the General Accounting Office report, the number of provisions that are not neutral with respect to marriage has most likely increased. These would include a number of provisions enacted in the Taxpayer Relief Act of 1997, including the child tax credit, educational credits, and Roth individual retirement accounts.

2. In many other countries, the individual is the filing unit for the income tax, and each spouse is taxed on his or her own income. As a result, the individual's tax liability does not generally change upon marriage in these countries. However, the United Kingdom has recently adopted an EITC-like tax credit (the Working Family Tax Credit) that is based on the couple's combined income, even though the individual is still the unit of taxation for the rest of the income tax.

3. There may be differences in ability to pay between two-earner and one-earner couples because the monetary value of the services, such as child care, provided by the stay-at-home spouse is not taxed. Through the child and dependent care tax credit and the exclusion for child and dependent care, the tax code adjusts for differences in ability to pay caused by work-related child-care expenses. Married couples generally cannot claim the credit unless both spouses work and they incur child-care costs in order to work.

4. Shortly before publication, the Economic Growth and Tax Relief Reconciliation Act of 2001 was enacted. The act includes several provisions that would simplify the EITC eligibility criteria, including a modification of the AGI tiebreaker. Beginning in 2002, the AGI tiebreaker rule will apply only when both parents file tax returns claiming the EITC using the same child.

5. Other types of households may also be affected by the AGI tiebreaker test. The AGI tiebreaker applies whenever a child satisfies the EITC relationship and residency tests with respect to more than one taxpayer. Under the relationship test, the child must be the taxpayer's son, daughter, grandchild, or foster child. Under the residency test, the taxpayer must reside with the child for more than six months (for twelve months if the child is the taxpayer's foster child). Thus, a three-generation household—child, mother, and grandmother, for example—could also be affected by the AGI tiebreaker. Under pre-2000 law, if a single mother lived with both her child and her mother, and her mother had the higher adjusted gross income, then only the grandmother could claim the EITC with respect to the child. The test may also apply when an unrelated individual shares a home with a parent and child, but newly enacted legislation limits the circumstances under which this may occur. Under pre-2000 law, a live-in boyfriend might have been eligible to claim his girlfriend's child from a previous relationship as his foster child if the boyfriend lived with the child for the full year and cared for the child as his own. In late 1999, Congress passed legislation to modify the definition of a foster child. Under this provision, a taxpayer is not able to claim a child as a foster child unless the taxpayer (1) is the sibling, aunt, or uncle of the child or the

child has been placed in the taxpayer's home by an authorized placement agency; (2) cares for the child as his or her own; and (3) lives with the child for a full year.

6. A more detailed discussion of the specific assumptions used to allocate dependents and income can be found in Bull et al. 1999. Our estimates are based on current law as of September 24, 1999. In late 1999, Congress enacted legislation to prevent the alternative minimum tax from reducing personal credits, including the child credit and the child- and dependent-care tax credit, in tax years 2000 and 2001. Our estimates do not reflect this temporary provision.

7. Tax return information could be used to directly allocate certain other forms of unearned income to each spouse. However, even pensions may be considered a marital asset that should be divided if the marriage ends.

8. This approach allows us to isolate the effects of the design of the EITC on marriage penalties and bonuses. It is consistent with our overall approach of estimating the marriage penalties and bonuses associated with the structural design of the individual income tax. We assume the continued existence of the income tax, and specifically the EITC, in the second step. Because of the interactions between the EITC and the $500 child tax credit, our results would have been qualitatively and quantitatively different had we assumed that the EITC did not exist in this step. For families with three or more children, the full amount of the child tax credit depends on the taxpayer's EITC as well as the taxpayer's income and payroll tax liabilities. Under the approach taken in this chapter, the measure of the effect of the EITC on marriage penalties reflects some changes in the child tax credit, but only to the extent that the EITC would change if the couple could file as unmarried individuals rather than filing a joint return. If we instead had assumed that the EITC did not exist, our estimates would include some changes in the child credit resulting solely from the repeal of the EITC. This is because the couple's child tax credit changes as a consequence of the repeal of the EITC, even if they file a joint return.

9. Two-earner couples are defined to include couples in which one or both spouses have social security or unemployment compensation benefits.

10. All other things equal, the existence of such large marriage bonuses might discourage separations and divorce. Our measure does not account for second-order changes, including the change, if any, in marital behavior that might occur in response to the presence of such large marriage bonuses.

11. Some taxpayers whose taxes are minimized by splitting custody of the children would fare equally well if they allocated all children to the lower-income spouse.

12. Shortly before publication, the Economic Growth and Tax Relief Reconciliation Act of 2001 was enacted. It contains a provision that is imilar to the EITC proposal included in the vetoed 1999 tax bill. Beginning in 2002, the phase-out range of the Earned Income Tax Credit will be extended. By 2008, the beginning- and end-points of the EITC phase-out range will increase by $3,000 for joint filers.

13. There are a number of other ways that a single filing option could be designed. Senator Daniel Moynihan (Dem.-N.Y.) recently proposed that each spouse would be able to claim the EITC based on his or her own income and that they each be allowed to claim up to two children in the family. Senator Moynihan's proposal effectively treats a married couple as if they were living apart and had divided custody of their children.

REFERENCES

Alm, James, and Leslie A. Whittington. 1996. "The Rise and Fall and Rise . . . of the Marriage Tax." *National Tax Journal* 49(4): 571–89.

———. 1997. "Income Taxes and the Timing of Marital Decisions." *Journal of Public Economics* 64(2): 219–40.

———. 1999. "For Love or Money? The Impact of Income Taxes on Marriage." *Economica* 66(261): 297–316.

Bittker, Boris I. 1975. "Federal Income Taxation and the Family." *Stanford Law Review* 27(4): 1389–1463.

Brazer, Harvey E. 1980. "Income Tax Treatment of the Family." In *The Economics of Taxation*, edited by Henry J. Aaron and Michael J. Boskin. Washington, D.C.: Brookings Institution.

Bull, Nicholas, Janet Holtzblatt, James R. Nunns, and Robert Rebelein. 1999. "Defining and Measuring Marriage Penalties and Bonuses." Paper 82. Washington: U.S. Department of the Treasury, Office of Tax Analysis.

Cilke, James. 1994. "The Treasury Individual Tax Model." Mimeo. Washington: U.S. Department of the Treasury, Office of Tax Analysis.

Dickert-Conlin, Stacy. 1999. "Taxes and Transfers: Their Effects on the Decision to End a Marriage." *Journal of Public Economics* 73(2): 217–40.

Dickert-Conlin, Stacy, and Scott Houser. 1998. "Taxes and Transfers: A New Look at the Marriage Penalty." *National Tax Journal* 51(2): 175–217.

Eissa, Nada, and Hilary Williamson Hoynes. 1999. "Good News for Low-Income Families? Tax-Transfer Schemes and Marriage." University of California, Berkeley. Mimeo.

Feenberg, Daniel, and Harvey Rosen. 1995. "Recent Developments in the Marriage Tax." *National Tax Journal* 48(1): 91–101.

Holtzblatt, Janet. 1997. "Comments on 'Taxes and Transfers: Their Effects on the Decision to End a Marriage.'" In *Proceedings of the Eighty-ninth Annual Conference on Taxation*. Washington, D.C.: National Tax Association, Tax Institute of America.

Scholz, John Karl. 1997. *Statement of the Deputy Assistant Secretary for Tax Analysis, U.S. Department of the Treasury, Before the U.S. House of Representatives, Committee on Ways and Means.* Hearing on the Internal Revenue Service's 1995 Earned Income Tax Credit Compliance Study. Washington, D.C., May 8.

U.S. Congressional Budget Office. 1997. *For Better or for Worse: Marriage and the Federal Income Tax.* Washington, D.C. (June).

U.S. General Accounting Office. 1996. *Income Tax Treatment of Married and Single Individuals.* GAO/GGD-96-175. Washington: U.S. Government Printing Office.

Chapter 5

The Optimal Design of the Earned Income Tax Credit

Jeffrey B. Liebman

The Earned Income Tax Credit (EITC) is unusual among U.S. cash transfer programs for several reasons: only taxpayers who work are eligible for the credit; payments initially rise with income; and the credit phases out gradually as a taxpayer's income rises. In contrast, typical transfer programs such as Temporary Assistance for Needy Families and Supplemental Security Income provide their highest payments to households with no other income and then reduce benefits rapidly as a household's income rises.

The EITC's distinctive budget constraint causes 75 percent of its dollars to be transferred to workers with annual earnings between $9,000 and $31,000 (the median recipient has earnings of around $15,400)—a much higher income range than in traditional transfer programs.[1] In addition, the budget constraint alters incentives, subsidizing work as the credit is phased in and taxing it as the credit is phased out.

A fundamental issue for any transfer program is whether it increases the well-being of its recipients by enough to outweigh the reduction in well-being that it causes for the higher-income taxpayers from whom the revenue for the program is raised. It general, the cost of providing one dollar's worth of utility gain to a transfer recipient can be substantially more than one dollar. This disparity occurs for two reasons. First, raising the revenue for the program involves deadweight loss; therefore, taxpayers lose more than a dollar's worth of utility for every dollar raised. Second, because transfer programs alter the incentives facing recipients, the value of the transfer to recipients may be less than if the same transfer were paid as a lump sum; therefore, beneficiaries may gain less than a dollar's worth of utility for every dollar they receive.

These two sources of leakage imply that society may have to value a dollar given to a transfer recipient at several times the value of a dollar in the hands of the typical taxpayer in order to justify using distortionary tax and transfer systems to redistribute income. These values may be acceptable when a program's benefits are narrowly targeted on a population that is particularly needy or deserving. However, as a program is expanded, either by increasing benefits to a fixed population or by widening the eligible population, the marginal social welfare value of additional transfers to beneficiaries will typically decline until it no longer exceeds the marginal cost to taxpayers. Thus the optimal design for a transfer program depends on both the degree of distortion created by the incentive effects of the program and on the weights with which society trades off dollars in the hands of different households.

While this basic logic applies to the EITC, the design of the EITC provides several exceptions to these general principles that make it interesting to study. First, it is not always the case that a dollar spent on the EITC produces less than a dollar's worth of utility gain to beneficiaries. Because the credit is available only to workers, the EITC offsets some of the distortions created by the rest of the welfare and tax systems, and taxpayers who leave welfare to claim the EITC can increase their well-being at the same time as government expenditures decline. Therefore, for some beneficiaries, the cost of providing a dollar's worth of utility is actually less than a dollar. Moreover, for some two-earner couples and for some EITC recipients receiving the maximum credit, the EITC is effectively a lump-sum transfer that does not produce any deadweight loss.

Because of these theoretical peculiarities and because even the more conventional features of the EITC apply to a very thick portion of the income distribution, choices about the structure of the EITC create important policy trade-offs. This chapter uses a microsimulation model calibrated to microdata from the 1999 Current Population Survey (CPS) to illustrate the trade-offs that arise in designing an Earned Income Tax Credit, focusing in particular on the choice of a maximum credit, a phase-in rate, and a phase-out rate.

The research underlying this chapter yields two basic results. First, in contrast with the findings of Edgar Browning (1995), I find that the overall efficiency cost of transferring income through the EITC is fairly low. While Browning found that it cost $4.03 to provide one dollar's worth of utility gain to recipients in the phase-out region and almost $2.00 to provide one dollar's worth of utility to recipients in the phase-in and constant regions, I find that it typically costs less than $2.00. An important reason for my lower results is that I take into account the impact of the EITC on the labor force participation of single parents. Recent research by Nada Eissa and Jeffrey Liebman (1996), Bruce Meyer and Dan Rosenbaum (1999; chapter 2, this volume), and David Ellwood (chapter 3, this volume) suggests that the EITC causes a large number of welfare recipients to enter the labor force. When the savings from reduced welfare spending are taken into account, the EITC appears to be a much more efficient way to accomplish income redistribution than when they are ignored.[2] In addition, a significant portion of the labor supply responsiveness of married couples is likely to be the result of secondary earners' leaving the labor force. My simulations indicate that much of this responsiveness derives from the income effect of the EITC rather than the substitution effect. Therefore, for these households, the EITC is effectively a lump-sum transfer.

Second, the optimal structure of the EITC depends heavily on society's taste for redistribution, something that is difficult to observe. For the current structure of the EITC to be optimal, taxpayers must value one dollar's worth of utility gain for a typical EITC recipient at roughly 2.5 times a dollar in the hands of the typical non-EITC taxpayer. If society places a relative welfare weight on EITC recipients of 3 or more, then the credit should be expanded substantially. In contrast, if society places a relative weight of less than 2 on EITC recipients, then the EITC should be reduced or eliminated.

WELFARE ANALYSIS OF THE EITC

There are five basic scenarios that illustrate the ways in which the labor supply behavior of an unmarried taxpayer could be affected by the introduction of an Earned Income Tax Credit.[3] First, a taxpayer might have had earnings greater than the EITC break-even point if there were no EITC but reduces his or her earnings in order to receive the EITC. Second, a taxpayer might have had income in the EITC phase-out range even in the absence of the EITC, but because both the income and substitution effects of the EITC encourage the taxpayer to reduce earnings, he or she moves to a lower level of earnings. Third, a taxpayer with earnings in the constant region might reduce his or her earnings because of the negative income effect from the EITC. Fourth, a taxpayer with earnings in the phase-in region might alter his or her earnings in either direction because the positive substitution effect and the negative income effect make the net impact on labor supply ambiguous. Finally, a taxpayer who would not have had any annual earnings in the absence of the EITC might decide to join the labor force because the EITC increases the average return to working. Such a taxpayer could enter the labor force at any level of earnings eligible for the EITC. In all of these cases the taxpayers receiving the EITC have higher utility than they did before the EITC was introduced.

In evaluating the impact of the EITC on economic welfare, it is helpful to convert these utility gains into dollars because it is easier to think about whether society wants to take five dollars from a high-income taxpayer in order to give one dollar to a low-income taxpayer than it is to think about transferring utils. Since thought experiments like the one just described usually pertain to lump-sum transfers among taxpayers, it is also important to separate the changes in economic welfare into components occurring because of lump-sum transfers and those owing to deadweight loss.

A standard method for evaluating the welfare implications of changes in economic policies is money metric equivalent variation (MMEV).[4] This method assigns a dollar amount to each indifference curve by calculating how many dollars would have to be transferred to the individual, starting at the prereform utility level and prices, in order for the individual to achieve the postreform level of utility. Thus, the money metric equivalent variation for a policy reform that increases a taxpayer's utility from U_0 to U_1 is

$$MMEV = e(p^0, U^1) - e(p^0, U^0),$$

where $e(\bullet)$ is the expenditure function, p^0 represents the initial price level, and U^0 and U^1 represent the initial and postreform levels of utility, respectively. Deadweight loss is the difference between the increase in government spending owing to the policy change and the MMEV, and it measures the extent to which the utility gain to the EITC recipient is less than if the same money had been transferred as a lump-sum payment. Figure 5.1 illustrates this measure of welfare gain for a taxpayer in the phase-out range who reduces his or her hours of work when the EITC is introduced. The increase in utility from U_0 to U_1 could have been achieved by a lump-sum transfer of BC. This is the money metric equivalent variation measure of the individual's increase in welfare owing to the introduction of the EITC. Since the individual receives EITC payments of AC that are greater than BC, there is deadweight loss from the transfer equal to $(AC - BC = AB)$. While similar analysis applies for most EITC recipients, for taxpayers whose original and post-EITC incomes are in the flat region of the credit, prices are not changed, so there is no deadweight loss from the transfer. Similarly, for taxpayers who were out of the labor force receiving welfare, the EITC offsets the negative incentives of the welfare system and often reduces deadweight loss on net; the increase in economic welfare for these taxpayers occurs even as the budgetary cost of the transfers they receive declines.

In addition to increasing the utility of recipients and producing deadweight loss, the EITC requires that tax revenue be raised from higher-income taxpayers in order to pay for the transfers. Raising this revenue produces a direct loss of utility from higher-income taxpayers as well as additional deadweight loss. Including both the welfare gains and revenue costs of the EITC, the net benefit to society of transferring income to EITC recipients is

$$\text{Net Benefit} = \sum_i [W_i B_i(\tau) - (1 + MEB)EITC_i(\tau)], \tag{5.1}$$

where i indexes all EITC recipients. The first term in the expression measures the benefit to society of transferring income to EITC recipients: W_i is the Bergson-Samuelson social welfare function weight for taxpayer i (the average welfare weight for the taxpayers from whom the revenue is raised is normalized to one),[5] and $B_i(\tau)$ is equal to $e[P^0, V_i(\tau)] - e[P^0, V_i(0)]$, where P^0 represents the budget constraint facing the taxpayer in the absence of an EITC, $V(\tau)$ gives the value of the indirect utility function under a particular EITC budget constraint indexed by τ, and $V(0)$ is the value of the indirect utility function in the absence of the EITC. The second term in equation (5.1) measures the utility loss to taxpayers from whom the revenue for the EITC is raised. MEB is the marginal excess burden of raising tax revenue,[6] and $EITC_i(\tau)$ is the amount of EITC received by taxpayer i when he or she maximizes utility under the particular EITC budget constraint indexed by τ.[7] Thus this term is simply total spending on the EITC multiplied by the marginal excess burden of taxation.[8]

FIGURE 5.1 / Dollar Measure of Welfare Gain from EITC

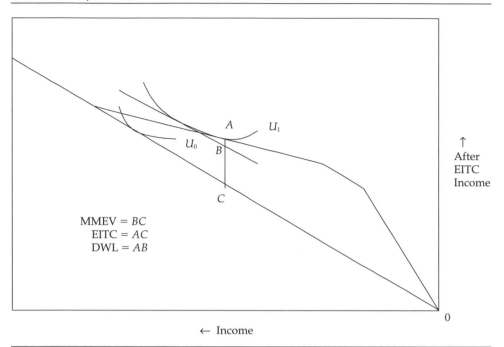

MMEV = BC
EITC = AC
DWL = AB

← Income

↑
After
EITC
Income

Source: Author's configuration.

Equation (5.1) can be rewritten as

$$\text{Net Benefit} = \sum_i \{W_i[EITC_i(\tau) - DWL_i(\tau)] - (1 + MEB)EITC_i(\tau)\},$$

decomposing the net utility gain to recipients into the utility gain from a lump-sum transfer of $EITC(\tau)$ minus the deadweight loss that comes from altering incentives facing recipients. Notice that this equation shows clearly that if there is deadweight loss from transferring income (that is, DWL and MEB are positive), then the net benefit to society of transferring income will be negative unless W_i is sufficiently greater than one. It is also worth emphasizing that $DWL(\tau)$ can be negative for taxpayers who participate in the labor force only in the presence of the EITC (and for whom the EITC offsets distortions created by the tax and welfare systems).

Simulation Methodology

To examine the trade-offs involved in the design of the EITC, I conduct simulations using a constant elasticity of substitution (CES) utility function, calibrated to individual-level data on hours of work, wages, unearned income, and family composition of single and married taxpayers with children from the March 1999 CPS.[9]

The CES utility function can be written as

$$U = [(1 - \alpha)Y^{-\rho} + \alpha (L - h)^{-\rho}]^{\frac{-1}{\rho}} - FC,$$

where Y is income after taxes and transfers, h is annual hours of work, L is the maximum possible annual hours of work (365×24), and FC is the fixed cost associated with work.[10] Three parameters need to be chosen in the utility function for each individual: ρ, α, and FC. Using results from N. H. Stern (1976), I set ρ for each individual to match the compensated wage elasticity chosen for the simulation. Then I choose α such that the individual's simulated hours choice (under a budget constraint designed to approximate the 1998 tax code and welfare system) matches the individual's observed hours worked for 1998 as reported in the CPS. For individuals with positive hours in 1998, fixed costs were randomly drawn from a uniform distribution with a lower limit of zero and an upper limit equal to the difference between the individual's utility at their observed hours of work and their utility at zero hours of work. These fixed costs were then divided by a scalar so as to produce labor force participation responsiveness to the EITC that is consistent with that measured in the empirical studies cited earlier. Fixed costs for people out of the labor force were chosen to be large enough so that none of them would choose to work under the 1998 budget constraint. Further details of the calibration methodology are in the appendix.

Once preference parameters are calibrated for each individual (separately for each simulation elasticity), it is straightforward to alter the budget constraint and simulate the individual's new hours choice by searching over all possible hours choices for the one that maximizes the individual's utility.

Social Welfare Weights

Because changes in the EITC budget constraint can alter the characteristics of the EITC population, it is desirable to have a method for valuing dollars transferred to different types of EITC recipients differently. For example, a reduction in the phase-out tax rate will cause higher-income taxpayers to receive the credit, and dollars transferred to these wealthier taxpayers presumably deserve less weight than dollars transferred to lower-income taxpayers. To weight dollars transferred to recipients with different incomes, I use a standard individualistic social welfare function that is additively separable in the utilities of each recipient:

$$W_i = v\left(\frac{U_i^{\mu-1}}{U_r^{\mu-1}}\right).$$

In this equation, the utility of each EITC recipient, U_i, is defined relative to the utility of an arbitrarily chosen reference EITC recipient receiving the maximum EITC, U_r.[11] I take as my reference EITC recipient a single parent with two children who works two thousand hours a year at $6.00 an hour. The parameter, v, represents the value of a dollar given as a lump sum to the reference EITC recipient relative to the value of a dollar given as a lump sum to the typical nonrecipient taxpayer from whom the revenue is raised (recall that the value of a dollar to the nonrecipient taxpayer has been normalized to $1.00 and that for simplicity I have taken all non-EITC taxpayers to be the same because the simulations do not have much impact on who they are). Thus, this first parameter reflects how much society cares about a full-time low-wage worker with children relative to the typical taxpayer.

The parameter μ (which can range from zero to one) reflects the heterogeneity within the recipient population. In particular, it measures how fast social welfare weights rise at utility levels below that of the reference EITC recipient and how fast they fall at utility levels above that of the reference EITC recipient. Under this standard social welfare function, μ close to one corresponds to a social welfare function in which all recipient taxpayers are weighted equally (at v), and μ close to zero corresponds to a social welfare function in which the lowest-income recipients receive much higher weights than higher-income recipients.

SIMULATION RESULTS FOR HEAD-OF-HOUSEHOLD FILERS

The EITC is often described by six characteristics: the maximum credit, the phase-in subsidy rate, the minimum income at which the maximum credit is received, the maximum income at which the maximum credit is received, the phase-out tax rate, and the maximum income at which any credit is received. However, the choice of any two of the first three parameters pins down the third, and the choice of any two of the last three parameters similarly pins down the third of that group. Therefore, the EITC can be defined by four parameters. While historically EITC parameters have been identical for married and unmarried taxpayers, there is no need for this to be so.[12] Indeed, recent concern about marriage penalties created by the EITC has led to proposals with a more generous credit for some married couples. Therefore, in this chapter I conduct separate simulations for head-of-household and married filers. This section presents the results for head-of-household filers and begins by focusing on three of the possible parameters (the maximum credit, the phase-in rate, and the phase-out rate) individually. These parameters are the ones than are most often discussed in the policy debate and serve to illustrate the full range of analytical issues. At the end of this section, I present results in which I search simultaneously over four EITC parameters in order to find the configuration of the EITC that maximizes social welfare.[13] The subsequent section of the chapter contains results for married taxpayers.

The Maximum EITC

The political debate over the size of the EITC tends to be dominated by two extremes. Critics of the program claim that the program has been growing out of control, noting that the growth of spending on the EITC has been faster than that of any other entitlement program.[14] These critics usually fail to mention that this growth is the direct result of legislation designed to expand the EITC and that recent Internal Revenue Service efforts to combat noncompliance have actually reduced expenditures below the level that was forecast when the EITC expansions were enacted. On the other side of the debate, a remarkable number of analyses on topics such as rising wage inequality or the impact of trade on low-wage workers conclude with a short section on policy recommendations that suggests increasing the EITC.[15] These calls for increasing the EITC seem to be independent of the level of the EITC, and in particular there is no sign that their prevalence is any lower with the maximum EITC for a family with two children at $3,816 than they were when it was $851.

What is missing from the public debate is an explicit recognition that there are trade-offs between the well-being of EITC recipients and that of the taxpayers from whom the revenue is raised. In particular, as the EITC increases, at some point the marginal benefit for each dollar spent on the program begins to fall and will eventually descend below the marginal cost of raising an additional dollar from taxpayers. The marginal benefit for each dollar spent falls for three reasons. First, at higher EITC levels, beneficiaries have higher levels of utility and therefore receive less weight in the social welfare function. Second, a higher maximum EITC implies a higher phase-out tax rate (holding constant the income level at which the maximum credit is received and the maximum income for eligibility for the credit), raising deadweight loss and reducing the utility gain to recipients for each dollar received. Finally, it is likely that participation elasticities decline as the credit increases and fewer people remain near the margin between work and welfare. Thus, the welfare savings for each dollar of EITC expenditure decline.

The simulations presented in tables 5.1 and 5.2 illustrate these trade-offs. They show the impact of raising the maximum EITC, holding constant the income range over which the maximum EITC is received. Thus, they involve increasing both the phase-in subsidy rate and the phase-out tax rate in proportion to the increase in the maximum credit.[16]

Columns 1 through 5 of table 5.1 show the distribution of head-of-household filers by EITC region. The top panel presents the results when the compensated wage elasticity is 0.1; the second panel presents the results when the wage elasticity is 0.3; and the third panel presents the results when the wage elasticity is

TABLE 5.1 / Impacts of Alternative Levels for the Maximum EITC: Head-of-Household Filers

| | Number of Taxpayers (Millions) | | | | | Dollars (Millions) | | | | | |
Percentage of Current Law Maximum	Zero Annual Hours (1)	In EITC Phase-In (2)	In EITC Flat Region (3)	In EITC Phase-Out (4)	Beyond Phase-Out (5)	Total EITC Payments (6)	Lost Income Tax Revenue (7)	Additional Welfare Spending (8)	Net Revenue Cost (9)	Welfare Gain (MMEV) from EITC Payments (10)	Cost per Dollar's Worth of Utility Gain (11)
Compensated wage elasticity of 0.1											
0	2.542	0.412	0.636	5.277	2.617	0	0	0	0	0	—
50	2.025	0.980	1.270	4.592	2.617	7,242	1,013	−1,906	6,350	6,432	0.99
100	1.703	1.484	1.721	3.959	2.617	15,009	2,309	−1,125	16,193	13,226	1.22
150	1.679	1.788	1.946	3.453	2.617	23,810	2,733	−547	25,996	19,487	1.33
200	1.621	2.365	2.051	2.830	2.617	33,205	3,246	−266	36,185	25,491	1.42
Compensated wage elasticity of 0.3											
0	2.819	0.281	0.516	5.221	2.647	0	0	0	0	0	—
50	1.929	1.120	1.570	4.249	2.617	7,022	1,176	−3,056	5,141	5,746	0.89
100	1.703	1.484	1.721	3.959	2.617	15,009	2,499	−2,792	14,717	11,764	1.25
150	1.644	1.706	1.926	3.591	2.617	24,393	3,247	−2,415	25,226	17,590	1.43
200	1.444	2.188	2.434	2.877	2.540	36,020	3,835	−2,980	36,875	23,599	1.56
Compensated wage elasticity of 0.5											
0	3.187	0.283	0.410	4.719	2.885	0	0	0	0	0	—
50	1.942	1.271	1.587	3.945	2.738	6,633	1,230	−4,094	3,769	5,233	0.72
100	1.703	1.484	1.721	3.959	2.617	15,009	2,762	−4,972	12,799	11,033	1.16
150	1.550	1.631	2.101	3.704	2.498	25,809	3,752	−5,350	24,211	17,904	1.35
200	1.482	1.817	2.679	3.257	2.249	38,311	5,029	−5,335	38,005	25,983	1.46

Source: Author's simulations.

0.5.[17] Recall that the simulations for each elasticity are calibrated to match the actual 1998 distribution of taxpayers under the EITC rules for that year.

The first row of each panel shows results in the absence of an EITC. At a compensated wage elasticity of 0.1, without an EITC 2.5 million single parents do not work at all and instead receive welfare, and relatively few taxpayers locate in the phase-in region of the credit, where marginal benefit-reduction rates from the welfare system are high. As the credit increases, welfare recipients enter the labor force. In the first panel the percentage of single parents who work at some point during the year increases from 78 percent in the absence of the EITC to 82 percent at half of the current maximum EITC and 85 percent at the current level of the EITC. The participation responsiveness with higher compensated wage elasticities is somewhat larger.[18] These levels of participation responsiveness are roughly consistent with the large increase in annual labor force participation among single mothers from 73 percent in 1984 to 87 percent in 1998 that has recently occurred[19] and with the findings of Meyer and Rosenbaum (1999), which indicate that EITC expansions were responsible for 63 percent of this increase. In addition, the results in all three panels show that as the EITC is introduced and then expanded, some taxpayers in the phase-out region reduce their hours and locate in lower regions (including the kink point at the upper end of the constant region). In the higher-elasticity examples, taxpayers from beyond the phase-out region reduce their hours and become EITC recipients.

The remaining columns of table 5.1 show the revenue and welfare implications of changes in the maximum value of the credit. As the credit expands, total expenditures on the EITC increase. In addition, the income effect of the credit and the higher phase-out tax rate causes people to reduce their hours of work, decreasing income tax revenue. However, this income tax effect is substantially offset by the savings from lower welfare payments for new participants in the labor force. Thus in many cases the net revenue cost of the program is less than total EITC payments. For example, with a compensated wage elasticity of 0.3, the current level of the EITC costs $15.0 billion and results in $2.5 billion of lost income tax revenue from those reducing their hours of work. However, these two budgetary costs are partially offset by $2.8 billion in savings on welfare spending, so the total budgetary cost is $14.7 billion.[20]

Because the EITC distorts incentives for recipients, they gain less in utility than if the payments were made as a lump sum. Comparing column 10 to column 6 in the top panel, we see that there is substantial deadweight loss from the transfers, ranging from 22 percent of spending at low levels of the EITC and a compensated wage elasticity of 0.1 to 34 percent at higher levels and elasticities. With higher elasticities we see greater amounts of deadweight loss. At current program levels, the welfare gain from EITC payments to single-parent households is 88 percent of EITC spending levels when the compensated wage elasticity is 0.1, 78 percent when the elasticity is 0.3, and 74 percent when the elasticity is 0.5. The welfare gain relative to the combined revenue cost from EITC payments and lost income tax revenue is 76 percent when the elasticity is 0.1, 67 percent when the elasticity is 0.3, and 62 percent when the elasticity is 0.5. In comparison, Browning (1995) calculates that the marginal benefit for each dollar of revenue cost is $0.46 in the phase-out range, roughly $1.03 in the phase-in range, and $1.00 in the plateau range when the compensated wage elasticity is 0.3. Weighting these three numbers by the total EITC dollars received by taxpayers in each of these ranges in my simulations produces an overall Browning estimate of $0.69—very close to my estimate of 67 percent. The similarity of the results up to this point serves to highlight that the difference in my overall assessment of the efficiency cost of the EITC from that of Browning does not come from the basic simulations of the benefits for each dollar transferred but rather derives from the fact that I incorporate the impact of people leaving welfare to participate in the labor market.

When the savings from reduced welfare spending are taken into account, the utility gains can actually exceed the revenue cost. For example, with a maximum EITC that is half the current level and a compensated wage elasticity of 0.3, the welfare gain is $5.7 billion while the net revenue cost is only $5.1 billion, indicating a cost for each dollar of utility gain of 89 cents. At higher compensated wage elasticities, the cost for each dollar of utility gain sometimes falls relative to lower elasticities because the higher wage elasticities also result in higher participation elasticities and therefore in higher savings on welfare spending.

As can be seen in the last column of table 5.1, the cost of each dollar's worth of utility gain (calculated by dividing the figure in column 9 by that in column 10) rises as the size of the maximum credit increases. This occurs for two reasons. First, the higher subsidy and tax rates that result from a higher maximum credit lead to more deadweight loss. Second, at higher credit levels fewer people are leaving welfare for each additional dollar spent on the EITC, so the cost of the program is not being offset by welfare savings.

As noted in the foregoing discussion on theory, the revenue effect does not represent the total cost of the program. There is also deadweight loss from raising the revenue through distortionary taxation. If we assume a marginal excess burden of 0.5, we find (by multiplying the numbers in column 11 of table 5.1 by 1.5) that in all cases the total cost of giving one dollar's worth of utility to an EITC recipient exceeds one dollar.[21] This implies that for the benefit of the EITC to outweigh its costs, society must value a dollar of utility for EITC recipients somewhat more than it values a dollar in the hands of the typical taxpayer.[22]

Table 5.2 illustrates how the net benefits of the EITC vary with the size of the maximum credit and with how much society cares about EITC recipients. These results use a compensated wage elasticity of 0.3. The three panels of table 5.2 correspond to three values of the parameter v, which represents how much society values a dollar in the hands of the reference EITC recipient (a person receiving the maximum credit) relative to the average taxpayer from whom the revenue is raised. For each value of v, results are also presented for three values of the parameter μ, which reflects how quickly the value of transfers fall at income levels above that of the reference taxpayer (recall that lower values of μ imply that the social welfare weight falls more rapidly as income rises).

In the first column of table 5.2 we see the cost for each dollar of utility gain.

TABLE 5.2 / The Costs and Benefits of the EITC at Different Levels of the Maximum Credit: Head-of-Household Filers (Compensated Wage Elasticity = 0.3)

Percentage of Current Law Maximum	μ = .05				μ = .50				μ = .95			
	Cost per Dollar of Utility	Benefit per Dollar of Utility	MMEV (Millions of Dollars)	Net Benefits (Millions of Dollars)	Cost per Dollar of Utility	Benefit per Dollar of Utility	MMEV (Millions of Dollars)	Net Benefits (Millions of Dollars)	Cost per Dollar of Utility	Benefit per Dollar of Utility	MMEV (Millions of Dollars)	Net Benefits (Millions of Dollars)
v = 1												
50	1.34	0.86	5,746	−2,793	1.34	0.92	5,746	−2,436	1.34	0.99	5,746	−2,016
75	1.69	0.85	8,766	−7,406	1.69	0.91	8,766	−6,819	1.69	0.99	8,766	−6,132
100	1.88	0.83	11,764	−12,271	1.88	0.91	11,764	−11,426	1.88	0.99	11,764	−10,433
150	2.15	0.81	17,590	−23,596	2.15	0.89	17,590	−22,158	2.15	0.99	17,590	−20,457
200	2.34	0.79	23,599	−36,705	2.34	0.88	23,599	−34,571	2.34	0.99	23,599	−32,025
v = 2												
50	1.34	1.71	5,746	2,126	1.34	1.84	5,746	2,840	1.34	1.98	5,746	3,679
75	1.69	1.69	8,766	4	1.69	1.82	8,766	1,176	1.69	1.98	8,766	2,551
100	1.88	1.67	11,764	−2,467	1.88	1.81	11,764	−776	1.88	1.98	11,764	1,210
150	2.15	1.62	17,590	−9,354	2.15	1.78	17,590	−6,476	2.15	1.98	17,590	−3,074
200	2.34	1.58	23,599	−18,097	2.34	1.76	23,599	−13,830	2.34	1.97	23,599	−8,738
v = 3												
50	1.34	2.57	5,746	7,044	1.34	2.75	5,746	8,116	1.34	2.97	5,746	9,375
75	1.69	2.54	8,766	7,413	1.69	2.74	8,766	9,172	1.69	2.97	8,766	11,234
100	1.88	2.50	11,764	7,337	1.88	2.72	11,764	9,874	1.88	2.97	11,764	12,853
150	2.15	2.43	17,590	4,889	2.15	2.67	17,590	9,205	2.15	2.96	17,590	14,308
200	2.34	2.37	23,599	511	2.34	2.64	23,599	6,911	2.34	2.96	23,599	14,550

Source: Author's simulations.

This is simply column 11 of table 5.1 multiplied by 1.5 to incorporate the excess burden involved in raising the revenue. The second column shows the social welfare benefit for each dollar of utility gain when μ equals .05. This number is calculated by weighting each dollar of utility gain provided by the EITC by the social welfare weight associated with the utility level of the person receiving the gain. These values are below the value of v because the average dollar transferred through the EITC to a head-of-household filer goes to someone with income above that of the reference taxpayer. The third column shows the total utility gains in millions of dollars, the MMEV (this column comes directly from column 10 of table 5.1). The fourth column multiplies the total utility gain by the difference between the benefits and costs for each dollar transferred to produce the net benefit of the EITC for a given level of the maximum credit.

In the top panel, v equals 1, meaning that society does not value dollars in the hands of EITC recipients any more highly than dollars to the average taxpayer. Under this assumption, we see that net benefits from the EITC are always negative. Although savings from reduced welfare spending is taken into account, the deadweight loss from raising the revenue and making the transfers implies that it costs more than a dollar to make a dollar's worth of transfers; so with dollars to EITC recipients valued the same as dollars to other taxpayers, the program's cost exceeds its benefits.

The second panel contains results for the case in which dollars in the hands of the reference EITC recipients receive twice the weight of dollars in the hands of the average taxpayer (v = 2). With this assumption, a maximum credit at around 50 percent of the current level yields the highest positive benefits for all three values of μ. In this set of results the net benefits eventually become negative as the size of the credit rises. As the program gets larger, the cost for each dollar transferred rises (because the subsidy and tax rates are rising and fewer additional people are leaving welfare for work), and the benefit for each dollar transferred falls (because each marginal dollar is adding less to social welfare since the recipients' incomes are rising).

In the third panel, we see that if EITC recipients receive three times the weight of other taxpayers (v = 3), then a program of roughly the current size can be optimal. More specifically, with μ equal to .05, a credit at 75 percent of current levels is optimal; with μ equal to .50, the current level is optimal; and with μ equal to .95 (and high-income EITC recipients receiving a welfare weight that is nearly as high as that of an EITC recipient at the current EITC maximum), a credit of 200 percent of the current level (or larger) is optimal. Additional results not shown indicate that if EITC recipients are given four times the weight of the average taxpayers, then the optimal EITC is at least 125 percent of current levels; if they are given five times the weight of the average taxpayer, then the optimal size is more than double the current size.

Given the changes under way in the U.S. welfare system and the sensitivity of the efficiency cost estimates to the amount of welfare savings that accrue when welfare recipients enter the labor force, it is worth examining how the optimal size of the EITC varies with the size of the basic welfare benefit. There are two

TABLE 5.3 / The Optimal Level of the EITC as a Percentage of the Current Level for Different Levels of the Welfare Guarantee (Compensated Wage Elasticity = 0.3)

	Welfare guarantee of $3,000			Welfare guarantee of $6,000			Welfare guarantee of $9,000		
v	$\mu = .05$	$\mu = .50$	$\mu = .95$	$\mu = .05$	$\mu = .50$	$\mu = .95$	$\mu = .05$	$\mu = .50$	$\mu = .95$
1	0	0	0	0	0	0	25	25	50
2	25	25	25	50	50	50	75	75	100
3	175	200+	200+	75	100	175	100	125	125
4	200+	200+	200+	175	200+	200+	125	150	200+

Source: Author's simulations.

potentially offsetting effects. As the rest of the welfare system becomes less generous, there becomes less of a need for the EITC to offset the negative incentives created by the welfare system. On the other hand, with smaller welfare benefits, people in the phase-in region are poorer, and therefore the EITC transfers are more valuable. In my basic results, I model the rest of the welfare system as providing a $6,000 guarantee that is phased out dollar for dollar with additional income. Table 5.3 shows how the optimal size of the maximum credit changes as the size of the basic welfare guarantee is reduced to $3,000 and then increased to $9,000.

With a lower welfare guarantee, the optimal size of the EITC is typically a bit smaller than in the basic results from table 5.2 when v equals 1 or 2 and larger when v equals 3 or 4. The intuition for this is fairly straightforward. With a lower welfare guarantee, few people are on welfare even in the absence of an EITC, and thus the welfare cost savings from introducing the EITC are small. With only a small cost savings to offset the revenue cost of the program, the cost for each dollar's worth of utility is higher than in the basic results. At low levels of v, this higher cost offsets the higher benefits of each dollar of transfer that occur because of low-income EITC recipients having lower levels of utility (because they receive small levels of welfare benefits). Only at the higher values of v do the higher benefits of each dollar of transfer outweigh the higher costs for each dollar and justify a larger program than in the base case.

With the higher welfare guarantee there are similarly offsetting effects. Welfare participation rates are much higher and are less responsive to increases in the EITC. However, with more people out of the labor force receiving welfare, EITC spending is significantly lower as well, and the cost of each dollar's worth of utility gain is generally a bit lower than in the base case, as we would expect given the presence of a large welfare system and therefore of more preexisting distortions for the EITC to offset. However, the large welfare system means that the lowest-income recipients have higher incomes than in the other simulations and the social welfare value of transfers to them is therefore lower. On net, the lower costs and lower benefits generally lead to a similar or slightly smaller optimal maximum size for the EITC than in the base case.

The Phase-In Subsidy Rate

For a given maximum level of the Earned Income Tax Credit, the phase-in rate determines the income level at which the maximum credit is received. In practice, this income level has remained relatively constant in real dollars, and therefore the EITC phase-in rate has grown essentially in proportion to increases in the size of the maximum credit. Although the phase-in rate has not been treated as an independent parameter in the United States to date, it is worth noting that in the United Kingdom's version of the EITC, the Working Families Tax Credit, there is no phase-in region at all. Taxpayers are ineligible for the U.K. credit unless they work at least sixteen hours a week. At sixteen hours a week they receive the maximum credit, and it is phased out as hours (and income) rise further. For a full-year worker earning the equivalent of $8.00 an hour, the credit would be equivalent to an EITC that was zero for incomes below $6,656 and jumped immediately to its maximum at that income level. Thus, the U.K. counterexample raises the question of why the United States has a phase-in region and whether the EITC should be designed differently.[23]

Presumably one reason why the U.S. system has a phase-in region while the U.K. system does not is that the United States bases the EITC on a full calendar year of income, while a worker can apply and receive the Working Families Tax Credit after three months of work. Thus to create a work incentive for workers who are entering the workforce in the middle of the year, the EITC needs to provide some payments for people whose earnings do not reach the level of full-time full-year work.

More generally, a higher phase-in rate (holding the maximum credit constant) will induce a greater number of nonworkers to enter the labor force but will also encourage additional higher-income workers to reduce their hours and take advantage of the generous credit at lower levels of earnings. The simulations shown in tables 5.4 and 5.5 illustrate these two offsetting effects.

Table 5.4 presents simulations using the same format as table 5.1. Thus, there are panels for each of the three compensated wage elasticities. In each panel, the first row shows the distribution of head-of-household taxpayers by EITC region in the absence of an EITC. The second row shows results for simulations in which there is no phase-in region and the credit jumps from zero directly to the current maximum at the point where the maximum credit currently begins. Subsequent rows show results for a 30 percent phase-in rate (a bit slower than the current rate), the current rate (40 percent for families with two children and 34 percent for families with one child), and then a phase-in rate of 60 percent. Comparing the second and fourth rows in the middle panel, these simulations indicate that eliminating the phase-in completely would greatly reduce the EITC's effectiveness in encouraging people to leave welfare for work. An extra 925,000 household heads would leave the labor force. Moreover, relatively few taxpayers in the phase-in region are induced to work a greater number of hours when the phase-in is eliminated. Only 343,000 extra workers locate in the flat

TABLE 5.4 / Impacts of Alternative Phase-In Rates: Head-of-Household Filers

	Number of Taxpayers (Millions)					Dollars (Millions)					
Phase-In Subsidy Rate	Zero Annual Hours (1)	In EITC Phase-In (2)	In EITC Flat Region (3)	In EITC Phase-Out (4)	Beyond Phase-Out (5)	Total EITC Payments (6)	Lost Income-Tax Revenue (7)	Additional Welfare Spending (8)	Net Revenue Cost (9)	Welfare Gain (MMEV) from EITC Payments (10)	Cost per Dollar's Worth of Utility Gain (11)
Compensated wage elasticity of 0.1											
No EITC	2.542	0.412	0.636	5.277	2.617	0	0	0	0	0	—
No phase-in	2.398	0.410	2.064	3.996	2.617	14,045	1,895	−867	15,073	12,530	1.20
30 percent	1.791	2.352	0.765	4.042	2.617	14,472	2,129	−1,651	14,950	12,769	1.17
Current law	1.703	1.484	1.721	3.959	2.617	15,009	2,309	−1,125	16,193	13,226	1.22
60 percent	1.703	1.366	1.839	3.959	2.617	15,273	2,293	128	17,694	13,432	1.32
Compensated wage elasticity of 0.3											
No EITC	2.819	0.281	0.516	5.221	2.647	0	0	0	0	0	—
No phase-in	2.628	0.197	2.046	3.996	2.617	14,065	2,231	−1,145	15,150	11,213	1.35
30 percent	1.703	2.393	0.765	4.140	2.617	14,400	2,377	−2,918	13,859	11,427	1.21
Current law	1.703	1.484	1.721	3.959	2.617	15,009	2,499	−2,792	14,717	11,764	1.25
60 percent	1.703	1.452	1.753	3.959	2.617	15,490	2,502	−1,679	16,313	12,106	1.35
Compensated wage elasticity of 0.5											
No EITC	3.187	0.283	0.410	4.719	2.885	0	0	0	0	0	—
No phase-in	2.546	0	2.325	3.996	2.617	14,993	2,438	−3,816	13,615	10,495	1.30
30 percent	1.762	2.334	0.765	4.183	2.617	14,294	2,606	−4,710	12,190	10,685	1.14
Current law	1.703	1.484	1.721	3.959	2.617	15,009	2,762	−4,972	12,799	11,033	1.16
60 percent	1.703	1.737	1.467	3.959	2.617	15,557	2,767	−3,443	14,880	11,566	1.29

Source: Author's simulations.

region, and only an extra 40,000 locate in the phase-out region compared with the rates under current law. Moving to the last column, we see that the cost for each dollar's worth of utility gain is noticeably higher (1.35 versus 1.25) without the phase-in.

Comparing the various phase-in rates, we see that for all three compensated wage elasticities, a phase-in rate of 30 percent produces lower costs for each dollar's worth of utility gain than do either lower or higher phase-in rates. This occurs because as the phase-in rate rises from zero to 30 percent, significant numbers of welfare recipients are entering the labor force. As the rate rises above current law, however, very few additional participants enter, and the main impact is to induce higher-earning taxpayers to reduce their earnings.

Because the phase-in rate has relatively little impact on the distribution of EITC dollars by income, we see in table 5.5 that the average benefit for each dollar of utility varies hardly at all with the phase-in rate. Therefore, the result that a 30 percent phase-in rate provides the lowest cost relative to utility gain carries through to imply that the 30 percent rate maximizes net benefits.

The Phase-Out Tax Rate

Sixty percent of EITC recipients have incomes of more than $12,300 and are therefore in the phase-out region of the credit. In 1999, these 9 million taxpayers received around $15 billion from the Earned Income Tax Credit. Taxpayers in the phase-out region with two children lose 21.06 cents of the EITC, and those with one child lose 15.98 cents, for every additional dollar they earn. Since these taxpayers face a 15.3 percent Old-Age, Survivors, Disability, and Health Insurance (OASDHI) payroll tax on earnings and many of them are also liable for federal and state income taxes, the cumulative marginal tax rates for phase-out rate taxpayers often exceed 45 percent. These marginal tax rates are among the highest in the current U.S. tax system. Congressional proposals introduced over the past few years to reduce the budgeted cost of the EITC by phasing it out more quickly would add as much as 12 percentage points to these marginal tax rates.

If taxpayers in the phase-out region perceive and respond to these incentives, then it might be possible to redesign the phase-out of the EITC in order to reduce its efficiency cost. It is not possible to tell on a priori grounds whether a faster or a slower phase-out will be preferable to the current rates. A more rapid phase-out reduces the utility of EITC recipients and causes some taxpayers to leave the labor force and return to welfare. Nonetheless, such a policy could be desirable if it made possible a tax cut for higher-income taxpayers that raised their economic welfare by more than the amount of the loss for the low-income EITC recipients.

Table 5.6 presents results from simulations of different phase-out rates (holding constant the current-law phase-in rate and the maximum credit, as well as the income level at which the phase-out begins). As in the previous results, the three panels contain results for three different compensated wage elasticities.

TABLE 5.5 / The Costs and Benefits of the EITC at Different Phase-In Rates: Head-of-Household Filers (Compensated Wage Elasticity = 0.3)

Percentage of Current Law Maximum	μ = .05				μ = .50				μ = .95			
	Cost per Dollar of Utility	Benefit per Dollar of Utility	MMEV (Millions of Dollars)	Net Benefits (Millions of Dollars)	Cost per Dollar of Utility	Benefit per Dollar of Utility	MMEV (Millions of Dollars)	Net Benefits (Millions of Dollars)	Cost per Dollar of Utility	Benefit per Dollar of Utility	MMEV (Millions of Dollars)	Net Benefits (Millions of Dollars)
$v = 1$												
No phase-in	2.03	0.83	11,213	−13,442	2.03	0.90	11,213	−12,599	2.03	0.99	11,213	−11,613
30 percent	1.82	0.83	11,427	−11,254	1.82	0.90	11,427	−10,416	1.82	0.99	11,427	−9,433
Current law	1.88	0.83	11,764	−12,293	1.88	0.91	11,764	−11,352	1.88	0.99	11,764	−10,432
60 percent	2.03	0.84	12,106	−14,378	2.03	0.91	12,106	−13,528	2.03	0.99	12,106	−12,530
$v = 2$												
No phase-in	2.03	1.65	11,213	−4,178	2.03	1.80	11,213	−2,492	2.03	1.98	11,213	−520
30 percent	1.82	1.66	11,427	−1,769	1.82	1.81	11,427	−91	1.82	1.98	11,427	1,874
Current law	1.88	1.66	11,764	−2,529	1.88	1.82	11,764	−647	1.88	1.98	11,764	1,193
60 percent	2.03	1.67	12,106	−4,242	2.03	1.82	12,106	−2,542	2.03	1.98	12,106	−545
$v = 3$												
No phase-in	2.03	2.48	11,213	5,086	2.03	2.70	11,213	7,616	2.03	2.97	11,213	10,573
30 percent	1.82	2.49	11,427	7,717	1.82	2.71	11,427	10,233	1.82	2.97	11,427	13,181
Current law	1.88	2.49	11,764	7,235	1.88	2.73	11,764	10,058	1.88	2.96	11,764	12,818
60 percent	2.03	2.51	12,106	5,894	2.03	2.72	12,106	8,444	2.03	2.97	12,106	11,440

Source: Author's simulations.

TABLE 5.6 / Impacts of Alternative EITC Phase-Out Rates: Head-of-Household Filers

Phase-Out Tax Rate	Number of Taxpayers (Millions)					Dollars (Millions)					
	Zero Annual Hours (1)	In EITC Phase-In (2)	In EITC Flat Region (3)	In EITC Phase-Out (4)	Beyond Phase-Out (5)	Total EITC Payments (6)	Lost Income-Tax Revenue (7)	Additional Welfare Spending (8)	Net Revenue Cost (9)	Welfare Gain (MMEV) from EITC Payments (10)	Cost per Dollar's Worth of Utility Gain (11)
Compensated wage elasticity of 0.1											
No EITC	2.542	0.412	0.636	5.277	2.617	0	0	0	0	0	—
10 percent	1.703	1.484	1.721	5.181	1.395	18,433	2,694	−1,125	19,974	16,684	1.20
Current law	1.703	1.484	1.721	3.959	2.617	15,009	2,309	−1,125	16,193	13,226	1.22
30 percent	1.703	1.484	1.760	2.822	3.715	12,738	1,974	−1,125	13,560	10,752	1.26
40 percent	1.703	1.484	1.760	2.005	4.532	11,470	1,767	−1,125	12,084	9,374	1.29
50 percent	1.703	1.484	1.763	1.621	4.913	10,849	1,680	−1,125	11,376	8,551	1.33
Compensated wage elasticity of 0.3											
10 percent	1.698	1.484	1.721	5.187	1.395	18,373	2,858	−2,824	18,407	15,409	1.19
Current law	1.703	1.484	1.721	3.959	2.617	15,009	2,499	−2,792	14,717	11,764	1.25
30 percent	1.703	1.484	1.763	2.790	3.744	13,208	2,244	−2,792	12,659	9,561	1.32
40 percent	1.703	1.484	1.789	2.080	4.427	12,372	2,020	−2,792	11,600	8,471	1.37
50 percent	1.703	1.484	1.950	1.649	4.698	12,316	1,966	−2,792	11,491	7,978	1.44
Compensated wage elasticity of 0.5											
10 percent	1.688	1.484	1.721	5.221	1.369	18,374	3,069	−4,989	16,454	14,859	1.11
Current law	1.703	1.484	1.721	3.959	2.617	15,009	2,762	−4,972	12,799	11,033	1.16
30 percent	1.703	1.484	1.765	2.732	3.799	13,571	2,466	−4,972	11,065	9,057	1.22
40 percent	1.703	1.484	1.892	2.131	4.274	13,194	2,318	−4,972	10,540	8,190	1.29
50 percent	1.703	1.484	2.168	1.556	4.573	13,002	2,115	−4,972	10,145	7,866	1.29

Source: Author's simulations.

Each row corresponds to a different EITC phase-out tax rate. With a phase-out rate of 10 percent (implying that taxpayers with two children can receive the credit at incomes up to $47,160), 1.7 million household-head filers are in the constant region (including those at the kink point at the beginning of the EITC phase-out), 5.2 million such taxpayers are in the balance of the phase-out region, and only 1.4 million have incomes above the EITC break-even point. With a 10 percent phase-out rate, total spending on the EITC is $18 billion, and an additional $3 billion in income tax revenue is lost by taxpayers' reducing their hours in response to the EITC. These costs are partially offset by $1 billion to $5 billion (depending on the compensated wage elasticity) in savings from reduced welfare payments owing to people entering the labor force in response to the incentives created by the EITC. With an elasticity of 0.3, the MMEV measure of the welfare gain for EITC recipients from the EITC is $15.4 billion, 84 percent of total EITC payments made as well as of the net revenue cost.

For all three elasticities, the cost for each dollar's worth of utility gain rises with the phase-out tax rate. The phase-out rate also has significant impacts on the characteristics of EITC recipients and total amount of expenditures. In particular, a lower phase-out rate implies that a higher fraction of EITC dollars are going to higher-income taxpayers and raises total expenditures substantially.

Table 5.7 presents estimates of the net benefit of the EITC that take both of these factors into account. With v equal to 1, the costs of the EITC outweigh the benefits, and therefore phase-out rates that are higher than the current level reduce the total costs of the EITC by minimizing the size of the program. With v equal to 2 and μ equal to .05 or .50, a phase-out rate of 30 or 40 percent is optimal because it combines a wide gap between benefits and costs for each dollar and fairly large expenditures on the program. With μ equal to 0.95 (so that a high-income EITC recipient with an income of $47,000 receives nearly the same social welfare weight as an EITC recipient at $15,000 of income), a slower phase-out rate is preferable since it allows additional taxpayers with high social welfare weights to receive the credit. With v equal to 3, even with social welfare weights that drop off with income, social welfare is maximized with a more gradual phase-out rate that allows additional taxpayers to benefit from the program.

Maximizing Four Parameters at Once

The results so far have focused on changes to a single EITC parameter, holding other features of the EITC constant. The results from such an approach could differ substantially from simultaneously optimizing over the entire set of EITC parameters. Table 5.8 shows the results from simultaneously maximizing over six possible phase-in rates (15, 30, 45, 60, 75, and 90 percent), eight levels of the maximum credit (25, 50, 75, 100, 125, 150, 175, and 200 percent of the current-law levels), five lengths for the constant region (0, $1,500, $3,000, $6,000, and $9,000), and six phase-out tax rates (10, 20, 30, 40, and 50 percent and a cliff). Thus for

TABLE 5.7 / The Costs and Benefits of the EITC with Different Phase-Out Rates: Head-of-Household Filers (Compensated Wage Elasticity = 0.3)

Phase-Out Tax Rate	μ = .05				μ = .50				μ = .95			
	Cost per Dollar of Utility	Benefit per Dollar of Utility	MMEV (Millions of Dollars)	Net Benefits (Millions of Dollars)	Cost per Dollar of Utility	Benefit per Dollar of Utility	MMEV (Millions of Dollars)	Net Benefits (Millions of Dollars)	Cost per Dollar of Utility	Benefit per Dollar of Utility	MMEV (Millions of Dollars)	Net Benefits (Millions of Dollars)
v = 1												
10 percent	1.79	0.79	15,409	−15,387	1.79	0.88	15,409	−13,990	1.79	0.99	15,409	−12,304
Current rate	1.88	0.83	11,764	−12,293	1.88	0.91	11,764	−11,352	1.88	0.99	11,764	−10,411
30 percent	1.98	0.87	9,561	−10,600	1.98	0.93	9,561	−10,063	1.98	0.99	9,561	−9,444
40 percent	2.06	0.90	8,471	−9,809	2.06	0.94	8,471	−9,425	2.06	0.99	8,471	−8,989
50 percent	2.16	0.91	7,978	−9,978	2.16	0.95	7,978	−9,658	2.16	0.99	7,978	−9,298
v = 2												
10 percent	1.79	1.57	15,409	−3,270	1.79	1.75	15,409	−475	1.79	1.97	15,409	2,897
Current rate	1.88	1.66	11,764	−2,529	1.88	1.82	11,764	−647	1.88	1.98	11,764	1,235
30 percent	1.98	1.74	9,561	−2,270	1.98	1.86	9,561	−1,195	1.98	1.98	9,561	42
40 percent	2.06	1.79	8,471	−2,209	2.06	1.88	8,471	−1,442	2.06	1.99	8,471	−569
50 percent	2.16	1.82	7,978	−2,724	2.16	1.90	7,978	−2,084	2.16	1.99	7,978	−1,363
v = 3												
10 percent	1.79	2.36	15,409	8,848	1.79	2.63	15,409	13,041	1.79	2.96	15,409	18,098
Current rate	1.88	2.49	11,764	7,235	1.88	2.73	11,764	10,058	1.88	2.97	11,764	12,882
30 percent	1.98	2.61	9,561	6,061	1.98	2.78	9,561	7,673	1.98	2.98	9,561	9,528
40 percent	2.06	2.69	8,471	5,390	2.06	2.83	8,471	6,541	2.06	2.98	8,471	7,850
50 percent	2.16	2.73	7,978	4,531	2.16	2.85	7,978	5,490	2.16	2.98	7,978	6,572

TABLE 5.8 / The Optimal EITC for Head-of-Household Filers: Varying All Four Parameters at Once

Parameter	$v = 1$			$v = 2$			$v = 3$			$v = 4$		
	$\mu = .05$	$\mu = .50$	$\mu = .95$	$\mu = .05$	$\mu = .50$	$\mu = .95$	$\mu = .05$	$\mu = .50$	$\mu = .95$	$\mu = .05$	$\mu = .50$	$\mu = .95$
Compensated wage elasticity = 0.1												
Phase-in subsidy rate (percentage)	15	15	15	30	15	30	30	30	45	45	45	45
Maximum credit (percentage of current level)	25	25	25	50	50	200	125	200	200	200	200	200
Length of plateau (dollars)	0	0	0	0	0	9,000	6,000	9,000	9,000	9,000	9,000	9,000
Phase-out tax rate (percentage)	cliff	cliff	cliff	cliff	20	10	50	10	10	20	10	10
Compensated wage elasticity = 0.3												
Phase-in subsidy rate (percentage)	15	15	15	15	15	15	30	30	30	30	45	45
Maximum credit (percentage of current level)	25	25	25	50	25	200	150	200	200	200	200	200
Length of plateau (dollars)	1,500	1,500	1,500	0	9,000	9,000	6,000	9,000	9,000	9,000	9,000	9,000
Phase-out tax rate (percentage)	40	40	40	10	10	10	10	10	10	10	10	10
Compensated wage elasticity = 0.5												
Phase-in subsidy rate (percentage)	15	15	15	15	15	15	30	45	45	45	45	45
Maximum credit (percentage of current level)	25	25	25	25	50	200	200	200	200	200	200	200
Length of plateau (dollars)	3,000	3,000	3,000	6,000	0	9,000	9,000	9,000	9,000	9,000	9,000	9,000
Phase-out tax rate (percentage)	10	10	10	40	10	10	10	10	10	10	10	10

Source: Author's simulations.

each elasticity, 1,440 different EITC configurations are analyzed, and then the one that maximizes social welfare for different values of v and μ is determined.

When v equals 1, a very small EITC is optimal. With a maximum credit that is 25 percent of the current-law level, the welfare saving from inducing additional people to enter the labor force offsets a sufficiently high fraction of the cost of the EITC to allow the net benefit from the EITC to be positive (even though the reference EITC taxpayer receives the same welfare weight as the taxpayers from whom the revenue is raised). When v equals 2, an EITC that is 25 to 50 percent of its current size is optimal (unless μ equals 0.95, in which case an EITC that is double current levels is optimal). With v equal to 3 or 4, the EITC should be substantially larger than current levels. These results (and additional results not shown) indicate that for the current EITC to be optimal, v must be around 2.5. With values much lower than that, a smaller EITC maximizes social welfare, and with higher values a larger EITC would be optimal. These results also indicate that the optimal value for a particular parameter depends heavily on the values that the other parameters take on. Therefore the conjecture that different results might be obtained from maximizing over all EITC parameters simultaneously was correct. For example, in table 5.7 we saw that a phase-out rate of 30 to 40 percent was often optimal given the current structure of the EITC. However, table 5.8 shows that at either the small values of the maximum credit that are optimal when v equals 2 or the larger values that are optimal when v equals 3 or 4, a phase-out rate of 10 percent is generally optimal.

SIMULATION RESULTS FOR MARRIED FILERS

The analysis so far has focused on the 66 percent of EITC recipients who have children and are not married. The optimal EITC for married taxpayers is likely to differ from that for single taxpayers for three reasons. First, married taxpayers who receive the EITC would rarely have been receiving welfare in the absence of an EITC, and therefore the welfare savings that played a big part in reducing the efficiency cost of the EITC for single taxpayers will not be present for married couples. Second, the empirical labor supply literature indicates that the labor supply of prime-age males is relatively inelastic and the labor supply elasticity of secondary earners fairly elastic, particularly on the participation margin. Therefore, we would expect to see most of the impact of the EITC for married couples to be on the labor force participation of the secondary earners.[24] Since the primary earner's earnings will usually be sufficient to reach into the constant region or even the phase-out region, the main labor supply impact of the EITC on married couples is likely to be a negative effect on the labor force participation of women in married couples (both from the income effect of providing more income and the substitution effect from the phase-out of the credit) rather than the positive participation impact that has been found for single EITC recipients. Finally, because the distribution of incomes for married couples is concentrated at the upper end of the phase-out range rather than in the constant region and the beginning of the phase-out, as it is for unmarried EITC recipients, changes in the EITC for married couples, particularly changes in the phase-out rate, will have a greater impact on the average social welfare weight of EITC dollars than they do for single taxpayers.

The simulation model for married couples is similar to that for head-of-household filers. However, two features deserve attention. First, the model assumes that the husband's earnings are fixed and that the household optimizes over the choice of the wife's hours of work. While analytically convenient, this classic "male chauvinist" labor supply model is unlikely to be a good description of the economic behavior of low-income households in which the wife's earnings are often a significant share of total household earnings. Therefore, the results presented here should be seen as illustrating some of the policy trade-offs facing these households, but they may not provide a good guide to the magnitude of the responses to policy changes that would, in fact, occur. Second, the model for married couples assumes that no public assistance is available to them. This assumption means that the lower bound on income for these households is zero rather than the $6,000 that it was for single-parent households. In some simulations, households in which the wife faces a large fixed cost of work end up optimizing at a very low level of income. These observations receive extremely high welfare weights and lead to optimal phase-in rates that would probably not occur in a more realistic model. For this reason, I limit the single-parameter analysis in this section to the maximum level of the credit and to the phase-out tax rate. Results for the phase-in rate are presented only in the context of maximizing four EITC parameters simultaneously.

The Maximum EITC

Tables 5.9 and 5.10 examine the impact of alternative levels for the maximum EITC for married filers. The format of table 5.9 is similar to that of table 5.1. However, the first column now shows the labor force participation rate of the second earner rather than the number of taxpayers with zero annual hours. This column illustrates one of the main differences between the impact of the EITC on household heads and its impact on married filers. For household heads, labor force participation increases as the EITC became more generous. For married households, expanding the EITC reduces the labor force participation of second earners owing to both income and substitution effects.[25] Thus, as table 5.9 shows, with a compensated wage elasticity of 0.3 the labor force participation rate of second earners declines from 78 percent in the absence of an EITC to 75 percent at current levels of the EITC. Additional simulations (not shown) find that simply giving each household a lump-sum transfer equal to their EITC payment would reduce the secondary-earner labor supply to 76 percent, indicating that the income effects are responsible for at least two-thirds of labor force participation responsiveness of these secondary earners.

Comparing the 11th columns of tables 5.9 and 5.1, we see that in many cases

TABLE 5.9 / Impacts of Alternative Levels for the Maximum EITC: Married Filers

Percentage of Current Law Maximum	Labor Force Partic. Rate of Second Earner (1)	Number of Taxpayers (Millions)				Dollars (Millions)					Cost per Dollar's Worth of Utility Gain (11)
		In EITC Phase-In (2)	In EITC Flat Region (3)	In EITC Phase-Out (4)	Beyond Phase-Out (5)	Total EITC Payments (6)	Lost Income Tax Revenue (7)	Additional Welfare Spending (8)	Net Revenue Cost (9)	Welfare Gain (MMEV) from EITC Payments (10)	
Compensated wage elasticity of 0.1											
0	0.772	0.619	0.418	4.512	14.078	0	0	0	0	0	—
50	0.760	0.558	0.630	4.420	14.018	5,350	694	0	6,044	5,287	1.14
100	0.754	0.591	0.874	4.200	13.906	11,447	1,297	0	12,744	11,179	1.14
150	0.696	0.633	1.285	3.906	13.802	19,844	2,191	0	22,035	18,193	1.21
200	0.656	0.717	1.577	3.708	13.624	29,645	3,106	0	32,751	27,062	1.21
Compensated wage elasticity of 0.3											
0	0.784	0.64	0.421	4.274	14.236	0	0	0	0	0	—
50	0.772	0.531	0.597	4.397	14.047	5,096	772	0	5,868	5,009	1.17
100	0.754	0.591	0.874	4.200	13.906	11,447	2,062	0	13,509	10,825	1.25
150	0.713	0.635	1.142	4.051	13.743	19,359	2,909	0	22,267	17,947	1.24
200	0.663	0.652	1.427	4.049	13.443	29,001	3,757	0	32,758	26,084	1.26
Compensated wage elasticity of 0.5											
0	0.796	0.581	0.383	4.377	14.232	0	0	0	0	0	—
50	0.779	0.595	0.590	4.257	14.131	4,950	880	0	5,831	4,739	1.23
100	0.754	0.591	0.874	4.200	13.906	11,447	2,296	0	13,743	10,447	1.32
150	0.684	0.714	1.254	4.192	13.413	20,972	3,795	0	24,767	18,210	1.36
200	0.646	0.731	1.456	4.339	13.049	31,168	5,816	0	36,983	26,734	1.38

TABLE 5.10 / The Costs and Benefits of the EITC at Different Levels of the Maximum Credit: Married Filers (Compensated Wage Elasticity = 0.3)

	μ = .05				μ = .50				μ = .95			
Percentage of Current Law Maximum	Cost per Dollar of Utility	Benefit per Dollar of Utility	MMEV (Millions of Dollars)	Net Benefits (Millions of Dollars)	Cost per Dollar of Utility	Benefit per Dollar of Utility	MMEV (Millions of Dollars)	Net Benefits (Millions of Dollars)	Cost per Dollar of Utility	Benefit per Dollar of Utility	MMEV (Millions of Dollars)	Net Benefits (Millions of Dollars)
$v = 1$												
50	1.76	0.80	5,009	−4,787	1.76	0.83	5,009	−4,613	1.76	0.98	5,009	−3,888
75	1.87	0.79	7,733	−8,370	1.87	0.82	7,733	−8,097	1.87	0.98	7,733	−6,911
100	1.88	0.78	10,825	−11,905	1.88	0.82	10,825	−11,456	1.88	0.98	10,825	−9,721
150	1.86	0.74	17,947	−20,115	1.86	0.80	17,947	−19,110	1.86	0.97	17,947	−15,890
200	1.89	0.71	26,084	−30,810	1.89	0.78	26,084	−29,026	1.89	0.97	26,084	−23,932
$v = 2$												
50	1.76	1.60	5,009	−783	1.76	1.67	5,009	−436	1.76	1.96	5,009	1,015
75	1.87	1.58	7,733	−2,268	1.87	1.65	7,733	−1,722	1.87	1.96	7,733	651
100	1.88	1.55	10,825	−3,514	1.88	1.63	10,825	−2,615	1.88	1.95	10,825	855
150	1.86	1.48	17,947	−6,849	1.86	1.59	17,947	−4,839	1.86	1.95	17,947	1,601
200	1.89	1.42	26,084	−12,322	1.89	1.55	26,084	−8,754	1.89	1.95	26,084	1,435
$v = 3$												
50	1.76	2.40	5,009	3,220	1.76	2.50	5,009	3,742	1.76	2.94	5,009	5,918
75	1.87	2.37	7,733	3,834	1.87	2.47	7,733	4,653	1.87	2.93	7,733	8,212
100	1.88	2.33	10,825	4,878	1.88	2.45	10,825	6,225	1.88	2.93	10,825	11,431
150	1.86	2.22	17,947	6,418	1.86	2.39	17,947	9,433	1.86	2.92	17,947	19,092
200	1.89	2.13	26,084	6,166	1.89	2.33	26,084	11,519	1.89	2.92	26,084	26,801

Source: Author's simulations.

the cost of each dollar's worth of utility gain for married filers is smaller than the same cost for household heads. At first this result may appear surprising since the EITC for married couples does not result in any budgetary savings from reduced welfare spending. Indeed, the lack of reduced welfare spending does explain why at low levels of the EITC, the cost of each dollar's worth of utility gain is higher for the married filers. However, at higher levels of the EITC a second factor dominates: in one-earner households under this male chauvinist model, the EITC is effectively a lump-sum transfer. Similarly, for some women who leave the labor force in response to the EITC, it is the income effect, not the substitution effect, that causes the response, and there is no deadweight loss associated with the EITC payment.

Table 5.10 incorporates social welfare weights to calculate total benefits from the transfers. The reference taxpayer for this table is a married couple with two children and income of $15,300.[26] In this table, we see that with v equal to 1, there should be no EITC. This is true if v is equal to 2, as well, unless μ is very high. Finally, with v equal to 3 an EITC larger than the current level is optimal.

The Phase-Out Tax Rate

Tables 5.11 and 5.12 present simulations of the impact of alternative EITC phase-out rates on married taxpayers. As in previous tables, the last column of table 5.11 shows the revenue cost of each dollar's worth of utility gain. This cost rises steadily with the compensated wage elasticity. Table 5.12 incorporates social welfare weights to calculate total benefits from the transfers. We see that the average benefit for each dollar of utility is lower relative to v for married couples (when μ equals .05 or .50) than it is for head-of-household filers. This occurs because the distribution of married EITC recipients is concentrated toward the end of the phase-out region, among taxpayers who receive lower social welfare weight owing to their higher incomes. The combination of these two factors implies that for v equal to 1 or 2, the costs of the EITC outweigh its benefits (except when v equals 2 and μ equals .95), and a rapid phase-out that minimizes the size of the program is optimal. When v equals 3, the current phase-out rate or one of 30 percent is optimal, so long as μ is not too large.

Maximizing Four Parameters at Once

Table 5.13 presents results from simultaneously maximizing over the same four EITC parameters as in table 5.8. Two results stand out. First, a high phase-out rate—even a cliff in which the entire EITC is eliminated immediately at the end of the plateau—is often part of the optimal EITC. Because the distribution of married taxpayers is quite thick at the end of the current phase-out region, increasing the phase-out rate saves a significant amount of money that would go to individuals with relatively low social welfare weights. Second, rapid phase-in

TABLE 5.11 / Impacts of Alternative Phase-Out Tax Rates: Married Filers

Phase-Out Tax Rate	Labor Force Partic. Rate of Second Earner (1)	Number of Taxpayers (Millions)				Dollars (Millions)					
		In EITC Phase-In (2)	In EITC Flat Region (3)	In EITC Phase-Out (4)	Beyond Phase-Out (5)	Total EITC Payments (6)	Lost Income Tax Revenue (7)	Additional Welfare Spending (8)	Net Revenue Cost (9)	Welfare Gain (MMEV) from EITC Payments (10)	Cost per Dollar's Worth of Utility Gain (11)
Compensated wage elasticity of 0.1											
10 percent	0.721	0.588	0.940	7.820	10.278	19,450	3,308	0	22,758	18,815	1.21
Current law	0.754	0.591	0.874	4.200	13.906	11,447	1,297	0	12,744	11,179	1.14
30 percent	0.746	0.588	1.007	2.581	15.450	9,101	994	0	10,095	8,462	1.19
40 percent	0.745	0.588	1.030	1.716	16.283	7,656	852	0	8,509	7,038	1.21
50 percent	0.746	0.588	1.030	1.048	16.951	6,875	788	0	7,663	6,330	1.21
Compensated wage elasticity of 0.3											
10 percent	0.714	0.591	0.795	7.955	10.231	19,493	4,604	0	24,097	19,033	1.27
Current law	0.754	0.591	0.874	4.200	13.906	11,447	2,062	0	13,509	10,825	1.25
30 percent	0.762	0.591	0.885	2.600	15.496	8,695	1,460	0	10,155	8,071	1.26
40 percent	0.763	0.591	0.885	1.744	16.304	7,223	1,311	0	8,534	6,622	1.29
50 percent	0.765	0.591	0.934	1.165	16.834	6,591	775	0	7,366	5,897	1.25
Compensated wage elasticity of 0.5											
10 percent	0.702	0.602	0.819	8.307	9.846	20,007	5,589	0	25,659	18,995	1.35
Current law	0.754	0.591	0.874	4.200	13.906	11,447	2,296	0	13,743	10,447	1.32
30 percent	0.766	0.602	0.896	2.579	15.480	8,826	1,359	0	10,185	7,600	1.34
40 percent	0.769	0.602	0.940	1.642	16.373	7,308	1,054	0	8,362	6,158	1.36
50 percent	0.767	0.602	1.012	1.004	16.894	6,837	813	0	7,650	5,492	1.39

TABLE 5.12 / The Costs and Benefits of the EITC with Different Phase-Out Rates: Married Taxpayers (Compensated Wage Elasticity = 0.3)

Phase-Out Tax Rate	μ = .05				μ = .50				μ = .95			
	Cost per Dollar of Utility	Benefit per Dollar of Utility	MMEV (Millions of Dollars)	Net Benefits (Millions of Dollars)	Cost per Dollar of Utility	Benefit per Dollar of Utility	MMEV (Millions of Dollars)	Net Benefits (Millions of Dollars)	Cost per Dollar of Utility	Benefit per Dollar of Utility	MMEV (Millions of Dollars)	Net Benefits (Millions of Dollars)
$v = 1$												
10 percent	1.91	0.60	19,033	−24,819	1.91	0.71	19,033	−22,811	1.91	0.96	19,033	−17,939
Current rate	1.88	0.78	10,825	−11,853	1.88	0.82	10,825	−11,420	1.88	0.98	10,825	−9,688
30 percent	1.89	0.84	8,071	−8,473	1.89	0.87	8,071	−8,270	1.89	0.98	8,071	−7,320
40 percent	1.94	0.86	6,622	−7,088	1.94	0.90	6,622	−6,882	1.94	0.99	6,622	−6,280
50 percent	1.88	0.91	5,897	−5,711	1.88	0.92	5,897	−5,638	1.88	0.99	5,897	−5,223
$v = 2$												
10 percent	1.91	1.20	19,033	−13,380	1.91	1.41	19,033	−9,364	1.91	1.93	19,033	381
Current rate	1.88	1.56	10,825	−3,410	1.88	1.64	10,825	−2,544	1.88	1.96	10,825	920
30 percent	1.89	1.68	8,071	−1,692	1.89	1.73	8,071	−1,287	1.89	1.97	8,071	613
40 percent	1.94	1.73	6,622	−1,362	1.94	1.79	6,622	−950	1.94	1.97	6,622	254
50 percent	1.88	1.81	5,897	−364	1.88	1.84	5,897	−219	1.88	1.98	5,897	611
$v = 3$												
10 percent	1.91	1.80	19,033	−1,941	1.91	2.07	19,033	3,140	1.91	2.89	19,033	18,700
Current rate	1.88	2.34	10,825	5,034	1.88	2.46	10,825	6,333	1.88	2.94	10,825	11,529
30 percent	1.89	2.52	8,071	5,090	1.89	2.60	8,071	5,697	1.89	2.95	8,071	8,547
40 percent	1.94	2.59	6,622	4,365	1.94	2.69	6,622	4,982	1.94	2.96	6,622	6,788
50 percent	1.88	2.72	5,897	4,982	1.88	2.76	5,897	5,199	1.88	2.97	5,897	6,445

Source: Author's simulations.

TABLE 5.13 / The Optimal EITC for Married Filers: Varying All Four Parameters at Once

Parameter	v = 1			v = 2			v = 3			v = 4		
	μ = .05	μ = .50	μ = .95	μ = .05	μ = .50	μ = .95	μ = .05	μ = .50	μ = .95	μ = .05	μ = .50	μ = .95
Compensated wage elasticity = 0.1												
Phase-in subsidy rate (percentage)	60	—	—	75	100	60	100	75	30	100	100	30
Maximum credit (percentage of current level)	50	0	0	200	75	200	200	200	200	200	200	200
Length of plateau (dollars)	3,000	—	—	3,000	9,000	9,000	6,000	9,000	9,000	6,000	9,000	9,000
Phase-out tax rate (percentage)	cliff	—	—	cliff	cliff	cliff	cliff	cliff	10	cliff	30	10
Compensated wage elasticity = 0.3												
Phase-in subsidy rate (percentage)	100	75	75	100	60	60	100	60	30	100	100	30
Maximum credit (percentage of current level)	50	25	25	200	50	200	200	200	200	200	200	200
Length of plateau (dollars)	0	0	0	1,500	9,000	9,000	6,000	9,000	9,000	9,000	9,000	9,000
Phase-out tax rate (percentage)	50	50	50	cliff	cliff	cliff	cliff	cliff	10	20	cliff	10
Compensated wage elasticity = 0.5												
Phase-in subsidy rate (percentage)	60	75	75	100	100	60	100	100	30	100	60	30
Maximum credit (percentage of current level)	25	25	25	200	100	200	200	200	200	200	200	200
Length of plateau (dollars)	0	0	0	0	1,500	9,000	6,000	9,000	9,000	9,000	9,000	9,000
Phase-out tax rate (percentage)	20	50	50	cliff	30	cliff	cliff	cliff	10	cliff	cliff	10

Source: Author's simulations.

rates are often part of the optimal structure for the EITC for married couples, though, as I discussed earlier, this result is likely to be a result of my modeling strategy and might not persist in a more realistic model.

CONCLUSION

This chapter has analyzed the optimal design of the EITC in the context of a simple static labor supply model. The results indicate that the efficiency cost of transferring income through the EITC is substantially lower than previous studies have found. It costs upper-income taxpayers only $1.88 to provide a transfer worth $1.00 to EITC recipients. The main reason for the difference among head-of-household filers is that this study takes into account the positive impact of the EITC on labor force participation of single parents and the savings on welfare spending that this labor supply response brings about. Among married filers, it appears that a substantial amount of the labor supply response to the EITC is likely to derive from secondary earners' leaving the labor force. The simulations indicate that this responsiveness is primarily a function of the income effects, rather than the substitution effects, of the credit and therefore that the EITC is effectively a lump-sum transfer for these households.

The chapter also illustrates that the optimal structure of the EITC depends heavily on society's taste for redistribution, something that is difficult to observe. For the current structure of the EITC to be optimal, taxpayers must value one dollar's worth of utility gain for an EITC recipient in the plateau region at roughly 2.5 times a dollar in the hands of the typical non-EITC taxpayer. If society places a relative welfare weight on EITC recipients of 3 or more, then the credit should be expanded substantially. In contrast, if society places a relative weight below 2 on EITC recipients, then the EITC should be reduced or eliminated.

There are two important caveats to keep in mind in interpreting these results. First, the simulations are based on a simple static model of labor supply and use a CES specification for utility. Results could differ with a different specification of preferences, particularly one that focuses on longer-term labor supply decisions such as choices of careers and human capital accumulation. Second, while this chapter has shown that the current design of the EITC may be close to optimal if one is limited to using an EITC-like program, there is a much broader range of policies that could be used to assist low-wage workers, and it is possible that some of them might be preferable to the EITC.

APPENDIX

This appendix describes the CPS data used for the simulations and the details of the calibration methodology.

DATA

Using the March 1999 Current Population Survey (CPS), two samples were created, one of single parents with children and another of married couples with children. For each single parent and each woman in the married couples, I calculated a wage as total annual earnings divided by total annual hours (with a minimum value set at the minimum wage). Wages for nonworkers were imputed as the average for women of their marital status and level of education. The total-hours variable was also used in calibrating the simulations. Nonwage income was calculated as the difference between the CPS measures of adjusted gross income and earnings. Itemized or standard deductions were determined by subtracting the CPS measure of taxable income from the CPS measure of adjusted gross income. Variables on family size and number of children were used both in constructing equivalence scales and in determining the value of the EITC that the family was entitled to. March supplement weights were used to weight the results up to the general population. The total number of EITC recipients in the simulations tend to be fewer than those in Statistics of Income data, in part because of the EITC compliance problem.

SIMULATION METHODOLOGY

The simulations use a CES utility function,

$$U = [(1 - \alpha)Y^{-\rho} + \alpha (L - h)^{-\rho}]^{\frac{-1}{\rho}} - FC,$$

where Y is net income, h is annual hours of work, and L is the total number of hours in a year. For each individual, a set of parameters (α, ρ, and FC) were chosen for each compensated labor supply elasticity. Stern (1976) shows that the first-order condition for maximization of the CES utility function with respect to a linear budget constraint ($Y = I + wh$) is

$$\left[\frac{L - h}{I + wh}\right]^{\rho+1} = \frac{\alpha}{(1 - \alpha)w},$$

where I is virtual income and w is the net wage. Logarithmically differentiating the first-order condition leads to expressions for the uncompensated wage elasticity,

$$\left(\frac{\partial h}{\partial w}\right)\frac{w}{h} = \frac{(I - wh\rho)(L - h)}{h(\rho + 1)(I + wL)}, \tag{5.2}$$

and the income effect,

$$\left(\frac{\partial h}{\partial I}\right) w = \frac{-w(L - h)}{(I + wL)}.$$

Plugging in each individual's wage, actual hours choice, and the virtual income implied by the budget constraint on which they located yields the income effects for the simulations. After choosing a compensated wage elasticity for the simulations, the uncompensated elasticity can be calculated as

$$\varepsilon_w = \varepsilon_c + w \left(\frac{\partial h}{\partial I}\right).$$

Then ρ can be found using equation (5.2) as

$$\rho = \frac{IL - hI - \varepsilon_w (hI + hwL)}{\varepsilon_w (hI + hwL) + wh - wh^2}.$$

In this linear case, α can be solved for as

$$\alpha = \frac{\kappa w}{1 + \kappa w}, \tag{5.3}$$

where

$$\kappa = \left(\frac{L - h}{I + wh}\right)^{\rho+1}.$$

Because, in general, labor supply elasticities depend on the particular budget constraint faced by an individual, the foregoing procedure uses a linear budget constraint so that the chosen compensated wage elasticity will represent a similar underlying responsiveness to changes in the net wage for each individual regardless of how close he or she is to a kink point. However, calibrating preferences using this linear approach and then having the individuals optimize under the true budget constraint resulted in many individuals choosing levels of hours that placed them on a different segment of the budget constraint than their actual choice. Therefore, instead of using equation (5.3) to calibrate α, I searched over values of α so as to match the true hours choice. Since neither the wage nor income elasticity depends on α, this approach preserves the desired labor supply responsiveness while matching the true hours distribution under the full non-linear 1998 budget constraint. However, for about 20 percent of individuals there was no value of α for which they would choose their actual level of hours. I dropped these observations from my simulations and reweighted the remaining observations to replicate the empirical distribution of EITC recipients by EITC region. The dropped observations were people who located at places at which economic theory suggests they should not locate. For example, some people's true hours placed them at places where the marginal tax rate from the welfare system was 100 percent and others located very near the kink at the end of the EITC phase-out. It is unclear what the direction of bias is from dropping these observations. On the one hand, these appear to be people who are not optimizing according to standard theory and therefore may not be very responsive to incentives. On the other hand, theory would suggest that they should make large changes in location from where they are, and it is possible that small perturbations in the budget constraint would cause them to locate far from their current location. Most likely, these observations simply represent an incorrect specification of the budget constraint or underlying model, and there is no obvious reason that the bias from these sorts of errors would go in one direction or the other.

With this sample restriction, my simulations result in all sample members locating at their true hours choice under the current-law budget constraint, and this is true for each compensated wage elasticity. The budget constraint includes the OASDHI payroll tax, the federal income tax, the EITC, and a simplified approximation of the welfare system that provides a $6,000 guarantee to a nonworking household head and then taxes away the benefit at a 100 percent rate as income rises. A more sophisticated model would have higher total welfare benefits (taking into account food stamps as well as Temporary Assistance for Needy Families) and would have marginal benefit-reduction rates below 100 percent owing to the various monthly income disregards that are taken into account in calculating benefit levels. The calibration of the parameter measuring fixed costs of working is described in the text.

NOTES

1. These numbers come from calculations using the 1995 Internal Revenue Services' Statistics of Income public-use data file, inflated into 1999 dollars using the growth rate of personal income.

2. Emmanuel Saez (2000) integrates labor force participation into an optimal tax model and shows that with sufficiently high participation elasticities, transfer schemes like the EITC can be optimal.

3. The impact on married taxpayers is discussed later.

4. See King 1987 and McKenzie 1983 for discussions of this concept.

5. For simplicity, this expression has a single welfare weight for each EITC recipient. In my simulations, the welfare weight for each dollar transferred through the EITC is based on the EITC recipient's utility level after the previous dollar of transfer.

6. For discussions and estimates of the marginal excess burden of taxation, see Ballard et al. 1985, Browning 1987, and Feldstein 1995.

7. In altering taxpayers' labor supply choices, the EITC also affects welfare spending and income tax revenue. The simulations presented in the next section incorporate these additional revenue effects.

8. Because total spending on the EITC is small relative to total government spending, I have made two simplifying assumptions. First, the marginal excess burden from raising revenue from non-EITC recipients to spend on the EITC does not vary with the size of the EITC. Second, the relative social welfare weight society places on non-EITC recipients does not change with the size of the EITC.

9. The CES utility function has been used in many previous labor supply studies. For examples, see Stern 1976, Blinder and Rosen 1985, Auerbach and Kotlikoff 1987, and Zabalza 1983. I use simulation rather than estimation because commonly used structural labor supply models such as the Hausman model have difficulty reproducing the in-sample distribution of hours. In contrast, the simulation methodology used in this chapter results in a distribution of preferences that can reproduce the empirical distribution of hours under the initial budget constraint. For related work on the EITC, see Robert Triest (1996), who conducts simulations using the Hausman model calibrated to the Panel Study of Income Dynamics.

10. This additively separable specification for the fixed costs of work can be thought of as representing the psychological stress associated with the uncertainty of leaving welfare to take a job. Alternatively, if fixed costs derive from purchasing a uniform or a new pair of shoes in order to work, then they would more appropriately be specified as part of Y. If they derive from lost leisure during the job search process, then they should be specified as part of h.

11. I further scale the utilities so that $U_r = 1,000$. This normalization ensures that the main curvature in the social welfare function occurs over the utility range of EITC recipients and that even at the end of the current EITC phase-out range, the welfare weight is still considerably greater than that of non-EITC recipients. For example, when the reference EITC recipient receives a weight of 3 (that is, $v = 3$), an EITC recipient with $30,000 of income receives a weight of 2.93 if $\mu = .95$, a weight of 2.37 if $\mu = .50$, and a weight of 1.92 if $\mu = .05$.

12. Ellwood (1996) explains that the current EITC parameters were designed to achieve President Bill Clinton's 1992 campaign promise that no full-time worker with children would be poor.

13. Many other reforms could be explored. For example, Triest (1996) studies an expansion of the EITC (starting from the 1987 level) in which the phase-in and phase-out rates are held constant but the income over which the phase-in rate is applied is increased. More generally, one could analyze broader reforms that consider the full range of tax benefits provided for families with children rather than simply treating the EITC as the marginal program. Ellwood and Liebman (2001) discuss options for integrating the EITC, child credit, and dependent exemption in order to reduce work and marriage disincentives.

14. For an example, see James K. Glassman, "A Program Gone Bonkers," *Washington Post*, October 12, 1995.

15. For examples see Peter Passell, "Rich Nation, Poor Nation: Is Anyone Looking for a Cure?" *New York Times*, August 13, 1998; Wolf 2001; Krugman 1996.

16. Note that because setting four EITC parameters automatically determines the other two, it is impossible to vary any one of the EITC parameters without varying at least one other. Thus an alternative to the simulation conducted in this subsection would

be to vary the maximum credit while holding phase-in and phase-out rates constant, but this would require me to vary the income range over which the maximum credit applies.

17. In early versions of this chapter I presented results for higher elasticities. However, under higher compensated wage elasticities the labor force participation elasticities became implausibly large (and the welfare cost of transferring income through the EITC became very small).

18. With the simple model of fixed costs used in this chapter, there was no way to set the participation elasticities to be equal across all three compensated wage elasticities (without setting fixed costs to be negative for some individuals—which would lead to a mass of people working exactly one hour a year).

19. Liebman (1998) presents the details of how these participation rates were calculated.

20. It is worth noting that average welfare savings for each new participant in my model is only $2,502 at current program levels and an elasticity of 0.3. Because I have a fairly simple model of the welfare system that does not take full account of food stamps and housing subsidies, it is likely that these savings are understated and that the efficiency cost of the EITC is even lower than these results indicate. Although I incorporate payroll taxes in calculating a person's budget constraint, my revenue calculations exclude payroll tax revenue, since changes in payroll tax revenue will be partially or fully offset by changes in future social security benefits.

21. A marginal excess burden of 0.5 is higher than the traditional estimates of 0.3, based on labor supply elasticities used by Ballard et al. (1985), but lower than some recent taxable income elasticities, such as those in Feldstein (1995), would imply.

22. In comparing my overall cost for each dollar of utility to that of Browning (1995), it is important to note that he assumes a marginal excess burden of taxation of 85.2 cents, while my estimates assume that the marginal excess burden is 50 cents. Even if I used his assumption my cost results would be significantly lower than his.

23. While for a particular individual with a fixed wage, an hours restriction and an earnings restriction can be equivalent, the two types of restrictions can have very different effects on a population with people earning different wages or if people increase their earnings by taking higher-wage jobs rather than by increasing their hours. Michael Keane (1995) argues that hours restrictions are more effective at encouraging work at a low cost. In the United States, however, there has been concern that it would not be possible to collect accurate data on hours worked.

24. Nada Eissa and Hilary Hoynes (1998) find that recent EITC expansions have reduced the labor force participation of married women by 1.2 percentage points.

25. For couples in which the primary earner has earnings in the phase-in range, the EITC can encourage the secondary earner to enter the labor force.

26. This income level was chosen by taking the $12,000 income level from the single-parent reference taxpayer and scaling it up according to the equivalence scale for family size recommended by the Panel on Poverty and Family Assistance (National Research Council 1995).

REFERENCES

Auerbach, Alan, and Lawrence Kotlikoff. 1987. *Dynamic Fiscal Policy*. Cambridge: Cambridge University Press.

Ballard, Charles L., Don Fullerton, John B. Shoven, and John Whalley. 1985. *A General Equilibrium Model for Tax Policy Evaluation*. Chicago: University of Chicago Press.

Blinder, Alan, and Harvey Rosen. 1985. "Notches." *American Economic Review* 75(4): 736–47.

Browning, Edgar K. 1987. "On the Marginal Welfare Cost of Taxation." *American Economic Review* 77 (1): 11–23.

———. 1995. "Effects of the Earned Income Tax Credit on Income and Welfare." *National Tax Journal* 48(1): 23–43.

Eissa, Nada, and Hilary Hoynes. 1998. "The Earned Income Tax Credit and the Labor Supply of Married Couples." Working Paper 6856. Cambridge, Mass.: National Bureau of Economic Research.

Eissa, Nada, and Jeffrey B. Liebman. 1996. "Labor Supply Response to the Earned Income Tax Credit." *Quarterly Journal of Economics* 111(2): 605–37.

Ellwood, David T. 1996. "Welfare Reform As I Knew It." *American Prospect* 7(26): 22–29.

Ellwood, David T., and Jeffrey B. Liebman. 2001. "The Middle-Class Parent Penalty." *Tax Policy and the Economy* 15: 1–40.

Feldstein, Martin. 1995. "Tax Avoidance and the Deadweight Loss of the Income Tax." Working Paper 5055. Cambridge, Mass.: National Bureau of Economic Research.

Keane, Michael P. 1995. "A New Idea for Welfare Reform." *Federal Reserve Bank of Minneapolis Quarterly Review* 19(2): 2–28.

Killingsworth, Mark, and James J. Heckman. 1986. "Female Labor Supply: A Survey." *Handbook of Labor Economics* 1: 103–204.

King, Mervyn A. 1987. "The Empirical Analysis of Tax Reforms." In *Advances in Econometrics: Fifth World Congress,* edited by Truman F. Bewley. Vol. 2. Cambridge: Cambridge University Press.

Krugman, Paul. 1996. "First, Do No Harm." *Foreign Affairs* 75(4): 164–70.

Liebman, Jeffrey B. 1998. "The Impact of the Earned Income Tax Credit on Incentives and Income Distribution." *Tax Policy and the Economy* 12: 83–118.

MaCurdy, Thomas, David Green, and Harry Paarsch. 1992. "Assessing Empirical Approaches for Analyzing Taxes and Labor Supply." *Journal of Human Resources* 25(3): 415–90.

McKenzie, George W. 1983. *Measuring Economic Welfare: New Methods*. Cambridge: Cambridge University Press.

Meyer, Bruce D., and Dan T. Rosenbaum. 1999. "Welfare, the Earned Income Tax Credit, and the Labor Supply of Single Mothers." Working Paper 7363. Cambridge, Mass.: National Bureau of Economic Research (September).

National Research Council. Panel on Poverty and Family Assistance. 1995. *Measuring Poverty: A New Approach*. Washington, D.C.: National Academy Press.

Saez, Emmanuel. 2000. "Optimal Income Transfer Programs: Intensive Versus Extensive Labor Supply Responses." Working Paper 7708. Cambridge, Mass.: National Bureau of Economic Research (May).

Stern, N. H. 1976. "On the Specification of Models of Optimum Income Taxation." *Journal of Public Economics* 6(1): 123–62.

Triest, Robert K. 1996. "The Efficiency Cost of Increased Progressivity." In *Tax Progressivity and Income Inequality*, edited by Joel Slemrod. Cambridge: Cambridge University Press.

Wolf, Edward N. 2001. "The Rich Get Richer; and Why the Poor Don't." *American Prospect*, February 12, 2001.

Zabalza, Antonio. 1983. "The CES Utility Function, Non-linear Budget Constraints, and Labor Supply: Results on Female Participation and Hours." *Economic Journal* 93(370): 312–30.

Part III

Compliance Problems

Chapter 6

Noncompliance with the Earned Income Tax Credit: The Determinants of the Misreporting of Children

Janet McCubbin

T he Earned Income Tax Credit (EITC) was created in 1975, largely to offset the burden and labor force disincentives associated with social security taxes levied on low-income workers (U.S. Senate 1975, 33). In keeping with these goals, the credit was set at 10 percent of earnings up to $4,000. The credit was reduced by ten cents for every dollar of income in excess of $4,000 and was therefore completely phased out when income reached $8,000. The creators of the EITC also hoped that the credit would offset the work disincentives inherent in the welfare system. Because individuals with children are the most likely to be eligible for welfare benefits, the credit was limited to workers maintaining a household for a dependent child under the age of nineteen. The EITC has been modified since 1975, but the credit is still targeted to low-income workers, particularly those with children.

As with all tax provisions (and all transfer programs), efforts to target EITC benefits to certain groups can exacerbate compliance problems and increase administrative costs. For example, very low-income persons have an incentive to overreport income, and those with moderately higher incomes face an incentive to underreport income. Persons with no children or only one child might benefit from overreporting the number of children. In addition, some taxpayers might misunderstand the EITC eligibility criteria and make unintentional reporting errors.

To some extent, noncompliance is merely a transfer from the government to individuals, which has little effect on economic efficiency.[1] However, if there are noncompliant taxpayers, then tax rates must be raised or government expenditures must be reduced. Higher tax rates generally do result in efficiency losses, and reductions in government expenditures may prevent the achievement of other social goals. In addition, when noncompliance is advantageous, individuals might divert resources from productive activities to cheating activities. Furthermore, the tax authority must use resources to prevent, detect and punish cheating; and compliant filers must spend resources on documenting their compliance. This diversion of resources is likely to lead to losses in efficiency. On the other hand, to the extent that noncompliance reduces the effective marginal tax rate, it might mitigate distortions introduced by taxation and improve economic efficiency.

There are equity effects to consider as well. When noncompliance is undetected, noncompliant taxpayers are better off than compliant taxpayers with the same income and family characteristics, violating horizontal equity. In addition, to the extent that cheating reduces the targeting of the EITC, it might reduce the progressivity of the tax system and reduce the value of the EITC to policymakers and taxpayers.[2]

In designing the EITC, policymakers must consider these effects, just as they consider the effects of the credit on labor supply, poverty rates, and so forth. Therefore in this chapter, I examine the extent and nature of EITC noncompliance in 1994 (the most recent year for which compliance data are available). I find that the misreporting of qualifying children is the most important EITC error and was associated with an estimated $3.1 billion in excess EITC claims. I then estimate the probability that a taxpayer erroneously claims an EITC-qualifying child as a function of the size of the EITC and other variables. I find that the probability of noncompliance is positively correlated with the size of the credit and that reducing the EITC by 10 percent would reduce the amount of EITC overclaimed attributable to child misreporting by about 14 percent. However, scaling back the EITC would also reduce the amount of credit that could be claimed by compliant taxpayers, who constitute the majority of EITC recipients. Therefore reducing the EITC would reduce the EITC overclaim rate (defined as the amount claimed in error divided by the total amount claimed) by only a negligible amount. Efforts to reduce the frequency of unintentional errors and enhance the effectiveness of Internal Revenue Service (IRS) enforcement activities might bring about greater improvements in EITC error rates, at a lower cost to compliant taxpayers.

NONCOMPLIANCE IN 1994

The Internal Revenue Service has not conducted a comprehensive study of taxpayer compliance since 1988.[3] However, the IRS's Criminal Investigations Division (CID) has more recently examined the returns of 2,046 randomly selected who filed EITC claims for tax year 1994. The sample represents a population of 15 million returns and $17.2 billion in EITC claims accepted by the IRS between mid-January and mid-April 1995. (During the entire filing year, 19 million tax return units claimed $21.1 billion in EITC; IRS 1997a, table A.)

The EITC errors identified in the study include both intentional noncompliance and unintentional reporting mistakes, and the two types of errors are not readily distinguishable in the data. However, returns were selected after mathematical and clerical errors were corrected, as part of routine IRS processing. Therefore these simple computational errors are not counted as noncompliance in this study.

It is important to keep in mind that the IRS audited only taxpayers who claimed the EITC. The IRS found that some taxpayers who claimed the credit had not claimed the full amount to which they were entitled. These taxpayers failed to claim an estimated $293 million, or 1.7 percent of the total EITC claimed for the same period. However, this estimate of unclaimed EITC excludes the amount that should have been claimed by taxpayers who did not claim any EITC at all. (John Karl Scholz [1994] estimates that for tax year 1990, 13.6 to 19.5 percent of eligible taxpayers failed to claim the EITC.) Because the IRS study excluded all nonparticipants, the data can be used to estimate the amount of EITC that was claimed (and the portion that was claimed in error), but they cannot be used to estimate the total amount of EITC that should have been claimed. Therefore in the remaining analysis, estimates of erroneous EITC claims and error rates reflect excess amounts of EITC only (and not excess claims net of amounts that were not claimed).

Error Rates in the EITC

The results of these examinations indicate that $4.4 billion in excess EITC was claimed during the January to April study period.[4] This accounted for 25.8 percent of the total EITC claimed for the same period. About 12 million taxpayers claimed the credit for workers with EITC-qualifying children during the study period. These taxpayers claimed an estimated $4,368 million in excess EITC amounts, resulting in an overclaim rate of 26.1 percent for this group. About 3 million taxpayers claimed the smaller credit for workers without EITC-qualifying children during the study period. The CID data indicate that these taxpayers claimed $81 million in excess EITC, resulting in an overclaim rate of 15.7 percent for this group.[5]

These estimated error rates are for amounts claimed rather than amounts paid and do not reflect the effect of IRS enforcement activities. The IRS and the Treasury Department estimated that if IRS enforcement procedures in effect during the 1995 filing season were taken into account, the error rate would have been reduced from 25.8 percent to about 23.5 percent. The IRS and the Treasury also estimated that if certain new enforcement procedures first in effect during the 1997 filing season had been in effect in 1995, the error rate would have been reduced further, to about 20.7 percent.

Errors Associated with the Qualifying-Child Criteria

Taxpayers with one or more qualifying children receive a substantially larger credit than taxpayers with no qualifying children. A qualifying child must be under the age of nineteen, a full-time student under the age of twenty-four, or permanently and totally disabled. The child must be the filer's own child (including an adopted child or stepchild), grandchild, or foster child.[6] The child must have lived with the filer in the United States for more than half of the tax year if the child is the taxpayer's own child or grandchild or for the entire tax year if the child is the taxpayer's foster child. If a child is the qualifying child of more than one person (because more than one person lived with and was related to the child), then only the taxpayer with the higher adjusted gross income (AGI) may claim the credit. The taxpayer must provide a taxpayer identification number (typically, a social security number) for each child claimed. For tax year 1994, children under the age of one were exempt from the social security number requirement.[7]

The sources of EITC overclaims among taxpayers with and without claims for EITC-qualifying children are summarized in table 6.1. The largest source of EITC errors was the failure to meet the qualifying-child criteria. Excess EITC claims on returns on which a qualifying child was claimed in error and for which no other error was detected amounted to $2,605 million (58.6 percent of the total amount overclaimed). Another $475 million in excess EITC (10.7 percent of the total) was associated with erroneous child claims on returns that also had income or filing status errors (or both).

The failure to meet the residency test was the most important qualifying-child error. An estimated $1,470 million in EITC was erroneously claimed by taxpayers who did not live with the qualifying child for the required length of time during the tax year and who did not make any other detected qualifying-child error. Another $254 million in errors was associated with failure of the residency test in combination with failure of some other qualifying-child criteria (most often the relationship test).

About $782 million in EITC overclaims occurred on returns filed by taxpayers

TABLE 6.1 / Sources of EITC Overclaims for Tax Year 1994 (Millions of Dollars)

Type of Return	Taxpayers Claiming Qualifying Children	Taxpayers Not Claiming Qualifying Children	All EITC Claimants
Returns with qualifying-child errors	3,080	—	3,080
Residency	1,724	—	1,724
Relationship	559	—	559
AGI tiebreaker	782	—	782
Age of child	202	—	202
Other	136	—	136
Returns with filing-status errors	1,362	32	1,394
Returns with income errors	445	49	494
All returns with EITC overclaims	4,368	81	4,448

Source: Author's tabulations of IRS's 1994 EITC compliance study data.
Note: The sum of EITC overclaims on returns with each type of error exceeds the total amount of EITC overclaims because some returns have more than one type of error.

who failed the AGI tiebreaker test. In these cases, both the taxpayer and another person were eligible to claim the same qualifying child, but the taxpayer included in the sample had the lower adjusted gross income and should not have claimed the credit. An estimated 38.0 percent of the overclaimed amount occurred in cases in which the taxpayer's parent had the higher adjusted gross income and was eligible to claim the credit. About 46.8 percent of the overclaimed amount occurred in cases in which the taxpayer's boyfriend or girlfriend had the higher adjusted gross income and was deemed eligible to claim the credit. (In a number of these cases, accounting for 24.9 percent of the total EITC error associated with the tiebreaker, it appears that the taxpayer's boyfriend or girlfriend was not the parent of the child.)[8] In the remaining cases, the taxpayer with the higher adjusted gross income was another friend or relative of the sampled taxpayer or was a person whose relationship to the taxpayer could not be determined.

The IRS did not collect additional information on the taxpayer with the higher adjusted gross income. Hence it is impossible to determine whether the filer with the higher income claimed the credit or was eligible to claim credit. (A taxpayer with a higher adjusted gross income but with no earned income or with adjusted gross income or earnings above the EITC threshold would not be allowed to claim the credit. In that case, no EITC for either taxpayer is allowed.) Because some taxpayers with higher adjusted gross incomes could have claimed the credit but did not, and because the IRS study did not account for EITC nonparticipation, the importance of violations of the AGI tiebreaker rule is probably overstated by these data.

An estimated $559 million in EITC overclaims occurred on returns in which the child failed the relationship test, and about $202 million in errors was associated with the failure of the age test. About $63 million in errors occurred in cases in which the claimed child did not appear to exist at all. I could not determine the nature of the qualifying-child error in some cases (because of missing or inconsistent data); these cases accounted for about $73 million in EITC overclaims.

Errors Associated with Filing Status

Another important source of error is the misreporting of filing status by married taxpayers. Taxpayers who use the "married filing separately" status may not claim the EITC. In addition, taxpayers who are married and filing jointly may receive a smaller credit than they would receive filing individually as unmarried persons. Suppose, for example, that taxpayers A and B are married and have three children, that taxpayer A has earnings of $20,000, and taxpayer B has earnings of $10,000. This couple is not eligible for any EITC in 1994, because their combined earned income exceeds $25,296. However, taxpayer A would be eligible for a credit of $596 based on one qualifying child or $932 based on two children; taxpayer B would be eligible for a credit of $2,038 based on one qualifying child or $2,528 based on two children. Therefore if taxpayers A and B misreport their filing status (and file as single persons or heads of households), then they can claim as much as $3,124 in combined Earned Income Tax Credit, even if they do not duplicate without duplicating their qualifying-child claims.[9]

The misreporting of filing status was associated with an estimated $1,394 million in EITC overclaims, or 31.3 percent of the total amount overclaimed during the study period. (Some returns with filing-status errors also had income or qualifying-child errors that contributed to the EITC reduction or denial.) About three-fourths of these errors occurred on returns for which the IRS changed the filing status of the sampled taxpayer from single or head of household to married filing separately, resulting in a complete denial of the credit. In the remaining cases, the IRS changed the filing status to married filing jointly, and the addition of the spouse's income to the sampled return resulted in a reduction or the denial of the credit. The IRS did not record any additional information about the spouse who was not sampled, and it is not known whether the other spouse also claimed the EITC.[10]

Income-Reporting Errors

The EITC initially increases with earned income, then remains constant as income rises, and finally decreases with rising income until it is completely phased out. The phase-in rate applicable for tax year 1994 was 7.65 percent on earnings up to $4,000 for filers with no qualifying children; 26.3 percent on earnings up to $7,750 for filers with one child; and 30 percent on earnings up to $8,425 for filers with two or more children. Hence the maximum credit ranged from $306 to $2,528, depending on the number of qualifying children. The credit for taxpayers without children was phased out once earnings or adjusted gross income reached $5,000, at a rate of 7.65 percent, and was completely phased out once income reached $9,000. The credit for filers with one child was phased out at a rate of 15.98 percent applied to income over $11,000 and was completely phased out at income of $23,755. The credit for filers with two or more children was phased out at a rate of 17.68 percent of income over $11,000 and was entirely phased out once income reached $25,296.[11]

Income underreporting (excluding amounts added to the sampled taxpayer's return but initially reported by a spouse who filed separately) was associated with about $432 million, or 9.7 percent, of the excess EITC claimed. Wages account for the largest amount of unreported income ($1.5 billion), followed by self-employment earnings ($1.3 billion) and unemployment compensation ($476 million).

Because a taxpayer must have earned income to receive the EITC, and because for very low-income workers the amount of the credit increases with earned income, some taxpayers may be induced to overreport income. This possibility has concerned a number of policymakers and researchers, particularly as the EITC phase-in rate has increased to exceed the self-employment tax rate of

15.3 percent (see, for example, Steuerle 1993). However, income overreporting was rarely observed in the tax year 1994 data, being associated with only about 1 percent of the EITC overclaim.[12]

The reason that income overreporting occurs much less frequently than income underreporting is not clear. It is possible that taxpayers in the phase-out range find it relatively easy to increase the EITC amount by failing to attach one W-2 form, while taxpayers with earnings in the phase-in range find it more difficult to increase the EITC amount by fabricating a W-2 form or self-employment income (which would entail fabricating a schedule C or F and a schedule SE). In addition, a taxpayer is probably more likely to unintentionally omit earnings (by, for example, misplacing a W-2 form from a temporary or part-time job) than to unintentionally overreport earnings (by, say, double-counting income from a W-2 form).[13] Third, while the EITC increases with earnings for recipients in the phase-in range, Aid to Families with Dependent Children and food stamp benefits decrease with earnings. Low-income EITC recipients might not want to overreport income for fear of jeopardizing eligibility for other benefits.[14] Finally, because overreported self-employment income would be subject to self-employment tax, the net benefit of overreporting a dollar of earnings for taxpayers in the phase-in range (about 12 cents for a taxpayer with one child) is less than the benefit of underreporting a dollar of income for taxpayers with income in the phase-out range (about 30 cents for a self-employed taxpayer with one child, or 45 cents if the taxpayer is subject to income tax).

Complexity, Refundability, and Other Issues

Some tax professionals have suggested that complexity in the definition of a qualifying child—in particular, differences in the definitions of dependent children and EITC-qualifying children—contributes to errors (see, for example, American Institute of Certified Public Accountants 1997). The definitions of dependent children and EITC-qualifying children have never been identical, and they were made less similar in 1990, primarily in an effort to simplify the administration of the EITC. However, at least 16.4 million (or 93.9 percent) of the EITC-qualifying children claimed during the study period were also claimed as dependents.[15] In 13.1 million of the matched cases, both the EITC claim and the dependent exemption were allowed. In 1.7 million cases, both the EITC-qualifying child and the dependent claim were denied. In about 1.0 million cases, only the EITC claim was denied; and in about 0.7 million cases, only the dependent exemption claim was denied. When both the EITC claim and the dependent exemption were denied, the failure of the residency test was the most common reason for the denial of the EITC claim (accounting for 1.1 million cases). The IRS did not record the reason for denying the dependent exemption. When only the EITC was denied, the most common reason for denying the EITC child was the failure of the AGI tiebreaker (about 0.4 million cases).

Given that different determinations were made about the EITC child and dependent claims in 1.6 million cases, it is possible that confusion about the different definitions is contributing to EITC and dependent exemption errors. However, the denial of both the EITC-qualifying-child claim and the dependent claim in 1.7 million cases highlights the fact that many of the errors that cause EITC overclaims also result in mistakes on other parts of the tax return. The misreporting of income, marital status, and information about children affects the tax return filer's entire tax liability, not only the EITC. From the CID data on EITC claimants alone, it is difficult to determine how important EITC noncompliance is relative to noncompliance with respect to other parts of the tax code. In addition, it is difficult to determine the extent to which reporting errors are made in response to incentives created by the EITC and the extent to which they are attributable to other incentives.

More generally, it is virtually impossible, using the CID data, to distinguish taxpayer confusion from intentional misreporting. The IRS did ask agents to indicate whether they thought that each EITC overclaim was intentional or unintentional, and using this information, IRS officials have testified that "about 50 percent" of overclaims were attributable to unintentional mistakes (see Brown 1997). However, the terms "intentional" and "unintentional" do not correspond directly to the types of errors defined in the tax code, and IRS agents were given no specific criteria on which to base a determination of intent.

Perhaps as a consequence of the lack of specific instructions about taxpayer intent, there are observations that appear to involve similar circumstances but are coded differently. (It should be noted, however, that only part of the information available to IRS agents was transcribed and made available for analysis; hence unobserved differences in the cases could explain variation in determinations of intent.) In addition, some IRS examiners were much more likely than others to code errors as intentional; these differences in examiner behavior remain statistically significant, even after controlling for the size and type of error. Furthermore, errors made by men filing as single or as head of household were more likely to be coded as intentional than similar errors made by unmarried women and by married taxpayers. It is not clear why men would tend to make intentional mistakes, whereas women and couples filing jointly would be more likely to make unintentional errors. It is possible that the determinations about taxpayer intent reflect primarily the IRS agent's certainty about the presence of an EITC error rather than the nature of the taxpayer's behavior.

Lisa Schiffren (1995) and others have suggested that the refundable nature of the EITC (that is, the fact that the EITC may exceed the recipient's income and self-employment tax liabilities) invites noncompliance. The CID data on EITC claimants do not appear to support this theory. For example, the EITC overclaim rate among EITC claimants with no income tax or self-employment tax liability (before taking the EITC into account), who would have received the entire EITC in the form of a refund, was 12.7 percent. The overclaim rate among EITC claimants with some income or self-employment tax liability, who therefore would have received less than the entire EITC as a refund, was 37.7 percent. This suggests that taxpayers might be more likely to claim the EITC to avoid a tax liability than to generate a refund. (It is also possible that filers who are not eligible for the EITC are also not eligible to claim dependent exemptions, the head-of-household filing status, or other items that reduce taxable income and taxes and are therefore more likely to have a tax liability. The effect of refunds and balances due on compliance is examined more carefully later in this chapter.)

During the study period, 31.2 percent of EITC claims were filed electronically, and 68.8 percent were filed on paper returns. Some have worried that electronic filing will invite noncompliance, because the IRS has committed itself to processing electronic returns more quickly and might therefore have less time to check for errors (see Sparrow 1993 and Yin 1995 for examples). Others have hypothesized that the speed of the refund—the lure of quick money—makes cheating by electronic filing more attractive. In fact, electronic returns were subject to more rigorous verification of social security numbers in 1994 than were paper returns, and the CID data show almost no difference in the EITC overclaim rates for paper returns (26.1 percent) and electronic returns (25.3 percent). Perhaps the attraction of filing electronically and receiving the refund quickly is outweighed by the additional scrutiny applied to electronic returns in 1994.

Some financial institutions offer refund anticipation loans, whereby taxpayers use their expected tax refund as collateral for a short-term loan. The IRS data indicate that 47.9 percent of electronic filers applied for a refund anticipation loan, though the data do not indicate which filers actually received a loan. Some tax administrators have suggested that refund anticipation loans encourage noncompliance because they make it easier for filers to "take the money and run" (see Samuels 1995 and Sparrow 1993 for examples). The tendency to use a refund anticipation loan may also be correlated with noncompliance (but not actually cause noncompliance) if filers with a high rate of time preference are simultaneously more likely to overclaim the EITC and more likely to use refund anticipation loans. In fact, the gross overclaim rate among filers who applied for loans (26.6 percent) is not markedly higher than the rate among filers who did not (about 24.0 percent). This may be because faster refunds do not encourage noncompliance and are not associated with noncompliance or because lenders screen out some suspicious claims before they are filed.

In addition, the CID data show virtually no difference in the error rates of taxpayers who used paid preparers and those who prepared their own returns. An estimated 44.2 percent of EITC claimants filed their own returns; the error rate among these returns was 26.1 percent. About 54.2 percent of the taxpayers represented by the study used paid preparers, and the EITC overclaim rate among these returns was 25.7 percent.[16] However, a deeper analysis shows substantial differences in error rates across different types of preparers. About 8.9 percent of EITC claims during the study period were prepared by attorneys, certified public accountants, or enrolled agents. The EITC overclaim rate among these returns was 14.8 percent. Another 15.6 percent of EITC claims were prepared by large, nationally recognized tax preparation services. The error rate among these returns was 23.1 percent. About 29.7 percent of EITC claims were completed by other types of paid preparers. These other types of preparers include persons who are not attorneys, certified public accountants, or enrolled agents and who are self-employed or working for small local firms. The "other" category also includes cases in which the type of preparer could not be determined. The error rate among these EITC claims was 30.6 percent.

There do not appear to be substantial differences in the types of errors made by different kinds of preparers. Rather, some types of preparers appear to be better than others at comprehending and applying all of the EITC eligibility criteria to their clients' situations. In a number of cases, the IRS agents reported that the tax return preparers had not asked the taxpayers for all of the information needed to determine their EITC eligibility. It is also possible that differences in the overclaim rates reflect different characteristics of the clients who choose different kinds of preparers.[17]

MODELING THE DETERMINANTS OF QUALIFYING-CHILD MISREPORTING

Findings from the 1985 and 1988 Taxpayer Compliance Measurement Program studies influenced decisions to modify the EITC eligibility criteria in 1990 and subsequent years.[18] Noncompliance rates estimated from the TCMP data and these new estimates for tax year 1994 continue to influence policy debates about the appropriate size and structure of the EITC. For example, in 1995, the U.S. Senate proposed reductions in the EITC to prevent the abuse of the credit (U.S. Senate 1995). It is not immediately clear, however, how taxpayer noncompliance is expected to change with the size and structure of the EITC. Therefore, I estimate the probability that an ineligible taxpayer claims an EITC-qualifying child, given the resulting EITC and tax benefits and other variables.[19]

Creating a Data Set of Ineligible Claimants and Nonclaimants

Data for ineligible EITC claimants alone tell us little about the determinants of EITC noncompliance. Rather, a sample containing both taxpayers who are not eligible for the EITC and do not claim the credit and taxpayers who are not eligible for the EITC but do claim it—that is, a sample of both compliant and noncompliant taxpayers—is needed to estimate the determinants of EITC noncompliance. The EITC compliance study does not include data on taxpayers who do not claim the EITC, and the IRS has not conducted a study of compliance among the larger population of all individual income tax return filers since 1988. The IRS's Statistics of Income Division (SOI) does collect tax return data for a large stratified sample of returns in every year. These returns are not audited, but I can identify taxpayers who do not claim the EITC, even though they report income and other characteristics that would make them eligible for the credit if they had a qualifying child.[20] These observations can be combined with the observations from the CID study to construct a sample of compliant and noncompliant taxpayers without qualifying children with which to examine the determinants of erroneous EITC claims.

The sample of audited EITC claimants includes 534 taxpayers who erroneously claimed a qualifying child and reported income and other characteristics in such a way that they appeared eligible for the credit given one qualifying child. These 534 ineligible claimants represented 2.2 million returns for tax year 1994, with excess EITC claims of $3.0 billion (see the top panel of table 6.2). To identify their compliant counterparts in the SOI data, I eliminate taxpayers who claim EITC-qualifying children. I also eliminate taxpayers who, based on their reported income and other characteristics, would not be eligible for the EITC even if they had a qualifying child; returns filed for years other than 1994; and returns filed before mid-January or after mid-April. The result is a sample of 7,596 observations, representing 24.8 million tax returns (see the bottom panel of table 6.2).

On average, each of the 534 observations in the noncompliant portion of the sample represents 4,064 returns, whereas each of the 7,596 observations in the compliant portion of the sample represents 3,266 returns. If I modeled EITC noncompliance using unweighted observations, my estimates would be biased, because compliant filers are sampled at a higher rate and therefore are over-represented relative to noncompliant filers.[21] Therefore I use weighted observations for the remaining analysis. The combined weighted sample indicates that for tax year 1994, 27.0 million low-income filers were ineligible for the EITC because they did not have a qualifying child, and 2.2 million (or 8.0 percent) of these ineligible filers erroneously claimed the EITC.

It might seem problematic to combine observations from two different data

TABLE 6.2 / Sample of Noncompliant and Compliant Low-Income Taxpayers Ineligible to Claim EITC-Qualifying Children, Tax Year 1994

Gender and Reported Filing Status	Unweighted Number	Weighted Number
Noncompliant (claiming EITC qualifying-child)	534	2,170,000
Males filing as single or head of household	404	1,020,000
Females filing as single or head of household	116	901,000
Married couples filing jointly and widowed filers	14	249,000
Compliant (not claiming EITC-qualifying child)	7,596	24,807,000
Males filing as single or head of household	2,986	11,523,000
Females filing as single or head of household	2,876	10,333,000
Married couples filing jointly and widowed filers	1,734	2,951,000
Total number of ineligible filers	8,130	26,978,000

Source: Author's tabulations of IRS's 1994 EITC compliance study data and 1994 Statistics of Income individual income tax return data.

sets in this way. If the observations from the two data sets differed in some way that was correlated with the benefit of claiming a child, then the estimated effect of the EITC on compliance would be biased. However, the key information source for both sets of observations is the tax return as it was filed by the taxpayer. Both data sets employ stratified random samples with known selection criteria, and nearly all of the variables in the econometric model are defined identically for observations in the two data sets (exceptions are addressed in the discussion that follows). Estimates about the population of EITC claimants made from the two data sets are quite similar. Therefore I am confident that the combined data set adequately represents the population of low-income workers who do not have EITC-qualifying children.[22]

A Theoretical Model of Noncompliance

Now consider the choice of whether or not to report a child for a fully informed taxpayer who does not have a child. Suppose that the taxpayer's utility maximization problem is

$$\text{Max}_{y_r, x_r} [1 - p] \, U \, (y_t - \tau[y_r - \delta x_r] + E(y_r, x_r)) + pU(y_t - \tau [y_r - \delta x_r]$$
$$+ E(y_r, x_r) - \pi(y_t - y_r, x_r - x_t, T, \gamma)),$$

subject to

$$0 \le x_r \le 2,$$

where the variable y_r is reported income, x_r is the reported number of children, y_t and x_t are the true values of income and the number of children, p is the probability of detection, τ is the income tax rate, δ is the amount of income exempt from tax for each reported child, $E(y_r, x_r)$ is the EITC as a function of reported income and the reported number of children, π is the penalty for noncompliance, T is the tax underreported plus the EITC overreported—that is, $T = \tau[y_t - \delta x_t - y_r + \delta x_r] + E(y_r, x_r) - E(y_t, x_t)$—and γ is a vector of demographic characteristics.[23]

In this example, the specification of the penalty function is crucial to the theoretical predictions of the model. There are essentially five possible outcomes when an individual tax return filer is found to have understated his or her federal tax liability: no penalty, a civil penalty equal to 20 percent of the tax understatement, a civil penalty equal to 75 percent of the tax understatement, criminal sanctions, or a combination of criminal and civil penalties. A taxpayer is subject to the 20 percent penalty if the tax understatement exceeds the greater of 10 percent of the required tax or $5,000 or if the understatement is the result of "negligence or disregard of rules or regulations" (Internal Revenue Code, section 6662). The taxpayer is subject to the 75 percent penalty if the understatement is "attributable to fraud" (Internal Revenue Code, section 6663). Potential criminal sanctions include fines of up to $100,000 and imprisonment of up to three years for statements on a tax return that the taxpayer "does not believe to be true and correct as to every material matter" (Internal Revenue Code, section 7206). Hence a fraudulent tax return statement could yield a civil sanction of 75 percent of the tax understatement plus additional criminal penalties, whereas a taxpayer who has not made a substantial understatement and who has not made an understatement attributable to negligence, disregard, or fraud will be liable only for the understated tax and interest.[24]

Given this penalty structure, the taxpayer's diligence and intent (and the tax authority's determination about the taxpayer's diligence and intent), as well as the tax understatement and EITC overstatement, determine the marginal penalty that is assessed. Therefore taxpayer demographic variables (which might include the taxpayer's age, education, household composition, filing history, and the complexity of the tax situation) enter into the penalty function, $\pi(\cdot)$. In addition, I specify the penalty as a function of the variables $y_t - y_r$ and $x_r - x_t$ to reflect the possibility that the tax authority's determination about the filer's diligence and intent is influenced by the size of the reporting error, regardless of the size of the net tax understatement, T. The terms $y_t - y_r$ and $x_r - x_t$ also serve to distinguish income-reporting errors from child-reporting errors and thereby allow for the possibility that the tax authority's determination about the filer's diligence and intent is influenced by the type of error, regardless of the impact on T.

The first-order condition describing the optimal number of children reported is

$$[1 - p]U'_1 \left[\tau\delta + \frac{\partial E(y_r, x_r)}{\partial x_r}\right] + pU'_2 \left[\tau\delta + \frac{\partial E(y_r, x_r)}{\partial x_r}\right]\left[1 - \frac{\partial \pi}{\partial T}\right] - pU'_2 \frac{\partial \pi}{\partial x_r} = 0,$$

where the first term is the expected marginal benefit of misreporting a child (weighted by marginal utility in the unaudited state, denoted 1) and the second and third terms represent the expected marginal cost of misreporting a child (weighted by marginal utility in the audited state, denoted 2). The optimal number of reported children will be positive if the first-order condition is positive when evaluated at reported income equal to y_r and reported number of children equal to zero.[25] Because the taxpayer chooses reported income as well as the reported number of qualifying children, the EITC and other variables conditioned on reported income may be endogenous. The model estimated here assumes that all of the explanatory variables are exogenous. The results are not markedly different when a simultaneous equations model that accounts for the possible endogeneity of income is estimated.

Tax Variables

The key explanatory variable is $\partial E(y_r, x_r)/\partial x_r$—the increase in the EITC that a taxpayer with no child can receive by reporting one child, conditional on reported income. Based on the theoretical model previously outlined, I expect the incidence of noncompliance to increase with the size of the EITC benefit. The average increase in EITC obtainable by reporting one qualifying child among taxpayers who do not report a child is $1,101; the average EITC benefit of claiming one child among taxpayers who do report at least one child is $1,290.

Taxpayers who report a qualifying child might reduce their income tax liability before credit, in addition to obtaining the EITC. In fact, nearly all of the taxpayers who erroneously claimed a qualifying child also claimed one or more dependent exemptions; 83 percent of taxpayers who erroneously claimed a qualifying child also claimed the head-of-household filing status. Given their reported incomes, compliant taxpayers (those who did not claim a qualifying child) could expect an average benefit of $288 from misreporting a dependent and filing status; noncompliant filers would receive an average benefit of $276 from misreporting a dependent and filing status. This tax benefit variable corresponds to the term $\tau\delta$ in the theoretical model.[26]

In the preferred specification of the model, I impose the assumption that a dollar of EITC benefits will have the same effect on compliance as a dollar of other tax benefits obtainable by reporting a child. The average of EITC and other tax benefits from claiming a qualifying child among taxpayers who did not claim a qualifying child is $1,389; the average benefit among taxpayers who did claim a child is $1,566 (see table 6.3).

I also expect opportunities for child misreporting to be an important determinant of taxpayer noncompliance. Indications of child-misreporting opportunities might include whether or not a taxpayer resides with a child at any time during the year, whether the taxpayer is a noncustodial parent, and whether a taxpayer has access to a child's social security number and other information about a child with which to support an EITC claim. This information is not available in the tax return data. However, I do observe whether or not taxpayers claimed a dependent or the head-of-household filing status, and, for EITC claimants, I observe whether the dependent and filing-status claims were denied or allowed. I include a dummy variable equal to one for taxpayers with a dependent or the head-of-household filing status, as reported if the taxpayer did not claim the EITC and as determined by the audit if the taxpayer did claim the EITC, as an indication of greater opportunity for misreporting an EITC-qualifying child.[27]

Most states and the District of Columbia also tax individual incomes. Because some information is shared by states and the IRS, and because some states require taxpayers to refer to items from their federal returns in completing their state returns, there is likely to be a correlation between misreporting on federal returns and misreporting on state returns and thereby a correlation between

TABLE 6.3 / Weighted Means for Low-Income Taxpayers Ineligible to Claim EITC-Qualifying Children

Variable	Filers Not Claiming EITC: Unweighted, $N = 7,596$, Weighted, $N = 24,807,000$		Filers Claiming EITC: Unweighted, $N = 534$, Weighted, $N = 2,170,000$	
	Mean	Number With Value Greater Than 0	Mean	Number With Value Greater Than 0
EITC increase and tax decrease from reporting one child, given reported income	1,389.37 (751.50)	24,807,000	1,566.31 (706.38)	2,170,000
Dummy variable = 1 if filer may claim dependent or head-of-household status	0.0583) (0.2342)	1,445,000	0.3560) (0.4788)	773,000
Dummy variable = 1 if filing from a state with income tax	0.8038 (0.3971)	19,940,000	0.7934 (0.4048)	1,722,000
Maximum state EITC, given one child	41.81 (149.53)	3,698,000	50.01 (190.67)	260,000
Dummy variable = 1 if filer is self-employed	0.0681 (0.2520)	1,691,100	0.0513 (0.2207)	111,000
Income not subject to losses less withheld taxes, as reported to taxpayer on information returns	9,998.13 (8,276.70)	24,121,000	9,071.81 (5,880.65)	2,013,000
Income not subject to losses less withheld taxes, if self-employed (0 if not self-employed)	729.07 (3,842.32)	1,526,000	249.76 (1,751.94)	67,000
Other income, as reported for taxpayer on information returns	689.13 (26,417.38)	2,512,000	261.30 (3,802.88)	131,000
Other income, if self-employed (0 if not self-employed)	310.14 (25,802.78)	799,000	52.48 (515.03)	35,000
Refund filer receives with no qualifying child (negative if taxpayer has a balance due)	327.46 (493.60)	22,125,000	152.24 (548.12)	1,559,000
Wealth, imputed from income on information returns	9,137.83 (52,168.04)	10,270,000	699.87 (4,837.93)	389,000

(Table continued on p. 252.)

TABLE 6.3 / *Continued*

Variable	Filers Not Claiming EITC: Unweighted, N = 7,596, Weighted, N = 24,807,000		Filers Claiming EITC: Unweighted, N = 534, Weighted, N = 2,170,000	
	Mean	Number With Value Greater Than 0	Mean	Number With Value Greater Than 0
Dummy variable = 1 if filing from the Western region	0.1404 (0.3474)	3,483,000	0.1603 (0.3669)	348,000
Dummy variable = 1 if filing from the Southwest region	0.1381 (0.3450)	3,425,000	0.1379 (0.3448)	299,000
Dummy variable = 1 if filing from the Midwest region	0.1485 (0.3556)	3,685,000	0.0982 (0.2975)	213,000
Dummy variable = 1 if filing from the Central region	0.1355 (0.3423)	3,362,000	0.0561 (0.2302)	122,000
Dummy variable = 1 if filing from the Southeast region	0.2017 (0.4013)	5,005,000	0.3297 (0.4701)	716,000
Dummy variable = 1 if filing from the Mid-Atlantic region	0.1196 (0.3245)	2,968,000	0.1259 (0.3318)	273,000
Fraction of housing units in filer's zip code that are in an urban area	0.6103 (0.4603)	16,445,000	0.7143 (0.4311)	1,622,000
Fraction of adults in zip code with less than a high school education	0.2487 (0.1212)	24,796,000	0.3263 (0.1354)	—[a]
Age of the primary filer	34.77 (16.91)	24,807,000	35.18 (11.02)	2,170,000
Dummy variable = 1 if filer is male filing as single or head of household	0.4645 (0.4987)	11,523,000	0.4702 (0.4991)	1,020,000
Dummy variable = 1 if filer is female filing as single or head of houshold	0.4165 (0.4930)	10,333,000	0.4153 (0.4928)	901,000

Source: Data from IRS's 1994 EITC compliance study; IRS's 1994 Statistics of Income individual income tax return data; IRS's information returns masterfile data; Social Security Administration; U.S. Bureau of the Census 1992; Board of Governors of the Federal Reserve System 1995; and Wheeler 1996.
Note: Standard deviations shown in parentheses.
[a]Data from cells based on fewer than three observations (or from cells for which the complement is based on fewer than three observations) are not disclosed, to protect taxpayer confidentiality.

misreporting on federal returns and state tax rates. Therefore I include a dummy variable equal to one for filers living in states with income taxes.[28]

Similarly, several states have an Earned Income Tax Credit, usually equal to a fixed percentage of the federal credit; I include an estimate of the value of the state EITC as an explanatory variable.[29] To avoid introducing another potentially endogenous variable, I use the maximum value of the state EITC given one child. Nearly 15 percent of filers who did not claim a qualifying child lived in a state with an EITC and could have received an average state credit of up to $281. Twelve percent of taxpayers who did claim a child lived in a state with an EITC; the average maximum state credit among these filers was $418. (Unconditional means are shown in table 6.3.)

Income and Wealth Variables

The theoretical model also suggests that the incidence of noncompliance will depend on the taxpayer's true after-tax income. A change in income affects the taxpayer's incentives in several ways. First, under the usual assumption of decreasing absolute risk aversion, an increase in income will increase the taxpayer's willingness to accept risk and thereby increase the willingness to engage in noncompliance. Second, an increase in true income (holding the reported values of children and income constant) could increase the size of any tax understatement and EITC overstatement and thereby increase the expected total penalty for noncompliance. Third, the marginal penalty for noncompliance might be increasing with true income and with the net tax understatement.[30] The first factor tends to increase the probability of noncompliance, whereas the second and third factors tend to reduce the likelihood of noncompliance. Therefore the total effect of an increase in true income on child misreporting is ambiguous in sign.

Recall that the returns obtained from the SOI sample are not audited, and true income is unobserved for these observations. Reported income is observed; but because some filers will understate (or, more rarely, overstate) income on their tax returns, reported income might differ from true income, and therefore reported income might be poorly correlated with the filer's degree of risk aversion and the expected penalties. In addition, if the decisions as to income reporting and qualifying-child reporting are correlated, then reported income will be endogenous in the model of qualifying-child reporting. Therefore I use income as reported directly to the IRS by employers, financial institutions, and other independent sources, on the W-2 form, 1099 forms, and other information returns, as the measure of income for both the audited and unaudited taxpayers.[31]

Income as reported on information returns may differ from the taxpayer's true income for several reasons. First, some types of income, such as substantial portions of business and farm income, are not independently reported to the IRS. Second, other types of income (such as sales of capital assets) may be reduced by legitimate losses or expenses that are not independently reported to the IRS. To account for some of the differences between true income and income as reported on information returns, I divide income into two variables.

The first variable includes forms of income that are virtually always independently reported to the IRS and are not typically offset by losses or other adjustments. This variable includes wages, interest, dividends, unemployment compensation, retirement account and pension distributions, social security benefits, and tax refunds. Because this variable is intended to reflect all of the taxpayer's income (that enters into the utility function and determines the taxpayer's degree of risk aversion), I include the full value of retirement distributions and social security benefits, even if these amounts are not fully taxable. In addition, I include nontaxed employer-provided dependent care benefits and deferred employee compensation.

The second component of income received during the year includes forms of income against which losses or expenses (the true values of which are not observed) might be deducted. This variable includes nonemployee compensation,[32] rents, royalties, the gross value of sales of stocks and bonds, income from futures contracts, capital gains distributions, the gross value of real estate sales, gambling winnings, prizes and awards, grants, agricultural subsidies, income from farmers' cooperatives, and other types of income from fiduciaries, partnerships, and S-corporations.

Information returns data tend to understate the earnings of self-employed persons, because many forms of business and farm income are not independently reported to the IRS. Self-employment income obtained from the information returns filed for these taxpayers is about $3.8 billion; self-employment income reported on tax returns by these taxpayers is $5.7 billion (and true income is likely to be higher still). If self-employed persons have less income (as measured by information returns) and are also less likely to claim EITC-qualifying children, then the estimated income effect might be biased downward. Self-employed persons might be less likely to claim qualifying children for two reasons. First, self-employed persons have greater opportunities to underreport income, and a variety of empirical research suggests that they are more likely to do so (see, for example, Clotfelter 1983, Feinstein 1991, Erard 1992, and McCubbin 1997, 1999). If income underreporting and child overreporting are substitutes, then self-employed persons will be less likely to overreport children (because they are more likely to underreport income). In addition, self-employed taxpayers might be more likely to be audited (because the IRS is aware of greater opportunities for noncompliance and higher levels of noncompliance among these taxpayers). Therefore self-employed taxpayers might be reluctant to misreport a child, even if they report income correctly. To examine the effect of self-employment income on child reporting and improve the estimation of the effect of income, I add a dummy variable equal to one for taxpayers who have self-employment business or farm income and interactions of the dummy variable with the two information returns income variables.[33]

Prior empirical research, as well as the examination of EITC errors, suggests that the taxpayer's withholding position might also be an important determinant of taxpayer compliance (see Robben et al. 1990, Martinez-Vazquez, Harwood, and Larkins 1992, and Carroll 1992). Therefore I subtract the amount of taxes withheld from income during the year from the income variables described earlier, and I include as a separate variable the additional income received at the end of the year in the form of a tax refund. (The refund variable will be negative if the taxpayer owes additional taxes at the end of the year.) The income variables can be thought of as after-tax income received during the year, and the refund variable can be thought of as additional income received (or taxes owed) at the end of the year.

The refund (or tax due) is conditional on reported income, no EITC-qualifying child, and no dependent or filing-status misreporting. A larger refund conditional on no EITC-qualifying child increases the filer's true after-tax income; under the assumption of decreasing absolute risk aversion, this additional income is expected to be positively associated with noncompliance. On the other hand, taxpayers who expect to receive a substantial refund when they accurately report their family characteristics might be satisfied with their refund and less likely to misreport than taxpayers who will receive a smaller refund. If so, the true refund will be negatively correlated with misreporting.[34]

The theoretical model presented earlier assumes that an individual receives utility from current-period income only. In fact, a taxpayer's degree of risk aversion might depend on wealth or permanent income rather than, or in addition to, current year income. Wealth and permanent income are not directly observable in tax return data. However, it is possible to estimate wealth by grossing up current-year asset income, using the annual rate of return to assets. I assume that wealth is equal to interest, dividends, and income from partnerships, S-corporations, trusts, and estates divided by their average rates of return. To avoid introducing an endogenous variable, or a variable that is downwardly biased for income underreporters, I gross up the income that is reported for the taxpayer on information returns rather than income as reported by the taxpayer on the income tax return.[35]

The difference in the mean of estimated wealth for compliant and noncompliant taxpayers is striking. Average wealth among EITC-ineligible low-income taxpayers who do not claim qualifying children is $9,138, whereas average wealth among those who do claim children is $700. Part of the difference in wealth between compliant and noncompliant taxpayers is associated with the difference in the age distributions of the two groups. Wealth increases with age, and about 9 percent of low-income taxpayers who do not claim a qualifying child but less than 2 percent of ineligible taxpayers who do claim a child are aged sixty-five or over. Estimated mean wealth is $4,669 among compliant taxpayers who are under the age of sixty-five and $669 among noncompliant taxpayers who are under the age of sixty-five. (In the regressions, I control for age as well as wealth.)[36]

As is often the case with distributions of income and wealth, the distribution of wealth among these taxpayers is highly skewed. The median level of wealth is zero, among both low-income taxpayers who claimed the EITC and those who did not. About 59 percent of taxpayers who do not claim EITC-qualifying children and 82 percent of taxpayers who do claim children have no estimated wealth.

Other Variables

The probability of detection and penalty rate, which are expected to be negatively correlated with the probability of erroneously reporting a child, are not available. However, IRS resources and practices vary across IRS regions, and taxpayers in some areas might have a higher expectation of being audited and penalized than taxpayers in other areas. Therefore I include six IRS regional dummy variables to control for variation in expected audit rates and penalties. Taxpayer behavior might also vary geographically, and these dummy variables would reflect that variation as well as variation in IRS practices.

I match the tax return data to 1990 Census Bureau data at the five-digit zip code level to obtain additional demographic information. Taxpayers who live in urban areas might be more likely to be noncompliant because they know many other people who claim the EITC. Therefore I include the fraction of households in the taxpayer's zip code that were categorized as being in an urban area according to the 1990 Census (see U.S. Bureau of the Census 1992, table H5).[37] Tax return filers who have less education might be more likely to make unintentional errors. Therefore I include the fraction of adults in the filer's zip code with less than a high school education, according to the 1990 Census (U.S. Bureau of the Census 1992, table P29). This variable is a measure of the education level of all adults in a taxpayer's neighborhood (rather than a direct measure of the taxpayer's education). Therefore the education variable, like the urban area variable, might reflect the likelihood that the taxpayer lives in a neighborhood with a large number of EITC recipients, as well as the probability that the taxpayer has less than a high school education.

Previous empirical research suggests that the level of noncompliance is higher among married taxpayers and among younger taxpayers. Therefore I also include age and gender, as reported in the Social Security Administration records. In the case of a joint return, I use the age of the first taxpayer listed on the return and assign gender of "joint" to the return.[38]

Results

The model is estimated using the probit procedure. The regression is weighted; however, key results from an unweighted probit are not substantially different. Table 6.4 shows the estimated coefficients from the probit and the estimated marginal effects of the independent variables on the probability of reporting a child for a taxpayer with the predicted probability of claiming a child equal to the actual fraction of ineligible taxpayers who claim a child (about 0.08).

TABLE 6.4 / Estimates of the Probability of Reporting an EITC-Qualifying Child

Variable	Coefficient	Marginal Effect
Intercept	-5.2021**	-0.7766**
	(0.2801)	(0.0418)
EITC increase and tax decrease from reporting one child, given reported income	0.0002**	$3*10^{-5}$**
	($3*10^{-5}$)	($1*10^{-5}$)
Dummy variable = 1 if allowed head of household or dependent	1.3905**	0.2076**
	(0.0680)	(0.0101)
Maximum state EITC for one child	0.0001	$1*10^{-5}$
	(0.0002)	($2*10^{-5}$)
Dummy variable = 1 if from a state with income tax	0.2140**	0.0320**
	(0.0709)	(0.0106)
Dummy variable = 1 if taxpayer is self-employed	-0.8969**	-0.1339**
	(0.1946)	(0.0290)
Income not subject to losses less withheld taxes, per information returns	$-2*10^{-5}$**	$2*10^{-6}$**
	($4*10^{-6}$)	($1*10^{-6}$)
Income not subject to losses less withheld taxes, if self-employed	$4*10^{-5}$**	$1*10^{-5}$**
	($2*10^{-5}$)	($3*10^{-6}$)
Other income, per information returns	$1*10^{-5}$	$2*10^{-6}$
	($1*10^{-5}$)	($1*10^{-6}$)
Other income, per information returns, if self-employed	-0.0001*	$-1*10^{-5}$*
	($3*10^{-5}$)	($5*10^{-6}$)
Refund filer receives with no qualifying child (negative if taxpayer has a balance due)	0.0009**	-0.0001**
	(0.0001)	($1*10^{-5}$)
Wealth, estimated from income on information returns	$-3*10^{-5}$**	$5*10^{-6}$**
	($1*10^{-5}$)	($1*10^{-6}$)
Dummy variable = 1 if from the Western region	-0.0017	-0.0003
	(0.1040)	(0.0155)
Dummy variable = 1 if from the Southwest region	0.1543	0.0230
	(0.1121)	(0.0167)
Dummy variable = 1 if from the Midwest region	0.0022	0.0003
	(0.1096)	(0.0164)
Dummy variable = 1 if from the Central region	-0.2018*	-0.0301*
	(0.1198)	(0.0179)
Dummy variable = 1 if from the Southeast region	0.5006**	0.0747**
	(0.0975)	(0.0146)
Dummy variable = 1 if from the Mid-Atlantic region	0.1683	0.0251
	(0.1059)	(0.0158)

(Table continued on p. 258.)

TABLE 6.4 / *Continued*

Variable	Coefficient	Marginal Effect
Fraction of housing units in zip code that are in an urban area	0.4097** (0.0594)	0.0612** (0.0087)
Fraction of adults in zip code with less than a high school education	2.2194** (0.1883)	0.3313** (0.0281)
Age of the primary filer	0.1568** (0.0134)	0.0234** (0.0020)
Age squared	−0.0020** (0.0002)	−0.0003** $(3*10^{-5})$
Dummy variable = 1 if male filing as single or head of household	−0.2876** (0.0949)	−0.0429** (0.0142)
Dummy variable = 1 if female filing as single or head of household	−0.1994** (0.0943)	−0.0298** (0.0141)
Log likelihood	−1,604.23	
$1 - [\Sigma_i \varepsilon_{li}^2 / \Sigma_i (Y_{li} - Y_m)^2]$	0.2208	
Average predicted probability of claiming a child	0.0794** (0.0026)	
Average predicted increase in probability of claiming a child due to 10 percent increase in the EITC	0.0030** (0.0005)	
Average predicted increase in probability of claiming a child due to 10 percent increase in EITC and tax benefit	0.0038** (0.0006)	

Source: Data from IRS's 1994 EITC compliance study; IRS's 1994 Statistics of income Individual income tax return data; IRS's information returns masterfile data; Social Security Administration; U.S. Bureau of the Census 1992; Board of Governors of the Federal Reserve System 1995; and Wheeler 1996.
Note: Standard errors are shown in parentheses.
*Significant at the 10 percent level.
**Significant at the 5 percent level.

The estimated effect of the size of the EITC and tax benefit on the probability of reporting a child is positive and statistically significant. The estimated coefficient is 2.3×10^{-4} (with a standard error of 3×10^{-5}), and the estimated marginal effect for the reference individual is about 3×10^{-5}. This suggests that a $100 increase in the benefit of claiming a child would increase the probability that the reference individual claims a child from about 8.0 percent to 8.4 percent. On average, a 10 percent increase in the EITC and tax benefit of claiming a child will increase the predicted probability of claiming a child from 7.9 percent to 8.3 percent (or by about 5 percent). Increasing only the EITC by 10 percent will increase the average probability of claiming a child by about 4 percent.

I cannot reject the hypothesis that a dollar of increased EITC or a dollar of decreased taxes obtained by reporting a child will have the same effect on compliance. When this restriction is relaxed, the estimated EITC coefficient is 2.4×10^{-4} (with a standard error of 4×10^{-5}), the estimated tax benefit coefficient is 1.8×10^{-4} (with a standard error of 1.3×10^{-4}), and the log likelihood is $-1,604.15$. (The log likelihood for the restricted model is $-1.604.23$.)

The estimated effect of the dependent or head-of-household dummy variable is positive and statistically significant, suggesting that taxpayers who can claim a dependent or the head-of-household filing status even though they cannot claim the EITC are more likely than other taxpayers to claim the credit in error. The estimated effect of the maximum state EITC is the same sign and order of magnitude as the federal EITC effect, but it is smaller and statistically insignificant at the 10 percent level. (The econometric results are essentially unchanged when I instead use the value of the state EITC conditional on reported income and one child.) The estimated coefficient of the state tax dummy variable is positive and statistically significant, suggesting that federal tax return filers who are subject to state income taxes are less compliant than individuals living in states without income taxes.

For taxpayers who are not self-employed, noncompliance decreases with income that is not subject to losses; other income is not statistically significant. The probability of noncompliance is lower for the self-employed, suggesting that they are subject to higher rates of audit or are substituting income misreporting for child misreporting. For self-employed taxpayers, the probability of child misreporting increases with income that is not subject to losses and decreases with income that is subject to losses (including forms of self-employment that are reported independently to the IRS).

The estimated effect of wealth is negative and statistically significant. (Higher-order income and wealth terms, included in an alternative specification of the model, are not statistically significant.) It is possible that higher permanent income and wealth are correlated with lower probabilities of child misreporting because a more affluent taxpayer can borrow or use assets to pay his or her tax bill in a low-income year. In addition, a wealthier taxpayer might not want to increase the risk of being audited in a later year (when taxable income might be higher) by cheating in the current year. Wealthier taxpayers might face a higher probability of audit in any given year because their financial situation is more complicated. On the other hand, taxpayers with more income and wealth might have greater opportunities for misreporting income or deductions and therefore choose to evade taxes in those ways rather than by erroneously reporting children. Finally, taxpayers with higher levels of income and wealth might be more educated or have better access to high-quality tax return preparers and therefore might be less likely to make unintentional errors.[39]

These estimated effects of income (and of wealth estimated from asset income) on compliance should of course be viewed with caution, because income as reported independently on information returns might be an inadequate proxy for true income, as it excludes certain forms of income and losses. Moreover, because the EITC is a function of income, it is difficult to identify the separate effects of the EITC and income on compliance in a cross-sectional model. Fortunately, the EITC varies nonlinearly with income, making it more likely that the EITC and income effects are correctly identified. Yet if noncompliance varies nonlinearly with income in a way that is correlated with the nonlinear shape of the EITC function, then the estimated EITC effect could reflect variations in compliance that are associated with income.[40]

The estimated probability of noncompliance increases as the net balance owed by the taxpayer when he or she is compliant increases. This might be because noncompliance is decreasing with income (in the form of a larger refund or smaller balance due). It might also be that taxpayers who receive larger refunds or owe smaller balances are more satisfied with the tax system and have less desire to be noncompliant. Furthermore, low-income taxpayers who face a balance due at the end of the year might be likely to be noncompliant because they are liquidity constrained and unable to pay their tax bills.

Jorge Martinez-Vazquez, Gordon Harwood, and Ernest Larkins (1992) suggest that individuals may react differently to an event perceived as a loss (such as having withheld an insufficient amount and owing taxes at the end of the year) than to an event perceived as a gain (such as having withheld an excess amount and receiving a refund), even when the events have the same effect on net wealth. In that case, responses to refunds and balances due will not be the same size. In addition, an inability to pay one's tax bill might also cause taxpayers with a balance due to file noncompliant returns, even though they would not otherwise do so. On the other hand, Schiffren (1995) suggests that the refundable nature of the EITC makes it more vulnerable to fraud. When I allow for different responses to refunds and balances due, I find that decreases in balances due have a slightly larger impact on compliance than do increases in refunds. However, I cannot reject the hypothesis that an increase in the tax refund and a decrease in the balance due will have the same effect on compliance. In the unrestricted model, the estimated refund coefficient is 7.7×10^{-4} (with a standard error of 9×10^{-5}), the estimated balance-due coefficient is 10.1×10^{-4} (with a standard error of 11×10^{-5}), and the log likelihood is $-1,602.88$.

Filers from the Southeast are more likely to erroneously claim a qualifying child and taxpayers from the Central region are less likely to erroneously claim a child. Filers living in urban areas and filers who live in areas where many adults have less than a high school education are more likely to claim a qualifying child. The probability of noncompliance increases with age but at a decreasing rate; compliance begins to improve after about the age of forty. Both male and female taxpayers filing as unmarried are less likely to be noncompliant than married taxpayers filing joint returns.

These econometric results suggest that some EITC-ineligible taxpayers intentionally respond to increases in the size of the EITC by deciding to claim a child.[41] On the other hand, the results also indicate that the incidence of noncompliance is positively correlated with lower levels of education, income, and wealth, perhaps because less educated and less affluent taxpayers are more likely to make unintentional errors. The model also suggests that the size of the EITC, tax rates, and observable taxpayer characteristics can explain only a fraction of noncompliance. Unintentional errors might account for a substantial portion of the unexplained variation in the model. However, it is also likely that some of the noncompliance that is not explained by the econometric model is the result of unobserved variations in expected penalties, unobserved tendencies to engage in intentional noncompliance, or other factors associated with intentional noncompliance.[42]

REDUCING THE COSTS OF EITC COMPLIANCE

One way to reduce total EITC costs (and also benefits) is to simply reduce the size of the credit or the size of the eligible population. In 1995, both the House and Senate proposed reductions in the EITC. The most substantial reductions were proposed in the Earned Income Tax Credit Fraud Prevention Act (U.S. Senate 1995). The bill proposed freezing the credit for taxpayers with two or more children at tax year 1995 levels rather than allowing the full increase provided for by the Omnibus Budget Reconciliation Act of 1993. The bill also reduced the income levels at which the phase-in range ends and the phase-out rate begins, eliminated the indexation of these levels for inflation, eliminated the credit for workers without children, counted the full amount of social security benefits in income for purposes of phasing out the credit, and made other changes to the definition of income for EITC purposes. The Treasury Department estimated that these changes would affect 19 million taxpayers, who would lose an average of $602 in EITC (Samuels 1995).[43] Although the sponsors of the bill indicated that the primary purpose of the changes was to "prevent fraud and abuse" involving the credit, opponents of the bill characterized the EITC reductions as unfair tax increases on the working poor that would do little to improve compliance, and the proposed changes were not enacted.

The model estimated in this chapter provides a means for estimating the likely effect of, for example, a 10 percent reduction in the EITC on EITC noncompliance. The model predicts that under the tax year 1994 provisions, child misreporting by 2,143,000 taxpayers resulted in $2,987 million of EITC overclaims. In the absence of any change in taxpayer behavior, a 10 percent reduction in the EITC would reduce the estimated amount claimed in error by these taxpayers to $2,688 million. However, a reduction in the EITC is also expected to reduce the number of ineligible taxpayers who claim a child from 2,143,000 to 2,073,000 and thereby to further reduce the amount claimed in error to $2,577 million. Hence a 10 percent reduction in the EITC would reduce the amount of EITC erroneously claimed by taxpayers who do not have qualifying children by an estimated 14 percent.[44]

However, eligible recipients, who constitute the majority of EITC claimants, would also have their credit reduced by 10 percent; most of the revenue from reducing the EITC would come from these eligible taxpayers. As a result, the reduction in erroneous claims would have only a small impact on the usual measure of EITC noncompliance: the amount claimed in error as a percentage of the total amount claimed. Assuming that the behavior of eligible EITC claimants is as observed in the 1994 data, the model predicts that erroneous claims of qualifying children in 1994 amounted to 16.7 percent of the total amount of EITC claimed ($3.0 billion out of $17.8 billion). If the EITC were reduced by 10 percent, erroneous qualifying-child claims would fall only to an estimated 16.2 percent of the total amount of EITC claimed ($2.6 billion out of $16.0 billion). Because the behavioral response to changes in the EITC is modest in size, and because scaling back the EITC reduces the total amount claimed as well as the amount claimed in error, reducing the EITC is likely to have a negligible impact on the EITC overclaim rate.[45] Perhaps more important, reducing the credit would diminish the effectiveness of the EITC in inducing labor force participation and in providing income support to low-income families.

More direct efforts to strengthen IRS enforcement activities and to reduce the frequency of unintentional errors might bring about greater improvements in error rates at a much lower cost to compliant taxpayers. In response to the findings of the tax year 1993 and 1994 studies on EITC compliance, the Treasury Department proposed a number of changes to the EITC eligibility criteria and administrative procedures. These changes were designed primarily to provide the IRS with more information with which to evaluate EITC claims before refunds are paid and to make it less costly for the IRS to deny erroneous claims.

For example, the Personal Responsibility and Work Opportunity Reconciliation Act of 1996 requires all EITC claimants to provide a valid social security number for themselves and their qualifying children. (Before tax year 1996, social security numbers were not required for children under the age of one, and taxpayers who could not obtain a social security number because they were undocumented workers could still claim the EITC.) Using Social Security Administration data, the IRS can verify that the taxpayer and child exist and are the individuals to whom the social security numbers were issued. The IRS can also verify the ages of the taxpayer and child, confirm that the child's age matches the year of birth reported on schedule EIC, and detect multiple uses of the same social security number. The 1996 act also allowed the IRS to treat the failure to provide a valid social security number as a mathematical or clerical error. Using the math error procedures, the IRS can deny or reduce the credit before any tax refund is paid and without auditing the tax return. Taxpayers who are denied the credit through the math error procedure may obtain the EITC if they subsequently provide a valid social security number.

The Taxpayer Relief Act of 1997 provided for several new EITC penalties that may be levied in addition to existing taxpayer penalties. Under the 1997 act, a taxpayer whose EITC is disallowed or reduced, and whose error is determined to be the result of negligence or intentional disregard of the EITC provisions, is not allowed to claim the EITC again for two subsequent years. A taxpayer who is found to have fraudulently claimed the EITC is not allowed to claim the credit for ten subsequent years. In addition, a taxpayer whose credit is reduced or disallowed for any reason (other than for correction of a mathematical or clerical error) must provide additional information to the IRS regarding the validity of the EITC claim before receiving the credit again. These provisions are intended to deter taxpayers from filing erroneous claims and to provide the IRS with additional information before the IRS must pay the EITC to previously noncompliant taxpayers.

The 1997 act also included new due diligence requirements for paid preparers. A paid preparer who cannot show that he or she was diligent in filing a taxpayer's EITC claim may be assessed a $100 penalty (even if the taxpayer's EITC claim is not disallowed). To demonstrate due diligence, a preparer must ask the taxpayer certain questions in order to ascertain his or her eligibility for the credit and retain this information for a period of three years. By placing the burden of proof of due diligence on the preparer and allowing the IRS to levy fines without auditing the client's return, the provision makes it less expensive for the IRS to penalize preparers. The new requirement is also intended to educate preparers about the EITC eligibility criteria by spelling out exactly what information is necessary to evaluate a taxpayer's claim.

The Taxpayer Relief Act of 1997 provided the IRS with two new sources of information with which to evaluate the accuracy of EITC claims and select potentially erroneous returns for audit. The first is the Federal Case Registry of Child Support Orders. This registry will allow the IRS to identify noncustodial parents, who are likely to fail the EITC residency test. In addition, the Social Security Administration will be required to obtain the social security numbers of parents when they apply for a social security number for a minor child. This information will allow the IRS to identify individuals who are likely to fail the EITC relationship test.

The Balanced Budget Act of 1997 increased the discretionary appropriations cap for fiscal years 1997 through 2002, to provide additional funding for EITC compliance improvement efforts. The IRS appropriation for fiscal year 1998 included $138 million, and the 1999 budget $143 million, for EITC compliance improvement efforts. The IRS has used these funds to implement the provisions of the 1996 and 1997 acts by, for example, developing new forms and regulations, changing the computer programs to automatically deny the EITC to taxpayers with social security number problems, and updating or developing databases. Because many EITC errors are unintentional, the IRS has also used the appropriation to improve the clarity of EITC related forms, notices, and publications and to increase the availability of taxpayer assistance. Finally, the IRS has used a portion of the funds to audit more returns with EITC claims. The IRS estimated that it spent $101 million on administering EITC math error adjustments and conducting audits and criminal investigations related to EITC claims during fiscal year 1998, and that as a result, it prevented or recovered $977 million in EITC overpayments. The IRS spent about $87 million on these activities in 1999 and saved an estimated $1,123 million in EITC overpayments (IRS 1999, 2000).[46] The IRS is also conducting research to ascertain the effect of these efforts on EITC compliance rates.

CONCLUSIONS

Efforts to target the EITC and other tax benefits to certain types of taxpayers create opportunities for unintentional taxpayer errors and incentives for intentional taxpayer misreporting. Internal Revenue Service data for 1994 indicate that $4.4 billion in excess EITC was claimed, primarily attributable to the misreporting of qualifying children. In this chapter I test the hypothesis that taxpayers respond to increases in the marginal benefit of misreporting by engaging in noncompliance. I find that the probability that an ineligible taxpayer claims a qualifying child increases with the size of the EITC. The results suggest that reducing the EITC by 10 percent would reduce EITC overclaims attributable to child misreporting among ineligible taxpayers by about 14 percent. However, reducing the size of the EITC would also reduce the amount of EITC that could be claimed by compliant taxpayers; the EITC overclaim rate (defined as the amount claimed in error divided by the total amount claimed) would be reduced by a negligible amount. Efforts to reduce the frequency of unintentional errors and enhance the effectiveness of IRS enforcement activities might bring about greater improvements in EITC error rates at a lower cost to compliant taxpayers.

Since 1993, virtually all of the IRS's compliance research has focused on EITC claimants. The sampling of only EITC claimants precludes the study of EITC nonparticipation (probably the largest source of unclaimed EITC). The EITC study design also creates sample selection bias and precludes the econometric modeling of some forms of EITC noncompliance. Furthermore, the errors made by EITC claimants (including misreporting filing status, misreporting family and household characteristics, and underreporting income) can also be made by taxpayers who do not claim the EITC. Without comparable data on taxpayers who do not claim the EITC, it is impossible to fully understand the extent to which EITC overclaims are the result of the EITC itself and the extent to which they are part of a more general compliance problem. The absence of broader compliance data also makes it difficult to evaluate the importance of the EITC compliance problem relative to other tax compliance problems and to efficiently allocate IRS enforcement resources.

Views and opinions expressed in this chapter are those of the author and do not necessarily represent the policies or positions of the Department of the Treasury.

NOTES

1. See Skinner and Slemrod 1985 for a broad discussion of the effects of tax evasion on economic efficiency and equity.

2. See McCubbin 1999 for a description of the characteristics of compliant and noncompliant EITC claimants for 1994. See also chapter 7 of this volume for a description of ineligible EITC recipients and a discussion of how the social value of the EITC might depend on the nature of EITC noncompliance.

3. The IRS postponed indefinitely a Taxpayer Compliance Measurement Program (TCMP) study planned for tax year 1994, citing budget constraints. The IRS is also aware that TCMP audits are burdensome to the selected taxpayers and unpopular with many politicians. The Treasury and General Government Appropriations Act as passed by the Senate in 1998 included a nonbinding Sense of the Senate Resolution stating that "the Internal Revenue Service should not conduct random audits of the general population of taxpayers or tax returns" (U.S. Senate 1998).

4. Results from this compliance study were released by the Internal Revenue Service (1997b) and Scholz (1997). The U.S. General Accounting Office (1998) reviewed the IRS study and subsequent Treasury analysis.

5. All estimates regarding taxpayers who claimed the credit for workers without qualifying children should be used with caution, as they are derived from a sample of only ninety-nine returns.

6. Under 1994 law, a foster child was any child who resided with the taxpayer for the full year and whom the taxpayer cared for as his or her own child.

7. The EITC-qualifying child need not be the taxpayer's dependent. To claim the credit, the taxpayer must reside with the child and must have the highest adjusted gross income of all taxpayers who would otherwise be allowed to claim the child. To claim the dependent exemption, the taxpayer must generally provide more than half of the support for the child. Therefore a welfare recipient who does not provide more than half of the total support for the child may not claim a dependent exemption for the child but may still claim the EITC. On the other hand, a noncustodial parent may be allowed to claim a dependent exemption for a child that he or she supports, but a noncustodial parent may not claim the EITC.

8. The IRS did not record the relationship of the taxpayer to the qualifying child on the corrected return, when the EITC claim was disallowed. However, it is likely that in some cases, IRS agents denied the credit claimed by a parent in favor of a "foster parent" who was not related to the child biologically or by marriage. It is not at all clear that policymakers intended for parents to be ineligible for the credit in these cases. Largely in response to this finding, the definition of a foster child was modified, effective for tax year 2000. Under the new law, a foster child is a child with whom the taxpayer resides for the full year, whom the taxpayer cared for as his or her own child, and who is also the taxpayer's sibling, a descendant of the taxpayer's sibling, or a child placed in the taxpayer's care by a court or child placement agency.

9. On the other hand, the EITC can create a marriage bonus if, for example, a low-income taxpayer with earnings marries a nonworker with children. Stacy Dickert-Conlin and Scott Houser (1998) find that a substantial portion of low-income persons who lose welfare benefits by marrying receive a marriage bonus through the tax system. See also chapter 4 of this volume for a discussion of measuring EITC marriage penalties.

10. The failure to account for the nonsampled spouse's behavior can lead to erroneous estimates of the EITC overclaim rate when the filing status is changed to married

filing joint and both the sampled taxpayer and the spouse claimed the EITC. In that case, the excess EITC amount associated with the new, joint return should include any amount claimed by the spouse who was not sampled. In addition, the weight associated with the corrected joint return should reflect the joint probability that either member of the couple was sampled (rather than only the probability that the selected taxpayer was sampled). The failure to include the EITC overclaim of the spouse leads to the underestimation of the error rate; the failure to correct the weight for the observation leads to the overestimation of the error rate. In part because of these weighting difficulties, the data from the Taxpayer Compliance Measurement Program (last collected for tax year 1988) excluded taxpayers whose filing status was changed to married filing jointly from any other status during the course of the audit. Hence the TCMP estimates of EITC error rates and of the overall tax gap exclude a potentially important form of noncompliance.

11. If the taxpayer's adjusted gross income is less than the point at which the phase-out begins, then the credit is computed based on earned income. If the filer's adjusted gross income is greater than the point at which the phase-out begins, then the credit is computed using the income concept (earned income or adjusted gross income) that results in the smaller credit. Earned income is the sum of wages, self-employment income, and certain nontaxable earned income less one-half of any self-employment tax. Nontaxable earned income includes deferred or reduced compensation (such as employee contributions to a 401[k] retirement savings plan or a cafeteria benefits plan), excludable dependent care benefits, housing and subsistence allowances for U.S. military personnel, and any other nontaxable employee compensation.

12. This estimate should be used with caution, as it is based on very few observations.

13. About 94 percent of wage underreporters had received income from more than one job.

14. The federal tax code provides for the disclosure of tax return information by the Social Security Administration and the IRS to child support enforcement agencies and agencies administering Temporary Assistance for Needy Families (formerly Aid to Families with Dependent Children), food stamps, unemployment compensation, and other programs (Internal Revenue Code, section 6103[l]).

15. It is likely that additional qualifying children were claimed as dependents but could not be matched to the dependent information because of limitations in the EITC and dependent data extracted from the returns.

16. Another 1.6 percent of taxpayers who claimed the EITC during the study period used IRS assistance or volunteer assistance programs to complete their returns. The estimated error rate among these returns is unreliable, as it is based on a very small number of observations.

17. Brian Erard (1993) finds that self-selection across preparation modes increases the observed level of noncompliance.

18. See Holtzblatt 1992 and McCubbin 1999 for a discussion of findings from the IRS's TCMP data for 1985 and 1988 and how these findings have shaped EITC policy.

19. I focus on the problem of the misreporting of EITC-qualifying children because it accounts for more than two-thirds of the amount of EITC overclaimed. In previous work (McCubbin 1997, 1999) I examined income underreporting by eligible EITC claimants. The design of the EITC compliance study makes it virtually impossible to

model other forms of EITC noncompliance, such as the underreporting of income by ineligible EITC claimants and the misreporting of filing status.

20. Although the SOI data are not audited, they are corrected for computational errors and other internal inconsistencies; see IRS 1997a for a description of the tax year 1994 study of individual income tax returns.

21. In addition, the CID sample overrepresents male taxpayers, and the SOI sample over-represents married taxpayers and taxpayers with certain types of income. In the em-pirical model I condition on gender and reported filing status. I do not condition on the SOI income-sampling criteria.

22. See IRS 1997b and McCubbin 1999 for discussions of the SOI and CID sample designs and comparisons of EITC population estimates obtained from the two samples. One disadvantage of this approach is that it requires me to assume that filers in the SOI sample who did not claim EITC-qualifying children did not have EITC-qualifying children. Scholz 1994 has estimated that for tax year 1990, 13.6 to 19.5 percent of eligible taxpayers failed to claim the EITC. However, many EITC nonparticipants do not file tax returns and therefore would not appear in the SOI sample. Hence I argue that the SOI sample includes few taxpayers who were eligible for the EITC but failed to claim it.

23. This specification is written as though the marginal income tax rate is constant. The empirical specification of the model allows the income tax to vary nonlinearly with income and family characteristics. The theoretical model also assumes that the EITC is a continuously differentiable function of income and the number of children. The EITC is not a continuously differentiable function, and $E(y,x)$ is appropriately viewed as a continuously differentiable approximation of the actual EITC. More important, this specification allows the reported number of children to be a continuous variable, whereas a taxpayer must in fact report a discrete number of children. Specifying $E(y,x)$ as a continuous function and x_r as a continuous variable allows me to more easily examine the optimal reporting decision and to explore how the optimum will change with tax policy parameters, but it should be recognized that actual taxpayers might be unable to reach the optimum. In addition, this specification assumes that all children who are claimed for EITC purposes are also claimed as dependents. This need not be the case; and while the taxpayer may claim a maximum of two EITC-qualifying children, the number of dependents is not limited. However, specifying different child variables complicates the theoretical model without adding additional insight.

24. In addition to these penalties, there are several new EITC-specific penalties for non-compliance, which were not in effect for tax year 1994. There are also other penalties, such as sanctions for failure to file a return and for failure to make estimated tax payments, that are not likely to apply to EITC claimants.

25. In other words, a positive first-order condition (when evaluated at $x_r = 0$) is a neces-sary condition for child reporting to occur. Because the taxpayer cannot report a frac-tion of a child, a positive first-order condition is not a sufficient condition for child reporting to occur. Examination of the first-order condition for reported children about $y_r = y_t$ and $x_r = x_t$ (full compliance) demonstrates the importance of the pen-alty function specification. Given $y_r = y_t$ and $x_r = x_t$, child overreporting will occur if

$$\tau\delta + \frac{\partial E_r}{\partial x_r} > p \left[\tau\delta + \frac{\partial E_r}{\partial x_r}\right] \frac{\partial \pi}{\partial T} + p \frac{\partial \pi}{\partial x_r}$$

That is, child misreporting will occur if the marginal benefit exceeds the expected marginal cost. If the penalty is a function only of T and not also a function of x_r, then the second term on the right-hand side vanishes, and this condition can be reduced to $1 > p[\partial\pi/\partial T]$. In other words, the incidence of noncompliance will depend on the marginal penalty and probability of detection only and not on the EITC or tax rate. However, when the penalty is also a function of x_r, then $1 > p[\partial\pi/\partial T]$ is a necessary but not sufficient condition for misreporting to occur. Moreover, it is now possible that an increase in the EITC will cause an increase in the incidence of misreporting. See McCubbin 1999 for examples of other cost functions (in which the probability of detection and disutility from noncompliance are functions of the number of children overstated) that can generate this result. See also Shlomo Yitzhaki (1974), who first noted that the substitution effect of a tax rate vanishes when the penalty is a function only of understated taxes.

26. Because the SOI data are not audited, I do not know whether filing statuses and dependent exemptions were correctly reported by taxpayers who did not claim the EITC. However, only 5 percent of taxpayers who did not claim a qualifying child claimed a dependent, and only 4 percent claimed the head-of-household filing status, whereas most of the filers who erroneously claimed the EITC also claimed dependents and the head-of-household filing status. Therefore it seems reasonable to assume that the ineligible taxpayers who refrained from claiming the EITC also correctly reported their filing statuses and dependent exemptions. I adopt this assumption and calculate the reduction in income tax liability resulting from claiming an additional dependent and the head-of-household filing status relative to what is reported by taxpayers who did not claim an EITC-qualifying child and relative to what is allowed for taxpayers who did claim a qualifying child. (I employ the same assumption in specifying the head-of-household and dependent dummy variable.) The econometric results are not very different when alternative assumptions (including the assumption that none of the taxpayers in the sample should claim a dependent or the head-of-household filing status) are imposed.

27. There are several other reasons why taxpayers who are eligible to claim a dependent or the head-of-household filing status might be more likely to erroneously claim the EITC. Some taxpayers who have a dependent or who are heads of household might choose to claim the EITC because they feel entitled to it (having provided support for a dependent or maintained a household for a child). Taxpayers who have a dependent child might also be more aware of the EITC (and of the size of the benefit of claiming the EITC). In addition, taxpayers might not understand the differences in the definitions of EITC-qualifying children and dependent children or children that qualify the taxpayer for the head-of-household filing status. Once a taxpayer has determined (near the beginning of filling out the tax form) that he or she is eligible to claim a dependent or the head-of-household filing status, the taxpayer might assume that he or she is also eligible for the EITC (which is reported near the end of the tax form), without carefully evaluating the EITC eligibility criteria. In addition, noncustodial parents who are allowed to claim a dependent exemption as part of a separation agreement or divorce decree might fail to understand that these agreements do not apply to EITC-qualifying children. Finally, it is possible that the IRS did not detect all of the dependent and filing-status errors among the taxpayers who erroneously claimed the EITC. If erroneous head-of-household filing status and dependent claims

were allowed, then the tax benefit variable is too low for some noncompliant observations, causing the coefficient to be biased downward.

28. The states without individual income taxes in 1994 were Alaska, Florida, Nevada, South Dakota, Texas, Washington, and Wyoming. The federal tax code allows for the disclosure of federal tax return information to state tax agencies (Internal Revenue Code, section 6103[d]).

29. In 1994, these states were Iowa, Maryland, Minnesota, New York, Rhode Island, Vermont, and Wisconsin.

30. For taxpayers in the EITC phase-in range, an increase in true income would reduce the EITC overstatement and thereby reduce both the total and marginal penalties for reporting a child. An increase in income is most likely to lead to an increase in child misreporting for these taxpayers.

31. Unlike the CID and SOI tax return data, the information returns data are unedited, and discrepancies between the information return and the tax return may reflect errors in the information returns data, as well as taxpayer noncompliance. I correct the information returns data for some obvious errors, including duplicate and amended information returns and mismatches attributable to misreported social security numbers.

32. Nonemployee compensation is a payment for services made by a firm or an individual engaged in a trade or business to an individual who is not an employee. It is a form of self-employment income reported to the recipient and to the IRS on the 1099-MISC form.

33. If income- and child-reporting decisions are correlated, then these variables may be endogenous, because the self-employment dummy variable is based on income as observed on the tax return. However, because I use a dummy variable and the dummy variable interacted with exogenous income measures, rather than the amount of reported self-employment income, the variables are only endogenous if taxpayers have self-employment earnings and do not report any of it (or have no self-employment earnings but report a nonzero amount).

34. The empirical specification allows for the possibility that the amount of withheld taxes is misreported by the taxpayer. Conditional on reported income and the true number of children, total after-tax income is equal to $y_t - \tau[y_r - \delta x_t] + E(y_r, x_t) - w_t + w_r$, where w_t is the true amount withheld and w_r is the reported amount. Therefore I subtract the true amount of taxes reported from independent sources in deriving the measures of income received during the year ($y_t - w_t$), and I use withheld taxes as reported by the taxpayer in calculating the refund variable ($w_r - \tau [y_r - \delta x_t] + E(y_r, x_t)$).

35. This wealth measure excludes some important assets, such as owner-occupied housing and corporate stocks that do not generate dividend income, because unrealized capital gains income is not observed in either the tax return or the information returns data. In grossing up observable asset income, I assume that the nominal rate of return on government bonds is equal to 7.41 percent. I assume that the rate of return on tax-exempt securities is equal to the average yield of tax-exempt money-market funds, state and local government bonds, and municipal bonds (weighting each rate of return by the amount of money held in that form), or 5.70 percent. I assume that the rate of return on other interest-bearing assets is equal to the weighted average return of savings accounts, negotiable orders of withdrawal, and certificates of deposit, or

3.16 percent. I assume that the ratio of dividends to price on corporate common stock is 2.82 percent. See Board of Governors of the Federal Reserve System 1995, tables 12 and 18. I assume that the rate of return on partnership, S-corporation, and fiduciary assets is equal to the amount of income distributed to partners in the finance, insurance, and real estate industry divided by the amount of assets held by these partnerships, or 3.12 percent. See Wheeler 1996, figure D and table 5. I limit the calculation to partnerships in the finance, insurance, and real estate sectors because based on my review of the information returns, most partnership and S-corporation income for the taxpayers in my sample appears to be associated with the real estate sector.

36. Note that some of these relatively wealthy but low-income taxpayers would not be eligible for the EITC for 1996 and later years, even if they had a qualifying child. Beginning in 1996, taxpayers with investment income in excess of $2,200 are not eligible for the credit, and taxpayers must add certain losses and tax-exempt income to adjusted gross income in calculating the credit. The econometric results are largely unchanged when taxpayers who would not be eligible for the EITC under current law are excluded from the sample. The results are also unchanged when taxpayers over the age of sixty-four are excluded from the sample.

37. This fraction is essentially a dummy variable equal to one if the filer's neighborhood was classified as urban, because few zip codes contain both urban and nonurban areas.

38. Note that because only EITC claimants were audited, the gender variables are based on filing status as reported by the taxpayer rather than as determined by audit. About 17 percent of the EITC-ineligible EITC claimants who filed as single or as head of household should have filed as married. To the extent that filing-status errors are correlated with child-reporting errors, the gender variables are endogenous. The econometric results are largely unchanged when the gender variables are excluded.

39. I have not included the effect of paid preparers, because the use of a paid preparer (and the type of paid preparer) might be endogenous to the compliance decision. In addition, the EITC data suggest that compliance varies substantially across different types of paid preparers. I cannot identify the type of paid preparer in the SOI data for taxpayers who do not claim the EITC. When I include a dummy variable equal to one for taxpayers who use any type of paid preparer, the estimated paid-preparer effect is positive and statistically significant, and the average effect of a 10 percent increase in the EITC is reduced by about 8 percent.

40. Jeffrey Liebman (1995) suggests that taxpayers in the EITC phase-in range might be less likely to be noncompliant because they are likely to be younger and have less complicated family situations. Taxpayers in the plateau might have more complicated family circumstances and be more likely to make errors. Taxpayers in the phase-out range might tend to be older, have more stable family situations, and be less likely to make errors. If so, then the estimated EITC effect will reflect the correlation between these taxpayer characteristics and income rather than (or in addition to) any behavioral response to the EITC. The tax data for 1994 do show an increase in age and a decrease in the use of the single filing status, correlated with increases in income. However, the data do not show clear differences between taxpayers in the EITC plateau (where the benefit of claiming a child is highest) and taxpayers with higher or lower incomes. For example, the average age of both ineligible taxpayers in the phase-in range and those in the plateau is thirty-three years; 14 percent of ineligible

taxpayers in both the plateau and the phase-out claim the head-of-household filing status.

41. Liebman 1995 also finds that erroneous EITC claims are increasing with the size of the credit and concludes that this response is evidence of taxpayer fraud.

42. The foregoing estimates assume that all of the explanatory variables, including those conditioned on reported income, are exogenous. However, income as well as family characteristics may be misreported, and the qualifying-child- and income-reporting decisions may be correlated. If there is an unobservable tendency toward both types of misreporting, then the estimated EITC effect might be biased upward. This is because income underreporting by taxpayers in the EITC phase-out range (and income overreporting by taxpayers in the phase-in range) increases the benefit of reporting a child. As a result, we might observe a spurious correlation between a higher EITC benefit and a propensity for child misreporting. (If income misreporting and child misreporting are instead negatively correlated, perhaps because income underreporting increases the expected penalty for child misreporting, then we would expect the estimated EITC effect to be biased downward.) Similarly, income misreporting might increase the taxpayer's refund. If so, we might observe a spurious, positive correlation between large refunds and the incidence of child misreporting.

    Therefore I have also modeled income and child reporting as a simultaneous equations system. I find evidence that the estimated magnitude of the EITC and tax benefit effect is somewhat smaller (and the refund effect is more negative) than that estimated in the single equation models. For example, the simultaneous equations model suggests that increasing the EITC benefit by 10 percent will increase the number of ineligible EITC claimants by about 2.8 percent. Using the single equation model, I estimate that increasing the EITC benefit by 10 percent will increase the number of EITC claimants by about 3.8 percent. The reduction in the estimated EITC effect (and increase in the refund effect) after accounting for reported income suggests that income underreporting and child overreporting are positively correlated. However, the difference in the coefficient estimates is small relative to their standard errors, and not likely to be statistically significant. See McCubbin 1999 for details.

43. The estimated amount of EITC reduction reflects 1996 income levels and deindexation through 2000.

44. Estimated standard errors for the effects presented in this paragraph are as follows: the estimated change in the number of claimants is about seventy thousand, with a standard error of about thirteen thousand. The total reduction in erroneous EITC amounts is about $410 million, with a standard error of about $27 million. The estimated reduction in the amount of EITC claimed is 13.7 percent of the initial amount, with a standard error of 0.6 percent. This simulation assumes that 30 percent of taxpayers who are expected to claim at least one qualifying child will claim two children. In addition to reducing the amount of EITC claimed by $410 million, a 10 percent reduction in the EITC would reduce the amount of tax underreported because of child overreporting among ineligible taxpayers by an estimated $29 million.

45. This result is obtained under a variety of econometric and simulation specifications, including simulations that incorporate changes in income underreporting by EITC-eligible taxpayers.

46. It is possible that some of the EITC payments that were prevented or recovered as a part of the compliance effort were in fact claimed by compliant taxpayers. (This may be particularly true of the EITC claims that were denied after taxpayers failed to respond to IRS requests for additional information.) In addition, it is possible that increased audit rates and publicity about new enforcement procedures and penalties have reduced EITC claims by eligible taxpayers. However, in addition to intensifying enforcement efforts, the IRS has allocated resources to new outreach activities and improvements in taxpayer service that are expected to increase the EITC participation rate.

REFERENCES

American Institute of Certified Public Accountants. 1997. *Statement Before the U.S. House of Representatives, Committee on Ways and Means.* Hearing on the Internal Revenue Service's 1995 Earned Income Tax Credit Compliance Survey, Washington, D.C., May 8.

Board of Governors of the Federal Reserve System. 1995. *Annual Statistical Digest, 1994.* Washington, D.C.

Brown, Ted. 1997. *Statement of the Assistant Commissioner of Criminal Investigation of the IRS Before the U.S. House of Representatives, Committee on Ways and Means.* Hearing on the Internal Revenue Service's 1995 Earned Income Tax Credit Compliance Survey. Washington, D.C., May 8.

Carroll, John S. 1992. "How Taxpayers Think About Their Taxes: Frames and Values." In *Why People Pay Taxes: Tax Compliance and Enforcement,* edited by Joel Slemrod. Ann Arbor: University of Michigan Press.

Clotfelter, Charles T. 1983. "Tax Evasion and Tax Rates: An Analysis of Individual Returns." *Review of Economics and Statistics* 65(3): 363–73.

Dickert-Conlin, Stacy, and Scott Houser. 1998. "Taxes and Transfers: A New Look at the Marriage Penalty." *National Tax Journal* 51(2): 175–217.

Erard, Brian. 1992. "The Influence of Tax Audits on Reporting Behavior." In *Why People Pay Taxes: Tax Compliance and Enforcement,* edited by Joel Slemrod. Ann Arbor: University of Michigan Press.

———. 1993. "Taxation with Representation: An Analysis of the Role of Tax Practitioners in Tax Compliance." *Journal of Public Economics* 52(2): 163–97.

Feinstein, Jonathan S. 1991. "An Econometric Analysis of Income Tax Evasion and Its Detection." *Rand Journal of Economics* 22(1): 14–35.

Holtzblatt, Janet. 1992. "Administering Refundable Tax Credits: Lessons from the EITC Experience." In *Proceedings of the Eighty-fourth Annual Conference on Taxation.* Washington, D.C.: National Tax Association.

Internal Revenue Code as Amended Through December 31, 1997. 1998. New York: Research Institute of America.

Liebman, Jeffrey B. 1995. "Noncompliance and the EITC: Taxpayer Error or Taxpayer Fraud?" Harvard University (November). Mimeo.

Martinez-Vazquez, Jorge, Gordon B. Harwood, and Ernest R. Larkins. 1992. "Withholding Position and Income Tax Compliance: Some Experimental Evidence." *Public Finance Quarterly* 20(2): 152–74.

McCubbin, Janet. 1997. "Non-Compliance and the Design of the Earned Income Tax Credit." In *Proceedings of the Eighty-ninth Annual Conference on Taxation.* Washington, D.C.: National Tax Association.

———. 1999. "Non-Compliance and the Optimal Design of the Earned Income Tax Credit." Ph.D. diss., University of Maryland.

Robben, Henry S. J., Paul Webley, Russell H. Weigel, Karl-Erik Warneryd, Karyl A. Kinsey, Dick J. Hessing, Francisco Alvira Martin, Henk Elffers, Richard Wahlund, Luk Van Langenhove, Susan B. Long, and John T. Scholz. 1990. "Decision Frame and Opportunity as Determinants of Tax Cheating: An International Experimental Study." *Journal of Economic Psychology* 11(3): 341–64.

Samuels, Leslie B. 1995. *Statement of the Assistant Secretary for Tax Policy, U.S. Department of the Treasury, Before the U.S. House of Representatives, Committee on Ways and Means, Subcommittee on Oversight, and Subcommittee on Human Resources.* Hearing on the Earned Income Tax Credit, Washington, D.C., June 15.

Schiffren, Lisa. 1995. "America's Best-Kept Welfare Secret." *American Spectator* 28(4): 24–29.

Scholz, John Karl. 1994. "The Earned Income Tax Credit: Participation, Compliance, and Antipoverty Effectiveness." *National Tax Journal* 47(1): 63–85.

———. 1997. *Statement of the Deputy Assistant Secretary for Tax Analysis, U.S. Department of the Treasury, Before the U.S. House of Representatives, Committee on Ways and Means.* Hearing on the Internal Revenue Service's 1995 Earned Income Tax Credit Compliance Survey, Washington, D.C., May 8.

Skinner, Jonathan, and Joel Slemrod. 1985. "An Economic Perspective on Tax Evasion." *National Tax Journal* 38(3): 345–53.

Sparrow, Malcolm K. 1993. *Fraud in the Electronic Filing Program: A Vulnerability Assessment Prepared for the Internal Revenue Service.* Washington, D.C.

Steuerle, Gene. 1993. "The IRS Cannot Control the New Superterranean Economy." *Tax Notes* 49 (June 28): 1839–40.

U.S. Department of Commerce. U.S. Bureau of the Census. 1992. *Census of Population and Housing, 1990: Summary Tape File 3 on CD-ROM.* Washington, D.C.

U.S. Department of the Treasury. Internal Revenue Service (IRS). 1997a. *Individual Income Tax Returns 1994.* Statistics of Income Division. Publication 1304. Washington: Internal Revenue Service.

———. 1997b. *Study of EITC Filers for Tax Year 1994.* Washington, D.C.

———. 1999. *IRS Tracking, Earned Income Tax Credit Appropriation, Annual Report: FY 1998.* Document 9383. Washington, D.C. (January).

———. 2000. *IRS Tracking, Earned Income Tax Credit Appropriation, Annual Report: FY 1999.* Document 9383. Washington, D.C. (February).

U.S. General Accounting Office. 1998. *Earned Income Credit: IRS's Tax Year 1994 Compliance Study and Recent Efforts to Reduce Noncompliance.* GAO/GGD-98-150. Washington, D.C. (July).

U.S. Senate. Committee on Finance. 1975. *Report Accompanying H.R. 2166, the Tax Reduction Act of 1975.* S. Rept. 94-36. Washington, D.C.

U.S. Senate. 1995. *The Earned Income Tax Credit Fraud Prevention Act.* S.899.

———. 1998. *Treasury and General Government Appropriations Act, 1999.* Amendment 3345 to S.2312 (July 28).

Wheeler, Timothy D. 1996. "Partnership Returns, 1994." *Statistics of Income Bulletin* 16(2): 76–126.

Yin, George K. 1995. *Statement Before the U.S. Senate, Committee on Government Affairs: Hearings on Effectiveness and Design of the Earned Income Tax Credit.* Washington, D.C., April 5.

Yitzhaki, Shlomo. 1974. "A Note on Income Tax Evasion: A Theoretical Analysis." *Journal of Public Economics* 3(2): 201–2.

Chapter 7

Who Are the Ineligible Earned Income Tax Credit Recipients?

Jeffrey B. Liebman

T his year, 19 million families are expected to receive the Earned Income Tax Credit (EITC) at a total cost to the federal government of $30 billion (U.S. House 1998; Office of Management and Budget 2000). The cost of the EITC now exceeds total federal and state spending on Temporary Assistance for Needy Families. Research on the EITC suggests that the program succeeds in transferring income to needy families while maintaining low administrative costs, encouraging the labor force participation of single parents, and having little or no impact on hours conditional on working.[1]

Research has also shown, however, that many EITC recipients are ineligible for the credit. Janet Holtzblatt (1991) and John Karl Scholz (1990), who first presented the tabulations from the 1985 and 1988 Taxpayer Compliance Measurement Program (TCMP) surveys, have found that one-third of EITC recipients were not eligible for the credit, primarily because they did not have eligible children. More recent estimates from tax year 1994 returns suggest that 21 percent of EITC dollars are currently being paid in error, including payments to ineligible taxpayers and overpayments to eligible taxpayers (Scholz 1997; GAO 1998; chapter 6, this volume).[2] In comparison, quality control data suggest an overpayment rate of 6 percent for Aid to Families with Dependent Children (AFDC).[3]

Given the excess burdens involved in income transfers, a program that transfers one-fifth of its dollars to the wrong population could be prohibitively expensive.[4] However, it is far from certain that these overpayments are reaching families that are very different from the eligible families. Internal Revenue Service (IRS) rules regarding filing status and the claiming of children are complicated, and it is possible that many ineligible EITC recipients are making innocent errors in claiming the EITC.

To determine what share of EITC payments are erroneously going to families without children and the characteristics of these ineligible families, this chapter uses an exact match of the March 1991 Current Population Survey (CPS) to information from the 1990 tax returns of CPS adults. This match makes it possible to estimate the number of taxpayers who claimed the EITC but did not have any children living with them. In addition to providing an independent assessment of the extent and nature of the largest part of the EITC compliance problem, this analysis yields two other benefits that go beyond what can be learned from IRS compliance studies.[5] First, it directly answers an important policy question: what share of EITC dollars are reaching households with children? For many purposes this is a more relevant number than the noncompliance rate, and it is a number that is not available from the government studies. Second, the analysis provides a much richer description of the demographic characteristics of both eligible and ineligible EITC recipients than is available from tax data alone.

I find that between 11 and 13 percent of all tax year 1990 EITC recipients did not have a child in their CPS households at the time that they received the credit. By further matching back to the March 1990 CPS, I determine that 10 percent of EITC recipients also did not have a child in their households one year before they received the credit and therefore were very unlikely to have been eligible for the credit. Noncompliance rates appear to be particularly high among males filing as household heads. One-third of male household heads claiming the EITC lacked children in their CPS households.

THE EVOLUTION OF THE EITC COMPLIANCE PROBLEM

In the decade since the EITC compliance problem was first recognized, important changes in the EITC have altered the nature of the problem. The large expansions of the credit, legislated in 1990 and 1993, have increased the return to erroneously claiming the credit; modifications of eligibility rules have simplified enforcement; and the IRS has taken important steps to reduce EITC errors and fraud.

In tax year 1988, a taxpayer was entitled to claim the Earned Income Tax Credit if he or she met three requirements. First, the taxpayer must have had earned income (wage and salary income plus business and farm self-employment income) above 0 and below $18,576 as well as an adjusted gross income below $18,576. Second, the taxpayer must have had a child living with him or her for more than half of the year.[6] Third, the taxpayer was required to use a filing status of married filing jointly, head of household, or surviving spouse.

Married taxpayers were generally required to claim their children as dependents to be eligible for the EITC.[7] Thus the taxpayer must have provided at least half the cost of supporting the child. The head-of-household and surviving-spouse filing statuses require that the taxpayer provide half the cost of maintaining a home for the child.[8] Therefore, a support test applied for all EITC claimants. Income from AFDC is counted as support provided by the state, not the taxpayer. This means that a taxpayer who received $8,000 in AFDC benefits and $6,000 in earnings would have failed the support test and would not have been eligible to receive the EITC.

Estimates from the 1988 TCMP imply that one-third of the 10.5 million taxpayers claiming the EITC in that year were not eligible for the credit (see table 7.1).[9] The 3.4 million ineligible taxpayers received $1.9 billion of the $5.6 billion

TABLE 7.1 / Earned Income Tax Credit Audit Status of All Tax Returns in 1988
TCMP

	Returns		Total EITC Claimed	
Audit Status	Number	Share of Total (Percentage)	Amount (Billions of Dollars)	Share of Total (Percentage)
All tax returns	104,319,102	100.0	5.627	100.0
EITC not claimed	93,822,851	89.9	0.000	0.0
EITC established	95,467	0.1	0.000	0.0
EITC claimed	10,400,784	10.0	5.627	100.0
EITC not adjusted	5,600,237	53.8	3.056	54.3
EITC increased	428,040	4.1	0.172	3.1
EITC decreased	1,016,412	9.8	0.544	9.7
EITC disallowed	3,356,095	32.2	1.855	33.0

Source: IRS Taxpayer Compliance Measurement Program 1988.
Note: "EITC established" refers to tax returns that are eligible for the EITC but do not claim
the credit.

spent on the EITC. Forty percent of head-of-household filers claiming the EITC
were not entitled to the credit, compared with 21 percent of married filers. These
head-of-household returns accounted for almost three-quarters of the taxpayers
who had their EITC claims disallowed. Table 7.2 displays a tabulation of the
filing status claimed by the taxpayer as against the filing status determined by
the IRS auditor for all returns on which an EITC claim was disallowed. The table
shows that most of the head-of-household filers in this population should have
filed as single because all of their dependent child claims were disallowed. The

TABLE 7.2 / Claimed and TCMP-Established Filing Status of EITC-Disallowed Tax
Returns in 1988 TCMP Survey

	TCMP = Established Filing Status					
Claimed Filing Status	Single	Married Joint	Married Separate	Head of Household	Qualifying Widow	All
Single	262	0	0	0	0	262
Married joint	29,638	797,187	28,418	796	0	856,039
Married separate	18,263	0	0	0	0	18,263
Head of household	1,959,836	0	363,590	143,262	0	2,466,688
Qualifying widow	0	0	0	14,506	337	14,843
All	2,007,999	797,187	392,008	158,564	337	3,356,095

Source: IRS Taxpayer Compliance Measurement Program 1988.

filing status of married taxpayers whose EITC claims were disallowed was usually not changed by the TCMP auditor because losing dependent child exemptions does not affect a taxpayer's eligibility for the married filing status.[10]

The TCMP computer file does not explain why EITC claims were disallowed. However, it does include information on income, filing status, and dependent child exemptions both as claimed by the taxpayer and as revealed in the audit. In most cases, the disallowance of all dependent exemptions would mean that the taxpayer was not entitled to claim the EITC.[11] Table 7.3 uses the available evidence in the 1988 TCMP to explain why EITC claims were disallowed. Eighty-two percent of taxpayers whose EITC claims were disallowed were determined by the auditor either not to have any dependent children or not to be

TABLE 7.3 / Reasons for Disallowance of EITC Claims, 1988 TCMP

	Returns		Total EITC Claimed	
Reason	Number	Share of Total (Percentage)	Amount (Billions of Dollars)	Share of Total (Percentage)
No dependents and improper filing status, income eligible	1,925,104	57.4	1.126	60.7
No dependents only	376,832	10.2	0.201	10.8
Improper filing status only	435,910	13.0	0.264	14.2
AGI above $18,576 or earned income above $18,576, filing status and dependents eligible	386,471	11.5	0.157	8.5
Negative or zero earnings filing status and dependents eligible	16,550	0.5	0.011	0.6
(No dependents or improper filing status) and (AGI above $18,576 or earned income above $18,576)	66,113	2.0	0.027	1.5
Cannot explain why EITC was disallowed	149,415	4.5	0.069	3.7
Total returns with EITC disallowed	3,356,395		1.855	

Source: IRS Taxpayer Compliance Measurement Program 1988.

eligible to use a filing status entitling the taxpayer to the EITC (or both). Only 11.5 percent had income exceeding the maximum levels for EITC eligibility but were otherwise eligible. Fewer than 1 percent lacked positive earned income. Two percent had both excessive income and either no dependent or an improper filing status, and 4.5 percent of the disallowed EITC claims do not fit into any of these categories.

The basic TCMP data suggest that most noncompliance on EITC tax returns involves the reporting of dependent children. Most of the disallowed EITC claimants had income levels that would have made them eligible for the credit. However, these basic data are open to a number of interpretations.

First, it is possible that the TCMP does not accurately measure noncompliance. A study by the U.S. General Accounting Office (GAO) of erroneous dependent claims tried to examine the original audit sheets of 958 tax returns that were coded in the 1988 TCMP computer file as having the number of dependents altered in response to the audit. The GAO found that 180 of the audit sheets were missing, 51 had been miscoded on the computer file, and 85 contained dependent exemptions that were disallowed by default because the taxpayer never responded to the audit request (GAO 1993). In addition to doubts about data quality, TCMP-based estimates of EITC noncompliance are likely to be biased owing to the limits of what auditors can learn in an audit. On the one hand, TCMP audits generally occur two to three years after a tax return is filed, and some low-income taxpayers who provided more than half the support for a child may not be able to document the support a few years later. This would imply that the TCMP has overestimated the number of noncompliant EITC tax returns. On the other hand, auditors are unlikely to uncover all taxpayer fraud (Graetz and Wilde 1985), so the TCMP may undercount the number of ineligible EITC recipients.[12]

Second, it is possible that most of the ineligible 1988 EITC claimants failed the support test but were otherwise eligible for the credit. If this were the case, then, ceteris paribus, current rates of EITC noncompliance would be much lower than 1988 rates because under post-1990 rules, the support test no longer applies. From the TCMP computer file it is usually impossible to determine the reason that a taxpayer's dependent child claim was disallowed. However, the original audit sheets do contain an explanation for why the claim was disallowed. Although I was unable to obtain access to the audit sheets, the 1993 GAO study examined 554 TCMP audit sheets from tax returns that had one or more dependent-child claims disallowed. If the GAO sample were representative of all returns with disallowed dependent exemptions, then roughly one-third of the GAO sample would be tax returns that claimed the EITC. The GAO study estimated that if the post-1990 EITC rules had been in effect in 1988, then 890,000 of the 4 million tax returns represented in their survey would have failed the support test and been ineligible to claim a dependent child while still being eligible for the EITC.[13] Extrapolating to the entire population of 6.21 million returns with disallowed dependents implies that 1.38 million EITC tax returns would have been ineligible for the credit under the 1988 rules but eligible under the post-1990 rules. Thus, this small GAO sample suggests that the support test accounted for 59 percent of the 2.3 million EITC tax returns on which all dependent claims were disallowed and 41 percent of all disallowed EITC returns.[14]

Third, it is possible that ineligible EITC claimants did not have children living with them. One way in which this could occur is if noncustodial parents claimed their children. Since 1985, the custodial parent has been entitled to claim the dependent-child exemption so long as both parents combined paid more than half the child's support. Only if the custodial parent releases his or her right to the exemption (or did so under a pre-1985 divorce or separation agreement) may the noncustodial parent legally claim the exemption. Noncustodial parents are required to claim the children as dependents living away from home. In the TCMP, fewer than half of 1 percent of ineligible EITC returns contained claims for children living away from home. However, the IRS auditors I interviewed suggested that noncustodial parents are savvy enough to realize that claiming a child living away from home without providing the required paperwork would attract IRS attention, so that noncustodial parents may claim their children as living at home. Another way in which a taxpayer without children might claim a dependent child is to invent a fictional one. The strongest evidence for this possibility is that in 1987, the first year in which taxpayers were required to list social security numbers of dependents on their tax returns, 7 million fewer dependent children were claimed than in the previous year (Szilagyi 1991). Further evidence that nonexistent children may have been claimed comes from the 1988 TCMP. In 1988, taxpayers were required to list on their tax returns the social security numbers of all dependents who were at least five years of age. On tax returns on which the TCMP auditor disallowed an EITC claim, 39 percent of the disallowed dependent-child claims were dependents for whom the taxpayer checked the box stating that the child was under the age of five and did not provide a social security number—possibly because the child did not exist.

As has already been noted, the 1990 legislation simplified EITC rules by removing the support test and replacing it with a residency test and an adjusted gross income (AGI) tiebreaker. The EITC residency test requires that the child live with the taxpayer for more than six months during the year (twelve months for a foster child). The AGI tiebreaker rule states that if a child could potentially be claimed by two taxpayers, only the person with the higher adjusted gross income is eligible to take the credit.

While eliminating the support test may have made some previously ineligible taxpayers eligible for the credit, it has also created a new source of errors. The 1994 IRS compliance study found an overall overclaim rate of 21 percent, substantially lower than the 35 percent rate for 1988. Claims by taxpayers without children continued to be a problem, with 39 percent of EITC overclaims resulting from taxpayers' claiming children who did not meet the residence test. However, an additional 18 percent of overclaims were owing to the failure to correctly follow the new AGI tiebreaker rules (GAO 1998).

In addition, the 1994 study identified a large source of errors that had not been nearly as important in the 1980s—married taxpayers who by law are supposed to file married returns but do not. Thirty-one percent of EITC overclaims were attributable to these filing-status errors, which occur among separated couples who have not obtained a legal separation agreement or among couples who are living together but erroneously file separate returns with the filing status of single or head of household (perhaps deliberately avoiding EITC marriage penalties).[15] When these separate returns are combined into a joint return, the income rises, usually reducing the amount of the EITC the household receives or eliminating eligibility altogether.

Over this period, the IRS adopted a number of new enforcement procedures, including verifying the social security numbers of children claimed on tax returns before making payments. At first glance, it might appear that these enforcement efforts have been highly successful because the overpayment rate has fallen by roughly one-third. However, such a judgment is complicated by the removal of the support test that may have simply redefined many previously ineligible taxpayers as eligible taxpayers. Indeed, the 1993 GAO study indicates that the support test may have been responsible for 41 percent of ineligible EITC claims in 1988. This would imply that removing the support test directly reduced the level of EITC noncompliance to around 20 percent, raising the possibility that recent enforcement initiatives have had no effect.

While it is impossible to be certain, it seems likely that recent IRS efforts have indeed had a substantial impact. First, errors associated with the AGI tiebreaker have most likely replaced some of the support-test errors. Second, there is good reason to expect that in the absence of new IRS efforts, the error rate would have increased dramatically. The findings of an earlier work (Liebman 1995), in which I use the 1985 and 1988 TCMP surveys to study how EITC noncompliance responded to the 1987 expansion of the EITC, indicate that a 45 percent increase in the EITC increased the noncompliance rate by 14 percent. It is highly speculative to extrapolate from these results to the most recent EITC expansions. Nonetheless, between 1990 and 1994 the real value of the EITC more than doubled, raising the payoff to erroneous claims. Thus, we might have predicted an increase in noncompliance of 33 percent from this increase. So even if we assumed that elimination of the support test directly reduced the noncompliance rate to 21 percent, the expansion in the generosity of the credit would have raised the noncompliance rate to 28 percent. If recent reforms have reduced the rate of noncompliance back to 21 percent, then they have eliminated one-quarter of EITC noncompliance. If the impact of eliminating the support test was less than assumed here, the impact of IRS efforts may have been even greater.

DATA AND IMPUTATION METHODOLOGY

To produce an alternative measure of EITC noncompliance, I became a special sworn Census Bureau employee and used a data set that matched the March 1991 CPS to tax return data.[16] These data allowed me to estimate the percentage of taxpayers who were likely to have claimed the EITC on their 1990 tax returns

TABLE 7.4 / Details of Match Between 1991 Current Population Survey and 1990 IRS Individual Master Files

	Unweighted Number of Observations	Weighted Number of Observations
Individuals in the March 1991 CPS	158,477	248,807,213
Children (aged less than fifteen years)	37,157	55,347,888
Adults (aged fifteen and older)	121,320	193,459,325
Adults without valid social security numbers	15,803	25,155,698
Adults with valid social security numbers	105,517	168,303,627
Filers (adults matching to a tax return)	81,620	130,118,292
Nonfilers (adults not matching to a tax return)	23,897	38,185,335

Source: Author's calculations, from a match of the March 1991 CPS and the 1990 IRS individual master file.

(the returns most taxpayers filed in April 1991) who told the Current Population Survey that they did not have a child living with them in March 1991. Since the 1990 EITC rules were identical to those for 1988 (except that the credit amounts were adjusted for inflation), this provides a comparable estimate of the number of EITC claimants who wrongly claimed to have a dependent child when they did not have a child living with them. Since the support test is no longer a requirement for claiming the EITC and has been replaced by a residency test, the number of EITC claimants who do not have a child residing with them is also a relevant number for thinking about the current magnitude of child-related EITC noncompliance.

The March 1991 CPS contains information on 158,477 individuals, of whom 121,320 were adults (aged fifteen and older) and were asked for their social security numbers during the CPS interview (see table 7.4). The CPS obtained social security numbers for 87 percent of the adults in the sample. Of the adults providing social security numbers, 77 percent matched tax returns in the IRS's individual master file, which contains selected information on every tax return filed for tax year 1990. The taxpayers who have valid social security numbers but do not match to tax returns are considered nonfilers.

The IRS individual master file (IMF) contains information from every tax return filed during the year. Unfortunately, the 1990 IMF extract created for the match does not record whether or not the taxpayer claimed the Earned Income Tax Credit. However, it does contain the number of dependent children claimed (separate categories for children claimed as living at home and for children living away from home), adjusted gross income, wage and salary income, and a total income variable that can be combined with indicators from schedules C and F to calculate self-employment income.[17]

I assume that a taxpayer claims the EITC if the taxpayer both has income qualifying him or her for the EITC and claims a dependent child living at home.

I have tested my methodology for identifying EITC returns using the 1990 Statistics of Income sample of tax returns. The sample contains all of the variables that I use to predict whether a taxpayer claims the EITC as well as the actual amount of EITC that the taxpayer claimed. I find that my methodology successfully identifies 95 percent of tax returns that claim the EITC and that only 2 percent of the taxpayers whom I predict to claim the EITC did not claim it.[18] Thus, the measurement error introduced by not having a direct measure of EITC claims could at most bias my estimates of improper claims upward by 2 percentage points (if 100 percent of the people claiming dependent children living at home but not claiming the EITC did not have children at home). Most likely, the impact of this measurement error is negligible. For example, if improper child claims were twice as high among the people whom I wrongly predict to claim the EITC as among true claimers, my overall estimate of wrong claims would be biased upward by less than three-tenths of a percentage point.

To account for the 13 percent of CPS sample members who did not provide a valid social security number to the CPS and therefore could not be matched to a tax return, I estimated the probability of supplying a social security number to the CPS conditional on the individual's observed CPS characteristics and then reweighted the complete-data part of the sample by the inverse of this probability. I used the method of moments to produce standard errors that incorporate the extra uncertainty that the reweighting procedure introduced into the estimates.[19]

Even after accounting for nonmatches, the CPS-IMF sample has fewer EITC recipients than would be expected based on IRS Statistics of Income data. The last two rows of table 7.5 show the weighted number of EITC returns from the CPS-IMF match and from the Statistics of Income data by filing status. The total number of EITC returns in the CPS-IMF match is about 12 percent too low, and most of the discrepancy is found in a shortage of head-of-household returns.[20] There are a number of possible explanations for why the number of EITC tax returns filed by the entire March 1991 CPS sample is less than the number that were actually filed for 1990. First, it is possible that the CPS undercounts low-income families with children. Second, it is possible that some people file more than one tax return or file without proper social security numbers. Third, it could be that people who do not give their social security numbers to the CPS are more likely to file as heads of household than the prediction equations indicate. Whatever the cause, my inability to match the aggregate totals implies that my results are only representative of the 88 percent of EITC claims that are accounted for in the entire CPS sample, including imputations.

THE NUMBER OF CHILDLESS EITC RECIPIENTS

Using the CPS-IMF match, I estimate the proportion of tax returns predicted to claim the EITC in which the taxpayer was in a CPS household that did not contain any children. In my methodology, a child must be under the age of

TABLE 7.5 / Estimates of the Percentage of EITC Claimants in the CPS-IMF Match with Children Present

Category	Married Joint	Female Head of Household	Male Head of Household	Total
Percentage with no child in March 1991 CPS household	9.0 (0.4)	11.2 (0.6)	33.2 (1.8)	13.2 (0.4)
Percentage with no child in March 1991 CPS subfamily	11.3 (0.4)	15.7 (0.7)	45.9 (1.9)	17.8 (0.4)
Percentage with no child in the March 1991 CPS household and no child in March 1990 household	8.7 (0.8)	6.8 (0.9)	25.4 (3.3)	10.1 (0.6)
Percentage with no child in the March 1991 household or multiple tax returns in household and more dependents claimed on tax returns than there are children in CPS household	13.7 (0.5)	19.9 (0.8)	53.2 (2.0)	21.4 (4.9)
Percentage with no child and no adult child in the 1991 CPS household	7.1 (0.7)	9.2 (0.5)	32.3 (1.8)	11.3 (0.3)
Weighted number of EITC claimants in CPS-IMF match (millions)	4.739	4.754	1.452	10.978
Weighted number of EITC claimants in Statistics of Income estimates (millions)[a]	4.539			12.540

Source: Author's calculations from a match of the March 1991 CPS and the 1990 IRS individual master file.
Note: Standard errors in parentheses.
[a] Statistics of Income data do not give separate figures for female and male heads of houshold. The Statistics of Income estimates 7.944 million EITC claimants using the head of household filing status.

nineteen (or under the age of twenty-four if a full-time student) but does not have to be the child (or even a relative) of the taxpayer in the CPS household who claimed the EITC.[21] This is a lower-bound estimate of the degree of non-compliance, since there are a number of reasons (most importantly the AGI tie-breaker) why a taxpayer with a child in the household may not be entitled to claim that child for the purposes of the EITC. I also estimate the number of EITC claimants who do not have a child in their CPS subfamilies.[22] This alternative estimate gives an indication of families in which the choice of which adult claims the child for EITC purposes may be ambiguous.[23]

The first two rows of table 7.5 show the percentage of (predicted) 1990 EITC tax returns by gender and filing status in which there was no child in the CPS household or subfamily. Nine percent of couples filing married joint tax returns claiming the EITC did not have a child in their CPS household. This estimate has a standard error of 0.4. An additional 2.3 percent had a child in the household but not in the taxpayers' subfamily. For returns filed by female heads of household, the numbers are similar to those for married couples filing joint returns: 11.2 percent had no child in their household (with a standard error of 0.6), while an additional 4.5 percent had no child in their subfamily. For male household heads, the numbers are much larger; 33.2 percent of male household heads claiming the EITC did not have a child in their CPS household, and an additional 12.7 percent did not have a child in their subfamily. Among all tax returns claiming the EITC, 13.2 percent did not have a child in the CPS household and 17.8 percent did not have one in the subfamily.

Further Estimates

These results indicate that at the time EITC-claimant taxpayers receive their tax refunds, a sizable portion do not have children living in their households. While this fact may itself be of policy relevance, since the EITC aims to raise the living standards of families with children, it is not necessarily a good estimate of the number of EITC-claimant taxpayers who are noncompliant because they claim children who do not live with them. On the one hand the estimate is too low, since the requirements for being a qualifying child are stronger than simply residing in the same household or even the same subfamily. On the other hand, the estimates could overstate noncompliance to the extent that household composition might have changed between the tax year and the time of the CPS survey. In addition, it is possible that adult children may have qualified some taxpayers for the credit whom I categorize as ineligible. To investigate these considerations, I perform three additional calculations. First, when possible, I match EITC taxpayers who lack a child in the March 1991 CPS back to the March 1990 CPS. It is unlikely that a taxpayer would lack a child in both of the CPS surveys and still have had a child who met the six-month residency requirement for claiming the EITC.[24] Second, I calculate the number of EITC-claimant taxpayers who lived in households in which more than one tax return was filed and in which the total number of dependent children claimed on all the tax returns exceeded the number of children present in the CPS household. Third, I calculate a lower bound on the percentage of ineligible EITC recipients by counting some taxpayers with adult children in their households as eligible for the credit.

There were 1,010 observations in the March 1991 CPS who were predicted to claim the EITC but did not have a child in their households. In theory, roughly half of them (those with months-in-sample greater than four) can be matched to observations for the same individual in the March 1990 CPS. In fact, I was able to match only 60 percent of the potentially matchable individuals to individuals in the March 1990 CPS.[25]

Since sample attrition in the CPS is not random (Welch 1991), I estimated a logit regression to obtain the conditional probability that someone with given characteristics who was a March 1991 CPS adult and in his or her last four months in the sample would also be present in the March 1990 CPS. I then reweighted the 1991 observations that matched back to 1990 by the inverse of the probability that they were in both samples.

In the third row of table 7.5, I present estimates from this procedure. Of the tax returns claiming the EITC for 1990, 10.1 percent were filed by taxpayers who lacked children in both their March 1990 and March 1991 households. Thus my estimate of noncompliance is 25 percent lower when I use this more restrictive measure. Female household heads show a much lower noncompliance rate with this measure—6.8 percent rather than 11.2.

One reason that my basic estimates of noncompliance might be too low is that the same CPS child could be claimed by more than one taxpayer. Therefore, I estimate the percentage of households with EITC returns in which more than one return claimed a dependent child living at home and the number of children in the household was less than the total number claimed on all the tax returns filed by the household. For this estimate, I used only households in which all adults supplied social security numbers to the CPS. Of the 59,929 households in the March 1991 CPS, 49,878 included social security numbers for all adults. The percentage of EITC tax returns in this subsample that were in households that lacked children was 12.8 percent compared with 13.2 percent for the entire sample, so these households seem to be reasonably representative of all households. Of the EITC tax returns in this subsample, 32 percent were in households in which more than one tax return was filed. In roughly 40 percent of the EITC households in which more than one tax return was filed, more children were claimed on the tax returns than were present in the household. Thus, the total percentage of EITC tax returns that were in households with no children or that were in households in which multiple tax returns were filed that claimed dependent children and in which the total number of children claimed on tax returns exceeded the number of children present in the household in March 1991 was 21.4 percent (row 4 of table 7.5). The rate for married tax returns was 13.7 percent, the rate for returns filed by female household heads was 19.9 percent, and the rate for male household heads was 53.2 percent. While it is of course possible that the tax return in the household claiming the EITC was in fact eligible to claim the children while the other tax returns were not, these estimates suggest at the very least that there is sizable overreporting of dependents on tax returns filed by EITC households, if not necessarily on EITC returns.[26]

Under pre-1991 EITC rules, there was no age restriction on children claimed for the EITC. However, a married taxpayer generally had to claim his or her child as a dependent to receive the credit, and the rules for dependent children do contain age restrictions. Moreover, since all of the children in my EITC sample were also claimed as dependents, the age requirements for dependent children apply even for the head-of-household returns. Under the requirements for claiming dependent children, the child must be under the age of nineteen (or under the age of twenty-four if a full-time student) or the child's gross income must be under a certain limit ($2,100 in 1990). To eliminate households containing an adult child with income of less than $2,100 from my estimates of EITC noncompliance, I identified taxpayers with an adult child in the household (using the CPS parent-pointer variable). If the adult child either did not file a tax return or filed one with an adjusted gross income of less than $2,100, then I assumed the taxpayer could claim the child as a dependent and qualify for the EITC. For adult children who did not give social security numbers to the CPS, I used their total CPS income as a proxy for gross income. Since I do not impose the support test or the joint-return test, this measure overestimates the number of EITC-eligible households. Accounting for adult children lowers the estimates of EITC noncompliance for married taxpayers and female household heads by roughly 20 percent. However, it lowers the estimates of EITC noncompliance for male household heads by only 3 percent (row 5 of table 7.5).

Demographic Characteristics of Eligible and Ineligible EITC Recipients

Past descriptions of the characteristics of EITC recipients have had either to make do with the limited information available in samples of tax returns or to impute EITC recipiency based on survey information.[27] The estimates presented here are likely to give a much more accurate picture of who received the EITC in tax year 1990 and allow us to examine how the characteristics of eligible and ineligible EITC recipients differ. Tables 7.6 and 7.7 present demographic and economic characteristics of taxpayers who were predicted (based upon information from their tax returns) to claim the EITC in 1990. Table 7.6 contains information on taxpayers who had at least one child in their March 1991 CPS households, and table 7.7 presents the same information on taxpayers who did not have a child in their households. The tables also present separate characteristics by filing status and gender (the demographic characteristics of the married taxpayers are the average of the characteristics of the two spouses).

Table 7.6 shows that 52 percent of eligible 1990 EITC taxpayers are married, 30 percent are formerly married, and 18 percent have never been married. A little more than half are white, a quarter are black, and 18 percent are Hispanic. Of eligible EITC recipients, 74 percent have a high school education or less; 44 percent live in the South; and 36 percent live in a central city. Fifty-eight percent work fifteen hundred hours or more, though this average is brought down by married couples in which one spouse does not work. Sixteen percent of EITC-eligible tax returns are filed by individuals in households that receive welfare income during the year, and 25 percent are in households receiving food stamps.

Compared with eligible taxpayers, ineligible EITC recipients are less likely to be currently married and are more likely to have never been married. Ineligible taxpayers are also more likely to be black, to have less than a high school education, to live in the South, and to be at least thirty years of age. Ineligible taxpayers are much less likely to live in a household that received public assistance

TABLE 7.6 / Demographic and Economic Characteristics of Taxpayers Predicted to Claim the 1990 EITC Having Children in Their March 1991 CPS Household, by Tax Return Filing Status

Characteristic	Married	Male Household Head	Female Household Head	All
Marital status (percentage)				
Married	92.1	35.6	15.5	52.3
Widowed	0.7	2.4	5.1	3.0
Divorced	0.9	20.9	35.7	18.2
Separated	3.5	9.2	13.5	8.5
Never married	2.8	31.8	30.3	17.9
Race (percentage)				
Non-Hispanic white	66.1	34.6	46.2	54.0
Non-Hispanic black	9.1	35.7	37.6	24.5
Hispanic	19.8	26.9	13.8	17.9
Non-Hispanic other	4.9	2.8	2.4	3.6
Education (percentage)				
Less than high school	33.2	39.2	24.5	30.0
High school	42.4	41.0	46.9	44.2
More than high school	16.3	14.7	23.2	19.2
College degree	5.1	3.0	3.4	4.1
More than college	3.0	2.1	1.9	2.4
Geographical region (percentage)				
Northeast	13.1	14.7	16.5	14.8
Midwest	19.7	14.6	23.3	20.7
South	44.0	46.3	43.6	44.0
West	23.2	24.5	16.6	20.4
Central city (percentage)				
In central city	27.1	43.7	44.1	36.2
Balance of Metropolitan Statistical Area	37.1	31.5	33.5	35.0
Not in Metropolitan Statistical Area	35.8	24.8	22.4	28.8
Farm (percentage)				
Farm	3.3	0.8	0.5	1.8
Nonfarm	96.7	99.2	99.5	98.2
Age (percentage)				
Fifteen to nineteen	1.9	4.1	2.7	2.5
Twenty to twenty-four	13.0	15.5	13.2	13.4
Twenty-five to twenty-nine	20.1	24.9	19.7	20.5
Thirty to thirty-nine	34.6	32.0	40.2	36.8
Forty to forty-nine	19.7	16.3	17.6	18.4
Fifty to sixty-four	9.6	6.9	6.3	7.9
Older than sixty-four	1.0	0.4	0.3	0.6

(Table continued on p. 288.)

TABLE 7.6 / *Continued*

Characteristic	Married	Male Household Head	Female Household Head	All
Hours worked last year (percentage)				
0	22.0	5.7	6.7	13.5
0 to 500	9.2	5.6	8.1	8.3
501 to 999	8.5	5.0	9.2	8.5
1,000 to 1,499	9.8	13.7	14.0	12.1
1,500 to 1,999	11.7	15.7	18.1	14.9
2,000 to 2,499	28.7	45.1	39.8	35.3
2,500 to 2,999	5.4	5.1	2.6	4.1
3000 or more	4.8	4.0	1.5	3.2
Migration status (percentage)				
Same house last year	73.8	65.5	71.5	71.9
Different house last year	26.2	34.4	28.5	28.1
Labor force status (percentage)				
Working	61.3	74.5	75.4	68.5
With job not working	2.4	2.4	3.6	2.9
Unemployed looking	7.2	9.2	6.6	7.1
Unemployed on layoff	1.7	4.2	1.1	1.7
Not in labor force	27.4	9.7	14.2	19.7
Income on tax return (percentage)				
Phase-in	25.8	35.7	38.3	32.3
Flat	15.2	16.0	20.7	17.7
Phase-out	58.9	48.3	40.9	49.9
Household public assistance (percentage)				
Yes	11.2	20.0	19.8	15.9
No	88.8	80.0	80.2	84.1
Household public assistance mean for receiving households (dollars)	3,185	2,868	2,707	2,878
Household food stamps (percentage)				
Yes	22.0	25.7	27.5	24.8
No	78.0	74.3	72.5	75.2
Household food stamps mean for receiving households (dollars)	1,593	1,686	2,514	1,631
Household Medicaid (percentage)				
Yes	20.6	29.4	29.3	25.4
No	79.4	70.6	70.7	74.6
Weighted number of tax returns	4,240,106	1,008,069	4,087,243	9,355,391
Unweighted observations	4,978	603	2,552	8,146

Source: Author's calculations from a match of the March 1991 CPS and the 1990 IRS individual master file.
Note: The weights for the married tax returns are split between the two spouses.

TABLE 7.7 / Demographic and Economic Characteristics of Taxpayers Predicted to
Claim the 1990 EITC Having No Children in Their March 1991 CPS
Household

Characteristic	Married	Male Household Head	Female Household Head	All
Marital status (percentage)				
Married	71.3	14.1	19.2	32.7
Widowed	0.1	2.0	14.2	6.7
Divorced	4.4	21.7	35.3	21.4
Separated	11.7	14.7	7.9	11.2
Never married	11.7	47.5	23.4	28.0
Race (percentage)				
Non-Hispanic white	55.7	23.8	42.3	40.3
Non-Hispanic black	13.7	52.0	45.5	38.1
Hispanic	27.7	22.2	10.6	19.5
Non-Hispanic other	2.8	2.1	1.6	2.1
Education (percentage)				
Less than high school	46.6	41.5	36.1	40.9
High school	35.7	36.4	38.4	37.0
More than high school	11.2	14.8	20.1	15.8
College degree	4.3	5.1	3.2	4.2
More than college	2.2	2.1	2.1	2.2
Geographical region (percentage)				
Northeast	12.9	11.5	18.3	14.5
Midwest	16.0	21.7	15.3	17.6
South	41.7	49.4	54.8	49.2
West	29.4	17.4	11.6	18.7
Central city (percentage)				
In central city	26.8	46.1	44.1	39.4
Balance of Metropolitan Statistical Area	44.0	29.8	32.9	35.2
Not in Metropolitan Statistical Area	29.2	24.0	23.0	25.4
Farm income (percentage)				
Farm	4.2	2.5	0.4	2.2
Nonfarm	95.8	97.5	99.6	97.8
Age				
Fifteen to nineteen	0.5	2.3	0.2	1.0
Twenty to twenty-four	3.6	15.6	7.9	9.2
Twenty-five to twenty-nine	12.2	20.5	11.5	14.7
Thirty to thirty-nine	24.1	38.4	21.6	27.9
Forty to forty-nine	20.9	11.0	28.1	20.3
Fifty to sixty-four	29.8	10.6	27.4	22.5
Older than sixty-four	8.8	1.6	3.3	4.4
Hours worked last year				
0	26.9	5.6	5.1	11.9
0 to 499	6.7	3.4	4.2	4.7

TABLE 7.7 / *Continued*

Characteristic	Married	Male Household Head	Female Household Head	All
500 to 999	7.8	7.7	8.8	8.1
1,000 to 1,499	9.2	12.6	12.1	11.5
1,500 to 1,999	14.0	18.5	21.0	18.0
2,000 to 2,499	24.1	43.8	43.6	37.8
2,500 to 2,999	6.3	5.6	2.5	4.7
3000 or more	5.1	2.8	2.6	3.4
Migration status				
Same house last year	75.9	69.0	75.3	73.4
Different house last year	24.1	31.0	24.7	26.6
Labor force status (percentage)				
Working	59.2	69.7	84.3	71.9
With job not working	3.3	3.8	1.9	2.9
Unemployed looking	9.3	9.2	4.4	7.4
Unemployed on layoff	1.0	6.2	0.9	2.7
Not in labor force	27.2	11.1	8.4	15.0
Income on tax return (percentage)				
Phase-in range	33.8	36.3	31.1	33.6
Flat range	20.5	18.0	19.7	19.3
Phase-out range	45.7	45.7	49.1	47.2
Household public assistance (percentage)				
Yes	2.3	3.8	3.1	3.1
No	97.7	96.2	96.9	96.9
Household public assistance mean for receiving households (dollars)	2,152	1,588	2,083	1,881
Household food stamps (percentage)				
Yes	8.1	8.6	6.4	7.6
No	91.9	91.4	93.6	92.4
Household food stamps mean for receiving households (dollars)	1,134	718	862	888
Household Medicaid (percentage)				
Yes	13.2	11.3	8.1	10.7
No	86.8	88.7	91.9	89.3
Weighted number of tax returns	419,902	482,713	518,785	1,430,718
Unweighted observations	402.5	273	328	1,010

Source: Author's calculations from a match of the March 1991 CPS and the 1990 IRS individual master file.
Note: The weights for the married tax returns are split between the two taxpayers.

(3 percent), food stamps (8 percent), or Medicaid (11 percent) during the previous year. This is further evidence that no child was living with the taxpayer during the previous year and that the discrepancy between the number of children claimed on the tax return and the number present in the CPS household is not caused by CPS measurement error.

The marital status tabulations in table 7.7 indicate that a substantial percentage of taxpayers who filed head-of-household returns reported to the CPS that they were in fact married. This is consistent with the results of the 1994 IRS compliance study that found that many married taxpayers erroneously used a nonmarried filing status.

IS THE EITC AN EFFECTIVE WAY TO TRANSFER INCOME?

The estimates in this chapter indicate that in 1990, between 11 percent and 13 percent of EITC recipients did not have a child living with them at the time they received the credit. Thus it seems likely that almost 90 percent of EITC dollars are reaching families with children.[28]

However, some of these families appear to have incomes above the intended range. Relatively few EITC taxpayers underreport income, but because households often contain more than one tax-filing unit, the income measured on a tax return may not correspond well to the total resources of the household. More than one-third of EITC recipients in the 1990 data lived in households with multiple adults filing separate tax returns, and many lived in households with total incomes above the EITC maximum. Moreover, data from the 1994 IRS compliance study indicate that errors associated with the AGI tiebreaker and with married taxpayers' wrongly splitting their incomes among two nonmarried returns are responsible for almost half of EITC overclaims, accounting for about 10 percent of EITC dollars.[29]

The difficulties that arise in verifying the residency of children claimed on tax returns and the imprecise measure of household resources provided by a tax return are two drawbacks to using the tax system to transfer income to low-income families. In contrast, traditional welfare programs employ caseworkers to verify eligibility and often use more comprehensive measures of household resources in determining eligibility. However, the greater accuracy of the welfare system comes at a cost. Administrative costs of the AFDC program were 16 percent of benefits paid in 1996 (U.S. House 1998), while administrative costs for the EITC, although hard to isolate from the rest of the IRS budget, appear to be less than 3 percent of total credits received by taxpayers, probably substantially less.[30]

Moreover, the welfare system is generally thought to impose a greater burden on beneficiaries than the tax system, both because the time cost of regular meetings with a caseworker is larger than the marginal cost of adding an additional form to one's tax return and because of the stigma associated with welfare receipt.[31] These cost differentials are likely to be part of the reason that take-up rates appear to be higher for the EITC than for traditional welfare programs.[32] Moreover, even within the EITC itself it is clear that recent efforts at improving compliance have increased administrative costs and have most likely discouraged some eligible recipients from applying for the program.

Is it more cost-effective to administer payments to low-income working families through the tax system with low administrative costs and high error rates or through the welfare system with high administrative costs and lower error rates?[33] The answer depends heavily on how dollars transferred to ineligible taxpayers are valued.

With an overpayment rate of 21 percent and administrative costs of 3 percent, every dollar that is transferred to an eligible EITC recipient leads to 27 cents of payments to ineligible taxpayers (.21/.79) and administrative costs of 4 cents (.03 × 1.27).[34] In contrast, if it were possible to administer the EITC through the welfare system with an overpayment rate of 6 percent and administrative costs of 16 percent, then every dollar transferred to eligible recipients would lead to 6 cents in payments to ineligible taxpayers (.06/.94) and administrative costs of 17 cents (.16 × 1.06).[35]

If both the administrative costs and the transfers to ineligible taxpayers are treated as having zero value, then administering the program through the welfare system is cheaper; transferring $1.00 to an eligible taxpayer costs $1.23 through the welfare system and $1.31 through the tax system.[36] However, if many EITC errors are inadvertent and involve payments to low-income families with children, we may want to place some value on the transfers to ineligible taxpayers, perhaps assigning them the same social welfare weight as a dollar given to the average taxpayer. In that case the dollars that go to the ineligible taxpayer are not a cost (though the transfer does still require administrative costs), and transferring $1.00 to an eligible taxpayer costs $1.17 through the welfare system and $1.04 through the tax system.[37]

CONCLUSION

The IRS estimates that more than 20 percent of EITC payments are made in error. However, by matching the CPS to tax return data, this chapter finds that a large portion of the overpayments went to families with children. Depending on the exact measure used, only 11 to 13 percent of EITC recipients lacked children in their household at the time they received the credit. While some of these erroneous payments to households with children are going to households with multiple adults and combined incomes that exceed that of the typical EITC family, many of these ineligible families with children are likely to be quite similar to EITC-eligible families.

NOTES

1. On administrative costs, see GAO 1995 and Scholz 1997. On labor force participation, see Dickert, Houser, and Scholz 1995; Eissa and Liebman 1996; Meyer and Rosen-

baum 1999; chapter 3, this volume. On hours worked, see Triest 1996; Holtzblatt, McCubbin, and Gillette 1994; Dickert, Houser, and Scholz 1995; Eissa and Liebman 1996; Eissa and Hoynes 1998; Meyer and Rosenbaum 1999.

2. From the 1994 study, the Treasury Department has released figures only on overpayment rates and not on the number of ineligible taxpayers. However, in the 1988 TCMP data, the percentage of ineligible taxpayers and the overpayment rates were quite similar, suggesting that in 1994 around 20 percent of EITC recipients were ineligible for the credit.

3. Quality control audits of AFDC recipients may not be of the same intensity as IRS audits. Evidence of possibly higher AFDC error rates come from the work of Kathryn Edin (1993), who finds that essentially all AFDC recipients in a Chicago housing development had unreported income (although not necessarily enough to make them ineligible for the program), and Carolyn Hill and colleagues (1997), who match administrative welfare and earnings data for four California counties and find that at least 14 percent of AFDC recipients underreport earnings to the welfare system.

4. In an earlier paper (Liebman 1995) I provide a simple framework for calculating when it is more efficient to make transfers through the tax system than through the welfare system in light of differing administrative costs, participation rates, and noncompliance rates. The IRS estimates a noncompliance rate of 16 percent for the overall tax system (IRS 1996), so the estimated EITC overpayment rates are not that far above the overall noncompliance rate.

5. The analysis reported in this chapter was completed well before the data from the 1994 compliance study were available, at a time when it was unclear how much of an EITC compliance problem remained after the elimination of the support test in 1990.

6. Under pre-1991 EITC rules, a child was the taxpayer's son, daughter, stepchild, legally adopted child, or descendant of the taxpayer's child. In addition, married taxpayers could claim foster children who under IRS rules are children "you cared for as you would your own child." However, the foster child (which for married taxpayers includes grandchildren) had to live with the taxpayer for the full year.

7. Married taxpayers were entitled to claim the EITC without claiming a dependent exemption if the taxpayer's spouse was not the child's parent and the child's other parent was allowed to claim the exemption under a divorce agreement.

8. Surviving spouses also had to be able to claim their children as dependents to claim the EITC, as well as meeting a household maintenance test.

9. The Taxpayer Compliance Measurement Program samples roughly fifty thousand individual tax returns every three years. Internal Revenue Service auditors conduct line-by-line audits of the sampled tax returns to assist the IRS in designing methods for predicting which tax returns are efficient to audit. The 1991 TCMP was canceled owing to budget cutbacks. Tax returns were selected for the 1994 TCMP, but the audits never occurred, first because of budget cutbacks and then because of congressional opposition to the "audits from hell."

10. The TCMP dropped from the sample nonmarried filers who, in response to the audit, opted to file as married. From the 1994 IRS study we know that such filers are rare.

11. A taxpayer could have legitimately claimed the EITC without claiming a dependent child if the taxpayer had given up the dependent exemption in a divorce agreement.

12. Two IRS auditors I interviewed told me that it is difficult to catch a taxpayer who hides AFDC income, since the auditor generally cannot obtain information from the state on benefits paid (Kevin Belanger and Sean Schomer, interview with author, Boston, September 6, 1994). Another complaint about using TCMP estimates to measure EITC noncompliance comes from Robert Greenstein (1995), who argues that not all taxpayers who erroneously claim the EITC receive the EITC, since the IRS manages to catch some erroneous claims before mailing out refund checks. Greenstein's point is more relevant for recent years, when the IRS has begun using computerized matches of social security numbers before sending out refunds, than it is for the 1980s, when it was often many months after a refund check was mailed out that the IRS discovered that the return was suspect.

13. The GAO sample represents only 4 million of the 6.21 million tax returns with disallowed dependent exemptions. The sample does not represent the entire tax-filing population because some audit sheets could not be found and because discrepancies were found between some of the audit sheets and the TCMP computer file.

14. The 1993 GAO report estimates that 57 percent of returns that failed the support test failed because the claimant had not provided half the support, while 43 percent failed because the claimant had not kept adequate records. According to the auditors I interviewed, a taxpayer's dependent claim is often disallowed for not having kept adequate records when the auditor suspects but cannot prove that welfare income exists but can show that spending is greater than reported income. This implies that it is likely that many of the taxpayers whose claims were disqualified for insufficient documentation in fact did not meet the support test.

15. It seems likely that most of these errors involve married spouses who are separated from each other, because the IRS study found that the appropriate postaudit filing status for most of these households was married filing separately, not married filing jointly. While technically ineligible for the EITC, some of these separated households may be very similar to the eligible single-parent households to which the EITC aims to transfer money.

16. In order to protect census respondents, U.S. law does not permit the Census Bureau to share with the IRS microdata in which individuals can be identified. Therefore, research matching census microdata with tax return data can only be done by Census Bureau personnel.

17. The total income variable is the sum of wage and salary, total interest (taxable and tax exempt), taxable dividends, alimony received, business income, farm income, pensions and annuities, net rents, royalties, estates, trusts, unemployment compensation, and social security benefits. The file contains separate items for the amount of wage and salary income, interest income, rent and royalty income, and social security income. For tax returns that contained a schedule C, a schedule F, or a schedule SE, I define self-employment income as the difference between total income and the sum of the separately listed components of income. To the extent that these self-employed taxpayers have alimony, pension, or unemployment compensation income, my measure of self-employment income is incorrect.

18. Three-fourths of the EITC claims that I miss are head-of-household filers who do not claim a dependent child. If I were to include all head-of-household filers with appropriate income in my sample of EITC filers, then my sample would include 99 percent

of all EITC claims. However, 6 percent of my sample would be taxpayers who did not claim the EITC.

19. An earlier version of this paper (Liebman 1996) compares the estimates from the reweighting procedure with those from two multiple imputation techniques and presents the full details of all three methods. The results were extremely similar across the three procedures.

20. About one-fifth of the undercounting is attributable to my method of identifying EITC returns. In the Statistics of Income sample, my method identifies 12.2 million EITC returns while there are in fact 12.5 million.

21. Currently a child must be under the age of nineteen, under the age of twenty-four and a full-time student, or permanently or totally disabled to be an EITC qualifying child. However, under 1990 rules some older children could have qualified their parents for the EITC. In the next subsection, I explore the possibility that taxpayers are claiming adult children in order to claim the EITC.

22. I include the primary family (excluding any subfamilies that belong to it) as a subfamily. Thus, in this portion of the analysis a child will qualify only one of the household's subfamilies for the credit.

23. There are two main cases in which children in different subfamilies might entitle a taxpayer to the EITC. First, in a multigenerational family a grandparent who was in a different subfamily (as defined by the Census Bureau) could be eligible to claim the child for the EITC. Second, under the foster-child rules (which in this period apply only to married taxpayers), a taxpayer can claim a child for the EITC if the child lives with the taxpayer for the entire year and if the taxpayer treats the child as if he or she were the taxpayer's own child.

24. While family dynamics are often complicated, for my methodology to miss a child who qualifies the taxpayer for the EITC the child would have to have made two moves between March 1990 and March 1991—a first move into the household after March 1990 and a second move out of the household more than six months later but before March 1991. Even if this possible measurement error makes my estimates less than ideal measures of EITC noncompliance, the estimates are still relevant for the question of whether EITC payments are reaching households that have children living in them at the time the payments are made.

25. Within households, I first matched individuals in the March 1991 household to individuals who were one year younger, of the same gender, and on the same CPS line number in the March 1990 household. If no match was found, I then dropped the line-number requirement. If there was still no match, I matched the March 1991 individual to an (unmatched) individual in the March 1990 household of the same gender who was either the same age as the March 1991 individual or two years younger.

26. There is another source of child-related EITC noncompliance that is not picked up in these estimates. Even when each child is claimed only once, if there are multiple tax returns filed by adults in the household the wrong taxpayer (the one with the lower adjusted gross income) could erroneously claim the child in order to receive the EITC.

27. Scholz (1994) matches the 1990 Survey of Income and Program Participation (SIPP) to a file that allows him to determine which SIPP individuals filed tax returns. He presents the characteristics of people who are predicted, based on SIPP information, to be

eligible for the EITC and who file a tax return. He also presents characteristics of people who told the SIPP that they received the EITC but who do not appear to be eligible for the credit, based upon other SIPP information.

28. If the noncustodial parents who are erroneously receiving the EITC make income transfers to their children, the percentage of EITC dollars reaching families with children could be even higher.

29. It is likely that a substantial share of the married taxpayers who filed nonmarried returns involve cases in which the spouses are separated and therefore that the incomes on the two returns are not accruing to a single household.

30. This number is based on Scholz 1997; see Liebman 1998 for a discussion. To the extent that AFDC administrative dollars are spent on services beyond eligibility verification and benefit payments, the administrative costs of the two programs are not directly comparable.

31. According to Scholz (1997), most EITC recipients would file a tax return even in the absence of the EITC.

32. Scholz (1994) shows, using a variety of data sets and methodologies, that between 80 and 86 percent of EITC-eligible taxpayers receive the EITC. In comparison, Rebecca Blank and Patricia Ruggles (1993) estimate that AFDC-eligible families received 75 percent of the total dollars to which these families are entitled.

33. Holtzblatt and Liebman (1999) discuss the United Kingdom's recent conversion from a welfare-based system of in-work benefits to a tax-based system.

34. There is also excess burden from raising the revenue, but in this simple example it is simply proportional to the direct costs and does not affect the comparison.

35. As I discussed in note 3, there are reasons to suspect that AFDC noncompliance rates are higher than the official quality control estimates would suggest.

36. Placing a low or even negative weight on the dollars transferred to ineligible recipients could be justified if their activity might encourage others to evade taxes or is simply distasteful. An earlier paper (Liebman 1995) finds that improper claiming of children rose after the 1986 expansion of the EITC, indicating that at least some ineligible EITC recipients are responding to the economic incentive to wrongly claim children.

37. This analysis ignores the different participation rates of the two programs. If the social-welfare value of dollars to eligible taxpayers is high, the tax system could be preferable even at a higher cost because it manages to reach a higher percentage of its intended beneficiaries. Liebman 1995 contains a more elaborate analysis of this issue that includes differential participation rates.

REFERENCES

Blank, Rebecca M., and Patricia Ruggles. 1993. "When Do Women Use AFDC and Food Stamps? The Dynamics of Eligibility Versus Participation." Working Paper 4429. Cambridge, Mass.: National Bureau of Economic Research.

Dickert, Stacy, Scott Houser, and John K. Scholz. 1995. "The Earned Income Tax Credit and Transfer Programs: A Study of Labor Market and Program Participation." *Tax Policy and the Economy* 9: 1–50.

Edin, Kathryn. 1993. *There's a Lot of Month Left at the End of the Money: How Welfare Recipients Make Ends Meet in Chicago.* New York: Garland Publishing.

Eissa, Nada, and Hilary Hoynes. 1998. "The Earned Income Tax Credit and the Labor Supply of Married Couples." Working Paper 6856. Cambridge, Mass.: National Bureau of Economic Research.

Eissa, Nada, and Jeffrey B. Liebman. 1996. "Labor Supply Response to the Earned Income Tax Credit." *Quarterly Journal of Economics* 111(2): 606–37.

Graetz, Michael J., and Louis L. Wilde. 1985. "The Economics of Tax Compliance: Fact and Fantasy." *National Tax Journal* 38(3): 355–63.

Greenstein, Robert. 1995. "The Earned Income Tax Credit: A Target for Budget Cuts." Washington, D.C.: Center on Budget and Policy Priorities.

Hill, Carolyn J., V. Joseph Hotz, Charles H. Mullin, and John Karl Scholz. 1997. "EITC Eligibility, Participation, and Compliance Rates for AFDC Households: Evidence from the California Caseload." University of Chicago. Draft Report.

Holtzblatt, Janet. 1991. "Administering Refundable Tax Credits: Lessons from the EITC Experience." In *Proceedings of the Eighty-fourth Annual Conference on Taxation.* Washington, D.C.: National Tax Association.

Holtzblatt, Janet, and Jeffrey B. Liebman. 1999. "The EITC Abroad." In *Proceedings of the Ninety-first Annual Conference on Taxation.* Washington, D.C.: National Tax Association.

Holtzblatt, Janet, Janet McCubbin, and Robert Gillette. 1994. "Promoting Work Through the EITC." Washington: U.S. Department of Treasury (June).

Liebman, Jeffrey B. 1995. "Noncompliance and the Earned Income Tax Credit: Taxpayer Error or Taxpayer Fraud?" Unpublished paper. Harvard University.

———. 1996. "The Impact of the Earned Income Tax Credit on Labor Supply and Taxpayer Compliance." Ph.D. diss., Harvard University.

———. 1998. "The Impact of the Earned Income Tax Credit on Incentives and Income Distribution." *Tax Policy and the Economy* 12: 83–118.

Meyer, Bruce D., and Dan T. Rosenbaum. 1999. "Welfare, the Earned Income Tax Credit, and the Labor Supply of Single Mothers." Working Paper 7363. Cambridge, Mass.: National Bureau of Economic Research.

Office of Management and Budget. 2000. *Budget of the United States Government, Fiscal Year 2001.* Washington: U.S. Government Printing Office.

Scholz, John K. 1990. "The Participation Rate of the Earned Income Tax Credit." Discussion Paper 928-90. Madison: University of Wisconsin, Madison, Institute for Research on Poverty.

———. 1994. "The Earned Income Tax Credit: Participation, Compliance, and Antipoverty Effectiveness." *National Tax Journal* 48(1): 63–85.

———. 1997. "Internal Revenue Service's 1995 Earned Income Tax Credit Compliance Study." Hearing before the Committee on Ways and Means, U.S. House of Representatives, 105th Cong., 1st sess. Serial 105–26. Washington, D.C. (May 8).

Szilagyi, John. 1991. "Where Some of Those Dependents Went." In *1990 Research Conference Report: How Do We Affect Taxpayer Behavior.* Washington: U.S. Department of the Treasury, Internal Revenue Service (March).

Triest, Robert K. 1996. "The Efficiency Cost of Increased Progressivity." In *Tax Progressivity and Income Inequality,* edited by Joel Slemrod. Cambridge: Cambridge University Press.

U.S. Department of the Treasury. Internal Revenue Service (IRS). 1996. *Federal Compliance Research: Individual Income Tax Gap Estimates for 1985, 1988, 1992.* Washington: U.S. Department of the Treasury.

U.S. General Accounting Office (GAO). 1993. *Tax Administration, Erroneous Dependent and Filing Status Claims.* GAO/GGD-93-60. Washington, D.C. (March).

———. 1995. *Earned Income Credit, Noncompliance, and Potential Eligibility Revisions: Statement of Lynda D. Willis Before the U.S. Senate, Committee on Finance.* GAO/T-GGD-95-179. Washington, D.C. (June 8).

———. 1998. *Earned Income Tax Credit: IRS's Tax Year 1994 Compliance Study and Recent Efforts to Reduce Noncompliance.* GAO/GGD-98-150. Washington, D.C. (June).

U.S. House of Representatives. Committee on Ways and Means. 1998. *1998 Green Book.* Washington: U.S. Government Printing Office.

Welch, Finis. 1991. "Matching the Current Population Surveys." *Stata Technical Bulletin* 12: 7–11.

Part IV

How Recipients Use Their Credit

Chapter 8

The Earned Income Tax Credit: Expectation, Knowledge, Use, and Economic and Social Mobility

Timothy M. Smeeding, Katherin Ross Phillips, and Michael A. O'Connor

The largest targeted tax-credit program for low-income families is the Earned Income Tax Credit (EITC). In 1997, the EITC cost the federal government $30.0 billion, more than was spent on food stamps or Temporary Assistance for Needy Families in that year. More than 19.8 million taxpaying units benefited from the EITC in 1997. About 80 percent of the benefits were returned to claimants in the form of Internal Revenue Service (IRS) tax refund checks in 1998, and the remainder went directly to reduce tax liability (IRS 1999c). Despite its fiscal size, little is known about the impact of the EITC on the families who receive it.[1] Unlike other income transfer programs, the EITC is received by almost all families as an annual lump-sum tax refund check paid sometime in the spring of the year after wages are earned (IRS 1999b). Because of the form and generosity of the EITC, it is liable to have very different behavioral and economic effects than if the benefits were received on a monthly basis throughout the year, as is the case with most other means-tested transfers.

This chapter examines how the EITC influences recipients' expenditure patterns by asking a number of questions. Does expectation of a refund affect how EITC funds are used? Are EITC checks used to pay bills or to make new purchases, or are they primarily saved for later use? Does the EITC mainly help finance current consumption, or does it affect savings and investment behavior, helping low-income beneficiaries build assets and equity and therefore improve economic and social mobility?[2]

RECENT STUDIES OF THE EITC: BEHAVIORAL AND ECONOMIC EFFECTS

The EITC was enacted in 1975 to provide refundable tax credits to low-income workers and, originally, to refund some fraction of their social security taxes (Eissa and Hoynes 1998). The EITC was significantly expanded in the Tax Reform Act of 1986 and the Omnibus Budget Reconciliation Acts of 1990 and, especially, 1993. The most significant changes in the EITC have taken place in benefit generosity to families with two or more children.[3] The 1993 Omnibus Act expanded the maximum credit for families with two or more children from $1,511 in 1993 to $3,556 in 1996. As a result, the earnings subsidy for low-earnings families with two or more qualifying children doubled over three years, from 19.5 percent of earnings in 1993 to 40 percent of earnings in 1996. Because of this growth, the EITC benefits a wide range of families, from those who might be cycling on and off welfare (Temporary Assistance for Needy Families) to those with near median incomes. Faced with this broad range of beneficiaries, we would expect to find different types of behavioral and economic effects for different types of recipients.

Most, if not all, previous studies of the behavioral effects of the EITC have concentrated on labor supply, family formation, or differential design of employment-based subsidies. The EITC offers a powerful work incentive for low-income parents with children—for example, the Temporary Assistance for Needy Families population—with an earnings subsidy of 40 percent for each dollar of pay up to $8,890 in 1996. One recent econometric study (Meyer and Rosenbaum 1999) concludes that the EITC has been the primary driving force in increasing employment by single mothers over the period from 1984 to 1996. Nada Eissa and Jeffrey Liebman (1996) reach a similar conclusion for the period from 1984 to 1990, using different data, and the Council of Economic Advisers (1998, chart 6) demonstrates that increased labor force participation among low-income mothers closely tracks changes in the maximum EITC benefit level over the past decade. The federal EITC for families with two or more children in 1996 declined at a rate of 21.06 percent for each dollar earned from $11,610 to $28,495, the phase-out range. Eissa and Hilary Hoynes (1998) find that the phase-out reduces work effort by married women. Thus, higher-earning families in the phase-out region of the EITC may have different labor supply responses than do lower-earning families in the phase-in or plateau ranges.[4]

All of these studies treat the EITC as an income subsidy and, for the most part, do not deal explicitly with its delivery mechanism, timing, and form of benefit receipt or its effects on expenditures. In fact, recent studies of the substantial antipoverty effect of the EITC (Greenstein and Shapiro 1998; Council of Economic Advisers 1998) estimate the effect of the EITC on poverty during the year in which earnings are received as income, not during the following year, when the EITC tax refunds based on these earnings are actually received. Counting the EITC as income in one period when the benefit is not received until the following year suggests a degree of liquidity and consumption spreading that may be beyond the means of many recipient families. Looking at the timing and form of benefit receipt also raises the question of whether the EITC should be viewed as an income transfer or as an asset transfer.

Because of its unique administration through the income tax system and its "lumpy" character, the EITC offers a rare opportunity to examine the economic impact of a tax refund program on recipients. Nicholas Souleles (1999) also studies the response of household consumption to income tax refunds from 1979 to 1990 but does not separate the EITC from other refunds. He finds that roughly 20 percent of all income tax refunds is used for purchases of durable goods.[5]

The lumpy nature of the EITC arises from several factors. First, only a portion of the EITC can be received as an ongoing transfer during the year in which income is earned. An employee who submits a W-5 withholding form to his or her employer can receive an advanced payment of up to 60 percent of the maximum allowable amount of the credit for a worker with one qualifying child. This translates into a maximum amount of advanced payment in 1998 of $26 a week (IRS 1999b). By receiving the credit as a lump sum at tax time, however, a worker with two qualifying children could be eligible for as much as $72 a week, nearly three times the maximum advance-payment amount.[6] More than 99 percent of recipients do not use the advance-payment option and instead receive a lump-sum amount when they file their income taxes in the following year (Scholz 1994; IRS 1999a, 1999b).

There are several possible explanations for the observed preference for a lump-sum transfer over the advance-payment option, including employers' unwillingness to participate in the program; employees' unwillingness to inform the employer of EITC eligibility because of stigma effects or fears of lower pretax wages; instability and variability of earnings among the likely EITC population that raises the probability of having to repay the EITC advance at tax time; recipient indifference toward the choice between lump-sum and monthly payments with the added cost of compliance, with monthly payments tipping them in favor of the lump sum; and employees' desire for the forced savings aspects of the EITC that result from receipt of the entire benefit in a lump sum. While there is some evidence that recipients prefer the forced savings aspects of the EITC (Romich and Weisner 1999; Olson and Davis 1994), the relative impacts of each of these factors on the form of EITC receipt have yet to be thoroughly examined.

Regardless of the reason for the type of benefit receipt, the lumpy nature of the EITC benefit and its benefit generosity create an opportunity to study the effects of the program on household expenditure patterns and on asset behavior (that is, debt, credit, and savings).[7] Little has been written about the way households use EITC benefits, despite the fact that federal EITC benefits can be as high as 40 percent of the previous year's income. One small study (based on telephone interviews with two hundred to three hundred taxpayers) shows that the EITC is frequently used to pay overdue utility bills (Gallup Poll 1993). A *New York Times* news story (Sara Rimer, "Cutting Tax Credit Means Much to Those with Little," *New York Times*, October 16, 1995, 1) suggests that some recipients make interesting and creative use of the EITC to improve transportation to and from a job, to move to a safer neighborhood, or to put children into better schools. However, Rimer does not examine the extent to which these uses are typical or idiosyncratic. A recent ethnographic study of forty-two low-income families in Wisconsin examines the use of tax refunds (Romich and Weisner 1999).[8] The authors conclude that families use lump-sum tax refunds to improve family well-being and to make large purchases. Finally, Lisa Barrow and Leslie McGranahan, in chapter 9 of this volume, find that the EITC induces changes in seasonal expenditure patterns for durable goods. Using survey data specifically designed to address these questions, our study describes the way families plan to spend or save their EITC benefit.

THE CENTER FOR LAW AND HUMAN SERVICES STUDY

Our data are drawn from a sample of five thousand low-income Chicago-area taxpayers who utilized the free tax preparation services provided by the Center for Law and Human Services (CLHS) in the winter and spring of 1998. The CLHS has ten centers in the Chicago metropolitan area, almost all in low-income neighborhoods. Low-income taxpayers can receive free assistance in preparing their tax returns from professionally qualified volunteers at a CLHS center.[9] We designed the survey instrument and employed five interviewers who visited seven of these sites from January 1998 through April 1998 to interview EITC beneficiaries at the time their tax returns were filed. More than 90 percent of the taxpayers interviewed were willing to discuss their refunds, producing a sample of 1,226 total respondents, 1,121 of whom were expected to receive a federal refund and 846 of whom expected to benefit from the EITC.

For this chapter, we selected a sample of tax units that the CLHS calculated would have a federal tax refund and also receive the EITC. These selection criteria produced a sample of 823 returns. From these we excluded single persons receiving the EITC. Our main analytic group is the subset of the tax units that receive the EITC as part of a federal tax refund and that also have dependent children, a total of 650 respondents (table 8.1).

The CLHS database contains two types of information. First, we have access to data from the federal tax returns of all recipients who filed through the CLHS in 1998. For our sample this includes filing status, number of dependents, and all sources of income reported to the IRS. In addition, we constructed an interview with each respondent about the intended use of the EITC. The CLHS interview asked recipients about their knowledge of and expectation of the EITC and their priorities and anticipated use of the EITC to pay bills (several categories), purchase items (several categories), or to save the EITC checks for future use. They were also asked about their ability to carry out their spending or saving priorities were it not for the EITC. A subset of the actual questions used in the survey is included as an appendix to this chapter.[10]

Sample Characteristics

In this study we restrict our analyses to families with children: single parents or two-parent filers. According to IRS data for 1996, of the 19.5 million filers who claimed the EITC, 7.8 million claimed one child while 8.0 million claimed two or

TABLE 8.1 / Expectation of Tax Refund and EITC Among CLHS Sample, by
Refund Status

Refund Status	Overall	Expecting a Refund	Expecting a Refund and EITC	Expecting a Refund and EITC, with Children
Tax refund (dollars)[a]				
Minimum	0	1	17	40
Median	772	927	1,724	2,240
Average	1,326	1,450	1,800	2,173
Maximum	5,023	5,023	5,023	5,023
EITC alone (dollars)				
Minimum	0	11	11	14
Median	432	1,351	1,403	1,898
Average	1,019	1,477	1,502	1,850
Maximum	3,656	3,656	3,656	3,656
EITC as share of federal tax refund (percentage)				
Minimum		0	1	1
Median		76	88	91
Average		65	87	90
Maximum[b]		1,884	1,884	1,884

Source: Authors' tabulations from 1998 survey of Center for Law and Human Services tax
filers.
[a]Overwithholding plus EITC.
[b]The EITC acts both to offset a recipient's tax burden and as a refundable credit. In the
absence of the EITC, tax filers who overwithhold during the year would receive a tax refund
at the end of the year. For these tax filers, the EITC as a share of the federal tax return will be
less than 100. On the other hand, in the absence of the EITC, tax filers who underwithhold
during the year would owe taxes at the end of the year. For this group of tax filers, the EITC
as a share of the federal tax return will exceed 100.

more children (IRS 1999a). More than 97 percent of the total cost of the credit for
tax year 1996 ($28.2 billion) went to the 82 percent of the filers who claimed one
or more eligible children (IRS 1999a). Of our sample of EITC returns from households with children, 47 percent had one child and 53 percent had two or more
children. These figures are comparable to national figures of 49 percent with one
child and 51 percent with two or more children.

Our sample of filers with children is 48 percent African American, 32 percent
Latino or Hispanic, and 20 percent Caucasian or other. The 1990 census indicates
that among those families with children under the age of eighteen in the Chicago central city, 43 percent of families were African American, 27 percent Hispanic, and 30 percent white or other ethnic group (U.S. Bureau of the Census
2000). About 65 percent of our total sample who received the EITC and a refund
were single parents (as determined by head-of-household filing status), while 15

percent were married filing a joint return and 19 percent were single-person filers.[11] National samples from 1997 divide EITC beneficiaries into two major groups: about 70 percent are single parents filing as heads of households or single persons, and almost 30 percent are low-earning two-parent households (U.S. House 1998, 871, table 13-13). Other IRS data suggest that 18 percent of filers in 1996 were single filers without children (IRS 1999c). Assuming the same fraction of single filers in 1997 as in 1996, this means that 52 percent of national filers were single-parent heads of households in 1997.

These characteristics suggest that our total sample population is more likely to be made up of single parents than the national sample (65 percent for our sample as against 52 percent nationally). Our sample, however, is more restrictive than the IRS national sample: tax units in our sample not only receive the EITC but also have a positive federal tax refund. We know of no national data on the ethnicity of EITC recipients, but our sample is representative of the 1990 Census Bureau data on the racial and ethnic composition of the Chicago central-city area.

Classification of Expenditure and Savings Bundles

In this study, we examine two important types of uses for the EITC: making ends meet (or consumption use) and improving economic and social mobility (or investment use). The survey instrument permits us to go into considerable detail in classifying how recipients say they will use their EITC (see appendix 8A, section C). Respondents were given several categories of future purchases for goods or services, for paying off existing bills, and for saving the refund for future anticipated or unanticipated needs. While several other bundles of categories of uses could be created, we selected these two categories for a variety of reasons.

MAKING ENDS MEET   The EITC is targeted on low-income working families with children, many of whom also receive other means-tested transfers (see table 8.A1). This suggests that much of our head-of-household population could be a population that is struggling to make ends meet. They may have unmet consumption needs, or they may use the EITC mainly to spread their consumption over the year. Chapter 9 of this volume finds some evidence that EITC recipients smooth consumption. Hence, the EITC may provide the means for recipients to buy clothing, food, and durables, pay off outstanding bills, and meet other urgent consumption needs.

In the making-ends-meet bundle we include payment of regular bills (rent, utilities, food, groceries, personal expenses), purchases of clothing, appliances, or household furniture, and other personal or regular household expenses.[12] To the extent that the EITC helps meet current consumption needs, it may be no different from other types of income subsidies, child-care subsidies, and similar benefits (for example, food stamps) in terms of its impact on recipients' expenditure patterns.

IMPROVING ECONOMIC AND SOCIAL MOBILITY   In a recent study of low-income working mothers, Kathryn Edin (1998) finds that a majority of her sample were credit constrained and had little leverage to borrow money. The recent literature on asset holdings by the poor and by minorities (for example, Sherraden 1991; Edin 1998; Oliver and Shapiro 1995; Shapiro 1998; Ziliak 1999) suggests that when presented with incentives and opportunities to save, low-income families are willing to postpone current consumption to improve their long-run economic well-being.

The large size of the EITC relative to current income may present an opportunity for otherwise credit-constrained low-income families to move beyond current consumption and to use the EITC to build assets. Thomas Shapiro (1998) refers to this as "asset building" or "improving social mobility." We adopt the term "economic and social mobility" here to describe several equity-enhancing uses of the EITC that improve longer-term economic mobility and well-being. Most of these are consistent with Edin's (1998) findings and those of Rimer ("Cutting Tax Credit Means Much to Those with Little") and Jennifer Romich and Thomas Weisner (1999) in their more limited set of interviews. They are also consistent with the evidence on spending on vehicles from general income tax refunds (Souleles 1999).

Our economic-and-social-mobility bundle includes all forms of debt repayment, savings, and other expenditures that increase chances for improved mobility, including all forms of work-related expenses.[13] These include payment of credit card, automobile, or personal debt as well as human capital building (for example, payment of tuition, medical bills), expenses for cars (purchases, repairs, insurance), moving expenses, and home improvements.[14] Sharing money with family members is also classified as an equity expense in that it builds bonds to family members who could help the donor unit in time of need.[15]

RESULTS OF THE CENTER FOR LAW AND HUMAN SERVICES STUDY

Does expectation of a refund affect financial planning, especially planning of how EITC funds will be allocated? Are EITC checks used to pay bills or to make new purchases, or are they primarily saved for later use? Does the EITC mainly help finance current consumption, or does it affect savings and investment behavior, helping low-income beneficiaries build assets and equity and therefore improve economic and social mobility? In the tables in this chapter, we categorize respondents along three axes: expectation of receiving a refund, income level, and the three ranges of EITC benefit receipt—those with lower earnings that provide less than the maximum benefit are in the phase-in (or subsidy) range, those with the maximum benefit are at the plateau, and those with higher incomes are in the phase-out range. Expectations of refunds should be an important determinant of planned uses. Those with knowledge of the EITC should have made better long-run plans for spending and have a clearer set of prioritized uses than those who do not have such knowledge. Different income levels may help explain involvement with financial intermediaries. First, we examine the average size of the EITC and tax refunds among our sample.

Tax Refunds or EITC?

Owing to overwithholding, our recipients could receive tax refunds other than the federal EITC. Overwithholding, not the EITC itself, could be the driving factor influencing the expenditure decisions we observe. Table 8.1 presents information on the distribution of total refunds as well as EITC benefits for four groups: all taxpayers interviewed in the CLHS study, all those expecting a refund, all those expecting a refund and the EITC, and our main sample, all those with children expecting both a positive refund and the EITC. The EITC is the largest source of refund for all recipients, particularly those with larger total refunds (see table 8.1) and families with children. In our sample, the average EITC payment is $1,850, and, on average, the EITC constitutes 90 percent of the total federal tax refund.[16] We conclude that the EITC is the main driving force in our analyses and the major source of the associated economic impacts examined in this chapter.

Expectation and Knowledge of the EITC

To some extent, many findings in this study are dependent on the assumption that our clients expected to receive a refund and then considered how those refunds would be used.[17] We find a surprisingly high level of expectation of a tax refund and some evidence that the EITC program was the primary source of the expected tax refund (figure 8.1). A full 83 percent of our sample expected to receive a refund when they came to the CLHS. Among those expecting a refund, about one-third seemed to be familiar with the EITC itself. That is, they used the term "EITC" for the refund or told the interviewer that they were eligible for the refund because it was intended for low-income people or because they had worked all year and had a qualifying child or a similar response.[18] We deliberately did not include the EITC as a category in the survey, preferring that the recipients identify the program themselves. The remaining responses were scattered among other categories, particularly "received a refund last year" and others.[19] Since respondents were allowed to provide only one reason for their expectation of a refund, some who did not identify the EITC may also have had knowledge of the EITC but answered in other categories. Table 8.2 indicates that the expectation of a refund increases across the EITC range; the greatest percent-

FIGURE 8.1 / Knowledge of EITC Among Respondents Getting a Refund and EITC and With Dependent Children

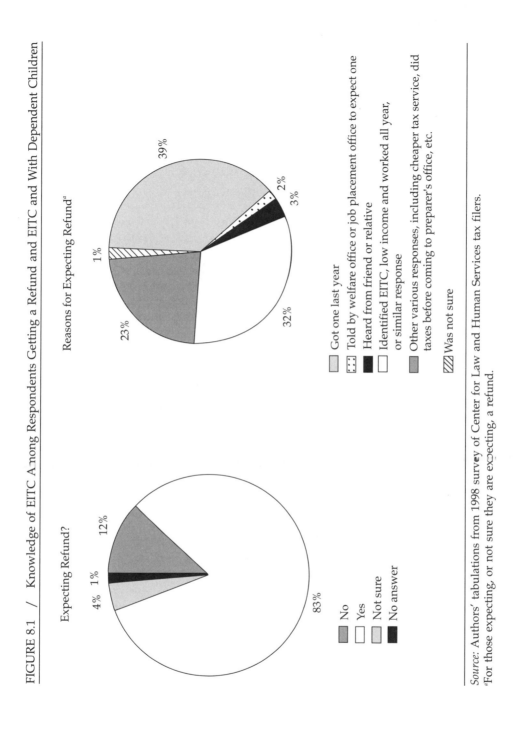

Source: Authors' tabulations from 1998 survey of Center for Law and Human Services tax filers.
[a]For those expecting, or not sure they are expecting, a refund.

TABLE 8.2 / Expectation of EITC Receipt, by EITC Range (Percentage)

EITC Range	Expecting EITC	Not Expecting EITC
Phase-in	74.9	25.1
Plateau	82.6	17.4
Phase-out	82.0	18.0
N	513	137

Source: Authors' tabulations from 1998 survey of Center for Law and Human Services tax filers.

age with expectations are at the plateau level, where the refund level is highest both in dollars and as a percentage of income, and in the phase-out range, where incomes are higher. A large majority of recipients in our sample anticipated refunds and may have factored the refunds into their household financial planning. The data in table 8.3 suggest how important the tax refund is to our sample of survey respondents.

Importance of the EITC

Respondents who expected to receive a refund of $200 or more were asked to list, in order of importance, up to three important uses of the refund. They were then asked if they could afford to carry out their first priority in the absence of the tax refund (table 8.3).[20] Almost half of the respondents (48.7 percent) said that they would not be able to meet their first priority unless they received the refund, and another 43 percent stated that without the refund they would be

TABLE 8.3 / Importance of EITC Refund, by Expectation of Receipt and EITC Range (Percentage)

In absence of refund, could respondent do first priority?	Expected a Refund		EITC Range			
	Yes	No	Phase-In	Plateau	Phase-Out	Overall
Yes	7.1	6.6	5.4	5.6	10.0	7.1
No	48.7	47.3	49.8	47.7	47.3	48.5
Lesser amount	14.7	18.7	18.2	13.1	12.9	15.3
With some delay	28.4	24.2	24.7	32.7	28.9	27.7
Lesser amount and some delay	0.2	0.0	0.0	0.0	0.5	0.2
Not sure	0.8	3.2	1.9	0.9	0.5	1.2
N[a]	476	91	259	107	201	567

Source: Authors' tabulations from 1998 survey of Center for Law and Human Services tax filers.
[a]More than 12 percent of respondents (83) of the sample (650) did not answer this question.

forced to spend (or save) a lesser amount or to delay their top priority for some time. Those with the lowest incomes (in the phase-in and plateau regions) are slightly more likely to have difficulty. The inability to carry out first-priority objectives in the absence of the EITC, however, is evident across all three EITC ranges and does not differ by expectation of a refund. Only 7 percent could definitely achieve their primary objective if they did not receive the EITC, and the ability to find alternative sources of income for the stated purpose increased in the phase-out ranges. Respondents who did not expect a refund were less likely to be able to meet their first-priority uses. The large majority of beneficiaries, whether expecting a refund or not, could not readily meet their priority uses unless they received the EITC.

Priority Uses of the EITC

Of our sample, 81 percent had at least a first-priority use for the EITC, while 46 percent also had a second priority and 14 percent a third priority use as well (figure 8.2). These priority declarations were separate from questions regarding the detailed use of refunds, which followed (see appendix 8A). These responses indicate that bill paying was the single most important use of the EITC for one-half of all beneficiaries; among the smaller fraction of respondents who listed second- and third-priority use levels, purchases were the second most important use. Across all three priority levels, bill paying was a priority use for 83 percent of respondents, and purchase of some commodity was a priority for 74 percent. Clearly the EITC helps pay bills and to make ends meet.

However, fully one-half of all respondents with qualifying children also stated that their priorities included saving some or all of their EITC checks. Moreover, in our earlier paper (Smeeding et al. 1999) we identified three key uses of the EITC to enhance social mobility: moving, paying tuition, and purchasing or repairing a car. Each of these uses is also presented in figure 8.2. While moving seems to be an all-or-nothing decision (with only 2 percent listing it as a secondary or tertiary priority compared with 4 percent who list it as a primary priority), paying tuition and purchasing or repairing a car are more evenly spread across the priority ordering. Altogether, 16 percent of the sample stated they would use the EITC to pay tuition, while 22 percent would make a car-related use of the refund. These uses suggest that the EITC also plays a large role in improving economic and social mobility. All other priority uses of the EITC are included in the final column of figure 8.2 and amount to only 10 percent of primary priorities and 13 percent of secondary priorities.

Bundles of Use

In addition to asking respondents to list anticipated uses for their refunds, in order of importance, we also asked them how they specifically intended to use

FIGURE 8.2 / Self-Reported Important Uses of Refund Among Respondents Getting a Refund and EITC and With Dependent Children (Percentage)

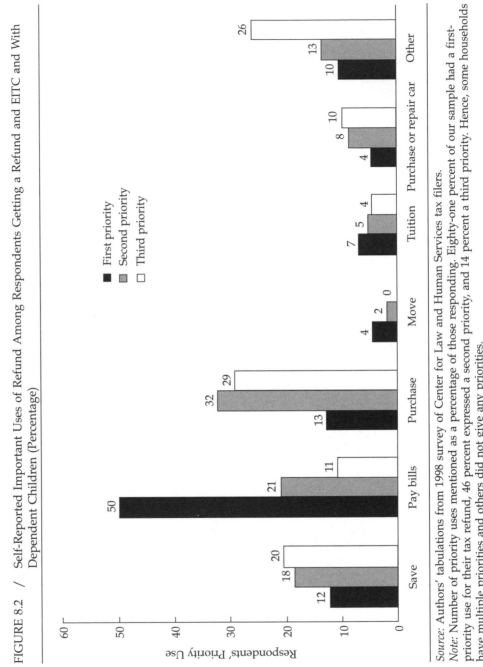

Source: Authors' tabulations from 1998 survey of Center for Law and Human Services tax filers.
Note: Number of priority uses mentioned as a percentage of those responding. Eighty-one percent of our sample had a first-priority use for their tax refund, 46 percent expressed a second priority, and 14 percent a third priority. Hence, some households have multiple priorities and others did not give any priorities.

the EITC. Respondents could, and usually did, have more than one expected use for their credit refunds. Because a first-priority use (for example, paying an over-due bill) may differ from the largest source of expense or use, these questions were designed to have the client give us as much detail as possible about the categorical breakdown of the refund. We then disaggregated respondents by ex-pectation of refund to arrive at our best overall snapshot of EITC use.[21]

Almost 70 percent of all beneficiaries with children had a use for the EITC related to economic and social mobility (table 8.4). Those who expected a refund were much more likely than those not expecting a refund to have such a use (75 to 49 percent). Cars and schooling were the most important specific spending uses listed under mobility uses. Among respondents who had a mobility use but did not expect a refund, the majority planned to save at least a portion of their refunds. Those not expecting a refund were also most likely to have no plans for the EITC (34.3 percent).[22] Because expectations lead to a high probability of mo-bility use (as well as making-ends-meet use), the EITC appears to be more than a

TABLE 8.4 / Anticipated Use of the EITC Refund, by Expectation of Refund (Percentage)

Category	Expecting Refund	Not Expecting Refund	Overall
Households receiving EITC	78.9	21.1	100.0
Economic- and social-mobility use	75.4	48.9	69.9
Move	6.4	0.0	5.1
Car or transportation	18.7	5.8	16.0
Save	34.3	25.6	32.5
Tuition and other schooling expense	11.1	6.6	10.2
Making-ends-meet use	68.8	49.6	64.8
Utilities	40.0	24.8	36.8
Rent	36.5	24.8	34.0
Food	23.0	12.4	20.8
Clothes	23.0	19.7	22.3
Durables	10.2	14.0	13.2
Plans for EITC			
None	7.4	34.3	13.1
Economic- and social-mobility use only	23.8	16.1	22.2
Making-ends-meet use only	17.2	16.8	17.1
Both uses	51.7	32.9	47.7
N	513	137	650

Source: Authors' tabulations from 1998 survey of Center for Law and Human Services tax filers.
Note: Owing to rounding, totals may not add up to 100 percent. The sample is the 650 respondents who are getting both a tax refund and EITC and have dependent children. Number of households mentioning each specific use with a specified dollar amount allocated to each use. Additional questions were asked to further break down bill and purchase priorities into subcomponents. See survey questions C.1 to C.3 in appendix.

simple consumption-spreading transfer.[23] That is, the EITC does seem to provide opportunities for investments that might not be as likely were those beneficiaries to receive a smaller but continuous transfer during the previous year.

About 65 percent of all EITC clients with children had a making-ends-meet use: 69 percent of those expecting a benefit and one-half of those not expecting a benefit. Overall, utilities and rent were the most important expenditure categories, followed by food and clothing. Only 13 percent mentioned purchasing a durable good (other than a car) as a specific use of the EITC refund. Almost one-half of all beneficiaries, and more than one-half of those expecting a refund, had both types of uses planned for their refunds. Among those choosing either mobility uses only or making-ends-meet uses only, the former was a stronger preference for those expecting a refund.

Use of the EITC, by Number of Children

One important determinant of the use of the EITC may be the number of children in the family (table 8.5). Among our sample of 650 EITC clients with children, 19 percent had three or more children, 34 percent had two children, and about 47 percent had only one child. Larger families were more likely to have at least one making-ends-meet use and less likely to have an economic- and social-mobility use. A full 20 percent of those with three or more children had only making-ends-meet uses. This pattern suggests that larger families are more likely to spend the EITC on a consumption-related use.

Access to Credit

It is important to understand how EITC recipients relate to financial institutions. Low-income respondents who use check-cashing services and have no formal relationship with financial service providers—for example, no checking or savings accounts and no credit cards, loans, or mortgages—are less likely to be able to keep a large EITC refund intact for future needs. Moreover, access to credit (and therefore to debt) is important for consumption smoothing, whether through credit cards or through formal loans. If we think of the EITC as an expected lump-sum transfer, access to credit may be crucial to consumption-smoothing behavior. In our sample it is not clear how debts and the timing of purchases are related. Even if the recipient chooses the ongoing payment option for the EITC, the maximum benefit may be as little as one-third of the actual refund, given the constraints of the advance-payment option. Therefore, access to credit and debt are an important aspect of EITC usage.

Access to financial and credit markets differs markedly across the income levels of our sample population (table 8.6). Only 42 percent of those with adjusted gross incomes of less than $7,500 had access to one or more of the common types of financial services. Only 27 percent had a checking account. In

TABLE 8.5 / Planned Use for EITC by Number of Dependent Children (Percentage)

| | Number of Dependent Children | | | |
Planned Use	1	2	3 or more	Overall
Plans for EITC				
Any economic- and social-mobility use	70.2	72.3	64.8	69.9
Any making-ends-meet use	58.0	70.9	70.4	64.8
Priority Plans for EITC				
None	13.1	11.8	15.2	13.1
Economic- and social-mobility only	28.9	17.3	14.4	22.2
Making-ends-meet use only	16.7	15.9	20.0	17.1
Both uses	41.3	55.0	50.4	47.7
N	305	220	125	650

Source: Authors' tabulations from 1998 survey of Center for Law and Human Services tax filers.

contrast, 81 percent of those with incomes of $15,000 or more had some contact with financial services, and 56 percent had checking accounts. Use of checking and savings accounts, credit cards, bank loans, and mortgages all increase with income. In contrast, use of a check-cashing service declines steadily with rising income, with 59 percent of those in the lowest income range using such services

TABLE 8.6 / Respondents' Access to Financial and Credit Services, by Adjusted Gross Income Range

| | Adjusted Gross Income | | | |
	$7,500 or less	$7,500 to $15,000	$15,000 or more	Overall
N	260	219	171	650
Average number of children	1.8	1.8	2.0	1.8
Assets and formal credit				
Checking account	26.5	42.0	56.1	39.5
Savings account	14.2	31.5	51.5	29.9
Credit card	19.2	32.9	40.4	29.4
Bank loan	1.9	4.1	5.3	3.5
Mortgage	3.5	8.7	11.1	7.2
Opening account with refund	1.2	1.4	0.0	0.9
Any of the above	41.5	66.2	81.3	60.3
Planning to use check-cashing service for EITC	59.2	42.5	24.6	44.5

Source: Authors' tabulations from 1998 survey of Center for Law and Human Services tax filers.

compared with only 25 percent in the highest income group. Most of our sample who have plans to save (64 percent) already have access to financial institutions.[24] Very few (1 percent of the sample) told us they planned to use the EITC to open a bank account. Tabular comparisons indicate that the breakdowns in table 8.6 are similar to those found by other researchers using national samples to investigate use of credit cards and checking and savings accounts among low-income populations (for example, Bird, Hagstrom, and Wild 1998; Carney and Gale 1998).

CONCLUSION

This chapter presents an exploration of how families use our largest targeted refundable tax credit, the Earned Income Tax Credit. The EITC is a unique income support program both because of its administration through the income tax system and the nature of its lump-sum, once-a-year delivery. While there is an option to have a portion of the EITC paid intrayear as a form of negative withholding (the advance-payment EITC option), only about 1 percent of taxpaying units receive the advanced EITC. A once-a-year benefit may provide a key pathway for families to overcome a short-term liquidity crisis and to move beyond support of current consumption to meet more strategic long-term goals. This chapter classifies uses of the EITC according to making ends meet (supporting consumption patterns) or improving economic and social mobility (strategic uses that can be expected to have a long-term payoff). When our sample of EITC recipients with dependent children went to the Center for Law and Human Services for tax assistance, they expected to receive tax refunds, and they planned to use the EITC not only to fund current consumption but also to invest in their families' futures.

Most of our sample mentioned multiple uses when we asked about how they planned to use their tax refunds. Nearly 65 percent planned for consumption spending (making ends meet), and almost 70 percent planned for economic and social mobility uses. This is a larger response for durables expenditures than that found by Souleles (1999) for income tax refunds in general. The majority of recipients who expected refunds have plans for both consumption and mobility uses. Paying utility bills and rent, along with purchasing food and clothing, are the most commonly mentioned consumption uses. Spending on cars and schooling were the most frequently identified mobility uses of the EITC funds, though cars can be thought of as having consumption- as well as work-related uses. Among respondents who were not expecting a refund but who plan to use the funds to improve economic and social mobility, the majority planned to save at least a portion of their refund.

Family size appears to be associated with plans for EITC use. Families with more children are less likely to specify a mobility use and more likely to plan to use their EITC funds for consumption spending. This pattern reflects the greater consumption needs of larger families. Former president Bill Clinton's proposal to expand the maximum credit for families with three or more children, an expansion that would help larger low-income families invest in economic and social mobility, as well as meet consumption needs, was not passed. However, the large tax reduction recently signed into law by President Bush provides additional help to many large low-income families, particularly those who are married and those who can now receive refundable child tax credits (Greenstein 2001).

Recipients with greater access to financial institutions were more likely to save part of their EITC refunds. The relationship between access to financial services and EITC use, however, remains unclear and puzzling. For instance, we also found that about a quarter of our overall sample have credit cards, and of these, 80 percent have credit card debt averaging about $2,400.[25] Yet only 18 percent of these respondents list paying off credit card debt as a priority use for the EITC refund they will receive. Because of growing interest in access to financial services for low-income families, the effects of asset testing on savings, and the movement toward electronic benefit transfer, these topics should be high on the EITC-related research agenda.[26]

The results presented in this chapter suggest that the EITC does more than spread consumption across time periods. It also allows recipients an opportunity to make changes in economic behavior. Without the EITC, almost one-half of recipients could not have met their first-priority use for the EITC, while most of the rest could have met their need only to a lesser extent or with some delay. Many EITC recipients are explicitly aware of the program, and the vast majority who expect a refund can articulate several specific uses for their refund, including investments in higher current and future earnings by such means as schooling, improved transportation, and moving. Recipients who did not expect a refund were the most likely to have no plans for the EITC. Continued outreach and greater general knowledge of the EITC should increase both participation in the program and use of the benefit for upward economic and social mobility.

To move beyond our results, we would encourage further research of this type in a dynamic context. Many families who receive the EITC in one year receive it again in the next. Indeed, about one-quarter of our sample indicated that they had received the EITC in the previous year, while another 32 percent expected a refund because they had received one in the previous year. Our findings (and those of others) suggest that the EITC may play an important part in assisting families who are moving from welfare to work to move beyond "working poor" status, possibly to middle-class status. Of course, many other factors also affect this transition. Following a sample of recipients over time would help identify the pathways from dependency on means-tested transfers to economic independence and the role of the EITC in these transitions.

APPENDIX 8A: CENTER FOR LAW AND HUMAN SERVICES QUESTIONNAIRE

The following questions were excerpted from the in-person interview and the telephone follow-up survey. Both instruments in their entirety are available from the authors.

A. EXPECTATIONS AND KNOWLEDGE QUESTIONS

[Figure 8.1 is based on responses to these questions.]

A.1. Did you expect to receive a refund *before* you came to the tax center?

a. _____ Yes (go to #A.2)
b. _____ No
c. _____ Didn't know (wasn't sure about receiving the refund or not)
d. _____ Wouldn't answer / Not applicable

A.2. Why did you expect to receive a refund *this year?*

a. _____ Got one last year
b. _____ Was told I would get one by welfare office or job placement center
c. _____ Heard from a friend or relative
d. _____ Other (specify and write EITC if that is mentioned; otherwise write their comment) _____
e. _____ Wasn't sure
f. _____ Wouldn't answer / Not applicable

B. PRIORITY USES OF THE EITC

[Figure 8.2 and table 8.3 are based on responses to these questions.]

B.1. Thinking of the next few months, what are the *most important* things you plan to do with your tax refund? (Name up to three)

a. Most important use of tax refund _____
b. Second most important _____
c. Third most important _____
d. _____ Not sure / Don't know
e. _____ Wouldn't answer

(Note: Question gets at priorities, not amounts.)

B.2. Would you have been able to . . . (read B.1.a., the first most important use) . . . anyway if you did not get this tax refund?

a. _____ No
b. _____ Yes, but of lesser amount

c. _____ Yes, but with some delay
d. _____ Other _____
e. _____ Don't know / Not sure
f. _____ Wouldn't answer / Not applicable

(Note: Question repeated for second and third priority uses.)

C. USE OF EITC

[Tables 8.4 and 8.5 are based on responses to these questions.]

C.1. Now we want to try to determine how you will allocate the refund among the important uses you have given us. Please identify one or more of the following options.

(Interviewer note: if more than one option is selected, prompt individual to make approximate percentage or dollar allocation among various options.)

PERCENTAGE or
USE | AMOUNT OF REFUND

a. _____ Savings (for unexpected costs or a specific
goal)   _____

b. _____ Pay bills (or save refund to pay future expected bills)
(see #C.2 after)   _____

c. _____ Purchase household / personal items (see
#C.3 after)   _____

d. _____ Move / Get new apartment   _____

e. _____ Pay tuition for a family member   _____

f. _____ Purchase / repair car   _____

g. _____ Other (specify) _____ _____

h. _____ Not sure (see question 14 [of the original questionnaire] after this)

i. _____ Wouldn't answer

C.2. What bills will you pay?

PERCENTAGE or AMOUNT
TYPE OF BILL | PAID FOR EACH BILL

a. _____ Rent   _____
b. _____ Child-care bills   _____
c. _____ Utility bills   _____
d. _____ Grocery bills   _____
e. _____ Car payments   _____
f. _____ Bank loan   _____

g. _____ Personal loan from family or friend _____
h. _____ Medical bills _____
i. _____ Other (specify) _____ _____
j. _____ Not sure (go to question 14 [of the original questionnaire].)
k. _____ Wouldn't answer (go to question 14 [of the original questionnaire].)

C.3. What items will you purchase?

TYPE OF PURCHASE   AMOUNT OF PURCHASE
a. _____ Household furnishings, e.g., rugs,
          drapes
          (What _____) _____
b. _____ Household appliances, e.g., T.V.,
          dishwasher
          (What _____) _____
c. _____ Clothing for family members _____
d. _____ Other
          (What _____) _____
e. _____ Not sure
f. _____ Wouldn't answer

TABLE 8.A1 / Summary Demographic Data, All Interviewees and Sample

	All Interviewees			Sample[a]			Sample with Children[a]		
	Number	Percentage	Percentage of Total, Minus Those Who Did Not Respond	Number	Percentage	Percentage of Total, Minus Those Who Did Not Respond	Number	Percentage	Percentage of Total, Minus Those Who Did Not Respond
Ethnicity									
African American	487	39.7	43.3	384	46.7	50.2	313	48.2	51.5
Hispanic or Latino	376	30.7	33.5	239	29.0	31.2	206	31.7	33.9
Caucasian	94	7.7	8.4	60	7.3	7.8	43	6.6	7.1
Asian or Pacific Islander	50	4.1	4.4	25	3.0	3.3	13	2.0	2.1
Native American	19	1.6	1.7	10	1.2	1.3	6	0.9	1.0
Other	98	8.0	8.7	47	5.7	6.1	27	4.2	4.4
Did not respond	102	8.3	—	58	7.1	—	42	6.5	—
Total	1,226			823			650		
Filing Status									
Head of household	582	47.5	47.5	539	65.5	65.5	531	81.7	81.7
Married, filing jointly	188	15.3	15.3	125	15.2	15.2	119	18.3	18.3
Married, filing singly	26	2.1	2.1	0	0.0	0.0	0	0.0	0.0
Single	430	35.1	35.1	159	19.3	19.3	0	0.0	0.0
Did not respond	0	0.0	—	0	0.0	—	0	0.0	—
Total	1,226			823			650		
Other Demographic Data									
Male	482	39.3	39.5	260	31.6	31.8	159	24.5	24.6
Female	737	60.1	60.5	558	67.8	68.2	487	74.9	75.4
Did not respond	7	0.6	—	5	0.6	—	4	0.6	—
Total	1,226			823			650		
TANF receipt	232	18.9	—	217	26.4	—	194	29.9	—
Food stamp receipt	279	22.8	—	251	30.5	—	214	32.9	—
Medicaid receipt	237	19.3	—	206	25.0	—	186	28.6	—

Source: Authors' tabulations from 1998 survey of Center for Law and Human Services tax filers.
[a]Sample includes those receiving both the EITC and a net positive refund.

APPENDIX 8B: COMPONENTS OF IMPROVING-SOCIAL-MOBILITY AND MAKING-ENDS-MEET BUNDLES

Improving Social Mobility

- Savings
- Paying off bank loans
- Making car payments
- Paying credit card bills
- Paying medical bills
- Purchase or repair of car
- Sharing money with family members
- Fixing up home
- Moving expenses
- Tuition and other school expenses
- Child-care bills
- Paying off personal loans

Making Ends Meet

- Rent
- Utility bills
- Other bills
- Purchase of groceries and paying grocery bills
- Purchase clothing for self or family
- Purchase of household appliance
- Purchase of household furniture
- Other personal or household expenses

The authors owe many thanks to Susan Lloyd and Caren Grown, and to the MacArthur Foundation for their support of this research. The Center for Law and Human Services provided the opportunity, site staffing, and encouragement to carry out the survey and assemble the data. Nada Eissa, Janet Holtzblatt, Jeff Liebman, Bruce Meyer, Lisa Barrow, Bob Greenstein, Doug Holtz-Eakin, Michael Wiseman, Eric Toder, and two anonymous referees provided helpful comments. Martha Bonney, Kati Foley, Esther Gray, Ann Wicks, and Jim Williamson provided excellent assisstance in preparing the chapter. The authors alone assume responsibility for all errors of omission and commission.

NOTES

1. Small ethnographic studies of the EITC include Sara Rimer, "Cutting Tax Credit Means Much to Those with Little," *New York Times,* October 16, 1995, 1; and Romich and Weisner 1999. Lisa Barrow and Leslie McGranahan, in chapter 9 of this volume, use the Consumer Expenditure Survey (CE) from 1982 to 1996 to examine the effects of the EITC on purchases of consumer durables by low-income households.

2. An earlier paper (Smeeding et al. 1999) uses a different sample and concentrates on the policy implications of EITC uses. Here we concentrate on families with children only and examine how use of refunds is related to expectations and other characteristics.

3. The EITC is also available to single persons but at a much lower level. In contrast with the treatment of families with children, the level of EITC benefit for single filers has not changed in real terms since 1994. In our analysis, we focus on families with qualifying children.

4. Other recent research suggests that the EITC has ambiguous effects on the decision of a female head to cohabit or to marry (Ellwood 1999; Dickert-Conlin and Houser 1998). Stacy Dickert-Conlin and Douglas Holtz-Eakin (1999) compare the EITC to employer-based wage subsidies and cite evidence that the EITC fosters high participation rates and produces increased labor force participation among groups at risk of long-run labor force detachment. Rebecca Blank (1998) also finds the EITC is better targeted on low-income families than equivalent-cost employer-based wage or earnings subsidies.

5. Nicholas Souleles (1999, table 5, 955) defines durables as "consumption minus strictly nondurables," thus including vehicles, appliances, education, and all other investment goods.

6. In 1998, an EITC-eligible earner with two qualifying children and an expected annual income of between $9,400 and $12,200 would ultimately receive a benefit averaging $72 a week ($3,756 divided by 52) once the tax return had been filed and the EITC benefit check received. If the earner had one child and between $6,700 and $12,200 of earnings during the year, the maximum benefit could amount to $44 a week, or 70 percent more than the $26 maximum allowed by law.

7. Ideally, one would like to separate the economic effects of the EITC using a comparison group to parse out behavioral effects. Because the EITC is a national program open to all low-income, low-wage taxpayers, however, there is no natural control group. One could examine year-to-year changes in outlays using, for instance, the Consumer Expenditure (CE) Survey, as in chapter 9 of this volume. However, the CE survey does not collect tax data and is not designed for assessing the effects of the EITC on its respondents. Furthermore, nonparticipants of the EITC are likely to be a nonrepresentative and biased group. As a substitute, we devised the questions regarding ability to make spending or saving decisions if the tax refund was not given. These results are reported later in this chapter, and the questions are presented in appendix 8A.

8. Romich and Weisner (1999) do not have access to tax returns, but they estimate that thirty-six of their forty-two families are eligible for the EITC. While their conclusions rely on comments from only a sample of their families, additional interviews are planned. Our larger sample and direct knowledge of EITC receipt complement the analyses of Romich and Weisner (1999) and Rimer, "Cutting Tax Credit Means Much to Those with Little." It is encouraging that our findings are generally similar.

9. While the CLHS offers one venue for data collection of this type, it is not the only such venue or vendor. Two types of paid tax preparers also help EITC recipients, 65 percent of whom used tax preparer services in 1990 (Scholz 1994). One type are large, national, for-profit tax preparation services, such as H&R Block. Another type are small, informal temporary services that are provided by self-employed persons. Both types differ from the CLHS in that, unlike the CLHS, they charge fees for tax preparation services. A second difference is that at least some of these services also charge customers for the right to receive their refunds in advance of the federal returns (which usually take four to six weeks to be processed). The CLHS does not provide this service. To the extent that clients differ by preparer type, our sample may be biased away from those with higher personal discount rates and therefore perhaps away from those with greater immediate need for the EITC refund. In addition, we obviously do not include those who file without a formal tax preparer's assistance. Little, if anything, is known about this group.

10. About one-quarter (208) of the 823 families in our sample also completed a follow-up phone interview six weeks after filing to verify their receipt of the EITC and to answer the same questions posed to them earlier on their use of the EITC. While we rely on the questionnaires filled out at the time of the tax filing, the 208 call-back interviews provide verification of intended use of the refunds. Call-backs were limited to those with refunds of $1,000 or more, and we obtained a 50 percent response rate. About 90 percent of the call-back interviewees received the refund amount calculated by the CLHS when the tax forms were submitted. Differences derived from federal inquiries regarding the legitimacy of the returns or lower refunds owing to garnishment for school loans or outstanding child-support payments. Among this 90 percent, there was a high (85 percent) correspondence between intended use of refund (sample used here) and actual use (once the check arrived), with no systematic change in the distribution of tax return use by type of use. Call-back interviewees were remarkably consistent in their preferences for EITC use in the phone and the face-to-face interviews. Additional detailed comparisons across samples are available from the authors, as is the entire survey instrument.

11. For detailed demographics of our sample, see table 8.A1, in appendix 8A.

12. Appendix 8B lists all of the expenditures included in the making-ends-meet bundle.

13. Only in our call-back interviews did we ask savers what they intended to do with the savings. Only 44 percent said they were saving for expected future bills (a consumption spending use), while more than 60 percent were saving for at least one of the equity-building purposes listed in appendix 8B, some of whom were also saving to pay expected future bills (multiple responses were allowed). All forms of savings were classified as behavior that enhanced social mobility.

14. We consider repayment of debt, for example, credit card debt, as increasing social mobility. We also believe that future studies of the EITC should further investigate the issue of debt repayment. This topic is discussed more fully later in this chapter.

15. The complete bundles are listed in appendix 8B. Considerable time and effort were spent to reduce arbitrariness in creating the bundles. Some amounts of EITC savings will no doubt be used to help make ends meet in coming months and hence may be misclassified. Even then, however, EITC savings become a form of self-protection and, for many low-income EITC clients, may replace reliance on welfare to meet these expenses. Similarly, sharing benefits with extended family might be construed as continued reliance on traditional networks of support and not on improved social mobility. In these cases we may overestimate items relegated to this category. In contrast, purchases of household appliances and other durables among low-income families, which are treated as making ends meet, often produce the physical capital necessary to start small businesses (Edin 1998). In this case durable purchases classified as making ends meet are actually improving social mobility by providing opportunities for self-employment. However, these particularly controversial uses were not critical to the overall patterns that emerged from the analyses that follow. We checked the sensitivity of our results to the bundle classification by placing household furniture and appliance purchases (durables) in the improving-social-mobility bundle and moving sharing money with family members into the making-ends-meet bundle. The correlation between the original bundles and the reclassified bundles is 0.91 for improving social mobility and 0.93 for making ends meet.

16. Because of overwithholding, the maximum amount of the refund can exceed $3,656 (see table 8.1). Since Illinois does not have a state EITC, the federal maximum of $3,656 is also the state maximum. Unpublished tabulations indicate that even at the 25th percentile, the EITC was about 70 percent of the total refund received.

17. For the majority of our respondents we do not know whether they received the EITC in the previous year. We asked those who were going to receive a refund in the year under study whether they were expecting a refund. If they did expect the refund, we asked them why (see the appendix 8A). About 39 percent said they had received a refund in the previous year. We did not, however, probe for whether the refund was the result of the EITC, overwithholding, or some other cause. Another 32 percent of the sample that expected a refund mentioned the EITC, low income, or work as a reason for expecting a refund. We cannot be sure, however, whether any of these respondents, or those who did not expect the refund, received the EITC in 1996. About one-third of our respondents also had used the CLHS in the previous tax year, and many of these appear to have received the EITC as well. The majority of these repeat CLHS filers are among those who said they expected a refund because they had received one the previous year; the rest are among those mentioning the EITC or related reasons. As a result we chose to split the sample by whether or not clients expected a refund.

18. Those with low income could expect a refund based on low earnings and withholding from the regular federal income tax withholding system or from the EITC. Because the large majority of these expected a much larger refund than that due them for normal withholding, and because the EITC is 90 percent of the average refund received by our sample, we interpret this response as an indication of knowledge of the EITC.

19. On many of the surveys, "other" was not filled in. Two of the more common responses were that the filer had already done his or her taxes before coming to the

CLHS office and that the filer had gone to H&R Block (or another commercial tax preparer) before coming to CLHS office.

20. Appendix 8A includes these questions as B.1 (priorities) and B.2 (importance). The reader should note that only figure 8.2 (priorities) is based on question B.1 and only table 8.3 (importance) is based on question B.2. Our analysis of actual uses of the EITC in tables 8.4 and 8.5 are based on the more detailed questions in section C of appendix 8A.

21. See questions C.1, C.2, and C.3, in appendix 8A, which form the basis for table 8.4. "Other uses" responses were not listed in table 8.4. They totaled 16.4 percent for improving-social-mobility uses and 11.2 percent for making-ends-meet uses.

22. Our earlier paper (Smeeding et al. 1999) and Jason DeParle ("Life After Welfare, First Filers: On a Once Forlorn Avenue, Tax Preparers Now Flourish," *New York Times*, March 21, 1999, 1) find that those with no plans for use of the EITC were those with smaller refunds and lower earned incomes and were on the phase-in range of the EITC.

23. This breakdown is consistent with a recent study by Souleles (1999) of household consumption from income tax refunds more generally, and with Barrow and McGranahan's study of the effects of the EITC on the purchase of durables (chapter 9, this volume).

24. Our data indicate that there is a positive correlation between having a financial instrument and saving (0.453) among families with children, but that correlation is not significantly different from zero at the 5 percent level.

25. See also Hurst, Luoh, and Stafford 1998 on patterns of asset accumulation and debt and changes in these patterns over a ten-year period (1984 to 1994) among whites, blacks, and other groups.

26. For more on electronic benefits, see Stegman 1998. On using EITC benefits for subsidized savings uses, such as individual development accounts or universal savings accounts, see Boshara 1999 and Seidman 1998. On the topic of means-tested benefits and negative effects on asset accumulation, see Hubbard, Skinner, and Zeldes 1995, Gruber and Yelowitz 1997, Powers 1998, and Ziliak 1999.

REFERENCES

Bird, Edward, Paul Hagstrom, and Robert Wild. 1998. "Credit Card Debts of the Poor: High and Rising." University of Rochester, Department of Public Policy. Unpublished manuscript.

Blank, Rebecca. 1998. "Enhancing Opportunities, Skills, and Security of American Workers." Washington: Council of Economic Advisers. Unpublished manuscript.

Boshara, Raymond. 1999. "Individual Development Accounts: A Tool for Building Savings and Wealth." Washington, D.C.: Corporation for Enterprise Development (February).

Carney, Stacie, and William Gale. 1998. "Asset Accumulation Among Low-Income Households." Brookings Institution. Unpublished manuscript.

Council of Economic Advisers. 1998. "Good News for Low-Income Families: Expansions in the Earned Income Tax Credit and the Minimum Wage." Washington (December).

Dickert-Conlin, Stacy, and Douglas Holtz-Eakin. 1999. "Helping the Working Poor: Employer- vs. Employee-Based Subsidies." Center for Policy Research Policy Brief No. 14. Syracuse, N.Y.: Syracuse University.

Dickert-Conlin, Stacy, and Scott Houser. 1998. "EITC, AFDC, and the Female Headship Decision." Syracuse University, Maxwell School, Center for Policy Research. Unpublished manuscript.

Edin, Kathryn. 1998. "The Role of Assets in the Lives of Low-Income Single Mothers and Non-Custodial Fathers." Paper presented to the Ford Foundation, Conference on Assets and the Poor. New York (December 10–12).

Eissa, Nada, and Hilary Williamson Hoynes. 1998. "The Earned Income Tax Credit and Labor Supply of Married Couples." Working Paper E99–267, Department of Economics, University of California (April).

Eissa, Nada, and Jeffrey Liebman. 1996. "Labor Supply Response to the Earned Income Tax Credit." *Quarterly Journal of Economics* 111(2): 605–37.

Ellwood, David, T. 1999. "The Impact of the EITC and Social Policy Reforms on Work, Marriage, and Living Arrangements." Working Paper 124. Chicago: University of Chicago, Joint Center for Poverty Research (November).

Gallup Poll. 1993. "Survey of EITC Hotline Users and HEAP Outreach Program." Conducted for the Public Service Gas and Electric Company. Princeton, N.J.: Gallup Organization (November).

Greenstein, Robert. 2001. "The Changes the New Tax Law Makes in Refundable Tax Credits for Low-Income Working Families." Report 01–120. Washington, D.C.: Center on Budget and Policy Priorities. Revised June 18, 2001.

Greenstein, Robert, and Isaac Shapiro. 1998. "New Research Findings on the Effects of the Earned Income Tax Credit." Paper 98-022. Washington, D.C.: Center on Budget and Policy Priorities (March 11).

Gruber, Jon, and Aaron Yelowitz. 1997. "Public Health Insurance and Private Savings." Working Paper 6041. Cambridge, Mass.: National Bureau of Economic Research.

Hubbard, R. Glenn, Jonathan Skinner, and Stephen P. Zeldes. 1995. "Precautionary Savings and Social Insurance." *Journal of Political Economy* 103(2): 360–99.

Hurst, Erik, Ming C. Luoh, and Frank P. Stafford. 1998. "The Wealth Dynamics of American Families." *Brookings Papers on Economic Activity* 1: 267–337.

Meyer, Bruce D., and Dan T. Rosenbaum. 1999. "Welfare, the Earned Income Tax Credit, and the Labor Supply of Single Mothers." Northwestern University, Department of Economics. Unpublished manuscript (September 15).

Oliver, Melvin, and Thomas Shapiro. 1995. *Black Wealth, White Wealth.* New York: Routledge.

Olson, Lynn M., and Audrey Davis. 1994. "The Earned Income Tax Credit: Views from the Street Level." Working Paper WP-94–1. Evanston, Ill.: Northwestern University, Center for Urban Affairs.

Powers, Elizabeth. 1998. "Does Means Testing Discourage Savings? Evidence from a Change in AFDC Policy in the United States." *Journal of Public Economics* 68(1): 33–53.

Romich, Jennifer, and Thomas Weisner. 1999. "Earnings, Refund, Windfall, or Equity: How Families View and Use the EITC." Paper presented at the annual meeting of the Population Association of America, New York, March 26.

Scholz, John Karl. 1994. "The Earned Income Tax Credit: Participation, Compliance, and Antipoverty Effectiveness." *National Tax Journal* 46(1): 59–81.

Seidman, Lawrence. 1998. "Assets and the Tax Code." Paper presented to the Ford Foundation, Conference on Assets and the Poor, New York, December 10–12.

Shapiro, Thomas. 1998. "Assets and the Poor: An Introduction." Paper presented to the Ford Foundation, Conference on Assets and the Poor, New York, December 10–12.

Sherraden, Michael. 1991. *Assets and the Poor*. New York: M. E. Sharpe.

Smeeding, Timothy, Katherin Ross, Michael O'Connor, and Michael Simon. 1999. "The Economic Impact of the EITC: Consumption, Savings, and Debt." Paper presented at the Conference on the Earned Income Tax Credit: Early Evidence. Evanston, Ill.: Northwestern University (October 7–8).

Souleles, Nicholas. 1999. "The Response of Household Consumption to Income Tax Refunds." *American Economic Review* 89(4): 947–58.

Stegman, Michael. 1998. "Electronic Benefit Transfer's Potential to Help the Poor." Policy Brief 32. Washington, D.C.: Brookings Institution.

U.S. Department of Commerce. U.S. Bureau of the Census. 2000. *1990 Census of Population and Housing Data*. Accessed from the Internet on February 1 at: *venus.census.gov/cdrom/lookup*.

U.S. Department of the Treasury. Internal Revenue Service (IRS). 1999a. "All Individual Income Tax Returns: Selected Income and Tax Items, in Current and Constant 1990 Dollars." *Individual Income Tax Returns 1996*. Publication 1304, 05-12-00. Washington: U.S. Government Printing Office.

———. 1999b. "EIC Advanced Payment Allowances." Internal Revenue Code section 3705(c)(2)(B)i, as amended by Public Law 103-66, sec. 13131(d)(5)(i). Washington: U.S. Government Printing Office.

———. 1999c. "Individual Income Tax Returns: Selected Income and Tax Items for Specified Tax Years, 1975–1998." *Statistics of Income Bulletin* 18(4): 164, table 1.

U.S. House of Representatives. Committee on Ways and Means. 1998. *Green Book: Background Materials and Data on Programs Within the Jurisdiction of the Committee on Ways and Means*. Committee Print 105-7. Washington: U.S. Government Printing Office.

Ziliak, James. 1999. "Income Transfers and Assets of the Poor." Working Paper 1202-99. Madison: University of Wisconsin, Institute for Research on Poverty (November).

Chapter 9

The Effects of the Earned Income Tax Credit on the Seasonality of Household Expenditures

Lisa Barrow and Leslie McGranahan

From humble beginnings in 1975 as a small program designed to offset the payroll taxes paid by low-income workers, the Earned Income Tax Credit (EITC) has grown into a major income support program. In 1996, the EITC transferred a total of $28.8 billion to more than 19 million families (IRS 1998).

In contrast with social programs that transfer benefits evenly over the calendar year, including Supplemental Security Income, Food Stamps, and Aid to Families with Dependent Children or the newer Temporary Assistance for Needy Families, the great majority of EITC benefits are paid during the tax-filing period in the calendar year following the year of eligibility. Most EITC benefits are paid in one of two forms: reductions in tax liability that accrue to recipients when taxes are paid (between January 1 and April 15) and increases in tax refunds that accrue when refunds are received (between the end of January and the end of May). As a result, the one-time payment received is larger than the periodic payments of other income support programs. For example, while the average EITC refund among recipients receiving refunds in 1996 was slightly more than $1,500, the average welfare (Aid to Families with Dependent Children) monthly check was $374, and the average December Supplemental Security Income benefit was $363 (U.S. House 1998).

The substantial size of EITC refund checks is sufficient to assist low-income consumers in purchasing big-ticket items. In this chapter we ask whether there is evidence that the lumpy nature of EITC payments induces changes in expenditure patterns among recipients. In particular, we think that the EITC payment might alter the seasonal pattern of expenditures on durable goods among its recipients, since many big-ticket items are classified as durable goods. How and when EITC payments are used may shed some light on the effects of proposals to alter the timing of EITC disbursements and may help explain why nearly all recipients choose lump-sum disbursements. To address these issues, we use data from the Consumer Expenditure Survey and exploit the monthly nature of the expenditure data and the concentrated payment period for EITC benefits.

Many researchers have explored the sensitivity of consumption to predictable changes in household income arising from sources other than the Earned Income

Tax Credit. Among studies looking at the effects of short-term income fluctuations on contemporaneous consumption, some, such as Christina Paxson's, find that households are not sensitive to the timing of income, while others, including studies by Jonathan Parker and Nicholas Souleles, find that households do not perfectly smooth expected income. Paxson (1993) finds that seasonal consumption patterns in Thailand result from seasonal variations in preferences or prices rather than from seasonal fluctuations in income. In contrast, both Souleles (1999) and Parker (1999) find that U.S. household consumption contemporaneously increases in response to predictable increases in income. Souleles looks at the consumption effects of tax refunds generally, while Parker primarily focuses on the effect of changes in social security withholding within the calendar year that affect high-income households. In contrast with Parker, in particular, we look at spending among an economically disadvantaged sample. Economically disadvantaged families may respond to income changes differently both because they live closer to subsistence and because they have less access to formal financial institutions. In addition, while many other studies have been interested in testing the implications of the life cycle and permanent income hypothesis, we are mostly concerned about the effects of the EITC's program features on recipient behavior.

Our research bears upon the policy decision to structure the program so that most EITC benefits are paid out in one yearly lump sum and the decision of most beneficiaries to take their entire payment in one lump sum. In late 1999, members of Congress proposed taking EITC lump-sum payments that would normally be paid to beneficiaries in spring and distributing them instead in twelve monthly payments. These payments would commence after the filing of the previous year's taxes (U.S. House 1999). How this change would influence recipient families depends on how and when EITC payments are spent. If families perfectly smooth consumption forward and do not earn interest on the lump-sum payment, they will be unaffected by the congressional proposal. On the other hand, if families spend the money upon receipt, they will be negatively affected by the policy change.

Under current law, EITC recipients have the option of receiving a portion of their benefits as supplements to their paychecks during the tax year of eligibility (before filing taxes). This policy option, known as the Advance Earned Income Credit (AEIC), has been in effect since 1979, when the Revenue Act of 1978 made the EITC a permanent program.[1] Since then, the AEIC has experienced minuscule levels of participation despite the fact that recipients might be expected to prefer receiving the same nominal dollar amount earlier rather than later because of the time value of money.[2] In 1996, 192,000 families received $76 million in AEIC payments, representing only 1 percent of recipient families and 0.3 percent of benefit payments (IRS 1999).

The decision of most recipients to take the EITC in a single payment may derive from their desire to purchase big-ticket items. This leads us to expect that the seasonality in income induced by the EITC may affect most profoundly seasonal patterns in expenditures on durable goods. Recipients who plan to use the

EITC to fund large purchases and have limited access to credit and to formal financial markets may be better off waiting to receive their EITC as a large check. If instead recipients desire to purchase small items, they would be better off receiving their money earlier because they could purchase these items earlier. In addition, people with savings accounts who wanted to purchase large items would be better off receiving payments earlier because they could earn interest until the purchase was made. However, for individuals with limited ability to store money safely and the desire to make a substantial purchase, the EITC may serve as a safe mechanism for savings. One further indication that EITC recipients lack access to formal credit networks, contributing to little interest in the AEIC, is the fact that only 21 percent of EITC recipients in tax year 1994 had any taxable interest earnings, compared with 56 percent of filers who did not receive the EITC (GAO 1996; IRS 1997).

If the EITC affects expenditure seasonality, we expect recipient households to increase expenditure soon after refund checks are received. Fortunately, refunds are received during a concentrated portion of the calendar year. Individuals must file taxes between January 1 and April 15, and the Internal Revenue Service (IRS) reports that most refunds are sent out between four and six weeks after filing.[3] This suggests that most refund checks should be received between February 1 and May 30. Data on the timing of both the refundable portion of the credit (that is, the portion of the EITC that exceeds a filer's tax liability) and individual income tax refunds bear out this prediction. Figure 9.1 shows the percentage of total IRS payments of each type paid out each month in 1998. The great majority of payments occurred between February and May, with 92.4 percent of EITC payments and 85.0 percent of individual income tax refunds occurring during this period. The data also show that EITC refunds are received earlier than other refunds. While EITC refunds peak in February (45.6 percent) and March (30.1 percent), individual income tax refunds are highest in March (24.1 percent), April (23.1 percent), and May (24.1 percent).[4] In addition, we note that the graph in figure 9.1 probably represents a distribution of the timing of payments that is slightly later than the distribution of the receipt of refunded dollars by tax filers. About one-half of EITC recipients file returns completed by paid preparers (GAO 1996). Most professional tax preparation services offer high-interest refund anticipation loans that allow filers to receive money as soon as two days after filing. Therefore, EITC recipients may well be receiving their refunds somewhat earlier than indicated in the IRS data displayed in figure 9.1.[5]

To investigate whether EITC recipients spend relatively more on all types of goods, and durable goods, in particular, during the tax refund season, we utilize the empirical strategy of Paxson (1993) to estimate expenditure equations that allow differences in income seasonality to affect seasonal consumption patterns. The empirical model estimated is derived from an expenditure model that allows for imperfect ability to smooth consumption across seasons such that actual expenditure in each season is a weighted average of income in that season and desired expenditure in that season.

In looking for effects of the EITC on seasonal expenditure patterns, we find

FIGURE 9.1 / Timing of Federal Income Tax Refunds and EITC Payments, 1998, by Month

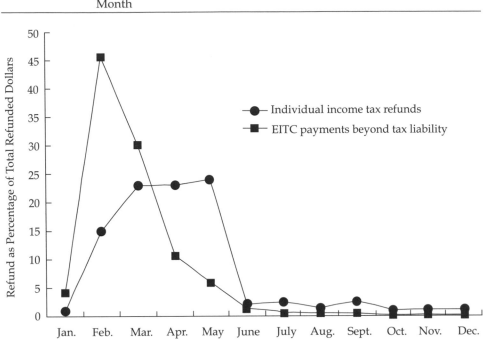

Source: Data from U.S. Department of the Treasury, Financial Management Service, 1998, various months.
Note: Data points in the figure represent the percentage of income-tax refunds and EITC payments sent out in a given month during 1998.

that the EITC leads to increased levels of expenditure during the tax-filing season. In particular, we find that EITC-eligible households spend approximately 3 percent more in total during February, the modal month of EITC refunds, and 9 percent more on durable goods. This supports our conjecture that the EITC facilitates the purchase of big-ticket items by low-income families. These estimates also suggest that EITC recipients smooth expenditure somewhat, since when we translate these increases into dollars, the average increase in expenditure is less than the average refundable EITC amount.

DATA DESCRIPTION

To explore the effect of the EITC on consumption seasonality, we use data from the 1982 through 1996 waves of the Consumer Expenditure Survey (CES). The CES surveys a nationally representative sample of consumer units with questions about their monthly expenditure patterns and limited questions about their income, assets, and family structure. The CES unit of analysis, the consumer unit, is an individual or group of individuals living together who are related either by blood or by legal arrangements or who use their income to make joint expenditures in two of three categories: housing, food, and other living expenses. Throughout the remainder of this chapter, we use the terms consumer unit, family, and household interchangeably. The CES surveys consumer units four times in consecutive three-month increments about their expenditure over the previous three months.[6] For example, one consumer unit may be questioned in February about expenditure in November through January, in May about expenditure in February through April, in August about expenditure in May through July, and then finally in November about expenditure in August through October. New units enter the sample every month. Most questions refer to the amount spent in each of the previous three months. However, a limited set of questions ask about the combined amount spent in the entire three-month period and then record monthly amounts that are these quarterly amounts divided by three. The categories surveyed at the quarterly level include food, alcoholic beverages, gasoline and motor oil, reading, personal care, tobacco, and fees and admissions. We structure all expenditure data in a monthly format and do not adjust for the smoothing induced by dividing some quarterly totals by three. We do not believe that this is a problem because expenditure in these categories is likely to be relatively constant from month to month—a fact that in part explains why expenditure in these areas is not asked separately for each month.[7] All expenditure data are converted to 1998 dollars using the monthly personal consumption expenditure (PCE) total-price index.[8]

Calculating EITC Eligibility and Payment Values

The CES does not ask the consumer unit any questions relating specifically to the EITC. Therefore, we need to predict the value of the EITC payments that the consumer unit is eligible to receive, using data on children, earnings, and household structure. We do this using the CES member files, which provide information on the earnings, relationship to reference person, and age of the individuals that constitute the consumer unit. The need to use the member rather than the consumer-unit information arises from the fact that for families with complicated structures (which lower-income families often are), the consumer unit can be different from the tax-filing unit. From the member file data, we create tax units, determine eligible children in those units, calculate tax-unit earnings, and impute EITC payments based on the program schedule. The consumer-unit EITC is then defined as the sum of the calculated EITCs for the tax units that make up the consumer unit.

To calculate tax-unit earnings we use the responses to questions about the member's salary, nonfarm, and farm income asked during the first and fourth waves of questioning. These questions refer to income during the previous twelve-month period, which corresponds to the calendar year (and tax year) only if the recipient is questioned during January. We calculate earnings data that corresponds to the tax year by taking a weighted average of the earnings reported in the first and fourth interviews; the weights are based on the months for which the tax and interview year overlap. We define consumer-unit income as the sum of salary, nonfarm, and farm income.[9] Most assessments point to earnings underreporting in the CES income data. To the extent that we are underestimating earnings, we are also overestimating EITC eligibility.

Having calculated tax-unit income and the number of eligible children, we impute EITC payments for each tax unit within the consumer unit, based on the EITC program schedule. We calculate EITC benefits based on our best estimate of earnings and family structure for the calendar year preceding the year in which we observe February expenditure. In this way, we are predicting EITC payments that will be received in the same time frame during which we observe expenditure. We deviate from program rules for defining EITC eligibility in that we assume all childless workers are ineligible, despite the introduction of a small credit for this group in 1994. We do this so that our EITC-eligible sample represents a more homogeneous recipient group with a more substantial credit.[10]

It is important to note that between 1982 and 1996 the EITC increased in generosity numerous times. In particular, Congress enacted major programmatic expansions in both 1990 and 1993. Between 1990 and 1991, the maximum credit grew by 25 percent for families with one child and by 30 percent for families with two or more children. In addition, the credit rate increased from 14 percent of earned income for all families with children to 16.7 percent for families with one child and 17.3 percent for families with more than one child. As a result, the average credit grew from $601 to $813 (nominal) for each recipient family (U.S. House 1998). The second major expansion occurred between 1993 and 1994 (although the changes were not fully phased in until 1996), when the maximum credit increased by 42 percent for households with one child and 67 percent for households with two or more children. At this time, a small credit for families without children was introduced as well. As mentioned earlier, we define these childless households as ineligible for the EITC for estimation purposes.

Consumer-Unit Income

In our estimates, income is defined as total consumer-unit before-tax income from the fourth interview plus imputed EITC benefit. The before-tax income measure from the CES family files is more comprehensive than the income data available from the member files that are used to calculate EITC eligibility. Unlike the member file, which contains only earnings information, the family file includes measures of income from other sources such as interest income, welfare, and child support. We use the income measure from the fourth interview because it represents income over the same horizon as the consumption data. Ideally we would be using a reliable measure of after-tax income. However, after-tax income in the CES is calculated as before-tax income minus reported tax payments net of refunds. Unfortunately, the measures of both tax payments and tax refunds do not appear to be accurate. In contrast with IRS reports that 70 percent of tax-return filers received overpayment refunds in 1996, the CES reports positive refunds in fewer than 40 percent of consumer units in the same year. This underreporting of refunds in the CES appears to be especially pronounced among low-income filers. While the IRS reports positive refunds for more than 70 percent of tax units with incomes of less than $15,000, fewer than 20 percent of consumer units with before-tax income of less than $15,000 (and more than $1) report any refund amount to the CES (IRS 1998).[11] In light of these data issues, we do not use the refund data from the CES in our analyses. Also, we have not adjusted the income data to account for the underreporting in the CES.

Consumer-Unit Expenditure

We look at consumption expenditure in three different categories: total expenditure, durable-goods expenditure, and nondurable-goods and services expenditure. Durable goods comprise expenditures on household furnishings and equipment, televisions and other home electronics, and vehicle purchases. Nondurable goods and services includes expenditures on food, clothing, and entertainment.[12] Expenditures on health care, education, shelter, utilities, vehicle finance charges, vehicle insurance, and other household operations are included in the total expenditure category but in neither durables nor nondurables. We are most interested in the big-ticket items represented in the durable-goods category and use nondurables as a comparison group. One indication that this definition of durable goods represents the big-ticket items we are most interested in is that consumer units spend less on durable goods in the average month, but durable-goods expenditure has a higher standard deviation across consumer unit-months.

Summary Statistics

Variable means and standard deviations for the estimation sample are presented in table 9.1. Note that a consumer unit is labeled EITC eligible if any tax unit within the consumer unit was imputed to be eligible for any EITC amount. We drop observations with negative or zero expenditure for total expenditure, durable goods, or nondurable goods and services. In addition, we drop all consumer units with income less than or equal to zero, and then we drop the consumer-unit months in the bottom 3 percent of the income distribution.[13] Our final sample consists of 117,801 consumer units and 587,294 consumer-unit months. In approximately 9 percent of the remaining family-month observations, we impute the family as EITC eligible in that year. In addition, among eligible families the average amount of the imputed credit was $844.

We present summary statistics separately by imputed EITC eligibility in table 9.1.

TABLE 9.1 / Variable Means and Standard Deviations

Variable	All Families	EITC-Eligible Families	Noneligible Families
Dummy = 1 if eligible for EITC	0.090	1	0
	(0.286)	(0)	(0)
Predicted yearly EITC Benefit	75.769	844.109	0
	(317.635)	(689.518)	(0)
Before-tax income	45,108.06	22,963.74	47,291.81
	(34,978.91)	(16,245.11)	(35,567.27)
Total expenditure	2,817.268	2,209.189	2,877.233
	(3,059.400)	(2,352.438)	(3,114.029)
Durable-goods expenditure	505.835	394.504	516.814
	(2,215.755)	(1,764.206)	(2,255.096)
Nondurable-goods expenditure	1,165.292	936.990	1,187.806
	(1,281.098)	(1,001.382)	(1,303.276)
Dummy = 1 if family has unmarried children under the age of nineteen	0.435	1	0.379
	(0.496)	(0)	(0.485)
Family size	2.765	3.941	2.649
	(1.512)	(1.482)	(1.465)
No high school diploma	0.185	0.281	0.176
	(0.389)	(0.450)	(0.381)
High school graduate	0.308	0.393	0.300
	(0.462)	(0.488)	(0.458)
Some college	0.243	0.232	0.244
	(0.429)	(0.422)	(0.430)
College graduate	0.263	0.094	0.280
	(0.441)	(0.291)	(0.449)
Number of unmarried children under the age of nineteen	0.840	1.951	0.730
	(1.172)	(1.085)	(1.122)
Northeast	0.193	0.169	0.195
	(0.394)	(0.375)	(0.396)
Midwest	0.234	0.210	0.237
	(0.424)	(0.408)	(0.425)
South	0.262	0.291	0.259
	(0.440)	(0.454)	(0.438)
West	0.228	0.219	0.229
	(0.420)	(0.414)	(0.420)

TABLE 9.1   /   *Continued*

Variable	All Families	EITC-Eligible Families	Noneligible Families
Rural	0.083	0.109	0.081
	(0.276)	(0.312)	(0.272)
Dummy = 1 if household head is white	0.880	0.780	0.890
	(0.325)	(0.414)	(0.313)
Dummy = 1 if household head is male	0.689	0.529	0.705
	(0.463)	(0.499)	(0.456)
Family type is husband, wife, and own children only	0.572	0.437	0.585
	(0.495)	(0.496)	(0.493)
Family type is male parent and own children only	0.007	0.017	0.006
	(0.084)	(0.129)	(0.078)
Family type is female parent and own children only	0.053	0.257	0.033
	(0.225)	(0.437)	(0.180)
Family type is single persons	0.213	0	0.234
	(0.409)	(0)	(0.423)
Other family types	0.155	0.289	0.141
	(0.361)	(0.453)	(0.348)
N (number of family months)	587,294	52,717	534,577

Source: Authors' calculations based on data from the Consumer Expenditure Survey, 1982 to 1996.
Note: All dollar valuations are in real 1998 dollars. Standard deviations are in parentheses.

Families eligible for the EITC have lower incomes than those who are not eligible for the credit: $22,964 (in 1998 dollars) as against $47,292. As expected, EITC families spend less each month, on average, on both durable and nondurable goods. For all families, monthly durable-goods expenditure represents approximately 18 percent of total monthly expenditures, while spending on nondurable goods represents approximately 41 percent. Finally, while all of our EITC families have children, only 38 percent of noneligible families have children. As a result, average family size among EITC-eligible families is 3.9 persons, compared with 2.6 persons for families that are not eligible. Among EITC-eligible families, we note that average annual total expenditures are greater than average annual total income. This is a common feature of CES data and arises from the underreporting of income and the exclusion of some income-support-program money from the income definitions. To address this issue, we control for a number of demographic characteristics in the following regressions that may be correlated with income.

MODEL AND ESTIMATION STRATEGIES

We investigate the role of the EITC in the expenditure patterns of recipients using the model of consumption and income seasonality utilized by Paxson (1993). Paxson begins with a perfect consumption-smoothing model and extends the model to allow for the imperfect ability of households to smooth consumption by permitting expenditure in a given period to partially track income from that period. As a result, actual expenditure by individual i in month m, E_{im}, is written as a weighted average of desired monthly expenditure, E^*_{im}, and monthly income, Y_{im}:

$$E_{im} = E^*_{im} (1 - \pi) + Y_{im}\pi, \tag{9.1}$$

where π is between 0 and 1 and measures the extent to which seasonal expenditure tracks seasonal income. When $\pi = 0$, expenditure is independent of the timing of income; when $\pi = 1$, expenditure perfectly tracks seasonal income patterns.

A key feature of Paxson's consumption-smoothing model is that the allocation of consumption across months is only a function of prices and preferences. Given the assumptions that individuals face identical prices and have identical preferences, desired monthly expenditure becomes a constant fraction of income for all individuals in a given month. Let β_m equal the share of annual income that all individuals wish to consume in month m: $\beta_m = E^*_{im} / Y_i$, where Y_i is annual income for individual i. Let A_{im} equal the share of annual income received in month m by individual i: $A_{im} = Y_{im} / Y_i$. Thus, equation (9.1) can be rewritten as follows:

$$E_{im} = Y_i[\beta_m(1 - \pi) + A_{im}\pi]. \tag{9.2}$$

The β_m values sum to one across months and measure the effects of preferences and prices on expenditure, and the sum of A_{im} across months equals one for each individual and reflects the timing of income. As above, if $\pi = 0$, the only determinants of the seasonal pattern of expenditure are prices and preferences.

For estimation purposes, Y_i is redefined as average monthly income (total annual income divided by 12), and β_m and A_{im} are multiplied by 12 so they average one across seasons. Equation (9.2) may then be rewritten as follows by taking the natural logarithm:

$$ln(E_{im}) = ln(Y_i) + ln[(1 - \pi)\beta_m + \pi A_{im}]. \tag{9.3}$$

Taking the first-order Taylor series expansion of equation (9.3) around $\beta_m = 1$ and $A_{im} = 1$ yields

$$ln(E_{im}) = ln(Y_i) + (1 - \pi)\beta_m + \pi A_{im} - 1. \tag{9.4}$$

If households perfectly smooth consumption spending, the coefficient on A_{im} will be zero.

With good information on seasonal income and expenditure, equation (9.4) can be estimated to generate predictions of π. However, Paxson is concerned about possible measurement error in A_{im} and so also develops a reduced-form model of seasonal expenditure. This is done by rewriting the share of annual income received in month m, A_{im}, as a combination of a component that is common to all individuals, A_m, plus an additional month effect, $Z_i A^Z_m$, for individuals with a particular characteristic, Z, that affects the timing of income, and an error term, e_{im}:

$$A_{im} = A_m + Z_i A^Z_m + e_{im}. \tag{9.5}$$

Combining equations (9.4) and (9.5) generates the following reduced-form equation:

$$ln(E_{im}) = ln(Y_i) + (1 - \pi)\beta_m + \pi A_m - 1 + \pi A^Z_m Z_i + \varepsilon_{im}. \tag{9.6}$$

For this analysis, we also have concerns about the measurement of A_{im}. In particular, income is reported on a yearly basis only, and we do not know the month in which the EITC refund is received by a given consumer unit. However, we can predict whether a household is EITC eligible, and this indication of eligibility becomes our Z. Specifically, $Z_i = 0$ for households that are ineligible for the EITC, and $Z_i = 1$ for EITC-eligible households. We utilize the following empirical specification of equation (9.6):

$$ln(E_{im}) = \alpha_1 ln(Y_i) + M\gamma + (M \times R)\phi + \varepsilon_{im}. \tag{9.7}$$

E_{im} is expenditure by individual i in month m for the given category of expenditure (durable goods, nondurable goods and services, or total); Y_i is average monthly income for individual i; α_1 is the elasticity of expenditure with respect to income, which we do not restrict to equal one; M is a vector of monthly dummy variables; and γ is the parameter vector of monthly effects that captures preferences, prices, and income seasonality common to all households. Specifically, each element of γ is defined as $\gamma_m = (1 - \pi)\beta_m + \pi A_m - 1$. R is a dummy variable equal to one if the family is EITC eligible, and ϕ is the added monthly effect for EITC-eligible families. Each element of ϕ is defined as $\phi_m = \pi A^Z_m$. Finally, ε_{im} is the household-month error term. Thus, testing that short-term changes in income induced by the EITC do not affect expenditure patterns, $\pi = 0$, is equivalent to testing that the values of ϕ_m are jointly insignificant.

In estimating equation (9.7), we also control for year-specific fixed effects, family size, education level of the reference person, number of unmarried children under the age of nineteen, region, an indicator for the sex of the reference person, and an indicator equal to one if the household head is white. For confidentiality reasons, region is not defined for consumer units residing in rural areas. In estimation, we use rural as the omitted category; therefore, the interpretation of the region effects is relative to rural households located in any region. In addition, we include a set of indicator variables for family type: husband, wife, and own children only; male parent and own children only; female parent and own children only; single persons; and other family types. We also incorporate a constant and omit September from $M\gamma$. We choose September as the baseline month because it is a month when almost no EITC payments are made (fewer than 1 percent) and is also before the Christmas shopping season. Throughout, we calculate standard errors that are robust to observing the same consumer unit multiple times. In the concluding section, we discuss implications of the mismeasurement of R caused by our imputation procedure.

In the estimation section, we estimate equation (9.7) focusing on the coefficient estimates of the interaction between month and EITC eligibility, ϕ. These coefficients measure the extent to which the expenditure pattern of EITC-eligible families differs from that of other families. If EITC receipt affects expenditure patterns—in other words, if individuals are unable to perfectly smooth consumption—we expect the coefficients ϕ to be largest during the EITC refund season. Similarly, if the EITC leads to the purchase of big-ticket items, the difference in the coefficients should be greater for durable goods than for nondurable goods.

RESULTS

In table 9.2 we present results for a simple regression of log expenditure (by expenditure category) on log income, a set of month dummy variables, and the demographic and regional covariates described earlier. In addition, we include a constant and control for year-specific fixed effects. The following categories are omitted: September; high school diploma; rural; female; nonwhite; and family type is husband, wife, and own children only. Note that these estimates do not include any measure of EITC eligibility.

We estimate that the elasticity of expenditure with respect to income is approximately 0.32 and find evidence of seasonality in expenditure.[14] In figure 9.2 we graph the estimated monthly coefficients relative to September (the omitted month throughout this chapter). Looking at the monthly pattern of total expenditure, we observe low relative levels of expenditure in the first third of the year. Total expenditure is especially low in February, a month that is shorter than others and also follows on the heels of the Christmas spending season. This is followed by increased expenditure in the summer months and a slight decline in October and November. Finally, there is a large rise in December that accompanies the Christmas season. Looking again at table 9.2, the coefficient on family size (0.101) indicates that a one-person increase in the number of people in the family increases expenditure by 10 percent; however, each additional child within the family decreases total expenditure by 5 percent, holding family size constant. Thus, on net each child increases total spending by 5 percent. We also

TABLE 9.2 / Seasonal Expenditure Patterns

Category	Log Total Expenditure	Log Durable-Goods Expenditure	Log Nondurable-Goods Expenditure
Log income	0.316	0.343	0.317
	(0.003)	(0.004)	(0.003)
January	−0.027	−0.083	−0.054
	(0.003)	(0.010)	(0.003)
February	−0.057	−0.099	−0.058
	(0.003)	(0.010)	(0.003)
March	−0.025	−0.036	−0.012
	(0.003)	(0.010)	(0.003)
April	−0.020	0.002	0.003
	(0.003)	(0.010)	(0.003)
May	−0.012	0.124	0.008
	(0.003)	(0.010)	(0.003)
June	0.004	0.089	0.028
	(0.003)	(0.010)	(0.003)
July	0.017	0.054	0.037
	(0.003)	(0.010)	(0.003)
August	0.041	0.032	0.053
	(0.003)	(0.009)	(0.003)
October	−0.018	0.0005	−0.011
	(0.003)	(0.009)	(0.003)
November	−0.021	0.071	−0.001
	(0.003)	(0.010)	(0.003)
December	0.112	0.517	0.165
	(0.003)	(0.010)	(0.003)
Family size	0.101	0.077	0.137
	(0.003)	(0.005)	(0.003)
No high school diploma	−0.127	−0.090	−0.141
	(0.004)	(0.008)	(0.004)
Some college	0.091	0.050	0.081
	(0.003)	(0.008)	(0.004)
College grad	0.221	0.116	0.181
	(0.004)	(0.008)	(0.004)
Number of unmarried children under the age of nineteen	−0.050	−0.047	−0.070
	(0.003)	(0.006)	(0.003)
Northeast	0.092	0.028	0.071
	(0.006)	(0.012)	(0.006)

(Table continued on p. 342.)

TABLE 9.2 / *Continued*

Category	Log Total Expenditure	Log Durable- Goods Expenditure	Log Nondurable- Goods Expenditure
Midwest	0.049 (0.005)	0.067 (0.012)	0.025 (0.006)
South	0.095 (0.005)	0.079 (0.012)	0.054 (0.006)
West	0.142 (0.005)	0.079 (0.012)	0.090 (0.006)
Dummy = 1 if household head is white	0.096 (0.004)	0.065 (0.009)	0.115 (0.005)
Dummy = 1 if household head is male	0.040 (0.004)	0.046 (0.007)	0.093 (0.004)
Family type is male parent and own children only	0.003 (0.016)	−0.054 (0.034)	0.058 (0.019)
Family type is female parent and own children only	−0.064 (0.007)	−0.081 (0.015)	−0.003 (0.008)
Family type is single persons	−0.204 (0.005)	−0.176 (0.010)	−0.212 (0.006)
Other family types	−0.046 (0.004)	−0.025 (0.009)	−0.030 (0.005)

Source: Authors' calculations based on data from the Consumer Expenditure Survey, 1982 to 1996.
Note: There are 587,294 consumer unit–month observations and 117,801 consumer units. Each regression also includes a constant and year fixed effects. The omitted categories are September; high school graduate; rural; family type is husband, wife, and own children only; and year equals 1995. Standard errors are Huber-White standard errors allowing for dependence within consumer units. All dollar values are in real 1998 dollars.

find that expenditure increases with educational attainment, probably reflecting higher permanent income as well as some of the measurement error in income. The region categories indicate that rural consumer units consume less than urban consumer units and that midwestern urban consumers spend less than urban consumers in all other regions. Households headed by a male consume 4 percent more in each month than female-headed households, and not surprisingly, families headed by a single female parent consume 6 percent less than families with both parents present. In addition, households headed by white persons consume 10 percent more than nonwhite households.

The monthly pattern of durable-goods expenditure is quite similar to that for total expenditure, although the magnitudes of the coefficients tend to be larger. Durable-goods purchases are also low in the first part of the year and highest in December. In fact, December expenditures are more than 50 percent higher than expenditures in September. Durable-goods spending also increases noticeably in

FIGURE 9.2 / Overall Yearly Expenditure Patterns, by Month

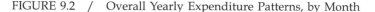

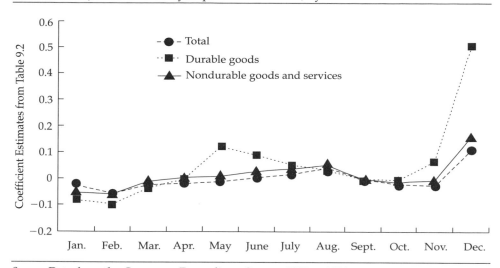

Source: Data from the Consumer Expenditure Survey, 1982 to 1996.
Note: For each series we plot coefficient estimates on month dummy variables from a regression of log expenditure on log income, a set of month dummies, demographic characteristics, and year fixed effects. See table 9.2 for a detailed list of the covariates. The dependent variables are log total expenditure, log durable goods expenditure, and log expenditure for nondurable goods and services. In each case, September is the omitted month.

May and June. Not surprisingly, the results for nondurable goods and services are nearly identical to the results for total expenditure.

The remainder of the coefficient estimates in the regressions for durable goods and nondurable goods and services are similar to the coefficient estimates in the total expenditure results, although durable-goods expenditure is less sensitive to most of the demographic characteristics. In the remainder of this chapter we present coefficient estimates only for the monthly effects and for the interaction between the monthly effects and EITC eligibility (and in some cases other categories). In these additional regressions, the coefficient estimates for the demographic characteristics and income are broadly similar to those in these preliminary regressions.

We now turn to the results comparing EITC-eligible households with those that are not eligible for the credit. Tables 9.3, 9.4, and 9.5 present monthly effects for each of the three expenditure categories. Each table represents a different expenditure category: total expenditure (table 9.3), expenditure on durable goods (table 9.4), and expenditure on nondurable goods and services (table 9.5). The first column of each table presents the estimates of the monthly effects for the noneligible population. The third column presents the additional monthly effects for the EITC population and represents the difference in expenditure in each month between the eligible and noneligible populations. Therefore, the pre-

TABLE 9.3 / Log Monthly Total Expenditure, by EITC Eligibility

Month	Noneligibles		Eligibles	
	Coefficient	Standard Error	Coefficient	Standard Error
January	−0.029	(0.004)	−0.018	(0.009)
February	−0.061	(0.004)	0.004	(0.009)
March	−0.027	(0.004)	−0.015	(0.009)
April	−0.022	(0.004)	−0.015	(0.009)
May	−0.012	(0.003)	−0.026	(0.009)
June	0.006	(0.003)	−0.056	(0.009)
July	0.019	(0.003)	−0.050	(0.009)
August	0.040	(0.003)	−0.031	(0.009)
September			−0.034	(0.009)
October	−0.018	(0.003)	−0.036	(0.009)
November	−0.022	(0.003)	−0.022	(0.009)
December	0.111	(0.004)	−0.023	(0.009)

Source: Authors' calculations based on data from the Consumer Expenditure Survey, 1982 to 1996.
Note: The dependent variable is the logarithm of monthly total expenditure. In addition to the covariates listed, the regression also includes all covariates included in the regressions presented in table 9.2. There are 587,294 consumer-unit-month observations. Standard errors are Huber-White standard errors, allowing for dependence within consumer units. All dollar values are in real 1998 dollars.

TABLE 9.4 / Log Monthly Durable-Goods Expenditure, by EITC Eligibility

Month	Noneligibles		Eligibles	
	Coefficient	Standard Error	Coefficient	Standard Error
January	−0.088	(0.010)	−0.029	(0.025)
February	−0.110	(0.010)	0.050	(0.026)
March	−0.043	(0.010)	0.002	(0.026)
April	−0.008	(0.010)	0.026	(0.026)
May	0.123	(0.010)	−0.067	(0.026)
June	0.088	(0.010)	−0.068	(0.026)
July	0.051	(0.010)	−0.048	(0.026)
August	0.031	(0.010)	−0.071	(0.026)
September			−0.082	(0.026)
October	−0.003	(0.010)	−0.041	(0.026)
November	0.069	(0.010)	−0.059	(0.025)
December	0.523	(0.010)	−0.145	(0.024)

Source: Authors' calculations based on data from the Consumer Expenditure Survey, 1982 to 1996.
Note: The dependent variable is the logarithm of monthly durable-goods expenditure. In addition to the covariates listed, the regression also includes all covariates included in the regressions presented in table 9.2. There are 587,294 consumer-unit-month observations. Standard errors are Huber-White standard errors, allowing for dependence within consumer units. All dollar values are in real 1998 dollars.

TABLE 9.5 / Log Monthly Nondurables Expenditure, by EITC Eligibility

Month	Noneligibles		Eligibles	
	Coefficient	Standard Error	Coefficient	Standard Error
January	−0.055	(0.004)	0.0001	(0.009)
February	−0.062	(0.003)	0.0215	(0.009)
March	−0.013	(0.003)	−0.0076	(0.009)
April	0.002	(0.003)	−0.0114	(0.009)
May	0.007	(0.003)	−0.0116	(0.009)
June	0.029	(0.003)	−0.0407	(0.009)
July	0.038	(0.003)	−0.0331	(0.009)
August	0.051	(0.003)	0.0005	(0.010)
September			−0.0199	(0.009)
October	−0.011	(0.003)	−0.0221	(0.009)
November	−0.002	(0.003)	−0.0104	(0.009)
December	0.161	(0.004)	0.0267	(0.009)

Source: Authors' calculations based on data from the Consumer Expenditure Survey, 1982 to 1996.
Note: The dependent variable is the logarithm of monthly nondurable-goods-and-services expenditure. In addition to the covariates listed, the regression also includes all covariates included in the regressions presented in table 9.2. There are 587,294 consumer-unit-month observations. Standard errors are Huber-White standard errors, allowing for dependence within consumer units. All dollar values are in real 1998 dollars.

dicted seasonal pattern for EITC recipients is the sum of the first and third columns. Table 9.6 reports the *p*-values for five different tests applied to each expenditure category. The first statistic reported is the *p*-value for the test of whether there is any seasonality in expenditure for the population that is not eligible to receive the EITC:

TABLE 9.6 / Tests of Seasonality in Spending of EITC-Recipient and Non-EITC-Recipient Households (*p*-Values)

Test	Total	Durable Goods	Nondurable Goods and Services
No seasonal pattern spending of nonrecipients	0.000	0.000	0.000
No seasonal pattern spending of recipients	0.000	0.000	0.000
No difference in seasonality between recipients and nonrecipients	0.000	0.000	0.000
Constant difference in monthly effects between recipients and nonrecipients	0.000	0.000	0.000
Constant difference in monthly effects between recipients and nonrecipients from January to October	0.000	0.002	0.000

Source: Authors' calculations based on data from the Consumer Expenditure Survey, 1982 to 1996.

$$\gamma_1 = \gamma_2 = \ldots = \gamma_8 = \gamma_{10} = \ldots \gamma_{12} = 0.$$

We are testing whether all values of γ_m equal zero, with September being the omitted month. The second statistic is the p-value for the test of whether there is any seasonal pattern in expenditure for the EITC population:

$$\gamma_1 + \phi_1 = \gamma_2 + \phi_2 = \ldots = \phi_9 = \gamma_{10} + \phi_{10} = \ldots = \gamma_{12} + \phi_{12} = 0.$$

The third statistic is the p-value for the test of whether there is a difference in expenditure seasonality between the EITC and non-EITC populations:

$$\phi_1 = \phi_2 = \ldots = \phi_{12} = 0.$$

In other words, are the coefficient estimates for the month-EITC-eligibility interactions jointly insignificant? If there is no difference in the monthly effects between EITC and non-EITC families (we fail to reject the null hypothesis), then we would be unable to argue that the EITC is affecting seasonal expenditure patterns. The fourth statistic is for the test of whether the difference in monthly expenditure between the two population is constant over the entire year:

$$\phi_1 = \phi_2 = \ldots = \phi_{12}.$$

This tests whether the pattern of expenditure for EITC and non-EITC families is the same across months without requiring that the level of expenditure, controlling for other characteristics, be identical. This may be a better test of the effect of the EITC than the third test if we have omitted variables such as those that capture differences in how consumer units allocate expenditure between durable goods and nondurable goods and services. The fifth test statistic is for the test of whether this difference in monthly expenditure is constant from January to October. We construct this test statistic to determine whether there are nonconstant differences in monthly expenditure excluding the effects of Christmas. We are most interested in these final two test statistics because if we can reject the possibility that the difference in the expenditure patterns is constant, we may be observing an EITC-induced change in expenditure patterns.

As displayed in table 9.3, for total expenditure, we find evidence of strong seasonality in expenditure for all households, similar to that presented in table 9.2 and figure 9.2. We also easily reject the hypothesis that there is no expenditure seasonality for EITC-eligible households (the second test). Our results show that the seasonal pattern for EITC recipients is different from the pattern for nonrecipients. This is evident in the p-value of 0.000 for the third test. More important, we can also reject the hypothesis that the monthly differences in expenditure between the two populations are constant over the entire year or constant for the first ten months of the year.

Three particular months stand out when assessing the differences between the eligible and noneligible populations in these total expenditure estimates. First, while EITC-eligible households spend an average of 3 percent less each month (the average of the twelve coefficients), they spend 6 percent less than other households in June and 5 percent less in July. This may be because the income of EITC recipients limits their ability to take vacations or buy cars, two activities that are concentrated in the spring and summer months. Second, EITC-eligible households spend the same amount in February as other consumers. Additional tests (not shown in this chapter) demonstrate that EITC recipients consume more in February, relative to nonrecipients, than in any other month. This may be the result of expenditure patterns induced by the EITC. As already discussed, February is the modal month of EITC refund payments. The other major EITC months, March and April, appear to be more typical, although the coefficients are next highest after February. These suggestive results are investigated in more detail later.

In table 9.4 we present results for durable goods. For durable goods, we also see evidence of differential expenditure seasonality among EITC recipients relative to nonrecipients. Again, we easily reject all five of our hypotheses. We see that EITC-eligible households spend more on durables in February than in any other month relative to noneligible households. The February difference stands out more for durable goods than it does for total expenditure, with a difference between EITC eligibles and noneligibles of 5 percent relative to an average difference of -4 percent (the average of the twelve interaction coefficients). The only other months in which we see EITC eligibles spending more than noneligibles are March (0.2 percent) and April (3 percent). We can reject the hypothesis that the difference in February is equal to the difference in each other month (at the 99 percent level) except March and April. This provides support for our hypothesis that the EITC may induce increased spending on durable goods. Recipients of the EITC appear to concentrate a higher portion of their durable-goods spending during the period when most EITC payments are received. For durable goods, we also see a pronounced difference in expenditure in December, with spending 15 percent lower among EITC eligible households than noneligible households. We think it is unlikely that lower December expenditure is caused by EITC receipt, and this affect is attenuated when we allow for seasonality by income level and child status.

The pattern for nondurables expenditure, displayed in table 9.5, is similar to that for total expenditure. We continue to see high relative spending levels in February among EITC-eligible households and lower relative levels in June and July. For nondurables, the coefficient estimate on the February EITC interaction is slightly less exceptional than was the case for durable goods, with a difference in expenditure of 2 percent, relative to an average difference of -1 percent. However, we can reject the hypothesis that the February effect equals that in each other month at standard levels of significance with the exceptions of August and December.

While the EITC may induce the expenditure patterns we observe in February for all three categories of expenditure and in February through April for durable-goods spending, other factors correlated with EITC eligibility—namely, children and income—may be related to seasonal preferences in expenditure. If this is the case, the coefficients on EITC eligibility are partially capturing these differences in preferences. In addition, it is possible that there are systematic differences in income seasonality between EITC-eligible households and other households owing to factors other than EITC receipt. In particular, the seasonal income pattern for poorer families may differ from that of more well-to-do families. If this is the case and the difference in income seasonality corresponds to the timing of EITC receipt, then we may be assigning causality incorrectly to the EITC.

Differences in Income Seasonality and Preferences

Two possible reasons for the difference between EITC and non-EITC families in their monthly expenditure are differences in seasonal preferences for spending and differences in income seasonality. The specification of equation (9.7) assumes that seasonal preferences, as represented by γ, are constant across all families and that the only difference in income seasonality arises through the EITC.

Families that receive the EITC are different from other families in two major ways that may be correlated with preferences. First, EITC-eligible families are much more likely to have children (see table 9.1). Second, to receive the EITC families must have income below a certain threshold. As a result, EITC-eligible families are, on average, much poorer than noneligible families. We think it may be possible that the seasonal spending preferences of families with children or with low incomes may be different from those of other families. For example, families with children may wish to purchase more during the back-to-school shopping season (August) than families without children.

In addition to having different preferences for monthly expenditure patterns, low-income families may have different income seasonality. There are other forms of income seasonality observed during a calendar year in addition to that induced by the Earned Income Tax Credit. Other forms of tax refunds, particularly federal tax overpayment refunds, are also mostly paid out between February and April, and most tax filers receive a refund. In 1996, approximately 70 percent of filers received an average refund of $1,335 (IRS 1999). While this is a substantial sum, it amounts to only approximately 3.5 percent of average adjusted gross income among all filers. In contrast, the 1996 average refundable portion of the EITC of $1,506 represented more than 10 percent of the adjusted gross income of EITC recipients, and EITC refunds were nearly 15 percent of adjusted gross income for those EITC recipients with incomes of less than $20,000 (IRS 1999). As mentioned earlier, we do not use the refund data from the CES in our analyses, but the presence of these other refunds is important to keep in mind.

A second potential source of income seasonality is seasonality in earnings from employment. To look at the pattern of earnings over the calendar year, we investigate the monthly pattern of earnings using the outgoing rotation group (ORG) files from the monthly Current Population Survey for 1995 and 1996.

FIGURE 9.3 / Monthly Earnings Patterns, by Income

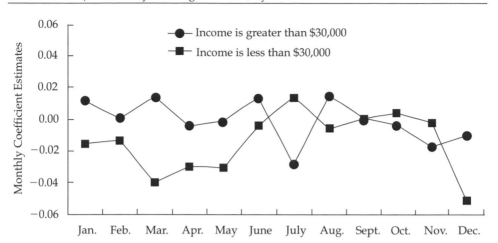

Source: Data from Current Population Survey Outgoing Rotation Group files, 1995 and 1996.
Note: The graph shows the monthly coefficient estimates from regressions of log earnings on a series of month dummies. The separate regressions are for individuals with annual income above and below $30,000. In both cases, September is the omitted month.

These years are chosen because they are in the middle of an expansion and therefore the data are unlikely to be confounded by business-cycle effects. We estimate separate regressions for households with annual incomes of more than and less than $30,000, regressing log income on a series of monthly dummies (excluding September). Figure 9.3 shows the monthly dummy coefficients from these two regressions. The earnings measure is earnings last week.[15]

Two patterns emerge from this figure. First, while there is some earnings seasonality, especially among low-income workers, it follows a pattern quite distinct from that induced by the EITC. In particular, the earnings of low-income workers peak during the summer and fall months and are low during spring and December. Second, the income change induced by the EITC dwarfs these other income changes. We conclude that differences in income seasonality between low- and high-income individuals are unlikely to generate the seasonal differences observed in the expenditure regressions. That said, in the next set of regressions we allow for income-level expenditure differences that will capture both preference differences and the potential for systematic differences in income seasonality.

We address the potential for preferences to be correlated with income and child status by simultaneously allowing low-income households and households with children to have different seasonal spending patterns. In particular, we reestimate equation (9.7), including a series of month-child interactions and month-low-income interactions. The new estimation equation is as follows:

$$ln(E_{im}) = \alpha_1 ln(Y_i) + M\gamma + (M \times R)\phi + (M \times \text{Child})\kappa$$
$$+ (M \times \text{Low Income})\eta + \varepsilon_{im}.$$

Once again, R is the measure of EITC eligibility. Child equals one if there are any unmarried children under nineteen years of age living in the consumer unit. Low income equals one if the consumer-unit income is in the bottom 40 percent of the income distribution (less than $29,032 a year). The vector κ represents the marginal monthly effects of having children in the household, while η represents the marginal effects of being low income.

We present the results from these regressions, separately by expenditure category, in tables 9.7, 9.8, and 9.9. In each table, the first column presents the coefficients on the month dummies. The second column presents the added monthly effects for EITC-eligible households. The third column presents the added monthly effect for households with unmarried children under the age of nineteen. The final column presents the added monthly effect for low-income households.

For total expenditure (table 9.7), we observe that families with children spend an average of 8 percent more in each month than families without children (the average of the coefficient estimates in the third column). Two months stand out from these results: August and December. In both of these months, families with children spend 12 percent more than families without children. These tables also show that low-income households spend 2 percent less on average than higher-income households (the average of the coefficient estimates in the fourth column). This difference is especially pronounced in December, during which low-income households spend 7 percent less. In both cases, the February effect is about average, indicating that different seasonal expenditure preferences among low-income households and households with children are not driving the effects presented in table 9.3. This is confirmed by the fact that February continues to be the largest coefficient estimate in the second column. While EITC families consume 4 percent less, on average, each month than non-EITC families, controlling for the child-month and low-income-month interactions, in February they consume only 1 percent less. Based on the results of the first test in table 9.10, we reject the hypothesis that there is no seasonality in expenditure for the base group (noneligible, childless, higher-income households). In the second, fourth, and fifth tests, we reject the hypothesis that there is no difference in monthly effects between the base group and the EITC eligible, households with children, and low-income households, respectively. In the third test, we reject the hypothesis that there is a constant difference in monthly effects between EITC-eligible families and the base group.

For durable goods (table 9.8), as was the case for total consumption, we find that households with children spend more in December relative to households without children, while low-income households spend relatively less in December than higher-income households. The other months, including February, are much less remarkable than December. For the EITC interactions, the February effect continues to be the largest; while EITC recipients spend 5 percent less than

TABLE 9.7 / Log Monthly Total Expenditure, Allowing Different Seasonality for Households with Unmarried Children Under the Age of Eighteen and for Poor Households

Month	All Families	EITC Eligible	Children	Low-Income
January	−0.036 (0.006)	−0.037 (0.010)	0.072 (0.007)	0.005 (0.007)
February	−0.065 (0.006)	−0.012 (0.010)	0.075 (0.007)	−0.008 (0.007)
March	−0.034 (0.006)	−0.036 (0.010)	0.079 (0.007)	−0.003 (0.007)
April	−0.028 (0.006)	−0.034 (0.010)	0.076 (0.007)	−0.003 (0.007)
May	−0.008 (0.006)	−0.030 (0.010)	0.062 (0.007)	−0.018 (0.007)
June	0.015 (0.006)	−0.054 (0.010)	0.061 (0.007)	−0.030 (0.007)
July	0.025 (0.005)	−0.055 (0.010)	0.076 (0.007)	−0.037 (0.007)
August	0.026 (0.005)	−0.068 (0.010)	0.122 (0.007)	−0.027 (0.007)
September		−0.045 (0.010)	0.077 (0.007)	−0.021 (0.007)
October	−0.003 (0.005)	−0.025 (0.010)	0.051 (0.007)	−0.035 (0.007)
November	−0.020 (0.006)	−0.032 (0.010)	0.080 (0.007)	−0.030 (0.007)
December	0.114 (0.006)	−0.039 (0.009)	0.120 (0.007)	−0.072 (0.007)

Source: Authors' calculations based on data from the Consumer Expenditure Survey, 1982 to 1996.

Note: The dependent variable is the logarithm of monthly total expenditure. In addition to the covariates listed above, the regression includes all covariates included in the regressions presented in table 9.2. A consumer unit is defined as having a child if there is an unmarried child under eighteen living in the unit. A consumer unit is defined as low-income if total income for the unit is in the bottom 40 percent of the sample. There are 587,294 consumer unit-month observations. Standard errors are in parentheses. Standard errors are Huber-White standard errors allowing for dependence within consumer units.

TABLE 9.8 / Log Monthly Durable-Goods Expenditure, Allowing Different
Seasonality for Households with Unmarried Children Under the Age of
Eighteen and for Poor Households

Month	All Families	EITC Eligible	Children	Low-Income
January	−0.100 (0.016)	−0.055 (0.028)	0.066 (0.018)	−0.003 (0.017)
February	−0.106 (0.016)	0.049 (0.028)	0.034 (0.018)	−0.015 (0.017)
March	−0.045 (0.016)	−0.008 (0.029)	0.041 (0.018)	−0.003 (0.017)
April	−0.027 (0.016)	−0.011 (0.029)	0.074 (0.018)	0.013 (0.017)
May	0.129 (0.016)	−0.073 (0.029)	0.079 (0.018)	−0.069 (0.017)
June	0.101 (0.016)	−0.061 (0.029)	0.053 (0.019)	−0.060 (0.017)
July	0.051 (0.016)	−0.058 (0.029)	0.060 (0.019)	−0.030 (0.018)
August	0.029 (0.016)	−0.083 (0.029)	0.053 (0.019)	−0.016 (0.018)
September		−0.090 (0.029)	0.054 (0.019)	−0.024 (0.017)
October	0.022 (0.016)	−0.013 (0.029)	0.016 (0.019)	−0.054 (0.017)
November	0.082 (0.016)	−0.060 (0.028)	0.095 (0.018)	−0.103 (0.017)
December	0.574 (0.016)	−0.116 (0.026)	0.181 (0.017)	−0.301 (0.016)

Source: Authors' calculations based on data from the Consumer Expenditure Survey, 1982 to
1996.
Note: The dependent variable is the logarithm of monthly durable goods expenditure. See
notes for table 9.7.

nonrecipients in the average month, they spend 5 percent more in February. In
addition, we find that EITC-eligible households spend only 1 percent less in
March. For durable goods, we perform the same set of tests as we did for total
expenditure and continue to reject easily the null hypothesis in each case. Most
important, we can reject the hypothesis that EITC recipients have the same
monthly expenditure patterns as nonrecipients and that the difference in monthly
effects is constant.

TABLE 9.9 / Log Monthly Nondurable-Goods and Services Expenditure, Allowing Different Seasonality for Households with Unmarried Children Under the Age of Eighteen and for Poor Households

Month	All Families	EITC Eligible	Children	Low-Income
January	−0.0594 (0.006)	0.004 (0.010)	0.019 (0.007)	−0.039 (0.007)
February	−0.0644 (0.006)	0.026 (0.010)	0.024 (0.007)	−0.050 (0.007)
March	−0.0207 (0.005)	−0.010 (0.010)	0.033 (0.007)	−0.043 (0.007)
April	0.0033 (0.005)	−0.002 (0.010)	0.022 (0.007)	−0.056 (0.007)
May	0.0123 (0.005)	0.004 (0.010)	0.012 (0.007)	−0.056 (0.007)
June	0.0369 (0.005)	−0.023 (0.010)	0.019 (0.007)	−0.071 (0.007)
July	0.0428 (0.005)	−0.020 (0.010)	0.030 (0.007)	−0.077 (0.007)
August	0.0280 (0.005)	−0.030 (0.010)	0.090 (0.007)	−0.062 (0.007)
September		−0.011 (0.010)	0.023 (0.007)	−0.054 (0.007)
October	−0.0001 (0.005)	0.003 (0.010)	0.002 (0.007)	−0.063 (0.007)
November	−0.0041 (0.005)	−0.006 (0.010)	0.030 (0.007)	−0.056 (0.007)
December	0.1504 (0.006)	0.009 (0.010)	0.098 (0.007)	−0.103 (0.007)

Source: Authors' calculations based on data from the Consumer Expenditure Survey, 1982 to 1996.
Note: The dependent variable is the logarithm of monthly nondurable goods and services expenditure. See notes for table 9.7.

For nondurable goods (table 9.9), we find that households with children spend 3 percent more than households without children in the average month. Notably, however, they spend 9 percent more than households without children in August and 10 percent more in December. These increases in August and December may be the result of higher spending for back-to-school merchandise and Christmas gifts among families with children. Low-income households spend an average of 6 percent less each month than higher-income households

TABLE 9.10 / Tests of Seasonality in Spending, Allowing Different Seasonality for Households With Unmarried Children Under the Age of Eighteen and for Poor Households (p-Values)

Test	Total	Durable Goods	Nondurable Goods and Services
No seasonality in base group (not low income, not EITC recipient, no children)	0.000	0.000	0.000
No difference in month effects between EITC group and base group	0.000	0.000	0.001
Constant difference in month effects of EITC group and base group	0.004	0.001	0.000
No difference in month effects between consumer units with children and base group	0.000	0.000	0.000
No difference in month effects between low-income consumer units and base group	0.000	0.000	0.000

Source: Authors' calculations based on data from the Consumer Expenditure Survey, 1982 to 1996.

but 10 percent less in December. This decrease in December may reflect the fact that lower-income households are not able to increase Christmas spending as much as higher-income households. Turning to the EITC coefficients, we continue to see that EITC-eligible households have the highest relative consumption in February. Finally, we once again easily reject all five hypotheses presented in table 9.10.

As shown in the results in tables 9.7 through 9.9, the larger relative size of the February and March interaction-coefficient estimates in the regressions presented in tables 9.3 through 9.5 cannot be explained by preferences or income seasonality correlated with the low-income or child status of eligible families. However, we find that some of the lower December expenditure among EITC households can be explained by lower levels of Christmas spending among families of limited means.

Program Expansions

Before concluding, we look at the effects of the EITC on expenditure from one additional angle by taking advantage of the program expansions that have taken place since 1982. If EITC receipt, rather than the combination of being low income and having children, is causing the expenditure pattern observed in the data, we expect to observe different expenditure patterns for households that were eligible when sampled from the patterns of households that were not eligible when sampled but would be eligible under the new program rules. Similarly, the effect of the EITC on expenditure seasonality should become more pronounced as the program's generosity increases.

To address the first of these ideas, we take advantage of the EITC program changes by comparing families that received the EITC with the set of families with children that would have received the EITC in 1995 but were ineligible in the year in which they were sampled. These families are low income but had earnings above the phase-out ending income in the year in which they were sampled. We examine this by estimating the following equation:

$$ln(E_{im}) = \alpha_1 ln(Y_i) + M\gamma + (M \times E_{1995})\Psi + (M \times E_{1995} \times R)\phi + \varepsilon_{im}, \quad (9.8)$$

where $E_{1995} = 1$ if the consumer unit is eligible for the EITC under 1995 rules, independent from whether it is EITC eligible when sampled. The vector Ψ represents the marginal difference of being EITC eligible under 1995 rules relative to being ineligible under the 1995 rules, independent of the eligibility of the consumer unit in the year in which it was sampled. The parameter ϕ represents the additional effect of actually being eligible when sampled. If the EITC affects expenditure, we expect to see a seasonal pattern in the ϕ parameters that corresponds to the timing of the EITC. However, we expect that any seasonal pattern in the Ψ parameters will not correspond to the timing of the EITC.

The results for equation (9.8) are presented in tables 9.11, 9.12, and 9.13. We show three sets of monthly interactions. In each of these tables, the first column

TABLE 9.11 / Log Monthly Total Expenditure, Accounting for Change in Eligibility Rules

Month	All Families		Added Pattern for Eligible Under 1995 Rules		Added Pattern for Eligible When Sampled	
	Coefficient	Standard Error	Coefficient	Standard Error	Coefficient	Standard Error
January	−0.028	(0.004)	−0.060	(0.014)	0.037	(0.016)
February	−0.060	(0.004)	−0.050	(0.014)	0.049	(0.016)
March	−0.027	(0.004)	−0.043	(0.014)	0.023	(0.016)
April	−0.022	(0.004)	−0.032	(0.015)	0.013	(0.017)
May	−0.011	(0.004)	−0.071	(0.015)	0.039	(0.017)
June	0.007	(0.003)	−0.076	(0.016)	0.014	(0.018)
July	0.020	(0.003)	−0.079	(0.016)	0.023	(0.018)
August	0.041	(0.003)	−0.062	(0.016)	0.026	(0.018)
September			−0.044	(0.015)	0.005	(0.017)
October	−0.016	(0.003)	−0.079	(0.015)	0.036	(0.017)
November	−0.022	(0.004)	−0.041	(0.014)	0.013	(0.016)
December	0.111	(0.004)	−0.033	(0.013)	0.006	(0.015)

Source: Authors' calculations based on data from the Consumer Expenditure Survey, 1982 to 1996.
Note: The dependent variable is the logarithm of monthly total expenditure. In addition to the covariates listed above, the regression includes all covariates included in the regressions presented in table 9.2. There are 587,294 consumer-unit-month observations. Standard errors are Huber-White standard errors allowing for dependence within consumer units.

shows the expenditure pattern of all families, γ, the third column shows the marginal effect of being eligible according to the 1995 rules, Ψ, and the fifth column shows the marginal effect of being EITC eligible when sampled, ϕ. In table 9.14 we present three test statistics. First, we test whether individuals eligible under 1995 program rules have different expenditure patterns from those of the ineligible, $\Psi = 0$. Second, we test whether there is a difference in monthly effects between those eligible according to 1995 program parameters and those eligible when observed in the sample, $\phi = 0$. Finally, we test whether this difference between monthly effects for the eligible according to the 1995 rules and for those who were eligible when sampled is constant.

For total expenditure (table 9.11), we reject the first of our hypotheses and marginally reject the second. We fail to reject the hypothesis that the difference in the monthly effects for the eligible when sampled relative to the eligible under 1995 rules is a constant. We find that the marginal effect of being interviewed in a year in which a person is eligible relative to being eligible under 1995 rules is largest in February, but we cannot reject the possibility that it equals the coefficient estimates for a number of other months.

For durable-goods expenditure (table 9.12), we can easily reject our first hypothesis and marginally reject the second; however, we cannot reject the test of constant difference between eligibility under 1995 rules and eligibility when sampled. We continue to see the strongest effect of eligibility in February. The

TABLE 9.12 / Log Monthly Durable-Goods Expenditure, Accounting for Change in Eligibility Rules

Month	All Families		Added Pattern for Eligible Under 1995 Rules		Added Pattern for Eligible When Sampled	
	Coefficient	Standard Error	Coefficient	Standard Error	Coefficient	Standard Error
January	−0.087	(0.010)	−0.129	(0.043)	0.088	(0.048)
February	−0.109	(0.010)	−0.130	(0.044)	0.170	(0.050)
March	−0.045	(0.010)	−0.048	(0.045)	0.042	(0.050)
April	−0.011	(0.010)	0.007	(0.046)	0.013	(0.052)
May	0.122	(0.010)	−0.087	(0.043)	0.011	(0.049)
June	0.087	(0.010)	−0.084	(0.046)	0.007	(0.052)
July	0.051	(0.010)	−0.122	(0.046)	0.064	(0.052)
August	0.033	(0.010)	−0.174	(0.047)	0.091	(0.052)
September			−0.104	(0.045)	0.013	(0.051)
October	−0.003	(0.010)	−0.118	(0.044)	0.065	(0.050)
November	0.069	(0.010)	−0.101	(0.044)	0.033	(0.049)
December	0.524	(0.010)	−0.134	(0.040)	−0.021	(0.045)

Source: Authors' calculations based on data from the Consumer Expenditure Survey, 1982 to 1996.
Note: The dependent variable is the logarithm of monthly durable goods expenditure. See note for table 9.11.

TABLE 9.13 / Log Monthly Nondurables Expenditure, Accounting for Change in EITC Eligibility Rules

Month	All Families		Added Pattern for Eligible Under 1995 Rules		Added Pattern for Eligible When Sampled	
	Coefficient	Standard Error	Coefficient	Standard Error	Coefficient	Standard Error
January	−0.055	(0.004)	−0.055	(0.013)	0.049	(0.015)
February	−0.061	(0.004)	−0.057	(0.013)	0.072	(0.015)
March	−0.012	(0.004)	−0.060	(0.014)	0.047	(0.016)
April	0.003	(0.003)	−0.059	(0.014)	0.042	(0.016)
May	0.008	(0.003)	−0.059	(0.014)	0.042	(0.016)
June	0.031	(0.003)	−0.071	(0.015)	0.024	(0.017)
July	0.040	(0.003)	−0.090	(0.014)	0.050	(0.016)
August	0.051	(0.003)	−0.048	(0.015)	0.043	(0.017)
September			−0.033	(0.014)	0.008	(0.016)
October	−0.010	(0.003)	−0.074	(0.014)	0.045	(0.016)
November	−0.001	(0.003)	−0.049	(0.013)	0.033	(0.016)
December	0.161	(0.004)	−0.019	(0.013)	0.041	(0.015)

Source: Authors' calculations based on data from the Consumer Expenditure Survey, 1982 to 1996.
Note: The dependent variable is the logarithm of monthly nondurable goods and services expenditure. See note for table 9.11.

TABLE 9.14 / Tests of Seasonality in Spending, Accounting for Change in Eligibility Rules (*p*-Values)

Test	Total	Durable Goods	Nondurable Goods and Services
No difference in spending seasonality of EITC eligibles and noneligibles according to the 1995 rules	0.000	0.000	0.000
No difference in spending seasonality of EITC recipients and those eligible according to the 1995 rules	0.079	0.091	0.000
Constant difference in monthly effects between EITC recipients and those eligible according to the 1995 rules	0.330	0.274	0.084

Source: Authors' calculations based on data from the Consumer Expenditure Survey, 1982 to 1996.

results for nondurable goods and services (table 9.13) are very similar to the results for total expenditure.

In sum, we find weaker results when we compare all families who would have been eligible under the 1995 rules to those families who were eligible when sampled. In particular, we cannot reject the hypothesis that the coefficients on the interactions between month, eligibility according to 1995 rules, and eligibility when sampled are constant. However, if we look at the monthly patterns, for the group that is eligible when sampled (the sum of the coefficient estimates in the third and fifth columns), we still observe that the eligible when sampled have larger relative levels of consumption in February. Coefficient estimates for households eligible under 1995 rules do not exhibit the same pattern. Together, these results suggest that EITC receipt affects expenditure patterns but that we lack sufficient statistical power to identify the effect.

Next, we take advantage of the increasing maximum credit by looking at whether the expenditure pattern is different among EITC recipients before and after the program expansions that occurred between 1990 and 1991. We expect that expenditure will be more responsive to EITC receipt in the later years, when the benefits are more generous. Between 1982 and 1990, the average credit was $549, while between 1991 and 1996 the average credit was $1,197 (both credits in 1998 dollars) (U.S. House 1998). To look at the effect of the expansion in generosity on expenditure patterns, we add a set of monthly interactions that allow the seasonal pattern of expenditure to differ across EITC recipients before and after the 1991 expansions. The new estimation equation is

$$ln(E_{im}) = \alpha_1 ln(Y_i) + M\gamma + (M \times R)\phi + [M \times R \times (\text{Year} > 1990)]\tau + \varepsilon_{im},$$

where Year > 1990 is an indicator variable equal to one if the consumer unit is observed after 1990 and τ is a vector of additional monthly effects arising from being EITC eligible after 1990. The results for the three expenditure categories are presented in tables 9.15, 9.16, and 9.17. In table 9.18, we use a slightly different set of test statistics that focuses on the difference between EITC families before and after the expansions. The first is a test of whether there is any difference between the two eligible groups—that is, are the coefficients on the month-eligibility-year interactions, τ, jointly equal to zero? The second is a test of whether this difference is constant—that is, are all the values of τ equal (but not necessarily equal to zero)?

For total expenditure (table 9.15), we can reject the hypothesis that there is no difference between the effects of the EITC during the two time periods and can marginally reject the hypothesis that the difference is constant. The February coefficient estimate in the fifth column is the largest and is significantly different from that in all other months at the 10 percent level except for March and July.

For durable goods (table 9.16), we can easily reject both tested hypotheses: that there is no difference between the effect of the EITC during the two time periods and that there is a constant difference between the two time periods. From these results, we can see that the increase in February and March spending

TABLE 9.15 / Log Monthly Total Expenditure, Accounting for 1990 EITC Program Expansions

Month	All Families		Added Pattern for All EITC Recipients		Added Pattern for EITC Recipients After 1990	
	Coefficient	Standard Error	Coefficient	Standard Error	Coefficient	Standard Error
January	−0.029	(0.004)	−0.002	(0.012)	−0.030	(0.017)
February	−0.061	(0.004)	−0.010	(0.012)	0.029	(0.017)
March	−0.027	(0.004)	−0.016	(0.012)	0.001	(0.017)
April	−0.022	(0.004)	−0.012	(0.012)	−0.006	(0.017)
May	−0.012	(0.003)	−0.018	(0.013)	−0.017	(0.017)
June	0.006	(0.003)	−0.048	(0.013)	−0.016	(0.018)
July	0.019	(0.003)	−0.049	(0.013)	−0.003	(0.018)
August	0.040	(0.003)	−0.021	(0.013)	−0.022	(0.017)
September			−0.026	(0.013)	−0.016	(0.017)
October	−0.018	(0.003)	−0.017	(0.013)	−0.037	(0.018)
November	−0.022	(0.003)	−0.001	(0.012)	−0.044	(0.017)
December	0.112	(0.004)	−0.009	(0.011)	−0.029	(0.016)

Source: Authors' calculations based on data from the Consumer Expenditure Survey, 1982 to 1996.
Note: The dependent variable is the logarithm of monthly total expenditure. In addition to the covariates listed above, the regression includes all covariates included in the regressions presented in table 9.2. There are 587,294 consumer-unit-month observations. Standard errors are Huber-White standard errors allowing for dependence within consumer units.

observed in the earlier results is being driven by the expenditure patterns of EITC-eligible households in the later program years. In particular, we do not observe February or March effects for EITC recipients before 1991 (see the results in the third column); however, the additional marginal effect for February is substantial and statistically significant for EITC recipients in the post-1990 period. The March effect in the post-1990 period is smaller but also positive. Post-1990 EITC families spend 13 percent more in February on durable goods and 4 percent more in March than pre-1990 eligible families. In the average month, post-1990 EITC families spend 5 percent less.

In the case of nondurables expenditures (table 9.17), we can reject the hypothesis that there is no difference in the monthly effects for pre- and post-1990 families but cannot reject the hypothesis that their difference is constant. In contrast with the durable-goods results, for nondurables the pre-1990 period February coefficient estimate for all EITC recipients is among the largest of all the monthly effects. That said, the overall nondurables monthly pattern for pre-1991 EITC eligibles does not as clearly suggest an EITC expenditure effect as some other results presented. More similar to the durable-goods results, the additional marginal February effect for post-1990 EITC recipients is the largest of the additional monthly effects. In addition, it is the only positive coefficient estimate.[16]

TABLE 9.16 / Log Monthly Durable-Goods Expenditure, Accounting for 1990 EITC
Program Expansions

Month	All Families		Added Pattern for All EITC Recipients		Added Pattern for EITC Recipients After 1990	
	Coefficient	Standard Error	Coefficient	Standard Error	Coefficient	Standard Error
January	−0.088	(0.010)	−0.003	(0.035)	−0.052	(0.047)
February	−0.110	(0.010)	−0.016	(0.035)	0.131	(0.049)
March	−0.043	(0.010)	−0.018	(0.035)	0.042	(0.049)
April	−0.008	(0.010)	0.056	(0.035)	−0.062	(0.050)
May	0.123	(0.010)	−0.020	(0.036)	−0.099	(0.049)
June	0.088	(0.010)	0.001	(0.036)	−0.142	(0.049)
July	0.051	(0.010)	−0.031	(0.036)	−0.034	(0.049)
August	0.031	(0.010)	−0.033	(0.037)	−0.077	(0.049)
September			−0.060	(0.035)	−0.043	(0.048)
October	−0.003	(0.010)	0.013	(0.036)	−0.109	(0.049)
November	0.069	(0.010)	−0.009	(0.035)	−0.101	(0.047)
December	0.523	(0.010)	−0.129	(0.031)	−0.034	(0.044)

Source: Authors' calculations based on data from the Consumer Expenditure Survey, 1982 to
1996.
Note: The dependent variable is the logarithm of monthly durable-goods expenditure. See
notes for table 9.15.

This investigation into changes in expenditure induced by expansions in the
EITC lends further credence to our hypothesis that the EITC increases spending
during the month when most EITC payments are received. One conclusion we
can draw from these results is that the seasonal expenditure effect of the EITC is
measurable exclusively in the post-1990 period, when the EITC program is more
generous.

Assessing Magnitudes

The results point to the conclusion that the EITC leads to increased spending on
durable goods and to a lesser extent on nondurable goods and services during
the month of February, the most common month for EITC refunds during the
most recent and most generous years of the EITC. Based on the results presented
in table 9.4, we find that for durable goods, the EITC increases February expenditure for all eligible families by 9 percent (a coefficient of 0.05 relative to an
average coefficient of −0.04). According to table 9.16, this breaks down into no
increase for families eligible before 1991 (a coefficient of −0.016 relative to an
average coefficient of −0.021) and an increase of 18 percent for families eligible
after 1990 (a sum of coefficients of 0.115 relative to an average sum of −0.069).
For nondurable goods and services, based on table 9.5 we find that EITC eligi-

TABLE 9.17 / Log Monthly Nondurable Expenditure, Accounting for 1990 EITC Program Expansions

Month	All Families		Added Pattern for All EITC Recipients		Added Pattern for EITC Recipients After 1990	
	Coefficient	Standard Error	Coefficient	Standard Error	Coefficient	Standard Error
January	−0.055	(0.004)	0.0069	(0.012)	−0.014	(0.016)
February	−0.062	(0.003)	0.0175	(0.012)	0.006	(0.016)
March	−0.013	(0.003)	0.0066	(0.012)	−0.030	(0.017)
April	0.002	(0.003)	0.0030	(0.012)	−0.030	(0.017)
May	0.007	(0.003)	−0.0096	(0.012)	−0.005	(0.017)
June	0.029	(0.003)	−0.0327	(0.012)	−0.017	(0.017)
July	0.038	(0.003)	−0.0214	(0.012)	−0.024	(0.017)
August	0.051	(0.003)	0.0120	(0.013)	−0.023	(0.018)
September			0.0087	(0.012)	−0.056	(0.017)
October	−0.011	(0.003)	0.0004	(0.012)	−0.045	(0.017)
November	−0.002	(0.003)	0.0117	(0.012)	−0.045	(0.017)
December	0.161	(0.004)	0.0337	(0.012)	−0.015	(0.016)

Source: Authors' calculations based on data from the Consumer Expenditure Survey, 1982 to 1996.
Note: The dependent variable is the logarithm of monthly durable goods expenditure. See note for table 9.15.

bility increases expenditures by 3 percent. This breaks down into an increase of 2 percent before 1991 and 5 percent after 1990. Similarly for total expenditures, presented in table 9.3, EITC eligibility increases spending by 3 percent. This corresponds to an increase of 1 percent before 1991 and 5 percent after 1990, according to the results presented in table 9.15. If we assume that the EITC increases durable-goods expenditure by 9 percent, nondurable goods and services expenditure by 3 percent, and total expenditure by 3 percent, these increases translate into February spending increases by EITC-eligible families of

TABLE 9.18 / Tests of Seasonality in Spending, Accounting for 1990 EITC Program Expansions (*p*-Values)

Test	Total	Durable Goods	Nondurable Goods and Services
No difference in spending seasonality of EITC recipients before and after 1990 changes	0.049	0.002	0.032
Constant difference in month EITC effects before and after 1990 changes	0.087	0.008	0.129

Source: Authors' calculations based on data from the Consumer Expenditure Survey, 1982 to 1996.

$33, $25, and $63, respectively. If we further assume that of the $844 average estimated EITC payment, 76 percent is refunded (the average refundable portion over the period from 1982 to 1997) and 46 percent is paid out in February, this yields an average expected payment among EITC recipients of $295 in February. A comparison between these two calculations suggests that EITC recipients are spending about one-fifth of their refunds in the month in which the refund is received.

We believe that the estimate that families spend approximately one-fifth of their EITC refund in February may be biased downward owing to imperfect EITC imputation. We know that some of the families imputed as EITC eligible are not actually receiving the EITC. This could be attributable either to their failure to file taxes or fill out the necessary schedule or to the underreporting of income in the CES. Income underreporting implies that some families with earnings above the ending income of the phase-out range report earnings in the eligible range to the CES. For these nonrecipient families, the EITC should have no effect on their income seasonality and therefore no induced effect on their expenditure pattern. By including them in the eligible group we are underestimating the effects of the EITC on expenditure.

IMPLICATIONS

Our results suggest that EITC receipt induces a change in seasonal expenditure patterns. In particular, we observe an increase in February expenditure relative to that in other months, with results that are strongest for durable goods. These results suggest that EITC recipients do not smooth expenditure perfectly. However, the evidence also implies that recipients spend less than the full amount of their refund in the month of receipt. In effect, some smoothing does occur.

Our finding that EITC recipients spend approximately one-fifth of the refundable portion of the EITC during the month of receipt suggests that if the advance EITC were costless, the average EITC household would be better off taking the Advance Earned Income Credit. This is true even if recipient households are relying on the refundable portion as a forced savings mechanism. We draw this conclusion since the AEIC only allows employers to remit up to 60 percent of the total EITC as a supplement to pay. As a result, it would seem that households could use the nonadvanced refundable portion of the EITC as a savings mechanism while using the AEIC to greater smooth their income. As discussed earlier the AEIC is not costless because of the basic paperwork required, exacerbated by the greater employment instability among its targeted beneficiaries. Thus, any policy changes to reduce the costs of receiving the AEIC may lead to increases in its take-up rate and improved welfare for EITC-recipient households.

Our results also have some implications for a plan considered by Congress in the fall of 1999. Republican members of Congress proposed to pay out EITC benefits in twelve monthly installments following the filing of taxes rather than as a lump-sum refund. The finding that EITC-eligible households appear to be engaging in some consumption smoothing with their EITC payments does not imply that this plan to smooth benefit payments would advantage low-income households. In particular, the congressional plan would have served only to delay payments to beneficiaries. In addition, to the extent that EITC recipients choose to use the EITC as a forced savings mechanism, they would lose the option to save.

The work in this chapter shows that income seasonality caused by EITC receipt leads to changes in seasonal expenditure patterns, particularly for durable goods. In future work we hope to expand this analysis to look at narrower categories of expenditure. In this way, we hope to better understand the specific ways in which EITC refunds are spent. In addition, we plan to investigate measures of savings and credit to determine what mechanisms facilitate consumption smoothing observed in the data.

NOTES

1. Note that even if EITC recipients opt to receive the Advance Earned Income Credit, they may receive only a portion of their projected EITC in advance, such that at least 40 percent of their EITC is paid out in a lump-sum payment.

2. We note that it is not entirely costless to receive AEIC payments: eligible recipients must file IRS form W-5 with their employers, the estimated time of completion of which is forty-three minutes (IRS 2000). To the extent that low-income households have unstable employment relationships it may be difficult for them to keep this form on file. We return to this issue in the final section of this chapter.

3. Taxpayers can request extensions and file their taxes following the April 15 deadline, but this option is rarely taken by low-income taxpayers. Only about 0.5 percent of taxpayers with incomes of less than $30,000 file extensions. In comparison, more than 20 percent of taxpayers with incomes in excess of $100,000 file extensions (IRS 1998).

4. Before 1992, the IRS made more EITC payments in March than in any other month.

5. Other evidence also suggests that low-income filers anticipating refunds file earlier than average (Slemrod et al. 1997).

6. The CES actually surveys families five times. However, data are reported only for surveys two through five. Throughout the chapter we refer to these as surveys one through four.

7. In an earlier version of this paper, we used only quarterly expenditure data. The results from that analysis were much weaker than the current results. We did not find significant effects of the EITC on expenditure seasonality. Using monthly expenditure data has much more power for identifying an effect of the EITC because we avoid smoothing monthly fluctuations over three-month periods.

8. A more detailed description of the data is available from the authors on request.

9. While the EITC eligibility rules depend on the adjusted gross income when it is greater than earned income, the member files do not contain the detailed information needed to calculate the adjusted gross income.

10. We have also performed the estimates including individuals who received the small childless credit in the EITC eligible sample. The results are substantively unchanged.

11. While some of these discrepancies can be explained by the fact that not all individuals are required to file taxes, the differences are too large and persist too high into the income distribution to be explained by this fact alone. For example, there is a gap of 30 percentage points in refund percentages even among individuals with incomes between $40,000 and $50,000.

12. According to our definition, nondurables comprise food, alcohol, apparel and services, gasoline, other vehicle expenses, public transportation, fees and admissions, pets and toys, other entertainment, personal care, reading, tobacco, cash contributions, and personal insurance and pensions. The interpretation of the regressions is robust to the exclusion of cash contributions and personal insurance and pensions from the nondurables category. This definition differs slightly from those used by other authors, such as Annamaria Lusardi (1996).

13. If we use all households, the shape of the log function leads us to estimate an unreasonably small elasticity of consumption with respect to income; however, our conclusions are not altered. We experimented with a variety of cutoff points and chose 3 percent (annual income of $1,582) because the gains in the elasticity estimates taper off at higher cutoff percentages. Each regression also includes a constant and year-specific fixed effects. The omitted categories are September; high school graduate; rural; family type is husband, wife, and own children only; and year equals 1995. Standard errors are Huber-White standard errors allowing for dependence within consumer units. All dollar values are in real 1998 dollars.

14. This elasticity is lower than expected because of the combination of the shape of the log function, low-income families, measurement error in income, and the inclusion of demographic characteristics that may be picking up some of the effects of income. If we exclude the demographic covariates, the elasticity increases to 0.45 for total expenditures. While still below the predicted value of one, it falls within the range of estimates presented in Paxson 1993.

15. The sample used is the earnings sample of the outgoing rotation group files. This sample excludes individuals who did not work any hours in the week preceding the interview. Variation in the probability of positive hours causes income variability that is not captured in these estimates. Therefore, we also look at monthly variation in the probability of working during the week preceding the interview. We find that higher-income workers are less likely to work positive hours during the summer months. Lower-income workers have much less seasonal variation in the probability of working positive hours. Individuals in neither income category have distinctive seasonal variation that corresponds with the tax refund season, suggesting that seasonality in income is not correlated with EITC refund payments.

16. We have looked at program changes in a more continuous framework by adding an interaction between the maximum EITC benefit in the sample year, our indicator of eligibility, and the month dummy variables. The results from estimating these equations lead to similar conclusions.

REFERENCES

Cruciano, Therese. 1998. "Individual Income Tax Returns, 1996." *Statistics of Income Bulletin* 18(2): 8–44.

Lusardi, Annamaria. 1996. "Permanent Income, Current Income, and Consumption: Evidence from Two Panel Data Sets." *Journal of Business and Economic Statistics* 14(1): 81–90.

Parker, Jonathan A. 1999. "The Reaction of Household Consumption to Predictable Changes in Social Security Taxes." *American Economic Review* 89(4): 959–73.

Paxson, Christina H. 1993. "Consumption and Income Seasonality in Thailand." *Journal of Political Economy* 101(1): 39–72.

Slemrod, Joel, Charles Christian, Rebecca London, and Jonathan A. Parker. 1997. "April 15 Syndrome." *Economic Inquiry* 35(4): 695–709.

Souleles, Nicholas S. 1999. "The Response of Household Consumption to Income Tax Refunds." *American Economic Review* 89(4): 947–58.

U.S. Department of the Treasury. Financial Management Service. Various months. *Monthly Treasury Statement of Receipts and Outlays of the United States Government.* Washington: Department of the Treasury, Financial Management Service.

———. Internal Revenue Service (IRS). Statistics of Income. 1997. "1994, All Individual Returns: Sources of Income, Adjustments, and Tax Items, by Size of Adjusted Gross Income." *Individual Income Tax Returns, 1994.* IRS Publication 1304. Washington, D.C. (April 16).

———. Internal Revenue Service (IRS). Statistics of Income. 1998. "Individual Income Tax Returns, 1996." *Statistics of Income Bulletin.* IRS Publication 1136. Washington, D.C. (November).

———. Internal Revenue Service (IRS). Statistics of Income. 1999. "All Individual Income Tax Returns: Selected Income and Tax Items, in Current and Constant 1990 Dollars." *Individual Income Tax Returns, 1996.* IRS Publication 1304. Washington, D.C. (May 12).

———. 2000. *Circular E: Employer's Tax Guide.* Publication 15. Washington, D.C. (January).

U.S. General Accounting Office (GAO). 1996. *Earned Income Credit: Profile of Tax Year 1994 Credit Recipients.* GAO/GGD-96-122BR. Washington, D.C.

U.S. House of Representatives. Committee on Ways and Means. 1998. *1998 Green Book.* WMCP: 105–7. Washington: U.S. Government Printing Office (May 19).

———. Committee on Appropriations. 1999. *H.R. 3037: Making Appropriations for the Departments of Labor, Health and Human Services, and Education, and Related Agencies for the Fiscal Year Ending September 30, 2000, and for Other Purposes.* Washington, D.C. (October 7).

Chapter 10

How Families View and Use the Earned Income Tax Credit: Advance Payment Versus Lump-Sum Delivery

Jennifer L. Romich and Thomas S. Weisner

In 1990 and again in 1993, Congress approved significant expansions of the previously modest Earned Income Tax Credit (EITC). These increases targeted working families with children. In a 1993 event publicizing the administration's role in the increases, President Bill Clinton lauded the expansions and celebrated this policy that made work its primary goal. "[The EITC is] not about more governmental or social workers, or more services. It's about more groceries and a car, more school clothes for the kids and more encouragement and hope to keep doing the right thing" (Clinton 1998).

Analysis of the policy's effectiveness must examine the extent to which these hopes are being realized. As the EITC gains prominence in the national budget and policy debate, researchers are starting to investigate the credit's policy effects and possibilities. A picture of the credit's impact on labor supply and well-being is emerging. Most significantly, the EITC accounts for the largest share of the increase in the formal work participation of single mothers over the past two decades (Meyer and Rosenbaum 1998). The credit also seems to have caused a slight decrease in labor force participation by secondary wage earners while having no empirically discernible impact on marriage decisions (Eissa and Hoynes 1998). Furthermore, the credit lifts more families with children out of poverty than any other government transfer program (Council of Economic Advisers 1998; Blank 1999; Greenstein and Shapiro 1998).

Creating a link between the EITC and well-being also requires an examination of how families spend the credit. Are low-income families purchasing the projected groceries, cars, and school clothes? There is also a puzzle about *when* families choose to spend the credit. The vast majority of families receive it in the form of a lump sum after the end of the tax year, even though they could get the bulk of their credit advanced in increments over the course of the year (GAO 1992). These concerns motivate the questions we examine.

- What are the thoughts and decisions of low-income families when filing their taxes?

- If they receive a check, how do people allocate it between consumption and savings? What do they buy?

- How, if at all, does information about tax refunds and credits influence planning, work participation, and consumption at other times during the year?

Understanding the decisions people make to use (or, more commonly, not use) the advance payment requires an examination of behaviors at tax time within the context of year-round spending, savings, and work decisions.

THE STUDY

In this chapter we draw on intensive qualitative data to provide a detailed description of how families view and use the EITC. We spoke with urban low-income families in Wisconsin, which has a large state earned income credit. Qualitative empirical work on EITC recipients is relatively rare, and this is the first work we know of since the credit's expansion in the mid-1990s.[1] We rely on theories of household consumption behavior to frame the trade-off between the lump-sum and advance options and conclude that an augmented form of the basic life-cycle consumption hypothesis best predicts the observed behavior. We hope this present work complements other work on the EITC and sparks quantitative investigations of our findings (see, for example, chapter 9, this volume). We assume that readers are familiar with the federal EITC. To understand the specific circumstances of our Milwaukee sample and issues involved in the trade-off between lump-sum and advance delivery, we provide background information on the Wisconsin credit as well as the federal and state advance-payment options.

Wisconsin is one of several states that offers an EITC. Like most state EITCs, Wisconsin's is based on the federal qualifying restrictions. The Wisconsin EITC is available only to families with children and is prorated by number of children. Families with one qualifying child receive a credit equivalent to 4 percent of their federal amount; having two qualifying children increases the credit to 14 percent. The federal credit is capped at two children, but the Wisconsin benefit is most generous for families with three or more qualifying children. Such families receive a refundable credit equal to 43 percent of their federal amount. A family with three children and earnings in the maximum credit range will receive a $1,600 Wisconsin credit and a total of more than $5,000 from state and federal EITCs combined (Wisconsin Department of Revenue 1998a).

In 1979 the federal government initiated an advance-payment option through which workers can receive a portion of their projected EITC credit in every paycheck. Only workers with children are eligible. The amount advanced is based on projected income and cannot exceed 60 percent of the projected total credit for a one-child family. This cap applies to families of any size, essentially limiting families with two or more children to a hybrid advance payment–lump-sum payment structure. In 1999, eligible workers could earn up to an additional $1,387 with their paychecks (IRS 1999a, 1999b).

Receiving an advance credit involves coordination with an employer. The employee files a form W-5, the Earned Income Credit Advance Payment Certificate, with the employer. The employer then includes a portion of the credit in each paycheck. The total advance received is reported on the employee's year-end W-2. All who use the advance-payment option are required to file a tax return (U.S. House 1998).

Wisconsin offers an option, the Working Family Tax Credit, that allows working members of families to benefit from the credit in advance of year-end filing. By completing form WT-4B and registering it with the employer, workers who qualify for the Working Family Tax Credit can be exempted from all state income tax withholding. This option serves as an advance equivalent to the nonrefundable portion of the credit. Families who qualify for credit beyond the value of the exempted income tax then file for the additional amount (Wisconsin Department of Revenue 1998c).

There is some concern over whether the federal advance-payment form is underutilized. More than 98 percent of families receive all of the credit as a lump sum along with their income tax refund (chapter 6, this volume). In the 1993 Omnibus Budget Reconciliation Act, congressional attention focused on the low use of the advance. A report commissioned by Congress recommended increasing public awareness of the advance option, a call that has been echoed by not-for-profit organizations (GAO 1992; Center on Budget and Policy Priorities 1998). The decision to claim the advance credit makes a difference in household income flow. For an earner with two children who earned $15,000 in 1998, the decision to receive the EITC in one lump sum of $3,174 rather than an advanced payment of $115 a month, with the balance of $1,794 paid at tax time, means forgoing a 9 percent increase in monthly income. Whether the smoother income pattern enabled by the advance-credit option raises family utility is a question of theoretical concern.

Household Consumption Theory

Discussions of optimal spending often implicitly invoke a life-cycle model of savings. Is that the most appropriate conceptualization? Theoretical explanations of households' consumption uses of the EITC must account for two choices: which delivery mechanism gives greater utility, the advance-payment option or the lump sum, and what kinds of purchases will be made with the respective payment forms. We outline predictions using life-cycle theory and then a modified life-cycle model that incorporates psychological aspects of saving.

The life-cycle hypothesis of savings and consumption provides a useful starting point for understanding the relationship between a household's income, current consumption, and savings.[2] This theory holds that current consumption is a function of the present value of projected lifetime earnings. Anticipated future income will be factored into current consumption decisions. Under common assumptions, an increase in future income will raise both current and future consumption.

In the life-cycle hypothesis, a worker who knows he or she will get a large tax credit will consume with that credit in mind. In the simplest view, timing of income is neutral. A $120 payment today is equal to $120 in twelve months time or $10 a month for a year. Life-cycle theory is often augmented to reflect credit constraints and future discounting (Thaler and Shefrin 1981). With the plausible assumption that a low-income family faces high interest rates for borrowing or credit constraints, timing is no longer neutral.[3] Now a monthly payment is superior to the year-end lump sum. Furthermore, economists often assume that people are impatient and would prefer money now to money in the future, all other things being equal. With slight and sensible modifications, the life-cycle hypothesis makes a prescriptive statement about timing of payment: the advance form of the EITC is superior to the year-end lump sum.

In some situations, the life-cycle hypothesis holds for households yet they still do not use the advance-payment option. For instance, persons who do not know about the advance will not claim it. Attempts to claim might also be stymied by an employer who does not know about the credit or actively discourages workers from taking advantage of it.[4] In all these situations, the advance payment would raise the family's utility, as theory predicts, but is not feasible because of other constraints.

A second explanation for the low reported use rates is that the life-cycle theory does not adequately predict household behavior. Citing the life-cycle theory's mixed empirical success in a number of different areas, Richard Thaler and Hersh Shefrin (1981) propose an augmented version of the hypothesis that incorporates psychological concerns, the behavioral life-cycle model.

The behavioral life-cycle model incorporates three aspects of human behavior: self-control, mental accounting, and framing. In this model, self-control has a cost, and persons are willing to pay a price to not have to exercise self-control.[5] Consumers act as if they have separate funds within their accounting system by separating income into current income and wealth. Finally, the marginal propensity to consume from different income sources (salary as against bonus, for example) varies, even if the action that results in the income (work) is the same. People are more likely to build assets or savings with money they view, or "frame," as wealth, relative to money they view as current income. An emerging collection of theoretical and empirical work builds on this model (see, for example, Zimmerman, Eason, and Gowan 1999; O'Donoghue and Rabin 1999; Souleles 1999), particularly in the area of saving for retirement (Bernheim, Skinner, and Weinberg 1997; Lusardi 2000; Levin 1998).

In the case of the EITC, the behavioral life-cycle model has different predictions and prescriptions concerning the decision of when and how the credit will be spent. The theory is no longer neutral with respect to timing and form. The cost of self-control suggests that persons might prefer the lump-sum payment over the advance form, particularly if they have lumpy consumption needs.

Mental accounting and framing suggests that a lump sum will be seen as different from additional income received in a paycheck. Specifically, the marginal propensity to save from a lump-sum payment is greater. Unlike the life-cycle model, the behavioral life-cycle hypothesis does not suggest that the advance form of the credit necessarily enables a household to reach greater utility.

Examining these predictions requires data on household income and consumption streams. In this study we draw on ethnographic data to provide a detailed description of low-income families' spending over time. Our design precludes explicit hypothesis testing and cannot reject one theory in favor of another. Rather, we aim to richly describe and analyze household behavior around the EITC. In doing so we raise questions about household consumption theory.

Data

The ethnographic data used in this analysis comes from a much larger study integrating multiple research perspectives and methods. For context we briefly describe the larger study. Our sample is a subset of 1,357 households who volunteered for the New Hope Project, a community-initiated antipoverty program in Milwaukee, Wisconsin. New Hope enrollees faced a random assignment and agreed to participate in a program evaluation run by the Manpower Development and Research Corporation. Additionally, 812 households with young children were identified to be part of a more in-depth child and family study. Project data used for descriptive purposes in this chapter comes from New Hope intake forms and a survey administered after the first two years of the program. We also use administrative data from unemployment insurance records, the federal Internal Revenue Service, and the Wisconsin Department of Revenue.[6]

Ethnographic Sample

A subset of sixty families was randomly drawn from the families with young children and assigned to fieldworkers.[7] A Spanish-speaking fieldworker is assigned to families in which Spanish is spoken as the primary language in the home. Families who agree to take part are paid $50 for each quarter they remain in contact and participate in interviews and field visits.

Of the families contacted, 77 percent (forty-six of sixty) were located and agreed to participate. Some families had moved away from Milwaukee, and so they could not be included in the ethnographic study. Excluding cases outside of the Milwaukee-Chicago metropolitan areas, the ethnographic sample includes 87 percent of those families contacted. An additional four families were excluded from this analysis because fieldworkers had completed fewer than three visits with them as of April 15, 1999. This leaves forty-two households for the purposes of this descriptive analysis.

Demographics of our sample are presented in table 10.1. When applicable we compare our sample to the comprehensive national distribution of all 1994 EITC recipients as described by the U.S. General Accounting Office (GAO 1996). Although this work predates our study, this comparison with publicly available data illustrates that our sample is a policy-relevant subgroup of possible EITC recipients rather than a nationally representative group. Overall our sample seems to be more persistently economically disadvantaged than an average federal EITC recipient, most likely reflecting the persistent poverty that characterizes the particular Milwaukee neighborhoods targeted by the New Hope Project.

TABLE 10.1 / Sample Demographics

Characteristic	Ethnographic Sample (N = 42)	1994 Federal EITC Recipients (N = 14.9 million[a])
Primary respondent characteristics		
Gender (percentage)		
Female	95.3	—
Male	4.7	—
Age		
Under twenty-five (percentage)	11.9	13.1
Twenty-five to forty-five (percentage)	85.7	68.8
Over forty-six (percentage)	2.4	18.4
Average age (years)	32.7	—
Race or ethnicity (percentage)		
African American	52.4	—
Hispanic	33.3	—
White, non-Hispanic	14.3	—
Household structure		
Number of children (percentage)		
One	10.0	54.3
Two or more	90.0	45.6
Three or more	47.5	—
Household members (percentage)		
Spouse	12.5	—
Partner	10.0	—
Other adult relative	23.8	—
Filing status (percentage)		
Married	—	33.3
Head of household	—	63.6
Single	—	3.0

Source: Authors' calculations based on data taken from survey during twenty-fourth month of New Hope Project participation, roughly six to twelve months before the beginning of ethnographic data collection; 1994 federal EITC data from GAO 1996.
[a]Households with children only.

In most cases the primary respondent is a woman. Four-fifths are between twenty-four and forty-six years of age, with the average age at the two-year follow-up being slightly over thirty-two. About half are African American. One third of the ethnographic sample are Hispanic, a category that contains a diverse mixture of Puerto Ricans, Mexican Americans, and immigrants from other Latin American countries.

Family structure, particularly number of children, is an important indicator of the amount of EITC credit a family receives. Most families in our survey had two or more children, and about half had three or more, hence qualifying for the maximum-level Wisconsin EITC credit. At the time our data was collected, about one-eighth were married and living with a spouse; slightly fewer reported living with a partner. A significant number also were living in households with other adult relatives. Our sample seems to be less likely to be married than the nationally average EITC recipients; the General Accounting Office (1996) reports that one-third of 1994 EITC recipients filed as "married."

Labor market characteristics of the sample are reported in table 10.2. Between signing up for the New Hope Project and the two-year follow-up survey, 92.9 percent of respondents worked in a job for which earnings were reported to the unemployment insurance office. Among those who worked, average earnings were between $8,000 and $9,000 a year, which places them within the phase-in or early plateau portion of the credit for families with children. They also reported working more than fourteen hundred hours a year on average. The respondent's earnings were not the only source of income for these families. Many households had other wage earners or received transfer payments such as W-2 (Wisconsin Works, the Wisconsin welfare program) or Supplemental Security Income. The last line of table 10.2 reports that on average less than two-thirds of a sample member's household income came from earnings. This partial reliance on transfer income further illustrates economic disadvantage.

TABLE 10.2 / Work and Earnings of Sample ($N = 42$)

Characteristic	Statistic
Percentage ever worked	92.9
Among those who ever worked ($N = 39$)	
Average annual earnings	$8,364
Average annual hours	1,444
Ratio of earnings to cash transfer[a]	62.8

Source: Authors' calculations, data from New Hope twenty-four-month survey and administrative data from State of Wisconsin unemployment insurance and public assistance records.
Note: Figures reflect work and earnings during first two years of participation in the New Hope Project, ending roughly six to twelve months before the beginning of ethnographic data collection.
[a]Includes primary and, when applicable, secondary wage earner.

Ethnographic Analysis

This analysis uses ethnographic data on the way of life of economically poor families and children in the program and control groups, situated in their neighborhoods and work settings. Several techniques are used to gather data. Fieldworkers undertake focused, semistructured interviews and participant observation in homes and community settings. Interviews are focused on work, child care, budgets and incomes, health care, social supports, family history, children's schooling, and a common list of related topics.

Fieldworkers also prepare questions on specific topics that are circulated to other fieldworkers, answered by fieldworkers following visits with their families, and posted on the web site. This was the approach used to gather information on the EITC and related family-budget data. Common topics and questions regarding the EITC, budgets, and related topics were explained to the group of fieldworkers, and preliminary findings were discussed during meetings. Abridged versions of both the general fieldwork template and the EITC questions as presented to fieldworkers are included in the appendix to this chapter.

The product of all these field visits are field notes, which are organized according to the common topics and then used in analysis. Analysis of qualitative data is an iterative process. We start by reading through the complete field notes to identify themes and patterns. Notes are then coded and tallied according to these preliminary findings. Narrative summaries including all relevant information are written for each case. Summaries are double-checked by a research assistant and by each case's fieldworker. New hypotheses emerge in the course of analysis, prompting notes to be recoded and summaries revised.

Study Limitations

As in any similar endeavor, both our choice of data set and our methodology involve certain trade-offs. Our sample is drawn from one geographic area; it is not a nationally representative sample and cannot be generalized as such. However, it is a strong sample for addressing questions concerning the EITC and low-income families. The sample is drawn from Milwaukee, a unique and interesting site for research on income tax credits and workers at the lower end of the earnings distribution. Because of the relatively generous state earned income credit, Wisconsin residents are eligible for a larger total EITC than persons from other states. Wisconsin was also among the first set of states to receive a waiver for reform of the Aid to Families with Dependent Children system and started its statewide welfare reform two years before Congress passed the Personal Responsibility and Work Opportunity Reconciliation Act in 1996.

It should also be noted that the sample consists largely of low-income persons who voluntarily signed up for a work based program. We believe that the volunteer nature of the program does not corrupt our sample and is actually a benefit for analyzing EITC knowledge and use. Demographically, New Hope participants were relatively similar to the general population of the targeted neighborhoods (Brock et al. 1997). Within the volunteer sample the individual participant families were randomly selected. This is different from some ethnographic work that relies on word-of-mouth and participant referrals to build a sample. Finally, our sample consists of the types of families targeted by the EITC (low income and able to work) while having been selected without pretesting for any prior knowledge or use of the EITC.

The use of ethnographic data separates this analysis from most other work on the EITC. Strengths of our ethnographic data lie in its longitudinal and personal nature. We follow families over time, both hearing plans and observing behavior. Collecting data in the form of an ongoing relationship, one fieldworker visiting a family every four to eight weeks, also encourages honest responses on touchy subjects such as noncompliance and purposeful misreporting. However, fieldworkers do not ask the exact same questions of every family. Owing to idiosyncrasies of individual households, the depth and thoroughness of data on any given topic varies. Our goal in presenting data from intensive qualitative work with a small number of households is to provide a complement to other types of analysis.

FINDINGS: FAMILY FINANCES AND TAX TIME

Thoughts and decisions surrounding taxes and credits are one element in a family's total financial picture. Overall, our data shows that making ends meet is a difficult and time-consuming task for low-income families. This is congruent with the findings of Kathryn Edin and Laura Lein (1997), who interviewed more than 350 low-income single welfare-reliant and working women in the late 1980s and early 1990s. The Edin and Lein study documents the careful accounting that goes into managing a low-income household. Mothers know the sources of their income and where all of it goes. Although our sample includes married households and allows for slightly higher household income, the same financial acumen is present.

Like the wage-dependent women in Edin and Lein's sample, the working mothers and fathers in our sample have many conflicting demands on their time and money. Problems that all working parents face—arranging day care, finding time to spend with children, completing housework—are worsened by reliance on public or undependable private transportation, working evening and weekend shifts, and living in neighborhoods that lack reasonably priced shopping and medical services.

Although most support themselves primarily through work, few have predictable work lives. Most primary contacts have held several jobs over the past two years. Only eight (19 percent) have worked at the same job over the duration of our contact with the family. Additionally, more than a quarter (11 respondents) have held formal or informal second jobs at some point.

Income varies, but bills remain a constant. Seventeen families (40 percent) have debts other than mortgages. Among families with whom we have discussed outstanding debt, one-third owe more than $400. Estimated total debt ranges from $200 to $10,000, with the median between $1,000 and $3,000. This includes car, credit card, and furniture payments that families make, as well as bills families are not currently paying. Back utility bills are the most common forms of outstanding debt, followed by medical bills.

Money-related stress varies among families; many (40 percent) feel comfortable with their financial situations. Respondents from these families often cite their ability to budget limited money. One woman describes herself as a "penny pincher," another says that she would rather cut back than go into debt. A significant number—24 percent—feel the opposite; bills are constantly overwhelming them. Parents say they "can't get ahead" or are constantly short on money. Finally, the remaining 36 percent fall somewhere in the middle—generally surviving but always close to financial problems. Field notes describe one women who commented, "As long as things were going okay, then [I] could make it." Another woman feels stressed by bills and the costs of helping a sick relative, yet she says, "I believe it will work out. . . . It's tight now, but we got a roof over our head, we got food. You know we don't have a lot of little splurging or anything."

It is this financial background—less-than-stable work and constant budgeting with various degrees of success—against which families decide how to receive and use the EITC. How does the credit fit into these families' budgets?

Tax Time

Not all families in our sample were eligible for the EITC. Two households held two jobs and clearly earned too much; several others were close to the total phase-out limit of the credit. Two were wholly self-employed in cash businesses and did not file taxes.[8] Another four had no earned income, three relied on welfare, and one was receiving Supplemental Security Income disability payments. This leaves thirty-four of the forty-two (81 percent) potentially eligible for the credit. This percentage is higher than the administrative estimate of the actual percentage of recipients reported in table 10.3 suggests.[9]

Not all of these working families get their income taxes refunded. Six households (14 percent) had their tax refunds and EITC garnished automatically in one or both years because of outstanding debts incurred in government administered programs. Three participants report owing back student loans, the most common reason for garnishment. The others have their refunds garnished for back taxes, overpayment of unemployment insurance, or convictions for welfare fraud.

The people in our survey use a variety of tax preparation methods. Among

TABLE 10.3 / Knowledge and Use of the Earned Income Tax Credit Among Sample ($N = 40$)

Measure	Statistic
Survey questions (percentage responding yes)	
Have you heard of the earned income tax credit?	89.7
If so, in the last year, have you used it on your federal or state tax return?	71.9
Administrative Records	
Estimated percentage filing in 1996	76.2
Estimated percentage eligible for EITC	45.2
Among those who received the credit, 1996 EITC amount (dollars)	
Wisconsin	481
Federal	1,036
Total	2,772

Source: Data from New Hope two-year survey and tax administrative data from Internal Revenue Service and Wisconsin Department of Revenue.
Note: To preserve anonymity, individual tax records were not provided. However, we have group-level data for subgroups of approximately fifteen families stratified by experimental status, income level, and family structure. This data allows us to consistently describe the mean filing rate and level of EITC credit received by sample members.

respondents who discussed how they prepared their tax forms, 10 percent completed the forms themselves, 60 percent used commercial services, 15 percent relied on nonprofit community agencies or the free tax assistance offered by the government, and another 15 percent relied on friends or relatives. Informal preparers—relatives and acquaintances—frequently charged a small sum, $15 or $20. Most who used commercial services did so because they could get the money more quickly. As noted by Lynn Olson and Audrey Davis (1994), participants use terms featured in advertisements for commercial tax preparation firms, most notably H&R Block's "rapid refund."

Among those persons who file, most think about tax time far before W-2 forms arrive. Sample members generally look forward to their tax check, often planning in advance what they will do with the money. Tax time is an exciting time of year for most of the low-income working families in our sample. As one sample member exclaimed, "I tell people, 'I can't wait for January,' and when they ask why, I tell them it's so I can file my taxes." Generally, respondents view tax time as a time when they can get caught up on their bills and feel a little ahead for a while. Field notes describe the thoughts of one woman who is counting on a $4,000 combined refund and credit: "She can pay off all her [back] bills, be caught up with all her bills and not feel stressed. . . . All she has to do is keep working until December. Then in January she can turn in her tax form so she can get that money."

Up to this point, we have lumped tax money together with the EITC. This reflects the views of our sample members. The delivery mechanism that links the EITC with the income tax system is reflected in people's views of the credit.

Awareness of the EITC

Most people have heard of the EITC. In 1997, only three respondents (8 percent of filers) had never heard of the credit, and a year later, only two sample members were unaware of it. Without tax records, we have no way of knowing whether or not these families claim the EITC, although the dollar amounts of their combined federal and state tax checks ($2,900 and $4,000) suggest that they received the credit. An additional one-fifth of the sample members recognize the EITC with slight prompting. Participants often note that they heard about the credit through the New Hope Project (if they were in the New Hope sample group), another community agency, or family members and friends.

Most families (53 percent of 1998 filers) were aware of the credit but could not give an exact breakdown of how much they get from the EITC as against how much comes from their refund. Field notes describe a typical response from October 1998: "Although [she] could not recall if the money she got at tax time was EITC money or not, she does recall how much she got and what she has done with it. Last year [she] said she got about $4,000."

Finally, about 10 percent recognized that part of their tax check comes from the EITC program and can give a dollar breakdown of the amounts. The explanation of one working mother with four children is typical of this group—she educates a fieldworker (notes translated from Spanish): "[She] knows pretty well what [the] EITC is, she showed me her tax forms and explained to me what [the] EITC was. According to the tax form that she showed me, last year she got $1,350 thanks to the EITC. In the end she got almost $3,000 refunded from her income taxes." Knowledge of the EITC is widespread.

Marginal Incentives

How sophisticated is this understanding? The EITC credit structure decreases the rate of supplement as families move beyond the upper end of the plateau into the phase-out structure. Economists' concerns about the work disincentives on the phase-out portion of the credit is not reflected in the descriptions most of our families give of the relationship between how much they work and how much credit they get. With an average income of less than $9,000, most of the families in our sample are in or below the plateau area. This limited experience drives their understanding of the credit.

Overall, people commonly describe a linear relationship between the amount of time they work and the total dollar amount of their refund check. Among participants who discussed the relationship between the amount they work and the amount of the check, one-third of the cases could be described as holding a "more work, more money" view—accurate for those in the phase-in part of the credit. One woman describes her thoughts on the issue to a fieldworker in this way: "[She] said that sometimes when she thinks about whether she is going to work overtime, she does think that if she works more her tax check will be bigger, but that thought really doesn't sway her to work too much more."

The perception of marginal incentives may be related to work experience. Recent welfare reforms and a strong labor market in Milwaukee have drawn many of our sample members into full-time work over the past few years. Some of the respondents who think their combined refund and EITC will increase with increases in work have entered the workforce over the past two years. Consider one mother of four children, who moved off welfare into a relatively well-paying office job in the fall of 1997: "Once she had done her taxes [for 1997] and figured out how large her return would be, she realized that it was only for four months' worth of work, 'Four months! I was wondering why I didn't have a job the entire time!' She got a very big tax return—$4,000, $2,000 of which she thinks was the EITC. . . . [She] estimates she will get about $6,000 this year."[10]

Most likely she is overestimating, but not drastically so. The perception that more work will continue to increase the check at tax time does not reflect the phase-out structure of the EITC but is consistent with overwithholding. For such families who are new to the workforce, it will be interesting to observe the yearly learning process and its implications for labor supply as we follow them over two more years.

Only two families in our sample know they need to earn a certain amount to maximize their credit. One family, with two parents in their late thirties and five children, generally subsists on informal labor ("junking") but also aims to have about $12,000 in reported earnings. Field notes from the other respondent, a single mother with two children and five years of heavy employment (often working two jobs), illustrate her understanding of the credit. The fieldworker asked if the EITC makes her work more. "No, she explains that she actually tries not to work too much. One year a few years ago she was working a lot the whole year and ended up actually owing money. I ask how much work is too much. She doesn't give a specific amount but does tell me that it depends on family size. She keeps her hours down because 'I work hard for my money and I want all of it.'" These families with long work histories describe a decreased labor supply in response to the phase-out of the credit.

Misunderstandings and Strategic Use

In addition to a general understanding of implicit marginal tax rates based solely on previous experience, there are a few families at both ends of the knowledge distribution—those misinformed and those highly informed. Three members of the sample misunderstood the eligibility rules surrounding the credit. One person, the only working adult in her household, makes $6.25 an hour yet thinks she earns too much for the credit. Another believed she had to be unemployed part of the year to qualify. Another mother thought that she was ineligible because she did not work an average of twenty-five hours a week.

In contrast, some families understand the marginal incentives offered by the EITC and income tax structure thoroughly enough to engage in strategic behavior beyond adjusting labor supply. Three families plan their tax-filing status to maximize total refunds. In extended families in which multiple adults share child-raising responsibilities, different people may file returns identifying different children as dependents. For example, one woman relies on her mother to baby-sit her younger daughter every weekend. The grandmother also buys school clothes for the child. In return for this care, the grandmother "gets hers back at the end of the year" by (illegally) filing the child as her dependent and receiving an EITC.

Use of the Advance

Consistent with general perceptions and the General Accounting Office report (GAO 1992), most of the families in our sample receive their credit in a lump sum. Four of the taxpayers chose the advance-payment option in 1997; three continued to claim the advance in 1998. One woman claims the advance as a way of preventing her EITC from being garnished for outstanding welfare overpayments. Another works for a community not-for-profit agency and was encouraged to take the "W-5 plan" at work. The woman who discontinued taking the advance ended up owing money in 1997 and switching employers at the end of the year. She did not file a W-5 with the new employer. One additional sample member who had received the advance at a previous job was told the option was not available with her current employer.

Among the sample members who do not claim the advance, most do not know much about the option. When asked generally about the EITC, six mentioned that they got the credit in a lump or that they had not taken the advance. Others did not volunteer knowledge about the advance-payment option. In the cases of some families that received the lump sum and did not seem to know about the advance, fieldworkers told them about the option. Most continued to express preference for the lump sum—generally saying they wanted to get all their money at once. Upon learning of the advance option, no one said they would prefer it to the lump sum. These findings are consistent with the more systematic analysis presented by Olson and Davis (1994).

This description of families' generally stressed financial state, awareness of the EITC, and eagerness to get a tax check makes the preference for the lump-sum delivery over the advance form seemingly more puzzling. If some families are constantly struggling to make ends meet and most know that the EITC is a helpful source of income, why do so few choose the advance option? Wouldn't the advance option increase families' well-being?

FINDINGS: BEHAVIORAL LIFE-CYCLE HYPOTHESIS

Several pieces of evidence support the use of the behavioral life-cycle hypothesis as an explanation for household behavior. Like Thaler and Shefrin (1981), we find that a need for self-control drives spending and saving patterns; we also find support for Thaler and Shefrin's assertion that people keep money in separate mental accounts. We argue against the assumption that people do not use the advance merely because they do not know about it. Recipients' uses of the lump-sum credit are consistent with the predictions of the behavioral life-cycle theory, and, according to our findings, delivery of the EITC through a lump sum actually serves to maximize some families' utility.

Budget Problems and Solutions

Some families in our sample express difficulty with exercising self-control in spending. Among families with whom we have discussed or observed budget decisions, more than half (58 percent) have trouble budgeting money. One woman wishes she could set money aside, but, she says, "the majority of money when I do get paid is going to bills." Savings accounts get whittled down easily. This leads to different coping mechanisms. One woman "had to take money out of the bank that she had been trying to save, 'not to get things that I want, but to get things that I need. It's like uh! Sometimes you can't win for losing.' She explained that she purposely opened a bank account far away so she wouldn't take her money out so often."

Another mother tried to work out a payment plan with her day-care provider that meshed with her pay schedule: "She said that she has tried to make an arrangement in which she pays a lump sum every two weeks when she gets her check, because if she waits she won't have any money left on the week she doesn't get paid." In light of strained resources, persons in our sample choose to use various self-control mechanisms.

Mental Accounts: "Tax Time" and the EITC

Applying Thaler and Shefrin's (1981) behavioral adaptations to the life-cycle consumption theory results in distinct predictions about how people view and use the EITC. In their theory, households act as if they explicitly divide money into mental accounts. Separating money in this way allows for greater self-control over that part of the money seen as wealth.

Earlier we described how people view tax time as a unique season of the year—a time in which they can momentarily catch up or even get ahead. Similarly, they talk about the money from taxes in different terms from those used to describe paycheck money. Often people will discuss tax time in a ritualistic manner: "I always buy furniture with my tax money," or "When I get my check I buy a car." People will splurge during tax time in ways they would not normally. One family goes out to dinner a few times, "to all the places they could never normally afford."

Consistent with the behavioral life-cycle assertion of mental accounts, people see tax money as different from periodic income. However, they do not generally distinguish the EITC from the rest of their refund. This lack of a distinction between the two sources raises a question about the relation between knowledge and the use of the lump sum. Are people not using the advance because they do not know about it? Recall that this would be consistent with the low reported use rate and the life-cycle hypothesis.

Information and Use

There are two possible interpretations of the relationship between not knowing about and not claiming the advance-credit form. One common argument, consistent with the life-cycle hypothesis, is that people do not claim the credit because they do not know about it; with sufficient information and education, people would claim and benefit from the advance. Along these lines, Olson and Davis (1994) argue for increased education about the advance option.

While we agree that increased education will do no harm and may very well inform people who could benefit from the program, we argue for a second interpretation of the lack of information. People do not know about the advance-payment option because it is not useful knowledge.

It is interesting to compare knowledge of the advance with knowledge of another tax-based benefit available to the members of our sample. The Wisconsin State Homestead Credit provides a tax credit for low-income households with earned income who own or rent homes or apartments. This credit was not originally a topic in the ethnographic template: hence fieldworkers did not ask about it. However, respondents mentioned the Homestead Credit voluntarily when talking about taxes. Field notes from an early visit show one woman educating a fieldworker. The fieldworker's later comment is italicized:

> She is looking into something called the Homestead program *(which I had never heard of, so if this sounds fuzzy, it is probably due to my lack of understanding; She seemed to have a pretty good grasp of what it was)*. This is a program that is offered to low-income families . . . whereby they will pay you back for up to half of your rent. You don't qualify if you are getting subsidized housing. She thought that for example, [if] you were paying $500 a month, that the Homestead program would pay you up to $250.

This participant's understanding is basically correct for her family income. In 1999, a family with two children and an annual income of $15,000 who paid $500 a month for a heated apartment would qualify for a $290 refund from the Homestead Credit (authors' calculations using Wisconsin Department of Revenue 1998b). Other sample members displayed similar knowledge of this credit. This included familiarity of the process needed to claim the Homestead Credit— namely, saving rent receipts and having a landlord fill out a rent certificate to attach to the state income tax return. Widespread knowledge of the Homestead Credit—a program with clear financial benefits—contrasts with the scant knowledge of the EITC advance-payment option.

The life-cycle hypothesis would hold if information had no cost. That is not true, however; people have limited time to pass on and absorb information. The most useful information gets passed on first, and useless information may not be passed on at all. This suggests a different interpretation of the lack of knowledge of the advance. The absence of information on the advance-credit delivery form arguably demonstrates that the option does not represent a valuable benefit for low-income working families. To understand why the advance might not be a benefit we turn to the marginal consumption patterns enabled by the credit.

Postreceipt Consumption

Not only does the behavioral life-cycle theory suggest that people think about tax money and paycheck income differently, it also predicts that they will spend it on different things. According to Thaler and Shefrin (1981), people are likely to spend current income on current consumption and save wealth (lump-sum) income or spend it on big-ticket goods.

Again, this violates the life-cycle hypothesis of fungibility. A life-cycle hypothesis suggests that income is neutral with respect to source. Thaler (1994) has contradicted this in a study of employee compensation, showing that marginal propensity to save from bonuses—even expected bonuses—is greater than the propensity to save from paycheck earnings. We should expect more savings and big-ticket purchases from the EITC money than from normal income.

We find that families' plans for and uses of tax checks generally parallel the findings of Timothy Smeeding, Katherin Ross Phillips, and Michael O'Connor (chapter 8, this volume). We concentrate our discussion on two aspects of family well-being: expenditures on children and asset accumulation. The former confirms the policy intention that the program benefit children. The latter shows support for the behavioral life-cycle hypothesis.

Two-thirds of the parents in our ethnographic sample who receive the EITC or a substantial tax refund cite expenditures on children as a priority use of check. Among the eight families who did not specifically mention buying items for children, four were using the check as a lump-sum down payment on a house or a car (two instances each). Clothes are the most commonly cited child-specific purchase. The mother of a preschool-age child and a kindergarten-age child explains that "when my taxes come . . . I'll take the kids shopping because my kids really need to go shopping, especially [my older son]. He has no clothes. He needs clothes. . . . I can't send my son to school like this. I need to

[go] shopping for him really bad. Once I get the money, you know send in all the papers—my W2 thing, I [am] most definitely going shopping for my son. Go to Wal-Mart and Kmart and just stock up." The lump-sum payment enabled purchase of a child's wardrobe—a full set of socks, underwear, and school uniforms—rather than a few items at a time.

Other child-specific uses of the credit are to pay private school tuition (three instances) and establish savings accounts in a child's name (two instances). People also take joy in being able to give their kids money to spend or take the family out for a special treat—some of the credit is used for "fun money" or to "fool with." Most child-oriented expenditures are nondurable consumption, but purchases of durable goods actually are a more visible part of postcheck consumption.

Whenever taxes are discussed, family members can often point to some item in their lives purchased after the last tax time—furniture, a car, appliances, or a house. Furniture is the most common postcheck purchase. Among the families who received tax checks, 60 percent bought couches, tables, beds, or other furniture. Appliances are also another necessary asset. Inexpensive Milwaukee apartments generally rent without stoves, refrigerators, washers, or dryers. The first two are crucial; the latter two are important time-savers for working families (Edin 1998). Our respondents have used their tax checks to buy washers, dryers, refrigerators, and a deep freeze. Entertainment equipment such as televisions, video-cassette recorders, and videos are another popular purchase; 29 percent report such purchases.

Transportation and housing are the next two most common uses of the refund and credit check. Just over one-quarter of our sample have used or plan to use their credit on a car. This includes buying cars outright, making a substantial down payment, or repairing current cars. One person's only planned use of her refund is personal transportation: "I don't care what I get back as long as it's enough to get me a car . . . get me a car that can take me around for . . . at least a year or two."

Nine members of our sample (21 percent) own a home, and three explicitly said they had used a previous tax refund and EITC check for a down payment. Five more were house shopping in 1999, including two who planned to use their 1998 tax checks as part of a down payment. These asset-building uses of the lump-sum credit check are consistent with the behavioral life-cycle theory.

Many families hope to save a portion of the tax check; some are able to. Among the twenty-eight families who received a net positive EITC and refund and whose subsequent spending we tracked, nineteen (68 percent) did not have cash savings left from their most recent check after two months. As one woman lamented, "With bills and seven kids, the money didn't last long enough. Now it's back to week-to-week." Three of these rapid spenders arguably used the money for savings-like purposes—one paid for a land contract on her house, another made a loan to a friend. The third, a woman from a close-knit extended family, gave money to family members to make an insurance payment, knowing that they would help her if needed. Three others paid several months' worth of rent in advance.

Nine families (32 percent) had money in the bank more than two months after receiving their checks. These families were split between having large savings goals—such as saving for a down payment on a house—and keeping the money in the bank for future emergencies. The nine include four families who admit to generally having problems saving money. Consistent with Thaler and Shefrin's (1981) prediction of a lower propensity toward current consumption with lump-sum payments, we find that people use their EITC and tax refund checks to buy larger-item goods, accumulate assets, and create savings.

Expanding the Total Resource Pie

The use of the lump-sum tax refund and EITC check as a self-control mechanism to enable big-ticket purchases and savings follows the predictions of the behavioral life-cycle model. Ethnographic data give insight into a secondary, interesting, and less conventionally visible aspect of this phenomenon. Following a family over time helps us figure out how they do make ends meet in the eleven months a year when they do not get a large refund. Their coping mechanisms actually serve to expand the total resources available to the family.

We find both formal and informal labor supply increases to cover budget shortfalls or to cover special expenditures. People can and do choose to work more hours when they need extra money. One woman paid for holiday gifts this way: "[In] October and November [she] had extra time to spend at work. On certain days she worked twelve hours a day, but it wasn't so bad because her job keeps her active and it is not boring. The money she made was used for Christmas gifts." A more subtle form of increased labor supply happens informally—the extra labor of tightening the belt when finances are very short. Pinching pennies is often extra work. Field notes describe how one woman dealt with an unexpected shortage: "[She] said that she had to go down to the food pantry to get food for the kids to eat for the week. . . . She hadn't been to the food pantry in a long time, but she had no choice."

Other nonmarket strategies include cooking inexpensive meals at home (49.6 percent of the survey sample reported having "enough food, but not always the kinds of food we want to eat"), being more vigilant about collecting child support from noncustodial parents, borrowing from relatives, and being very frugal with utility usage. These nonmarket methods of providing in hard times parallel many of those documented by Edin and Lein (1997).

All of these techniques require extra labor—which is obvious when talking with women. Given their low incomes, the lack of benefits associated with most jobs, and high job turnover, struggling to make ends meet drives such informal work much of the year. In effect, the lump-sum format of the EITC creates an informal, unseen labor incentive for nearly all of the year. A family's income constraint is expanded as people cope with shortfalls that would be covered by the advance.

CONCLUSION

The very-low-income members of our sample generally know about the EITC and other specific programs, yet they either do not know much about or do not choose to use the advance credit. Evidence suggests that this is a response to rational optimizing behavior that follows a behavioral life-cycle description of household income and consumption. People view the combined income tax refund and EITC check differently from paycheck income. In particular, they display a higher propensity to consume durable goods and make large purchases with the lump-sum payment. Also, in the short run, people will put EITC money into savings. Finally, the use of the EITC as a self-control mechanism actually serves to increase the total amount of consumption available to the families as they substitute market and nonmarket labor during months when they do not receive credit payment.

The preference for the lump-sum delivery is puzzling in the context of the life-cycle model. Our study design is not a rigorous test of household consumption theories, but findings imply that many aspects of how families view and use the EITC align with the predictions of the behavioral life-cycle theory. Recent empirical work has investigated similar discontinuities between household behavior and the life-cycle model in the areas of consumption around the time of retirement (Bernheim, Skinner, and Weinberg 1997; Lusardi 2000; Levin 1998) and spending of tax refunds (Souleles 1999). Although our study focuses on low-income families, it is important to note that the tenets of the behavioral life-cycle model apply at all income levels, as reflected in other current work.

This work suggests that a lump-sum EITC can help very-low-income families manage larger purchases such as furniture, cars, and homes, a finding congruent with that of Lisa Barrow and Leslie McGranahan (chapter 9, this volume), who look at a more representative range of EITC-eligible families. It also seems that self-control in spending habits might be an important predictor of asset accumulation. In the face of a universal program such as the EITC, any relationship between asset accumulation and choice of EITC delivery system is difficult to interpret. Households with lower perceived costs of self-control might choose the advance-payment option and save on their own to purchase assets. There is no way to identify spending patterns related to delivery mechanism.

Current and possible future variation between state EITCs could allow more conclusive investigation of some of the hypotheses suggested by this research. One currently testable hypothesis involves the savings level of low-income working families. If a large lump-sum income tax refund and EITC is more likely to be saved than paycheck income, we would expect low-income households in states with more progressive EITC and income tax packages to hold more assets and have larger savings accounts than families with the same net income in less progressive states. Another testable hypothesis concerns the link between timing of the credit and labor supply. Do households cut back their work hours temporarily when they get their checks? Both these issues could be addressed with large, nationally representative data sets.

If the EITC does indeed allow families to save and build assets, another link must be made between these behaviors and family well-being. There has been some recent attention to asset accumulation as a way of promoting well-being (Sherraden 1991; Oliver 1997; Edin 1998; Canedy 1998). However, further specification of how assets contribute to functioning and eventually to well-being is necessary to inform policy trade-offs. Are assets a better buffer for children in low-income families than more cash income on a monthly basis? What is the developmental trade-off between a more stressed-out parent during the year and a mattress to sleep on or a home in a safer neighborhood? Given that income is not timing neutral for low-income families, steps to identify parameters for an optimal mixture of regular and lump-sum income must include specification of how money translates into family welfare.

This work has also led us to consider how the advance-credit option ought to be publicized. Should service agencies and advocacy groups encourage credit-eligible earners to take the advance, as some have done? Based on these data, we argue that people should be made aware that the option is available but not necessarily encouraged to use it. Better would be a frank discussion of possible pros and cons.

Finally, systematic investigation of the role played by employers and for-profit tax preparers would complement this family level work. We cannot reject the hypothesis that some people would benefit from the advance but do not use it because of employer resistance. This suggests continued vigilance is due. It would be useful to further investigate what kinds of information commercial firms provide concerning the advance option. Larger lump sums mean potentially greater revenue from refund loans. Hence commercial tax services have no incentive to inform people about their advance options.

These findings, consistent with Thaler and Shefrin's (1981) behavioral life-cycle theory, suggest that the spacing of income over time is not neutral, even during a time period as small as a year. For the families in our sample, the combination of periodic wage income and lump-sum EITC checks allows for both daily living and accumulation of large durable goods and assets. This research is suggestive, and we hope it encourages additional work on household consumption theory, well-being, and issues surrounding EITC delivery and use.

APPENDIX: FIELDWORK TEMPLATES

A general set of themes guided fieldwork collection. Tom Weisner and Cindy Bernheimer, of the University of California at Los Angeles, compiled themes based on previous work with low-income working families, focus groups, and input from the New Hope advisory boards and staff. An abridged version is presented here. Among the influences on New Hope take-up are:

- family background
- work history and values of participant and relatives
- education of participant and relatives
- the role of religion and spirituality
- paths to employment and patterns of work at entry, including the role of the underground economy
- the number of and relationships with case representatives, W-2 caseworkers, and other social service workers
- the role of ethnicity
- beliefs about and the use of child care
- gender roles and relationships with the participant's partner or spouse
- life goals and ambitions, including attitudes or values about work

Outcomes of New Hope participation include:

- stability in participant's life
- feelings of success and evidence of planfulness rather than procrastination
- participant's future orientation, including investment in further education or training
- the meaning of work: job as against career, resource as against constraint
- equity[11]
  —purchase of a home, a car, an appliance, or furniture
  —possession of checking or savings account
  —the ability to deal with unexpected expenses
  —receipt of Earned Income Tax Credit
- social networks and community bridging, including involvement in a child's school
- children and child rearing
- political ideology
- job barriers or facilitators
- daily routine

The New Hope research team also identified specific areas—such as the EITC—for more intensive data collection. Background information on the credit was provided to the fieldwork team, as well as the additional questions presented here.

Financial picture, with specifics:[12]

- What are your current debts?
- What are your assets?
- What other sources of money do you have?

Tax thoughts:

- Are you planning to file a return? If no, why not?
- When and how will you file a return? (prepare by yourself, use a tax preparation service?) What did you do last year?
- Are you expecting to get money back? Why? [See if they mention the EITC.]
- How much do you think you will get back in total? What makes you think that? (For example, got one last year, heard that I could get one from W-2 or New Hope office, a friend told me, and so on.)

EITC knowledge and opinions:

- Do you know about the EITC?
- How did you find out about it?
- How much of what you get back is from the EITC?
- Is there a street name for the EITC? How do people discuss it with one another?
- Are there things you do differently because of the EITC?

Receipt and use of check:

- When do you think you'll get the check?
- How will you cash the check?
- What will you use the money for?
- [If pay bills] Did you allow bills to build up knowing that you would get a refund?
- What would happen if for some reason you did not get the check or money?
- [Try to get at long-term meaning of purchases.] What difference will this couch, chair, vacation, bills paid off make for you in the next few months?

Preference for lump sum over advance:

- Are you aware that you can get some of your refund in every paycheck, the advance?
- If you are already aware of the advance option, do you use it? Why or why not?
- If you were not previously aware of the advance option, would you want to use it? Why or why not?

NOTES

1. See Olson and Davis 1994 for an earlier interview-based investigation of knowledge of the credit and the advance-payment option.

2. Franco Modigliani and Richard Brumberg (1955) receive credit for development of this theory. Milton Friedman's (1957) permanent income hypothesis mirrors the life-cycle hypothesis (Frank 1997). We refer only to the life-cycle hypothesis for the sake of simplicity.

3. Another way to conceptualize the difference is to calculate the interest earned on the money if it were invested. The actual forgone interest is modest. A household that qualifies for the maximum advance of $115.58 a month and faces a 10 percent interest rate loses $89.60 in net future value by choosing a pure lump-sum delivery rather than the advance payment.

4. See GAO 1992 and chapter 8, this volume, for an additional discussion of employer-level explanations of low uptake rates of the advance payment option.

5. The term "self-control" is meant to evoke connection to a body of work in economic literature, not as a moral characterization. The term is used in the economic work that seeks to explain seemingly inconsistent and present-biased consumption patterns, a phenomenon that spans all income levels. See O'Donoghue and Rabin 1999 for a review of how economic theory specifies self-control.

6. Interested readers may consult Brock et al. 1997 and Bos et al. 1999 for additional information on the New Hope program and study.

7. The sample was stratified by experimental status, ethnicity, number of parents in household, and date of program entry. New Hope recorded ethnicity as African American, Latino, white, and "other." Many of the latter group were Asian, mostly recent Hmong refugees resettled to Milwaukee. Because of the complexity of Hmong culture and language and the need for a specialized study of this group, Hmong were excluded from the ethnographic subsample.

8. Of these, one acknowledges that she is noncompliant and fears audit.

9. This most likely represents the difference in timing between the administrative and ethnographic data. Many sample members were not working in 1996 but had joined the formal labor market by the time of our study. Additionally, part of this discrepancy is owing to sample members who—legally or illegally—do not file taxes.

10. This woman worked steadily in 1998. Her combined tax refund and EITC for 1998 was $3,500. She did not complain about the smaller-than-expected check, perhaps because tax time coincided with a promotion from $8 an hour to a salaried job at $28,000 a year.

11. The equity section of this list is expanded. Most other categories have a similar level of detail in the unabridged template.

12. These questions were asked before the EITC was mentioned.

REFERENCES

Bernheim, B. Douglas, Jonathan Skinner, and Steven Weinberg. 1997. "What Accounts for the Variation in Retirement Wealth Among U.S. Households?" Working Paper 6227. Cambridge, Mass.: National Bureau of Economic Research.

Blank, Rebecca. 1999. "What Public Policy Research Should We Be Doing?" Paper presented to the Institute for Policy Research. Northwestern University (February 22).

Bos, Hans, Aletha Huston, Robert Granger, Greg Duncan, Tom Brock, and Vonnie McLloyd. 1999. *New Hope for People with Low Incomes: Two-Year Results of a Program to Reduce Poverty and Reform Welfare.* New York: Manpower Demonstration Research Corporation.

Brock, Thomas, Fred Doolittle, Veronica Fellerath, and Michael Wiseman. 1997. *Creating New Hope: Implementation of a Program to Reduce Poverty and Reform Welfare.* New York: Manpower Demonstration Research Corporation.

Canedy, Dana. 1998. "Down Payment on a Dream." *Ford Foundation Report.* New York: Ford Foundation.

Center on Budget and Policy Priorities. 1998. Earned Income Tax Credit Outreach Campaign Kit. Washington, D.C.

Clinton, William J. 1998. Remarks by the President at Income Tax Credit Event. Washington, D.C. (December 4).

Council of Economic Advisers. 1998. "Good News for Low-Income Families: Expansions in the Earned Income Tax Credit and the Minimum Wage." Washington, D.C. (December).

Edin, Kathryn. 1998. "The Role of Assets in the Lives of Low-Income Single Mothers and Non-Custodial Fathers." University of Pennsylvania. Mimeo.

Edin, Kathryn, and Laura Lein. 1997. *Making Ends Meet: How Single Mothers Survive Welfare and Low-Wage Work.* New York: Russell Sage Foundation.

Eissa, Nada, and Hilary Williamson Hoynes. 1998. "The Earned Income Tax Credit and Labor Supply: Married Couples." Working Paper. Berkeley: University of California.

Frank, Robert H. 1997. *Microeconomics and Behavior.* 3d ed. New York: McGraw-Hill.

Friedman, Milton. 1957. *A Theory of the Consumption Function.* Princeton: Princeton University Press.

Greenstein, Robert, and Isaac Shapiro. 1998. "New Findings on the Effects of the EITC." Washington, D.C.: Center on Budget and Policy Priorities.

Levin, Laurence. 1998. "Are Assets Fungible? Testing the Behavioral Theory of Life-Cycle Savings." *Journal of Economic Behavior and Organization* 36(1): 59–83.

Lusardi, Annamaria. 2000. "Explaining Why So Many Households Do Not Save." Working Paper 203. Chicago: University of Chicago, Joint Center for Poverty Research.

Meyer, Bruce D., and Dan T. Rosenbaum. 1998. "Welfare, the Earned Income Tax Credit, and the Employment of Single Mothers." Working Paper 32. Evanston, Ill.: Northwestern University, Joint Center for Poverty Research.

Modigliani, Franco, and Richard Brumberg. 1955. "Utility Analysis and the Consumption Function: An Interpretation of Cross-section Data." In *Post-Keynesian Economics*, edited by Kenneth Kurihara. London: Allen and Unwin.

O'Donoghue, Ted, and Matthew Rabin. 1999. "Doing It Now or Later." *American Economic Review* 89(1): 103–24.

Oliver, Melvin L. 1997. "Building Assets: Another Way to Fight Poverty." *Ford Foundation Report.* New York: Ford Foundation.

Olson, Lynn M., and Audrey Davis. 1994. "The Earned Income Tax Credit : Views from the Street Level." Working Paper 94–1. Evanston, Ill.: Northwestern University, Institute for Policy Research.

Sherraden, Michael. 1991. *Assets and the Poor: A New American Welfare Policy.* Armonk, N.Y.: M. E. Sharpe.

Souleles, Nicholas S. 1999. "The Response of Household Consumption to Income Tax Refunds." *American Economic Review* 89(4): 947–58.

Thaler, Richard H. 1994. "Psychology and Savings Policies." *American Economic Association Papers and Proceedings* 84(2): 186–92.

Thaler, Richard H., and Hersh M. Shefrin. 1981. "An Economic Theory of Self Control." *Journal of Political Economy* 89(2): 392–406.

U.S. Department of the Treasury. Internal Revenue Service (IRS). 1999a. *The Earned Income Tax Credit (EITC)*. Washington, D.C. Accessed November 12, 1999 on the World Wide Web at: *www.irs.gov/prod/ind—info/eitc4.html*.

———. 1999b. Form W-5. Washington, D.C.

U.S. General Accounting Office (GAO). 1992. *Earned Income Tax Credit : Advance Payment Option Is Not Well Known or Understood by the Public*. GAO/GGD-93-145. Washington, D.C. (February).

———. 1996. *Earned Income Tax Credit : Profile of Tax Year 1994 Credit Recipients*. GAO/GGD-96-122BR. Washington, D.C. (June).

U.S. House of Representatives. Committee on Ways and Means. 1998. *Green Book: Background Material and Data on Programs Within the Jurisdiction of the Committee on Ways and Means*. Washington: U.S. Government Printing Office.

Wisconsin Department of Revenue. 1998a. *Form 1A and WI-Z Instructions*. Madison: State of Wisconsin.

———. 1998b. *Wisconsin Homestead Credit Schedule H and Schedule H Instructions*. Madison: State of Wisconsin.

———. 1998c. *Wisconsin Tax Bulletin 111*. Madison: State of Wisconsin (October).

Zimmerman, Raymond A., Patricia Eason, and Mary Gowan. 1999. "Taxpayer Preference Between Income Tax and Consumption Tax: Behavioral Life-Cycle Effects." *Behavioral Research in Accounting* 11(0): 111–42.

Index

Boldface numbers refer to figures and tables.